Personality and Mood by Questionnaire

A Handbook of Interpretive Theory, Psychometrics, and Practical Procedures

Raymond B. Cattell

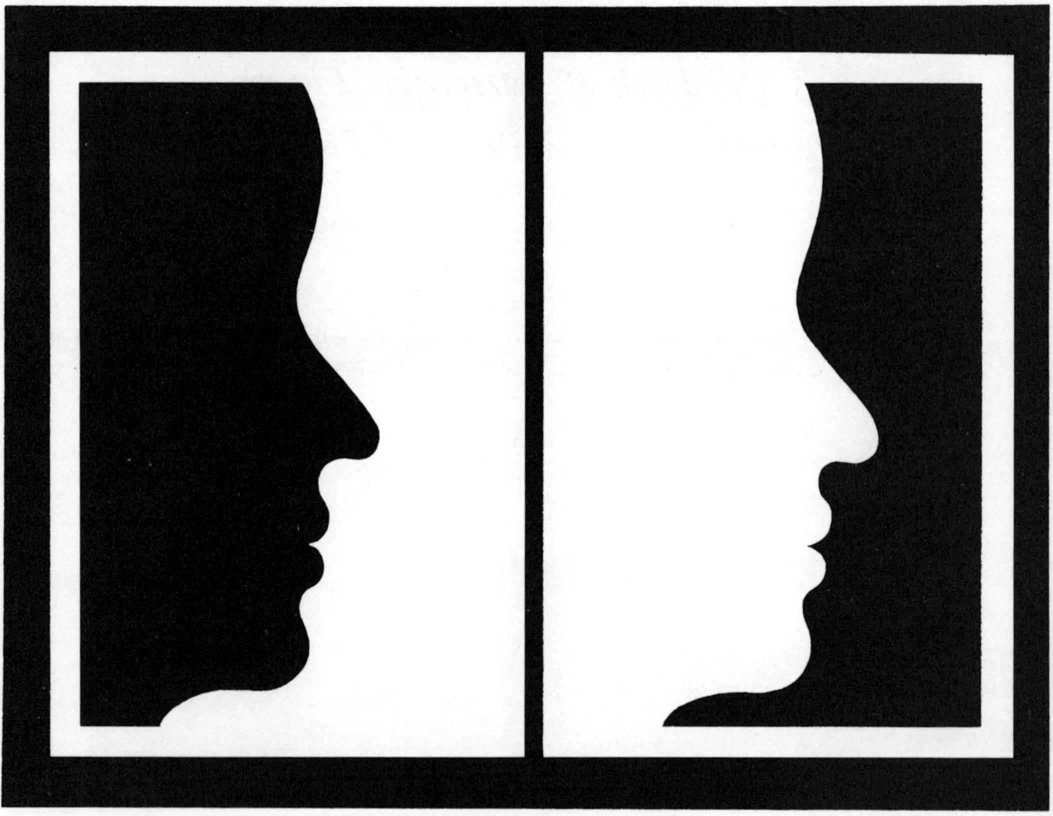

PERSONALITY AND MOOD BY QUESTIONNAIRE

Jossey-Bass Publishers
San Francisco • Washington • London • 1973

PERSONALITY AND MOOD BY QUESTIONNAIRE
A Handbook of Interpretive Theory, Psychometrics, and Practical Procedures
by Raymond B. Cattell

Library of Congress Catalogue Card Number LC 73-1853

International Standard Book Number ISBN 0-87589-181-0

Manufactured in the United States of America

JACKET DESIGN BY WILLI BAUM

FIRST EDITION

Code 7323

The Jossey-Bass

Behavioral Science Series

Preface

The primary object of *Personality and Mood by Questionnaire* is to report on the present status of the theory and practice of personality measurement by questionnaire. A publication of this scope in the questionnaire field is overdue from two points of view. First, the psychologist has not had available for some time an even remotely up-to-date and comprehensive book about the theory of questionnaire measurement. Second, the publications and concrete findings of some 50 research psychologists with whom I have coauthored articles and another 50 well known in the field with whom I have been in touch in the common enterprise of research have never before been brought together in easily accessible form. At the cost of a rather fearsome bibliography I have tried to list all these publications.

Since the last paragraph risks misunderstanding I hasten to add that there is no lack of excellent catalogs of questionnaires in texts for the testing practitioner and in Buros' *Mental Measurement Yearbook.* What is lacking is an integrative effort to develop a complete and advanced theory from available research. And as to possible misunderstandings of my second point, likely to take the form of charging me with undue emphasis on the work of the "school" of psychologists with which I have been associated in planned, programmatic research for more than 30 years. I can give only some frank though possibly not soothing answers. Except for certain social faddist groups in the American Psychological Association there are no longer schools in psychology since all researchers accept the criteria of empirical science; but some groups develop certain techniques and build what they hope are bodies of new knowledge. These cities become the targets of nomads who construct nothing, and the term *schools* may be bandied about. Any definite theoretical position is then ipso facto attacked but at least these attacks do not deny to my colleagues and myself a certain pride and pleasure in having constructed so substantial a target. For, indeed, the most substantial part of the integration presented by these theories is due to the cooperation, the planfulness and the unremitting toil of a group of researchers well coordinated in methodology and exchange of data. No one's work has been excluded from this survey because he happened not to belong to that group (approximately the membership of the Society for Multivariate Experimental Psychology). For example, research from New Zealand, India, Germany, Sweden, France, Japan, and from all approaches has been given prominence at appropriate points. The exclusion that has taken place, unquestionably, has been of those numerous studies that cannot be integrated because they do not meet minimal scientific standards. The reasons for rejection are explicitly stated, and I stand by them. This is the principal difference between this book and the good catalog (and also some painstaking histories) mentioned above: if a questionnaire is published and widely used the catalogs are compelled to list it, even though it was made up overnight and with complete disregard of scientific canons. But if one has to build rather than make a catalog, the pieces have to meet certain requirements of workmanship that permit them to fit together. Since my intention is to build the firmest and roomiest structure that present architecture and materials permit, I give in the text my reasons for rejecting certain materials—for example, ratings based on interview; studies in vacuo that carry no marker variables from careful earlier research; unfactored, arbitrary questionnaire scales; and even factor scales clearly derived from ill-planned and technically defective experiments.

At least it cannot be asserted that I have a biased approach to the questionnaire through an infatuation with my subject. One or two reviewers have noted with an ironic chuckle that I began 40 years ago by rejecting the questionnaire as a test form and turning whatever creativity I possessed to the invention of objective personality tests—that is, to measures of actual behavior (T-data in this book). The latter I still regard as the foundation of personality research with which psychologists should be most seriously concerned. But I have had to come to terms with the fact that this generation of psychologists, although moving slowly toward objective tests, is predominantly attached to the convenience of the questionnaire. Many paddle up to their ankles in the sea of personality measures and even edge toward response-set and cognitive-style approaches to objective tests; but relatively few have taken the bold theoretical plunge to swim freely in the new domain of objective personality testing.

Thus, it behooves personality researchers to get the utmost possible out of the questionnaire. To do so, however, requires considerable development of technical concepts and mathematical statistics. An author is therefore faced with the dilemma of doing a sincere and thorough job on the necessary problems for an effective science of questionnaires or publishing a book that will sell widely. As is evident from the tables and diagrams that attempt to tell much of the story in *Personality and Mood by Questionnaire,* I have aimed unswervingly at the former. Questionnaires are a prominent feature of current psychology, and enough professional psychologists are seriously concerned to make the best use of them to justify a presentation of the technical issues. Moreover the oncoming students in our universities are, one hopes, going to demand more realistic technical education than some of their predecessors thought sufficient.

Since questionnaires are, next to intelligence tests, the most widely used psychological tests, *Personality and Mood by Questionnaire* should function as the student's second textbook in any thorough course on psychological testing. And it is equally relevant in two other types of courses. First, in personality courses it offers a comprehensive and thoroughly documented introduction to personality and state structure with both formal precision and comprehensive illustration. Second, it offers a sufficiently rich illustration of the many uses of multivariate and especially factor-analytic concepts to supplement any course in these areas. It can be a useful adjunct to courses on multivariate statistics, for the old Herbartian adage remains as true as ever: students progress most happily when they approach the abstract via the concrete. And almost every point in the factor-analytic model, and in some other multivariate statistics besides, is concretely illustrated in the substantive psychology here.

Of course, this book is not only for student courses. Indeed, it offers, as no other contemporary available source does, the perspectives and the suggestive leads necessary for those who are doing research in this area. At each of several frontiers it offers directions for the next most likely break through. Incidentally, let no undiscerning critic fail to recognize the line clearly offered here between well checked knowledge and the nuances in the extra data frequently offered to the researcher as a new starting point! Finally, *Personality and Mood by Questionnaire* offers an indispensable shelf reference book for the practicing psychologist—in clinic, school and industrial selection unit. Two major chapters are directed specifically at the practitioner's problems, but an intelligent and constructive handling of those problems requires cognizance of principles and findings throughout the book.

My plan of presentation is obvious from the chapter titles. I am compelled in the interests of logic to begin with some relatively difficult, abstract concepts of personality structure and the methodology that investigates them. I then proceed with a systematic description of findings on normal adult structure, childhood development of structure, and the structure in pathological behavior. Recognizing that to this point only primary factors have been described, I next introduce and explore higher-order structures.

Having presented a comprehensive and measurable taxonomy, I then turn to the natural history of the development and interaction of traits. Some understanding of these abstractions having been gained, I discuss the taxonomy of emotional states and their questionnaire measurement. With the taxonomy thus completed in questionnaires, I ask how the personality constructs in questionnaires compare with those in the other two media of observation—ratings and objective tests.

Recognizing that the treatment to this point has been toward presentation of the most coherent possible theory, I then deal with those assertions in the battle of the questionnaires that seem to produce incoherence. Here I examine all important divergent views and propose a theory that encompasses their differences. In this attempt at integration I find it appropriate to include findings from different countries.

Finally, in the last two chapters I move from a basic examination of structure and general development of theory to practical concerns, first with methods of examining the psychometric properties of actual questionnaires and second with the use of questionnaires in education, industry, and clinical work so that one may make use of their full potential.

I must apologize for some difficulties of style and presentation: these are inevitable when severe condensation has to be the first consideration. The layman may marvel that a whole book can be written on the subject of questionnaires; the psychometrist will be astonished at the temerity of undertaking to encompass the field in one book. Condensation is not the sole cause of a certain difficulty of style. Another obstacle has been the constant need to keep text and numerous tables marching together with explicit interconnections; and that much in the tables is left unsaid in the text may give difficulty to some.

As for the general personality theory that is written large across *Personality and Mood by Questionnaire*—though often between the lines and in tables or equations—one must envy theorists of the Freudian era who could develop a personality theory in subtle (if not well founded) statements without a single table or equation to be explained—or reconciled with the statements. Today, every theoretical point must be expressed in numbers that any psychometrist can examine for sample size, statistical significance, and possible clerical errors; such theoretical points can be misunderstood when space is lacking to describe all the underlying algebraic matrix calculations. My intention has not been to satisfy every obsession by carrying to three decimal places but to present adequate data for the psychologist who wants to see for himself the general magnitude of the support. If these charts suffice to indicate the essential position today and to give profitable direction to future exact studies in these fields, I shall be satisfied.

I owe an immense debt to contributors of data for this book, both to psychologists remote from my laboratory, such as Herbert Eber, Saul Sells, Pral Hundal, Bien Tsujioka, Gundo Schröder, Ray Shrader, Porter Schaie, Graham Vaughan, Ralph Dreger, Peter Saville, and John Kear-Colwell, and to those who made analyses and prepared tables in my laboratory. Among the latter are Charles Burdsal, Keith Barton, Geritt DeYoung, Theodore Dielman, Carl Finkbeiner, Samuel Krug, Kenneth Nichols, David Vaughan, Timothy DeVoogd, and last but not least my secretaries, Deborah Skehen and Dorothy Wilder. Every one of them has played a substantial part in making the extensive analyses necessary to present a comprehensive overview of the subject, and I am grateful to them.

I dedicate this book to my wife, Karen, whose editorial care, scientific foresight, and sheer devotion to fulfilling the ideals of psychologists contributing in the Institute for Personality and Ability Testing have given psychology the substance and means for testing and applying the structural theories here discussed.

Champaign, Illinois
March 1973

RAYMOND B. CATTELL

Contents

Personality and Mood by Questionnaire

A Handbook of Interpretive Theory, Psychometrics, and Practical Procedures

I

Personality Structure: Principles Common to Q-, L-, and T-Data

Asking a man questions about himself is an ancient, though not necessarily reliable, way of finding out about his personality and behavior. Its unreliabilities I focus on in due course, but asking questions remains the method whereby the man in the street tries to find out about personality and mood. Some time ago I (Cattell, 1936) ventured to suggest that psychologists were disappointingly simple-minded in leaning on this method and that far more subtle and potent approaches were possible by measuring actual behavior in standard miniature situations. The latter method has duly developed, as in such batteries as the Objective-Analytic Personality Test (Cattell and others, 1955b) and in such recondite methods as observing response to music and humor (Cattell and Warburton, 1967). But psychologists' questionnaire scales have come to stay, notably in the clinic and school and in vocational guidance. They endure because they are quick and easy to administer and because they continue to show useful concrete validity. Meanwhile sufficient progress has been made in understanding the weaknesses and vices that reduce their validity to make cures for these distortions a reasonable hope. I give questionnaire scales serious study here on this belief that suble concepts and scoring devices are capable of rendering them effective instruments in applied psychology and in basic research on personality structure.

1. Relation of Questionnaire Measurement to Life Observation and Objective Laboratory Test Data

Measurement is the foundation of science. But, in personality, measurement worth anything at all must begin with our finding out the natural forms of human behavior patterns. We must define the naturally unitary traits—for example, anxiety, conscientiousness, ego strength, surgency of temperament—that constitute the topography (or taxonomy) of personality. Then and only then are we ready to set up scales and batteries to measure these traits. The first step I call research on *structure* (or taxonomy) and the second, *structured instrument scale construction.* Constructing questionnaires on a priori bases, naming scales by fiat—this is one of the easiest traps for a psychologist to fall into, and as the bulging volumes of Buros (1972) witness, there seems to be scarcely a psychologist who has not set up his questionnaire at one time or another.

Structural questionnaires, on the other hand, betoken basic research into taxonomic theory, to which they relate as a man's clothes relate to the structure of his body. And whereas arbitrary questionnaires are tossed off the press with no more than a few day's work of making up items, and an uninspired grinding of computers to get homogeneity by itemetric principles, the task of building structured questionnaires is as wide as the science of psychology and as deep as theories of human personality. Scales derived from such work are not just "tests," but ambassadors for a theory of personality, boldly given to the experimental world as hostages for the truth of the theory.

These developments are all the more important because personality theory throughout the first half of this century was a rank proliferation of essentially untestable theories. Nor did the movement toward quantification immediately clean the stable, for many psychologists naively assumed that one man's anxiety scale must measure the same thing as another's. It has taken forty years for the need of factor-analytic and other multivariate methods to be understood as an essential part of the education of the PhD, and judging by some comments in a recent review of the High School Personality Questionnaire the difference between structures uniquely determined by programmatic research and those arbitrarily set by fiat is still not widely realized as scientifically fundamental.

Indeed, the basic strategy of science that a thorough elucidation of taxonomic structure must precede any precise and profitable study of development, or of the effect of this or that learning, has itself only slowly penetrated and informed the premature and fruitless onslaughts on such problems. As Dahlstrom (1972) has well said, "the diversity of human behavior is prodigious" and the failure of psychologists to appreciate the value of "personological systematics, its purpose, and potential contributions" in the light of "taxonomic schemata in zoology and botany is almost unbelievable."

Throughout this book, whether I am dealing with traits or states, roles or types, my primary focus will be on evidence about personality structure per se. And in contrast to such writers as Gough, Howarth, Jackson, and Rorer, I shall consider it more desirable to measure the right factor with a test still in its infancy than an arbitrary, theoretically ill-founded entity with a test of high itemetric reliability (as, say, Sir Bernard Whittle in 1939 considered it more important to construct a jet plane that was initially less efficient than a piston-engined plane reaching the prescribed current ideals).

While dealing with the past we should perhaps go back to still more conservative positions and recognize that the very idea of measuring personality has been ridiculed by some philosophers and literary men. Again one may return to Thorndike's common-sense observation that "whatever exists, exists in some quantity, and can (theoretically) be measured." If any reader should feel that trait structures are too intangible for measurement one must remind him that he is then being inconsistent every time he uses an adjective, saying Smith is highly intelligent or Jones is not very conscientious. Apparent qualitative statements generally turn out to be quantitative —with respect, however, to dimensions needing to be defined as qualitatively different. Whether some aspects of personality are too subtle for our present trait-discovery methods to locate is quite a different matter, as also are such questions as the definition of the units to be used in our scales.

To put questionnaire use in perspective let us recognize that our possible sources of information about a personality are comprehensively and exhaustively three: *Q-data,* questionnaire responses in which the individual himself is the observer and describer of his behavior and feelings in words (as in the consulting room, too); *L-data,* in which an observer assesses the individual's behavioral traits from looking at what the subject does in his everyday life (hence L-) situations; and *T-data,* in which an observer measures the subject's (S's) behavior in a standard, contrived laboratory or test (hence T-) situation, accepted voluntarily by the subject as a "test."

Possible superordinate classifications, of these three bring to our notice other features of their essential natures. For example, L- and Q-data can be brought into one class in that they deal with natural responses, whereas T-data require an artificial, laboratory setting. But T- and L-data are the same in that they involve external observers who can be compared for reliability, whereas Q-data involve introspection, forever private to the individual.

There are also subclassifications of media to consider, most noteworthy of which is the subdivision of Q-data into what I call Q′- and Q-data. In the first case we *believe what the person says,* we treat his statements as evidence of the behavior to which they refer. For example, if he, or more probably she, says "I have a headache," we take it as scientific evidence that she does; and if she, or more probably he, says "I'm the smartest man in town," we credit him with high intelligence. But in treating the same responses as Q-data, we consider only the verbal, symbol-using behavior as the true behavior, and we may find by investigation that "have a headache" correlates with "I don't want to go out," and "I'm smart" correlates with vanity rather than intelligence. As a behaviorist I here place ultimate faith only on questionnaire responses treated as Q-data, using the Q′-

approach as an intuitive aid, not as a basis for scientific systems. The difference become especially clear when I deal with distortion and sabotage.

Similarly a subclassification is possible within L-data—*life* observation—according to whether S's behavior in his everyday life is given a score by the brain of an observer (estimating a trait) or by a mechanical counting and recording of some specific behavior, for example, number of car accidents, in which the human abstractions made in rating do not apply. In the former, which I briefly index as L (R)-data, a trait such as sociability or accident proneness is rated; in the latter, L (O), there is an objective score —the number of times S speaks to people in the office in a day or the number of convictions for drunkenness he has had in twenty years, for example.

These three sources of personality inference—Q-, L-, and T-data—and their subforms, have diverse advantages and disadvantages. The psychologist is just beginning to evaluate these properties and a brief summary is given in *Table 1*.

The aim of this book is to make a thorough investigation of what can be inferred about personality—in its general structure and regarding each

Table 1

Properties of the Three Observation and Measurement Media

	Modality	*L-Data* [*L(R)/L(O)*]	*Q-Data*	*T-Data*
Effectiveness for Various Modalities of Trait	Ability	R Approximate O Exact	Invalid	Exact
	Personality	R Approximate O Exact	[a] Approaching exactness when distortion corrected	Exact
	Interest-motivation	R Approximate O Exact	Inefficient	Approaching exactitude
Properties	Gathered in a "cooperating" test situation only		[a] X	X
	Dealing with actual behavior	X	X	
	Behavioral, not introspective	X	[b]	X

[a] This square delimits the area of concentration of the present book.

[b] When Q-data are treated only as verbal behavior without dependence on the usual symbolic reference, they fit this category also.

particular case—from Q-data.[1] At the same time it does not neglect the given findings in L- and T-data, for the same personality is being seen by all three approaches and it should therefore be possible to knit the Q-data findings with L- and T-data in an integrated interpretation, as surely as we integrate the sound, sight, and feel of an object. Regarding this last point, since I start with the axiom that a real personality exists out there to be seen, I reject the position of some psychologists that Q- and L- and T-systems of observation deal with such separate domains of behavior that the traits are distinct. These psychologists accept the axiom "never the trio shall meet." Here I fully recognize, however, that the properties of each are peculiarly different and that in consequence substantial technical developments are needed to correct the "distortion" of each. Some mutual translation of the media has to take place if they are to be fitted together to present the person as he exists.

A second basic proposition that the reader should be prepared to recognize is clearly expressed above: that scientifically functional measurement scales must be aimed at the natural unitary structures in human traits. The greater part of the first four chapters is devoted to debating methodological standards in ascertaining what this structure is and how it may be conceived and defined for measurement. There are two distinct worlds of questionnaire construction: one in which these technical developments are respected and one in which anarchy prevails from a persisting belief that a clinical eye and subjective conviction are enough to decide on the scales. Regarding the second, which we leave outside our laboratory doors, let us be clear that nothing stops anyone from making up questionnaires for any trait he cares to imagine. And since there are an indefinitely large number of conceivable traits and roughly fifty thousand psychologists, questionnaires have in fact been the prolific rabbits of the psychometric world.

But on general evidence we know that there are unitary common traits or dimensions in personality, that is, personality has a structure, as the human body does in its organs. Consequently, some traits are more important, less subjective, and more functionally unitary than others, and an enlightened system of psychological measurement, here in Q-data as in other realms, will direct its measurement scales to these traits. Thus Charles Spearman shaped intelligence tests to measure his g-factor; Louis Thurstone aimed batteries at such primaries as verbal and numerical abilities, and I

[1] The only other thorough current treatment of the personality theory derivable from questionnaires is that of Eysenck and Eysenck (1969) since Guilford (1959) keeps close to psychometric issues only. However, the title of their work is misleading in that it claims to cover personality structure, whereas in fact its new contribution (all but the first two chapters) is personality as seen through questionnaire data only and largely through the Eysencks' EPI (formerly the MPI). Nevertheless, it is a systematic attack, as distinct from the numerous articles and handbooks on questionnaires that describe a particular questionnaire or factor analysis without addressing themselves in the least to an examination of the basic developments and structural theories involved in Q-data. Although, as we shall see, I am compelled to doubt the specific conclusions about structure in that book, its attention to general principles is consistent with mine.

developed objective test batteries for such factors as anxiety, ego strength, exuberance, regression, and extraversion (U.I. 24, 16, 21, 23, and 32).[2]

2. Factors and Correlation Clusters: Source Traits and Surface Traits

The preceding discussion points to two essential postulates of this book—and indeed of all the personality research conducted since the 1940's by coworkers in my laboratory and many other well-known investigators. They are that research on personality structure must precede instrument construction and that claims for the existence of particular unitary trait structures must present objective evidence that the behavioral parts of the total trait concept covary, as parts of a unity should. This building upward from a foundation of structural knowledge to experimental work based on measurement and so to the developmental and other laws discoverable by measurement has characterized all mature sciences. Chemistry located and identified its compounds and ultimately its elements before proceeding to its present vast superstructure of lawful generalizations; medicine had its Vesalius, establishing the anatomy of organs; biology had its Linnaeus, presenting a reliable taxonomy of species and genus, upon which Darwin was able to build his theories of evolution.

As several philosophers of science have noted, psychology had a frustrated and misspent childhood attempting to burgeon with grand theories before it had established the measurement basis by which any theory could be developed and checked. However, there is no longer any excuse for such flimsy theory in the personality field; the taxonomy of traits and states has greatly advanced, and there are now several reasonably thorough expositions on taxonomic methods and findings to which any reader can be referred (Burt, 1940; Cattell, 1957, 1965a; Eysenck, 1960; Fiske, 1971; Guertin and Bailey, 1970; D. N. Jackson, 1966; Mahrer, 1970; Messick and Ross, 1962; Thurstone, 1938; Goldberg, 1973).

The path to structural knowledge can perhaps best be briefly introduced and illustrated by the historical instances in which it first became

[2] For greater speed and precision of reference, throughtout this book I use index numbers as well as names for factorial source traits. Names vary from subculture to subculture and are often deceptive. Often they already connote an interpretation peculiar to the author and still under theoretical debate. For example, Eysenck calls UI 23 neuroticism and UI 25 psychoticism, whereas my laboratory finds irrefutable evidence that neurotics and psychotics differ as significantly from normals *on certain other factors as they do on these*. Consequently these popular labels mislead, and I have instead given them universal index (UI) numbers and terms in implying specifically analytical interpretations—regression and tense inflexibility—describing their particular role in the neurotic or psychotic process. The universal index series (running in ability factors from UI 1 to UI 15 and in personality from UI 16 to UI 36 Hundleby, Pawlik, and Cattell, 1965) enables different investigators to be sure they are referring at any time to the same factorial behavior pattern. Thus one eliminates confusion from different fashionable interpretations and holds the identity firmly while interpretive research proceeds for years. The UI series is for objective test, T-data, factors. The indexing of Q- and L-data factors has been somewhat different and is described shortly.

important: the recognition of structure in abilities by Spearman (1927) and in finer detail by the later work of Thurstone (1938). Correspondingly in personality one sees great attention given to structures by Freud (1920) and McDougall (1932) at the premetric stage, and by Burt (1940), Cattell (1957), Eysenck (1960), Guilford (1959), and many others in the metric phase, starting in the 1930's. When intelligence was the greatest issue in individual difference research, Spearman tackled the question of whether there is a single general intelligence or several independent abilities by asking which performances go together. However, he went beyond the principles of functional unity by general association, which the philosopher Mill (1863) had clarified, to the technical use of the correlation coefficient, developed by Galton (1883). Thus he took perhaps forty ability performances (measured on, say, two hundred people) in all possible pairs and correlated them in all possible combinations. By studying this correlation matrix Spearman was able to see which forms of behavior obviously go together—for example, performance on synonyms and on problem arithmetic—in what could be called correlation clusters. Later he developed the sophisticated examination by factor analysis, which shows how many factors —independent influences each causing covariation of elements—are actually needed to account for the correlational observations. The demonstrated success of these methods caused them to be applied (after the period of Freud and McDougall) to personality structure data.

Since correlational and factor-analytic concepts are a necessary part of all psychological education beyond the elementary level today, there is no need to reiterate them. However, the connection of my personality concepts operationally with correlational methods is central, so I shall run over essentials in a few paragraphs and refer the reader to the several excellent books on factor analysis and multivariate methods for the rest.

The most direct reminder of what correlation clusters and factors mean is provided by diagrams. Let us recognize that if we let an experimentally obtained correlation between variable 1 and variable 4 or 1 and 11 be represented by the cosine of the angle between the lines 1 and 4, or 1 and 11 in Figure 1, then a high correlation, say 0.8, exists between tests 1 and 4, and a zero correlation between variables 1 and 11. If a set of variables correlate mutually in all pairs highly then each such set forms a correlation cluster, as with variables 6, 7, 8, 9, and 10, mutually in all pairs in set *B*, or 17, 18, and 19 in set *D*. Six such correlation clusters stand out in the plots in Figure 1: *A, B, C, D, E,* and *F*. The factors among these same variables would, by contrast, be represented by just two dimensions and therefore by coordinates, as put in at F.I and F.II. If the correlations among the variables had been such that 4 and 5 correlated +0.7, 5 and 6 correlated +0.7, and 4 and 6 correlated +0.7, then the vectors 4, 5, and 6 would not have lain down in the plane of the paper. Number 5 would have stood up in the air and a third coordinate, beyond I and II in Figure 1 standing up vertically to the plane of the paper, would therefore have been necessary to take care of positioning all the points. All the correlations (angles) given by the experiment in Figure 1 allow all points to be explained by two coor-

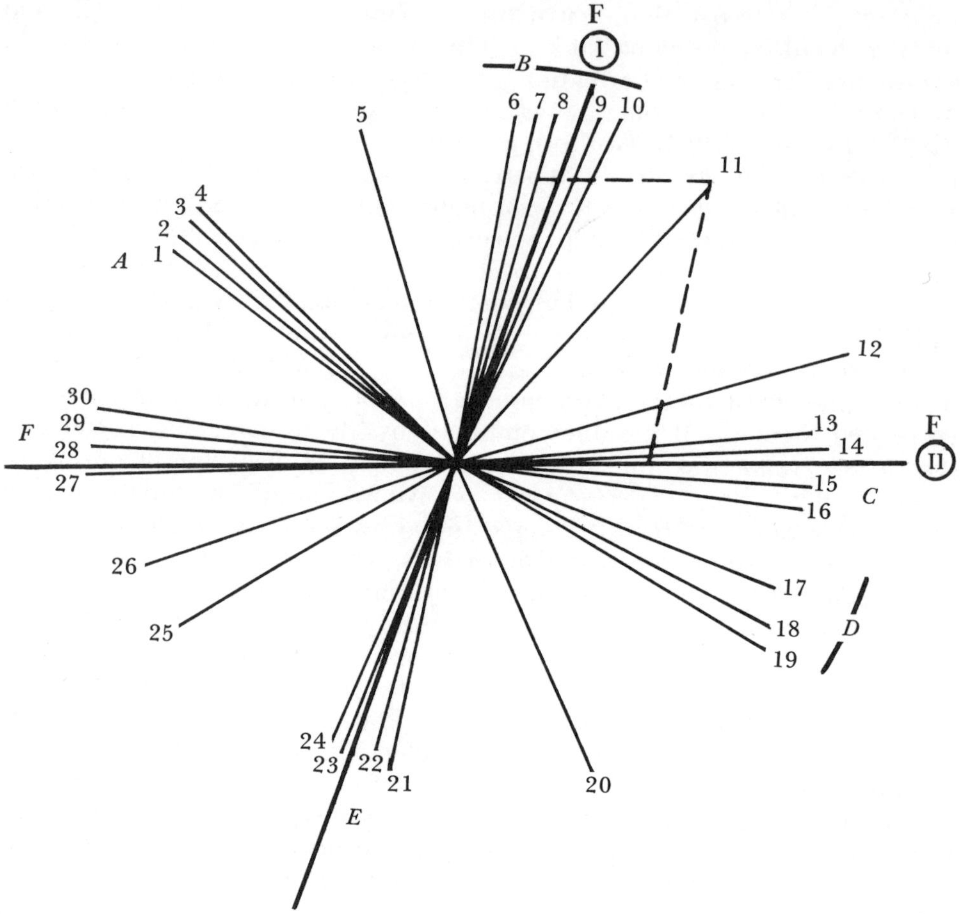

Figure 1. Diagramatic representation of correlation clusters and factors among variables representing specific measured behaviors.

dinates (sources of variance) only. These two factors (drawn obliquely instead of at right angles, for reasons given later) therefore suffice to explain and predict the performance of people on all thirty variables. The beginner in this field must be referred elsewhere for the way in which factor analysis finds these factors from the given correlation matrix (Child, 1970; Gorsuch, 1973; Guertin and Bailey, 1970; Harman, 1967; Rummel, 1970). But familiarity with the computations is not necessary provided that the basic principle is understood, namely, that we can find underlying influences—perhaps not immediately and directly measurable— that can be regarded as accounting for the numerous effects we see in the experimental variables. Thus in a concrete example (Cattell and Dickman, 1962) a prediction of scores on thirty-two ways in which eighty balls behave—for example, bouncing, rolling down an inclined plane—can be made from only four extracted factors—weight, length of attached cord, size and elasticity.

In short, given the correlation matrix from an experiment (in this case a square of 30 × 30 correlations) factor analysis enables us to find the number of factor coordinates (two is usually too few) needed to account for the correlations and the projection scores of all variables on the factors in a factor matrix (30 × 2 in this case). Geometrically the factors can be represented by dimensions (which may be somewhat correlated, as the obliqueness of F.I and F.II in Figure 1 shows). But—although not all factorists agree—many psychologists, including me, assume also the correctness of an underlying scientific model that recognizes the factors to be more than dimensions—in fact determiners, influences, or causes. Thus when we factor the experimentally obtained correlations among, say, fifty questionnaire items, we are (if we insist on simple structure, as defined later) discovering the number and nature of the underlying structural influences that account for observations being related the way they are. For example, the degree of inhibition the individual has acquired would account for his level on all the variables (See Table 4, Chapter Two) in the surgency-desurgency factor, *F*. Although the primary factors are thus to be recognized as real psychological influences on observed variables, this does not preclude their being in turn partly at the mercy of other causal influences, notably in the second-order factors considered later.

In many fields of complex multivariate covariation—in psychology, sociology, economics, meteorology, and medicine, for example—the human mind unaided by analytic computation (and the blessing of the electronic computer) is overwhelmed and becomes confused and arbitrary when attempting to isolate the underlying concepts. This has been true in psychology, particularly of the unaided clinical observation of personality structure, and here factor analysis has made very valuable clarifications (Lorr, 1966; Degan, 1952; Cattell and Schmidt, 1972). But these findings seem to most psychologists to be at a less finished stage than they are in the area of abilities, where the unique definition of intelligence and the primary abilities by Spearman and Thurstone came comparatively early.

3. Common and Unique, Broad and Specific Traits

My concern here is with what factor analysis has to say about personality structure, but except where certain hotly debated issues call for refined argument the reader will be able to follow with no more abstract treatment of factor analysis than that already given. The use of correlation-cluster and factor-analytic principles is implicit in a lot of thinking, including clinical thinking, not commonly thought of as multivariate statistics. Thus when Bleuler (1911) described the schizophrenic syndrome, or Howard Ricketts described the symptom complex of Rocky Mountain spotted fever, a correlation cluster was being recognized—by sharp observation and a good memory instead of measurement and a computer. The good clinician said, "When I see this, I tend also to see this and this and this. Therefore they must have a common underlying cause—a factor." And when Freud introduced the superego and the ego into psychoanalytic theory he was describing two underlying factors or influences that accounted sufficiently for relations he observed from patient to patient or from sitting to sitting with the same patient.

Certainly known unitary influences definitely appear in calculations as factors (Cattell and Dickman, 1962), and an argument can be made for a model which says that what we find as factors are influences. Factors may, however, be either one of two kinds of influence: a *present* influence, as when the sun simultaneously accounts for an increase during the morning in such variables as light, heat, cosmic rays, and evaporation, or when a state of anxiety accounts for present tremor, fall in skin resistance, change in muscle tone, and hesitation; and a *past* influence, as when a correlation pattern of limited vocabulary, poorness at arithmetic, and ignorance of history found among adults, is traceable to the number of months absent from school long ago. In one case the observed structure is due to a presently active function; in the other, as when we look at the unmistakable form of an extinct volcano, the unitary influence inferred is one that took place earlier and has now disappeared—except as a measurable pattern of effects.

On this hypothesis of structure it is not enough to talk about a factor as a merely mathematical concept. Lykken (1971) does well to doubt the value of such mere abstractions as orthogonal factors to psychology. In this book factors on such a basis, fitting only mathematical conditions, will not be considered valid evidence. Instead we deal with a scientific model, in which the unity of a trait is due to a unitary influence—something substantive—that will express itself as an oblique, simple- structure factor appearing simultaneously in different situations and also as a developmental pattern. Such traits can be divided broadly into those in which a learning influence has produced the unity (an environmental mold trait, Cattell, 1946a) and those in which a genetic, maturational action has produced the unity.

Because the unitary loading pattern caused by a factor represents an influence or source, I and my colleagues have consistently (here and in two hundred publications) called it a source trait. Intelligence, ego strength, surgency, and characterological anxiety (not the *state* of anxiety) are source traits. But correlation cluster is called a surface trait, which, as its name suggests, is simply the things directly seen to go together. However, as Hundleby's more complete discussion (1972) shows, deep probing by factor analysis might show that the cluster elements go together because of more than one influence. Talkativeness, impulsiveness, and poor self-control may be observed to increase together (a correlation cluster). But a manic temperament, alcohol, and fever may be three distinct influences capable of causing these elements to increase together. And if these three source traits or states are present together, the surface trait may be prominent indeed. Characteristically, in any case, there are somewhat more surface traits than source traits—as there are six recognizable clusters but only two factors in Figure 1.

The trouble with the surface trait, as an attempt at a precisely delimited and measurable unitary concept, is that often a sharp line cannot be drawn between one surface trait and another. As Figure 1 shows, the presence of a single extra variable between 16 and 17 would cause us to consider clusters *C* and *D* as *one* big cluster. Mere accident could have decided whether the experimenter included that variable. In practice the problem can be as difficult as trying to separate straggling clouds in the sky (except that we may have to work in ten or twenty dimensions instead of three). Consequently, although the concept of surface trait needs to be recognized and clinicians find it useful in denoting syndromes, I do not use it often in precise description and calculation here.

The structural concepts here discussed not only are basic to study in the questionnaire medium but apply equally to L- and T-data. Indeed they must also be the means of our later integration of personality concepts from Q-data, (questionnaires), L-data (life observation), and T-data (objective or laboratory tests). For my postulate is that the same real-personality trait structures, dressed in somewhat different patterns of expression, should appear in all three media.

In all these domains of trait expression we must recognize a second dichotomy of concepts, one which cuts orthogonally across that of source and surface. This is the distinction of common and unique. If a trait such as intelligence is established by correlating across many people in what is called R-technique factorization, that is, correlations on the basis of the individual difference domain, it is called a common trait. Most psychologists are content to do most of their work with common traits, which can be measured on the same battery for everyone. Use of common traits does not, for that matter, lose the uniqueness of the individual any more than the use in astronomy of common dimensions of distance, weight, rotation speed, and light emission denies the uniqueness of individual stars. The individuality of a person can be set out as a unique *combination,* a profile, of common source-trait scores. Geometrically he is firmly ensconced as a unique point in the multidimensional space of factors. When one recognizes nevertheless that the particular "flavor" of *A*'s intelligence is different from *B*'s, it is generally quite unnecessary to depart from a common dimension by setting up a different trait scale of intelligence for *A* and *B*. One quickly recognizes that *A* and *B,* although perhaps equal in intelligence, differ on other comon trait scores. For example, *A*'s intelligence may be more deliberate and less mercurial because he is higher on ego strength and lower on premsia.[3] The unique quality of, say, intelligence lies in a particular combination of common trait scores.

Some psychologists are likely to get mystical about uniqueness and unique traits, and fail to give any experimental, operational, and even logical basis for such ideas (as Allport, 1961, and many of his students have done). The fact is that in the realistic and demanding realm of applied psychology, substantial predictions of important criteria are made by questionnaires and intelligence tests that deal entirely with common traits. Nevertheless a real meaning can also be given to unique traits. Moreover,

[3] Premsia versus harria is a primary dimension of protected (or overprotected) emotional sensitivity (hence the acronym *pr-em-sia*) versus hard reality (*harria*) upbringing. (See Chapter Five.) An intelligent person also high in premsia has a "sensitive intelligence," whereas if he is low (harric) he would strike us as having a tough, practical "variety of intelligence." The intelligence contribution itself is the same.

psychologists are not alone among scientists in encountering the pains of having to do something about unique traits. If the size of a man's car or the capacity of a cow to yield milk has to be measured, we strictly have to consider the differing shapes of cars or the changing sugar, butterfat, and other contents of the milk from different breeds. A Guernsey would rightly be insulted at having its milk production compared in pints with that of a Holstein!

However, the only operational way in which the unique "shape" can be recognized in the case of a trait in an individual is through *movement*. The variables concerned in the possible unique trait factor must either fluctuate from day to day or change with growth. Then they can be correlated and factored over time, in a way to be described as P-technique (Chapter Five). The historical outcome of P-technique is that it has first yielded essentially the same factors as those already recognized by R-technique as common traits, for example, anxiety and intelligence. When unique trait patterns are found, they are sometimes, but rarely, genetic since almost any gene repeats itself over many people. Uniqueness of pattern is most frequently found in the dynamic domain of acquired interests and where personal history has brought contact with environmental pressure patterns no other individual has met. Thus Macbeth could be measured on an emotional attitude of preoccupation with Birnam Wood, which it would scarcely be useful to include in a battery for, say, Japanese high school students.

Such practical aspects are not considered when such writers as Allport (1961) or Mischel (1968) denigrate common traits in favor of unique traits; it is not unreasonable to ask them to produce statistical proof of better predictions of criteria from using unique traits. The matter should not in any case be viewed as an all-or-nothing philosophical issue. Both patterns exist, and all we need are quantitative answers about their relative importance in various prediction situations.

A distinction often confused with that between common and unique trait patterns is the antithesis of common and specific traits—or, as we shall call it, *broad and specific* traits. The first of these distinctions concerns commonness or uniqueness with respect to people; the second with respect to behavioral variables. To the mathematician a common trait is one affecting two or more variables in a matrix of variables, and often he calls it a *general* factor when it affects *all* variables. But since this definition is peculiar to the choice of variables in a matrix it is a local mathematical not a general scientific basis of definition. In the latter domain, assuming a stratified sample of variables from the personality sphere, we shall not speak of common or general factors, which invites confusion, but of broad traits, on the one hand, which influence two or more (usually many more) variables, and specific traits which are factors peculiar to one piece of behavior. And even then a danger sign must be attached to the term specific. One must not fall into the assumption that it really is specific to the one variable. Often it remains specific only because one has not experimented with the right second or third variable to share the variance. It may be a broad factor not yet explored. However, in general it is conceptually acceptable to believe that some factors may really be specific to a narrow, specific behavior.

4. What Are Mood States? Definition by P-Technique

A taxonomy of behavioral patterns must encompass states as well as traits. Psychometrists, fully engrossed with trait definition problems, neglected states until comparatively recently. (The first P-technique[4] analysis of states as such was made in 1945 and published by Cattell, Cattell, and Rhymer, 1947). Yet in the prediction of behavior, knowing whether a person is in a good or bad mood or angry or amorous may well be more useful than knowing his particular trait scores.

Introspectively we have no problem recognizing obvious states and moods, and as far back as Wilhelm Wundt systematic psychologists had considered putting them on dimensions. The question is: What dimensions? McDougall decided on dimensions of the primary drive expressions—for example, fear, pity, lust, anger—and considered more subtle moods as secondary emotions formed by combining these as an artist forms his quiet, subtle tints by combining three primary colors.

This is a reasonable approach, but what are the primary drives or ergs, and how do we measure their levels of tension or emotional excitation? The only answer yet given at an operational level—and it seems an adequate one—for locating the independent, unitary sources of state change lies in the experimental design we have just called P-technique, aided by what is described below as dR-technique. Althought both of these are taken up in technical detail in Chapter Six, the state chapter, the principles of each can be briefly introduced at this point. To describe the *longitudinal* P-technique so far mentioned let us suppose we measure Mary Jane on Monday on some 30 (say four-choice answer) questionnaire items concerning anxiety and also on pulse rate, electrical skin resistance and other hypothesized measures of anxiety, as well as on three or four items believed to be measures of, say, elation. Let us suppose that we repeat these measures daily for the next six weeks and plot the results as in Figure 2 (there extending to only a couple of weeks). During that time, either through some stress stimuli the experimenter has brought to bear or through the mood pressures of everyday life, the state levels of anxiety and elation, as distinct unitary emotional responses, will have gone up and down from day to day. If the manifestations we hypothesize to be expressions separately of anxiety and elation are indeed expressions, those of anxiety will follow a mutually roughly parallel course. Those of elation, we may expect, will also change together but follow different courses from those of the anxiety expressions, as shown in Figure 2.

If we had set up an experiment to find the relations among expressions of many emotions (instead of just two as in Figure 2), the tangled skein of plots would not permit us to separate them by eye as easily as in this

[4] P-technique is so named because it is factor analysis of the single person in contrast to R-technique, the usual factor analysis done with a representative array of people. (See Chapter Six.)

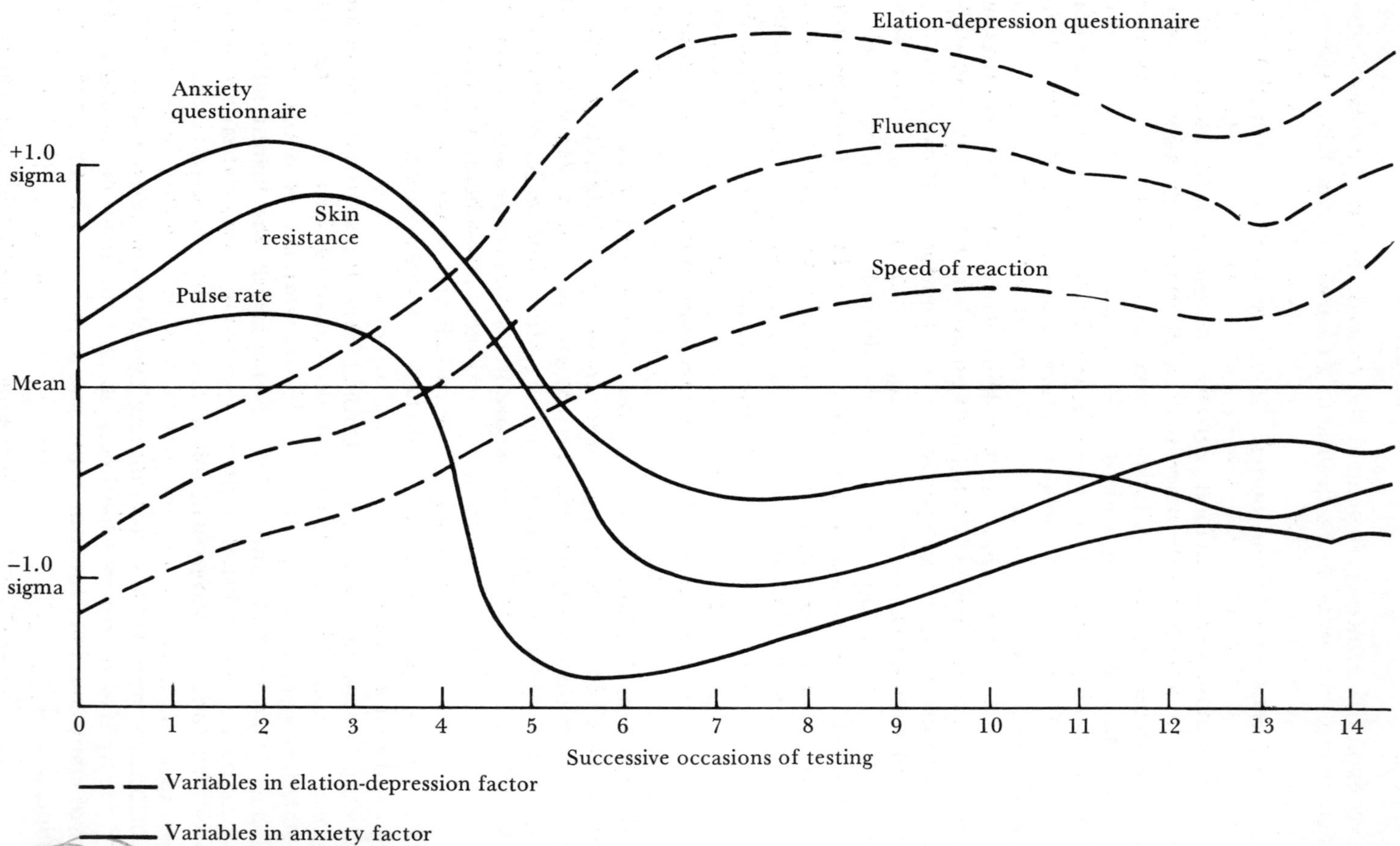

Figure 2. Basic Principles in P-technique analysis of mood dimensions.

example, and we would have to resort to calculation. Indeed, plots are seldom as "pretty" as in Figure 2. That calculation would take the form of correlating the series of scores (over fourteen entries in Figure 2 but one hundred in a good experiment) for the anxiety questionnaire items with the variables of pulse rate, skin resistance and so on. On looking at a matrix of correlations among, say, forty variables carried over one hundred days, one should be able to pick out certain correlation clusters of variables that go together, just as is done with traits (over people instead of over occasions) in Figure 1.

By analogy with traits any such correlation cluster found would be called a surface state, for although clusters and factors sometimes coincide, there are in general more particular clusters than there are general factors. However, instead of searching for often ill-defined surface clusters we would proceed to factor the correlation matrix and find how many independent sources are in the daily variation of mood conditions. This approach was given the label "P-technique" because it is factoring of the individual *person* over many occasions of course.

Chapter Six, on states and their discovery by P- and dR-technique, shows that some nine or ten independent dimensions—source states as I call them—are sufficient, in their combinations, to account for the large variety of human mood expressions so far measured. (The dynamic, drive states are not included.) Regarding these nine or ten "general" state dimensions, one would naturally next ask whether the P-technique analysis of different individuals leads to the same patterns. The essential answer is yes (although the Laceys, 1958, and some others are questioning this as it seems to me on a misconception of what statistical results would be expected). However, the patterns of response that constitute anxiety, for example, stress, depression, and fatigue as they are initially revealed by P-technique can strictly claim only the status of unique states. Immediately on comparing the patterns, however, one finds they are highly similar from person to person, and hence are common states. Further, when dR-technique [5] is brought to bear, the patterns it reveals correspond to the central source state pattern in the P-technique experiments.

Since the supposedly fixed traits in human beings almost certainly also vary in level a bit from day to day, we must recognize that a factor found in P- or dR-technique, especially if of small variance, is not necessarily a state. As far as present knowledge goes, however, states shift by quite a different order of magnitude, and they probably swing more definitely in response to external stimuli, wheras traits may show change in more steady growth and decline. Further, if we average state measures across many occasions, people probably will not differ much in their average values, whereas in traits they would. But the important point in recognizing, indexing, interpreting, and naming a unitary state pattern is its factorial unity

[5] dR-technique is short for *differential R-technique,* that is, a factoring of correlations over a representative sample of people, as in R-technique; but the scores used are *differences* between one occasion and another. Thus the dimensions found must by their origin deal with directions of change, that is, with state factors.

in P-technique or dR-technique. It is not enough, as Spielberger and others have done, to find particular variables that oscillate considerably and then arbitrarily call them anxiety or depression or whatever. These merely changeable items could be measures of complexly mixed states—or merely unreliable items. Nor is it satisfactory to identify and name state response patterns by what triggers them since different people respond (for example, with anxiety) to different stimuli. The recognition of a repeating pattern of response as a common source state is the first step in naming and ordering state phenomena. After the pattern is recognized as a particular replicable psychophysiological response process, the stimuli that commonly trigger it in a given culture can be observed and listed as a secondary piece of information about the natural history of the given state dimension.

To complete this brief initial definition of the structure of states (Chapter Six expands on the whole matter) we need only remind ourselves that like traits they are logically cross-classifiable into (a) both surface (cluster) and source (factor) state entities, and (b) both common and unique state patterns. These concepts are summarized for convenience in Table 2 in the perspective of traits, types, and processes, although the two last need yet to be discussed to complete our overview of basic taxonomy.

5. Completion of Taxonomy by Types and Processes

After unitary traits and states any psychological taxonomy must move for completeness to a study of types and processes, as indicated in the lower part of Table 2. The main problem in regard to type is that, as shown elsewhere (Cattell, 1957), people have used it in about forty-five different ways. A class of uses that has little to recommend it outside popular speech—because other, simpler ways of handling the inherent concept exist—consists of referring to people at the poles of an asymptotic normal distribution curve as types. For example, extraverts and introverts, idiots and geniuses are made "types" instead of "scores" as illustrated in Figure 3 (a). Among a million people only two qualify, the rest being incorrectly described or subjected to type assignment by introducing some quite arbitrary cutoff point. This classification is crude because we have available the more precise alternative of giving each individual in the distributions an exact score on a single, defined trait continuum.

A true type—by any consistent use of language—is statistically a mode—a particular, discrete value or combination of values applicable to many cases, which form one of nature's "fashions," as in the case of a biological species or a product repeatedly manufactured in the same way. Thus the words *robin, blackbird,* and *gull* are useful descriptive terms because they form discrete modes and do not blend into one another statistically. However, we may find continuity of distribution on certain scores and yet have some tendency to distinct modes, as in the distribution illustrated in Figure 3(b). However, although plotting distributions and locating modes looks like a simple solution to finding types, the figure 3(b) procedure is not very apt because most type recognitions rest on several variables. And

Table 2

Taxonomic Concepts in Personality and Their Operational Bases

	Designation	*Analysis Operation Model*	*Experimental Design for Data*
Traits			
Common	Source trait	Simple-structure factor	R-technique on individual difference measures
	Surface trait	Correlation cluster	R-technique on individual difference measures
Unique	Source trait	Simple-structure factor	P-technique on growth or fluctuation in one person
	Surface trait	Correlation cluster	P-technique on growth or fluction in one person
States			
Common	Source state	Simple-structure factor	dR-technique on fluctuation measures
	Surface state	Correlation cluster	dR-technique on fluctuation measures
Unique	Source state	Simple-structure factor	P-technique on fluctuation data
	Surface state	Correlation cluster	P-technique on fluctuation data
Types			
Univariate	Modes	Modes on a distribution	
	asymptotes	Extremes on a distribution	
Multivariate	Homostats (stats)	Centroid of a group of persons all with a mutual resemblance above a given r_p	
	Segregates (aits)	Centroid of a group of overlapping stats separated from other aits by absence of overlapping stats (an "island" in person space)	
	Dendritic segregates	Segregates related as branches on a tree, in a large overall schema	

Processes

A process may be considered a characteristic type in a time sequence of measurement. It is represented by a $p \times n$ score matrix in which there are p occasions and n state or other dimensions studied in the process.

the grouping of individuals according to one variable may be quite different from that according to another. Thus grouping flowers by color and by the number of petals would yield inconsistent groupings. Consequently, as Chapter Ten illustrates, the recognition of a type must be based on a pattern of consistent modes in a whole set of variables, for example, all sixteen factors in the 16 PF. This pattern is seen in Figure 3(c).

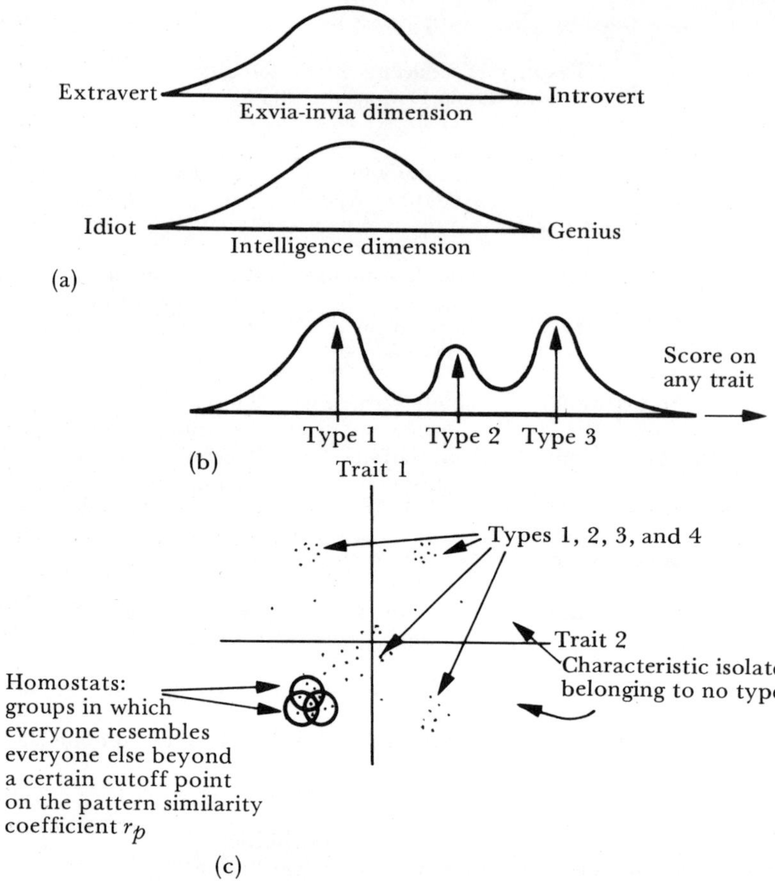

Figure 3. Taxonomy of types: (a) superfluous or rough usage of type as asymptote; (b) usage of type as mode on one variable; (c) best usage of type as multidimensional mode—a segregate—based on discovery of homostats by the taxonome program.

In its true sense then type refers to and is defined by the central tendency in a discrete group of individuals who resemble one another strongly (by the pattern similarity coefficient r_p) over *a whole pattern of scores* on independent dimensions. Moreover such a group of individuals must not merge, like one crowd straggling into another, because many of them have vaguely intermediate patterns. That is to say, if represented in two dimensions as in Figure 3(c), these people must constitute distinctly recognizable and separated clusters that can be picked out with the technical aid of a computer program, using the operational definition of a segregate. (The taxonome computer program that handles such sorting for the busy psychologist first finds homostats—stats for short—and then finds segregates —aits for short—as overlapping sets of stat (Bolz, 1972; Cattell and Coulter, 1966; Cattell, Coulter and Tsujioka, 1966). Space forbids pursuing further here the complex issues of defining and discovering segregate types by such mathematical-statistical procedures, but I hope the general concept of a type as a segregate is clear.

Table 2 shows one other basic concept necessary for psychological description and analysis—that of process. Individual difference psychology has hitherto got along mainly on concepts of traits and types, but if thoroughly treated it shares with all psychology the need also to define and recognize processes. A process is a sequence of several activities waxing and waning in a standard order over time, like the sound of instruments in a symphony. Mathematically it can be represented by the path a point weaves in multidimensional space along a time axis, the dimensions being those of stimuli and responses. Although any process is of interest and measurable, we are usually most interested in processes that characteristically repeat themselves on many occasions, either for everyone or for the sample person, with the same elements and order. Thus adolescence is a process, preparing for and going through a school examination is a process, and falling in love is a process. We already know (see Chapter Five) something about the concerted pattern of age changes on the various personality factor scales that characteristically occurs in ten years of adolescence, from 12 to 22. This understanding—or at least description—of a process rests on questionnaire measurements of traits, but, through the use of questionnaire measurements of *states,* we also know about the typical sequences of anxiety, stress, and fatigue in, say, the school examination process. According to this model the central process that constitutes this experience could be plotted by points in time-space. In short, we have theoretical and methodological resources to study processes along with traits and states to obtain a comprehensive grasp of the taxonomic quantification of human behavior.

Recognition and evaluation of the similarity of two vectors (series) of scores, whether they be sixteen different factor scores on two people or ten steps in a process apparently repeated itself twice in the same person, require calculation by the profile similarity coefficient r_p, a more exact equivalent of putting the succession of elements alongside each other to find by eye whether the patterns agree. The elements in the profile vector are either trait or state measures, depending on whether types or processes are sought.

Regardless of whether types or processes are involved, the success of such taxonomic work depends on the soundness with which the elements are measured. For example, to gain an exact concept of the developmental process of adolescence we must have questionnaires capable of measuring essentially the same traits at quite different age levels. The goal of making such a factored series available has so far been partially achieved, except for the two (adult and child) EPIS (Eysenck Personality Inventories), which unfortunately cover only three factors, only the complete IPAT (Institute for Personality and Ability Testing) series of questionnaires covering the same fourteen or more personality dimensions from five years of age to old age. These we shall examine later as the PSPQ (Pre-School Personality Questionnaire, 4–6), the ESPQ (Early School Personality Questionnaire, 6–8), the CPQ (Child Personality Questionnaire, 8–12), the HSPQ (High School Personality Questionnaire, 12–18) and the 16 PF for 18 years and older. The age trends shown on these source traits individually in Chapter Five form the basis for developmental process analysis.

The taxonomic concepts set out briefly in this chapter may be examined intensively elsewhere (Cattell, 1946b, 1957; Dreger, 1962; Eysenck, 1964; Fiske, 1971; Mahrer, 1970). The reader eager to get to substantive psychological results may indeed wonder why he is asked to pause in the first three chapters to strengthen his grasp of these theoretical concepts. I can only reply that while it is possible to go home and construct a questionnaire overnight on some arbitrarially chosen trait, this is not science. Nor is it helpful to clutter the field with such pseudoinstruments. The central theme here—that questionnaire construction should be directed to previously well-established unitary source traits—is a necessary condition for integrating measurement with dynamic theories of personality and personality development; for utilizing the power of learning and genetic laws in psychology in research and practice; for relating to clinical and other criteria; and for providing a bridge to measurements made in the other two media—L- and T-data.

6. Model for Integration of Traits in Total Personality

The psychologist entering this area should recognize that taxonomy is no mere museum exercise in classification. Taxonomy may seem at first glance only to pull the personality into pieces, losing the whole. Certainly its first goal is to find and measure as many common and unique source traits (first- and second-order) as experiment is capable of recognizing. But the second step is to proceed to a model that puts these measurements together for use in predicting and understanding the action of the total integrated personality. This integration is done centrally by using the behavior specification equation below and also by using those measures of total integration that tell us how well the specification equation operates in the given case.

It is a commonly repeated misconception that the factor analyst analyses but cannot synthesize. The same initial criticism has arisen in the early days of chemistry and physics and is a general misunderstanding of the meaning of analysis in science. Of the two integrative concepts just mentioned the basic one is the specification equation (below) which tells us with what weights—b's, called behavioral indices—to put the components of personality together in predicting and understanding any act of the total personality. The trait and state scores are those of the given individual; the weights are universal. The second and modifying principle is that a trait of sheer capacity to integrate must be introduced to say how well the specification equation will work in a given case, leading either to action of the kind indicated or to partial dispersal in anxiety. These two parts of the model apply, of course, without regard to the particular medium of trait measurement—Q-, L- or T-data—being use. They are general laws of personality.

In the behavioral specification equation (or simply behavioral equation) any act, response, performance, or decision is estimated for a given individual by taking his personal score on each of the known source traits and weighting it according to its peculiar importance for the given criterion behavior.[6] These contributions from the various traits are then simply added together. Thus, to make an estimate of an individual i's score on a performance or act j, the behavioral equation is

$$a_{ij} = b_{j1}T_{1i} + b_{j2}T_{2i} + \ldots + b_{jk}T_{ki} + b_jT_{ji} \qquad (1.1)$$

where there are k source traits, written serially as T_i through T_k, giving the individual's standard score on each of the k traits. The k weights written as bs to express that they are behavioral indices, are the factor pattern loadings given by a factor analysis. They can also be obtained from correlating T scores—for example, surgency, intelligence, exvia, anxiety—as a questionnaire or test scale, with the given performance or response a_j of individuals (over the whole series of people). Thus if Smith's score on intelligence is +1.5 (in standard score, that is, an IQ of about 124) and on ego strength is −1.0 in standard score), and the weights—bs—for these on j (say, freedom from automobile accidents) are respectively +0.2 and +0.7, then from these measures alone our estimate of his accident-proneness would be $a_j = 0.2 \times 1.5 + 0.7 \times -1.0 = -0.4$. A standard score of −0.4 on proneness means that he is a better than average risk. T_j is a specific trait, not mentioned in this calculation.

As will be seen when we come to experiment, the result of appropriately adding weighted scores on the 16 PF questionnaire scale in such specification equations is that we predict the resultant behavior tolerably well. In statistical terms the specification equation belongs to the class of *multiple correlations,* which sum up, like an ordinary correlation, into statements of how much of the criterion is predicted. Depending on the criterion the multiple R from personality factor Q measures inserted in the specification equation has a range from about 0.2 to 0.8. As the various educational and clinical criteria in Chapter Ten show, the results today bring psychology within the circle of effective applied sciences. Of course, every psychologist recognizes that the specification equation—in mathematical terms a *linear* and *additive* model—does not always tell the whole story. Relations of increments of traits to increments of performance may sometimes be curvilinear. The model is thus simplified relative to reality so that psychologists can handle it readily in calculation. For example, the specification equation may be in some cases a linear approximation to a nonlinear relation; school performance may not go on steadily increasing with increase in intelligence. Indeed, we know (Cattell, 1941, 1957) that motor-perceptual rigidity is related in curvilinear fashion to the ego strength

[6] A complete study of the stimulus-response prediction equation requires a taxonomy of situations balancing that of the present taxonomy of persons studied by trait. The brevity of my reference here to situations does not mean I am underestimating the importance of a taxonomy of cultural situations but am leaving the reader to study it later; first in Chapter Eight and then elsewhere (Sells, 1963). Actually the bs in Equation (1.1) are statements about the nature of the stimulus situation. It is, for example, an intelligence-demanding situation if the b_j for stimulus-response j is large and positive on the intelligence source trait T_g; it is an emotional-stability-demanding situation if the behavior index (b or loading) is high on the ego-strength factor C.

source trait, so that lower ego strength is associated with both very high and very low rigidity. However, instances that require equation (1.1) to be changed to a polynomial form are quite uncommon. Several studies have shown, moreover, that we usually do not improve significantly by going nonlinear and introducing T^2 or T^3 or such products as $(T_a\ T_b)$ into the equation.

The chief reasons why some psychologists have reached relatively disappointing multiple correlation magnitudes with the specification equation are: (1) Stopping at only three to ten trait factors when all the evidence points to twenty to thirty being necessary for completeness of survey of personality and ability, and (2) The conservatism of some psychometric schools in disregarding *states* (temporary emotions, moods) over and above *traits*. The latter, which is remedied in Chapter Six below, requires us to take stock of state terms from the beginning in the specification equation if we are not to start with false premises. Thus the behavioral equation (1.1) must immediately be extended as follows:

$$a_{ij} = b_{j1}T_{1i} + \ldots + b_{jk}T_{ki} + b_jT_{ji} + b_{js1}S_{1i} + \ldots + b_{jsp}S_{pi} \qquad (1.2)$$

where p state scores S_i through S_p—for example, anxiety, fatigue, arousal—are taken into account over and above the $(k + 1)$ trait terms. It should now be evident why "personality and mood," indicating concern with both trait and state, enter the title of this book.

7. Summary

(1) The questionnaire is one of three possible media for the observation and measurement of personality, hereafter called Q-, L-, and T-data realms of measurement.

(2) Measurement in psychology is pointless and can get lost in an infinity of arbitrary trait notions unless the psychologists' scales are aimed at meaningful unitary structures—source traits and states—first established by correlations on experimental observations and forming part of general personality theory.

(3) A comprehensive taxonomy established on such an operational basis must include four main types of structure—traits, states, processes, and species types. Traits must be recognized as existing operationally as surface and source, common and unique, broad and specific; and we recognize parallel categories for states.

(4) Unitary state dimensions are to be recognized and verified as independent internal *state response patterns* by longitudinal experiments over occasions either by P-technique or dR-technique (single-person analysis or differential analysis). In form these parallel the familiar R-technique done on individual differences over people. The formal equivalence arises from substituting different stimulus occasions for different people in the data score matrix.

(5) The behavior of the total personality is predicted from the integration of the trait and state score in the total *behavioral specification equa-*

tion. Here the combination of a vector of individual scores (*T*s and *S*s) with a vector of behavioral indices (*b*s) peculiar to the given act estimates the individual's standard score on the given response act or performance. Later this score needs to be qualified by an expression for the individual's degree of personality integration.

II

Research Basis of the Primary Source Traits in Normal Adults

As we now turn to the light thrown on personality structures by many years of research, let us not forget our frame of reference. What is revealed in questionnaire analyses is only one leg of the tripod of Q-, L-, and T-data, and our basic theoretical concepts must always be referred to support from all three. In concentrating first on Q-data I am not joining the school of thought—or unthought—that continues to handle questionnaires wholely by questionnaire item analyses, as if no other evidence had to be considered. However, the questionnaire evidence itself must be sufficiently strong and sufficiently consistent if it is to play its part.

1. A Brief History of the Diversity of Questionnaire Development

To the confusion of the student, a shocking disparity undeniably exists between the ideal application of multivariate experimental concepts in strategic and programatic research and what has happened in questionnaire development over the last 50 years.

The intense activity in questionnaire construction in the twenties, thirties, and forties of this century took little note of the taxonomic and theoretical canons discussed in the preceding chapter. Researchers proliferated questionnaires for ad hoc, applied psychological purposes, and although they learned much about item construction, the effect of various answer systems, the calculation of scale homogeneities and reliabilities, and even something about "social desirability" distortions—much of this learning falling in that branch of psychometrics which may be called *itemetrics*—they contributed next to nothing to structural concepts.

No one would object to these methods insofar as they aimed at special scales for predicting specific performances—for example, success as a janitor, performance as a machine-gunner, freedom from road accidents. But a fair amount of work by these methods purported to be a contribution to personality theory and to the study of the genesis and development of personality traits. Unfortunately few joined such men as Burt, Eysenck, Flanagan, French, Gibb, Guilford, Mosier, Reyburn, Thurstone, Vernon, and my colleagues (see summary in Cattell, 1957, 1965a) in the realization that one could not arbitrarily take some trait word out of the dictionary or some favorite idea from one's mind and assume it—without investigation—to be a unitary, independent, operationally-identifiable trait structure. Countless scales were based on current fashions ("authoritarianism") or on special preoccupations (notions such as "intropunitiveness" and "self-realizing capacity"). To some extent these scales still mingle with the present flow of research, just as Stone Age implements continued for centuries into the Bronze Age. These comments are no denial of the importance of inspiration. They suggest only that inspiration should take off from a higher level of technical knowhow than exists in popular psychology and that it should be verifiable against results in an exact model. The alert reader must examine for himself the credentials of various questionnaires that are still popular, and he must not be surprised to find that some of them rest on no original correlation work demonstrating that the alleged scale is even a surface trait, let alone a source trait.

In 1945 when I surveyed the field for my 1946 book on the subject, the popular questionnaires were Wadsworth (1933), Woodsworth's Personal Data Sheet (1938), Maslow's "dominance" test (1940), C. R. Rogers' child adjustment items (1939), Strong's Interest Test (1943), Bernreuter's "social behavior patterns" (1935–1938), Bell's Adjustment Inventory (1934–1939), Allport's Ascendence-Submission Scale (1928), and many others—none of which claimed to be, or could be considered, a factored test (Cattell, 1946b). In the following ten years, however, several important questionnaires on an extensive factor-analytic basis appeared: the Guilford-Zimmerman Questionnaire (1949–1955), the Cattell 16 PF (1949b), and the Thurstone Temperament Schedule (1949–1953), as well as Remmers and Schimberg's SRA Junior Inventory (1956–1960). In this creative midcentury moment the well-known MMPI also appeared (Hathaway and McKinley, 1951), which, although not factored, had a definite, objective, statistical rationale intended to obtain maximum separation of clinical groups. Other questionnaires appeared, many based purely on clinical insights: Mooney's Problem Check

List (1950), Gough's well-known California Personality Inventory (1957), and a host of lesser instruments now disappeared—though replaced each year by fresh crops of arbitrary scales.

Between that decade and the present, several important factored instruments appeared, notably the Comrey scales (1970); the Edwards Personal Preference Schedule (1957b); Dielman, Coan, and Cattell's Early School Personality Questionnaire (1973); Eysenck's EPI (formerly MPI scales, 1959); D. N. Jackson's PRI Scales (1966); Porter, Cattell, and Schaie's Child Personality Questionnaire (1966); Sells and Cattell's Clinical Analysis Questionnaire (Cattell and Sells, 1973); Barratt's Impulsivity Scales; Byrne's Repression and Sensitization Scales (1961); Schutz's FIKO Scales (1957); Stark's Polyfactorial Study of Personality (1959); Shostrom's Personal Orientation Inventory (1966); Rotter's Internal and External Control Scale (1966); the Triadal Equated Personality Inventory (United Consultants, 1963); and so on—in all, probably over two hundred printed "scales."

Sells and Demaree have attempted the gargantuan task of correlating some 134 such scales (1972) to see what this endless crop of scales around arbitrary concepts might mean in terms of the unitary factorial source traits that are represented in them. Harman and French (1972) have similarly breasted the unrelenting deluge with an attempt at a representative factoring. I am prepared to hypothesize that they will all be encompassed by the 23 normal (and possibly some of the 12 abnormal) source traits derived from programatic personality structure research, most of which were carefully defined in the literature before these publications began. For example, Byrne's Repression versus Sensitization Scale has been shown in a factorial study by Pieszko (1967) to contain nothing that is not already defined by the general second-order anxiety factor, QII. However, it is close to and a good measure of this factor, whereas preliminary correlations suggest that this is not true of some other such arbitrary scales. The latter lie in the comprehensively defined space of the factored scales, but they seem unlikely to be clear measures of any *one* of the uniquely rotated primaries.

Decades do not define stages in technical development since obsolete procedures have a habit of persisting in backwaters. But by and large the period from 1960 to the present has been marked by acceptance of the need to demonstrate the unitary structure of the trait before constructing a scale for it, as was stressed by Thurstone, Guilford, and myself in our scale constructions of the late 1940s. Although Edwards' EPPS (1957b) was based on the arbitrary need categories of Murray and others (1938)—a type of test construction that Goldberg (1972b) oddly calls rational scale design, although nothing could be more irrational than subjectivity in science—it came in for factoring, as also did the MMPI and some of the earlier arbitrary scales. But more encouraging, several scales appeared in this decade for which the personality structure research had reached reasonable consummation: the Comrey scales (1970), Dielman, Coan, and Cattell's Early School Personality Questionnaire (ESPQ) (1973), Porter and Cattell's Child Personality Questionnaire (CPQ) (1959), Eysenck and Eysenck's EPI (1963) (formerly MPI, 1959), the High School Personality Questionnaire, and Sells and Cattell's Clinical Analysis Questionnaire, which rests on the analyses of clinical structure by Delhees 1971). Important advances were also made by several factorings of questionnaires that did not lead to questionnaires, as in the work of Adcock and Adcock (1972), Sells, Demaree, and Will (1970), Eber (1967), and Harman and French (mentioned above).

At present we therefore have a great variety of Q-data instruments, some factored, some unfactored, some doing their best to integrate with general personality theory, some concentrating on sheer internal itemetric properties regardless of wider theory, some special-purpose and oriented to one concrete "applied" criterion, and some general-purpose and oriented to basic traits and states. Any conscientious psychologist who delves into the two volumes of the 1972 *Mental Measurement Yearbook* will probably be overwhelmed by the number of alternative instruments; but, more relevantly, he will be absolutely appalled at the mutually contradictory, inaccurate, and often theoretically obsolete criteria (for example, those of itemetrics alone or of high homogeneity) by which the reviewers seek to sort out the significance and well-researched instruments from the rest.

At first sight—if one desires progress in the methods of objective, operational, factor-analytic research, leading to the concept system of the last chapter—it is disappointing to find that some reviewers make the confusion seem as prevalent among the factored scales as among others. As I hope to show in this book, however, the methodological means and criteria exist to proceed in the factored domain to testable common concepts; and the findings of a dozen or so of the most careful and sophisticated investigators, covering the most important questionnaires in use, are about to awake from this illogical nightmare by offering decidedly more clear and convergent results.

2. Definition of the Present Field of Study: Principles of Selection.

Noting my emphasis on the nature and variety of existing questionnaires, the reader may ask whether this book is to be concerned with questionnaires as such or with personality theory as illuminated by and expressed in questionnaires. The answer already indicated is that the second is my concern: the nature of personality and mood structure as it shows itself in questionnaires, but aided by such broader evidence as comes from L- and T-data. Beyond basic theory I aim also to explain how questionnaires may be used in both basic research and the applied psychology of schools, industry, and clinics.

Several excellent and comprehensive volumes are available—notably those of Anastasi (1961), Buros (1972), Dunnette (1966), Ghiselli (1966), Kleinmuntz (1967), Nunnally (1959, 1967), Thorndike and Hagen (1955)—for those who want an extensive cataloging of all types of test. Consequently, I can afford here, without accusation of arbitrary bias, to concentrate only on the outstanding examples that indicate the theoretical development.

To anticipate and justify the selection that must occur in realizing this aim, let me be explicit about the criteria to be applied.

(1) Dependence on Nonsubjective, Correlational-Experimental Personality Concepts. My concern is with factored tests only—or at least tests that have criteria other than definition of a scale by fiat; or, alternatively, by collection of items that show only high internal itemetric homogeneity about some arbitrary special-purpose criterion. As Ashton and Goldberg (1972), Dawes, and others have shown, an arbitrary scale defined by a trait term and a set of items can have items written for it by nonprofessional, item-writers—items that are on the average as valid as those written by professionals. It is questionable whether the same holds true for trait concepts rooted in theoretical understanding of personality structure. But the fact that items can be successfully written does show that acceptance of a concept is no guarantee that it is a factorially pure trait. If we drop such unfactored tests (as is inevitable in good psychometric practice) we lose mainly little-known and obsolescent tests but also one or two well-known ones such as the CPI. Unfortunately it does not help much if such tests, for example, the Bernreuter or the Humm-Wadsworth, get factored after they have been constructed and are in use. The result is by no means the same as when they are designed from the beginning on objective structural concepts. Such exclusions leave us to study, among leading tests, mainly Comrey's Eight Factor Questionnaire, Edwards' PPI, Eysenck's EPI, the Guilford-Zimmerman, the IPAT questionnaires (16 PF, HSPQ, CPQ, and others), the MMPI, Jackson's PRI, Thorndike's questionnaire, and Thurstone's Temperament Schedule. Unfortunately we can have little to say about Thurstone's and R. L. Thorndike's questionnaires because psychologists have not done the research to link them to any other questionnaires with factor matchings, as Gibbons (1966) did for the Guilford-Zimmerman scales and the 16 PF or Specht for the 16 PF and the MMPI. Undoubtedly these links will soon be sought with the central patterns and scales I hope to clarify here.

(2) Exclusion of Ability and Interest Modalities as Unsuitable for Questionnaires. Althought my concern is with general personality and mood, readers might well ask whether I can extend my survey of questionnaire measurements to ability and interest motivation. Psychologists have long accepted the division of traits into three modalities: (1) abilities, (2) temperament (or general personality) traits, and (3) dynamic traits (or interests). A precise operational theory has been suggested elsewhere for distinguishing them (Cattell and Warburton, 1967). Any particular behavior is commonly determined by traits from all three modalities, but the traits we extract can be wholly of one modality; on common-sense grounds psychologists have little difficulty in agreeing on these modalities, although the operational distinction is subtle (Cattell and Warburton, 1967). The basic question at this point is: For which of these modalities is the questionnaire a suitable measuring device? Obviously not for the first modality: one cannot depend on a man's being prepared to report that he is of below-average intelligence; nor would he be able to state his percentile score on a test of spatial or verbal ability with much validity. (We have tried this, and item validities around

0.2 can generally be obtained.) However, no psychologist seems seriously to have proposed that we measure abilities by Q-data rather than T-data.

But it has not been so frankly recognized that the questionnaire may be almost as unsuitable for measuring interest strength as it is for measuring ability level. Everyday life shows that people's self-conscious estimates of their interest and motivational strengths are apt to be wildly inaccurate when compared with subsequent performance. Further, in the light of what psychologists assume about the Freudian censor and the unconscious, as well as the folk wisdom of a familiar French proverb about the aim of words being to hide our intentions, common sense must conclude that if people did know the strengths of their drives, intentions, and interests they would still be unwilling to disclose them. The distortions that we know exist in the personality questionnaire, and shall study later, are almost certainly larger in the modality of interests and motivations.

Fortunately the research that shows this has at the same time led to better ways than the questionnaire to measure motivational strength. The work of Burdsal (In preparation), Horn (1966a), Krug (1971), Cattell, Radcliffe and Sweney (1963, 1967), Cattell, Kawash and DeYoung (1972), and many others (see summaries in Cattell, Horn, Radcliffe, and Sweney, 1964, and in Cattell and DeYoung, 1973b,c), has compared the validities of over a hundred different objective devices for measuring motivational strength and has shown that the half dozen most valid are almost as simple to administer, even to groups, as the questionnaire. They are also more valid than any inventory, for the typical self-evaluation of interest strength in a questionnaire correlates only about 0.3 to 0.4 with the total of the many motivation-testing devices that psychologists have considered. Compared with the battery of objective interest measures built into the MAT (the IPAT Motivation Analysis Test) and the SMAT (School Motivation Analysis Test), the inventory approach could thus be accounting for a bare 10 to 20 percent of the total real interest variance.

From the substantial research with the MAT and SMAT against a variety of real-life criteria by Butcher, Burdsal, Barton, Bartsch, Dielman, DeYoung, Sweney, and others (see references in Cattell and Child, 1973), it seems that these properties of greater reliability and concept validity in the *objective* devices continue to show themselves also in predicting life criteria (Horn, 1966a; Sweney, 1967). The difference between the questionnaire and the objective-test approaches to interest measurement is one of dependability of scores, not one of structures. As far as can be ascertained from the labels of the authors and the item content itself, the factorings of interest based on inventory responses by Guilford and others (1954), Kuder (1953), Edwards (1957a,b), and Jackson (1966) do yield concepts essentially congruent (see Cattell, 1957, as far as Guilford's results are concerned) with those based on objective tests in the MAT (Cattell, Horn, Sweney, and Radcliffe, 1964), the SMAT (Sweney, Cattell, and Krug, 1970), and the Child Motivational Analysis Test (Burdsal and Cattell, In preparation, 1973). However, the factorial techniques in some of the former—for example, orthogonal rotations and no test for number of factors in several cases—are such that precise mutual alignments of concepts would scarcely be expected. The next problem therefore is not that questionnaires give the wrong structure in interests, but that they are too vulnerable to motivational distortion and other sources of invalidity. By definition the traits in motivation and interest are different from those of general personality. People can have the same personalities with totally different interests; Eysenck, for example, has shown that extreme radicals and conservatives resemble one another in personality more than they resemble the group with middle-of-the-road political beliefs. Conversely, people can have the same interest fixations with very different personalities. The source traits in personality are fully discussed below. Those in the dynamic motivation domain are the drives or ergs (for example, sex, fear, curiosity) and the sentiments (such as attachment to home, career, country, sports, a hobby). Only when dynamic traits cease to be attachments to objects and ergic goals and become complex systems of check and control, do they achieve the status of general personality characteristics, as in the psychoanalytic ego and superego concepts. It is precisely these two factors—the *C* and *G* factors in the 16 PF questionnaire, and the corresponding ego and superego strength factors in the MAT—that correlate sufficiently across these different media to suggest that they are the same entities.

In the realm of questionnaires, the Edwards PPI, the Jackson PRI, and the Kuder Interest Test are the principal instruments seeking dynamic measures. All three have exemplary bases, except that Edwards and Jackson accept Murray's arbitrary needs (why not McDougall's, Freud's, Robach's, or Drever's, all on the same pre-MAT basis?), whereas Kuder rests on a straight factor analysis. As Anastasi (Buros, 1972) points out, Jackson's scales have faultless itemetric properties, although Edwards' scoring is on an ipsative basis, thus producing spurious (negative) correlations among the scale scores. However, because this book is concerned with general personality traits, I do not include these scales systematically in my survey. They belong to the measurement of interest and motivational strength (Cattell and Child, 1973). Every thorough study to date has shown that (with the exception of ego and superego dynamic structures) the general personality and the dynamic interest modalities are in factor-space domains as distinct as those of the personality factors and the ability factors.[1] For example, both Cattell and

[1] My rejection of the questionnaire as a means of measuring abilities will be gainsaid by few psychologists, and casts doubt on no great investments. But my indicting of it as a means of measuring strength of interest, attitudes and dynamic traits collides with much vested construction research, in such instruments as the Allport-Vernon-Lindzey Study of Values, the Edwards PPI, Jackson's PRI (1966), the Kuder Preference Blank (1953), the Strong Interest Blank (1943) and several other more or less accepted uses. The reason's for doubting the validity of people's statements about their own motivations are obvious to a psychoanalyst, and have been demonstrated to reach no better than a 0.3 to 0.4 validity by Cattell, Radcliffe, and Sweney (1963). Incidentally, validities of this order have been obtained for questionnaire self-evaluations of intelligence, which no psychometrist will use! However, the main argument for rejecting measurement of need strength by questionnaire as a practical procedure is that decidedly better and less fakable means are available in *objective* methods, as used in the Motivation Analysis Test (Cattell and Horn, 1964), the School Motivation Analysis Test (Sweney, Cattell,

Butcher (1968) and Barton, Dielman, and Cattell (1971) have shown that factor measures for the ability, the personality, and the motivational-interest modalities are in virtually uncorrelated domains. Furthermore, this noncorrelation agrees with the finding that each modality contributes about one-fourth of the variance in school achievement, so that a multiple correlation using the three adds up to nearly three-fourths of the observed variance. The operational means whereby the dictionary definitions of ability, motive, and personality can be brought to objectively separable concepts are set out elsewhere (Cattell and Warburton, 1967).

Osgood's semantic differential approach to evaluating persons and

---

and Krug, 1970) and the Family Attitude Measure. The research bases for this conclusion are set out in Horn (1966) and Cattell and Child (1973). As a tentative hypothesis at this stage of research I would suggest that the second order factors coming out of primary dynamic trait factor measures are personality traits. That is to say, personality variance contributes to expressions of dynamic, interest traits as commonly measured. The support for this is Nesselroade and Baltes (1972), finding that the second order factors in Jackson's PRI approach those long established in the HSPQ and 16 PF.

Although Chapter Ten deals with the additive action of personality questionnaires with measures of motivation in general prediction, the field of personality and temperament factors itself is nowadays so large that motivation per se must be excluded.

The reader who wishes to go beyond the brief "boundary interaction" inquiries in this book is referred to my *Abilities: Their Structure, Growth and Action* (1971a). In regard to interaction with dynamic structures, there are now intensive and extensive experimental analyses by Delhees (1968), Horn (1966a), Cattell, Radcliffe, and Sweney (1963), Guilford (1959), Cattell and Child (1973), Cattell and Butcher (1968), Dielman, Barton, and Cattell (1971), and many others with less rigorous models. We may pause to glance at this list long enough to note that the programatic interlocking research of Barton, Bartsch, Burdsal, Butcher, Child, Delhees, Dielman, Horn, Radcliffe, Sweney, and others has led to the conclusion that interest measures can be consistently resolved into about 12 basic drives (technically ergs), such as sex, fear, hunger, gregariousness, and curiosity, and an indefinite number of acquired sentiments, depending on the culture (home, career, country, and so on). But these drives and sentiments must be measured by objective tests, for despite every corrective device that can be added, the questionnaire approach to motivation is likely to be inferior to the objective test approach.

Osgood's semantic differential as a personality measurement device is also omitted from any extensive consideration here. In the semantic differential approach the nature of the associations that the subject is asked to make, for example, "good" or "strong" or "weak" to specific terms, makes any subsequent factor analysis essentially an isolation of value dimensions. This devise is no inquiry about the individual's behavior, but only an oblique study of his feeling reactions to a variety of objects and concepts (see Chapter Seven). As such, it should yield components somewhere between the esthetic values and the primary emotion dimensions. Furthermore, to the extent that choice of variables and rotation procedures approaches the latter, the same dimensions should be found in reactions to objects (such as tiger, girl, night) as to trait objects (such as courage, miserliness). Such a nonspecific dimensionality in fact is what accumulating evidence seems to show. It is perhaps for this reason that the semantic differential is omitted from the comprehensive survey of personality tests in the *Seventh Mental Measurement Yearbook* (1972). A sound factor-analytic check on the number of dimensions required in the semantic differential appears never to have been made. Any score therefore belongs in the domain of feeling, which, as part of the dynamic-interest modality, is not included in this book (see, however, Cattell and Child, 1973). Curiously no attempt has been made to relate the semantic differential scores to the main dimensions of personality in the 16 PF, HSPQ, Comrey, Eysenck, and Guilford scales.

objects (Osgood, 1962), must also be considered an attempt at evaluating the subject's affective (interest, value) reactions to the object, rather than the description of the person in terms of his own inherent standards, which we seek here.

(3) Emphasis on Programatic Research. It is scientific practice to attempt to refer to all published data. While observing this principle, anyone familiar with the present state of the field will recognize that—like, say, chemistry in the eighteenth century—psychology is in a phase of such variance of technical standards and methodological fremeworks that integration in a true sense (excluding the lip service often paid in survey articles) is possible only within a moderately sized subset of technically coordinated research. Even within factor-analytic experimentation, there are so many different possibilities of approximation that, for example, orthogonal rotations should not and cannot yield the same results as those of maximum simple-structure oblique rotations.

Equally important is the use of common marker variables, variables that in past research have been highly loaded on particular factors. Without them experiments are isolated. Systematic, programatic research of the kind indicated above and shown to be capable of integrating action has developed only in two or three laboratories in this generation. My colleagues form one such integrating laboratory. I hope that no carping spirit will take advantage of this historical situation to accuse me of a disproportionate emphasis on this programatic work accomplished, with enormous labor, by some forty researchers in various parts of the world working on the integrated development of the 16 PF, HSPQ, CPQ, ESPQ, PSPQ, and other interrelated trait and state scales. Guilford and Zimmerman, Thurstone, Eysenck and Eysenck, Comrey, and a few others (including Nesselroade, Curran, and Barton on states) alone offer similar systematic work based on common and careful standards suitable for an integrative survey. One-shot (or even three-shot) studies without replication, without tests of invariance, and without bridging studies to the work of others (such as that which Sells, Demaree, and Will; Specht; Hundleby; and others have valiantly performed) will get us nowhere in this area.

(4) Relation to General Personality Theory. One mystery that some historian may eventually explain is the division that still persists between psychometrists and personality theorists. The neglect of quantitative, psychometric evidence by personality theorists has been perhaps sufficiently pilloried in my books; this neglect of the evidence extended from the heyday of Freudian, Jungian, Adlerian, and Allportian insouciance in the 1930s and 1940s to now. However under such impacts and the launching of quantitative, experimental personality journals this neglect has steadily diminished. On the other side, the indifference of supposedly scientifically trained psychometrists to theory is harder to explain. One guesses that this indifference may be due to (1) their largely mathematical training, which makes them satisfied with mathematical models and solutions and even mere computer procedures, regardless of wider psychological considerations, and (2) the growth in psychometry of purely technical games with questionnaire items—statistical games that I have called itemetrics (Cattell, 1957; 1966a). What is missing is the comprehensive, flexible, and meaningful use of mathematical models that constitutes true psychometrics and relates to personality theory. Defect (1) shows itself in such assertions as that unrotated and rotated factors are equally acceptable; defect (2) appears in antlike industry intended to produce numerous highly homogeneous, "reliable" scales, regardless of their meaning in validities, the fitness of the questionnaire to measure the traits concerned, or their standing as concepts in the light of clinical, physiological learning and social psychological evidence.

The positions of Barton, Coan, Comrey, Dielman, Digman, Delhees, Dreger, Eber, Eysenck, Horn, Howard, Meredith, Nesselroade, Schaie, Schmidt, Schneewind, Sells, and myself, to name a few who have written on personality theory in relation to factored questionnaire scales, stand in marked contrast to the bulk of psychometric literature on questionnaires. The four principles above constitute the rationale for greater attention to some developments than others.

3. Some Necessary Common Technical Foundations of Factor Analytic Experiments: The Personality Sphere

The reader with only an introductory education in psychological statistics has been promised that he can read this book without having to master factor-analytic computations, provided that he knows the principles. However, in all science considerable differences of theoretical opinion can hang on some precise technicality—as Einstein's relativity did on the Michelson-Morley result or very exact measures of the transit of Mercury. Similarly, certain disputes on first- and second-order factor theory between Eysenck and me, or between Howarth and Browne concerning the very existence of such dimensions as surgency, ego strength, and ergic tension can be explained and settled only by resorting to complex technical points. Thus I intend to devote the remainder of this chapter to the technical foundations of the main conclusions to be drawn later.

The issues that come up for debate most often in the discovery and definition of unitary traits by questionnaire are the following: (1) Was the choice of the original pool of items adequate? Was it biased? Was it guided by some basic principle, such as that of the personality sphere? (2) Was the design of the factor analysis itself adequate, with respect to person sampling, decision on number of factors, communalities, objectivity, and uniqueness of rotational resolution? (3) Was the result of the factor analysis checked for invariance of pattern against other research in a programatic plan with the same variables? And as part of this programatic quality was it examined for consistency of its second-order factors, its agreement with L- and T-data factors, and some demonstration of independent characteristics of the source traits in manipulative and developmental studies?

These requirements will be examined shortly, but first I must deal with a basic point: the adequacy of the factor-analytic model itself for the data and the expected theory. Little discussion is necessary because critics of the method have been answered fully during the past thirty years (Spearman, 1927; Thurstone, 1938; Harman, 1967; Cattell, 1952), although such criticism perennially recurs, for example, in the paper by Lykken (1972).

First, it is admitted that the relation of factors to variables and to one another could be to some degree curvilinear, instead of linear. Curvilinear relations are demonstrably infrequent, but if they occur, factor analysis gives only a first approximation to the pattern of entities. These patterns of determiners then have to be sharpened by being examined separately in their relations to variables, by nonfactor methods, in the usual successive approximations of science. Thus both the factor score and the form of the specification equation (Chapter One may need to be modified after their initial discovery with the aid of factor analysis.

Second, the critic may object that simple structure alone is not proof that the factors correspond to causal influences. True, this is only a probability. Confactor rotation (Cattell and DeYoung, 1973a) and ordinary bivariate manipulative experiment may be needed for further support. An apparent primary factor could conceivably be a product of other factors (see Chapter Four). Theory must here admit two or three main possibilities. However, as Eysenck has well said in his criticism of Burt, the concept of factors merely as classificatory principles is one interpretation that misses the most important use. That factors are sometimes—perhaps generally—determiners or causes is shown by the factoring of physical data "plasmodes" by Cattell and Dickman (1962), Cattell and Gorsuch (1963), Cattell and Sullivan (1962), and Coan (1959).

Many criticisms of the limitations of fit of factor analysis to conceivable needs of personality theory apply only to the earlier, unimaginative, and undeveloped use of factor analysis. The critics are here in agreement with my strictures on "mathematician's" factor analysis. But when the scientific model of factor analysis is concerned, with the flexible use of P-, dR-, and other special techniques, and with the special conditions of simple structure and confactor rotation, the issue is entirely different. Besides, the critics have no substitute to offer, in clinical observation or bivariate research, that will find source-trait structures as efficiently as factor analysis does (Cattell, 1966a).

One hardy annual with the critics is the assertion that you get out of factor analysis only what you put in. That is, you don't find the possibly important relations existing among variables that you neglected to put in. Unfortunately no form of science—not even traditional bivariate experiment—can claim the conjuring trick of proving relations to exist among variables it has not used. All one can say is that one covers the field of possible relations more quickly by multivariate than bivariate experiment (Cattell, 1966a). This criticism is a boomerang. However, the issue does alert us to the first requirement in a good factor-analytic experiment: proper sampling.

(1) Sampling of People and Variables. What needs to be said about the sampling of people has been covered in a hundred textbooks. One needs to note only two points: that special selections will yield the same factors though with changes of pattern (except in covariance terms: Cattell, 1970a, 1972a), relative variance, and intercorrelation; and that the number of people sampled should bear a relation (ratios from 2:1 to 5:1 as minima have been suggested) to the number of variables.

The sampling of variables in experiments to find the main questionnaire factors needs more discussion. In a hypothesis-testing use of factor analysis one will choose them according to hypotheses. In a representative experiment—and this is the real beginning, to create the hypotheses later to be tested—one will seek some principle to define a total population of human behavior from which items are to be set up in a stratified sample. The principal systematic contributions to representative sampling have been made by Allport and Odbert (1936), Burt (1940), Brunswik (1956), Cattell (1946b, 1957), Kaiser (1960), and Sells (1962). In regard to personality, the solution proposed 30 years ago has been the personality sphere, and a good deal of programatic experimentation has been based on it. Its basis can be either (1) the language of the dictionary (the total of personality-describing words has altered little in the nearly four hundred years since Shakespeare) or (2) behavior time sampling in our culture, round the clock. Beginning with (1) and using Allport and Odbert's (1936) approximately 4000-word list from the dictionary, I reduced them by objective steps described elsewhere first to 180 terms (1946) and then by correlation to a standard rating checklist of 45 (1957). These terms seem to yield a factor dimensionality of 12 or more (perhaps extending to 16 or 17), according to the precision of ratings (Coan and Cattell, 1958; Cattell and Digman, 1964; Cattell and Gruen, 1953; Peterson and Cattell, 1958, 1959; Hammond, 1965, 1973; Kelly and Fiske, 1951; Norman, 1963; and Tupes, 1957).

To switch the personality sphere "map" from L-data to Q- and T-data certain transformations obviously have to take place, although the transformation from L- to Q-, standing in the verbal domain on both sides, is easier than from T- to L- or Q-. In essence, but not entirely, the questionnaire personality sphere for what I call the IPAT questionnaires (the PSPQ, ESPQ, CPQ, HSPQ, 16 PF, 16 PF Supplement, CAQ, and CTASK) [2] rests partly on this dictionary personality sphere (Allport and Odbert, 1936) simply translated into questionnaire items. (Precisely what this means can be misunderstood. Howarth and Browne (1971a, 1971b) suppose that the factors in Q-data are made to emerge by taking the markers from factors in L-data. Even if such actual high markers were taken, the questionnaire would still be free to go to its own unique resolution. Taking all the personality-sphere variables, however, leaves the dimensionality and the par-

[2] These questionnaires, for future reference, are the 12–factor PSPQ (Preschool Personality Questionnaire) 4–6 years, by Dreger and others; the 13–factor ESPQ (Early (Child Personality Questionnaire) 8–12 years, by Schaie and Porter; the 14–factor HSPQ (High School Personality Questionnaire) 12–18 years, by Cattell and Cattell; the 16–factor 16 PF 18–70 years, by Cattell, Eber, and Tatsuoka; the 6–factor 16 PF Supplement 18–70 years, by Cattell and Marshall; the 28–factor CAQ (Clinical Analysis Questionnaire), by Cattell and Sells; the 8–factor CTSQ Kit (Central Trait State Questionnaire; second order), by Barton and Cattell; and the 10–factor OATQ (Objective Analytic Trait Questionnaire), by Cattell and Vaughan.

ticular factor resolution to move to whatever is appropriate in the Q-data domain itself.)

In the end there is no other guarantee that the sphere has been fully explored than to explore it until one reaches diminishing returns. Thus the 16 to 19 dimensions found in 1949 have increased to 23 normal behavior dimensions and 12 abnormal ones. However, the personality sphere also contains a guard against "stretching" areas disproportionately, for by multiplying questionnaire items in some narrow area it would be possible to create artificial broad factors called bloated specifics. The history of the IPAT personality sphere set of items goes beyond the dictionary basis to a second check within psychology itself. In 1945 my *Description and Measurement of Personality* surveyed all questionnaire scales and research published to that date and made a best estimate that some 23 factors of the 90 singly reported in various research looked as if they had some replication and evidence of being independent, distinct dimensions. Accordingly, although in theory I expected these to be covered by the personality sphere representatives already provided, at least three markers for each were added to the proposed pool from which basic factoring was to begin. Finally, as described in Chapter Three, items from abnormal behavior were added 20 years later, and they proved to subtend 12 further factors. Since the initial pool of 1948, items have also been added to this basic adult pool from patterns becoming apparent in the factoring carried on over the same period throughout the child age range. In round numbers, between 8000 and 10,000 items have at some time been examined in the past 25 years of research on the 16 PF CAQ, HSPQ, CPQ, ESPQ, PSPQ, and CTS kit scales, of which about one-third (2896 at the latest count) have achieved status as scorable items on these seven instruments.[3]

It is proof of the power of the personality-sphere concept that the initial research (Cattell, 1948) showed that the markers for all the published questionnaires did not subtend more than three-fourths of the total space indicated by the personality sphere. The vagaries of psychological and clinical interest up to about 1950 had missed substantial areas of behavior. Indeed, such interests resembled the old Bostonian's map of America or Homer's account of the world as the Greeks saw it. The subsequent factor analyses, climbing from the 4-, 5-, and 6-factor scales before the 16 PF to the 16 to 19 of the 1949 16 PF and to more than 30 today, now support this early impression. The original estimate (Cattell, 1946b) that some 23 primary factors are indicated seemed absurd to the majority of "practical" questionnaire factorists and scale constructors of the next decade who, like Eysenck (1952) and Flanagan (1935), thought that personality could be encompassed

[3] A typical instance of the poor quality of scientific understanding and debate in this field is that, in the review of tests in Buros (1972), both Rorer and Jackson criticize the 16 PF and HSPQ for inattention to the item pool. I was afraid that with two books and 20 articles explicitly referring to the sampling basis I had repeated myself. It would be hard indeed to find another questionnaire in Buros' whole survey that is based on such a thorough collecting of an item pool as the 16 PF and its supplement—as the payoff in number of factors shows.

by three, four, or five factors. Current findings come very close to this first (1946–1948) estimate grasped through the mists of inadequate data and depending on early forms (Tucker; see Thurstone, 1938) of what is now essentially the *scree test* for the number of factors.

A new source from which the personality sphere was later enlarged (to a limited extent) has been the types of behavior found to be important in the objective test. Here, for example, the "regressive" behavior of factor UI 23 and the curious "cortically alert" (cortertia) behavior of UI 22 have been translated from those tests into comparable behavior open to questionnaire report from everyday life. It remains to be seen how far this translation has succeeded in bringing Q- and T-factors into a demonstrably common realm; but Chapter Seven shows by the OAQ scales that the majority of stable T-factors are now gaining representation in the Q-data medium. Regardless of source of items, the object is both to represent the personality sphere and to carry forward what have become recognized as high-loaded markers, so that hypotheses about the existence and nature of such factors can be progressively tested.

4. Some Necessary Common Technical Foundations in the Conduct of Factor Analysis

Having investigated planned sampling of items and people as the first requirement in sound factoring for questionnaires (including proper construction of the items as variables), let us now examine five further technical steps that are indispensable.

(2) Testing for Number of Factors. To an almost incredible degree theories in personality have been built on factor analyses wherein the number of factors has been decided by the personal predilection of the investigator. This phenomenon is taken up specifically in evaluating the discrepancy between my eight or nine second-order factors (in the 16 PF and CTS kit) and Eysenck's trio of second orders. It is also instanced by Howarth and Browne, who, after applying tests and disliking the result, then took out a number better fitting their views (1971a,b). In several instances, including a key study by Eysenck (1971), the number was decided by the capacity of the particular computing machine to extract factors.

Existing tests disagree on the number of factors by about ten percent, although in the hands of experienced investigators the influences causing error are sufficiently understood to lead to close agreement when two or three difference methods are applied. (The Kaiser-Guttman test, for example, overestimates with many variables and underestimates with few. Small *N*s yield superfluous common error factors.) The methods found most reliable have been the maximum likelihood (Lawley and Maxwell, 1963), the scree (Cattell, 1966b), Sokal's test (1959), and Tucker's test (see Thurstone, 1938). Although the theory of the scree remains to be debated and clarified, the test itself has been found to yield a correct statement of the number of factors in virtually every case where a plasmode has been made up from a known number of factors (Cattell and Jaspers, 1967); thus much of my work depends on the scree, always checked by some second method. It is not as conservative—in the sense of scientifically cautious and exact—to take out too few factors as some psychologists suppose. The variance thrown away leads to distorted patterns in the factors retained—*after the rotation.* This explains some discrepancies in analyses by Eysenck (1971; see Cattell, 1957) and by Tupes (1957) in ratings from results reached by Pierson, Finkbeiner, Dielman, Schaie and myself. If anything, it is better to overestimate and rotate out as Thurstone (1938) pointed out.

(3) **Estimating Communalities.** The correlation matrix given by the experiment lacks values in the diagonal, and these have to be estimated. Guttman (1950) and Roff (1953) have shown that these communalities (sharings of the common factors), calculated as a squared multiple correlation of each variable with all the others, are a lower bound for the true communality. Those using this approach often forget that it is a lower bound, not a best estimate. The best estimate is obtained by repeating the factor analyses several times—iterating—retaining the number of factors judged correct. Such iterating gives stable convergence (in due conditions) to values correct to several decimal places. All studies on the IPAT item pool have been so iterated. The use of unities or any other crude estimate of communalities does not give grossly misleading results when scales are used as variables (if there are 50 or more), but when items are factored it can play havoc with their loadings. Certain claims for factors from 16 PF items different from those basically recognized have been made by experimenters who have neglected this requirement.

(4) **Objectively Reaching a Unique Resolution.** Discrepancies among conclusions caused by neglect of these factors are trivial compared with the numerous instances of complete, chaotic disagreement through systematically wrong or, more commonly uncompleted rotation to the ultimate unique resolution. The nonmathematician should keep in mind that an infinite number of alternative rotations of the correctly extracted factors (by criteria (2)–(3) above) are mathematically indistinguishable in their power to restore the original correlations. The scientific, not the mathematical, model bids us find a unique resolution that by general objective principles (not specific psychological theories) is best. Two general principles are available: *simple structure,* which means that in a broad personality sphere each influence is likely to affect only a limited subset of variables, and *confactor rotation,* which means that when two experiments are compared we should find one position in each that gives a truly parallel structure to the other. This is like finding the position of two cylinders in a combination lock that opens it. Since a tentative but still computationally expensive solution for confactor rotation has only recently been found (Cattell and DeYoung, 1973a), virtually all research reported here depends on simple structure.

One must insist from experience (and it is recognized widely that more rotations have been carried out between 1940 and 1973 at the IPAT laboratory than anywhere else) that push-button computer program rotations will not yield the true, highest simple structure, except on oversimplified physical plasmodes. This is demonstrated in the comparison of methods by Dielman, Cattell, and Wagner (1972). Of the two types, *continuous analytical* and *nonparametric topological,* the former has faulty expressions for maximizing the hyperplane count,[4] and the latter is erratic.

The only satisfactory procedure—after getting a "lift on the way" by the topological maxplane program or by such analytical programs as oblimax (Pinska and Saunders, 1954) or the HK—is to rotate blindly (disguising variables by ciphers) so one's theories cannot affect outcomes—at least in new, exploratory studies—until a maximum hyperplane count is reached. This would take a year on a 200-item × 20-factor problem, using the methods one was compelled to use in the late 1940s, but the rotoplot (Cattell and Foster, 1963) now offers powerful computer aid to human judgment. A plot of successive percentages in the hyperplane—called a history of hyperplane—is the real basis for deciding on simple structure (see Figure 4). That is, one must find a plateau position in the curve such that after several attempts in different directions no improvement, but only loss, results from movement—much as one would locate the top of a hill by walking in all possible directions in the dark. This typically requires 20 to 30 overall shifts after one has taken a ride on the automatic program as far up the hill as possible. Cogent arguments have long been presented by leading factor analysts (e.g., Child, 1970; Guertin and Bailey, 1970; Gorsuch, 1973; Harman, 1967; Thurstone, 1938), that unique, optimal best simple structure is incompatible with orthogonal factors.

The reason for true simple structure being typically oblique is, of course, that influences in nature, operating in one universe, are seldom exactly uncorrelated. Later, in Chapter Seven, we discuss in some detail an experimental instance which clearly brings this out; but here we simply point to this demonstration of our present argument. In that experiment 80 balls of different weights, sizes and elasticities were measured on 32 forms of "behavior" (rolling, bouncing, etc.) The factoring of the 32 × 32 matrix yielded four factors, corresponding to real determiners, of which we need note only weight and volume here. Since balls of bigger volume tend (in spite of golf balls and beach balls) to be heavier in weight these two factors are positively correlated, as shown by the continuous lines in Figure 5. The varimax program, as shown by the orthogonal discontinuous lines, fails to find simple structure (the variables cluster on the true factor not the orthogonal lines).

[4] The hyperplane count is the percentage of all variables in the study that lie in hyperplanes, that is, have essentially zero loading on the factors. "Essentially" is commonly taken as within a loading of ±0.10, but a nicer calculation of twice the standard error of a zero loading, according to the N and inter-correlation values may suggest, say, ±0.06 or ±0.13.

The analytic methods maximize the variance of loadings, thus forcing many to the lowest possible value, but that value can be 0.15, 0.20, and so on. The topological method, however, maximizes those falling in a definite hyperplane belt, say ±0.08. In short, analytic programs do not maximize literally what the theory requires, and, despite their saving the investigator considerable time and energy, must be regarded as temporary approximations.

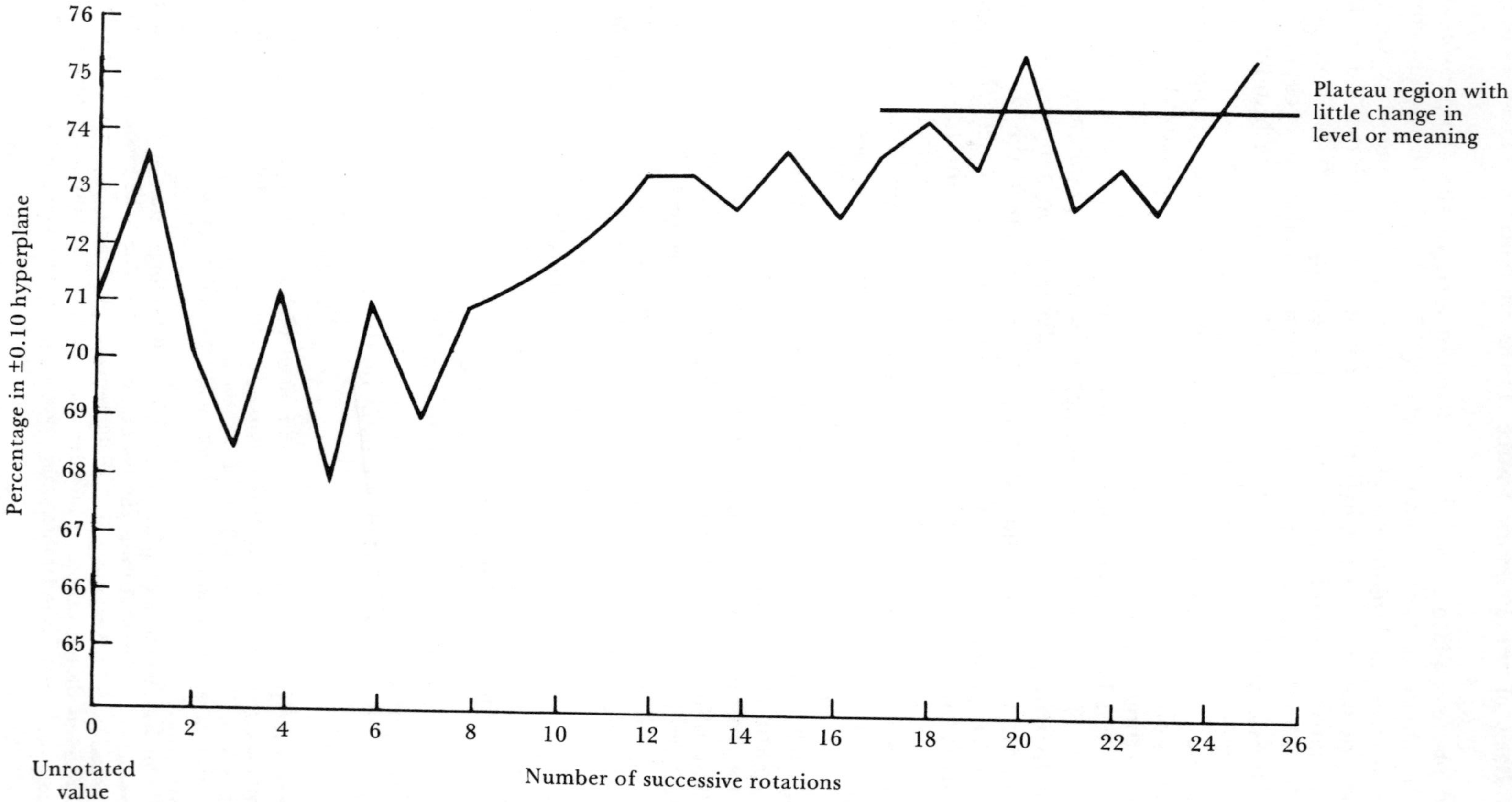

Figure 4. History of hyperplane. The oblimax solution at 1 was decidedly inferior in ± 0.05 loadings to the final position at the 25th rotation. It is not unusual for the count to fall initially as the oblimax is rotated from its extreme angles.

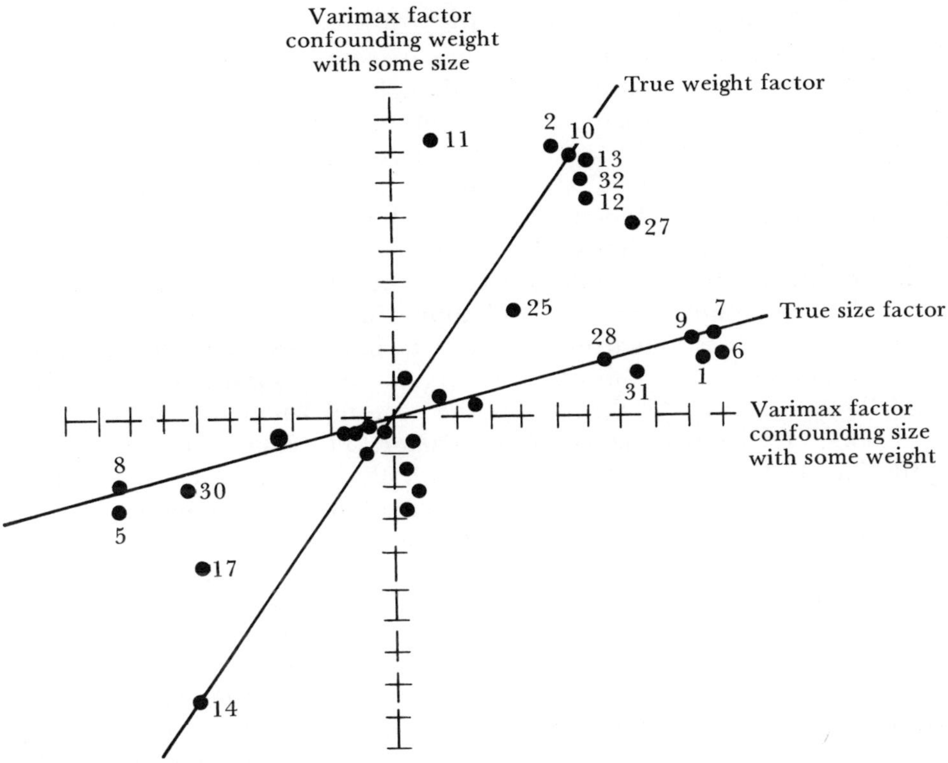

Figure 5. Orthogonal varimax analytic solution to ball problem (for size and weight factors). Identification of variables by number: (1) diameter, (2) weight, (5) rotations rolling, (6) distance from eye to cover circle, (7) diameter of shadow cast, (8) rotations to one rotation of tire, (9) number of squares covered by ball, (10) distance of weight from ball, (11) collision displacement, (12) paddle-wheel rotations, (13) springboard depression, (14) angular momentum, (17) croquet blow up in inclined plane, (25) inclined plane carpet friction, (27) weight of splash, (28) inclined plane impulse distance, (30) winding necessary to use up string, (31) size of eclipse shadow, (32) impact displacement by pendulum.

This page-length discussion of canons of rotation is justified by the disastrous discrepancy between the casualness with which some experimenters pursue it and its vital importance for theoretical concepts. The task of definitive rotation, being difficult and demanding of time, is all too frequently furtively evaded. The journal article records from which Table 45 (Chapter Eight) was built show that roughly four-fifths of editorially accepted articles are satisfied with computer push button outputs. They have seldom rotated visually even half a dozen times, or displayed a hyperplane progress history (Figure 4 above), or reached a final hyperplane count significant at the $P < 0.05$ level by Bargmann's test. The main instances of dispute over rotation with important implications for personality concepts are examined in Chapter Eight.

(5) Testing the Resolution for Inherent Statistical Significance. The only statistical test for significance of simple structure—Bargmann's test (1953)—has assumptions which although reasonable seem to make it, in practice, rather exacting. Probably only one-fifth of published research would meet the $P < 0.05$ level, and even with the greatest care it is unusual for all factors to reach the $P < 0.01$ level—see, for instance, the studies of Cattell, Schroder, and Wagner (1969) and Cattell, Wagner, and Cattell (1970). Nevertheless, before results of one study are quoted against another (as is done in Comrey and Duffy's criticisms of solutions differing from their own 1968), we should at least be told approximately where the significances lie. In the IPAT questionnaires it is usual to finish with virtually all factors at the simple-structure position at a Bargmann test significance level from $P < 0.05$ to $P < 0.01$. (See Cattell, Finkheiner, and Vaughan, 1973.)

(6) Testing Invariance of the Factor. The final test is a matching of the factors in one research project with those in another. Our interest here lies not in any given questionnaire scale but in the general concept of a source trait in personality theory. Such a source trait should show itself not just in one questionnaire research project but be demonstrable in all such research. Indeed, in this book I argue that the traits should also appear as patterns in L- and T-data, and that it does not suffice to have evidence only in Q-data—even if all our work is to be done with questionnaires.

Three approaches are possible (Cattell, 1962b, 1971b; Cattell, Balcar, Horn, and Nesselroade, 1969; Schneewind and Cattell, 1970) for evaluating the match of questionnaire factors across research: the congruence coefficient r_c; the configurative method; and the salient variable similarity index s. (The correlation coefficient if applied to loadings is quite erroneous.) The first is due to Burt (1940), the second to Kaiser (1971) and the third to Cattell (1949a, 1965b; Cattell and Baggaley, 1960). Significance tests for the first, specifically in the domain of relating factor-loading patterns, have been worked out by Monte Carlo methods (Schneewind and Cattell, 1970). The second is difficult in practice. The third, the s index, has the advantage of giving significance directly. Most of my work on matching has used both the r_c and s since their emphases are sufficiently different to be supplementary.

One would not expect the loading pattern for the same factor in two different experimental settings to be identical. Quite apart from random error, systematic effects from variance changes (and other influences if the population is different) are reduced only by changing from ordinary factor analysis to covariance factoring (Cattell, 1972a; Harman, 1967). Nor, conversely, would one expect the loading pattern of two distinct and different factors to correlate zero (that is, be correlationally insignificant). It is in the nature of psychological action that cooperative factors (Cattell, 1952) appear—factors such as superego (G) and self-sentiment (Q_3), or sympathetic and parasympathetic systems, which affect much the same subsets of variables. These wider considerations must be kept in mind when the reader inspects matching tables like Tables 23 and 24 (Chapter Four).

If one counts sampling of people and of variables as two distinct requirements, I have now cited six indispensable conditions of adequate factor analysis. Other, more specific points may be added by technicians. But if personality theorists (not to mention journal editors) had checked these criteria, there would have been far fewer pointless debates in the past and more effective concentration on progress in the essentials of personality measurement. To give two instances, Guilford's rotations are orthogonal and mine are oblique; yet many have wasted time conjecturing whether they are the same. Eysenck's early concepts are on orthogonal factors and would be expected to change when he accepted oblique rotation. These concepts cannot be the same, as long as geometry is respected. Again, from 1945 to 1965, Eysenck operated with 3 factors while I found 15 to 17. Such writers as Adcock (1965), Howarth and Browne (1971a,b), and Howarth and others (1972) who debated the relative correctness of these views might better have spent their time in sharpening the precision of tests for deciding the number of factors. Investigators are free to accept different models but not to condone gross inconsistencies within the accepted model.

5. Divergent and Convergent Emphases in the Chief Developments of 1945–1973

The advance of programatic research in the questionnaire area—prior to the late 1960s, when computers (and the pioneers' computer programs) became available everywhere—has (apart from Thurstone's brief entry into the field in his last years been concentrated in only five laboratories: those of Guilford, Eysenck, Hathaway and Meehl, and Comrey, and my own. Decidedly more than five researchers, however, have participated. For example, in my Illinois laboratory, questionnaire research has been pursued in publications by Barton, Bartsch, Beloff, Bolz, Burdsal, Delhees, DeVoogd, Drevdahl, Gruen, Peterson, Saunders, Scheier, Vaughan, Wagner, and others. Still more powerfully, it has been drawn forward by independent but programatically associated researchers in other universities such as Butcher (Sussex), Bjersted (Malmo), Coan (Arizona), Curran (Purdue), Dielman (Michigan), Dreger (Louisiana), Eber (Georgia), Gorsuch (Vanderbilt), Horn (Denver), Hundal (India), Karson (Eastern Michigan), Kear-Colwell (Glasgow), Nesselroade (Pennsylvania), Nichols (Calgary), Nuttall (Boston), Pichot (Sorbonne), Porter (Indiana), Radcliffe (Sydney), Rickels (Pennsylvania), Saville (London), Schaie (West Virginia), Schneewind (Trier), Schmidt (Saar), Schröder (Cologne), Sells (Texas Christian), Sealy (London), Shrader (Tennessee), Tatsuoka (Illinois), Tsujioka (Kansas), Warburton (Manchester), and other active investigators. Besides these, a far greater number have contributed from the applied field with a steady stream of concrete criterion relations (see Chapter Ten).

Because of the basic agreement among these investigators and perhaps among fifty more on the theoretical model and on technical standards, as well as because of the programatic way in which they have interrelated their research in regard to such questionnaire scales as the 16 PF, HSPQ, CPQ, ESPQ, CAQ, CTS kit, Eight-State Battery, the Anxiety Scale, and others,[5] what they have constructed must occupy the core of any modern presentation of the questionnaire domain. It is possible that one could accumulate as many published questionnaires around the world that do not follow the factor-analytic method or some systematic equivalent or do not follow it with the standards listed above; but they do not integrate either with this central core or with one another. Inasmuch as the search here has been representative of these many investigators, and insofar as a "democratic" approach nevertheless does not require in science that one give equal space, on the one hand, to rigorous and creative work, and on the other, to test publication which ignores goals of sound theory, no apology is necessary for omitting some publication that might be included in a catalog of the period 1945–1973.

In what follows I propose first to put forward the most coherent explanation of this strategic, programatic work and then to examine certain disputes among these laboratories and others. Before giving the history of work and conclusions in this core of programatic research, let me indicate the nature of the disagreements that are examined in Chapter Eight.

As to Eysenck's laboratory, the difference concerns the number of factors involved—his 3 against the 15 to 25 claimed here. This difference can be partially reconciled if one accepts Eysenck's conception that he is operating at the second order relative to the 16 PF, HSPQ, CAQ and others. But one must react to his regarding the first orders themselves as unnecessary (Eysenck, 1971). However, in accepting his three as close to three of my second orders I must insist that the researchers listed previously have consistently found eight or nine second orders against his three. Moreover, his lag in shifting from the earlier foundation of his theory in orthogonal to oblique rotation combines with other technical omissions to produce some weakness and distortion of meaning even in his first three factors.

As to Guilford and Zimmerman's alternatives, the issue is simple. We find approximately the same number of factors, and the bridging studies (see Cattell and Gibbons, 1968) show that even the domains (factor spaces) of these well-known scales—the G-Z and the 16 PF—substantially overlap. But as long as Euclid reigns it is absurd to say that orthogonal and oblique coordinates can be truly identical, although some four of his and my primaries come as close to defining the same factors as the slight departures of the orthogonal-oblique systems in those cases allow.

[5] The abbreviations for published questionnaires referred to in this book are: AS—IPAT (Scheier) Anxiety Scale; CAQ—The Clinical Analysis Questionnaire; CPQ—The Child Personality Questionnaire; CPS—Comrey Personality Scales; CTS Kit—The Central Trait and State Kit; EPI—Eysenck Personality Inventory; 8SQ—The Eight State Questionnaire; ESPQ—Early School Personality Questionnaire; G-Z—The Guilford-Zimmerman Temperament Survey; HSPQ—High School Personality Questionnaire; MMPI—Minnesota Multiphasic Personality Inventory; 16 PF—The Sixteen Personality Factor Questionnaire; STAI—Spielberger State-Trait Anxiety Scale; PSPQ—Preschool Personality Questionnaire.

As far as integration of findings from the two scale systems is concerned, a transformation matrix can be readily set up to transform scores on one to estimated scores on the other. My rejection of the orthogonal solution is purely on the grounds of basic general principles, on which, for example, Thurstone (1938) and I (1952, 1954, 1966) and now Eysenck (1960) apparently agree. Moreover, to the psychologist the important considerations are that orthogonality closes the door to any exploration of higher-order factors, and that although the factors are conceptually orthogonal, Guilford and Zimmerman are embarrassed by the paradox that their actual scales intercorrelate appreciably, thus losing the only advantage that orthogonality offered.

As to Hathaway, Meehl, and McKinley and their MMPI, my position is that their aim has not been to reach factored, independent scales. By using the same items in different scales, they produce artificial algebraic dependencies that make the scales unsuitable for finding whatever second orders exist among these clinically devised scales. However, one can make positive links of the present factors with this MMPI development, with its rich and comprehensive representation of pathological behavior, as is shown in Chapter Three.

As to Comrey's scales, there is a difference in emphasis on homogeneity as opposed to factor trueness compared with the main approach here. Briefly, the result is that his parcels (FHIB's in his terms) are probably close to being factors in a first-order space. Consequently, his eight scales approach the second orders in the 16 PF, those which Barton and myself set out as scales in the IPAT CTS questionnaire kit. In this connection there is a systematic difference between Comrey and me on the one hand, and Eysenck and Howarth on the other, as to whether factoring of items or factoring of homogeneous parcels is the more reliable. I contend that rotation of items is erratic, and the failure of Eysenck and of Howarth and Browne to rotate in the same space to the 16 PF factors may illustrate this variability. (Howarth and Browne's study, 1971a, failed to find by rotation even the general intelligence factor.)

In short, if one thus considers the differences of aim and the omission of technical requirements in some studies, the apparent deviations of certain studies from the central programatic findings to be described are not so chaotic as may first appear to the nonfactorist (who is all too ready to take the factions of factorists as fatal). These issues are taken up in detail in Chapter Eight along with the question of item versus parcel factoring. On this point, incidentally, I am between two camps: I agree with Comrey that parcel factoring is often desirable; therefore I disagree with Eysenck and Howarth that item analysis *alone* is correct. Yet I agree that each is permissible, and I have demonstrated (Chapter Eight) that in fact both yield the same result.

In addition to these debates, which have resulted in actual questionnaires to represent the given theoretical viewpoints, one must consider also such well-conceived comparative studies as that of the G-Z and the 16 PF together (Sells, Demaree, and Will, 1970). My conclusion is that because of limitations in rotation programs this important study resulted in a mixed series of first- and second-order factors, each compatible with the general findings now to be described.

6. Advances from Programatic Research 1945–1973

The long series of factor analyses of adult and child personality questionnaire items began with the preliminary delineation of the personality sphere in 1946. Throughout, these factor analyses used some alternation of factoring of parcels of items, used as variables, with factoring of items—in a tactic of alternation with advantages to be explained below. After delineation of the personality sphere an oblique simple-structure factoring was done on 80 representative items (in those days an outsize factor analysis) representing the sphere and other markers.

The result of this first factor-analytic attack, based on 370 male and female students, was 15–18 factors; these factors, rotated to the best simple structure, gave a hyperplane count (± 0.10 loadings) of 60 percent—satisfactory and well above average for item studies. To these factors an intelligence factor was added and the 16 PF was launched as a new *experimental* personality questionnaire in 1949.

After an indication of factor structure by key items had been obtained, a second factoring was carried out (Cattell, 1950c), taking factors in blocks of four (to reduce the size of factorings) and adding new items aimed at them. This factoring was designed to bring the number of items to 20 or 26 per factor. From this factoring the first edition of the 16 PF with Forms A and B, with either 10 or 13 items for each factor, was issued. Also at this point Saunders and I made an initial check of the relation of questionnaire factors to rating [L(R)-data] (Cattell and Saunders, 1950), the identifications having previously rested on psychological identification of content. The tentative conclusion was that rating factors *D, J,* and *K* had not yet appeared in questionnaires and that four questionnaire factors had not shown up in ratings. To indicate their purely Q-data character, these factors were labeled Q_1, Q_2, Q_3, and Q_4. The lettering system *A* through *P,* continuing to Q_1, Q_2, Q_3, and Q_4, has been retained to this day. The stagnation in behavior rating research (see Chapter Six) has meant that no adequately marked rating equivalents of these last factors can yet be indicated; but the questionnaire research described here has led to the finding of "mental interiors"—questionnaire factors—for *D, J, K,* and *P.* Thus Q- and L-data run parallel for factors *A* through *P.*

Because the validity of the new items in the second item-factoring research rested only on sectional factorings, two more basic factor analyses were planned immediately after the 1950 report. These analyses are designated the third (published in 1956) and the fourth (also published in 1956) validation and intensification factoring experiments. At that point my experience and reports from other laboratories began to throw doubt on the possibility of obtaining satisfactory invariance from study to study when items are used as the basis of research. The brevity of the response time per item, the high cultural specificity of the item behavior, and the grouping of the points close to the origin in the item plots for rotation militate against clean resolutions. Accordingly, after the first two analyses of items had given an approximate delineation of the number and nature of factors, I decided to factor parcels (clusters of items), and on this basis subsequent refinement of the definition of factors rested until the two 184-item factorings reported in Chapter Eight.

Factoring parcels or short scales requires that a few—say three to eight—items be grouped in a cluster that is in some sense and degree homogeneous, which is thenceforth scored as a single variable. If the items one begins with are taken from a broad sampling of the personality sphere, or designed to tap expressions of a personality factor in suitably diverse situations, the acceptable limit of intercorrelation of items for a parcel will tend to be about 0.5 or even down to 0.2. It is possible to get higher homogeneity, as Comrey (1970) and some others have done, by asking virtually the same question in several ways, or using the same trait adjective, e.g., anxious, repeatedly, as Spielberger has done. But this throws away the vitally important personality sphere sampling concept. Furthermore, as Chapter Eight will show, there is an important difference, previously unrecognized, between two varieties of homogeneous cluster—the *ordinary* and the *radial* —such that the former, in its "equal cut" form is unsuitable for determining simple structure.

The third factor analysis, conducted to check the necessity of 15 to 18 primary factors, took the 30 scales (A and B on 15 factors, intelligence omitted) and added 720 new items. These were reduced to 450 and then to 126 by eliminating (1) those not in the 16 PF space, that is, correlating with none of the 16 dimensions, and (2) those with extreme yes-no cuts. (Note that (1) was part of a strategy not only to increase the existing factors but also to locate seven missing factors; the items outside the 16 dimensions were preserved for later analyses.) The 126 items were grouped in 45 parcels, making 75 variables in all when added to the 30 scales (two markers per factor). On 295 undergraduates analysis yielded 15 factors, recognizable readily by the markers in all factors but *O*, which seemed to merge with Q_4. Simple structure reached 67 percent in the hyperplane.

A fourth factoring, not basic but designed to clarify and supplement factors—notably the weak members, *M, C, O,* and Q_2, which are harder to define—was pursued with 200 new items. As a result of the third and fourth factorings, items loading less than 0.15 were cut out and replaced by new ones, leading to strengthening of *M, C* and Q_2 and better separation of *O* from Q_4.

The fifth analysis (1956) is of special importance in that it lays down a series of 10 technical principles important for all questionnaire research and development. It brought two extension questionnaires of new items, one of 512 that was reduced by the preliminary technical requirements to 252, and another of 320 reduced to 200 (an initial pool of 1552 items in all). The main factoring of the 75 packages on 408 men and women (largely air force personnel, partly students) again yielded the theoretically expected

15 factors (plus intelligence). These factors were correlated with the extension items and the existing items by "undoing" the parcels. The percentage in the hyperplane at simple structure was 67 percent, factor correlations were moderate, and with the new items from the third and fourth analysis factor *O* was successfully separated from Q_4. On this basis the 1962 edition of the 16 PF (Forms A, B, and C) was developed.

The sixth factoring was carried out in parallel with a factoring of the Japanese translation of the 16 PF (Tsujioka and Cattell, 1965a, 1965b). Only Forms A and B were used (as variables), and 117 American undergraduates were tested. A simple-structure rotation on 16 factors (shown to be sufficient by the scree test) reached a 60 percent hyperplane and gave a clear separation of all factors which, incidentally, was as highly congruent (r_c) with the Japanese population results as with the other American samples. However, factors *L* and *N* still showed lower validities than others.

The seventh factoring took a new course by shifting to a population of older and nonstudent adults. The fifth had already shifted to general adults without any indication of significant change of structure, but it is a principle of factor analysis that changes of population are likely to bring out different emphases of factor pattern and even require some change of items to measure the same factors, so a second cross-age validation was made. On a sample of 606 men and women (mean ages of constituent groups: 20 to 46), all four forms of the 1962 edition were given. The scree test showed 19 factors, three after rotation being of small variance, and rotation produced a high simple structure with 83 percent in the hyperplane. All the usual 16 factors were well marked by the four markers for each but again the weaker factors were *E, M, N,* and *O*. The correlations among factors were moderate and matched those usually found. Karson and O'Dell (1973) have also factored the 1962 edition, though on a highly selected group—air control tower operators. From the extension items in this study some replacements were made for the 1967 edition of Forms A, B, C, and D. The structure at this stage can be seen from Table 3. The item-structure table is too large for reproduction (see Cattell, 1972c) and even the complete table for the four scales per factor would be expensive to reproduce, but a representative section in Table 3(a) shows the general nature of the simple structure and the regularity of the loadings on the correct markers.

There are some low loadings on other factors for the factor clearly designated by the four markers, those for factor *A*, for example, numbering 10 between 0.10 and 0.17. By now, both through the seven successive 16 PF factorings and the converging child analyses (Chapter Three), the psychological nature of the factors was becoming clear, justifying such half-way steps to interpretation as in the labels affectia (*A*), intelligence (*B*), ego strength (*C*), dominance (*E*), and surgency (*F*). The criterion associations found in different cultures and subcultures showed that broad personality source traits, powerfully operative in life, had been located. However, theories of psychological meaning must be deferred until the evidence on the structures themselves has been further examined. Despite the convergence among the results of those using oblique simple structure and factor number checks, other investigators intermittently claimed different interpretations. And despite cross-checks producing often repeated matchings superior to those found in the old field of abilities, the majority of psycholo-

Table 3

Representative Simple Structure and Marker Loadings
for the 16 Primary Factors (by scales)
(a) 1962 Edition of 16 PF[a]

Primary Factor	*A*	*B*	*C*	*E*	*F*	*G*	*H*	*I*
A: Affectothymia								
Form A	61			–10	11			16
B	93				–14			–10
C	57			18	12	18		
D	64							
B: Intelligence								
Form A		54				10		
B		54	–18			–13		
C		51						11
D	12	49	20			10		
C: Ego Strength								
Form A	–15		72					
B			51					
C			10	–15		–12		
D		12	21			–12		
E: Dominance								
Form A	12	12		25	14		24	–12
B	10			25			13	–11
C			11	68		–12	10	–14
D		–15		24	28	–31		
F: Surgency								
Form A					62		10	
B	17				68	–13		
C	–11		10		41	15	52	
D					74		11	
G: Superego Strength								
Form A				–12		23		
B				–17	16	54		
C		–11		–11		43	11	
D					–10	74		
H: Parmia								
Form A			11		23	16	69	
B							91	
C			–11	–10		–22	63	
D	13			15		14	81	
I: Premsia								
Form A	12		13				12	70
B	–11						–10	74
C			–10		20			55
D	15							62

[a] N = 606 men and women (general population).

(b) 1967 Edition of 16 PF [a]

Form	*Scale*	*A*	*B*	*E*	*G*	*I*	*M*	*O*	Q_2
A									
	A	68							
	B		66						
	E			48				12	
	G				73				11
	I	16				71			11
	M				−17	20	38		
	O		−14					63	
	Q_2								65
B									
	A	74							
	B		69						
	E			28 [b]			27		12
	G				65				
	I					70	14	12	
	M				11	27	55		
	O		−15					19 [c]	
	Q_2						−25		51

[a] N = 6476 general adults (general population, some college and 18-year-olds). Half (even-number) factors.

[b] 0.90 for women, 0.40 for men on separate group factoring.

[c] 0.42 for women on separate group factoring.

Note: Since the original matrix factor *A* and the next seven even-numbered factors are too large to reproduce here, this representation is based on Cattell (1972a).

In all correlation and factor loading tables the decimal points but not the signs have been omitted, all values being two decimal place numbers.

gists continued to assume that personality factor structure was more speculative than in the "firm" field of abilities.

Accordingly, an eighth factoring of the 16 PF, using the most recent techniques, was carried out in 1968 on a large sample of 6476 men and women of widely varying age. This factoring was done only on Forms A and B (two hours of testing). The simple structure showed these factors to persist with their markers (Cattell, Eber, and Tatsuoka, 1970) across this wide range, but not quite as clearly as in the more homogeneous early groups (see Table 3(b)). Factors *E, L, M, N,* and *O* remained at somewhat lower validities than others, and Q_3, self-sentiment, specifically had lower validity in this sample, presumably because of the changing meaning of the self-image across so wide an age range. Nevertheless this examination of the third and last edition of the 16 PF (1968) showed it to be functioning as planned across the broadest age and social range of adults, and for men and women. Chapter Seven brings out that the 16 primaries now located also retain their structure across cultures. Since the debates described in Chapter Seven involve assertions that more or less than 16 factors are involved in the 16 PF (Howarth, for example, says 10), it is desirable at this point to set out in Figure 6 the scree tests for the number of factors in three of the largest research projects discussed.

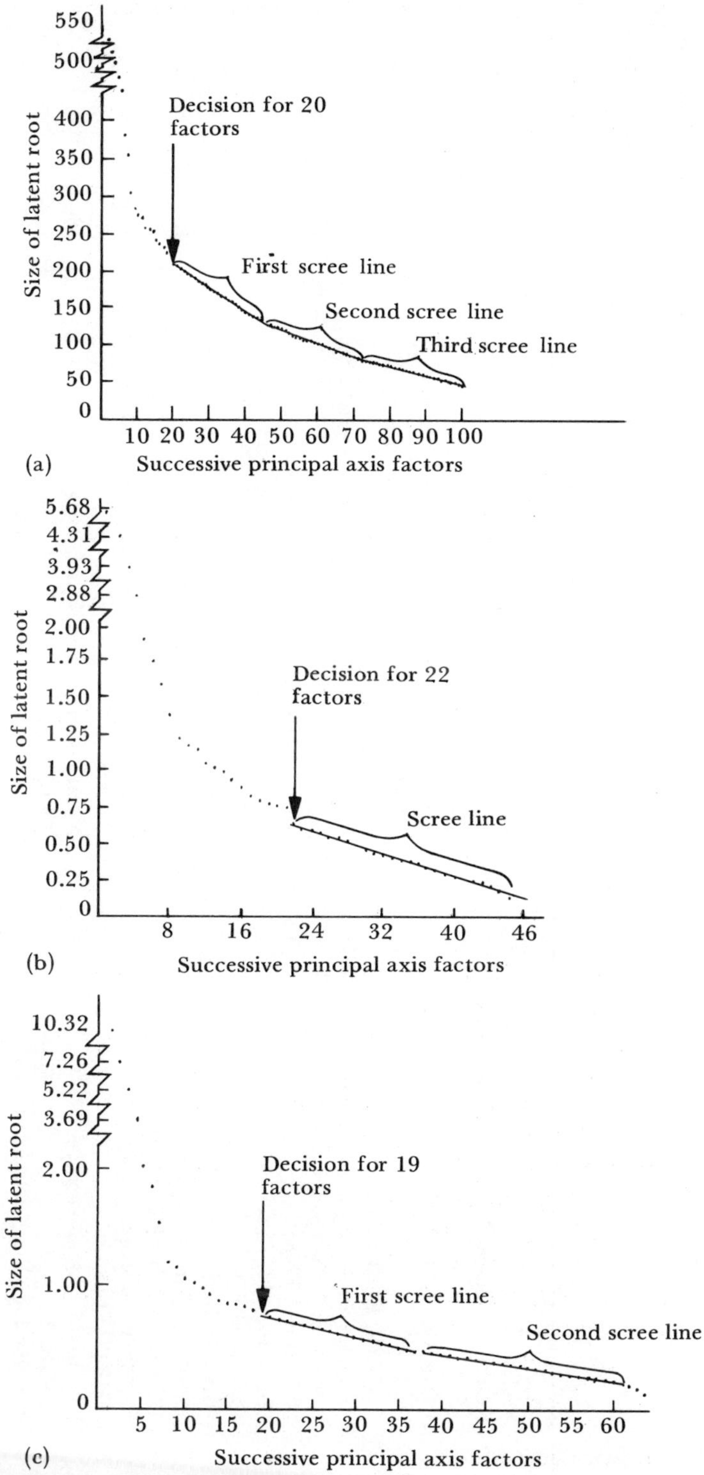

Figure 6. Decision on number of primary factors in initial personality sphere; (a) by item (Cattell, 1972a; N = 780 adults); (b) by parcel (Vaughan and Burdsal, 1973; N = 240 students); (c) by scale (Cattell, Eber, and Delhees, 1968; N = 606 mixed normal and clinical adults).

Table 4

First Fifteen Normal Questionnaire Primaries from a Programatic Attack over Eight Factor Analyses

Source-Trait Index	*Low-Score Description*	*High-Score Description*	*Number of Items in Each Form in 16 PF (HSPQ and CPQ essentially similar)*		
			AB	*CD*	*EF*
A	SIZIA Reserved, detached, critical, aloof, stiff	AFFECTIA Outgoing, warmhearted, easygoing, participating	10	6	8
B	LOW INTELLIGENCE Dull	HIGH INTELLIGENCE Bright	13	8	8
C	LOWER EGO STRENGTH At mercy of feelings, emotionally less stable, easily upset, changeable	HIGHER EGO STRENGTH Emotionally stable, mature, faces reality, calm	13	6	8
E	SUBMISSIVENESS Humble, mild, easily led, docile, accommodating	DOMINANCE Assertive, aggressive, competitive, stubborn	13	6	8
F	DESURGENCY Sober, taciturn, serious	SURGENCY Happy-go-lucky, gay, enthusiastic	13	6	8
G	WEAKER SUPEREGO STRENGTH Expedient, disregards rules	STRONGER SUPEREGO STRENGTH Conscientious, persistent, moralistic, staid	10	6	8
H	THRECTIA Shy, timid, threat-sensitive	PARMIA Venturesome, uninhibited, socially bold	13	6	8
I	HARRIA Tough-minded, self-reliant, realistic	PREMSIA Tender-minded, sensitive, clinging, overprotected	10	6	8
L	ALAXIA Trusting, accepting conditions	PROTENSION Suspicious, hard to fool	10	6	8
M	PRAXERNIA Practical, "down-to-earth" concerns	AUTIA Imaginative, bohemian, absent-minded	13	6	8

N	ARTLESSNESS Forthright, unpretentious, genuine, but socially clumsy	SHREWDNESS Astute, polished, socially aware	10	6	8
O	UNTROUBLED ADEQUACY Self-assured, placid, secure, complacent, serene	GUILT PRONENESS Apprehensive, self-reproaching, insecure, worrying, troubled	13	6	8
Q_1	CONSERVATIVISM OF TEMPERAMENT Conservative, respecting traditional ideas	RADICALISM Experimenting, liberal, free-thinking	10	6	8
Q_2	GROUP ADHERENCE Group-dependent, a "joiner" and sound follower	SELF-SUFFICIENCY Self-sufficient, resourceful, prefers own decisions	10	6	8
Q_3	LOW SELF-SENTIMENT INTEGRATION Undisciplined self-conflict, lax, follows own urges, careless of social rules	HIGH STRENGTH OF SELF-SENTIMENT Controlled, exacting will power, socially precise, compulsive, following self-image	10	6	8
Q_4	LOW ERGIC TENSION Relaxed, tranquil, torpid, unfrustrated, composed	HIGH ERGIC TENSION Tense, frustrated, driven, overwrought	13	6	8

Note: Factor *B*, intelligence, although not one of the 15 personality factors, being an ability measure, is kept in its usual position here in the 16 PF scales.

The results of these three scree tests are of special interest since they examine the same domain of behavior through three different kinds of variables—scales, items, and parcels. Despite differences of variable and population sample, these number-of-factor tests converge (19, 20, 22) on about 20 factors—something very different from the 3 (to 11) of Eysenck, the 8 or 9 of Comrey, or the 11 of Howarth. We have recognized through all our primary factor research that more than 16 factors (varying in different studies from 18 to 23) exist. The 16 PF was constructed conservatively on the largest and most reproducible of these.

Two more factorings of the 16 PF both carried out by items (184) and by parcels (46), have brought the total of systematically related factorings to 10 (or 12 if one counts both methods). These factorings are documented in Cattell (1972c) and Burdsal and Vaughan (1973) and are discussed as to convergence (which is satisfactory) in Chapter Eight. It has seemed desirable to summarize all 10 studies (on adults alone; the programatic link with child studies is in Chapter Three) since their scattering in separate journal articles has apparently prevented evaluators of different theories from realizing the weight of evidence, in size and number of samples, objective tests of number of factors, and replication of patterns, on which the theory of 16 primary factors (plus "stragglers") rests. The focusing of this series of foundations in experiment has been necessary not only for this reason but also to permit critical examination and comparison of evidence when we ask how steady these patterns are across different cultures and what the higher-order structure is.

A summary of notation, titles, and descriptions of the 16 factors that have maintained their meaning and validity throughout considerable research is given in Table 4. A discussion of the psychological meaning of these source traits follows in Chapter Five, where reasons are given for their technical titles. In any case, technical names are essential to avoid the pollution of meaning in scientific discussion—pollution caused by the inappropriate associations dragged in by popular terms.

7. Search for the Seven Missing Factors

For 20 years after the recognition of these 15 to 20 personality dimensions in Q-data in normal subjects (abnormals are another matter; see Chapter Three) there were glimpses of other factors in research going beyond the 16 PF dimensions. Thus while the checking, confirming, and intensifying of scales for the 15 was proceeding, the research of Gruen, Coan, Peterson, Beloff, and others (surveyed in Chapter Three) found certain patterns among children not clearly established in adult data; also, research outside my laboratory—for example, that of Sells, Demaree, and Will (1970) —showed two factors in the G-Z for which the 16 PF had no transformable equivalent; two uninterpretable factors in Comrey's scale; and so on.

The common-factor analyses ultimately incorporated in our programatic research to bridge with the Guilford-Zimmerman and the MMPI revealed a substantial common space staked out by at least three scales of virtually the same meaning. Thus the G-Z factor *M* is 16 PF *I; N* is *O;* and *S* is *H*. But the G-Z had some additional space to the 16 PF, notably a dimension of "arts interest" (*AA*) and suggestions of a second, unknown dimension. The programatic research described in the last section, as it explored new extension item data, commonly showed two or three factors (sometimes different from study to study) over and above the 15 for which reinforcing material was being sought. Research projects employing the Dwyer extension, which picks up new items in the existing dimension but adds no dimensions, do not reveal new dimensions in the new items, but the new factorings did turn up new dimensions. Furthermore, these two to four new factors in the 17 to 19 frequently indicated by the scree did not appear merely as common-error factors but had substantial congruence.

Accordingly, in 1965 a systematic search was undertaken, beginning with a careful harvesting of persistent markers that had been allowed to fall like shavings from the main workbench. The search revealed that (apart from some purely abnormal dimensions found in simultaneous factorings of MMPI items) seven missing factors could be hypothesized in the domain of normal behavior. An experimental check on these hypotheses was made by Cattell and Delhees (1973) by administering to 225 male and female undergraduates a battery consisting of two scales to mark each of the 16 PF factors, and two parcels of 5 to 12 items in each, employing the items believed to mark each of the seven new factors. Additionally, to confirm that none of the abnormal (depression) factors was among the seven missing factors, two marker scales were added for each of six depression factors. (The origin of these depression factors is described in Chapter Three.) Thus the factorization was one of 58 variables (parcels of 5 to 12 items each) hypothesized to mark 29 factors and covering 458 items. The scree test indicated either 26 or 29 factors, and when the larger number was taken out for safety, the rotation produced three trivial factors indicating 26 to have been the correct number. This reduction was caused by the collapse of the six depression factors found in abnormals into three second orders in normals (see Chapter Three). As far as the hypothesized seven missing factors are concerned the answer was clear: they indeed constitute new dimensions beyond the 16 PF and their natures are much the same as hypothesized by the initial markers, although some shifts in loading occurred.

As with the main 16 PF development, a programatic procedure was begun using what is described in Chapter Eight as progressive rectification. Thus two further factor analyses with extension items have been made, one with 240 undergraduate students (DeVoogd and Cattell, 1973) and another in progress with military subjects. The independence of the factor structure for these new factors is shown in Table 5.

The product is a seven-factor 16 PF Supplement (Cattell and Marshall, 1973) presenting equivalent Forms A and B of 10 items each for seven factors indicated in Table 6.

As to the index designation of these factors, there are indications that the "sanguine" casualness factor has already appeared in ratings (Cattell, 1957), so we have assigned it an ordinary [L(R)-data] notation as *P*. A rating

Table 5

Synopsis Showing Agreement of Two Studies to Check Independence of Seven Missing Factors

	Factor Pattern, Delhees Research (1972). Designations of Primaries as in Table 4										*Factor Pattern, De Voogd Research (1973). Designations of Primaries as in Table 4*										
Marker Variables	A	B	C	F	G	Q_2	D	K	Q_6	Q_7		H	I	L	O	Q_1	Q_3	D	K	P	Q_5
A_1	64	*									H_1	92									
A_2	50										H_2	60									
B_1		47			13						I_1		74								
B_2		36						−17	−26		I_2		78				−14				
C_1			76	14							L_1	13		41	37						
C_2		31	50						33		L_2			45			34				
F_1				80							O_1	−17	21	26	29		13		−17		
F_2		15	14	36							O_2	−16		−31	47						
G_1			−15	18	46		18				Q_1^1				−14	60					
G_2					64			13			Q_1^2				15	65					
Q_1^2						72					Q_2^1	17			14		53				
Q_2^2						53			−13		Q_2^2				−38		48				
D_1				24			32		15		D_1	−19						37	33		
D_2							80		−24		D_2	13						66	−31		
K_1				16				48			K_1			−24	15				30		
K_2		−20	−15					67		19	K_2			41			−14		57		
Q_6^1							39		26		P_1									72	
Q_6^2									13		P_2									32	
Q_7^1										52	Q_5^1			27							53
Q_7^2			15				20	45		15	Q_5^2	−15	24	−23							62

Note: Only loadings above 0.12 are given in these tables. To cover the relation to most 16 PF factors a different sample of the 16 PF part is taken in the two studies but all seven new source traits are taken from the missing factors part. (For matrices presented in full see Cattell and Delhees, 1973, and Cattell and DeVoogd, 1973.) There was no point in expending on pursuit of rotation to the utmost count on the old established factors, and such factors as H and O in the second study show broader hyperplanes than usual. In the new factors the markers for Q_6 and Q_7 are not satisfactory, but the others, D, K, P, and Q_5, are about as good as for old factors. The important point is that two research projects agree in showing the need for 22 dimensions, and confirm the intended markers. Actually, scales Q_6 and Q_7 and others have since been intensified by new item substitutions by Marshall for the 16 PF supplement, i.e., after intermediate scales used in the experiments here illustrated.

Table 6

Brief Designation of the Seven Missing Factors
(the 16 PF supplement in the normal behavior domain)

D: Insecure Excitability
I bubble over with ideas of things I want to do next.
(a) *Always* (b) Often (c) Practically never
The people I want never seem very interested in me.
(a) True (b) Uncertain (c) *False*

J: Coasthenia–vs–Zeppia
I enjoy getting a group together and leading them into some activity.
(a) True (b) Uncertain (c) *False*
People tell me I'm
(a) Apt to be noisy (b) In between (c) *Quiet and hard to understand*

K: Mature Socialization–vs–Boorishness.
I prefer plays that are
(a) Exciting (b) In between (c) *On socially important themes*
If I take up a new activity I like
(a) *To learn it as I go along* (b) In between (c) To read a book on it by an expert

P: Sanguine Casualness
I rarely let my mind stray into fantasies and make-believe.
(a) *True* (b) Uncertain (c) False
I most enjoy talking with my friends about
(a) *Local events* (b) In between (c) Great artists and pictures

Q_5: *Group Dedication with Sensed Inadequacy*
I like a project into which I can throw all my energies.
(a) *Yes* (b) Perhaps (c) No
In a situation which puts sudden demands on me I feel
(a) *No good* (b) In between (c) Confident of handling it

Q_6: *Social Panache*
I am good at inventing a clever justification when I appear in the wrong.
(a) *Yes* (b) Perhaps (c) No
I have never been called a dashing and daring person.
(a) True (b) Uncertain (c) *False*

Q_7: *Explicit Self-Expression*
I am not concerned to express my ideas at public meetings.
(a) True (b) Uncertain (c) *False*
In many undertakings I am in I don't seem to get a definite idea of what to do next.
(a) Yes (b) Perhaps (c) *No*

Note: Full justification of the titles is given in Chapter Five.

factor close to the next questionnaire factor meaning appeared as factor *K* in L(R)-data on the 350 student sample and the factor is so indexed. Factors *D* and *J* have appeared both in questionnaire factors at the child level (Chapter Three) and as L(R)-factors, previously so designated. We have used *A* through *P* in Q-data because we support the theoretical position that 15 factors in Q-data can also be found in L(R)-data, although no rating study has yet found all these primaries simultaneously. My conclusion is that seven factors, Q_1, Q_2, Q_3, Q_4, Q_5, Q_6, and Q_7 (the first four were in the 16 PF from the beginning) are established in the questionnaire medium only. This may mean only that their variances are small in the rating field and therefore that they are still likely to be found therein by superior methodology.

Psychological conceptions of these seven 16 PF Supplement factors must rest for the present on their content since as of 1972 there has been no time to explore such a rich array of criterion relations for them as have been found for the main 16 PF factors. However, the joint second-order structure with the main 16 PF (Chapter Four) tells us something, indicating, for example, by the high loading of *D* in anxiety (*Q*II) that the *D* excitability tends to be one of attention-getting insecurity; of *J* in invia (*Q*I) that the *J* trait participates somewhat in general introvert withdrawal; of *P*, sanguine casualness, negatively with anxiety and positively with independence (*Q*IV) showing that it is not just overcompensatory behavior; of Q_5, group dedication with superego (*Q*III), which is consistent; of Q_6 negatively with intelligence, suggesting that this is the compensatory panache of one used to failure. It is possible that Q_5 is a relatively narrow factor of training in group participation and that Q_7 is a pattern of bohemian self-expression that may be peculiar to our times.

Do these 23 primary source traits in Q-data exhaust the list of primaries in general normal personality? This question must undoubtedly be answered, in the name of caution, in the negative. The primary source traits found later in these systematic searches are for our culture of smaller variance than those found first. (The alphabetic position, it must be remembered, is intended to indicate diminishing variance, not order of discovery.) By variance ($\Sigma^n b^2/n$) a factor such as *N* is undoubtedly of less importance than *A*—affectia vs. sizia—which has long stood clinically as Bleuler's (1911), Kraepelin's (1921), and Kretschmer's (1921) cyclothymia versus schizothymia. Correspondingly Q_7 gives every indication of being less important than Q_1, radicalism-conservatism, or Q_2, self-sufficiency, with their large criterion predictions.

Indeed, the whole issue of questionnaire factors cannot be brought into perspective without recognizing that if investigators neglect an operational personality-sphere concept and put specialized questions together they can confuse themselves with an almost endless list of "common" factors, as some think has happened in Guilford's proliferation of ability factors. Moreover, if we include items covering abnormal behavior and pathological subjects, further dimensions undoubtedly remain to be considered (see Chapter Three). And when we move from these primaries to second orders a substanial riddle presents itself. For such matchings of Q- and T-data factors as have so far been successfully made have matched second-order Qs with first-order Ts. But this matching obviously cannot be carried to a one-to-one completeness because there are now some 20 first-order Ts and only about half that number of second-order Qs.

Our best perspective here is to remember that we are like a geographer mapping some mountain range. If he wishes to complete his map he will have to record eventually a diminishing series down to hillocks that scarcely merit a name.

With this closure of the theoretical research basis for the primary source trait identifications as such, it is appropriate to give a summary of the technical steps which follow in questionnaire construction as such (at least, as they have been followed in the IPAT series of questionnaires here and abroad).

First, a large number of items (in this case 1552) is made up by at least six different people (to avoid person-specific factors sometimes demonstrable in tests). The choice is made on the personality-sphere principles, and, for existing factors, from all that is known (in questionnaire, rating, and 16 PF criterion prediction data) about the number and nature of the emerging primary personality factors.

Second, these items are submitted to persons of different backgrounds and to word count surveys in order to eliminate uncommon words (Flesch word count) and items that are too long or ambiguous or too specific culturally.

Third, two population samples are taken, one toward the upper and one toward the lower half of the age and education range for which the test is intended, and correlation matrices are calculated among the items separately for these.

Fourth, in the light of the purpose (trait or state) and the population (age and so on) for which intended, a decision must be made between 2, 3, . . ., 6 alternatives in the multiple choice. The first examination of the data is to eliminate items with insufficient variance or extreme cuts (under 10 percent in one end category of three) before the calculation of correlation matrices. The phi coefficient or the tetrachoric is used. Phi divided by the maximum possible phi for the given extremity of cut has been used before and, like the tetrachoric, has the advantage of getting rid of difficulty factors, but since it is likely to yield non-Gramian matrices and since the alternative tetrachoric involves undue assumptions, the present studies have used generally the ordinary product moment (becoming phi for two categories).

Fifth, the *R* matrices from the two experiments are separately factored and rotated blindly to simple structure. It is important that the rotation be thorough, probably involving, as discussed under factor-analytic requirements, some 20 to 30 overall rotoplot rotations.

Sixth, items are picked for each factor having the highest correlations with the required factor, and, if possible, suppressing (positively and negatively canceling) correlations with another factor. At this point only those items are carried further that show emphatic consistency in their factor patterns in the two studies. For example, no matter how significant the positive loading on one study might be, the item would be rejected if it had insignificant or negative loading on the other. As the questionnaire progresses one examines the weight (V_{fe}) of the item rather than its simple correlation (V_{fs}) with the factor.

Seventh, to get suitable means, variance, and grading on each factor scale, the cuts (alternative response frequencies) are examined in regard to their summed effect. It is possible to predict both mean and variance of the resultant scale by certain assumptions from the combined cuts on the included items. The choice of items by cut should accordingly give a mean that is central on the possible scale range and a maximum scatter (near-even cuts) to an extent compatible with usefulness for extreme samples, as well as equal means and variances for the equivalent A and B forms.

Eighth, an even balance of counted yes and no responses is assembled from the surviving items, in regard to giving a positive score on each factor. By this balance one eliminates position or response-set effects.

Ninth, the items are symmetrically divided between A and B forms, as to factor loading, mean, variance, yes and no response, and so on, as determined above (partly to ensure the kind of equivalence cited in the seventh step). Then the items are arranged in the test layout in some form of cyclical order convenient for the scoring key, avoiding several items in sequence for the same factor.

Tenth, the scales are standardized with the usual attention to stratified sampling and other considerations.

8. Summary

(1) A brief survey has been made of the almost boundless development of questionnaire devices. Most are either devised ad hoc for some special trait of interest to some special investigator or else based on subjective concepts of trait structure. When consideration is limited to statistically and experimentally sound research, the field narrows to about a dozen developments: the scales of Barton, Comrey, Edwards, Eysenck, Guilford and Zimmerman, the IPAT series of questionnaires (16 PF, HSPQ, CPQ, and others), Jackson's PRI, the Kuder Inventory, the MMPI, the Thorndike scales, the Thurstone Temperament Schedule, and a few others.

(2) Among the technically advanced attacks on the problem there are still important divergencies that arise partly from deliberate differences of theoretical model, as in Guilford's aiming at orthogonal factors and my IPAT series (and Thurstone's scales) aiming at oblique factors, or in Comrey's factoring subscales instead of items and thus proceeding to second orders rather than primaries. When these effects of diverse methods are considered the situation is not so chaotic as it may first appear, and with attention to technical points a reconciliation on common conclusions can reasonably be approached.

(3) Nevertheless, to achieve integration within the compass of a moderately sized volume it seems desirable to confine discussion to approaches with programatic methods than can be integrated and to investigations strictly within the domain of general personality-temperament traits. The latter aim rests also on the argument that self-evaluation by the questionnaire approach is suitable (and even there has difficulties) only for that modality and not for abilities or interests and motivation. Abilities and interest can be more successfully measured by objective tests. Consequently the

Edwards, Jackson, Kuder, and Strong tests and the semantic-differential instruments are left for examination elsewhere.

(4) Confining the facts and concepts to those from personality questionnaires based on objective search for dimensions by obliquely rotated factor analyses (as in the Barton, Bartsch, Coan, Comrey, Curran, Dielman, Dreger, Eysenck, Porter, Schaie, Scheier, Sells, Shrader, Thurstone, and other scales), it becomes necessary to begin by defining the common conditions and standards for integratable factor analyses: (1) developing a stratified sample of items from the personality sphere (reducible to 46 variables); (2) carrying markers from any previously claimed factor; (3) using an objective statistical test to decide the number of factors to be taken out; (4) iterating to appropriate communalities; (5) rotating blindly to maximum, oblique structure, which involves pursuit beyond the point reached by an automatic rotation program; (6) applying the Bargmann test of significance to the simple structure believed to have been reached; and (7) basing conclusions about invariance with other research findings on the significance of a congruence or salient variable similarity index.

(5) The error or instability in a factor-analytic experiment that is caused by change of population, insufficiency of markers, and especially the wobble in simple-structure determination, makes any attempt to formulate source-trait concepts and personality scales on the basis of a single factorial experiment, however large, absurd. A programatic approach with coordinated sequences and interlocking variables and method is indispensable. Such research is found only in four or five laboratories, and in terms of sequences and publications the greater part of this has been accomplished by some 50 investigators whose convergence on common standards and models has permitted programatic, constructive interaction in research over the past 25 years. Accordingly this has been made the core of the exposition of development from 1948 to 1973 in this chapter. After the theoretical development is clearly set out it will be critically examined in relation to alternatives in Chapter Eight.

(6) The experimental work began with the adult domain and covered 12 successive factor analyses on 8000 to 10,000 items and several thousand subjects. This work proceeded with progressive clarification from the evidence of 15 primary factors in 1948 to their stabilization in four or five parallel forms (A, B, C, D, and E) for each factor in the 16 PF and its seven-factor extension. With so many variables involved in the rotational space a simple structure reached at one stage does not prejudice further movement to new simple structures in what has been called progressive rectification.

(7) Considerable overlap in the factor space covered is evident among the 16 PF and HSPQ scales, and the G-Z, Eysenck, and Comrey scales. However, the 16 PF and G-Z, in spite of substantial overlap, can only be tightly aligned on about four factors because one system is oblique and the other orthogonal. The Eysenck and Comrey scales seem to align quite well with second-order factors of the 16 PF. In earlier work—for example, in Eysenck's three-factor system and some research today—certain scales differ from the 16 PF in taking out too few factors; in Eysenck's scales this holds even at

the second order, where eight are indicated. Discussion of relation to the MMPI is deferred to Chapter Three.

(8) We conclude that 23 primary factors can be located and demonstrated as independent within the personality sphere of normal behavior; these include 7 missing factors located in the last decade. Probably 15 of the 23 are paralleled by factors found in L-data. These 15 are indexed *A* through *P,* in approximate order of diminishing variance, in order not to prejudice theoretical interpretation by premature interpretive labels.

(9) Factors Q_1 through Q_7 are so indexed to show that they have appeared only as "mental interiors." When factors sharpen concepts already known to clinical psychology—for example, *A,* affectia (or cyclothymia); *B,* intelligence; *C,* ego strength; *G,* superego strength—existing technical terms are preserved; but when new they are given new labels rather than battered popular terms. Thus such terms as surgency for *F,* premsia (protected emotionality) for *I,* protension (projection of tension) for *L,* self-sentiment for Q_3, and ergic tension for Q_4 have helped to keep better order than is possible with shifting popular terms.

III

Structure in Normal Child Development and in Pathology

With some 15 factor patterns (16 with intelligence) repeatedly defined as primaries among adults and the "seven missing factors" now checked and incorporated in scales of usable validity, one naturally inquires, "What should be the next step in a systematic and scientific investigation of human personality structure?" Diverse directions are conceivable. One could, for instance, pursue the relation of personality factors to life criteria. Or one could explore the degree of constancy across other cultures, that is, the universality of the concepts. Or one could look at instrument factors in measurement by comparing Q-data with L- and T-data factors. Or one could plot developmental curves and examine nature-nurture ratios. Criterion relations will look after themselves (see Chapter Ten) once the major task of locating the source traits and building good scales for them is done, for many investigators stand ready for this interesting task. And constancy across other cultures (see Chapter Eight) is surely an issue that can be left until matters nearer home have been taken care of. Indeed, from a basic psychological standpoint the important question is the developmental one. If we are to study not just the adult but humankind then obviously the first question is how often these source-trait structures found in adults appear also in children.

1. Research Strategy and Test Construction in Expanding from the Adult Core

The question is of basic importance if developmental psychology is to establish itself, as it now should, upon exact curves and quantitative laws; for the growth of a trait and its response to various influences cannot be followed unless it can be located and measured as the same entity over an appreciable age range. Allied to this expansion of research into childhood is the expansion from this same core of knowledge about normal adults into the abnormal, clinical area. Are these factors modified or increased in number as one enters the domain of abnormal behavior? In other words, are clinical cases deviant only on the same dimensions found in normals or do they show entirely new pathological dimensions constituting disease processes?

This chapter condenses the evidence on both these directions of natural exploration of structure—into childhood and into deviant behavior. In Chapter Eight I view other cultures and explore the relations of Q-data source traits to those in the other media—L- and T-data. To anticipate, let it be said that the excellent rating studies of Huffman, Lorr and Jenkins, Digman (1970), and others surveyed elsewhere (Cattell, 1946b, 1957) strongly indicate that the same observer rating factors will be found in children as have been listed for adults, covering about three-fourths of the factors identified in the questionnaire realm.[1] However, let us examine the Q-data in and of itself.

As in many areas of science, the best expository sequence is the historical sequence. And here we shall note that in truly programatic research the principle of spanning the personality sphere was again basic in the selection and creation of items. Also, markers were carefully introduced in the opening studies by Beloff, Coan, Gruen, Peterson, and others in the Illinois Laboratory of Personality Analysis to relate carefully to any factors previously revealed (sometimes only with orthogonal rotation) in existing research and from other laboratories. Thus the 1946 survey already showed a few sporadic correlational studies on children's questionnaire responses,

[1] Apart from these studies no adequate source-trait factorization of ratings in children existed. Actually, such a rating experiment still does not exist by the desirable standards for ratings given in Chapter Seven. But the work of Ackerson (1942), McDonough (1929), Flemming (1935), Cattell and Gruen (1953), Maurer (1941), Tryon (1943), Williams (1935), and especially Huffman (see Cattell, 1957) and Koch (1942) suggested by the early 1950s that 12 to 15 dimensions could be demonstrated and that they were similar in meaning to the L(R)-data patterns for adults. The later child-rating studies of Coan (Cattell and Coan, 1957a,b), Peterson (Peterson and Cattell, 1958, 1959), and others brought more definite evidence on the agreement with adults on such patterns as *A*, affectia; *B*, general intelligence; *C*, ego strength; *E*, dominance; *F*, surgency; and *G*, superego strength. Apart from the extent of agreement on the rating factors there remained the 45 to 50 rating variables (Cattell, 1957) to help guide the development of questionnaire items from the L(R)-medium of the *personality sphere for child behavior*.

such as those of Flanagan (1935) and Brogden and Thomas (1943); my survey one decade later (1957) picked up two or three more factors, although unfortunately not connected by common markers and methods.

By the time the third (checking) factor analysis of the 1949 Adult 16 PF (see Chapter Two) had been completed the time seemed ripe for a systematic attempt to relate the factor structure of adults to an integration of childhood data. This effort was begun with the work of Beloff in 1952 (Cattell and Beloff, 1953) in the 10-to-14-year range, with a cross-checking study by Cattell and Gruen (1954) in the same range (11 to 14 years in that case). These studies observed the five conditions of factor analysis essential for effective exploration of a new domain, special attention being given to proper sampling of the personality sphere.

Theorists have commonly supposed that factors would be fewer and broader in children. If any weight is given to this speculation one might ask why the experimental design of the Illinois group did not begin with the less complex child structure and work upward. There are several good reasons for the strategy of starting with the normal adult and feeling one's way to the earlier structures and to pathological modifications. In the first place, one does not want errors from complications in the purely cognitive field while exploring the personality field. With children there are problems of reading and verbal understanding that might force one to forego due representation of certain areas of behavior. Similarly, with clinical cases problems of misperception of language and irrationality of responses arise. Such distortions interfere with the confident matching of Q-data factors (mental interior views) with the corresponding L(R)-data patterns because of unreliability in the Q-patterns. Moreover, if the self-perceptions of children—quite apart from language difficulties—should prove to be naïve and unstable (low in reliability coefficients), it would be a poor place to start trying to define elusive basic structures. My own theory does not agree with the assumptions of the theorists mentioned. I do not hypothesize—except in the dynamic area—that trait structure will automatically become simpler in the young—indeed, through lack of integration and maturation there could be more factors. Inasmuch as the major factors are ones of temperament modality, my guiding hypothesis was that one should expect the dimensionality of the young child and the adult to be much the same. In the physiological and anatomical domain essentially the same number of organs and hormones function in the child as in the adult.

Because of these considerations the best strategy has seemed to start with adults and work down. This approach also gives the advantage that the personality sphere can include markers for the adult factors so deliberately and gradually modified for children that a continuity of variables might be established. We aimed to make these steps with (1) sufficient replicatory studies to consolidate source-trait patterns at any age before attempting precise bridging by comparing factor patterns and (2) the introduction of *direct bridging by setting up boundary* research projects between adjoining age periods of the groups in which factor structures have been separately established. In such a boundary study the younger group must not be too young to read the common test and the older group not so old as to regard its content as childish. The age periods ultimately chosen are four: the high school period, 12 to 18 years; the child period, 8 to 12 years; the early school period, 6 to 8 years; and the preschool period, 4 to 6 years. The abbreviations HS, C, ES, and PS will be used hereafter for these periods; for example, the high school personality questionnaire scales will be designated the HSPQ. These periods tend to shorten as one goes down the developmental range; this is a planned response to the more rapid development and the rapid change of environment that occurs in the earlier years.

There is a whole realm of item construction research and of craftsmanship in the modification of questionnaires for children. This fact has created problems in ensuring continuity of marker variables. Item marker identity is essential to comparative bridging, that is, for comparison of factor patterns; but by the direct-bridging (boundary-group) method the identity of a factor for 16-year-olds with that for 10-year-olds can be established by direct correlation of factor scores (even when all items are different).

There seem to be five chief matters for consideration in this age adaptation.

First is the appropriate reduction in the size of vocabulary and grammatical complication.

Second is a skillful psychological translation of the same styles of behavior (for example, the sociability of factor *A*, the aggressiveness of factor *E*, the moral struggles of factor *G*) into the new domains of interest, as from family economics, politics, and career to school, peer group, parent interaction, and games. This translation of essential personality pattern reactions from one world of interest to another brings out once more the independence asserted in Chatper Two for the *general personality modality* and the *interest-motivation modality*. (See discussion of the realm of Edwards' EPPS and Jackson's PRF in Chapter Two.) The whole domain of interest involvement and specific motivation extends to new realms, from the nursery floor to the professional-social-political interests of the developed adult; but the broadest personality traits—affectia, surgency, ego strength, intelligence—have a continuity of pattern, though changing somewhat in level, in the individual's life.

Third, an adjustment must be made of the form of presentation to the cognitive attention span. This has taken the form of shorter questions and a reduction of the number of alternatives from four (CTS kit) to three (HSPQ) and so to two (CPQ, ESPQ, and PSPQ). The evidence on the effect of number of multiple choices is still obscure, mainly because experimenters have examined only limited aspects of the desiderata (see Chapter Nine on these psychometric matters). For example, experimenters show that more alternatives increase the reliability; but they do not consider the increased testing time or the reduced validity that might result from the subject's fatigue and aversion to complication. A multifactor estimate of total efficiency (Chapter Ten) is needed. In any case our plan has reduced the number of choices to two at the lowest age (forced-choices create no difficulties here), and it has introduced a device to repeat the alternatives, avoiding dependence on a long immediate memory.

Fourth, the whole style of presentation must be altered. In the 8 to 12 CPQ range the first alteration is introduced: that of allowing the question to be read aloud to the group at lower ages (in the 6 to 8 group the reading aloud is required). Here also the child does not have to read the alternatives themselves or mark them on a special answer sheet. Instead he rings a drawing, for example, a dog or a cat, directly on the paper before him. For the CPQ and PSPQ the two alternatives are put in explicit antithesis form: "Do you like best to play old games? Or to try new games?"

For the youngest group of all (the Pre-School Personality Questionnaire—henceforth PSPQ—(4 to 6 years) the questions are on tape, issuing from a mechanical speaker in a standard modulation (a woman's voice), and the experimenter treats it as an individual test, making the record of the child's response himself.

Fifth and last, the change in attention and fatigue spans due to age needs to be respected in both item length and total test length. Here opposing principles have to be reconciled: with young children more items may be needed to get the same degree of reliability and validity (because their behavior has more specificity and because their Q-responses have more random error), yet fewer items can be done at a session. The distinction in test construction needs to be made here (as followed in IPAT tests) between equivalent *forms* that are long enough to yield a separate, valid *score;* and *sessions* or parts that are short enough for a single test sitting without undue fatigue. At the adult and high school ages these can conveniently be allowed to coincide; the 30- to 45-minute 16 PF Form A is appropriate for both score reliability and session convenience. But at the PSPQ and ESPQ levels the sessions must be cut shorter than the forms. Thus no one should use two sessions or parts of these tests A1 and A2 (listed where A in form 1 or 2 is part of session) as if they had the status of equivalent forms—for which they are too brief.

2. Evidence on Primary Source-Trait Structure in High School and Middle Childhood

Among those who contributed most to the exploration of Q-data factors in children, Beloff, Mary Cattell, Gruen, Porter, Schaie, and Wagner concentrated on the two upper levels—8 to 12 years and 12 to 18 years. The tactics of research called for developing some scale structure at the middle of this 8 to 18 range and then specializing the common set of factors discovered into expressions suitable for the HSPQ (12 to 18) and then into the somewhat more difficult adaptations needed for the 8 to 12 range in the CPQ.

I shall condense the history of the child research developments here because a series of published articles is available to the basic researcher who wishes to follow up specific technical issues, and because *the basic correlational and factor tables* have been deposited at the National Auxiliary Publication Service.[2]

In the opening of programatic research in this area, which began two years after the stabilization of the adult Q-factors, all three media—ratings, questionnaires, and objective tests—were used in an intensive study of 184 children by Gruen (Cattell and Gruen, 1953, 1954, 1955) at the Mooseheart Laboratory, Illinois. For the questionnaire analysis 149 boys and girls were added, giving an N of 333 at a mean age of 11.3. Elimination of items showing extreme cuts (beyond 70-30) or considered by the children to lack clarity cut the initial 295 items down to 103. Fourteen factors were indicated, which after 14 overall rotations settled down at a simple structure as satisfactory as is usually obtained with items—at 60 percent in ± 0.10 loadings (Cattell and Gruen, 1954). By content, 13 of these factors seemed reasonably identifiable with 13 of the 15 in the 16 PF, but this matching was later to be put to a more rigorous objective evaluation. The only noteworthy difference from the adult results that appeared in this and the next study was that factors *I, O,* Q_4, and perhaps *G* had stepped up from their adult alphabetical index rank to a decidedly larger variance, larger for example than the *A, C, E,* and *F* source traits. The issue of dependable inference regarding variance change is taken up below.

A second and a third factoring, combining the most factor-valid items with new extension forms (extensions) consisting of newly constructed items from the personality sphere, was carried out by Beloff. The 115-item extension led to the survival of sufficient items for a first published experimental set of scales for 12 factors (plus intelligence) on a 60 percent plus hyperplane basis with 12 items per factor (Cattell and Beloff, 1953). The factors beyond 12 were for the time being neglected. The third study shifted to a group of 240 16-year-olds used as a boundary group to enable us to match with 16 PF factors by giving the child and adult tests together. Beloff augmented the scale validities by replacing items of lower validity (henceforth "deadwood") with higher-loaded items from a new 128-item extension (see *progressive rectification* in Chapter Eight, Section 3).

The child factors believed by content to be *A, B, E, G, H, I, O,* and Q_3 had their best (and highly significant) correlations with the hypothesized matches in the 16 PF factors. But $C(-)$, Q_4, and possibly *O* showed a tendency to run together into a single factor—noticed again in later less exact factorings—and factors believed to be *L, M,* and *N* were poorly identified.

Some of the trouble with these five factors was almost certainly caused by shortcomings inherent in the boundary-age technique—high-

[2] This is a branch of the American Society for Information Service. Microfilms of matrices can be obtained relatively inexpensively from CCM Information Science, Inc., 22 W. 34th St., New York. Precise references for obtaining these matrix deposits are given in the 50 or so articles in the bibliography from the Illinois Personality Analysis Laboratory and in a few others.

school-age items cease to be psychologically apt for the 18-year-olds in the adult boundary-level group. Granting some difficulty from this source I still think there are some systematic, inherent problems with respect to (1) the substantial correlations that arise among $C(-)$, O, and Q_4 in both older and younger groups; (2) the tendency of items well loaded on one of these also to measure to some extent the others, that is, there is a tendency to a common *cluster;* and (3) the smaller variance and relatively poor definition of L, M, and N.

These problems will not be fully examined at this juncture, but it is possible that in the curious cooperativeness of loadings on $C(-)$, O, and Q_4—ego weakness, guilt proneness, and ergic tension—we have an instance of nonlinear relations that need further exploration outside the factor model. Later I show that the only second-order factor that covers them, anxiety, also covers H, L, and Q_3—which do not "cluster." But in $C(-)$, O, and Q_4 there may additionally be mutual positive feedback such that guilt proneness, O, and frustrated drive tension, Q_4, weaken ego strength, C, directly. The hypothesis will also be considered later that the effect could be due to state factors intruding on top of trait factor variance, for situationally we should expect guilt proneness, O, to become high at times when frustrated drive (ergic tension, Q_4) is high. At any rate, it is quite difficult to find behavioral responses that do not involve to some extent all three factors. This situation has repeatedly led factorists using coarse methods to assert that a single factor is all that is needed to account for $C(-)$, O, and Q_4, but tests of dimensionality show indubitably that three influences are at work; careful rotation replicates the $C(-)$, O, and Q_4 meanings. The weakness of factors M and N (autism and shrewdness), to which I later add Q_1 (radicalism versus conservatism), is almost certainly due to their taking more markedly different areas of expression in childhood than is customary with other factors.

After the third factor-analytic replication—with its general confirmation of patterns at the child level but uncertainty with particular emerging factors—the planned split was made into the development of one questionnaire for the years 8 to 12 (the CPQ) and another for the years 12 to 18 (the HSPQ). To strengthen definition and validity in the HSPQ a new personality-sphere-chosen set of 450 items was introduced, over and above the core of known marker items for 12 to 14 factors. These items were conceived and written jointly by Coan and myself in the United States and Beloff in Great Britain with the aim of fitting both cultures. After reduction to 365 items the test was given to 200 British children in a factor-to-item correlation design that found 251 new items relevant to these factors. This is not counted as an independent factor analysis in our series since the existing factors were accepted as referents in this item analysis.

The fourth factoring was done with the parceling method. Two (six-item) markers were set up for each of the 12 scales and 46 new homogeneous parcels (six-item) were added. Subjects were 168 12- and 13-year-olds in Indiana (with the help of Rutherford Porter). Thirteen factors were again indicated (scree test) and were rotated with great thoroughness (20 overall rotations) to a hyperplane maximum of 65 percent, a value well beyond the $P < 0.01$ significance level by the Bargmann test.

A published experimental 14-scale HSPQ with equivalent A and B forms of 10 items each resulted from this work, in which the following three conditions (discussed in Chapter Ten) were observed. First, no item was allowed to be involved in two scale scores (this had not been true of other current scales). Second, suppressor action of unwanted factors was sought; that is, if item *x* is loaded positively on the wanted factor *A* and positively on some unwanted factor *B,* it should be balanced by another item, *y,* still positively contributing to *A* but negatively loaded on *B* to suppress the contamination introduced by *x*'s loading on *B.* Third, a balanced score on each factor for yes and no response sets (acquiescence tendency) was maintained. At this point a boundary study with the 16 PF was again made to check that, with any progressive movement of factor axes that might have taken place in successive rotations, the matching identify with *A, B, C,* and so on, in the 16 PF stood firm. A substantial confirmation of identities together with an evaluation of the general psychometric properties (reliability, equivalence, factor validity) of the experimental scores (Cattell, Coan, and Beloff, 1958) justified at this point the publication of the HSPQ in a form to encourage further experimentation.

The fifth HSPQ factoring (published as a laboratory report) simply took the 28 forms (14 factors, A and B forms of each) and factored on 449 boys and girls from Boston, to 14 factors with a Dwyer extension calculation on 400 newly designed items. This yielded the present complete HSPQ of A, B, C, and D forms each with 10 items per factor. The determination of structure for these 56 scales in the sixth and seventh factor analysis constitutes the most thorough analysis to date. The sixth study was on 399 girls and the seventh on 401 boys, average ages 13.6 and 14.3, sampled from four states (Cattell, Wagner, and Cattell, 1970). The scree test gave 16 factors in both cases. A prolonged, blind rotation for simple structure reached plateaus at the hitherto unequaled values of 73.4 and 73.2 percent, the Bargmann significances being adequate except for factors *C, J,* and Q_2.

The congruence coefficients between the factor patterns thus independently reached for boys and girls ranged from 0.27 to 0.84. All but one (which stayed at $P < 0.05$ level) are above the $P < 0.01$ significance level. The congruences were highest for intelligence (*B*) and premsia (*I*) and lowest for excitability (*D*) and ergic tension (Q_4). From the large table of factor loadings available elsewhere (Cattell, Wagner, and Cattell, 1970) Table 7(a) reproduces six samples. At this sixth step in the factor-analytic series, despite the adequacy of simple structure and the indubitable recognition of factors by significant loadings on 23 of the 24 required markers, there is still much room for improvement. Some factors are loaded on scales they should not load; factor *A* in boys, for example, has two significant loadings on factor *E.* Conversely, some scales have loadings on factors they should not include;

scale D form A on boys, for example, has a —0.39 loading on ego strength, *C*.

One must distinguish between failure of the analysis to yield a particular, identifiable factor at the simple-structure position—which would be serious—and weakness of validity or presence of contamination in the scales—which occurs here as in most early constructions, and can be remedied. Note that the latter flaws rarely persist across both male and female groups, which suggests that they are local to the group and are not so much errors in the main scale as inappropriateness of the scale to certain kinds of groups. For example, something in the intelligence scale, B—form A, second row, Table 7(a)—perhaps verbal knowledge, is negatively (—0.29) connected with affectia in boys. But if we changed these items we might get more contamination with girl subjects because there the scale is already loaded positively (0.23).

The outcome (boys and girls in a single group; the main intended use) as shown in Table 7(b) is satisfactory, reaching validities for a single form typical of 10-item scales. If we use all four scales with boys or girls alone it is again satisfactory, validities of about 0.9 being the rule. Nevertheless there is "noise" in the measurements (that is, relatively random unwanted loadings), as shown by the number of loadings above 0.20 that scatter themselves in undesired places in Table 7(a). Consequently it seemed desirable to proceed to further programatic experiments beyond the six described in the initial development.

Table 7

HSPQ Factor Structure and Concept Validities
(a) Factor Structure (mean ages 13.6 and 14.3 years)

	401 Boys						399 Girls					
Scales	*A*	*B*	*C*	*F*	*G*	*H*	*A*	*B*	*C*	*F*	*G*	*H*
Form A												
A	39				—30		48			26		
B	—29	76					23	85				
C			49						71			
D			—39		—29							
E		—33		23						39		—61
F				57						72		
G					71				33		42	
H						52			43			35
I									23			
J			—32									
O			—38			—34			—31			
Q_2							—51		43			
Q_3				—22							29	
Q_4			—54			—33	21					
Form B												
A	28						73					

Table 7 (cont.)

Scales	*401 Boys*						*399 Girls*					
	A	*B*	*C*	*F*	*G*	*H*	*A*	*B*	*C*	*F*	*G*	*H*
B		[79]					−25	70				
C			[22]			39			70	−23		23
D											31	
E	−46			[32]	38							
F				37	−35				35	52		
G			−28		[68]	22					46	
H					−34	[49]	24		45			35
I												
J					−47		−31					
O							−26					
Q_2							−38					
Q_3						30	22					
Q_4		22	−32			20						
Form C												
A	[78]						[51]					
B	22	[59]						[74]				
C			[28]		21		−24		[65]			
D					24							
E	21			−35					23			21
F				[42]	−40				−22	[57]		
G				−26	[66]						[46]	
H					22	[45]	32				23	[32]
I				−24			31			−22		
J	23								29			
O							23		−26			
Q_2												
Q_3										−45		
Q_4									−38			
Form D												
A	[42]						[52]					
B	27	[64]					−27	[73]				
C			[21]						[66]			
D											−30	
E						26			34		−32	
F				[70]	−24					[60]		
G					[41]						[74]	
H						[17]	24		−27	43	25	[25]
I						33			−29			
J												
O							43		−68			−22
Q_2									22			
Q_3					−21							
Q_4											−38	

Note: This table instances two blocks of three factors each (*A, B, C* and *F, G, H*) and economizes also by reproducing no loading (presumably below significance) within ±0.20 inclusive. The factors other than *A, B, C, F, G,* and *H* in general load significantly on their appropriate columns which for economy are omitted here, though their off correlations are shown in the columns here.

Table 7 (cont.)

Factor Structure and Concept Validities of the HSPQ
(b) Concept Validities by Ordinary Key Scoring and by Computer Synthesis
(correlations of scales with pure factors)

Factor	1 Form A (Boys and Girls)	2 Forms A + B (Boys and Girls)	All 4 Forms A + B + C + D Boys	Girls
A	0.67	0.80	0.91	0.94
B	0.69	0.81	0.92	0.93
C	0.71	0.84	0.85	0.96
D	0.63	0.77	0.86	0.96
E	0.65	0.79	0.81	0.83
F	0.68	0.81	0.90	0.94
G	0.68	0.81	0.92	0.92
H	0.72	0.84	0.91	0.85
I	0.70	0.82	0.91	0.87
J	0.58	0.72	0.88	0.86
O	0.77	0.86	0.86	0.84
Q_2	0.61	0.74	0.93	0.92
Q_3	0.57	0.72	0.88	0.94
Q_4	0.74	0.85	0.88	0.93

Note: Columns 1 and 2 are on 200 boys and girls; columns 3 and 4 are on 401 boys and 399 girls. The first two use only the 10 items keyed for the given scale. The last two use all 560 items in the test in the computer synthesis method described in the text.

Three further studies have been carried out by Friel (1972), Burdsal and Cattell (1973), and Vaughan and Cattell (in preparation), aimed primarily at checking structure in different populations and intensifying certain subscales on factors *C, D, E, J,* and Q_4 that had weak loadings. The first study took 1836 subjects from rural West Virginia and created four groups (456 girls and 466 girls; 410 boys and 504 boys), each given a separate factor analysis using 42 variables (three parcels randomly set up from the 10 items of each factor). Fourteen factors were clearly indicated and a good simple structure with means of 61, 62, 63, and 63 percent in the ± 0.10 hyperplane for the four samples was obtained. The congruence coefficients were all highly significant across the pattern from the four unique resolutions. Friel (1972, p. 58) reports that "cross validation generally supports the HSPQ factors" but adds that correlations among the primaries were higher than previously found, particularly for *D* (excitability) and Q_4 (ergic tension). However, the second orders found by T. W. Klein (1973) from these primaries turned out to be as usually hypothesized.

The second study (eighth in the series) by Burdsal and Cattell (1973) was on a group of 600 boys and girls from Illinois. The uppermost end of the HSPQ age range was chosen for a boundary study in which matches with the 16 PF would be checked. The study yielded 16 factors that rotated at once by maxplane to a simple structure of 62 percent in the hyperplane, conclusively yielding the hypothesized structure at a Bargmann significance of $P < 0.05$. The Vaughan and Cattell analysis (the ninth) is still in progress.

Although the HSPQ has its imperfections—such as the apparently greater suitability of the factor *C* items for girls than boys—the work in this age range has produced at least four solid conclusions for theory, as well as reliable help where test practice has hitherto lacked measures.

First, by correlational matching at boundary studies the number and nature of source traits in the 12-to-18-year range have been demonstrated to be similar to those in adults.

Second, some factors nevertheless seem of smaller variance and definition, and three—*L, M,* and Q_1—are not reliably reproduced. On the other hand two new factors, labeled *D* (excitability) and *J* (asthenia), appear that were not reliably located in adults until 1972.

Third, the validities of the present factor scales are those expected from good 10-item scales in any pencil and paper test. It is reassuring that the validities for these personality factor scales, item for item, are not lower than those for the much-longer-established general intelligence factor (Scale B in the HSPQ). Indeed, roughly half the validities are higher than for the intelligence scale, using the same number of items. These validities are modest—about 0.65 for a single form, which is "par" for 10 items—but through the provision of more forms (A, B, C, and D) and by computer synthesis, the practitioner can reach high validities centering on 0.9 [Table 7(b)].

Fourth and last, there are indications that in some factors scales that are relatively strong for one sex are relatively weak for another, and the possibility must be faced that in some ideal future construction different scale-item collections should be set up for males and females.

With the assurance of essentially consistent structure at the 12-to-18-year level, research turned to the 8-to-12-year (CPQ) level. After the three common 11-to-12-year factorings previously described and a study by Schaie (1962) to check the relation of questionnaire to rating factors in the 8-to-12-year range, Schaie and Porter developed a preliminary 14-scale factor questionnaire in two equivalent A and B forms, with boys and girls averaging 11 years. A check for identification with the ESPQ at the lower boundary (157 third-graders) and with the HSPQ at the upper boundary (182 sixth-graders) showed much common space but relatively disappointing alignment of similarly indexed factors. Thus factors *C* (ego strength) and *F* (surgency) were poor in terms of the ESPQ factors *C* and *F* at the lower boundary analysis, whereas form A of factors *D* and *E* and form B of factors *A, G,* and Q_4 were weak in loading at the factors defined in common with the HSPQ at the upper boundary. The authors promptly advised caution in the use of the experimental CPQ to identify *C, E, F,* and Q_4 with similarly named factors in the other scales, at least for one form of the test.

Accordingly a fifth and more substantial factor analysis intended to intensify and rotate more precisely these weak scales was undertaken by Porter, Schaie, and myself between 1968 and 1972. We used the four equivalent form markers per factor, added a substantial extension block of 300 new items, and applied the test to a population sample of 330 boys and girls in grades 3, 4, 5, and 6. Results are shown in Table 8, which for economy condenses the full 15 factors to exemplification in a matrix of six factors. The simple structure is now distinctly high and the majority of markers load as they were hypothesized to do.

Table 8

Personality Source-Trait Structure in Q-Data at 8-to-12-Year Level

Test Forms As Numbered in Matrix	*Primary Factors*					
	B	*C*	*D*	*E*	*F*	Q_4
1 *B* Form A	63					18
2 *B* Form B	72	14		−13		
3 *B* Form C	90					
4 *B* Form D	70		20	15		
5 *C* Form A		76		−19		
6 *C* Form B		80				
7 *C* Form C	14	32		14		−12
8 *C* Form D	11	38	16		15	
9 *D* Form A		11	49	15		22
10 *D* Form B		−16	13		−19	
11 *D* Form C			11			
12 *D* Form D	14	−12	11			35
13 *E* Form A	13		48	31		
14 *E* Form B	17			30		
15 *E* Form C				24	16	
16 *E* Form D				46		30
17 *F* Form A			22		34	
18 *F* Form B	19		−15	25	25	
19 *F* Form C		−11		19	42	−22
20 *F* Form D		35		17	24	
53 Q_4 Form A			61			47
54 Q_4 Form B		−16		13		53
55 Q_4 Form C	21	11			22	11
56 Q_4 Form D		11				43

Note: Exemplified by four scales on each of six factors the CPQ; Schaie, Porter, and Cattell, 1973; N = 330.

The chief weakness at this stage of research in the CPQ was clearly in the *D* factor, especially in its relation to *E*. Connections of *D*, excitability, with *E*, dominance, have been observed before. All the published CPQ scales have been improved by item analysis since the results reached by this fifth factor analysis.

In summary of the 8-to-12-year-range studies a 14-factor structure is demonstrated although two or three more source traits are indubitably but less clearly present. The fact that *N*, dropped from the HSPQ (the scale stretching between the 16 PF and the CPQ), now reappears suggests that with care it can be located in the middle age range. However, it has not matched well with *N* in the ESPQ, which leaves open the possibility that although the factor is roughly orthogonal to the same 12 other factors in the CPQ and the 16 PF it might not be the same factor. Until the HSPQ *N* scale is constructed the requisite boundary study is impossible. Meanwhile the HSPQ preadult factors *D* (excitability) and *J* (asthenia) maintain themselves in this younger range and continue even below it.

3. Source-Trait Structure at the Early School Age Level

Since the change in administration technique—from written to oral presentation and from three to two response alternatives—on reaching these lower age levels might modify structure, the results of exploring these lowermost levels were awaited with much curiosity. As in the last two sections and age ranges, I deem it desirable to set out the actual programatic research, with sizes of samples, results of tests for number of factors, percentage reached in the hyperplane of rotation, and so on. A bald statement of conclusions might be easier, but the serious investigator still has to find his way among too many such poorly based and conflicting "conclusions" in the literature, so it is better to present sufficient evidence for him to reach his own conclusions. The first factoring at the 6-to-7-year level was begun by Coan in 1956 on 151 boys and girls (mean age 6.6 years), again basing items on a personality sphere. This factoring consisted of a representative basis of 200 items which he, an experienced child psychologist, had designed. The planned program of research called for obtaining the first indications of the number and positions of factors by *item factoring,* followed by more exact determination by parceled factoring using the progressive rectification process.

In order to keep within the capacity of computers and to avoid the number of variables *n* exceeding the number of persons *N,* (an impasse reached more readily with items than parcels), I introduced matrix meshing. This alternative to parceled factoring is designed to meet the problem of large numbers of items, but is more difficult. One hundred twenty-five of the 200 items were first factored to simple structure and then the 48 most salient markers from the simple structure thus obtained were added to the 75 items remaining to be factored in a second set of 123 items. The two factor analyses (both of which suggested 22 factors, ultimately rotated down to 18) are thus not independent in persons sampling but are independent in factoring and in the blind rotation process. These analyses gave an excellent mutual check in that the 48 common meshing variables moved to the same factor pattern in the second factoring and simple-structure rotation as in the first. The two studies were thus locked together. The hyperplane counts were 65 and 61 percent respectively, somewhat better than usual for item factoring (Cattell & Coan, 1958). Judged by content the factors resembled those already found for older children in the CPQ and HSPQ. Again those identified as *I* and *G* were larger in variance than for adults, and those for factors *A* and *F* were smaller.

The third and fourth factor experiments were carried out by Coan, as usual taking the best items from the previous work along with newly constructed extension items. One hundred and eighty-one mid-Western boys and girls aged 6 to 10 years (mean age 7.5) responded to 172 items, again factored by matrix meshing (111 items, the first 50 carried over to make new set of 111). Again 18 factors were indicated and the third and fourth independent rotational resolutions matched excellently, the congruence matching indices running from 0.57 to 0.86 (Coan and Cattell, 1958).

The only oddity about these four factor experiments was the appearance of 18 factors where 14 to 16 had sufficed before. Since only 13 or 14 of the 18 could be identified the most likely explanations are (1) that in younger children there is more error and that common-error factors therefore loomed larger, creating two extras, or (2) that Coan's search for new items had been more creatively pursued than usual and had unearthed dimensions not previously encountered. Recent evidence points to both explanations.

Four more factorings proceeded to the present scales, as follows. A fifth study primarily directed as a boundary research to identify labels was made by giving the scales of the 12 factors (13 with intelligence) of the proto-ESPQ (Early School Personality Questionnaire) along with the HSPQ (the CPQ had not yet matured) to two samples (105 and 92) of boys and girls of 9 and 10 years. (Each hypothesized factor was represented by two six-item scales.) From the correlations (Coan & Cattell, 1959), the factors known at higher ages as *A, B, C, D, E, F, G, H, I, K, O,* and Q_4 constituted the patterns found at this age, *C* and *F* being least definite, *I* and *G* being larger than usual, and *K* appearing here but not in adults. Another tendency noticed first at the child level was that some simple-structure rotations approached directly what had been seen at the adult level as second-order factors. For example, the marker parcels for factors *A, F,* and *E* in one exploration of the space came together in a single factor (defined as exvia in Chapter Four) while *C, H, O,* and Q_4 coalesced in what is today recognized as the second-order anxiety factor. The phenomenon of the same unrotated matrix going by simple-structure rotation either to the usual primary factors or to a mixture of these with second-order factors is now well known (see Chapter Eight). However, the prolonged pursuit of blind simple structure here resulted in the appearance of the pure primaries. From this point on, the validation and intensification at the early childhood (6-to-8-year) level was pursued systematically by Dielman, using parcel (small-scale) factoring in what I designate as experiments 5, 6, and 7.

The fifth intensification was made as part of the previously mentioned CPQ-ESPQ boundary study in the development of the CPQ by Porter, Schaie, and myself. Two forms of the CPQ, each designed to measure 14 factors, and the two-scale forms of the ESPQ, each designed to measure 13 factors, were administered to 157 8-to-9-year-old children. Seventeen factors were extracted from the 54 × 54 matrix of correlations among the scales (parcels having appreciable item homogeneity) and rotated to oblique simple structure with a 75 percent hyperplane count. The sixth study, profiting by some improved items aiming at the joint ESPQ-CPQ factors, was conducted by Coan and Baker on a sample of 289 8-to-9-year-old children. It involved administering the 28 CPQ scales (14 factors with two forms each) and the 26 ESPQ scales (13 factors with two forms each) along with 200 extension items intended for construction of two additional forms. The main 54 × 54 CPQ-ESPQ scale correlation matrix was factor-analyzed with an iterative principal-axis procedure. Nineteen factors by the scree test rotated to oblique simple structure with a final hyperplane count of 80 percent. The Dwyer extension then picked up higher-validity items for these factors from the extension material.

In the Coan and Baker study high correlational alignment was found only for factors *B, F, J,* and *O* across both forms. Factors *E, G,* and *H* were not satisfactorily aligned on either form; the remaining factors characteristically showed an adequate loading for one form but not for the other. Schaie's study met with more success: adequate identification was achieved for all factors across both forms, with the exception of factor *N,* which was reliably identified by only one form. Progressive rectification (see Figure 23, Chapter Eight) sometimes swings backward. Progress to higher validities occurs in a zigzag line, and any factor (say, *E* or *N* or Q_3) in one scale (say, the CPQ) will at one time align well and another time poorly with the corresponding scale in the adjoining scale (say, the ESPQ) as each proceeds by successive factorings toward the eventual true position.

These deviations in particular forms and at particular stages in the series of factor experiments are sometimes discouragingly large because of a systematic cause not yet mentioned. Although I take my theoretical stand that factors are real functional unities, matchable from sample to sample by having the same pattern of expression, I also recognize that an appreciable difference of pattern can arise from population to population—in this case between 6-to-8-year-olds and 8-to-12-year-olds tested on the same items as if they stood at the 8-year boundary.

Programatic research plans have here encountered a dilemma. Should one proceed through a series of exactly equivalent samples from the same population of, say, one sex, the age of 7, and rural schools? Or should one deliberately sample (in, say, the ESPQ construction) 6-, 7-, and 8-year-olds, boys and girls alternately, rural and urban groups? We chose the latter because our factoring processes were accurate enough to ensure cross-identification despite some factor variance; because we did not wish to remain ignorant of how large these changes might be; and because the scales would eventually have to be used on mixed and varied populations, so that it was just as well to start from the beginning to find items that would retain their validity across as many populations as possible. Nevertheless, this course presents some disconcerting initial fluctuations in validity.

The seventh ESPQ study (the fourth on an independent, different kind of sample) was conducted by Dreger and myself in a preliminary step toward the construction of the PSPQ for 4-to-6-year-olds, the work to which I shall return later. The 616 children in this study were 5 to 6 years of age and were tested on 560 items: 160 of the two forms of the ESPQ, 200 experimental ESPQ extension items, and 200 items from an earlier PSPQ study conducted by Meredith. The 17 factors indicated by the K-G and the scree tests were rotated to oblique simple structure with a final hyperplane count of 66 percent. All the ESPQ salients were now satisfactorily identified. Congruence coefficients were computed among the three boundary studies and significant congruences were noted for all but factor *N* between the Schaie and Dreger and Cattell studies and all but factors *E* and *G* between the Schaie and Coan and Baker studies. In the Coan-Baker and Dreger-Cattell studies, however, factors *A*, *D*, *E*, and *H* failed to show significant congruence.

Dwyer extension analyses were conducted on the boundary studies that utilized experimental extension items by Dielman and Wagner. Less valid items in the first two forms were replaced by extension items that consistently exhibited higher correlations with the factor. Other groups of extension items were formed and tried on the basis of the same high factor-correlation criterion. In addition, new extension items were written around these nuclei for a third extension testing. This third testing was conducted by Dielman on two new separate groups, bringing the total of 6-to-8-year Q-data factor analyses to eight (see Dielman and Cattell, 1973).

Forms and sessions have to be treated as distinct features of design when one comes to tests for young children. In this case it was decided to split each form into two sessions of six items for each factor in each session (except B factor with eight). These sessions are labeled A1, A2, B, B2 in the ESPQ, each of the two sessions for one form occupying about 20 to 30 minutes of attention. With four forms per factor and 13 personality factors this gives 56 scale forms in all. Thus about three to four hours of testing (eight sessions of 20 to 30 minutes each) are possible when the greatest validity is required (320 items covering 13 source traits, hence 24 per trait—except B with 32). In the research by Dielman that followed these forms were administered to 147 first-grade children and intercorrelated and factored, giving 16 factors rotated to a final oblique position with a hyperplane count of 65 percent. All the A1 and A2 scales were adequately marked, but the B1 and B2 scales met with varying degrees of success.

For this reason, a new extension set was constructed and a ninth factor analysis was carried out on 362 6-to-8-year-old children. In all, 560 items were administered, 80 in each of seven separate one-hour sessions. The items consisted of the existing 160 A1 and A2 items, 192 items found with acceptable loadings in the Coan and Baker and the Dreger and Cattell studies, and 208 new extension items. An initial factor analysis was conducted on the 26 A1 and A2 subscales plus 39 additional markers (three for each of the 13 scales) constructed by grouping six items (eight in the case of the intelligence scale) for each marker on the basis of acceptable loadings on the factor in previous studies, resulting in a total of 65 variables. Seventeen factors were extracted from the 65×65 matrix of intercorrelations and rotated to a final oblique position with 62 percent of the variables in the ± 0.10 hyperplane. A Dwyer extension analysis was subsequently conducted against the factors defined by the A1 and A2 subscales to determine the correlations of the 400 extension items with the 13 identified factors. On the basis of this and the previous extension analyses, 160 items exhibiting consistently high correlation with the factor were selected to form the new B1 and B2 subscales. These new B1 and B2 scales were then correlated with the 26 A1 and A2 subscales and a tenth factor analysis was conducted, rotating 14 factors to a final ± 0.10 hyperplane of 62 percent. In this analysis, all the A1 and A2 subscales exhibited satisfactory loadings. In the B1 form, scale H did not reach a satisfactory value, and scales A, C, and J were weak on subscale B2. Congruence coefficients between this study and the former Dielman study revealed adequate factor matches for all but factor *A*.

4. Source-Trait Structure at the Preschool Level

The fact that programatic research at the 6-to-8-year level had to proceed through no fewer than ten successive factorial experiments to achieve acceptable certainty of structure and a collection of items "hardy" enough to stand as markers across different samples, suggests that the questionnaire method is encountering difficulties at earlier ages that are not important in work with adults. This problem seems not to exist with objective tests (T-data). Indeed, the definition of factor structure in the objective-analytic batteries is better for children than adults. (Compare Bolz and Cattell, 1973, with Hundleby, Pawlik, and Cattell, 1965.) The sources of invalidity and instability should first be examined by research at the item level. My hypotheses are that 4-to-8-year-olds are incapable of high *reliability* (test-retest) of item response and that their self-concepts are insufficiently developed to give validity to generalized trait questions. Incidentally, although the latter questions permit seemingly high validity with adults when only a few items are used, I have argued that the most desirable items deal with specific behavior, not traits abstracted into a self-concept. Thus if adult scales were ideally constructed they would not have this advantage in apparent validity over child scales; but the unreliability would still persist in child questionnaires.

In view of these signs that more items need to be used at the younger levels and that factor patterns tend to crystallize less readily, Dielman and his coworkers deemed it necessary to proceed to an eleventh and a twelfth study. This study was done on a new group of 408 6-to-8-year-old children in which the 320 items from subscales A1, A2, B1, and B2 were administered along with 110 new extension items. The 52 scales were intercorrelated and 14 factors were extracted and rotated to a final ± 0.10 hyperplane count of 65 percent. In this study the weaknesses of form B noted in earlier studies were not apparent: all scales exhibited satisfactorily high factor-pattern values. A Dwyer extension analysis was performed using the 110 new extension items, however, and substitutions were made in scales where an item had a history of marginal or inconsistent performance. A twelfth factorization on a new group of 200 children was done to check these revised scales by extracting 14 factors from the 52×52 matrix of correlations and rotating to a final oblique position with 70 percent of the variables in the ±0.10 hyperplane. All salient variables were as correctly placed and as well loaded as is possible for scales of this length with children of this age.

Although the factor structure and the scale validity were now deemed as satisfactory as could be reached, it was possible that in the prolonged rotational processes some factor might have changed places in psychological meaning, for example, an *O* with a Q_4 scale. One must remember that the factor identification as *A, B, C,* and so on at this young age now has to be carried a long way from the 16 PF scales as the basic identification through the HSPQ and the CPQ to the ESPQ. Undoubtedly more boundary studies are desirable to check upon, and ensure the dependability of, this continuation of identity by a chain of adequate correlations—from adulthood to 4 years. Accordingly a final boundary study (bringing the number of factor analyses to 13 in the development of the ESPQ) was conducted with 285 8-to-9-year-old children. The 28 CPQ and 52 ESPQ scales were administered and the resulting 80 × 80 matrix of interscale correlations was factor-analyzed and rotated to oblique simple structure with a hyperplane count of 68 percent. Adequate loadings were exhibited on the appropriate factors by all scales, as shown in Table 9. Nevertheless there is some contamination (−0.47 and −0.53) in two of the *J* factor scales, and Q_4 has its problems with *D* and *G*. These are psychologically easy to understand. Excitability behaviors in *D* are not easy to distinguish in child language from the tension responses of Q_4 (ergic tension), and much *D* (excitable, impulsive) behavior is antisocial and likely to be negatively loaded on superego, *G*.

Table 9

Personality Structure and Concept Validities for Q-Data at the 6-to-8-Year Level
(a) Data from the Twelfth Factor Study (see text)

	B	*D*	*E*	*G*	*J*	Q_4
Form A1						
B	95			−28	−25	
D		62				36
E		36	69		−38	
G		−33		66		−42
J	−47	−23			41	
Q_4				−24	24	68
Form A2						
B	101					
D	28	58	−22			
E		25	71		−26	
G				74		−43
J	−25			23	50	
Q_4		37		−44		57
Form B1						
B	62				−25	43
D	−24	87		−26		

Table 9 (cont.)

E		−16	[54]			
G				[69]		
J					[64]	21
Q_4		−41		−25		[74]
Form B2						
B	[66]	27				40
D		[49]		−37		−33
E			[70]			
G				[44]		
J			−53		[30]	30
Q_4						[48]

Note: Hyperplane loadings of 0.20 or below are omitted from this table. The reader is reminded in looking at form A, session 2, *B* factor loading of 1.11 that *loadings* can exceed unity.

(b) Data from the Ultimate Analysis, Showing an Alternative Set of Factors

Scale Variables			*Primary Factors*			
	C	*E*	*F*	*I*	*N*	*O*
Form A1						
1 *C*	[49]	−26				
2 *E*		[27]				
3 *F*			[53]			
4 *I*				[62]		
5 *N*					[19]	
6 *O*						[47]
Form A2						
7 *C*	[44]					
8 *E*		[64]				
9 *F*			[49]			
10 *I*				[30]	32	38
11 *N*					[51]	
12 *O*			33			[32]
Form B1						
13 *C*	[16]					
14 *E*		[66]				
15 *F*			[37]			
16 *I*				[48]		
17 *N*					[48]	
18 *O*					30	[58]
Form B2						
19 *C*	[44]					
20 *E*		[36]				
21 *F*		24	[18]			
22 *I*				[54]		
23 *N*					[12]	
24 *O*					31	[32]

Note: Hyperplane loadings of 0.20 or below are omitted from off-diagonals (Cattell and Dielman, in preparation).

Turning to the systematic exploration at the youngest age reached—the preschool period of 4 to 6 years using oral tests—the first step was taken in 1956 by Peterson and me, guided as to choice of items first by the personality sphere for older children and second by Koch's 1942 well-designed factoring of preschool behavior. Thirty-two boys and 48 girls at Chicago University Nursery School were presented orally with 104 items (reduced to 90 when difficulties over understanding or "cut" eliminated 14 of the items), 15 items at a session. Even at this early age the correlation matrix indicated 16 dimensions, cut to 12 by collapses in rotation presumably due to the small sample and the subjects' unreliability.

This study was part of a wider cross-media study (Cattell and Peterson, 1958) with L- and T- data, and, as shown in the cross-media survey in Chapter Seven, the alignment across instrumentalities in this pioneer study was initially poor and perplexing. However, the Q-data by contrast gave good simple structure, and a 72-item, 12-factor (without intelligence) crude initial PSPQ was constructed. This PSPQ was given in 1964 to a fresh sample of 57 boys and 57 girls (mean age 6.5 years) but in 26 parcels (two marker parcels for each factor) along with 20 ability tests for "hyperplane stuff"—variables that create hyperplanes with respect to the domain concerned (Cattell, 1966). Seventeen factors were indicated of which four were abilities and 13 were the excellently reproduced initial PSPQ patterns. A third experiment in which some of the same children were included was carried out by Dreger and Nesselroade; 180 boys and girls were given the best of the items with others in a total of 200 items. Factored by Meredith, in parcels this set of variables again gave 13 factors (published only as a laboratory publication), and the item gain was used to prepare what was then named the proto-PSPQ.

At this point a boundary study was designed by Dreger, Coan, and Baker with the object of simultaneously checking the proto-PSPQ and identifying its factors with those of the ESPQ. This was done on 200 4- and 5-year-old boys and girls. A total of 560 items were administered as described. The final rotated factor matrix showed excellent factor identification with the exception of factor *M*. The Dwyer extension analysis conducted by Dielman and Wagner, in addition to the item-factor correlations from previous experiments, provided additional variables, and a further item-factor analysis of the ESPQ-PSPQ boundary data by Dreger on two split samples of 300 children each eventuated in some item substitution. The new scales were employed in a final check on the PSPQ structure by Dreger and Putnam in 1971 and 1972. This study is in the process of publication but it can be recorded that 200 4-to-5-year-old children were tested on 200 items. The 42 subscales were correlated and factored with oblique rotation to a final 70 percent hyperplane count. For the factor structure of the PSPQ as it stands the reader is referred to the forthcoming PSPQ handbook by Dreger, Putnam, and Cattell (in preparation). This structure does not seem to yield the degree of scale contamination that one would expect from projecting to 4–6 years the increase observed in going from 8–12 to 6–8 years. A possible hypothesis is that the switch from group testing to individual testing and personal contact, and to recording of responses by the experimenter rather than the young subject, has reduced error of measurement.

A summary of the factors for which there is evidence, and for which reasonably sound measurement scales have now been provided across these five age periods, is given in Table 10.

Table 10

Primary Source Traits Located Across Five Developmental Age Levels

Standard Label	*Symbol*	PSPQ *(4–6 yr.)*	ESPQ *(6–8 yr.)*	CPQ *(8–12 yr.)*	HSPQ *(12–18 yr.)*	*16 PF (18–adult)*
Affectothymia	*A*	*A*	*A*	*A*	*A*	*A*
Intelligence	*B*	*B*	*B*	*B*	*B*	*B*
Ego Strength	*C*	*C*	*C*	*C*	*C*	*C*
Excitability	*D*	*D*	*D*	*D*	*D*	
Dominance	*E*	(*E*?)	*E*	*E*	*E*	*E*
Surgency	*F*	*F*	*F*	*F*	*F*	*F*
Superego	*G*	(*G*?)	*G*	*G*	*G*	*G*
Parmia	*H*	(*H*?)	*H*	*H*	*H*	*H*
Premsia	*I*	*I*	*I*	*I*	*I*	*I*
Asthenia	*J*	*J*	*J*	*J*	*J*	
Acculturation	*K*		(*K*?)	(*K*?)		
Protension	*L*					*L*
Autia	*M*					*M*
Shrewdness	*N*	*N*	*N*	*N*		*N*
Guilt Proneness	*O*	*O*	*O*	*O*	*O*	*O*
Radicalism	Q_1					Q_1
Self-Sufficiency	Q_2				Q_2	Q_2
Self-Sentiment	Q_3			Q_3	Q_3	Q_3
Ergic Tension	Q_4	Q_4	Q_4	Q_4	Q_4	Q_4
Total Number of Factors		13	13	14	14	16 or 9

Note: Recent extensions (*D, J, K, P*, Q_5, Q_6, Q_7) bring the total number of factors in the 16 PF (with 16 PF Supplement) to 23. Factors in parentheses have questionable identification at this stage.

5. The MMPI and the Evidence for Extra Dimensions in Pathological Behavior

The purpose of the second part of Chapter Three is to see what extensions of personality dimensions may be needed in abnormal behavior. Formally the questions are roughly the same as for the extension into childhood: Do the existing factors suffice? Does a fresh conception of the personality sphere need to be developed for the new population?

Generations of students have tripped over the distinction between deviant statistically (abnormal) and "deviant in healthiness of function" (abnormal, pathological). Some behavior we call pathological may be only abnormal in the first sense, that is, yielding extremely deviant scores on normal processes or dimensions. Consistent with this one school of clinical thought has stressed understanding the neurotic or psychotic in terms of a tangled maladjustment operating nevertheless with truly normal processes. One suspects, however, that psychological medicine will, like physical medicine, eventually recognize two forms of pathology—imbalance of normal function as in diabetes or stress disorders, and distinct disease processes as in tuberculosis or cancer. The present examination of psychopathology will be open to both.

Regardless of the kind of dimensions used, a choice of diagnostic method is encountered here. It is that between describing a clinical case by a profile of scores on common dimensions on the one hand, and pigeonholing him into one of several all-or-none syndrome groups on the other. The real basis of this distinction has already been brought into the perspective of a precise model in Chapter One. This model is not the same as the one described above, but dimensions promise a more functional analysis, whether by normal or abnormal dimensions, than does labeling in paranoid schizophrenic, simple schizophrenic, and other terms. The confusion between what is done in Aristotelian or "type" diagnosis and Galilean "function measurement" appraisal has become endemic in clinical psychology largely because of the failure of psychiatrists to understand the distinction of trait and type as drawn in Chapter One or in Mahrer (1970) or Freedman and Kaplan (1967).

Even if we use types—and they have uses—the basic principle (if we accept that the present reliability and consistency of clinical typing is not impressive) is that the classificatory types must first be discovered (as Chapter One points out in general terms and Chapter Ten, Section 5, in exact illustrations) by objective, non-arbitrary procedures. That is many patients must have profiles measured on some multidimensional instrument, and the pattern-similarity coefficient applied to them to find their natural groupings, for example, by the Taxonome program. However, if all types are not included in the factoring from the beginning the necessary totality of dimensions for a satisfactory typing cannot be found by such factoring. This is precisely what has happened to most questionnaires, including the 16 PF and the G-Z, which have built their primary scales on items primarily concerned with normal behavior. New dimensions beyond the normal are found when an abnormal-behavior personality sphere of items is used. Furthermore, certain inadequacies of the 16 PF in clinical diagnostic work are overcome when the 12 new dimensions are added to it, converting it into what is now called the Clinical Analysis Questionnaire (CAQ).

Since the late 1950s there has been an increasing use of the 16 PF and HSPQ in clinical work, and valuable reports have come from some forty researches.[3] The general conclusion drawn from these researches is that it

[3] Research date that has systematically evaluated diagnosis includes Bendig (1961), Cattell (1966a, 1970c), Cattell, Komlos, and Tatro (1968), Cattell and Rickels (1964), Cattell, Tatro, and Komlos (1964), Court (1965), Eber (1964), Forbes (1969), Fuller

would be hard to find a measuring instrument—from the Rorschach to the MMPI—that can claim statistically better results than the 16 PF and HSPQ in separating from normals and from one another such groups as the distinct neurotic types, alcoholics, homosexuals, drug addicts, and problem children, but these same primary factors seem of little use when it comes to recognizing psychosis and its varieties. True, the 16 PF shows schizophrenics as significantly introverted, paranoids as high on the projection of tension by the protension factor *L,* and so on; but this can be regarded as merely recording the patients' contributory prepsychotic tendencies. There is no question that the 16 PF (in contrast to its high sensitivity to neurotic maladjustment and to class and cultural grouping) has a blind eye in regard to psychosis.

Even had this inadequacy of the 16 to 23 normal primaries for psychotic pathology not been demonstrated, one would have planned to find whether an extension into a pathological personality sphere of items would produce extra dimensions. The carefully planned pool of pathological behavior items used as the wider personality sphere in the research now to be described came from three sources: (1) behavior recorded in the symptomatology of psychiatric diagnostic literature (particularly, Freedman and Kaplan's *Comprehensive Textbook of Psychiatry,* 1967, and Sankar's *Schizophrenia,* 1969); (2) the MMPI, discussed below; and (3) such newly devised items as Delhees, Sells, and myself constructed on seeing the emergence of new factors from the proto-CAQ study on abnormals, as well as those appearing as markers in the work of Bjersted (Cattell and Bjersted, 1967), Nunnally (1967), Weckowicz, Cropley, and Muir (1971), and others on depression.

The most valuable single contribution to this "patho-sphere" is the work of Hathaway and McKinley on the MMPI (1951). The MMPI and the 16 PF were born in the same year—1949—but with totally different philosophies and purposes. The MMPI continued the prevailing empirical construction of questionnaires, with certain refinements, to distinguish among concrete criteria. The 16 PF introduced the more abstract conception of an oblique simple-structure factor as a source trait or influence. As history would teach one to expect, the less abstract concept, more comprehensible to the prevailing zeitgeist, had for twenty years a wider popular understanding and use. Although some critical observations must be made on the psychometric confusions in the MMPI, there can be no doubt that it deserved success because it was the most comprehensive and well-expressed array of items yet put forward to cover the pathological personality. Indeed, here

---

(1963), Gleser and Gottschalk (1967), Harburg and others (1964), Holt (1965), Hartman (1966), Howard and Diesenhaus (1965a, 1965b, 1965c), Hunt and others (1959), IPAT Information Bulletin No. 8 (1963), Joshi and Roy (1967), Karson (1960, 1965, 1967), Karson and Haupt (1968), McAllister (1966), Murthy (1965), Philip (1970), Pierson and Kelly (1963), Rickels and Cattell (1965), Skekelle and Ostfeld (1965), W. F. White (1965), Tamkin and Sonkin (1969), Walker (1966), and Walton (1968). An early summary on substantial samples is given in *The Meaning and Measurement of Neuroticism and Anxiety* (Cattell and Scheier, 1961).

it was so good that it has been ruthlessly cannibalized by later test constructors.

Psychometrically, however, the MMPI conforms to none of the basic concepts set out in Chapter One. Its scales are not directed to source traits, to surface traits, or to types. In intention it comes nearest to the last—to recognizing and locating clinical groups as types. But with this intention one would argue that the designers would have done better first to find the totality of factor dimensions spanning normals and abnormals, as in the CAQ, and *then* to locate types by Taxonome using the multiple-discriminant function finally to give greatest separation weights on the functionally meaningful scales. Instead they accepted the less precise and stable typology propounded by psychiatrists at the time and set out to pick items that gave maximum discrimination among these syndrome types. (Thus they anticipated discriminant functions but did not use such precise methods.) A psychometrist is likely to be unhappy about the 12 or more scales built out of these 600 or more items because they have a built-in artificial, algebraic correlation among them, the result of using many of the same items (with their specifics dragged in) in *different* scales. This scale construction has not prevented attempts to factor the MMPI (after its construction) by factoring correlations among these scales. As more than six such factorings (for example, Finney, 1961; Tyler, 1951) now show, the 13 or so scales seem to subtend only five dimensions (see surveys by Holzberg, 1960; Schneidman, 1965; Vernon, 1933; and others). An attempt to simplify the MMPI by clusters rather than factors was made by Tryon (1939, 1943). However, we are looking for source traits rather than surface traits and are not interested in the structure of the MMPI as such but only in the basic structure of the pathological realm of which its items are representative. Certainly both Tryon's clusters and the scale factorings that center on five dimensions are decidedly fewer than the real-source-trait dimensionality of the 554 or more items that could be factored.

The ordinary polity of science suggests that the relations between the scales of these contemporaries—the MMPI and 16 PF—should have their relations investigated. Among recent studies (Cattell and Bolton, 1969; Hundleby and Connor, 1968; LaForge, 1962; Odell and Karson, 1969) the verdict is clearly that the 13 MMPI and the 16 scales of the 16 PF have substantial overlap, although not as much as between the 16 PF and the G-Z (Cattell and Gibbons, 1968) or the CPI (Mitchell, 1961). The two latter have at least a 14-factor common dimensionality, whereas the MMPI has only 5 or 6. As would be expected from this restriction, no alignment of an MMPI with a 16 PF scale is close. Welch's combinations of MMPI scales to give an anxiety meanings investigated. Among recent studies (Cattell and Bolton, 1969; scales to give the second-order anxiety factor in the 16 PF. Cattell, Eber, and Tatsuoka (1970; p. 46) present a transformation table between MMPI and 16 PF scales that yields a multiple R prediction of the MMPI scales from the 16 PF ranging from 0.42 (hysteria) to 0.88 (social introversion).

What needed to be done was to factor the large item pool of the MMPI, not its algebraically restricted scales, with the 16 PF. However, with so enormous a correlation matrix—566 × 566—and the still larger subject pool it required, no one before 1968 had had the temerity to attempt an item factoring. The task was actually begun by Eber and Fowler, but heavy costs and difficulties in getting unambiguous rotations with such a swarm of items brought their work to a standstill.[4] At this point, however, the work of Adams and Horn (1965) and Hundleby and Connor (1968), and the rough factor positions I was able to get by further rotation of Eber and Fowler's data, combined to crystallize suitable groups of items for a *parceled analysis.*

The 45 reasonably homogeneous parcels of about 12 items each from the work by Hundleby and others were included with 19 marker scales from the 16 PF (one each except for *G, N,* and Q_1, which might not pick up communality in the MMPI) in a single-factor experiment. This experiment was concluded the following year by Cattell and Bolton (1969) in an attempt to structure the abnormal domain and to check the hypothesis that the 16 PF normal factors would necessarily, as primary dimensions, be found in the MMPI item span—although possibly in somewhat pathological dress and accompanied by extra clinical factors. The incomplete and unpublished study by Eber and Fowler had not been in vain (quite apart from the contributions to finding homogeneous clusters), for their results on 566 items checked with those on 64 parcels in agreeing on the number of factors in the domain, since 22 (21 to 23) were found in both. (This again illustrates the truth of the formal proposition that items and parcels of items should yield the same number of factors.) A prolonged simple-structure rotation of the Cattell and Bolton 64 × 21 matrix (after dropping one weak factor) was undertaken to test a variety of positions in this new domain in 27 overall shifts, and the unusually high ±0.10 hyperplane count of 79 percent was reached, beginning from 45 percent before rotation.

The first striking result of this analysis was clear support for the hypothesis that even in pathological behavior items the ordinary personality dimensions of the patients must show through. All the 16 PF factors (except intelligence, *B*) showed up, and since by no means all the MMPI items are highly pathological it was easy to recognize them by content, although the firm identification rested on the loadings on the 16 PF parcel scales. Additionally, however, there were definitely five factors which the 16 PF had not possessed. The last was uninterpreted and the fourth seemed to be religious interest, but *psychotic hypochondria, psychopathic behavior,* and *psychasthenia* stood out easily in the new dimensionality. A further check is possible on this 16 PF structure in the pathological items in that the second-order structure among the pathologically expressed normal primaries

[4] The most determined attack I know is this of Eber and Fowler, who spent some 50 hours of computer time on a proposed total-item-factoring structure on 23 factors. In accordance with what I have said about rotating items in contrast to parcels, Eber found the low communalities in the formless swarm about the origin to present insuperable difficulties to automatic rotations, which presented several equally good (or poor) solutions. Bolton and I were invited to use the data; although further clarification was gained we eventually took a new sample and proceeded by parceled factoring as here described.

came out as typically found in the 16 PF, with additional, new loadings by the newer scales, for example, on hypochondria, on anxiety, 0.54 (see Table 22, Chapter Four).

This discovery of four new pathological source traits was encouraging for the broader attempt to factor the pathology domain. One result was the Clinical Analysis Questionnaire which was designed to provide clinicians with a set of scales that would measure abnormals both on the 16 PF normal factors and on whatever new pathological factors might be found.

6. Depressive and Other Pathological Source Traits Included in the Clinical Analysis Questionnaire

As mentioned in viewing these analyses of the MMPI, the total personality sphere of pathological behavior variables used as the jumping-off place for a thorough treatment of pathological dimensionality was broader than the MMPI domain alone. Despite the excellent natural historical coverage of the MMPI, we thought it wise to add markers for other recently discovered "pathological" factors. For example, the MMPI has one depression scale whereas the Nunnally-Grinker and Cattell-Bjerstedt factoring indicated six or seven depression factors; so markers for these were also included in the pathology pool. After this we again added more than 300 items newly written from behavior covered in psychiatric textbooks.

In exploring items for this pathological extension of the personality sphere one runs into a problem scarcely encountered in normal traits. The question arises more pointedly here as to how far the dimensions are those of traits and how far of temporary states—catatonic excitement, depression, manic episodes. The formal treatment of states in Chapter Six has answers to such questions but we took the tentative position that there are probably parallel states and characterological trait structures so that no state behavior should be excluded (since it may also represent a trait).

We already recognized this fact in the state and trait of anxiety, which was first clearly defined as a second-order factor (Cattell and Scheier, 1961) involving the primary factors C, H, L, O, Q_3, and Q_4. This factor appeared both as a state and as a trait. In the work on depression factors in the 1960s it was already clear that whereas anxiety formed a clear-cut single factor, depression presented a whole complex of depression factors, probably six or seven. Although the position in pathology of the second-order anxiety factor (well measured also by Welch's scale from the MMPI, Eysenck's N, the MAS, with some contamination, and the IPAT anxiety scale) was clear, depression presented psychometry with a harder nut to crack. Indeed, it has become increasingly evident that the six or seven factors initially located in depression phenomena labeled D_1 to D_6 in the CAQ) actually have wider pathological meaning and enrich the domain of neurotic and psychotic pathological phenomena more than was first suspected.

If we scrutinize this depression domain we find that noteworthy attacks on factoring have been made in L-data by Grinker and others (1961) and in Q-data by Weckowicz and others (1967, 1971) and by Bjerstedt (Cattell and Bjerstedt, 1967) in the studies to be described. At an a prior, clinical, noncorrelational level scales have been put forward by Beck, Ward, and others (1954), Friedman (1963), the MMPI (1951), Hoch and Zubin (1954), M. A. Klein (1935), and especially Shapiro, Newfield, and Post (1962); many others have offered observations on key manifestations suitable for scales. But not a single factorization, as of 1965, had met the necessary conditions for a reliable outcome. The rough factoring contributions up to that point had sufficed mainly to prove that depression cannot be accounted for (as the MMPI single scale implies) by a single factor—or even by two or three.

A systematic attack on the structure of depression in Q-data, using all the cited research as a valuable source of markers to span the domain, was made by Bjerstedt, beginning in 1963 (see Cattell and Bjerstedt, 1967). First, the most representative set of 73 items from these depression scale sources was administered with 96 16 PF and HSPQ items (to check that the dimensions could not be accounted for by those already known, for example, desurgency, *F*(—), and guilt proneness, *O*) to a mixed sample of 78 male and female patients and 61 male and female normals to ensure proper range. Tsujioka factored the 73 items alone (on 139 cases), showing 9 or 10 factors by the scree although only seven or eight rotated to appreciable variance. Putting each depression factor into two marker parcels and each 16 PF similarly, a factoring was done on this group (on a new retest, after a month) and on a new group of 163 young adult males (66 students, 97 air force personnel). The new group was sufficiently different to promise generality to whatever factors eventually emerged from these three studies. The items were brought to 239 by the addition of items to test the hypotheses suggested by Tsujioka's factors; the HSPQ was submitted for the 16 PF for marking normal dimensions.

There were thus three independent factor analyses by parcel—$(16 \times 2) + (8 \times 2) = 48$ variables—after the first analysis by item. The congruences of the former in number and form of factors was such that they could be added to a single summary matrix. Every indication at this stage pointed to seven or eight distinct but mainly positively correlated depression factors ultimately named as in Table 10. At each successive factoring new extension items were tried; items with improved loadings were substituted in the depression scales. The replication of depression factors by congruence coefficients was at the same significance level as for the 16 PF-HSPQ normal patterns for four or five of the *D* factors and became satisfactory for seven when the improved items were added (Cattell and Bjerstedt 1967).

At this point, the analyses of the depression primaries eventually placed as scales in the CAQ were carried to the second order (along with a fourth matrix from scale correlations). These analyses yielded the familiar second orders for the 16 PF and HSPQ, and three second-order depression factors. Thus at this stage the four analyses (three entirely independent, the fourth overlapping) had answered our initial questions. The depression primaries, probably seven rather than eight in number, are quite distinct from the nomal 16 PF. Moreover, they cannot be resolved into a single general depression factor at the second order but suggest no fewer than three second orders. These pathological second orders are discussed with second-order factors in Chapter Four.

The problem remained of ascertaining whether these seven primary depression factors are also distinct from the four or five general pathological factors discovered by Bolton, Cattell, Eber, and Fowler in their study of MMPI item dimensionality. Until this distinction became clear we could not proceed to an interpretation of the factors in depression (set out in Table 9, Chapter Three) as independent. The relations were checked by Delhees on a mixed group of 254 male and female, normal and abnormal adults. Into the markers among which the depressions were to find their place when 32 parcel scales representing the 16 normal factors (two per factor to mark each as a primary) as in the 16 PF. (However, one of each marker pair was the normal scale and one was the normal as found in pathological dress.) Next came 14 parcels (two for each factor) as representatives of the depression factors (which we had reduced to seven by dropping one of doubtful replication) and 36 (two parcels for each hypothesized factor) from the general pathological findings described previously. The parcels averaged 12 to 14 items each and the whole covered five hours of testing (750 items).

A word is needed on this choice of variables since it represents a complex design in regard to hypotheses. First, the thirty-two 16 PF scales checked the hypothesis from the Bolton study that the 16 PF factors appear equally in 16 PF normal items and in the MMPI items—though in abnormal mode of expression in the latter. Sixteen of these representatives come from the abnormal expression emerging from the MMPI material and 16 were form A 16 PF scales. Next came the seven depression factors, each by two parcels. Then we added markers for every suspected purely pathological factor from every available factor indication (Lorr, Wittenborn, Grinker and Nunnally, our own earlier research, and others). These amounted to at least 18 possible abnormal factors and were represented as two parcels each. (These putative factors in pathology were taken at the rate of about 14 items per factor from the Bolton factoring (Cattell and Bolton, 1969), the Eber-Fowler unfinished factoring of the MMPI, the then unpublished MMPI item anaylsis by Adams and Horn (1965), and the other sources just mentioned.) The scree on this final 82 $\times$ 82 parcel matrix indicated 29 factors (Delhees and Cattell, 1971) which, after maxplane and 29 hand rotations, maximized at 80 percent in the ± 0.10 hyperplane. The abnormal dress parcels for the 16 PF proved in some cases to be poor equivalents but the seven depression scales were well marked and the six essentially MMPI-derived pathological factors were especially clear.

The independence of the pathological and the depression factors was clear with one exception: our factor for the hypochondriacal variety of depression proved to collapse on rotation, and become the same as the pathological hypochondriasis factor from the MMPI. *Thus about 13 factors in all, six of them still labeled as* Ds *(depressions), are needed to describe the pathological domain.*

To this point the pathological research had followed the canons of programatic research: a broad search for dimension markers in the literature, followed by an iterative series of factor analyses with gradual addition and substitution of extension items deliberately shifted across different types of population to ensure that item validity holds across all likely populations (high transferability). These five factorings—three specifically from the depression area and two broad pathological approaches (Cattell and Bolton, 1969; Delhees and Cattell, 1971) to the CAQ—could by now claim to have given reasonably firm evidence on the primary dimensions and indeed a reasonable picture of the higher-order structure (Chapter Four).

This is perhaps an appropriate occasion to point out that a clear picture of the source-trait structure, on the one hand, and the provision of valid and reliable scales for them, on the other, are two very different things. The experimental CAQ as of 1973 does not claim to have reached the routine psychometric standards of older and less theoretical scales. As Jackson has stated and as Ashton and Goldberg (1972) have in some respects shown, even an amateur can make up items that will have acceptable homogeneity, reliability, and validity for some ad hoc scale—immediately. By contrast it takes years of painstaking programatic research—first converging upon the meaning and replicable pattern of a newly discovered source trait and then shaping a scale to measure it—if one's aim is to discover personality structure and orient scales to that structure. The itemetric critic (for example, Rorer, 1972) who judges a scale not by its long-term theoretical value but by its immediate itemetric properties encourages the less responsible and far easier proliferation of ad hoc conceptual scales and holds back the intelligent development of personality theory. When the source-trait-oriented scale matures it is much more than a test. It is *the operational definition of a theory* that would otherwise float in air like the now obsolete personality theories so prevalent years ago. It is also a firm reference point for further developmental, genetic, and other growths of theory. Thus the experimental CAQ of 1973 cannot claim the immediate psychometric efficiencies of MMPI scales but it can offer the promise of ultimately more meaningful diagnosis, meanwhile staking out with its scales the dimensions for which efficient scales need to be developed by years of intensive psychometry.[5]

For example, although the scales for hypochondria, paranoia, and psychasthenia are of acceptable validity, those for schizophrenia, psychopathic tendency, and general psychosis are relatively weak. The appearance of psychopathic tendency as a primary is puzzling because one might expect it to appear as a second-order factor among the diverse psychotic scales—schizophrenia, manic tendency, depression, and others. Possibly it will prove to be the highest-loaded in a second-order general psychosis factor

[5] The unmistakable verdict of research history in this field is that the proliferation of *ad hoc* scales with the narrow, compulsive goals of an accountant has proved sterile in the broader perspectives of scientific, conceptual psychology. Unfortunately the capacity of ad hoc scales to gain a quick but superficial claim to precision (mainly homogeneity) has also repeatedly discouraged more fundamental, comprehensive, imaginative approaches. One is reminded of the analogous situation of the human infant, who has further to go, but is actually less able to cope with his world than is the young monkey at the same age.

(Chapter Four). Another shortcoming in our present knowledge of CAQ pathology factors concerns our failure to get an entirely consistent picture of the second-order factors in depression. In some studies, notably Curran's state research (Chapter Six), the three secondaries appeared at the first order, and even in some trait studies there has been a definite tendency for the seven depression factors to collapse to three with a second-order pattern.

Related to this problem of separating the seven primary depressions and defining their second orders is the perennial task of clinicians: separating anxiety and depression conceptually and in practical evaluation. The evidence that developed from the CAQ reference markers at this stage seemed to be that anxiety joined in the loading pattern with one of the second-order depression factors (see Chapter Four). To clarify such structural issues and to collect intensification items, Delhees and I undertook a sixth factorial study in this area by factoring a normal and a clinical group as separate samples and together. In this new item construction we frankly accepted that the MMPI does not cover all the abnormal personality sphere and that the new emerging factors—the six beyond the six from the MMPI and even some of the original six—need to be enriched by items created according to the sense of the emerging factors. Thus 200 new items were designed and evaluated in this sixth experiment. The defining factor pattern for the subscales in this research is set out in Table 11, the fuller basis for which is given in Cattell (1973).

In terms of satisfactory simple structure and freedom from undesirable off-diagonal loadings, the new pathological factors (eight of which are shown in Table 11) have reached about as good a definition by this sixth study as the normal primaries. Furthermore, the off-diagonal erratics are different in the normal and the pathological sample, which may indicate that they are not systematic weaknesses in the scales but only the emphases inescapable in different populations. In view of these promising findings Sells and I have begun a seventh research project to bring the CAQ from the experimental stage to a final, practical instrument for clinicians. Since the items and scales at present—in Part II, Pathological Section—show skewed distribution with inefficient checks on pathological alternatives, phase one of the research has been directed to new items and item selections to spread the distribution. Phase two will be a full-scale factoring of two subscales (odd and even items) for each factor—that is, a 56×56 matrix with extension items from which we plan to construct the equivalent B form for all 28 scales.

The primary source traits of clinically deviant behavior are summarized in Table 12. Other dimensions probably remain to be found but these source traits and their scales constitute a mapped area of comparative clarity from which further explorations can be firmly extended. In seeking new dimensions and checks on present structure, investigators should remember the indications we have given of peculiarly high correlations among the *D* factors, as well as the general warning that it now becomes necessary to discover the degree of distortion of trait variance possible from adding variance from states. It has seemed best to retain the symbols for the 16

Table 11

Patterns of 12 Pathological and 16 Normal Primary Factors in the Clinical Analysis Questionnaire (CAQ)
(a) Normal Sample (N = 265) [Cattell, 1973e]

Scale	Form	*Normal Primaries*							*Pathological Primaries*							
		A	*B*	*C*	*I*	*O*	Q_3	Q_4	D_1	D_2	D_3	*Pa*	*Pp*	*Sc*	*As*	*Ps*
Normal [a]																
A	A	52												−31	−30	29
A	B	60						45					45			−30
B	A		49	25		−36										−25
B	B		69													
C	A			33							26					
C	B			51												
I	A				76											
I	B				43	31										
O	A					48										−31
O	B					40				29						
Q_3	A						61									
Q_3	B						39									
Q_4	A							50								
Q_4	B							48		37						
Pathological																
D_1	A								42							
D_1	B								65							
D_2	A								48	43						23
D_2	B								57	48						
D_3	A							−23			74					
D_3	B										76					
Pa	A									22		45				
Pa	B											61				
Pp	A							27					55			
Pp	B												61	28		

S_c											52			27		
Sc	B							−35			46			45		
A_s													29		29	
As	B			−20											27	
Ps	A												33			31
Ps	B												25			30

[a] Values less than 0.20 are not shown.

Note: The normal primaries selected for illustration are those with which some pathology might theoretically be related (C, I, O, Q_3, and Q_4 are deviant in neuroticism). Only the first three of the depression (D) factors, but all of the remaining pathology factors, are illustrated. The full matrices showing the independence of all 16 + 7 + 5 = 28 factors may be seen in the original research.

(b) Abnormal Sample (N = 450) [Cattell, 1973e]

		Normal Primaries							*Pathological Primaries*							
Scale	*Form*	*A*	*B*	*C*	*I*	*O*	Q_3	Q_4	D_1	D_2	D_3	*Pa*	*Pp*	*Sc*	*As*	*Ps*
Normal [a]																
A	A	49							−37	52	−27				−31	
A	B	60					27	−24								
B	A		65						−21							
B	B		66													
C	A			24												
C	B		22	55						−40						
I	A				39			21		26	20				−21	
I	B				67			−20							46	
O	A					58								22		
O	B					54		28	25							
Q_3	A					−20	66		−28							
Q_3	B			−27			67								−24	
Q_4	A							39							28	
Q_4	B					26		49				26				

Table 11 (cont.)

Pathological										
D_1	A		39							
D_1	B		57							
D_2	A			75						
D_2	B			75		21				
D_3	A				60					
D_3	B				53		37	34		
Pa	A					47				65
Pa	B					56				45
Pp	A						49			56
Pp	B	20					27			59
Sc	A							72		
Sc	B			−28	48			52		
As	A								29	28
As	B		40						52	
Ps	A		25							70
Ps	B									59

factors in the 16 PF that constitute Part I (normal) of the CAQ and to continue the MMPI use of two-letter symbols—mnemonic to the psychiatric labels—for the pathological factors.

It may also be wise to continue using distinct subscripts to a letter (D_2, D_3, D_4, etc.) for the factors that originated in the depression studies. However, it must by now be clear that although these factors originated in depression items some of them prove to be source traits of wider pathological importance of which depression is one expression. The full interpretation of these source traits depends on the intensive physiological and etiological research that these scales now render possible.

7. Summary

(1) After developing and checking measures for the primary questionnaire source traits in adults it seemed desirable to explore first (a) the child development range and (b) clinically deviant, pathological behavior—in the same culture. The former required a translation to the distinctly different interests and environment of the child as well as important adaptations of test administration form and vocabulary. The pathological area likewise required appreciable adaptation, especially the search for a full personality sphere of varied pathological behavior.

(2) The extension to childhood was organized about a convenient division into four preadult phases of development—4 to 6 years, 6 to 8 years, 8 to 12 years, and 12 to 18 years—designed to give shorter intervals at the earlier levels. A programatic approach similar to that at the adult level proceeded through about 10 successive iterative factor-analysis experiments at each level, beginning with items and shifting to parcels, intensifying the parcel scales with more valid items in the usual steps of progressive rectification. At the same time steps were taken through boundary studies, that is, using tests for adjoining ranges together on an intermediate age population to identify positively the 16 PF labels through the age range in successive steps.

(3) The main findings are that source traits are not significantly fewer at the child level and that they appear to be of the same nature—behaving more like abilities than dynamic interest traits. Moreover, matching shows them to have essentially the same identities. However, they appear to change in variance magnitude in systematic ways, premsia (I) and excitability (D), for example, being larger in children and radicalism-conservatism (Q_1) and possibly self-sentiment (Q_3) showing greater range in adults. However, these findings must be treated, at present, only as indications for research because it is possible to get different variances for factors merely from different sampling of variables—actually, different *density* of sampling—at the ages compared. (The variance is the mean squared loading per item, and, with most in the hyperplane, inclusion of a few extra high-loaded variables at one age, ignoring personality sphere stratified sampling, could give a false impression of factor size.)

Because of this possibility and because a trait like N found for adults

Table 12

Primary Source Traits in Clinically Deviant Pathological Behavior (Part II of CAQ)

Source-Trait Symbol	Low-Score Description (1–3)	High-Score Description (8–10)
Hd or D_1	LOW HYPOCHONDRIASIS Is happy, mind works well, does not find ill health frightening	HIGH HYPOCHONDRIASIS Shows overconcern with bodily functions, health, or disabilities
Sd or D_2	ZESTFULNESS Is contented about life and surroundings, has no death wishes	SUICIDAL DISGUST Is disgusted with life, harbors thoughts or acts of self-destruction
Bd or D_3	LOW BROODING DISCONTENT Avoids dangerous and adventurous undertakings, has little need for excitement	HIGH BROODING DISCONTENT Seeks excitement, is restless, takes risks, tries new things
Ad or D_4	LOW ANXIOUS DEPRESSION Is calm in emergency, confident about surroundings, poised	HIGH ANXIOUS DEPRESSION Has disturbing dreams, is clumsy in handling things, tense, easily upset
Fd or D_5	HIGH-ENERGY EUPHORIA Shows enthusiasm for work, is energetic, sleeps soundly	LOW ENERGY, FATIGUED DEPRESSION Has feelings of weariness, worries, lacks energy to cope
Gd or D_6	LOW GUILT AND RESENTMENT Is not troubled by guilt feelings, can sleep no matter what is left undone	HIGH GUILT AND RESENTMENT Has feelings of guilt, blames self for everything that goes wrong, is critical of self
Md or D_7	LOW BORED DEPRESSION Is relaxed, considerate, cheerful with people	HIGH BORED MISANTHROPIC DEPRESSION Avoids contact and involvement with people, seeks isolation, shows discomfort with people
Pa	LOW PARANOIA Is trusting, not bothered by jealousy or envy	HIGH PARANOIA Believes he is being persecuted, poisoned, controlled, spied on, mistreated
Pp	LOW PSYCHOPATHIC DEVIATION Avoids engagement in illegal acts or breaking rules, sensitive	HIGH PSYCHOPATHIC DEVIATION Has complacent attitude toward own or other's antisocial behavior, is not hurt by criticism, likes crowds
Sc	LOW SCHIZOPHRENIA Makes realistic appraisals of self and others, shows emotional harmony and absence of regressive traits	HIGH SCHIZOPHRENIA Hears voices or sounds without apparent source outside self, retreats from reality, has uncontrolled and sudden impulses
As	LOW PSYCHASTHENIA Is not bothered by unwelcome thoughts and ideas or compulsive habits	HIGH PSYCHASTHENIA Suffers insistent, repetitive ideas and impulses to perform certain acts
Ps	LOW GENERAL PSYCHOSIS Considers self good, dependable, and smart as most others	HIGH GENERAL PSYCHOSIS Has feelings of inferiority and unworthiness, timid, loses head easily

Note: The notation suggested for pathological factors uses two letters mnemonically related to the name (for example, *Sd* = suicidal disgust) to distinguish them from the normal factors, which use the alphabet by order of approximate variance: *A, B, C, . . ., P,* Q_1, Q_2, and so on.

disappears in the HSPQ and reappears in the 8-to-12-year range, it seems that the apparent gaps in the alphabetical series at some ages are results of nothing more than item sampling. The 23 factors of normal adult behavior—*A* through *P* and so to Q_7—are even now being discovered at lower ages although some real reduction may occur at the earliest levels.

(4) The factor pattern of expression of a source trait, presumably the result of an inner maturational, genetic influence or of a social reinforcement schedule from an institution, will necessarily change continuously with development. Consequently, even if conditions allowed us to use identical items at different ages it would be methodologically wrong to seek to prove identification of, say, a 6 to 8 pattern by direct matching with an adult factor (with the same variables on a common population). The realistic concept of a source trait is one of continuous identity with change of expression. Although matching of patterns with proper allowance for change is an acceptable technique, a better one is correlating factor scores (or factoring together) using scales from two age levels on individuals between them in what are defined here as boundary studies. Boundary studies have been set up at four levels at the frontiers of adjacent tests, seeking to trace the adult factors step by step to the earliest years. Naturally the factor measures at the lower ages have not yet been brought to the precision and validity of those for the two uppermost ranges, as in the 16 PF and HSPQ.

(5) The first 16 to 19 of the 23 normal factors have been found adequate to indicate varieties of neurosis and acting-out behavior, the profiles for which turn out to be significantly and characteristically different from the normal. But these dimensions alone have proved inadequate to give diagnostic separation of psychotic types. Psychotic behavior, well represented by 566 MMPI items, had not been previously factored as items. Two research projects led to the conclusion that this domain is spanned by the normal 16 PF factors and by six entirely new pathological source-trait dimensions. However, the MMPI proves not to cover all pathological dimensions.

(6) A conception of a pathological behavior sphere can be set up on the same principles as for the normal personality sphere. We have attempted to define this sphere from three main sources: the span of the MMPI; the American Psychiatric Association's diagnostic syndromes and their associated behaviors; and the behavior examined and factored in a long series of studies of pathological depression. Depressive phenomena prove more complex than anxiety and cover seven factors of which one is identical with the hypochondriasis factor from the MMPI. Four successive factorings of the factors from the MMPI, jointly with data from the second and third source (depression) above point to 12 pathological factors over and above the 16 from the 16 PF. However, those in the 16 PF also account for part of the variance in abnormal expressions. The six *D* factors (hypochondriasis aside) collapse to three second orders in some groups. On this evidence of the necessary 28-factor structural basis, a Clinical Analysis Questionnaire (CAQ) has been set up; Part I consists of 16 normal factors in slightly pathological item dress and Part II covers 12 new pathological traits.

(7) It is not possible to say how complete this 28 factor dimensionality

is, and further corners of the pathological domain remain to be explored. With the seven missing factors now accepted as in the normal domain, the primary personality factors that must be recognized in questionnaire measurement amount to no fewer than 35. If the personality sphere concept has been sufficiently pursued as the basis of present work, the greater part of the variance in normal and abnormal behavior can, judging by initial estimates of communalities, be largely predicted from these 35 common trait scores. Although more specialized common traits will undoubtedly be uncovered, the main need at present is the development of extended, valid scales for these 35, particularly for items and item weights adapted to the variations of these factor patterns that occur in different sex, age, and sociocultural groups.

(7) The issue of factor patterns changing with population is taken up systematically in Chapter Eight, but we can say that one expects differences partly for statistical reasons (for example, changes of group variance) and partly for psychological reasons, namely, that the influence we posit to be the factor changes its form. We do not yet know the nature-nurture ratios and therefore to what extent the pattern changes shape according to social reinforcement influence or level of maturational development.

Regardless of the origin of differences in expression of a source trait or influence, it presents an identification or matching problem. Broadly, two methods are open to us in identifying factors found at different age levels: matching factor-pattern loadings on the same variables and matching factor scores when the same individuals, at an age boundary, are administered both tests in a boundary study. (Testing and then waiting for the group to age for retesting is not so satisfactory.) Such boundary studies have now been made throughout the child age range, between the HSPQ, the CPQ, and other tests, by Baker, Coan, Dielman, Dreger, Nuttall, Schaie, and myself on a hypothesis of change with continuity. These findings are reasonably clear. Thus even at an early research stage an HSPQ-16 PF boundary study by Nuttall on 449 15-to-17-year-olds, the loadings on the same factors of the HSPQ and 16 PF scale markers were: for factor *B,* 0.45 (HSPQ) and 0.66 (PF); for *F,* 0.67 (HSPQ) and 0.36 (PF); for *I,* 0.63 (HSPQ) and 0.85 (PF); but for *E,* only 0.13 (HSPQ) and 0.29 (PF). Perhaps we may conclude that even though the two *E* factor scales concur in having some mutual congruence and no significant congruences with any other of the dozen factors, there is such difference in the expression of dominance between early adolescence and adult maturity as to create difficulties. (I would conclude that present boundary studies are attempting to meet over too wide a no-man's land and that some "in-between scales" may be needed to establish exact continuity.) Further, with present imprecise research some studies indicated possible complete absences as when Schaie (N = 182) failed to find any CPQ equivalent for *C, G,* and *O* and Nuttall (with the HSPQ) for *G* and *O.* One reassuring trend, however, is that as the process of progressive rectification (Chapter Eight) applied to each age level defines factors more clearly, the later boundary studies have shown better cross-validation and identification between the age levels.

(8) The first aim of present research must be to establish whatever identities exist, despite intruding errors, and to continue developing the more psychometrically sound scales for such stable source traits (as is now proceeding, for example, in the work of Harman and French, Comrey, Sells and the IPAT group of investigators). But as soon as such initial stability and assurance of identity is reached the next stage is to seek out and understand the differences of source-trait expression with age, sex, and other population changes. In actual testing it must be understood that even the best scales will not preserve absolute identity of patterns, from population to population and that the 16 PF, HSPQ, and other tests would ideally ultimately put out different scales (or score weightings at least) for males, for females, for different social classes, and so on. In this connection the probability that dominance (*E*) changes its expression notably between adolescence and adulthood has been stated; and theoretically one could argue that a significant change of item pattern might be expected also on superego between the ages of 4 (the PSPQ) and 14 (the HSPQ) or in the kind of avoidance behavior that expresses threctia (*H*-, threat susceptibility). But the accuracy necessary for firm conclusions has not yet been reached.

Theoretically, since factors shown to be substantially environmental in origin seem to change no more than heavily genetic factors we can tentatively suppose that the institutions offering schedules of social reward and punishment—for example, for superego development, self-sentiment growth, desurgent inhibition, and so on—for some reason do not greatly change over the age ranges studied. However, such a theory can be more profitably pursued when other researchers have checked the form and relative variance of these source-trait structures across the ages investigated here.

IV

The Nature and Meaning of Higher-Strata Source Traits

With the preceding definition of primaries and the establishing of reasonably valid scales for measuring them, the reader is likely to be interested next in the developmental age curves, life-criteria relations, cross-cultural comparisons, etc., for these primaries. However, we are not through with structural matters. In that area the relations of traits to states can be left to Chapter Six, but the concept of higher-order structures must be developed here while the primaries are fresh in mind. First we have to recognize that it is not enough to view the primaries as just a string of source traits. For they interact in characteristic ways in the total personality which means that they have a setting within a structure of higher-order factors. To explore what is known about this higher-order structure is the object of the present chapter.

1. Varieties of Higher-Order Factors and Their Expression in Prediction Equations

Let us deal first with the important questions that spring to mind when second-order factors are mentioned. How does one get hold of them? Operationally they are factors that emerge from factoring the correlation matrix among primaries, exactly as primaries are found by factoring the experimentally given correlations among variables. When the most meaningful, unique simple structure is obtained among the primaries one invariably finds (in virtually any domain of observation) that the primary factors are oblique, that is, correlated with one another.[1]

The existence of correlation among primary source traits is not surprising to a psychologist. Terman, for example, found a positive association of emotional stability with intelligence, possibly because the children of intelligent parents are emotionally disciplined wisely. In the 16 PF there is a correlation among adults of self-sentiment strength Q_3 with superego strength G possibly because self-regard grows in an atmosphere of integrity. Similar examples could be found also in physics and chemistry—in many variables taken at various meteorological stations we might find a factor of altitude and a pattern of air pressure. However, when these meaningful unique rotation positions are reached we should expect the altitude and the pressure factors to be considerably negatively correlated.

Psychologically these second orders—or *secondaries*—tend to be broader and shallower, that is, of lesser variance, than the primaries. If we consider Thurstone's primary abilities, such as verbal ability, reasoning, and numerical ability, we find about one-fourth of their variance accounted for by fluid general intelligence and another fourth by crystallized intelligence (Cattell, 1971). And in personality, if we consider the second-order exvia (extraversion) or anxiety factors we find that each takes out less than one-sixth of the variance of the primaries and that all known eight or nine secondaries together account for no more than about 60 percent of the variances of these primaries. For the present a second order can best be considered some influence that affects several primaries at once, as a man's age might affect sensory acuity, metabolic rate, and intelligence, each of which could be a primary factor influencing many distinct variables.

Since there is much empirical evidence for believing that primaries get correlated (incidentally, they can beget no secondaries if we manipulate them to suppress correlation), then consistent observation and logic we must allow secondaries also to go oblique. This is supported empirically, and third orders have been located by factoring the correlations of second orders. In principle this regression toward higher-order influences each acting on those below could go on indefinitely, but one rarely goes beyond third orders. Since at each stage there are commonly about one-fourth to one-half as many factors as variables, the process is brought to a stop when

[1] The factor correlation matrix comes from the transformation matrix L, which shifts the unrotated matrix V_0 from the factor extraction to its final unique reference vectors. It does so by the calculation $V_{rs} = V_0 L$. Then R_{rv}, the correlation among these primary vectors, equals $L'L$. The correlation among factors, R_f, has to be derived from that among vectors by

$$R_f = D\, R_{rv}\, D \tag{1}$$

where the Ds are stretching tensors (see Harman, 1967; Gorsuch and Cattell, 1967). However, if we have made good scales for the primary factors we can get an approximation to the same R_f simply by correlating the scores of people on the primary factor scales. The relative virtues of these two approaches are discussed elsewhere.

one is left with two factors (assuming the one-fourth ratio, 16 variables might give four second orders and stop with one third order). Thus 12 Thurstone primary abilities give, as second orders, fluid and crystallized intelligence factors and one or two other second orders that in turn lead to one or two third orders.

Just as Equations (1.1) and (1.2) stated the breakdown of a variable into primaries so we can give a specification equation to express the contribution of second orders (secondaries) to primaries:

$$F_{gi} = b_{gI}F_{Ii} + b_{gII}F_{IIi} + \ldots + b_{gP}F_{Pi} + b_{g}F_{Gi} \tag{4.1}$$

Here the subscripts on the right are Roman numerals (or capitals in the case of general numbers) to indicate that the primary, on the left (with Arabic or lower case subscripts) is being split up into P broad second orders on the right, plus a specific second order F_G, exactly analogous to the first order equation (1.1) in Chapter One. As usual the b's are behavioral indices (factor loadings) and the i subscript indicates the value for a particular individual.

The F_G factor is that part of the primary which is not accounted for by any secondary. It is quite specific to the primary source trait and we shall find it convenient to call it the "stub" of the primary. Anxiety, as we shall see below, is a secondary, and its loading negatively on ego strength C, and positively on O, guilt proneness, and Q_4, ergic tension, means that it acts to reduce the growth of ego strength C, increase a sense of guilt O, and add to the undischarged drive tension Q_4. Similarly, we might say that temperature at a meteorological station, which is a primary factor affecting such variables as plant growth, evaporation of moisture, and expansion of metals, is itself affected by such secondaries as the altitude and latitude of the station. The picture in the formal model, when we have, say, three orders of factors at work—primaries, secondaries, and tertiaries—is as shown in Figure 7 requiring three factor matrices of different (and diminishing) sizes. In this case there are 6 primaries, 3 secondaries and 1 tertiary, but our symbolism for the general case will be with k, p, and l factors. The primary common factors account for as much of the variance of the variables as is given by the communalities (leaving specifics in variables). In turn the secondaries account for a certain communality of the primaries, leaving some variance in the stubs of the primaries. Finally the tertiary-factor influence contributes a certain variance to each of the secondaries, again leaving stubs, that is, something specific to each secondary.

A persistent misunderstanding of the meaning of secondaries, lies in considering the secondary system of factors as an alternative to primaries. Both are part of the detectable structure as also are the tertiaries. The orders (or strata as we shall later call them) are properly understood as supplementary systems of concepts and of calculation. The motion of the moon is best understood, for example, if conceived as a satellite's motion about the earth which is in turn seen as a satellite of the sun. Consider the second-order factor called exvia-invia (the core of substance in the popular terms extra-

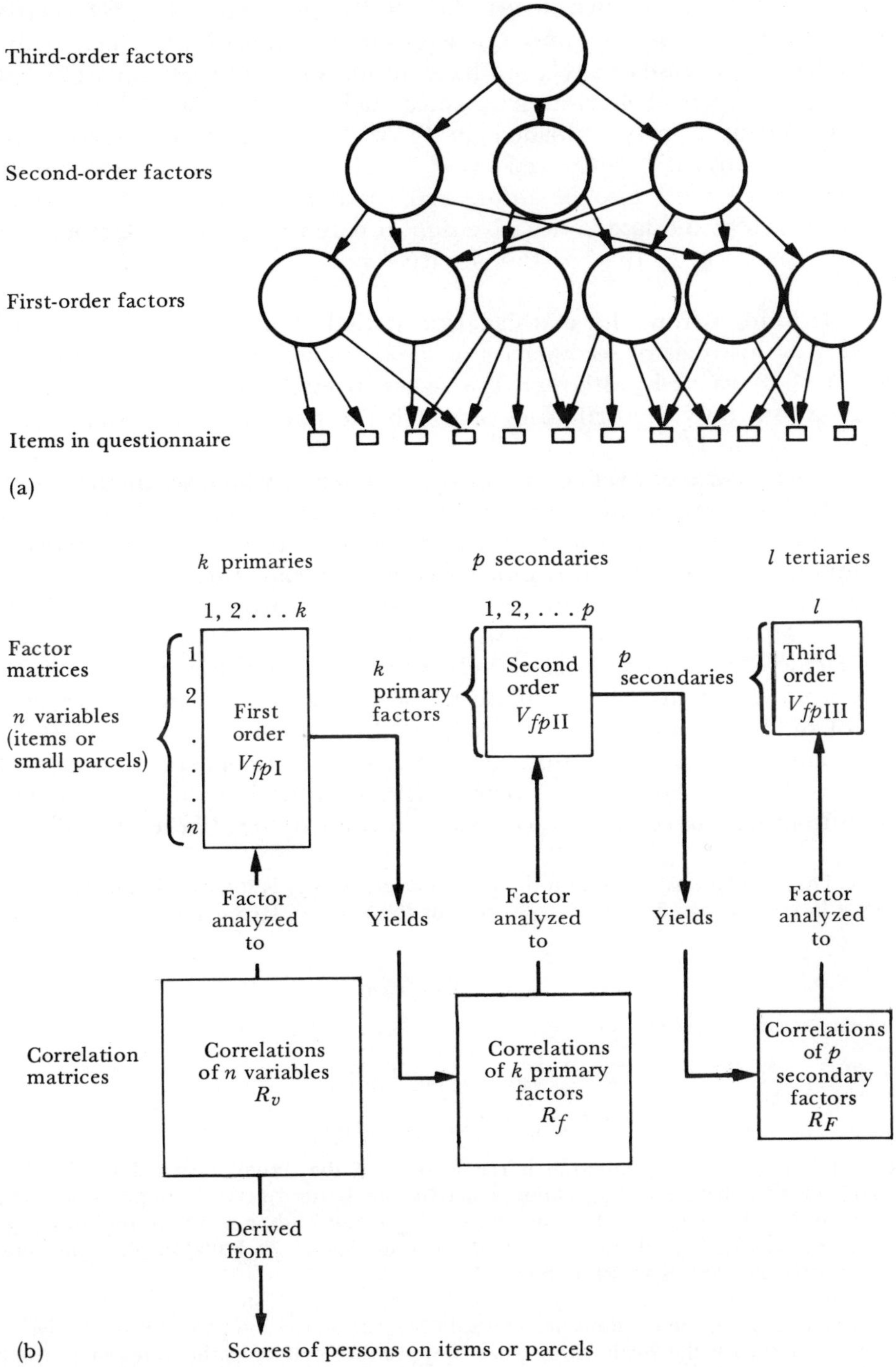

Figure 7. Main model and mode of calculation of higher-order factors: (a) model of action of influence, (b) mode of derivation of factors.

version-introversion), which loads the 16 PF primaries *A* (affectia-sizia), *F* (surgency), *H* (parmia), and Q_2— (group identification). This loading means that an increase in exvia produces an increase in development of both surgent and affectic behavior. And since such questions as, "Are you the life and soul of a party?" (loaded on *F*) or, "Do you prefer to keep your emotions to yourself?" (answered "yes" for *A*(—), sizia) are affected by the primaries, they must also be influenced to some degree by the common secondary. (Here and later a negative sign in parentheses after a factor means that the direction is that of the negative pole — *A*(—) means sizia not affectia.)

It follows from the mathematical-statistical model that we can find a pattern of loadings of secondaries on *items themselves* (called a grounded secondary) if we wish, although the secondaries do not *directly* influence the items, but only the primaries of which the items are the actual expressions (see Table 13).

Since we are not yet certain of the manner in which secondaries effect their contributions to the primaries in causal action terms we may prefer to state the connection of a secondary with an item in terms of statistical accountancy only, saying "this much secondary means this much increment in the following items," leaving the mode of action to future research. This system permits us to take the item scores of an individual and assign a second-order factor score to him. Alternatively we can work out his first-order factor scores from the items and calculate his secondary trait scores as weighted sums of his primaries.

The technicalities of this calculation need not concern most readers: it suffices that one can derive a new matrix showing how any second-order and third-order matrix affects (covaries with) an item.[2] There are different

[2] The calculations depend on the principle that if r_{jF_d} is the correlation of an item *j* with a factor primary F_d and r_{F_dFG} is that of the primary factor *d* with the secondary *G* then

$$r_{jFG} = r_{jF_d} r_{F_dFG} \tag{1}$$

In matrix terms this is written

$$V_{fp\mathrm{II.v}} = V_{fp1} \cdot V_{fp2} \tag{2a}$$

$$V_{fp\mathrm{III.v}} = V_{fp1} \cdot V_{fp2} \cdot V_{fp3} \tag{2b}$$

where the left side of the equation is the loading of the second order II or the third order III on the variable *v*; V_{fp1} is the primary-factor pattern matrix (simply written V_{fp} when no order distinction needs to be made); V_{fp2} is the loading of the second orders on the first orders, and V_{fp3} of the third on the second (Figure 7). Equation (2a) multiplies an *nxk* matrix by a *kxp* as shown in Figure 7.

This is the way the columns are calculated in the Cattell-White form. In the Schmid-Leiman form the columns are multiplied again by the uniquenesses of the factors concerned to reduce the loadings to what they would be if only the stubs of the first, second, and other order factors were at work. Thus the Schmid-Leiman equivalent of Equation (2a) becomes

$$V_{fp\mathrm{II.v}} = V_{fp1}\, U_2\, V_{fp2}\, U_3 \tag{3}$$

ways of expressing this called the Schmid-Leiman and the Cattell-White matrices, shown in Table 13. The difference is that the Schmid-Leiman matrix tells us what the stub of a first- or second- or third-order factor does to an item, whereas the Cattell-White matrix says what the whole factor does to the item. The difference can be indicated in notation by calling the Cattell-White factor F_x and the Schmid-Leiman factor F'_x. Although the Cattell-White representation has its use in practical situations it is the Schmid-Leiman that comes nearest to the true psychological model. According to that model, since nothing happens in the scientific world by accident, the obliqueness of two primaries—their correlation—requires that we recognize some influence that produces the correlation. Temperature is temperate and air pressure is air pressure; as two distinct factors there is no conceptual need for them to correlate. But if I measure temperature and air pressure at a hundred points on a mountain they will certainly have a positive correlation over the series. What is the second order affecting both of these primaries? Clearly it is altitude, and one could work out the effect of the altitude secondary directly on the variables—plant growth, rate of heartbeat—although it would be more scientific to seek to understand these as related to temperature and pressure.

In the psychological domain, despite some opinions to the contrary (Comrey, 1973; Eysenck, 1971; Peterson, 1960), the evidence is that the primaries examined in the last chapter are scientifically more important and constant and that the secondaries are more elusive and above all related to the accidental circumstances of the particular group. For example, the second-order factors of intelligence and anxiety are correlated −0.26 in

---

where U_2 is the diagonal matrix of unique loadings of primary factors as given in the second-order factor matrix and so on.

Proceeding from the calculation of loadings of higher-order factors directly on items to the reverse regression calculation of getting the weights of items on higher-order factors—to estimate those factors from items—we follow the usual rules.

To estimate second orders directly from primaries, as is often done with the 16 PF (Cattell, Eber, and Tatsuoka, 1970, p. 128) we use the equation

$$V_{fe2} = R_{f1}^{-1} V_{fp2} R_{f2} \tag{4}$$

where V_{fe2} is the required weight matrix, R_{f1} and R_{f2} are the correlations among primaries and secondaries, and V_{fp2} is the factor pattern of second orders on primaries. To do the same for the Cattell-White factor pattern of secondaries directly on items we proceed by

$$V_{feII} = R_{f1}^{-1} V_{fpII.v} R_{f2} \tag{5}$$

This is the formula used in computer synthesis when we want to use all items in such a questionnaire as the 16 PF or HSPQ to estimate an individual's second-order scores.

The amount contributed by the second orders, as shown by their communality across all variables, stands at its full value only when the pure-factor factorization rather than the scale factorization is used. The loadings in the latter are uniformly reduced down the column, compared with their true values, by a ratio r equal to the validity of the scale against the true factor; that is, we multiply the column by the concept (construct) validity. Table 16 estimates the true values from the pure factor studies, even though the pure factors V_{fp} rest on fewer studies, and Table 23 has no alternative to resting on pure factor angles at simple structure since prior to the Barton second order CTS Kit there were no scales for all secondaries.

Table 13

Contrast of Cattell-White and Schmid-Leiman Loadings of Higher-Order Factors on Variables

(a) By Cattell-White Formula

	First Order					*Second Order*			*Third Order*	
	1′	*2′*	*3′*	*4′*	h^2	*1″*	*2″*	h^2	*1‴*	h^2
1	.00	.00	.00	.50	.25	.00	.30	.09	.21	.04
2	.00	.50	.00	.00	.25	.00	.00	.00	.00	.00
3	.00	−.50	.60	.00	.61	.36	−.30	.09	.09	.01
4	.50	.60	.00	.00	.61	.25	.00	.06	.21	.04
5	−.50	.60	.00	.00	.61	−.25	.00	.06	−.21	.04
6	.60	.00	.50	.00	.70	.60	−.25	.24	.33	.11
7	−.60	.00	−.50	.00	.70	−.60	.25	.24	−.33	.11
8	.00	.00	.60	−.60	.79	.36	−.66	.28	−.16	.03
9	.00	.00	.00	.50	.25	.00	.30	.09	.21	.04
10	.00	.00	.00	.60	.36	.00	.36	.13	.26	.07

Intercorrelations of First-Order Factors (Cattell-White)

	1′	2′	3′	4′
1′	100	00	15	18
2′		100	00	00
3′			100	−08
4′				100.

Intercorrelations of Second-Order Factors (Cattell-White)

	1″	2″
1″	100	60
2″		100

(b) By Schmid-Leiman Formula

	First Order					*Second Order*			*Third Order*		
	1′	*2′*	*3′*	*4′*	h^2	*1″*	*2″*	h^2	*1‴*	h^2	Σh^2
1	.00	.00	.00	.40	.16	.00	.21	.04	.21	.04	.25
2	.00	.50	.00	.00	.25	.00	.00	.00	.00	.00	.25
3	.00	−.50	.52	.00	.52	.19	−.21	.08	.09	.01	.61
4	.43	.60	.00	.00	.55	.13	.00	.02	.21	.04	.61
5	−.43	.60	.00	.00	.55	−.13	.00	.02	−.21	.04	.61
6	.52	.00	.43	.00	.46	.32	−.18	.13	.33	.11	.70
7	−.52	.00	−.43	.00	.46	−.32	.18	.13	−.33	.11	.70
8	.00	.00	.52	−.48	.50	.19	−.47	.26	−.16	.03	.79
9	.00	.00	.00	.40	.16	.00	.21	.04	.21	.04	.25
10	.00	.00	.00	.48	.23	.00	.25	.06	.26	.07	.36

Note: In the S-L formula the projections of first orders on items is calculated by

$$\mathbf{V}_{fp\mathrm{I}} = V_{fp1}\, U_{\mathrm{II}}$$

where U_{II} is a diagonal matrix of first-order specifics (stubs) after the second orders are taken out. As is seen by comparing tables (a) and (b) the first-order factors in the C-W and S-L systems are individually simply proportional in their loadings. At higher orders the school children (Cattell and Cattell, 1969) and −0.31 in adults (Cattell, Eber, and Tatsuoka, 1970). But these correlations are on groups in a competitive, "achieving" (McClelland, 1955) society; indications from more casual societies are that low intelligence need not associate itself with high anxiety. In other words the higher- (third-) order structure is subject to social and economic conditions beyond the domain of personality and lacks the stability of meaning of the primaries.

Returning to our mathematical model and our calculation of factor scores, we see that it implies that the real primaries are the stubs—the parts of the primaries left over when the second-order contribution has been taken away—not the primaries as they first emerge from item factoring. The weights on items in estimating either of the original primaries or the stubs are the same (or simply proportional); so if the psychologist is unaware of the conceptual difference his ignorance is bliss. However, the split into a second order and a stub means that the Schmid-Leiman equation for estimating an item score requires attention both to the primary and to the secondary. That is, instead of considering the effect to be that of k oblique factors (say, 16 PF primaries) we regard it as the action of k orthogonal primary stubs plus p secondaries (anxiety, exvia, and others), as shown in Equation (4.2):

$$a_{ij} = b_{j1}F_{1i} + \ldots + b_{jk}F_{ki} + \mathbf{b}_{j21}\mathbf{F}_{21i} + \ldots + \mathbf{b}_{j2p}\mathbf{F}_{2pi} + \mathbf{b}_{j31}\mathbf{F}_{31i} + b_jF_{ji} \quad (4.2)$$

where a is the response act on item j by individual i as in Equation (1.1). The calculated result is the same; the only difference would be if one wished to extrapolate to some other situation, in which case the knowledge that the surgency stub and anxiety might change differently would give us more control by the Schmid-Leiman formulation.[3] There are now k primary stubs (**F**s), p secondary stubs ($\mathbf{F}_2$s), one tertiary ($\mathbf{F}_3$), and one item primary specific F_j. The communalities here as in the first-order specification are simply the sum of the squared loadings (loadings and correlations are the same here) since factors are orthogonal (see Table 13). The b_2 values here can be calculated (Schmid and Leiman, 1957; Cattell and DeYoung, 1973a) from the b loadings and the b_{II} loadings, that is, the loadings of the second order on the first order.

The reader need not bother with the details of Equation (4.2)—it is there for the psychologist who needs to calculate—but he should grasp the

relation is more complex (see footnote 2 and Cattell and DeYoung, 1973a). A systematic notation is needed in this domain; we represent C-W and S-L equivalents respectively by V and $\mathbf{V}$. The natural Vs, that is, the projection of each factor system on its next lower order are V_1, V_2, V_3, and so on; the projections directly on items become V_{I}, V_{II}, V_{III}. (In the C-W system $V_1 = V_{\text{I}}$ in one case.)

No correlation matrix is given for the S-L factors in table (b) because they are orthogonal. Only in the S-L do the squared summed loadings for a variable across the orders equal its communality.

[3] There is a mathematical objection to the Schmid-Leiman formulation—that it puts in more factors than we have evidence for, namely $k + p$. Indeed the string of first and higher orders from successive factorings ($k + p + q + \ldots$) can exceed the number of variables. Practically this means that factor estimates cease to be uncorrelated.

psychological concepts that correspond to the mathematical model. To reiterate, we do find primaries at simple structure to be significantly correlated, which requires some third influence to be acting on both (since at the same stratum they cannot act on each other). I have warned that this second-order influence need not be psychological: for example, mental age and emotional stability over childhood are both increased by chronological age. When the age of the sample is varied, this second-order variation brings variance to the primaries—intelligence and emotional stability. When age is kept absolutely the same for all children the observed variance in these two primaries is due to the stubs of the two factors F_g and F_e (using g for intelligence). But when we allow age F_{21}, a second order, to increase in variance, the variances of mental age and emotional stability increase from that of the stubs F_g and F_e to that of the full observed factor variance F_g and F_e (in the notation adopted). We *shall* see many instances where second-order factors are recognizable as *psychologically* real—anxiety, exvia—but it is necessary to be open to the possibility that they lie outside psychology.

The alternatives of writing the specification equation for oblique factors as in Equation (1.1) or in the Schmid-Leiman form as in Equation (4.2), in which the stubs F_g and F_e are with age F_{21} the total determiners, become clear in the preceding example.. We see that the second order—age in this case—does not directly affect arithmetic performance a_j. Intelligence and emotional stability affect accuracy of performance in arithmetic and age affects intelligence and emotional stability. It is thus only as a convenience of calculation that we write the final effects of different orders together directly on a variable as in the S-L equation (4.2). In short our real model is that the primary (stub) source traits directly affect item responses; that second orders act directly on primaries by expanding them; and that tertiaries in turn act on secondaries. The higher the order the broader the ultimate influence on items. One implication important for locating factors is that good simple structure of the higher orders directly on the items would not be expected to appear (see Chapter Eight). Higher orders must get their unique rotations directly from the next lower orders.

More remains to be said about the conceptual nature of higher-order factors and their interaction but that theme cannot be followed until psychological examples in Q-data are considered. This section concerns true second orders, not the *pseudo-second orders* which, as Chapter Eight brings out, are often put forward as true primaries or true secondaries (Eysenck, 1971; Howarth and Browne, 1971a, 1971b; Peterson, 1960, 1965). As DeYoung has shown, factoring items without taking out the full number of factors statistically required results in factors resembling the projections of true second orders directly on items. They are neither correct first orders nor dependable delineations of second orders on items. They may have fair hyperplanes and congruences with others similarly obtained but this does not justify them since the procedure inflates congruences. Viewing such studies one has to recognize that a crude approach to second orders characterizes the limbo in which inadequate or mutilated factors tend to end.

2. Congruence of 16 PF Second Orders Across Twelve Researches

Second- and third-order factors have regularly been found in all three modalities of trait and state measurement—abilities, personality-temperament, and dynamic interest. In personality they have been found alike in the rating medium L(R)-data (Cattell, 1957), in T-data (Pawlik and Cattell, 1964), and in Q-data.

In the oldest factored questionnaire, the Guilford-Zimmerman, factors are in principle orthogonal: no higher order can be built upon them. Nor have higher orders been explored with respect to the Comrey, Edwards, Eysenck, Jackson, and most other questionnaire scales. The higher orders in the 16 PF series of research, however, had their essential nature uncovered quite early (Cattell, 1955c, 1956d, 1957) and have since been brought to a high degree of confirmation and precision of form in over 28 independent studies. The most adequate 27 of these—14 in the adult 16 PF, 5 in the HSPQ, 4 in the CPQ, 2 in the ESPQ, and 2 in the CAQ—are summarized here. In the case of the Comrey questionnaire, the design of starting with variables that are factor-homogenous item parcels (but large ones, FHIDS, virtually equal to primary factors) leads one to expect that the factors on which its scales are based would be second orders. This conclusion is well supported by Comrey's own work (Comrey and Duffy, 1968) showing that the 16 PF primaries group themselves on his main factors closely to the second-order groupings. Although Gorsuch accepts this as an approximate statement he nevertheless concludes (1972) that there is doubt about the true order of some of the Comrey scales.

The early 1955–1957 studies brought out three important facts. First, that no fewer than four second orders appear with meanings that are psychologically clear and that even more exist. The concepts involved are anxiety (as shown by a pattern in the primaries of ego weakness, guilt proneness, ergic tension, and others); exvia (where the factors affectia *A*, surgency *F*, parmia *H*, and group dependence $Q_2(-)$ define the concept well), and two factors known as corteria and independence. Second, that these Q-data second-order patterns show a striking resemblance to the second orders found in L-data (Cattell, 1957). And third, that in the two largest—exvia and anxiety—there is virtually perfect alignment also with the simple-structure factors UI 24 (anxiety) and UI 32 (extraversion) in objective (T-data) measures.

In the following years 18 more second-order factorings of the 16 PF appeared: Conner (1968), Cattell (1965d), Karson and Pool (1958), Cattell and Horn (1963), Gocka and Marks (1961), Hundleby (1972), Klein (1973), Jenkins (1962), Karson and Wiedershine (1961), LaForge (1962), Michael, Barth, and Kaiser (1961), Mitchell (1963), O'Dell and Karson (1969), Tollefson (1961), K. White (1968), Gorsuch and Cattell (1967), Nichols (see Cattell and Nichols, 1972), and Cattell (1973a, c, and f). Since some studies used orthogonal (second-order) factors, unities as communalities, and so forth, Gorsuch (Gorsuch and Cattell, 1967) undertook to refactor the seven best studies to date. This was done by bringing all 1652 subjects covered in these studies into a single covariance-averaged correlation matrix. Because scree test was not yet available Gorsuch used a mean of the K-G, Sokal's (1959), and Bartlett's (1948) factor-significance test to determine the number precisely in this new realm. His verdict was eight factors. Twenty-six overall rotations yielded the results shown in Table 14. Except for some uncertainties in factors V and VI, intensive studies since Gorsuch's analysis have agreed closely with the patterns.

Table 14

Definition of Second-Order Structure from First Decade of Research [a]

		Factor Patterns of Secondaries							
Symbol	*Primary Factor*	*I*	*II*	*III*	*IV*	*V*	*VI*	*VII*	*VIII*
A	Sociable	46	—	−54	−23	—	—	—	—
B	Intelligence	—	—	—	—	—	—	87	—
C	Ego strength	—	−52	—	—	—	—	—	—
E	Dominance	44	—	—	36	—	—	—	—
F	Surgency	59	—	—	—	—	—	—	—
G	Superego strength	—	—	—	—	—	—	—	85
H	Adventurousness	62	−42	—	—	—	—	—	—
I	Sensitive	—	—	−66	—	—	−31	—	—
L	Paranoid suspiciousness	—	54	—	—	—	—	—	—
M	Unconcerned	—	—	—	38	—	44	—	—
N	Shrewdness	—	—	27	—	49	—	—	—
O	Guilt proneness	—	70	—	—	—	—	—	—
Q_1	Radical	—	—	—	46	22	—	—	—
Q_3	Self-sufficiency	−34	—	—	41	—	—	—	—
Q_2	Self-sentiment control	—	−54	—	—	25	—	—	—
Q_4	Ergic tension	—	76	—	—	—	—	—	—

[a] 1652 subjects; Gorsuch and Cattell, 1967. Only loadings above 0.20 are included. Decimal place omitted.

Note: The identification of these factors from content, criterion associations, and relations to objective test factors is as follows:

I. Exvia-invia
II. Anxiety-adjustment
III. Cortertia-pathemia
IV. Independence subduedness
V. Foxiness-secure naturalness
VI. Untamedness
VII. Intelligence
VIII. Moral background

In Table 14, as in many articles and books in this field, Roman numerals are used for the second order factors, more readily to distinguish them from the alphabetic symbols for the primaries. In both cases, of course, the aim is to permit debates on meaning and interpretive labels without losing exact reference to the identity of the pattern as such. Six years after Gorsuch's survey another major integration was made by Nichols with a change of method consisting of factoring the samples (ten studies) separately before coming to the central loading patterns.[4] Great care was taken with regard to such matters as number of factors, communalities, and especially rotation. Since 5 of his 10 studies extended to foreign language translations and foreign cultural samples they are discussed with the cross-cultural data in Chapter Eight. It may be said here, however, that the congruences were virtually as good across as within cultures. For example, Table 51(d) in Chapter Eight shows all congruences among all factor patterns for one English-speaking and one German sample. With the exception of the ninth factor (an unidentified or error factor) the agreement is about as high as for the same factor patterns compared for American men and women in Table 15 and the values are uniformly in the high nineties.

At first glance the off-diagonal values are sometimes said to be significant. Actually on 16 cases the highest value here—0.38—does not reach the $P < 0.05$ level, and it is one of 56 correlations. However, in some studies the loading pattern of one factor does resemble another beyond chance when the two factors are indubitably different, which constitutes the well-known phenomenon of cooperative factors: fluid intelligence g_f, crystallized intelligence g_a, and others. This tendency of two personality factors to affect the same variables is sometimes seen at the primary level in *A* and *H* or *C* and *O* and at the secondary level in exvia and independence. Its meaning is not yet clear. It can occur with complete orthogonality of the factors themselves.

Throughout these American and English studies (as in the others in Nichols' survey) the number of factors indicated by the scree was uniformly eight or nine; the ninth factor showed instability and seems sometimes a patently trivial error factor. Eight factors are consistently reported in Table 15 and elsewhere; the extras that occasionally appear are considered common-error factors or dim outlines of some smaller factor yet to be found.

Two additional studies should be mentioned because of the unusual feature that they are founded on item factoring of all 184 items in the 16 PF form. These studies were undertaken because of the disputes (on the one side Comrey and certain psychometrists, on the other Eysenck and Howarth and Browne) over parceled versus item factoring. My position is that both are legitimate and that they are mutually consistent. The first-order results are reported in Chapter Eight, but I want to point out here that those item-determined primaries gave second orders entirely consistent

[4] Taken from the following samples and studies: Cattell (1956d) N = 408; Cattell (1965c) N = 209 and 296; Cattell, Eber, and Tatsuoka (1970) N = 423 and 535; Cattell and Nesselroade (1965) N = 446; Cattell and Scheier (1961); Cattell and Warburton (1961) N = 202 and 604; DeAndrade, DeGodoy, and Ford (1969) N = 1325; Horn (1963) N = 172; Karson (1961) N = 96 and (1967) N = 124; Karson and Haupt (1968) N = 300; Karson and Pool (1958); Krug and Kulhavy (1973) N = 1000; Tsujioka and Cattell (1965b) N = 300; a single, large, composite group, Gorsuch and Cattell (1967) N = 1652; and Cattell, Schroder, and Wagner (1969) N = 1000 and 1800.

Table 15

Agreement by Congruence Coefficients of Second-Order Patterns

		Females[a]								
	Males[a]	*I*	*II*	*III*	*IV*	*V*	*VI*	*VII*	*VIII*	*IX*
		(a) Male and Female								
Exvia	I	[99]	−07	−12	24	14	−02	−01	−11	−19
Anxiety	II	−14	[99]	−00	09	−02	09	−10	−15	−17
Cortertia	III	−23	−14	[96]	01	−09	−23	−05	10	00
Independence	IV	34	03	−00	[98]	−25	11	−04	−06	−04
Foxiness	V	20	00	−13	−09	[96]	02	−12	03	−22
Untamedness	VI	−07	−11	−23	32	−13	[94]	09	14	19
Intelligence	VII	14	−09	−00	08	−13	−06	[96]	01	−19
Superego	VIII	−21	−15	−00	−09	12	01	−03	[97]	06
Unidentified factor	IX	06	−08	−38	−07	−12	08	04	−01	[86]
		(b) Across Diverse Populations								
Mean over 10 studies		92	97	89	83	85	64	76	85	−02

[a] American female students, N = 880; American male students, N = 1000.

The rows represent the male patterns and the columns the female. As in all correlation and factor loading tables the decimal points (but not signs) are omitted, all values being two decimal place values.

with those from other sources. These item-factoring-derived second-order patterns are matched in the congruence coefficients of Table 16(b). It is part of the grammar of science that a theory survives by its internal consistency as well as by its fit to external facts. The consistency with which the patterns of second orders appear upon first orders supports not only the significance of the second orders but also the reality of the first orders as consistently reappearing functional unities.

Lack of unlimited space prevents the setting out of full tables showing all possible factors [5] and congruences. Thus Table 16 sets out the best

[5] The unavoidable complexity in setting out statements about second-order factors lies in the fact that since they are oblique factors there are no fewer than eight forms in which the variable-factor V matrix can be set out. Since this matter is of importance in the field—if confusions are to be avoided—a brief exposition and systematic notation will be set out as follows: First we have the antithesis of the C-W and S-L modes of expression, as follows: (1) The *full second order* expressed on primaries (F_{21}, F_{22}, . . . , F_{2g}, . . . , F_{2p}). This is typically an oblique factor in a matrix V_{fp2}. In short each factor is here a column in the ordinary second-order kxp matrix. (2) *The (C-W model),* that is, the full second order expressed on items or variables. This model is the same as the oblique factor with its pattern expressed on variables (F_{I}, F_{II}, . . . , F_{G}, F_{P}). It is a column in the Cattell-White matrix. (3) The stub (specific part) of the second-order factor (what is left when third and higher orders are taken out) expressed in its loadings on primaries (F_{I}, F_{II}, . . . , F_{G}, . . . , F_{P}). This is a column in a matrix we have not defined but shall call the true second- (or higher-) order stub matrix V_{fp2}. This is the essential expression of what we have called elsewhere the ortho-strata model. (4) The stub second order projected on variables (F_{I}, F_{II}, and so on). Each such factor is a column in the typical Schmid-Leiman matrix. (Notations as above: V_{fpII}.)

The reader may note that only the fourth and last of these models permits an equation to be written in which factors of all orders can be set side by side with their loadings all contributing at once to the score on a variable. (1) and (2) are oblique systems in which estimate as a means of 14 studies in 9 matrices of the central pattern for all eight factors. Variations of pattern are given in Table 17. These 14 are the Gorsuch summary (five studies), the five from Nichols, the 423 male and 535 female adult samples reported by Cattell, Eber, and Tatsuoka (1970, p. 121), and the two item studies previously mentioned.

In considering higher-order structure the psychologist should recognize that second-order factoring can proceed from one of two bases: (1) pure factor intercorrelations obtained from a rotation of primaries to simple structure and (2) scale intercorrelations among the actual primary-scale scores. The former, which is the true-factor approach, would be preferable if rotation were perfect; but the fact that it is not has led psychometrists such as Cronbach to feel uncertain about the consistency to be expected from second-and third-order factors. When simple structure has been poorly pursued—which is all too frequently the case—these doubts are well founded and scale factoring, using correlations among the scales for primaries, would be safer.

However, the proof of the pudding is the eating, and, with simple structure commonly pursued from 15 to 20 overall rotations it turns out that the congruences are around 85 to 95 among the true-factor approaches and not significantly inferior between the results of the two methods, true primary and scale primary factoring. Indeed, on this basis it is reasonable to approach the third order with confidence.

The idea that we can escape from random (rotational) error by going to scales is false, however. We substitute inevitably defective validities for potentially perfect validities (unit length, but possibly not correctly oriented) and a new kind of random error. Inasmuch as designs for suppressor action among items commonly fall well short of the ideal, scale correlations are spoiled by intrusion into each scale score of some contribution from other scales.[6]

A consideration that should enter into this choice between two evils is the number of variables that have entered into the rotation of the pri-

---

there are five transformations of each—V_{rs}, V_{rp}, V_{fs}, V_{fp}, and V_{fe}—though only the three last are of importance other than as steps in calculation. Thus (1) above—the full second-order on primaries—can be written in five ways: as V_{fs2} the correlations of primaries with second orders, as V_{fp2} (loadings of second orders on primaries) and as V_{fe2} (weights of primaries when estimating secondaries), as well, of course, as two reference vector systems V_{rs2} and V_{rp2}. Since there are similarly three important versions of (2)—V_{fsII}, V_{fpII}, and V_{feII}—there are altogether eight *V*s to consider at the second order. $V_{feII.v}$ deserves special respect because it is our means of scoring second-order factors from the item responses.

[6] In the concept of the *consistency coefficient* there are three coefficients: *dependability* (test-retest reliability), *homogeneity* (internal consistency), and *transferability* (consistency across populations) (see Cattell and Warburton, 1967 and Chapter 9 here). It is incorrect to use the homogeneity (including the equivalence coefficient form) to correct for attenuation since the A and B forms of any scale include the second order and the primary factor variances, almost certainly in different proportions. The dependability coefficient falls short of unity only by error of measurement, and the question is whether primary *X* and primary *Y* correlate perfectly except for error of measurement. The answer is that they do not; this can be seen from factoring the pure-primary factors at simple-structure positions.

Table 16

Most Complete Available Statement (1973) of Eight Second-Order Source-Trait Patterns at Adult (16 PF) Level[a]

(a) *Pattern*

	I	*II*	*III*	*IV*	*V*	*VI*	*VII*	*VIII*
A	[58]	01	[−25]	01	[28]	00	−00	−01
B	−00	−02	00	−01	−01	00	[67]	−01
C	07	[−66]	10	−01	−02	−00	04	05
E	07	−00	01	[56]	−03	08	01	[−18]
F	[51]	−03	01	[30]	−02	−04	02	[−27]
G	06	−03	01	−03	00	−05	05	[67]
H	[50]	[−38]	[−14]	[34]	05	−01	−02	−00
I	07	00	[−73]	−03	01	04	01	02
L	05	[54]	06	[40]	02	−01	−06	04
M	12	03	[−47]	[20]	−05	[14]	−02	−08
N	−00	−02	00	03	[63]	00	−01	03
O	−02	[78]	−06	−05	−00	00	−04	03
Q_1	−02	−06	−01	07	06	[56]	05	−02
Q_2	[−65]	−01	−04	03	02	07	01	01
Q_3	−05	[−43]	01	02	01	03	−02	[47]
Q_4	−00	[80]	−05	10	−02	−03	09	−02

[a] Mean factor-pattern loadings from 14 studies and 9 summary matrices.

(b) *Goodness of Hyperplanes and Congruences Among Second Order Researches*

Even restricting to the congruences of one factor with its hypothesized counterpart in other studies there would be 11×6×8 = 528 congruences needing calculation here. We have cut down the 11×6 to 12 by taking only the congruences of each study with its adjacent study. Thus each of the eight entries is the *mean* of 12 examinations of the hypothesized identity from one research to another.

Identities of Source Traits

I Exvia
II Anxiety
III Cortertia
IV Independence
V Discreetness
VI Prodigal Subjectivity
VII Intelligence
VIII Good Upbringing

A. Congruences

Studies Compared*	*I*	*II*	*III*	*IV*	*V*	*VI*	*VII*	*VIII*
	Second Order Factors by Usual Notation							
1 with 2	100	100	96	95	96	94	97	98
2 with 3	99	98	97	95	93	94	85	92
3 with 4	99	100	99	97	99	99	99	97
4 with 5	96	98	94	52	97	86	98	59
5 with 6	91	97	79	57	85	41	76	60
6 with 7	91	97	88	92	87	56	65	83
7 with 8	97	99	97	89	92	72	61	96
8 with 9	78	96	84	81	89	23	51	95
9 with 10	88	98	93	96	86	60	58	95
Mean	93	98	92	84	92	70	77	86
Grand Mean 86								

* The studies are numbered as in Cattell and Nichols (1972).

B. Hyperplane Counts

	Researches									
	1	2	3	4	5	6	7	8	9	10
Percent in ±.10 Loading	72	76	78	78	73	70	74	72	71	68

Mean: 73.2%

maries. Rotation, like many other procedures, depends on size of sample. As the sample gets smaller, simple structure is forced to depend on representations of the hyperplanes by an insufficiency of variables to mark the structure clearly. This becomes a serious problem at the third order whether factors or scales are taken as the second-order basis because there are only about 8 to 10 points (second-order factors) on the plots.[7] Our significances may still look good since a high Bargmann significance requires fewer points with fewer factors, but there is reliability as well as significance to consider. Even at the second order, in two of the three preceding factors including anxiety itself the choice has to be made regularly between two simple structures that differ by only 10 to 20 percent in hyperplane count. Consequently the decision on higher-order rotations has been to adhere to the simple structure that is most consistently represented across many person samples. The main instance in which rotation and identity are in debate is an alternative rotation to cortertia that would drop sizothymia (*A*—) out of the cortertia pattern and leave it excessively correlated with exvia-invia. However, as the congruences show, factors V (discreetness) and VI (subjectivity) are also subject to a general variance from study to study because of almost equally satisfactory hyperplane alternatives.

Nevertheless if we accept that Eysenck's factors are rough approaches to second-order factors (*E* and *N* in the normal field and *P* in the pathological) it speaks for the effectiveness of these methods that they have produced with considerable consistency not three factors but eight. Of these, two are matchable by Eysenck's factors—exvia (I) by his *E* and anxiety (II) by his *N* (neuroticism). However, the precision with which this can be done in terms of congruence coefficients has never been shown to equal the precision of matching when they are taken out as true second orders, that is, from primaries instead of items, as shown in Table 17. From the results of 12 different samples and studies set out side by side, the reader can see the extent of variation of loadings [8] that occurs and can relate it to the magnitudes of the congruence coefficients in Table 16. (These Table 17 loading values are those from which the means of Table 16 were derived for exvia and anxiety.)

At this point the reader should recognize that *two* of these eight

[7] The generalization (1960) that I have called to the attention of those seeking unique hyperplanes—that with n variables and k factors a large number of perfect hyperplanes each of $(k - 1)$ variables can always be found—becomes especially relevant here. With five third-order factors from eight second orders there are 70 spurious hyperplanes each reaching the 50 percent count, that is, four points exactly in the hyperplane.

[8] The expression exvia-invia is used for the second-order factor covering *A, F, H,* and Q_2- found in both L- and Q-data. Since these factors closely match the UI 32 pattern in objective tests the same term will be used for UI 32. It has the same general meaning of going outwards versus going inwards that extraversion-introversion has but unlike that cliché it is a precise scientific concept. With the advance of science it has become possible to develop Jung's wordy concept into an exact psychometric operational concept—a particular second-order factor measurable with known validity from defined primaries. By a similar advance chemistry changed "dephlogisticated air" to "oxygen." Moreover the noun exvia and adjective exviant offer brief and neat communication.

Table 17

Degree of Modification of Exvia and Anxiety Factors with Change of Sample

	Exvia				*Anxiety*			
Factor	*1* [a]	*2*	*3*	*4*	*1*	*2*	*3*	*4*
A	61	61	51	66	−02	−02	10	06
B	−00	01	−06	−00	−02	−02	−04	−03
C	07	05	10	06	−80	−80	−80	−75
E	11	07	04	06	−04	03	02	03
F	63	61	64	53	−00	−04	−04	−08
G	07	05	09	09	−01	−01	−03	−05
H	55	49	63	56	−41	−41	−40	−38
I	12	13	−05	10	10	08	−06	00
L	−03	−01	−06	05	51	52	66	56
M	−11	−09	−03	−09	−13	−06	08	04
N	−00	00	−02	04	−01	−01	−10	−07
O	−07	−03	−07	−06	87	88	78	84
Q_1	00	02	−05	03	02	02	−08	−05
Q_2	−78	−78	−70	−70	−03	−02	00	−03
Q_3	07	−07	−09	−08	−47	−46	−44	−53
Q_4	02	04	00	−01	84	84	84	86

[a] Samples: (1) American 17-year-old boys; (2) American 17-year-old girls; (3) New Zealand 18-year-old boys and girls; (4) New Zealand 22-year-old men and women.

Note: If the reader compares these independent resolutions with those sometimes published resting on either automatic analytical or orthogonal rotation programs he will note that the latter diverge erratically from this central tendency. If these matrices claiming each its own unique analytical "truth" are averaged as in Table 16, the hollowness of the claim of each to have a viable alternative structure becomes evident from the blurred incongruences which result. Unlike Table 16, neither high salients nor clear hyperplane loadings emerge from such averaging.

second orders (and a third when we see how *N* behaves in the childhood series of second order) might appear to consist of a single primary. Thus VII is loaded only on *B;* VIII (except for slight loadings on *C*, *F*—, and Q_3) is *mainly* a high loading on *G*.

It is a rule of factor analysis (Cattell, 1965) that if a measure for a second-order factor is accidentally mixed with first orders it will stand out alone in a column of the second-order factor-pattern matrix, calling attention to its true rank. General intelligence—*g* in objective T-data work, *B* here—stands at the first order among T-data general personality factors and, according to my generalization that second order in Q-data is first order in T-data, should be a second order in Q-data. Indeed by every standard it should be second order, and the justification for its inclusion as a scale with the 16 PF primaries is practical: it is convenient for users of the 16 PF to have a brief intelligence test included.

Apart from this instance, however, there is every indication that the primary that appears to predominate is not the only significant loading. Its loading may be lower than it should be because the matrix lacks other variables that share enough communality to give a good estimate of its communality. But though it is king it has accompanying variables whose loadings are not zero. Occasional rotations of VIII (Cattell and Gorsuch, 1963) leave little but *G*. But the majority verdict of others (Cattell and Nichols, 1972) is that self-sentiment Q_3, desurgency *F*(—), and probably ego strength *C* and submissiveness *E*(—) regularly have some loading. This makes good psychological sense. The superego concept is properly restricted to the primary *G* but this second order VIII clearly suggests a pattern from exposure to a good upbringing that simultaneously raises superego, builds the social, self-respecting values of Q_3, and thus contributes to the soberness and prudence of desurgency (*F*—) and the modesty of *E*—. It must be added that when one extends research to primaries beyond the 16 PF, secondaries that appear here to have only one primary commonly pick up others (see Table 21).

3. Secondaries in the Preadult, High School, Adolescent Age Range

Because primaries and valid questionnaire scales at earlier ages have been established for only a short time, less higher-order research has been done on them. Consequently my account of the search for secondaries at the four preadult levels—the 12–18 year (HSPQ), the 8–14 year (CPQ), the 6–8 year (ESPQ), and the 4–6 year (PSPQ)—is condensed into this one section.

The first question is this: Do the secondaries exist in the same numbers and patterns as the primaries at the lower age levels? The evidence on the HSPQ, taken mostly from experiments at the 13-to-14-year-old level is clear and mostly affirmative. No fewer than 10 independent factor analyses can be marshaled for comparison. As at the adult level the initial analysis, with crude and now obsolete test forms for the primaries, was taken only to five or six factors but later studies agree on seven factors—one less than found in the 16 PF.

The first study by Cattell (1959) took 464 boys and girls at 13 years and factoring each by the scale method *and* by the pure-factor method found agreement on six factors of quite similar patterns. It was at once evident that four of these replicated the exvia (extraversion-introversion), anxiety, cortertia-pathemia, and possibly the independence factors. There followed two factorings on Morrison's Australian data, 209 12-to-14-year-old boys and girls, and on 296 12-to-14-year-old American boys and girls (Cattell, 1965c). A fifth and a sixth analysis were made on 401 boys and 399 girls separately on the data set out (Cattell, Wagner, and Cattell, 1970) for primaries. This study has superior psychometric properties in that it was on a large and socially stratified sample (800 in all) with a short range from $13\frac{1}{12}$ to $14\frac{1}{4}$ years and raises reliability by using all four forms of the test (A, B, C, and D, 52 variables, 560 items). This study yielded eight factors (seven interpreted) with good agreement of the boy and the girl patterns with the adult patterns (over that portion of the pattern *A, B, C, E, F, G, H, I, O,* Q_2, Q_3, and Q_4—12 primary loadings shared with the 16 PF). Other studies on thorough technical foundations but too recent for tabulation are those of T. Klein (1973) on 330 cases, of Nichols on about 600 Canadian children, and of Vaughan and Burdsal on nearly 1000. Klein's study has one factor not seen before but the rest of his factors and all those of Vaughan and Burdsal and Nichols converge closely on the outcome of the studies summarized with sample size and method in Table 18.

Table 18

Second-Order Source-Trait Patterns at 12-to-18-Year Adolescent Level [a]

	Summation of HSPQ *Research*						*Jackson's* PRF				
Factor	*I*	*II*	*III*	*IV*	*VII*	*VIII*	*I*	*II*	*III*	*IV*	*VIII*
A	74	−21	−30	06	01	00	33		−31		
B	01	01	00	−02	63	04					
C	05	−71	14	04	−05	15		−28			25
D	05	77	05	03	−01	01		27			−26
E	−03	−10	44	40	−06	−02	56		40	44	
F	56	03	02	31	07	−51				33	−53
G	03	15	−09	02	10	64		−46		−29	48
H	51	−60	03	31	−02	−00	44	−29		25	
I	03	04	−62	−05	−04	08			−38	−56	
J	−40	06	−00	19	−00	09			31		
O	13	69	−16	−04	−00	−07		25			
Q_2	−76	−07	07	05	06	01			43		
Q_3	−09	−38	03	−07	03	60		−44			43
Q_4	01	75	01	03	02	−03			−26		

[a] Mean loadings of seven independent samples and rotations. Decimals omitted. *All* loadings included to reveal exactly how many are near zero.

Note: As second-order source traits, V and VI load mainly on *M, N,* and Q_1 factors, which are not included in the HSPQ: they are not part of the visible pattern at the adolescent level. The seven samples are as follows: California and Illinois girls (N = 479); Crossnational girls (N = 1255); Friel (1972) West Virginia girls (N = 922); California and Illinois boys (N = 481); Crossnational boys (N = 1504); Friel (1972) West Virginia boys (N = 914); Canadian mixed sexes (N = 2513). In the Nesselroade and Baltes analysis of the Jackson PRF (right-hand side above) loadings below 25 have been omitted.

The similarity to the adult patterns is close. However, the absence of the primary *N* from the HSPQ has eliminated factor V, and information is added about the loadings of two new primaries *D* and *J* upon the secondaries. Measures of significance capable of telling us whether the slight observable differences are worth notice do not exist. Unlike the evidence at the lower and latency ages, however, which presents seemingly marked differences, this evidence suggests that the agreement of form is high. The new primaries, moreover, fit into the known secondaries in accordance with their hypothesized primary meaning. Thus *D* excitability, is a powerful component in the anxiety factor and enriches our grasp of the latter. Asthenia, *J*, as would be hypothesized from its group-rejecting nature, lines up largely in the invia pattern *I* — but also positively in IV, independence.

Although no clear evidence of significant differences from adult patterns exist at present, one or two indications deserve comment. Regarding anxiety, comparison of Tables 16 and 18 suggests a larger role of *A*— (sizia) and *H*— (threctia) at the younger level. The former finding suggests that emotional unity with the group is important for anxiety reduction in adolescence. The latter, which has been noted before even at levels below adolescence, has been interpreted to mean that anxiety is situational in the young and that high responsiveness to external threat (threctia) plays a larger role in anxiety than do inner conflicts—until later (see Spielberger, 1972).

No noticeable difference exists for exvia-invia (I) but cortertia (III) loads dominance (*E*) more than it does later in life. Cortertia—hypothesized as a level of cortical alertness in contrast to hypothalmic, pathemic feeling—is known to be advantageous in demanding situations. (It is high for successful air pilots, for nonneurotics in contrast to neurotics, and so on.) The advantage of quick effective response it gives in interpersonal relations may stimulate dominance during the competitive and insecure period of adolescence.

An indication also exists regarding good upbringing (VIII), which is more marked in adolescence than it is later by desurgency (*F*—) and submissiveness (*E*—). To maintain the framework of discipline in which the superego G and an organized self-sentiment Q_3 can grow, some docility in learning (*E*— correlates with school achievement; Cattell and Butcher, 1968) is necessary, although a high degree of inhibition (*F*—) is probably an inevitable consequence. The second-order good upbringing factor has proved useful in many contexts (see Gorsuch in Cattell and Dreger, 1973) and certainly fits well into the developmental evidence.

It has been pointed out that the absence of second-order factors V and VI at the 12-to-18-year level is fully accounted for by the absence of these salient primaries from the HSPQ scales. There is thus no evidence for any reduction of the number of second-order factors (from eight or nine in this domain).

A check on the second orders at the adolescent level has been made by Nesselroade and Baltes (1972), who used the HSPQ and Jackson's PRF on the same group, factored the PRF to the second order and then projected the seven secondaries they found on to the HSPQ primaries. Stricker (1973) brings essentially concordant findings. It is striking, aside from crudities due to an orthogonal rotation, how well this completely different source confirms the second orders in the series of studies mentioned here (see the right-hand side of Table 18). This finding suggests either that the PRF has missed its theoretical objective of covering interests (Murray's needs) and is operating, contrary to our and the designer's assumption, substantially in the area of general personality factors, or, alternatively, that the second-order *personality* factors project their variance into *motivation-interest* primaries as well as into personality primaries.

4. Secondaries in Childhood and Some General Methodological Problems in Clarifying Secondaries

Research on second-order personality structures below adolescence (8–12, 6–8, and 4–6) is at present rudimentary. There are only two studies in the CPQ and ESPQ range and none in the PSPQ range. Accordingly I shall treat the conclusions briefly and only as indications, and then pass on in this section to some general problems in second-order factoring covering all ages.

The second-order patterns at the CPQ level in Table 19 are derived from Krug, who added matrices from two studies (his own and that of Cattell, Porter, and Schaie, in preparation) with some frankly subjective emphasis in the light of the obsoleteness of certain scales in the earlier of these studies. The data collected from the revised scales by Schaie, Porter, and Cattell for the CPQ standardization should provide firmer ground.

Table 19

Second-Order Source-Trait Patterns at 8-to-12-Year Level

	Second Orders			
Primaries	*I*	*II*	*III*	*IV*
A	0.41	−0.48	−0.36	
B				
C		−0.40		
D		0.41	0.52	
E				0.21
F	0.47		0.29	
G		−0.20		
H	0.38			
I	−0.26		−0.33	
J	−0.21	0.31	0.23	0.25
N	−0.32			
O		0.47	0.21	0.21
Q_3		−0.21	−0.50	0.25
Q_4		0.24	0.23	

Note: All values below 0.20 omitted. This data is from the penultimate form of the CPQ (Schaie, Porter and Cattell, 1973).

Taking into account some single correlations from special studies not reproduced in Table 19, I infer that childhood anxiety (II) also influences surgency and low superego. Surgency has been found to load in Japan, where it is an almost ritualized expression for anxiety. Could childhood be in this respect a similar culture? Anxiety is heightened autonomic activity and energy creation, and in young children the impulsiveness and over-activity of $F+$ is accepted as a way of releasing it. The connection with $G-$ (low superego) has also been observed (Gorsuch, 1965; Horn, 1963) and explained (Cattell and Gorsuch, in press; Mower, 1966) as acting in the reverse causal direction; namely, effective expression of the superego reduces anxiety. Perhaps in early life this action is more prominent than it is later.

There is a suggestion of negative loading of Q_3 in exvia-invia (I) for which the hypothesis may be advanced that the introverted, thoughtful child develops a self-concept early and applies it to his behavior. The indications of parmia-threctia (*H*) and low superego entering into cortertia (III) will not be commented upon, pending confirmation. The appearance of dominance (*E*) and low self-sentiment (Q_3-) is more emphatic. A hypothesis for cortertia favoring dominance in the rough and tumble of childhood has been given; perhaps its reduction of concern for the self-concept is similar to that of exvia.

Independence-subduedness (IV) accrues loadings beyond its usual pattern, notably on naïveté ($N(-)$) and strength of self-sentiment (Q_3) and less clearly on ego strength (*C*) and guilt proneness (*O*).One can see that the child of strong temperamental independence will, like a Thoreau or a Rousseau, decline to acquire the petty shrewdnesses in competition of $N+$ and possibly develop early the self-standards and self-awareness of Q_3.

Although no psychologist expects a steady linear development through adolescence it is reasonable to expect that the changes from 12 to 8 will to some extent continue through 8 to 6 and 6 to 4. The second orders in the 6–8 range derived from analyses by Dielman following his first-order structuring (1973) are shown in Table 20.

Again the effect is deviation from the adult pattern, with conformity to the trend already noted in the other younger cross-sections. However, cross-validations on six different samples with the latest ESPQ primaries (Dielman, Coan, and Cattell, 1973) need to be made before clear hypotheses on trend can be formed.

Having surveyed the complete age range we have enough experience at this point profitably to attack more advanced methodological issues on the location of second orders and their separation from primaries. Later interpretations hinge on understanding these issues. Although a loading has been accepted as evidence of a second-order acting causally on a first order—for example, introversion to growth of self-concept—psychological interpretation has sometimes suggested the converse. For example, there are good reasons to hypothesize that a high sympathetic system reactivity to threat ($H+$, Threctia) is more responsible for generating anxiety in children than in adults. However, the issues that deserve study here are (1) why do some investigators (for example, Eysenck and Howarth, using "analytic" rotation programs) sometimes go directly to second orders from items, missing the first orders? and (2) what fraction of the full variance of oblique primaries is absorbed by secondaries; and how much remains in the true primaries—the stubs?

To answer the first question we must consider first how widely in nature the natural incidence of cooperative and correlated primary factors occur. Correlation is well understood, but cooperativeness (Cattell, 1952), is a concept not always fully grasped. In all realms of scientific data there are

Table 20

Second-Order Source Traits at 6-to-8-Year Level

				Secondaries			
Primaries	*I*	*II*	*III*	*IV*	*V*	*VII*	*VIII*
A	31		−65		−54		
B	13			18		37	
C		−27		13		−57	27
D				22		19	90
E			46	70	−16	44	14
F	50	−14		69		−18	
G				−32			62
H	29	−39			−04 [a]	13	−15
I		16	−59			−19	−13
J	−74			44		16	
N						−63	
O		76		01 [a]			−15
Q_4		55		−13	29	70	

Note: N = 408 boys and girls, grades 6 to 8, from Toledo, Illinois.

[a] Loadings normally fall at these two positions but are not present in this sample. Loading of ±0.12 or less has been considered to lie in the hyperplane. On this basis these two markers known at higher ages fail here; but of the two factors concerned—IV (independence) and V (foxiness)—one is well marked by other required salients and the other reasonably so. The real departure here lies in VII (intelligence) and VIII (moral upbringing) having several substantial salients that do not normally belong. One of the two other studies in progress, however, finds *D* (excitability) loaded on moral upbringing (VIII) and the possible explanation as an outlet for impulse suppressed at this early age in the stricter upbringing offers itself.

instances when distinct influences tend to hit the same target variables. Although they also affect variables peculiar to themselves the number of *common* loaded variables is far beyond that expected by chance alone. The factors are themselves nevertheless uncorrelated. For example, dampness and cold are likely to augment similar medical results—arthritis, infection, and so forth. Low intelligence and poor home conditions also produce similar results up to a point over a series of school learning variables, and in physiological psychology we recognize that the sympathetic and parasympathetic nervous systems affect the same organs (plus some peculiar to each) —mainly with opposite loading signs.

Among the primaries—and this is true of both rating and questionnaire factors—cooperativeness has been observed (Cattell, 1946b, 1957) between *A* and *H,* both of which favor approach behavior to groups of people; between *F* and *H,* which favor talkativeness and readiness to take risks; between *E,* dominance, and *I*(—), harria, both of which load tough social attitudes (death penalty, compulsory vaccination); between *G* and Q_3, which load considerate social behavior; and between Q_4 and *D* on a number of impatient responses that combine situational exasperation with temperamental excitability.

It is inessential that in more than half these cases cooperativeness is combined with positive correlation; for example, of *A, F,* and *H* as part of exvia and *G* and Q_3 as part of good upbringing, a second order. The difficulty of separating factors when cooperativeness is combined with correlation reaches a major challenge in regard to *C, O,* and Q_4, which have been lumped repeatedly into a single factor (not the full second-order anxiety factors, *C*(—), *L*(—), *O*, Q_3(—), and Q_4) by hasty factorizations. Certainly the best a priori even-density choice of items by stratified sampling from the personality sphere does not prevent the appearance of a relatively dense cluster of maladjustment items due to simultaneous ego weakness, guilt proneness, and high ergic tension from drive frustration (Q_4).

The reasons for insisting that they are nevertheless independent factors are (1) that tests for number of factors show three factors not one, (2) that although there is one *cluster* there are three significant hyperplanes, and (3) that the three distinct concepts make sense according to several other criteria; for example, Q_4 (ergic tension) is high in delinquents whereas guilt proneness *O* is not (Cattell, Eber, and Tatsuoka, 1970, p. 260).

Although rotation should be fixed by hyperplanes most analytical (not topological) automatic programs chase clusters. The reader should remember that clusters (surface traits) and independent factors (source traits) are totally distinct concepts. By a rough correlation, clusters tend to be on the perpendicular to hyperplanes (as reference vectors) so that the wrong principle happens to work most of the time. But it does not work all the time, and (especially when roughly applied) in the crucial cases considered here when both correlation and cooperation effects exist, cluster rotation will tend to pick out second-order factors, such as exvia (*A, F, H,* Q_2—) or clusters generated by *C, O,* and Q_4, as first-order factors. Certainly variables that enjoy the summed effect of several primaries will have high loadings that bolster the investigator's complacency. When cluster-chasing rotation is combined with underfactoring, which DeYoung (DeYoung and Cattell, 1973) has shown to favor the appearance of pseudo-second orders directly from variables, these second-order patterns will appear either as the main factor (when Eysenck extracts three factors instead of 15 or more) or mixed with primaries (when Howarth and Browne, or Sells, Demaree, and Will take 11 factors where statistical tests indicate 18 to 20).

A more confusing picture results when the existence of second orders is denied altogether, as when Eysenck considers his pseudo-second orders to be primaries and argues (Eysenck, 1971) that the variance of the true primaries given here is fully accounted for by the second orders found among them. This brings us to the second question above: How much primary variance is contributed by secondaries? Since the critics who claim *complete* sufficiency of second orders have set up their own restrictive condition (see Chapter Eight) that factoring must be of *items,* not *parcels,* (Eysenck and Eysenck, 1969; Howarth and Browne, 1971b) we respond with the 184-item factoring of form A of the latest 16 PF (Cattell, 1972g). Taking the pure-factor correlations and extracting no fewer than 10 secondaries to give the Eysenck position every chance, we find that the communalities are as follows:

	A	B	C	E	F	G	H	I	L	M	N	O	Q_1	Q_2	Q_3	Q_4
h^2	0.82	0.41	0.38	0.38	0.40	0.69	0.64	0.54	0.56	0.43	0.56	0.53	0.88	0.79	0.61	0.80

giving a mean contribution of all second orders to the primaries of 0.59. That is, with a full roster of 10 second orders (not three as Eysenck uses) not much more than one-half the primary variance is accounted for. The stubs are thus scientifically real, and the loading of a stub primary on a variable in Equation (4.2) could reach 0.64 that is, $\sqrt{0.41}$.

One's conclusion will depend on the sample and on which alternative base for second orders is used. By taking the correlation among pure factors in this example, the second-order contribution is probably higher than would be the case if correlations among primary scales were taken. The chance errors in rotational position in true factors increase communality as frequently as they decrease it. The experimental errors of measurement in scales, however, reduce their intercorrelations, and therefore their communalities, by the usual attenuation effect. Another influence acts in the opposite direction, however. If the items which score on factor X are contaminated by other common factors—that is, if suppression on unwanted factors fails—then scale intercorrelations are likely to be falsely increased, making second orders appear larger than they should from the factoring primary (see formulae in Chapter Nine) pure factors. Due to these possibilities of error the second orders are better derived from the latter procedure, though admittedly error of a different kind enters here, unless rotation to simple structure is extremely thorough. Just how well the two methods agree the reader can evaluate for himself by comparing the true-factor and scale-factor primary intercorrelation and factor tables from the handbook of the 16 PF (Cattell, Eber, and Tatsuoka, 1970, pp. 113–114). Clearly the second-order *factor patterns* and their *variance magnitudes* from the two sources are very similar. From the communalities of these cross-checking tables one sees also the unmistakable verdict that the primaries cannot be swallowed up in the secondaries. Moreover, since there is clear evidence (Chapter Six) that substantial parts of the second order factor variances are *state* (mood) rather than *trait* variance, the vital importance of the primaries in describing an individual's trait make-up is further supported.

Undoubtedly the most interesting light to be thrown on the nature of secondaries will come from the completion, by reaching more exact values, of the developmental comparisons of cross-sectional loading patterns begun in this section. Development, of course, includes both change of pattern and change of level. Logically change and identity of structure comes first as in this chapter, but in Chapter Five age plots are given for changes in levels on these factors from childhood to adulthood.

5. Secondaries on a Broader Basis Including That of Pathological Primaries

The number of second orders found in any domain tends to increase —simply because of more linkages—with the number of primaries included in the observations. It has seemed best to base the main presentation above in adult and preadult data, upon the 16 or so primary factors that have been longest established and around which many more years of research have accumulated. However, as Chapter Three brings out, this basis of primaries has been expanded since 1967, first by the addition of the seven missing factors among normals and second by the addition of 12 factors in the pathological domain. My aim in this section is to show how this expansion affects the roster of secondaries.

Consideration of some technical issues that affect limits of generalization is required here. According to a proposition first explicitly stated by Thurstone (1938) and amply proved by several examples, both substantive psychological and plasmodes, the addition of variables to a factor analysis—of primaries in this case—should not upset the simple-structure resolution found in the shorter lists used in earlier factorings. This is reasonable according to the causal-determiner theory of factors since an influence does not alter its action on variables *a* through *j* simply because *k* through *p* are not also considered. However, the proposition remains true only as long as certain limiting conditions are avoided. Restrictions on the size of the original variable sample can affect the outcome in two ways: (1) if there are less than two variables (often three in practice) for a factor then that common factor cannot appear, even though it affects the one marker present, and (2) since simple structure becomes a gamble when the number of variables to demarcate a hyperplane becomes too small the correct resolution of a factor may be missed in the absence of sufficient hyperplane stuff. Such a poorly rotated factor may then incur mistaken identity in matching. Regarding this mischance it is a minor miracle that the anxiety factor has continued to be picked up by truly blind rotations. For, since it is strongly loaded on seven primaries—*C, D, H, L, O,* Q_3, and Q_4—it leaves only a limited hyperplane, less than 60 percent of the primaries, to guide precise resolution.

Extending second-order analyses from 16 to a broader basis of 23 primaries in the normal domain (16 PF plus 16 PF Supplement) or the 28 factors (16 PF plus 12 pathological) in the CAQ could conceivably just alter some rotational resolution. Nevertheless, it could also improve them and the main reasons for pursuing these extended rotations are: (1) to increase the precision by extended hyperplanes (2) to see if any new second orders are indicated, and (3) to find how the new primaries load on and aid the interpretation of the existing secondaries. Note that the second-order factoring done here depends more on pure factor than on scale factoring because the newer factors are not always represented in scales with sufficient validity. However, this lack is by no means a disadvantage.

First we consider the result of extending the normal domain to 23 factors by the addition of the seven missing factors to the 16 PF in the form of DeVoogd's 16 PF Supplement. At present there exists only one study (Cattell, 1973c) on DeVoogd's scales although a second is in progress and interim findings will help decisions.

In this factoring of the 23 pure-factor correlations (N = 257 young

Table 21

Secondaries Across Full Span of 23 Primaries

Primaries, Old and New	*Old Secondaries*								*New Secondaries*				
	I	*II*	*III*	*IV*	*V*	*VI*	*VII*	*VIII*	*IX*	*X*	*XI*	*XII*	h^2
A	**58**	–27	**–39**		**28**	–42		17					71
B				–22			**66**				–16		51
C		**–66**		–23				–40					74
E				**90**									75
F	**62**									**41**	**25**		75
G	41			–33		–24		**76**					78
H	**59**	**–46**		**25**		**–06**				**27**			81
I			**–84**	–21		**(07)**							78
L		**38**		**35**		–23				–20			57
M		–21	**–21**	**53**		20		–24	25				60
N		–33		–30	**(–03)**		–33				–15		53
O	–28	**73**					–25						70
Q_1			20	**33**	–16	**41**							38
Q_2	**–73**		22	–16			36	16	**–29**				70
Q_3		**–58**	16			**–15**		**66**					78
Q_4		**78**		16									74
D		**24**								**–60**			50
J	**–22**				22						**66**		52
K									**74**				70
P				**–48**		21	30					**–64**	57
Q_5								**33**	–18	**–32**			49
Q_6		**73**											46
Q_7					**70**								68

Note: Values less than 0.15 and decimals omitted. Parentheses mark inadequate marker loadings. Usual markers in boxes. Data from Cattell and DeVoogd, 1973.

men and women) the scree and K-G tests for the number of factors definitely indicate the need for 11 to 12 factors—two more than have repeatedly been indicated for 16 primaries. As Table 21 shows, the answer to our question seems to be threefold. First, the factor structure found for 16 is not altered by the additions but is confirmed—and confirmed with the accuracy of an increased number of hyperplane zeros. Second, new second orders are perceived, here labeled IX, X, XI, and XII (Table 21). IX has slight loadings on *B, G,* and Q_2(—) and has substantial loadings on *K. X,* which loads *F* and *H* on the old primaries, has marked negative loading on *D* and less on Q_5. *XI* is largely *J* with some *F* and XII is largely *P* with some Q_6. Third, previously established second orders extend their meaning. Anxiety (II) has appreciable loading on *D* (excitability) and on Q_6 (social panache). Independence (IV) is negatively loaded on casual speculativeness (*P*) suggesting the latter to be more of an insecure compensation than a true confidence. Foxiness (V) continues to show its character of social skill by loading on explicit self-expression (Q_7). Finally the moral upbringing trait (VIII) discovers a further loading on Q_5 (felt inadequacy in group service).

Brief hypotheses for the new second orders are that IX may be called humanistic involvement, with intelligence, an empathic concern with others, and dependence on the group. (One thinks in modern times of

Dag Hammarsjold and other ambitious but idealistic group-devoted public types.) Second-order X may be designated tough stolidity with the toughness of *H* and *F* and low excitability and low response to the group. Second-order XI may be a genetic component, involving the schizoid *J* with excitability, *D* and *F*. XII is perhaps a hypomanic insecurity pattern.

Let us turn now from the new normal primaries to the old issue of which broad second orders lie in the domain of *pathological* primaries. The factorings of the MMPI cannot be said to answer this question because the scales are syndrome clusters, not factors, and, in any case, are spuriously algebraically dependent. With the establishment in the CAQ of true primary pathological dimensions—the six depressions and the six psychotic primaries—factoring of the CAQ primaries was therefore awaited with curiosity. From the uncorrelated factor space of these 12 scales with respect to the 23 normal dimensions it was already clear that the abnormal space in general must be new. But might there not be some sharing of the effect of a pathological second order with the normal primaries that systematically show up as powerfully diagnostic in neurosis, drug addiction, and so on? And what is the real nature of the three somewhat changeable second orders that have been seen in factorings of the six or seven depression factors? At present the answer given in Table 22 must be regarded as tentative; it is based on only one—though an extensive—normal-pathological population sample. (The agreement is reassuring, however, between Cattell and Delhees,[5] 1971, Table 2, and this newer data—Cattell, 1973i—in Table 22.)

As for the old theory of a general psychoticism factor, I have suggested that it is a general maladjustment of behavior that exists when that part of unrealism due to low intelligence is partialed out. Its essence is hypothesized as an inappropriateness of emotional response to stimuli in terms of survival (including group survival). As such it implies low integration in the precise dynamic formula given elsewhere (Cattell, 1957; 1973n) and might be expected to show up in low *C* (ego strength) in existing questionnaires. A puzzle now arises: we have found a clear-cut *primary* trait in pathological dimensions (Chapter Three) which from its content we interpreted as general psychosis. Since, as Table 22 definitely shows, we now have a second-order general psychosis factor spanning all six scales the question arises whether this primary *Ps* is really general psychosis. A similar problem appears in the ability field, where the four culture fair subtests form an apparent fluid intelligence general factor but are themselves engulfed in a broader factor at the higher order. It would seem safe to designate factor XIV in Table 22 as unquestionably a general psychosis factor and to investigate further whether the primary *Ps* is an approach to this at the first order or some specialized but not easily recognizable form of psychosis. If the former then *Ps* would be expected to load XIV most highly among the pimaries, and this it almost does; thus exact determination of this loading (attenuation corrected) is needed in a crucial experiment. A test corelation of the Eysenck psychoticism scale *P* with these two factors is called for. The present general psychosis factor includes ego weakness (a negative loading on *C*),

Table 22

Secondaries Spanning 28 Normal and Pathological Primaries

Primary	*Secondary*												
	I	*II*	*III*	*IV*	*V*	*VI*	*VII*	*VIII*	*XIII*	*XIV*	*XV*	12	h^2 [b]
A	35	–26	–18	44	10								35
B							64						41
C		–65										–41	56
E				34							24		52
F	21			33						–30		–40	48
G							32	43		–30			51
H	35	–20		35	–45	–41							48
I			–39		–46	–08							38
L				38				37					37
M			04	03		34	34		26				24
N		33			50		34						43
O		30			–42					25			45
Q_1	–31			17		59							69
Q_2	–73												58
Q_3		–35				–14		22					18
Q_4		40			28						–38	–35	45
D_1		55								50			60
D_2					45				60				55
D_3		–37	47										44
D_4				–42							–36		30
D_5				–34					39				34
D_6									55	36			43
D_7							–41						43
Pa					46					64			72
Pp										39	–65		47
Sc						–28		–36		27			33
As		47		–26						47			54
Ps									43	53			51

[a] XV is unrecognizable and might be an error factor. Parentheses indicate inadequate markers.

[b] Mean $h^2 = .46$.

Note: Boxes in upper half represent markers as commonly found in 16 PF secondaries. Boxes in lower half mark everything 24 or above as hypothesized markers in abnormal domain for factor research. All decimal points are omitted. The 12 recognized second-stratum factors in normal primary scales (Table 21) are indexed I through XII. Apparently new factors in pathological domain are designated XIII, XIV, and XV. At present XV is treated as an ill-defined entity with the tentative label of discomfiture. Data from Cattell, 1973i.

as my theory of *C* has led me to anticipate. It also shows that some depression or *D* factors are not depression alone, but psychotic in nature.

The second major finding in Table 22 is the existence of a second-order general depression factor XIII that is virtually clear of any connection with normal primaries. Where then are the other two or three second-order depression factors seen in three previous studies (see Cattell and Bjerstedt, 1967) when the seven *D*s are factored alone? The picture here is not so different from earlier views of four second orders only patchily covering the primaries. First general depression (XIII) is not entirely general, having low loadings on D_1, D_4, and D_7 precisely as in the Bjerstedt studies. Second there is agreement on a factor essentially like anxiety (QII) with loadings largely on D_1 but with strong loading also on asthenia. Third there is a pattern compatible with pathemia (III—) largely loaded on D_3; and lastly a subduedness pattern, IV(—), loading D_4 and D_5.

This analysis of the depression field is given—except for factor XIII, which is well checked—not as a finding but as a guide to save effort in further research. It is evident that if the seven *D*s are factored alone they yield only four second orders; if factored in wider company they add others. Only one comes near to being a general factor—XIII loading D_2, D_3, D_5, and D_6—and the others are second order but not general. Indeed as we have seen they appear to be familiar second orders partly responsible for some of the primary depressions. Thus part of the answer to the anxiety-depression riddle seems to be that anxiety is associated largely with hypochondriacal depression (D_1) and psychasthenia (A_s). Invia also slightly promotes hypochondria (D_1), anxious depression (D_5), and bored depression. Pathemia (III—) favors low-energy depression and boredom but is strangely negative on D_3 (restless, danger-seeking depression). Independence (IV) tends over Table 21 and others to oppose the depression of D_4 and D_5. Apart from these the most depression-relevant of the normal secondaries seem to be factor V with its loadings on suicidal disgust (D_2).

The remaining pathological second order, XV, is sketchy and suggests some inhibition of expression. Reversed it expresses ergic tension and psychopathic behavior ("manic-psycho-pathic"). A point not to be lost sight of in Table 22—and especially in unraveling the depressions and their relation to anxiety—is that the magnitudes and correlations of the factors alter appreciably according to whether relations are examined in wholly normal populations, wholly pathological populations, and a broad span including both. The last structure was used in Table 22 because the CAQ is intended to be applied in diagnostic separation of normals and abnormals. But this application is likely to give significantly more variance to the general psychology and general depression factors and may distort upward the loadings of pathological factors on normal secondaries. In concluding this survey of second orders it must be observed that in the pathological domain, as in the normal, much information is lost when the primaries are omitted in the interests of simplification by using the limited number of second-order scales.

6. Still Higher Orders: The Difference Between Orders and Strata

Just as primaries can be correlated and factored to give secondaries, so the correlations among secondaries can lead to tertiaries; and repetition of this process can lead to yet higher-order factors. At present these upper strata are likely to be reached on frameworks of pure-factor correlations since (except for the recent CTS kit with eight secondaries, Barton and Cattell, 1973a; the Comrey scales probably with seven; and the EPI with three) the construction of scales has not yet covered the second-order factors well enough to permit the more concrete approach by correlating scales. With careful rotation, however (say 20 overall rotoplots), the higher orders from pure factors should be better than those from scales.

The terms *order* and *strata* are sometimes used in the literature of secondaries and tertiaries almost interchangeably; but their real difference is such that to avoid conceptual stumbling in these higher-order climbs we must now recognize explicitly that difference. The former is simple: if one factors a matrix of first-order factors the result is by operational definition, a matrix of second-order factors. But suppose we have inadvertently or in ignorance already included one or two second-order factor scales among what we supposed to be first orders. If only one is included the error will become clear but if two or more are included—enough to give a higher order among them—our mistake will continue because we shall call any higher-order factor derived from them a secondary when it is in fact a tertiary.

Implicit in this statement about a stratum is the concept of some real level not fully dependent on the immediate operation, as has been indicated in Figure 7. The ultimate stratum can be inferred only from a combination of evidence, not a single experiment. To discuss in detail the possible inferences from a single experimental operation like the one described would require more space than is available but Figure 8 brings out the essentials. (This problem is fully discussed in Cattell, 1965 for the investigator who meets this problem in practice.)

Granted that we can distinguish between a *stratum,* which is a gen-

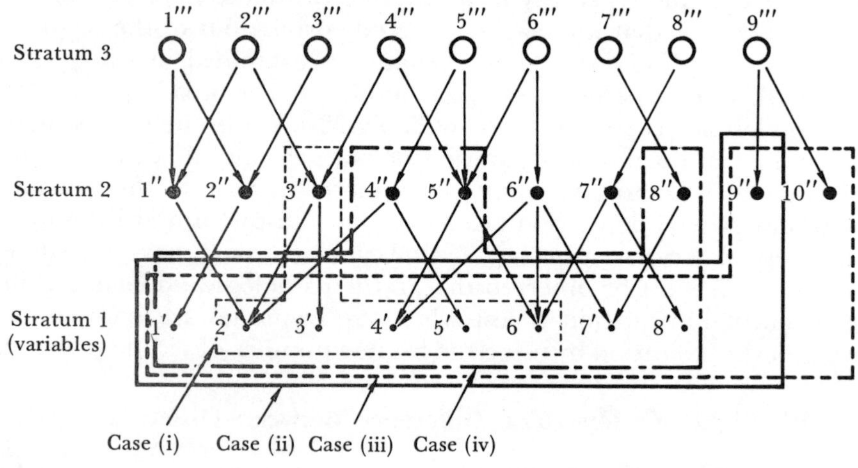

Figure 8. Possibilities of mistaking the stratum level of a factor. Case (i): One primary factor from stratum 2 is accidentally included with variables from stratum 1, and it has psychological representation in the other first-stratum variables. No problem arises. Case (ii): One primary factor from 2 is included in 1, and it has no psychological representation in stratum 1 variables. Case (iii): Two or more primaries from 1 are accidentally included in 2, with no psychological representation in first-stratum variables. Case (iv): Two or more primaries from 1 are included in 2, and they have psychological representation in first-stratum variables. For fuller discussion see Banks and Broadhurst (1965, p. 245). Distributed in the United States by Barnes & Noble.

eral psychological statement of the breadth and manner of influence of a factor, and an *order,* which is where it appears in a factor-analytic experiment, let us consider Figure 8, which starts with truly assigned strata. Here we see that if a second order mistakenly correlated into a set of primaries turns out to have no effect (Case ii) on these primaries it will either be lost from the next order as a single specific or, if by an unduly large communality estimate we take out an extra factor, it will appear after rotation in the next order as loading one primary only, namely, itself. Further, if it has some loading on the primaries in its company it will appear in its true place in the second orders, loading its own measure (Case i) mistakenly inserted among the primaries and loading a few others moderately. Thus one study may not suffice to give an unambiguous answer on strata but a correct idea of such strata can usually be reached from piecing together several studies, each giving only order, and also from extraneous evidence of the kind discussed below.

As a scientific model of influences the strata model is not the only one possible. As pointed out at the opening of this chapter there is also a *reticular model* that permits interactions backward and forward (even circular positive and negative feedback) in a completely irregular way. Except for the "interactive emergence" or spiral action invoked below, however, the reticular model and its variants are too complex for present methodology. Our compartive primitiveness in multivariate methods is regrettable since questions about this network model—even this question of whether a factor belongs to a first or higher stratum—are far from being artificial academic issues. Some of the head-on collissions and confusions we have encountered among the theories of Comrey, Eysenck, Howarth and Browne, and others could have been largely avoided by concern for the issue of first- versus second-stratum status of factors. For example, certain findings that Comrey and Eysenck cannot accept become reasonable if their supposed primary-scale factors are recognized to be at the second order. Further, the irreconcilability of Howarth's questionnaire and even some of Sells, Demaree, and Will's factors with Guilford's larger numbers and Eysenck's smaller numbers is due to several of these investigators interspersing primaries and secondaries in the same rotational resolution. The importance of attention to this issue can be evidenced from another field—that of ability structure and ability batteries—by the way in which the work of Horn (1972), Anderson and Cattell (1971a), and Hakstian (in preparation) has sorted out long known but confusedly conceived factors into consistent strata.

The inclusion of factor *B,* an intelligence scale, among the primary scales of the 16 PF is not an instance of such confusion. For the convenience of applied psychology, it was deliberately inserted among the primaries of the 16 PF and the fact that it again appears on its own among the secondaries as factor VII supports this interpretation. The tendency of primaries *J* (asthenia-zeppia) and *N* (shrewdness-naturalness) to emerge almost alone on certain rough second-order factorings has justifiably aroused the suspicion that they could be second-stratum traits. However, exact research always confirms their appearance in secondaries, for example, *N* in V and *J* in I along with other primaries.

Even if the psychologist takes his stand on the less chaotic strata model he must be prepared to recognize that the higher-stratum factors found in these studies, like those in other domains of multivariate analysis, may not be in the same domain as the primaries, that is, they may not even be *psychological* entities. (Narrower, subprimary factors that deviate in the opposite direction may also deviate from the psychologically fundamental but in the sense of going trivial. This latter overspecificity is recognizable since these narrow entities are clusters rather than factors, that is, they are defined by small, dense clusters rather than by an independent dimension with a definite hyperplane.) As an example of this transposition of domain I entertain a theory that a certain third-stratum factor is the effect of social status. If higher social status goes with higher intelligence, more attention to restraint in manners, inner development as in invia, and also more prodigal subjectivity (factor VI) through freedom from economic drugery, then these three second orders will be correlated and may well appear as a third-stratum factor pattern. One can descriptively, give some psychological unity to these three but it is not convincing as a necessary, organic connection and at present seems better explained by sociology than psychology. Elsewhere (1957), I have suggested that as higher strata are approached one is likely to enter neighboring sciences—sociology, economics, physiology. The psychologically organic and functionally unitary traits seem to be the primaries and to some extent the secondaries.

Because such questions of domain become clearer as concrete findings are revealed, we turn to discoveries at the third order that have become available since 1968. A rough picture that must be modified appeared in the 16 PF Handbook (Cattell, Eber, and Tatsuoka, 1970) but we now have available through the work of Nichols at least eight well-checked third-order analyses (Nicholas & Cattell, 1973b) for normal adults and adolescents. As Table 23 shows, the congruences among these studies from the second-order bases are satisfactory. The test for number of factors is consistent in indicating five factors across all studies for adults and four or five in the 12-to-18-year range.

The results in Table 23 are particularly interesting because critics have asserted that we are not ready to go to the third order, which must be guesswork. Moreover I have pointed out the problems to be overcome in rotating on a small sample of points. Nevertheless the congruence coefficients show that if research is pursued from sample to sample with constant markers and thoroughly, blindly pursued simple structure, high consistency of pattern can be reached.

Tentative titles have been given to the first four of these factors as follows: α, strength of contact; β, maladaptation; γ, readiness; and δ, antisocial unconcern. However, since these hypotheses must rest only on content (the absence of scales at present precludes criterion relations) the names are only conveniences.

To conclude this section by discussing the psychological interpretation of two or three of the most overdetermined higher orders, namely I (exvia), II (anxiety), III (cortertia), IV (independence), and VIII (good

Table 23

Source Trait Patterns and Congruences at Third Stratum

(a) Factor-Pattern Loadings (German H)

	ω	β	γ	δ	*(5)*
I	57	−06	−01	04	−39
II	01	65	−02	05	02
III	03	−06	60	04	03
IV	03	00	−02	73	−04
V	−02	−68	−24	05	04
VI	−36	−43	−04	19	−04
VII	−34	08	02	−00	−09
VIII	04	−40	−01	44	−02
(9)	02	−04	−01	−00	56

(b) Congruences [a]

	ω [b]	β	γ	δ	*(5)*
1–2	96	97	83	98	53
1–3	94	89	95	89	25
1–4	94	96	81	81	77
1–5	96	96	66	80	68
2–3	91	80	92	89	64
2–4	94	92	77	85	30
2–5	97	95	56	78	14
3–4	87	85	79	77	−11
3–5	86	80	67	77	27
4–5	90	92	89	89	67

[a] The studies compared are from Nichols and Cattell (1972): German high, German low, American boys, New Zealand (1), and New Zealand (2).

[b] This column is based on diagonals of matrices of 5 × 5 congruences. The pattern of factor 5 has not been firmly identified.

Note: Elsewhere (Cattell, Eber, and Tatsuoka, 1970) a single study has given emphases different from the five above; α (*strength of contact*) loads also on cortertia (III); β (*maladaptation*) loads also, negatively, on cortertia (III) and (intelligence) (VII); γ (*readiness*) loads also, negatively, on subjectivity (VI); δ (*antisocial unconcern*) loads on security and intelligence (VIII). As wider hyperplanes become available these lower loadings may be found to belong.

Factor alpha is one of strength of alert contact with other people. The term "strength" is preserved here because the Russian psychologist Nebylitsin and the English psychologist Gray have attempted to identify Pavlov's "strength of the nervous system" with an extravert pattern which I conclude is actually not extraversion but cortertia (alpha) (see Cattell, Nebylitsin, and Gray in Nebylitsin and Gray, 1972).

upbringing), it is necessary again to sharpen some concepts in regard to the possible models of factor interaction. One must note, for example, that a strata model does not necessarily imply that the upper factors become progressively fewer in the form of a pyramid of successively narrower strata on a broad base of variables. Factor-analytic experiments do produce such a pyramid of orders for the simple reason that one always takes out fewer (typically one-half as many) factors than variables (see Figure 7). Apart from this artifact it is possible that there are as many factors at one stratum as at another. The strata then simply define directions of causal action (always downward), and if enough primaries are taken one could have a large number of second-stratum influences.

To proceed with reasonably close relation to operations we have accepted the strata model rather than the reticular but, as Figure 9 shows, there are numerous models of mutual causal influence. The pan-general strata model (shown in Figures 8 and 9) and the general recticular model (No. V in Figure 9) are two that we have favored. But they are only two among many possibilities. In the case of the second-order anxiety factor we are tempted to abandon the classic conception of a second order acting on primaries and consider a peculiar model we call the spiral feedback.

One theory that has been in vogue among leading psychologists since Freud and is still the standby of most psychoanalysts rests on clinical observations but could just as well rest on the psychometric second-order evidence of Table 16. This theory proposes that anxiety is dynamically a result of ego weakness (our $C(-)$), unexpressed libido (which approaches the ergic tension concept Q_4), and superego pressure (which because of the psychoanalysts' abnormal population is better interpreted as guilt proneness O than straight G). To this explanation of anxiety by psychoanalysis our findings in the second order (Tables 16 through 20) now add temperamental high response to threat of any kind (threctia, $H(-)$), autonomic excitability (D), and poor self-sentiment integration ($Q_3(-)$). These clearly make harmonious additions. The problem for our second-stratum-as-a-cause theory is that all these factors are more easily understood in the psychoanalytic theory as causes rather than consequences of anxiety. True, there is nothing to prevent our considering the novelty of reversing psychoanalytic theory. Anxiety, situationally created in early development, could interfere with growth of ego strength C, deny ergic expression Q_4, and sensitize guilt proneness O and autonomic reactivity to threat H. An alternative to our position—that second-order anxiety is a cause—or to its reversal—the theory of psychoanalysis—is a spiral feedback to which I return in explaining the structure of anxiety (II) after illustrating it in the simpler case of exvia-invia (I).

Exvia-invia lends itself even less than anxiety to the possibility of the standard second-order causal action. It is not easy to imagine what could simultaneously increase affectia (A), surgency (F), parmia (H), and group dependency (Q_2-). For one thing surgency has a high inheritance (see Chapter Five) that is difficult to reconcile with its substantial loading on exvia if it is a dependent variable (although a close nature-nurture calculation might show it to be possible). Although I am by no means rejecting the standard strata model, other models are to be explored and one is the spiral feedback. Spiral feedback supposes that one factor—F in this case—is genetically high and propels the individual into situations where the three other primaries are favored in development. For example, since the high-F person seldom retreats from social difficulties he might become skilled

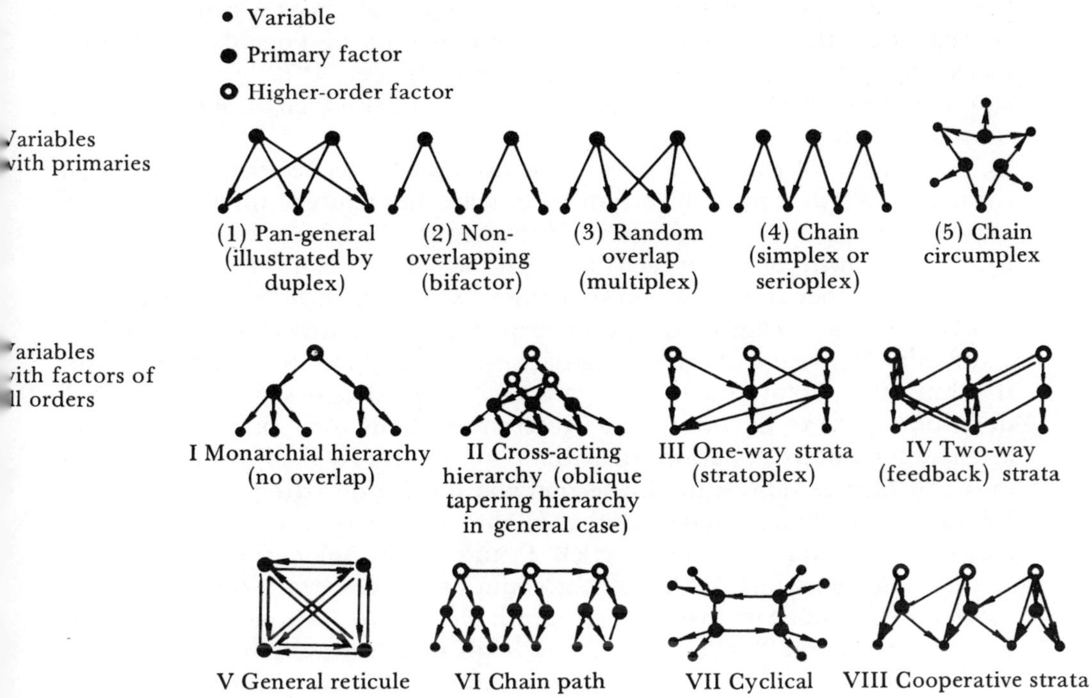

Figure 9. Possible mutual-influence models in factor relationships. The commonly assumed model in taking out higher-order factors is the multiplex, in which the loadings of the higher order on the lower order are free to assume any pattern of overlap (unlike, for example, the pan-general, No. 1, where every first order is loaded by every second order) or the Holzinger bifactor type of nonoverlapping loadings, No. 2. With an additional stratum this becomes the stratoplex. Contrasted with the pan-general and stratoplex models are a variety of special condition models; the general-reticule model is the major contrast to the stratoplex model. Therein, as illustrated by four factors, causal action—independent contribution to the variance—can run in all directions. As yet no analytic method can directly discover such a structure. At best a series of manipulative multivariate experiments is required. From Banks and Broadhurst (1965, p. 238). Distributed in the United States by Barnes & Noble.

in social intercourse as in the affectia factor *A*. This ability to empathize with people could in turn excite warm reactions from others and thus produce the sense of security seen in the *H* primary. Even with two factors of appreciable genetic determination like *F* and Q_2 there could be a statistical effect beyond additivity. The spiral-feedback theory proposes that by a series of mutual and partly serial interactions, beginning mainly with the most genetic primaries, a *common increase* is generated in the primaries. The unity that is statistically visible in the second order is here the unity of a process—a process of creating an "emergent" by interaction of existing primaries. It is a process of positive mutual or serial (spiral) feedback among the primaries in relation to life's situations, which makes the level of each primary a cause and a consequence. As determinations of loadings become more exact it should be possible, by watching changes of the pattern over age, to decide between the theory of the second order as a cause and as a consequence. In the case of anxiety it should even be possible by manipulative experiment (see model P. 169 in Spielberger, 1972) to see whether ego weakness, ergic tension level, and self-sentiment growth exercise direct mutual action.

In spite of these two prominent examples it seems likely from physical plasmodes that second-stratum factors are most often influences on primaries. Factor VIII, good moral upbringing, is such a case, where the common growth of super ego strength, social self-sentiment, general restraint, and other traits are best explained as the products of an emotionally satisfying home background combined with parental attention to behavioral standards. At present there is a restriction on interpretation of second- and third-stratum factors due to the absence of good scales for them. Their definition as pure factors permits inferences about their nature only from the loading pattern; relations to criteria, growth curves, and so forth become available only as valid scales for second and third orders are produced. Scales for exvia and anxiety have been available in the IPAT exvia and anxiety scales and presumably the Eysenck *E* and *N* for some time. Except for Comrey's scales, which by his own account are of uncertain order, no wide-spectrum second-order battery was available before Barton's CTS kit (with 8 secondaries) and Bartsch and Cattell's (in preparation) corresponding kit at the child level. Until these batteries and third-order scales from them have been in action many theoretical issues in social, clinical, learning, and physiological personality research cannot be handled with precision.

7. Summary and Discussion: Use and Meaning of Higher Strata Source Traits

Since the main presentations have been stripped to essential methodological data and evidence, some elements of a descriptive and interpretative nature must be offered here.

(1) There are eight or nine second-order factors across the 16 PF domain, fifteen if we include those that derive from the seven extension primaries and the pathological primaries (CAQ). Eight normal and two pathological secondaries have been shown to maintain their patterns with checked constancy across different analyses and age and sex populations. Their experimental consistency is essentially of the same significance by congruence coefficients as for the primaries. Four normal and one pathological call for further check, as indicated. Roughly in order of diminishing variance they have been named as follows. *Normal, checked:* *Q*I—exvia-invia; *Q*II—anxiety; *Q*III—cortertia-pathemia; *Q*IV—independence-subduedness; *Q*V—foxiness or discreetness–good-natured security; *Q*VI—untamedness or subjectivity; *Q*VII—fluid intelligence [9]; *Q*VIII—good home

[9] This may be viewed as the general intelligence factor introduced among the primaries or it could be, as suggested here, the fluid intelligence factor found at the second order from ordinary and culture fair intelligence tests (Cattell, 1971a).

upbringing. *Normal, requiring check:* QIX—dedication; QX—tough stolidity; QXI—isolatedness; QXII—hypomanic insecurity. *Pathological, checked:* QXIII—general depression; QXIV—general psychoticism. *Pathological, requiring check:* QXV—discomfiture. A majority of these factors gather their identity and designation not only from their questionnaire item content but also from criterion relations (described in Chapters Five and Ten), from relations to T-data factors (Chapter Seven), and from their age-curve developmental evidence (Chapter Five).

(2) The secondaries found at cross-sections down the age range in a thorough array of population samples and analyses for the HSPQ, but in only two or three studies at 8–12 (CPQ) and 6–8 years (ESPQ) and only one at 4–6, continue to show patterns essentially reproducing those found at the adult level. Some systematic change trends are indicated but the salient fact is persistence through the developmental period throughout the primaries and secondaries examined. The nature of the relations can be seen in Table 24, which sets side by side the central tendencies for each of the six largest secondaries taken at each of the four developmental periods. Worked out as congruences for each pattern across six age comparisons the results are shown in Table 24(b). Factors III and IV have the poorest stabilities.

(3) The third stratum has been examined across 10 studies. The results consistently indicate five factors (four stable; one too ill defined for titling) on the normal 16 primary basis with significant congruences, tentatively indexed and named as follows: α—strength of contact; β—maladaptation; γ—readiness; δ—antisocial unconcern.

(4) The same second- and third-stratum source-trait patterns are found whether one factors scale-score correlations or approaches pure factors by rotating to the best simple structure at the lower order taking the cosines of angles obtained. Their overall agreement is encouraging.

(5) The conceptual status and mutual relations of factors of different strata can be handled by two alternative models—the *strata* model (not necessarily hierarchical) and the *reticular* model. The appearance of a second-order factor is compatible with either. But a stratum is more than an order and nonfactorial experiments are needed to decide the best-fitting model. The strata model assumes, unless evidence dictates otherwise that higher-order factors act causally on lower order factors, contributing to their variance.

(6) Within the strata model the action of higher-order factors can be expressed statistically in two different ways—by the restricted oblique with obliquities only at the first order or by the ortho-strata model. With our preferred model—the ortho-strata model—mutually orthogonal influences exist at each stratum and observed obliquities of primaries and secondaries are due to the added contributions of common variance to stub factors that come from the orthogonal higher-strata factors.

Statistically the correlations between strata need to be expressed in no fewer than three alternative variable-factor relation systems (V_{fp}, V_{fs}, V_{fe}, and others). Among the additional systems are those in which the higher-

Table 24

Agreement of Preadult and Adult Second-Order Patterns in Main Culture

(a) Factor-Pattern Loadings on Factors Common to All Ages

	I Exvia				*II Anxiety*				*III Cortertia*			
Factor	*Adult*	*14 yr.*	*10 yr.*	*7 yr.*	*Adult*	*14 yr.*	*10 yr.*	*7 yr.*	*Adult*	*14 yr.*	*10 yr.*	*7 yr.*
A	58	74	52	33	01	−21	−18	−18	−25	−30	−28	−75
B	00	01	37	23	−02	01	−09	−18	00	00	35	−36
C	07	05	32	09	−66	−71	−53	−02	10	14	−19	−00
E	07	−03	25	19	00	−10	45	23	01	44	−12	47
F	51	56	72	37	−03	03	09	07	01	02	14	43
G	06	03	−00	05	−03	15	−01	−03	01	−09	07	−11
H	50	51	72	36	−38	−60	−21	−09	−14	03	−29	−40
I	07	03	−31	10	00	04	08	03	−73	−62	−12	−43
O	−02	13	−06	−08	78	69	39	84	−06	−16	02	07
Q_4	00	01	−32	63	80	75	17	27	−05	01	62	00

	IV Independence				*VII Intelligence*				*VIII Good Upbringing*			
Factor	*Adult*	*14 yr.*	*10 yr.*	*7 yr.*	*Adult*	*14 yr.*	*10 yr.*	*7 yr.*	*Adult*	*14 yr.*	*10 yr.*	*7 yr.*
A	01	06	10	02	00	01	23	07	−01	00	63	12
B	−01	−02	−01	02	67	63	39	72	−01	04	53	22
C	−01	04	−07	72	04	−05	−09	17	05	15	16	17
E	56	40	03	03	01	−06	22	16	−18	−02	−08	14
F	30	31	−01	46	02	07	39	−11	−27	−51	−04	07
G	−03	02	11	29	05	10	−03	15	67	64	99	59
H	34	31	00	37	−02	−02	−07	00	−00	−00	16	07
I	−03	−05	−13	18	01	−04	14	14	02	08	39	14
O	−05	−01	02	−08	−04	00	06	−20	03	−07	21	−08
Q_4	10	05	14	−04	09	02	14	07	−02	−03	−28	−24

(b) Congruences (diagonals)

	Factors					
Age	*I*	*II*	*III*	*IV*	*VII*	*VIII*
Adult with 14	98	96	81	97	97	92
Adult with 10	84	73	21	15	60	66
Adult with 7	67	71	58	36	91	65
14 with 10	80	73	09	18	59	61
14 with 7	63	64	67	49	82	64
10 with 7	50	68	23	−20	51	86

order scores are estimated from primary-factor scores and those in which they are estimated directly from items. To obtain loadings of higher orders directly on items we have the alternatives of the Cattell-White and the Schmid-Leiman formulas. The reverse regression—that for estimating factor scores from items—yields, according to which of the two models is used, the full-length (Cattell-White) and the stub (Schmid-Leiman) higher orders. Each has its convenience.

(7) Some psychologists teach that primaries and secondaries are nothing but alternative ways of regarding the same data; Eysenck (1971) has gone so far as to say that the secondaries, as in his EPI, account for all the important predictive variance regarding criteria. Even if the EPI covered the eight secondaries (as does Barton's CTS Kit) rather than only three, our data show that second-stratum factors would still, on 16 to 20 primaries, account for only about 60 percent of the primary variance. This figure defines not merely the contribution of the second orders but the total emanating from the second, third, and higher orders.

The primaries, secondaries, and tertiaries are not alternative ways of measuring individual differences in personality; they are supplementary ways. Thus to use secondaries alone is to ignore important information present in the stubs of the primaries. This can be illustrated by the psychological selection of research scientists (Cattell and Drevdahl, 1955). Creative scientists typically deviate significantly from the general population in the second-order factor I in an inviant (introvertive) direction. However, on the four primaries $A-$, $F-$, $H-$, and Q_2-, which would be scored together for the invia score on a second-order scale, H is positive in this group, that is, it deviates in the extrovert direction. Thus if the second-order invia score were used instead of the four primaries it would partly cancel H as a predictor. In analytical primary scores, H would act effectively because weighted oppositely to the others.

If the primaries, secondaries, and tertiaries are used as stub scores they are entirely independent and supplementary; if oblique primaries are used they include the even higher orders. The converse is not true: second-order scales omit primaries. As shown in Chapter Ten on applied psychology, an effective use of information from scales at all levels can be made in what I call *depth psychometry* (Cattell, 1970c). This approach has been independently developed by Vidal (1972) in France with the slightly different emphasis of interpreting each primary score in the light of its setting in the framework of secondary scores. The understanding of and prediction from a primary score is illuminated by knowing how much of that score derives from this or that secondary structure, for example, how much ego weakness ($C-$) in Smith is due to anxiety (II).

(8) Some psychologists continue to suggest that questionnaire users can get along with three to six scales and concepts. That this is a completely obsolete view of the true complexity of personality must be obvious from the many consistent primary studies organized above. Even at the second-order level, starting with a basis of 23 normal and 12 pathological primaries, no fewer than 15 secondaries are apparent, ten of them replicated repeatedly. By rough estimates the 35 primaries account for most of the variance of a personality sphere of specific behavioral items. The secondaries, tertiaries, and higher orders apparently account for slightly less than one-half of this factorially covered variance; the pure primaries (stubs) account for some-

what more than one-half. The 23 normal and 12 pathological primaries and the secondaries derived from them, while naturally open to additions, already contain scale dimensions—such as in the 16 PF, HSPQ, and CAQ—for which many omnibus scales in use have not yet begun to build up items. Alleged new concepts need first to be checked against these, by correlation.

Prediction from insightful psychological laws, which admits adding effects of time, circumstances, and background to prediction from merely statistical laws, will be augmented as our knowledge of the higher-order factors grows. The discovery of their numbers, patterns, appropriate measurement scales, and natural history continues to advance. However, careful attention to taxonomy, as here, is a necessary preliminary to advance in understanding development.

V

The Natural History of Traits and States: Interpretations in Personality Theory

To this point my concern has been to clarify structure and establish a firm taxonomy of traits. Now we are ready to see what light can be thrown on the natural history of these traits—their heredity, their development, their change with trauma and learning—by the use of meaningful scales raised to the best validities obtainable.

Some learning and personality theorists tend to regard questionnaire scales as mere tests. At least half of all published tests are admittedly just ad hoc tests—and often poor ones at that—but those developed as measures of structural unities found by painstaking research are conceptually quite different: they are the hostages the theorist has given into the hands of other experimenters for the truth of his theory. In the first place "they give to airy nothings" (if theory may sometimes be so described) "a local habitation and a name." Or, to transpose Shakespeare, they make a concept operationally testable. In the second place they permit us to discover much more about the concept from the relations of scores to experimental manipulations and criteria *provided that the work of aligning the scale and the trait factor, as in the last two chapters, has been thoroughly done.*[1]

1. The Heritability of Primary and Secondary Traits

Several more refined structural and technical issues remain to be tackled, among them the structure of states in relation to traits and the technical expression of identities across different media of observation. But it is time to let the reader satisfy his curiosity about the nature and history of the traits themselves. So far little more than the names of the individual primaries have been listed, leaving their nature largely implied as in Tables 4, 5, 12, 16, and 23. What we now propose to study under "natural history" covers (1) the origin of the patterns in heredity and environment, (2) their typical growth rates over the years, (3) the ways in which learning experiences affect them, (4) their interactions with ability and dynamic traits, and (5) interpretive theories of their essential nature.

Such an undertaking, if it is to be illuminating, has to relate to the whole domain of personality theory. Coming to grips with this in one chapter constitutes a challenge to quick perception I hope the reader will accept. It means that basic references must be assumed already known to the reader with respect to a number of general principles and concepts (Cartwright and Cartwright, 1971; Cattell, 1957, 1964; Eysenck, 1964, 1971; Fiske, 1971; Lindzey and Hall, 1970; Pervin, 1969). The five topics listed above are best pursued in the sequence set out. By the end of this chapter anyone who has spoken of the factor approach as yielding only "abstract mathematical factors" should recognize that each source trait has a demonstrable individuality and a life of its own as shown by characteristic patterns of growth, genetic origin, physiological basis, and relation to social learning situations. Source traits do not belong merely to the domain of individual differences and structural taxonomy; they belong to the dynamics of learning and the interactions of individuals and groups.

An axiom that it seems still necessary to state in giving attention to behavioral genetics is that all psychological structures are partly genetic and partly threptic. (Threptic is from a Greek root that permits it to be substituted for the cumbersome expression "environmentally determined"; see Cattell and Nesselroade, in preparation.) A second generalization—although not an axiom—is that virtually all personality and ability traits have a genetic basis that is polygenic, that is, quantitatively determined by the action of several genes. In few instances in psychology—mainly abnormal instances such as phenylketonuria, Down's syndrome, and Huntington's

[1] The formal steps involved here include use of the eight basic requirements in factor-analytic techniques mentioned in Chapter Two and Eight; replication of patterns as shown by congruence coefficients across a series of interlocking programatic experiments; refusal to recognize any factor as a new discovery unless it appears as an extra when the experiment has markers for all known factors; and demonstration that the supposed uniquely rotated primaries also give second- and higher-order patterns that likewise retain their relations to the primaries consistently over several studies.

chorea—does one find the simple situation of apparently a single specific gene action. In such source traits as intelligence, surgency, and ego strength we deal with dimensions that at least phenotypically show a continuous variation over a wide range—generally a normal distribution. Faced with this we abandon temporarily the aim of locating particular genes and settle for finding the relative contribution of heredity and environment to the observed variance of the trait in race and culture.

These nature-nurture or heritability ratios may not give all that we ultimately want to know but they are well worth knowing. If we learn, say, that intelligence is *largely* inherited we shall not make the mentally retarded unhappy by driving them to abstractions far beyond their capacity nor shall we neglect to search diligently for the environmental sources whereby defective ego strength (C) can be increased if our nature-nurture research assures us from the beginning that it depends largely on environment.

The basic model in this area (although nonadditive and interactive models are possible; Cattell and Nesselroade, in preparation) is a statement about how we suppose observed variation in a trait among people actually breaks down. The most practicable model is

$$\sigma_{xo}^2 = \sigma_{xwg}^2 + \sigma_{xbg}^2 + \sigma_{xwt}^2 + \sigma_{xbt}^2 + 2r_{wgwt}\sigma_{wg}\sigma_{wt} + 2r_{bgbt}\sigma_{bg}\sigma_{bt} \quad (5.1)$$

where σ_{xo}^2 is the measured variance on source trait x; w and b refer to *within*-family and *between*-family variance; and g and t stand for *genetic* and *threptic* components. The two correlations are those between the genetic and threptic effects within the family and between families. For example it is probable that for intelligence r_{bgbt} would be positive and appreciable, because there is a tendency—as *among* family averages—for genetically more intelligent parents to create a more intelligence-stimulating environment. On the other hand the correlation for dominance (E) is negative (Cattell, Blewett, and Beloff, 1955) because society likes to "cut down" individuals naturally too dominant and to help the humble inherit the earth.

The total environmentally determined threptic variance (combining within- and between-family sources of environmental difference) can be abstracted from Equation (5.1) and written

$$\sigma_{xt}^2 = \sigma_{xwt}^2 + \sigma_{xbt}^2 + r_{wgwt}\sigma_{wg}\sigma_{wt} + r_{bgbt}\sigma_{bg}\sigma_{bt} \quad (5.2)$$

Although we are concerned only with the environmental variance we have to take part of it out of a term that expresses the inevitably combined, interactive genetic-threptic covariance. The last term in Equation (5.1) is cut into two equal parts, one going to environment as in Equation (5.2) and one to the genetic part as follows:

$$\sigma_{xg}^2 = \sigma_{xwg}^2 + \sigma_{xbg}^2 + r_{wgwt}\sigma_{wg}\sigma_{wt} + r_{bgbt}\sigma_{bg}\sigma_{bt} \quad (5.3)$$

What is commonly called the heritability (H) is the fraction of the total measured variance of the trait x in the population that is due to hereditary differences in individual makeup. Remembering that xt and xg include interaction as in Equations (5.2) and (5.3) we may write this as

$$H_x = \frac{\sigma_{xg}^2}{\sigma_{xg}^2 + \sigma_{xt}^2} \tag{5.4}$$

or if we wish to have it as the nature-nurture ratio N to show the relative importance of the two then it can be written

$$N_x = \frac{\sigma_{xg}^2}{\sigma_{xt}^2} \tag{5.5}$$

Research on the behavior genetics of a source trait has to begin by attempting to calculate these variance contributions and it usually aims to summarize the conclusion in H or N values (easily transposed). Thus in the case of intelligence, estimates of H have ranged from Woodworth's (1938) 60 percent to Burt and Howard's (1956) 83 percent.

Information about the genetics of personality source traits is at present far more rudimentary than about intelligence. To appreciate the conclusions we shall reach about the primary personality factors it is necessary to keep in mind that three main investigatory methods have been used: the well-known twin method—comparing differences of identical and fraternal twins; the more comprehensive and up-to-date MAVA method (Cattell, 1953; Cattell and Nesselroade, in preparation; and attempts to discover association between measured traits and physical features known to be largely hereditary (such as eye color). The results of the first two methods will be brought together here in variance (H) estimates. The pioneer work on the primaries by Cattell, Blewett, and Beloff (1955), R. C. Nichols (1965), Gottesman (1963), Stafford (1965), Loehlin (1962), and Vandenberg (1965) and on the secondaries by Canter (1969), Eysenck and Prell (1951), and Shields (1962) shows internal consistency only in finding that a substantial level of heredity—with N values close to 50/50—runs through most of the personality factors including the primaries affectothymia, ego strength, surgency, parmia, self-sufficiency, and ergic tension and the secondaries exvia, anxiety, cortertia, and independence. Indeed, as Loehlin has pointed out, the apparent evenness of this balance is surprising. For the moment one cannot say whether this evenness is due to the approximations in measurement and method or whether genetic elements are evenly distributed across personality. I favor the former view. With the large samples of the Cattell, Blewett, and Beloff (1955) research and the use of MAVA rather than the twin method in the work of Klein and Cattell now proceeding, some traits such as intelligence, coasthenia, and surgency are beginning to show consistently high inheritances, whereas others such as ergic tension, guilt proneness, radicalism, dominance, and excitability are molded more by environment.

The greater variability of heritabilities for the secondaries in Table 25(b) when investigated by the EPI than by the IPAT scales may be due to the samples for the former being smaller. However, there is a central tendency for heritability to be higher for exvia and cortertia, the latter agreeing with Nesselroade's finding of higher stability coefficients. Anxiety is somewhat lower and independence (IV), even lower. The inheritance of neuroticism may be higher than for anxiety because it includes beyond anxiety the

Table 25

Approximate Heritabilities of Primaries and Secondaries in Q-Data

(a) Primaries

H estimated around 0.75	*B*	Intelligence
H estimated around 0.60	*F*	Surgency
	J	Coasthenia
H estimated around 0.50	*A*	Affectothymia
	I	Premsia-harria
	L	Protension
H estimated around 0.40	*C*	Ego strength
	G	Superego
	H	Parmia-threctia
	M	Autia-praxernia
	Q_3	Self-sentiment
H estimated around 0.25	*D*	Excitability
	E	Dominance
	N	Shrewdness
	O	Guilt proneness
	Q_2	Self-sufficiency
H estimated around 0.10	Q_1	Radicalism-conservatism
	Q_4	Ergic tension

Note: These rounded values for primaries are derived basically from Cattell, Blewett, and Beloff (1955); Canter (1969); Gottesman (1963); T. W. Klein and Cattell (1972, 1973). Scattered sources are not simple averages but include allowances for sample size, appraisals and reliabilities, and correction from within-family to total-population variance values.

(b) Secondaries

	Values on IPAT Scales			Values on EPI Scales			
Trait	*Klein and Cattell (1973)*	*Canter*[1] *(1969)*	*Other*[2]	*Canter (1969)*	*Shields (1953, 1962)*	*Eysenck and Prell (1951, 1970)*	*Mean of Columns*
I. Exvia-Invia	.39	.36	.46	.07	.50	.81	.45
	.38						
II. Anxiety	.54	.38	.33	.18	.30	.62	.35
	.10						
* Neuroticism	.55		.35				.44
	.43						
III. Cortertia	.48		.47				.45
	.41						
IV. Independence	.33		.30				.26
	.15						

* It will be noted that Neuroticism is not a second-order factor, but the mixture of anxiety and certain personality primaries which maximally distinguish neurotics from normals (Chapter Ten, Section 6). The upper figure in the Klein and Cattell (1973) is from monozygotic and the lower from dizygotic twins.

[1] The full data on Canter's studies are in Canter (1969), Mittler (1971), and Claridge, Canter, and Hume (1973).

[2] The values here are not from one sample, but from a compounding of the estimates for primaries finally reached in part (a) of this table.

characterological primaries *F, I, E,* and so on. Incidentally, the fact that secondaries have less distinctive heritabilities than the primaries supports the theory in the last chapter that they are combinations of primary action rather than distinct new influences underlying the primaries.

Regarding the third method of genetic study above, Cattell, Young, and Hundleby (1964) obtained indications at a suggestive statistical level that type A blood group is associated with raised *F* and *I* factor scores (compatible with higher *H* values in Table 25). Also, Matheny (1973) of the Louisville Twin Study found that a blue-gray as opposed to a brown iris is significantly (but slightly) associated with lower scores on surgency (*F*), dominance (*E*), asthenia (*J*), and shrewdness (*N*), and higher scores on superego strength (*G*), guilt proneness (*O*), and self-sentiment (Q_3). Thus although Table 25, which is a rough composite of twin and MAVA results, points to stronger hereditary action in intelligence, surgency, and coasthenia and indicates that we must look in the environment (probably the early family background) for the greater influence on self-sufficiency, guilt proneness, shrewdness, radicalism-conservatism, and ergic tension levels, even these latter traits have *some* genetic components.

These heritability estimates are on the whole in agreement with the indications from shifts under environmental influences recorded in the following section. But the idea that greater hereditary influence should show itself in smoother age curves is not borne out by comparing Table 25 and Figure 10. Sharp shifts at adolescence are evident, for example, in *A, F, I,* and *J,* which are among the highly genetic factors. The relation is more subtle. The theory that surgency (*F*) is degree of inhibition, that premsia (*I*) is raised by overprotection, and that *G* is affected by moral upbringing and *C* by exposure to anxiety is not incompatible with substantial hereditary contributions. However, the magnitude of recorded shifts related to known environmental events does seem greater in such traits as ego strength, superego strength, dominance, and ergic tension (shown in Table 25b).

2. The Normal Growth of Source Traits

For standardization if for no other reason, curves of the age trends of source traits need to be determined as soon as possible. For standardization they have to be known in order to make proper comparisons of endowment among individuals of different ages. Yet as of 1972 the IPAT questionnaires (16 PF, HSPQ, CPQ) are virtually the only scales for which age trends are well established or even sketched. In dealing with such a trait as intelligence we should feel lost without the IQ, which is after all nothing more than an allowance for age. But certain personality traits may need as much age correction as intelligence does in comparing the present standing and probable future standing of individuals. Beyond these practical considerations, dependable information about the development of personality traits is also fundamental for personality theory. As Angleitner and others (1971) have pointed out, this age dependency of personality scores shows in every culture yet examined.

Let us consider what personality theorists would like to know about these curves. Any age curve can be analyzed as the sum of an endogenous curve and an exogenous curve. The former describes what happens because of internally determined maturation and involution; it is virtually synonymous with the central tendency of the pure genetic component as it expresses itself over time. The rise and fall of innate capacities and temperamental reactions have the appearance of something set by an internally regulated clock. That curve is not, of course, immune to the viscissitudes of environmental effects on physiology, but in its pure form it is abstracted and averaged to free it of these environmental intrusions.

Conceptually both of these components—but most obviously the exogenous—can be divided again into an *ecogenic component* (representing what happens to all people as *an average across all historical human ecologies*) and an *epogenic component* (expressing the effect *peculiar to an epoch and a given culture*). We are of course dealing with averages; otherwise there would also be an idiosyncratic component. Changes of average personality with age have been well described throughout history; the fact that most ancient descriptions are still true points to their being endogenous and ecogenic effects. Yet of the French Revolution Wordsworth tells us "bliss was it in that dawn to be alive"; increased radicalism and affectia were normal in that epoch. The stress and crowding of the industrial revolution and the complexities of life in our own times may well have induced less-welcome personality trends. Within the period in which psychological testing has existed, the obvious change of environment ranging from the two world wars and a great economic depression for one generation to the comparatively placid and health and welfare regulated life of the young today might be expected to show in test results. The public sees the results in comparatively uninhibited youth, and, although not yet reliably documented, an upward shift in surgency (perhaps other exvia primaries too, along with anxiety reduction) is noticed by those who deal with personality testing. The upward shift in crystallized intelligence is well documented (Cattell, 1950b; Falek, 1972).

The special methodology for separating ecogenic and epogenic components has been discussed and set out by Baltes (1968), Cattell (1970b), and Schaie and Strother (1968a and 1968b) in terms of comparing simple longitudinal with cross-sectional data. However, cross-sectional data have been collected for most primaries and some secondaries, which means that we have averages for a particular decade and for groups of people at different age levels. The curves thus available confound the typical ecogenic age trend with the epogenic trends of our times, but the ongoing work of Baltes, Lynn, Nesselroade, Schaie, and others should separate them for the present factors shortly.

No matter what curve we are dealing with we must find a vertical scale that will be meaningful when we compare the age course of one trait with that of another. The natural raw scores cannot be considered meaningful and would not reliably indicate, for example, whether one trait changes with age more than another. Except for the proposal for true-zero factor analysis (Cattell, 1972a) still under adjudication, no convincing basis for a vertical scale exists other than that of using the units of standard scores (stens) established within a typical group at some one age level. Thus the basis of estimating between-age-group (mean) trends is the within-group variance at one age or an average for all ages. That is, if the sigma of true scores can be considered to stay the same at different ages we can take the sigma across individuals, averaged for all the age groups, as the basis for the vertical scale on which to plot the mean values for each age group. A refinement of this approach is Thurstone's method (1928) and my pan-normalization procedure (1972a). The latter has the advantage of not being restricted to the assumption that real differences of within-group sigma from age to age do not exist.

The curves of the primaries in four groups are presented in Figures 10, 11, 12, 13 and the secondaries in a block of four in Figure 14.

To cover the full age range it has been necessary to dovetail the evidence from four different instruments—the 16 PF, HSPQ, CPQ, and ESPQ—measuring the same factors over different age spans: 18+, 12–18, 8–12, and 6–8 years. Since not all factors are caught at each level some curves are less extensive than others. This dovetailing requires a clear procedure for joining the curves, which has been worked out as follows. The means for each year for any trait on one scale (for example, for the HSPQ, trait *C*) have been worked out in terms of stens (standard scores) from the distribution at the central age group for that scale, for example, 15.0 years in the case of the HSPQ as described above. Thus the age increments on the different instruments are in comparable units provided that the true sigma is equal at the different ages. The problem remains of joining the separate curve sections. This is done in this case by pegging the 12-year-old point at the lower end of the HSPQ curve to the 12-year-old point at the upper end of the CPQ and so on at all boundaries.

The zero on such a scale is arbitrary and since the 16 PF groups are largest we have taken the mean of 30-year-old men as the reference point on the vertical scales, calling it 5.5 stens (a standard score of zero) and letting the deviations of all other groups define their sten level relative to that. For each factor male and female plots are set out side by side for comparison. To permit comparisons among factors all factors are drawn on the same vertical scale; that is, stens are kept to the same graph size in all. Since this is the first time such complete life curves have been set out certain inadequacies naturally intrude. Although the total sample is substantial (16 PF: 4089 women and 5673 men; HSPQ: 3584 women and 3726 men; CPQ: 1420 women and 1414 men; ESPQ: 826 women and 827 men) the beginning (age 5) and the end (ages 50 and 60) of the curves are on small samples and less dependable. This has been shown by continuing those parts of the curve with a dashed line.

The plot of these extremities is a compromise between empirical fitting to less-certain point positions and an extrapolation by the mathematical expression found to fit the solid, central portion of the curve. The discrepancy is that the rough empirical points do not show such marked change

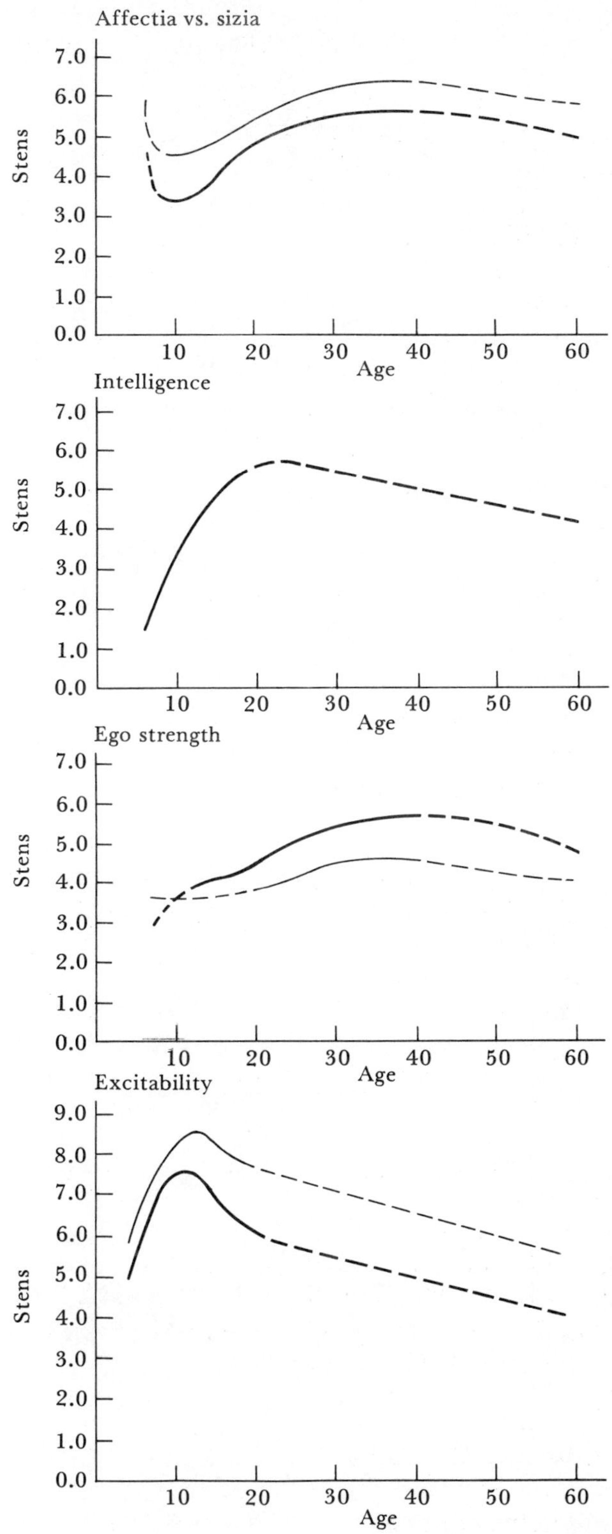

Figure 10. Age trends for primaries *A*, *B*, *C*, and *D*. Thin line is females; thick line is males.

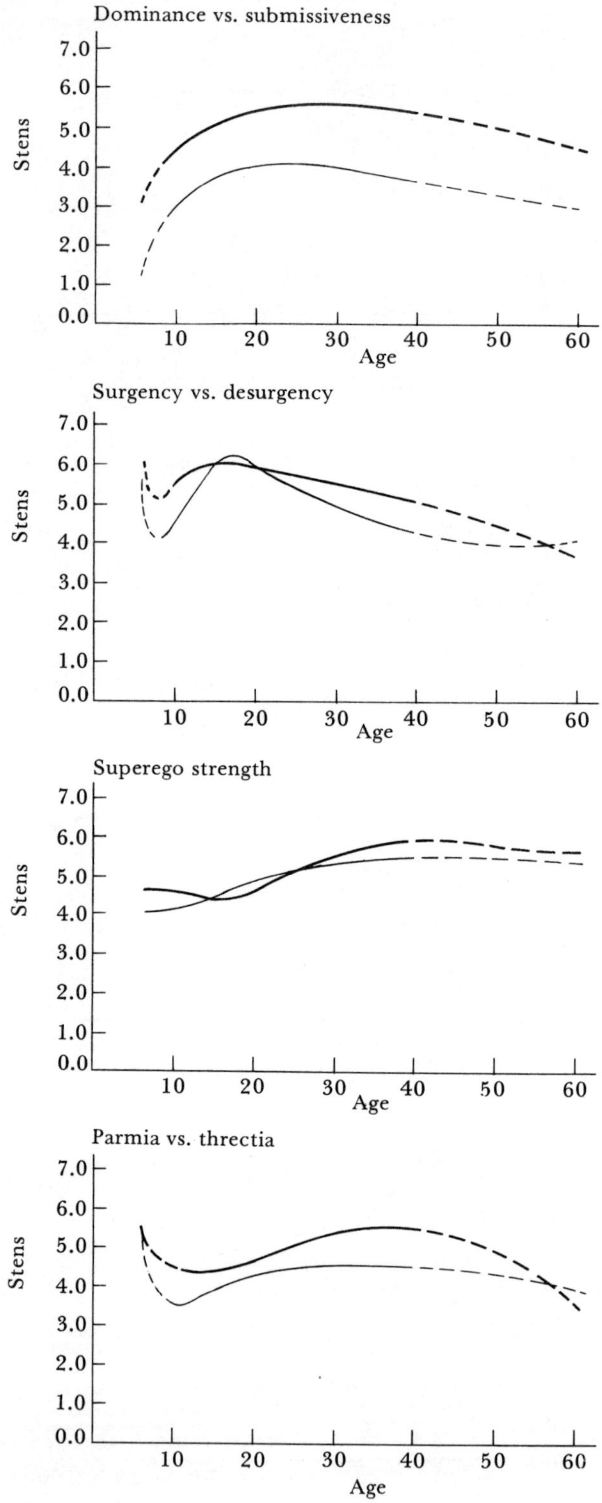

Figure 11. Age trends for primaries *E, F, G,* and *H*. Thin line is females; thick line is males.

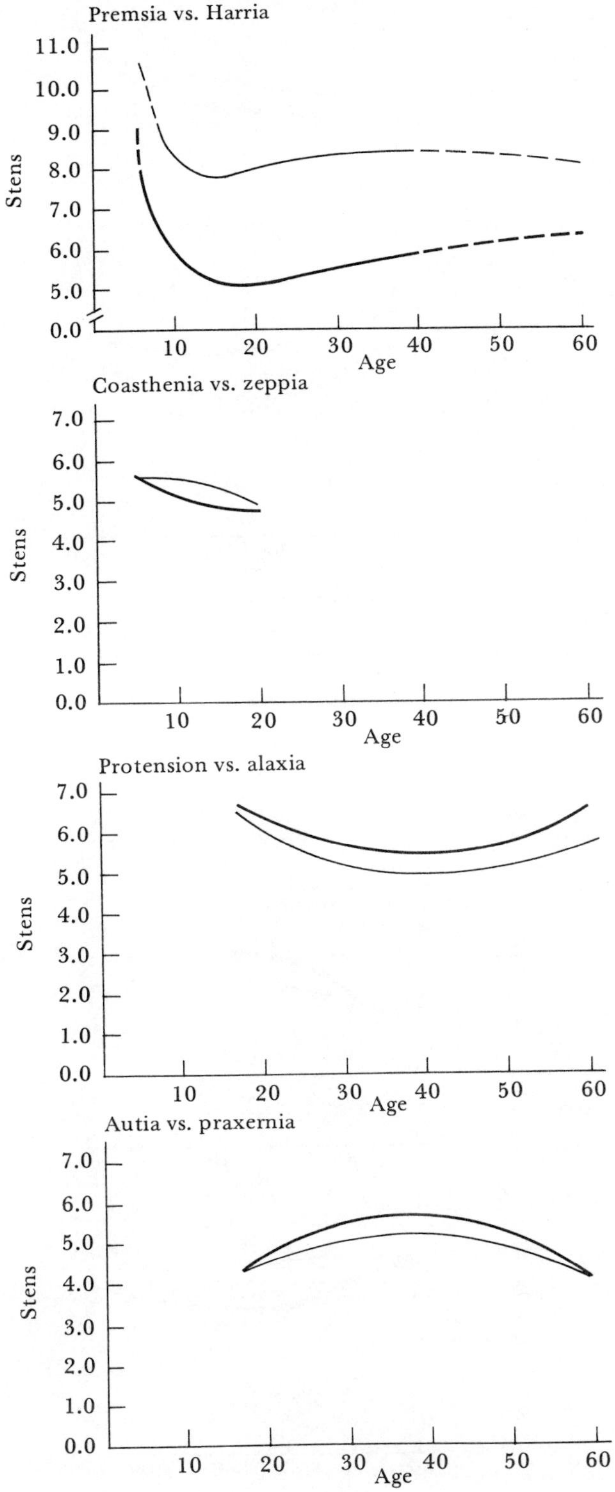

Figure 12. Age trends for primaries *I*, *J*, *L*, and *M*. Thin line is females; thick line is males.

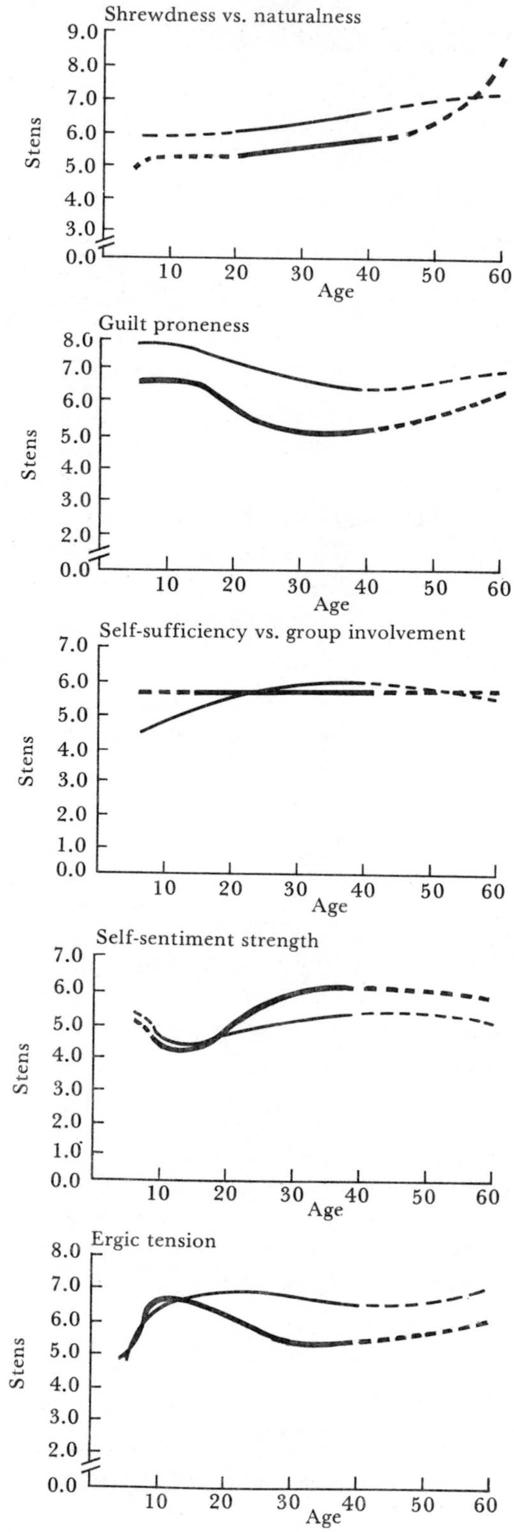

Figure 13. Age trends for primaries N, O, Q_2, Q_3, and Q_4. Thin line is females; thick line is males.

after 45 years as some of the mathematical extrapolations suggest. The mathematical functions of the best-fitting curves are usually quadratic for the middle range. For example, those for ego strength (C) in males and surgency (F) in females

$$C_n = C_{30} + 1.112\ (n - 30) - 0.015\ (n^2 - 30^2) \tag{5.6}$$

and

$$F_n = F_{30} - 0.610\ (n - 30) + 0.005\ (n^2 - 30^2) \tag{5.7}$$

where C_n is ego strength at year n and C_{30} is the normal value at age 30 (that found in the standardization tables) and similarly for surgency F.

As do the genetic findings these age findings support the theoretical concepts for these source traits emerging from clinical and other applied fields. If desurgency is an increase of general inhibition due to the usual preponderance of punishment or nonreward in trial-and-error behavior we should expect F to decline steadily from the beginning of adolescence, as it does. Ego strength C, at least for males, experiences a growth setback with the sexual and status disturbances of early adolescence but thereafter climbs markedly with increasing experience of mastery of impulse and discovery of acceptable outlets for ergic expression. The decline possibly indicated by present data after 40 years of age may be referred to physiological energy decline. Dominance E climbs steeply to the age of 20 (and virtually stops) as the growing individual is rewarded by increasing independence and adult status.

Shrewdness N grows steadily throughout life with increasing practice and skill in human relations. A curiosity to be noted is the rapid change on some factors at ages six and seven, which corresponds to the experience of entering school. We must suppose that the outgoing qualities of affectia A and surgency F are suddenly checked by the transfer from the warmly supportive home to the impersonal and competitive classroom. Conversely, ergic tension Q_4 shoots up in these first two school years, which suggests stimulation combined with frustration. In both cases things settle down steadily through middle childhood and then enter an entirely new phase in adolescence, again fitting classic personality theory.

Several contributions are made by these analyses to the understanding of sexual differences in development. The difference in effect on C of the relative strength of sex erg tension in males at adolescence has been mentioned. Another contribution is the fact that superego strength dips more in males in adolescence—presumably because of the stronger revolt against authority—than in females. A different effect probably accounts for premsia rising through adult life in males but being relatively steady in females. Here the male has further to go to catch up to the sensitive (and possibly effete) habits of sheltered culture, which constitute $I(+)$, and to become companion to the higher feminine level.

The results on radicalism-conservatism have been omitted from Figure 13 mainly because age change was nonexistent (see Supplement 1 to the 16 PF Handbook, where the technical bases of age corrections are shown in detail). However, the matter is complicated because there are local effects: radicalism increases in male college students but not in female students or nonstudents of the same age. Moreover the factor itself changes its pattern with age (Vaughan and Burdsal, 1973) to such an extent that comparisons become questionable. The surprise for most psychologists is that conservatism does not increase with age but this surprise arises from confusing rebellion with progressiveness. The conservatism of children is proverbial; the old, who are familiar with countless ways of doing things, may be more open to rational change.

This concentrated survey of new Q-data evidence on personality change with age needs to be completed by a view of trends on the secondaries. Figure 14 gives the curves separately for men and women, as in the primaries. Although the primaries that belong in one secondary tend to behave in their age trends in the same way, as would be expected from having perhaps one-sixth of their variance from the same source, a comparison of Figure 14 with Figures 10 to 13 shows that primaries still show the distinct idiosyncracies expected of independent stubs. For example, *A*, *F*, and *H* in exvia have similar curves but Q_2— behaves quite differently. The scores for secondaries in Figure 14 were obtained by adding the scores of the primaries with the usual weights for estimating secondaries. The curves plotted in stens are as for primaries.

The curve for anxiety fits that from direct use of anxiety scales (Cattell and Scheier, 1961) and shows the typical rise during adolescence, the decline through the middle years of established position, and the rise again with the loss of role and the increase of health problems in age. Exvia does not begin at the markedly higher level in early years that some might expect. It dips toward introversion in early adolescence and then rises and stays higher through later adolescence, declining thereafter steadily with age. The independence second order is similar. Cortertia—pathemia shows a more complex pattern of change not incompatible with the complex ratio meaning (high cortical activity versus living on the drift of feelings and intuitions) assigned to it by theory.

These trends have been separately examined for the equivalent *A*, *B*, *C*, and *D* scales. Otherwise some effect might be due to the large specifics in certain items. The fact that the curves are highly similar supports the conclusion that they are characteristic of the factor rather than of the particular sample of expressions taken.

3. The Natural History of Affectia, Ego Strength, Excitability, Dominance, and Surgency

We turn now from the mere names and index numbers to gain familiarity with and insight into the source traits themselves. Age trends and genetic roles have provided a beginning. Now we shall look at clinical, educational, occupational, and other statistically demonstrated criteria including evidence of changes brought about in the trait by particular environments. The general nature of each trait is illustrated by a few well-known

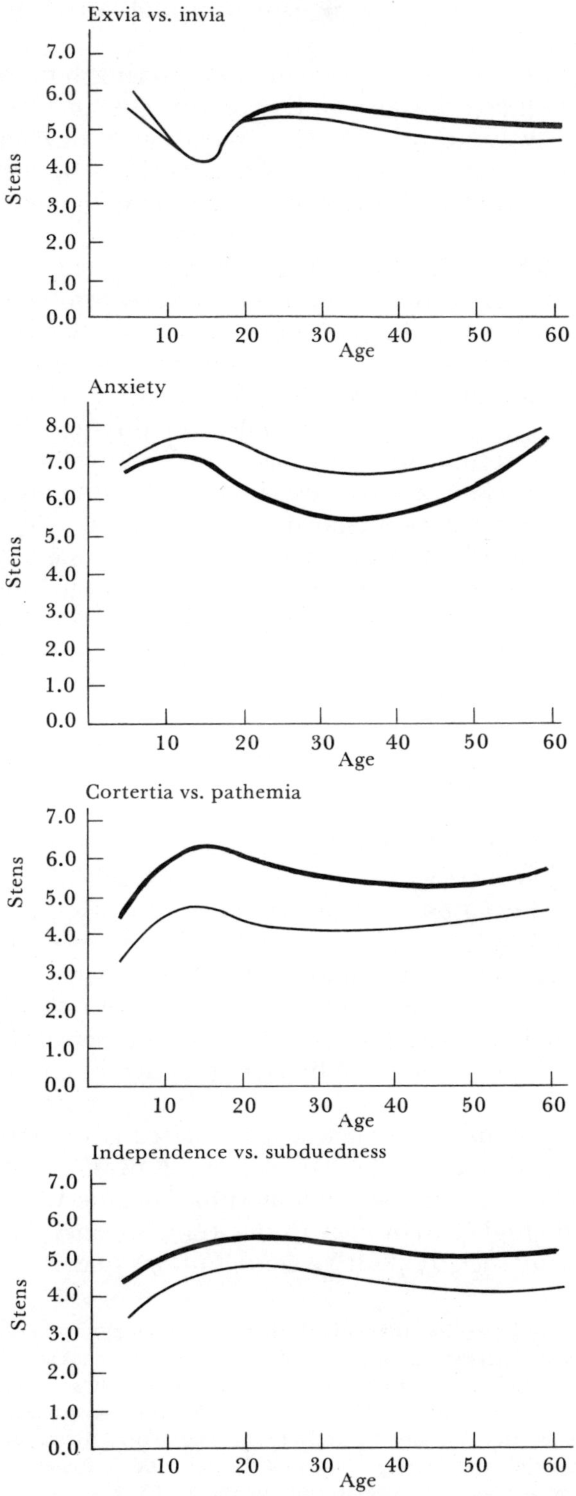

Figure 14. Age trends for secondaries I, II, III, and IV. Thin line is females; thick line is males.

personalities in whom it is prominent. Considering how recent the determination of the chief primaries and secondaries is, one cannot help being surprised at the volume of clinical, occupational, developmental, educational, and other criteria that have proved positive in the short time the scales have been available. These findings amply demonstrate that factorial source traits are no mere mathematical abstractions.

A: Affectia-Sizia. *History*. This pattern is an old one in clinical concepts and was formerly called cyclothymia-versus-schizothymia (Kretschmer, 1921). Kretschmer thus modified Bleuler's (1910) cyclic-versus-schizophrenic label of the functional psychoses to cover normal temperament. But because the pathological associations were still disliked and were in fact inapplicable to the normal range (psychosis is an added, modifying dimension) I introduced (1955a) the terms affectothymia-versus-sizothymia, finally shortened to affectia and sizia. The original terms signified a dimension ranging from warm and responsive emotion (showing ample affect) to an emotional flatness. The new term sizo, meaning flat, fully conveys the required meaning. As with other nouns used for primaries, modification to adjectives is simple —here to affectic and sizic. The symbol *A* was given because in rating studies and questionnaires this is the largest variance factor, confirming statistically the large role that Kraepelin (1921) and Bleuler recognized in abnormal manifestations.

H (Heritability). Around 0.50 (the range of *H* values for the following factors is from 0.25 to 0.75; hence this trait has a fairly substantial genetic component).

Age Trend. Trait decreases until about age 10; then there is a steady and relatively rapid increase to age 30, where it levels off.

General Associations. In general affectia is associated with a warm but not always tranquil home background.[2] The father is rated cheerful, the mother calm. Easygoing peer atmosphere. There is a correlation between low behavioral control in the family and more use of reasoning than punishment (Barton, Dielman, and Cattell, 1973). Such a person makes social contacts easily, is inclined to be sexually free, is active in church, displays high interest in schoolwork and sports, gets married early (in the twenties), has higher mean score than unmarried, when married is strongly devoted to the family (Barton and Cattell, 1972a; Barton, Kawash, and Cattell, 1972). There is a tendency toward an endomorphic, pyknic body build. Women score significantly higher than men in this trait. In small groups the affectic person makes many socially positive contributions and is voted a leader.

[2] Methodologically, these psychological descriptions rest not only on the content of the 40 to 60 loaded items but also on observer-related behavior (L-data) going with high scores, particularly on the life-criterion predictions. These criterion associations—instanced in the fields covered by Cattell (1957), Barton, Dielman, and Cattell (1971, 1972, 1973), Dielman, Barton, and Cattell (1971), Dielman, Cattell, and Rhoades (1972), Nichols (1973b), Cattell and Stice (1960), and Cattell and Butcher (1968)—are fully set out for several hundred research contributors in the 16 PF and HSPQ Handbooks (Cattell, Eber, and Tatsuoka, 1970; Cattell and Cattell, 1969).

Occupational and School Associations. This factor shows a curious inversion in relation to school achievement around the eighth grade. Before that time it is positive (Barton, Dielman, and Cattell, 1972; Cattell and Butcher, 1968); afterward and in college it is negative (Cattell and Butcher, 1968; Rothman and Flowers, 1970). Affectia is significantly high in salesmen, business executives, accountants, sales managers, priests, and social workers; it is significantly low in scientists (especially physicists and biologists), artists, musicians, writers, and creative people generally. The expressed job preferences agree with the means found in occupational surveys (see Cattell, Eber, and Tatsuoka, 1970). Affectic people generally receive more job promotions than do sizic.

Clinical Associations. Affectia is high in sociopaths and in the schizo-affective diagnosis. Affectia is high in coronary patients and low in attempted suicides, epileptics, criminals, paranoids, and in some chronic disorders, notably tuberculosis, speech defects, deafness.

Role in Behavior Specification Equations. The affectic person often gains success as a therapist, gets promoted early in business, tends to leave the parental home, makes a good teacher of children, marries early and is successful in marriage, earns more as salesman, and succeeds in school up through high school subjects. There is a negative loading in success as a police patrolman, scientist, or writer.

Change with Life Events. No statistically significant results have demonstrated that this factor is influenced by changes in one's life.

Eminent Illustrations. People high in affectia include: Falstaff, Dickens, F. D. Roosevelt, Cagliostro. Those with low affectia include Calvin, Woodrow Wilson, Edison, Coolidge, Newton, Cavendish, Austen Chamberlain, Carlyle, Milton, Henley, and Samuel Johnson.

Theory. It is wrong to see affectia as simple gregariousness. Sociability is equally evident in $F+$, $H+$, and Q_2-, although there is emotional warmth in it too. My hypothesis defines a genetic and a threptic component. The genetic component involves the hypothalamic area and its frontal lobe projections and represents a ready, apt, and easily controlled emotional expression as opposed to a rigid, inhibited but ardent emotional nature. The threptic component represents the extent to which emotional expression has been rewarded. Sizic people report more punishment and betrayal of emotional expression, and by the innate rigidity and depth of their emotional needs are likely to have a sense of being punished. The characteristic skeptical, critical, aloof behavior of the sizic person is thus an expression of low reward in human relations, which is due partly to rigid, ideal expectations and results in a turning to an orderly, impersonal world, such as science, logic, ideation. The lower reward hypothesized to lead to the increase of sizia is real enough; it is however, a summation of the effects of rigid temperament and whatever frustrations early life has brought.

B: *Intelligence.* This source trait is omitted as being amply treated in other texts.

C: Ego Strength-Dissatisfied Emotionality. *History.* (The bipolarity of this label is justified elsewhere.[3]) This pattern in questionnaire items and observer ratings is clearly the reality behind Freud's concept of ego structure strength. All clinical associations since the discovery of the factor in 1947 support this.

H (Heritability). Around 0.40 (low).

Age Trend. Increases strongly with age, then levels off at about 40.

General Associations. High for the oldest child, for small groups described as having high morale, and for group-approved persons. It is low in those from family backgrounds of matriarchal dominance and high among those who were disciplined by reasoning (as opposed to punishment) by the father. In marriage ego strength is positively related to greater satisfaction in sex; in development it is low with prolonged, chronic illness. Low scorers report profound discouragement and upset from such situations as an unhappy love affair or a job that has gone wrong. Low ego strength is associated with unemployment, truancy, and delinquency; high scores go with group participation and skilled occupations.

Occupational and School Associations. In school ego strength is positively related to achievement but only in later years. In occupations it is high in administrators, air hostesses, outstanding athletes, airline and military pilots, nurses, researchers; it is low in accountants, clerks, farmers,

[3] With certain exceptions (intelligence, anxiety, superego strength) the source-trait labels used here are bipolar. What are the implications of this? Factor analysis gives initially bipolar factors, that is, with about as many negative as positive loadings. The exceptions are ability traits where we have human preconceptions of what constitutes success, and dynamic traits where the strength, say, of memorizing a topic goes from zero to some positive quantity. Even these traits can be made bipolar as factors if we choose to rescore tests, for example, for number of mistakes instead of number right.

In temperament traits we do not know which direction of scoring is positive, in either an adaptive or a socially desirable sense. Indeed my hypothesis has been that the central tendency in a temperament trait is, in terms of the aims of natural selection, that which is most adaptive to the environment. Consequently no direction is more meaningful than another in the sense of being likely to be more often used predictively in practice in a positive sense. For example, desurgency $F-$ is about as frequently positive predictive of criteria as is surgency $F+$. Future research may relate temperament to degree of some physical entity (say, level of thyroxin or noradrenaline) but apart from this the direction called positive is as arbitrary as the names north pole and south pole.

The procedures most helpful to further research are thus to be constant and consistent in direction: affectia is $A+$, socially warm behavior; premsia is $I+$, protected emotional sensitivity (hence the acronym *pr-em-sia*). Moreover it is important to preserve a precise term for the opposite pole not only to be able to describe individuals at opposite extremes (affectic and sizic, premsic and harric) but also as insurance against the possibility that future research will find the opposite pole more meaningful.

Apart from these real considerations occurring in certain cases such questions as "Are traits bipolar or unipolar?" are mere semantics. To say that the word at one pole is not always the exact semantic opposite of the other misses the discoverer's aim, which is to enrich the usefulness of the bipolar designations by letting the second polar term convey important aspects that cannot be conveyed by the first. Thus C might be labeled high versus low ego strength, which, it is true, are exactly opposite; but by calling it, as here, ego strength versus dissatisfied general emotionality we provide a strict meaning at the conceptual and descriptive levels and can thus communicate with psychoanalysts and with psychometrists who have loosely called this factor emotionality.

artists, store clerks, professors, employment counsellors. Perhaps low ego strength is only a slight impediment to a routine job free of serious crises and confrontations and may aid in sympathizing with the maladjustments of others.

Clinical Associations. Psychopaths and some kinds of juvenile delinquents are the only high instances. Virtually all forms of pathology, neurotic and psychotic—as psychoanalytic theory would require—show statistically significantly lower *C*. Conversely *C* is the only trait with this generality across alcoholism, crime, all neuroses, psychoses, suicides, and drug addicts. Low ego strength also shows in some chronic physical disabilities and in marital instability.

Specification Equation. Positive loadings show up against criterion measures of success in marriage, performance as psychiatric technician, salesman, counselor, air hostess, and group leader (administrator).

Change with Events. This factor increases with marriage (compared with unmarried control groups). There is also an increase with church participation and some indication of an increase with reduction of anxiety by tranquilizers. There is a decrease under chronic anxiety most concretely shown in anxiety over disability and illness.

Eminent Illustrations. High: Washington, Alfred the Great, Bismarck, Lenin. Low: Baudelaire, Maupassant, Cellini, Nietzsche, Nero, Coleridge, Hamlet.[4]

Theory. This dynamic control structure grows from reward by experience of successful control over impulse, particularly by the reduction of the indecision component in anxiety (Cattell, 1972). This trait represents a high ratio of successful expression to drive tension level (hence its negative relation to Q_4 in the second-order anxiety factor *Q*II).

D: Excitability. *History.* This trait was demonstrated in ratings in 1947 and in Q-data soon after; its appearance in the childhood range was discovered later.

H (Heritability). Around 0.25 (only moderately heritable).

Age Trend. Increase to early adolescence and then a sharp decrease.

General Associations. Generally excitability is related more to conduct problems than personality disorders, conduct problems of a type that tend to clear up. It may be related to enuresis and truancy. High *D*s enjoyed family life, were rated "entertainingly expressive" and "self-confident." This trait is positively related to absence of demonstrative affection by parents, especially the father (Barton, Dielman, and Cattell, 1972).

Occupational and School Associations. (School interests: only investigated to age 18.) The excitable student does not settle down to classroom

[4] The reader may object that these collections of illustrations contain strangely diverse sets of people. So they do, because "types" have to agree on the *total profile* of traits whereas these men and women are chosen to be diverse *on all but* the factor concerned—to clarify what is essential to it. It is virtually impossible to find a set of people deviating on only one source trait and no others. For example, the mere fact that these men and women are eminent implies that most of them are also far above average in intelligence.

work, reading, or even steady sports participation, yet he is labeled creative and imaginative. Such people tend to be school dropouts.

Clinical Associations. Excitability is high in general conduct disorders with immaturity and acting out but not personality disorders; it is low in neurotics and drug addicts.

Specification Equation. This factor is slightly but significantly negative on most school achievement, achievement in sports, leadership, and interest in school.

Eminent Illustrations. High: Alexander the Great, Clive, Hitler, Strindberg, Mayer. Low: Duke of Wellington, Thomas Reed (speaker, House of Representatives), Emerson, Archimedes (by anecdote).

Theory. Excitability must not be confused with emotionality (as in *C, L, O*) or instability. It is a cognitive excitability, restlessness, and often antisocial expressiveness. There are indications of environmental contributions by family enouragement of "limelighting" (which gains attention by being entertaining) and also by early overprotection encouraging immaturity and dependence. Our theory, however, sees a basic emotional insecurity adding to this family dynamics effect. This insecurity arises from a lack or removal of real parental emotional support, bringing on a "demandingness," expressed ouwardly in immaturity and excitability, inwardly as "panic." (See the preceding relation to lack of demonstration of parental affection.) Some theories have related it to Degan's noneuphoric manic and to catatonic excitement. One reason for the difficulty of its recognition in adults may be that as genetic excitability declines in level and variance the acquired defenses or adjustments loom larger in the pattern. Environmental insecurity acting on a particular temperamental substrate seems to be the key to *D*.

E: Dominance-Submissiveness. *History.* Even within precise factorial work this trait has a long history (Maslow, 1940, 1954). It has a second tributary in animal ethology from McDougall (1932) to Ardrey (1966) and in hormone physiology and animal research (Scott and others, 1959; Seward, 1946).

H (Heritability). Around 0.25. Experimenters with man's mammalian relatives are inclined to dispute this low figure. Across the sexes and between species heritability is probably higher; within one sex, even in animal experiments, however, environment appreciably alters dominance (Mowrer, 1950; Harlow and Harlow, 1962), and in humans the heritability is as low as 0.25.

Age Trend. Increases rapidly in early life, then levels off and declines a little in the middle years.

General Associations. High in the oldest child. High *E*s are recorded as unconventional and rule-breaking in group behavior (heckling, bluffing, disturbing). There are significant relations to an early authoritarian family atmosphere and to stricter application of discipline (Barton, Dielman, and Cattell, 1972). Among 18-to-22-year olds there is a tendency to reject sexual restraints (Cattell and Nichols, in preparation; Barton and Cattell, 1972c; Maslow, 1940), to have a great number of social contacts, to drink immoderately, to have parents who criticize sexual behavior, to have less than average sleep needs (note the resemblance to manic behavior), to be inactive in church, and to be independent as a marriage partner (Cattell and Nichols, in preparation). Men average significantly higher than women.

Occupational and School Associations. In total school performance the association is significantly negative (perhaps due to a lack of docility). But in mathematics and in college the association is positive. This trait is high in airmen, competitive athletes, administrators, artists, engineers, psychologists, writers, and researchers. It is low in priests, counselors, farmers, physicians, professors, and clerks.

Clinical Associations. High in psychopaths and low in neurotics, alcoholics, drug addicts, all psychotics except manics, in stably married wives and unstably married husbands (Cattell and Nesselroade, 1968), and in the chronically ill.

Specification Equations. Positive predictions in creativity and research, and negative ones in sales success, stability of marriage, female counselor work, male teaching success, likelihood of election as a small-group leader, interest in school, participation in school sports, and poor results in all areas of school achievement below the graduate level.

Changes under Events. Lowered by chronic illness and raised by psychotherapy, leaving home, job promotion, and increased social contacts.

Eminent Illustrations. High in Kaiser Wilhelm II, Wagner, Clemenceau, Rutherford, Ghengis Kahn, Louis XVI, Hitler, Pasteur. Low in Saint Francis of Assisi and many Christian leaders, Gautama Buddha, Sydney Webb, Darwin, Edward the Confessor, Shakespeare.

Theory. This source trait is not to be identified with the strength of the self-assertive erg although it correlates positively with it: it is the extent to which the individual has the confidence and need to pit himself against social and material opposition. In all but the psychotic it shows constant realistic adjustment to the individual's success or failure, health or sickness, capacities or disabilities, and the relative outside forces. Although there are specific levels according to role, each individual has his distinct average level, somewhat genetically but substantially experientially settled. This confidence-ratio theory fits the known tendency of the pattern to change with subgroups.

F: Surgency-Desurgency. *History.* For some time this trait was confused with the second-order exvia factor although it is a distinct component not so different from one of the four components in extraversion conjectured by Jung. Since 1932 and more clearly since 1949 its special active, clever, fluent, impulsive pattern has been recognized both in L- and Q-data.

H (Heritability). About 0.60 (in some studies, lower). Some indications of blood group and physique support the higher figure.

Age Trend. Rising in adolescence but decreasing in adulthood.

General Associations. Generally this trait is related to high economic status of family, not being an only child, less illness, fewer work responsibilities, and early marriage. Surgent personalities frequently leave home in the 18-to-22-year range and leave their home town for a change of scene.

There is low restraint in sexual activities, there are many social contacts, and in small groups such a person is often voted an effective speaker and a leader. In home background desurgency significantly relates (Barton, Dielman, and Cattell, 1973) to parental exercise of a great degree of behavioral control over the individual concerned. In marriage the high *F*s show more than average mutual independence.

Occupational and School Associations. This trait tends to be slightly negative with school performance. Later this correlation becomes more significant (about 0.2) (Rothman and Flowers, 1970). This trait is high in athletes, soldiers, sailors, pilots, airline hostesses, musicians, salesmen. It is low in accountants, administrator, artists, engineers, clerical workers, priests, professors, scientific researchers, writers, cashiers.

Clinical Associations. Surgency is high in psychopaths and delinquents. Pumfrey and others (1972) noted persistent delinquents are high on *F* and *H* but not the other primaries (*A* and Q_2) in the exvia second order. Surgency is low in neurotics, alcoholics, psychotics (except manics), and physical illness, and notably low in coronary patients.

Specification Equation. There is a positive prediction of success in sales, counseling, and leadership in small groups but a moderately negative one for most scholastic achievement. There are appreciable cultural differences: this trait is high in Australians and low in the Chinese and Japanese.

Change with Events. Increases with the practice of a restrained sex life and with having a large circle of social contacts. Young adults who leave home and those who get married experience a significant shift toward desurgency compared with those who do not.

Eminent Illustrations. High surgency is found in Boswell, Whitman, Oscar Wilde, Whistler, Fluellen, H. G. Wells, Voltaire; low in Prospero, Lenin, Admiral Mahan, Pascal, Darwin, Emily Dickinson, Job, Harold Nicholson, Tennyson, Wilfred Owen.

Theory. Although one cannot help noticing a resemblance of surgency-desurgency to the manic-depressive axis (and such drugs as alcohol increase surgency) the antithesis is not so much one of mood as of habit. The desurgent person is prudent, sober-minded, and full of care; the surgent is happy-go-lucky and impulsive. A genetic contribution of irrepressibility, an ability to forget punishment easily, is certainly present, but equally important is an environmental training in general inhibition. Thus the disciplinary weight of experience is central to desurgency, which accounts for its steady increase throughout life, the association of desurgency with strong work habits, steady achievement, and deep creativity, as well as its confusion in some writings with superego. Several early researchers noted such strong associations of desurgency with conscience and surgency with delinquency that they hypothesized it to be superego. Desurgency is a more general inhibition than superego, which is concerned with moral inhibitions and positive commands. However, second-order factor VIII, hypothesized to be general moral upbringing although it loads *G* centrally, has a persistent negative loading on *F*. Desurgency thus represents the effect of a general severity of the economic, socio-ethical, and physical world, in terms of care and forethought required.

4. The Natural History of Superego, Parmia, Premsia, Protension and Autia

G: Superego. *History.* The concept of conscience is dateless; it is discussed by Hebrew prophets and Greek dramatists. But the dynamic developmental concepts are psychoanalytic, and the factor-analytic evidence of a distinct and measurable unitary structure in L-, Q-, and T-data is only 20 years old.

H (Heritability). About 0.40, which is too high to fit the general view of conscience as largely an environmentally acquired pattern and suggests that an appreciable predisposition is necessary. The investigation of psychopathic personalities supports this discovery of a hereditary component.

Age Trend. Moderate but decelerating increase with age.

General Associations. Higher G with: high regard for parents, election to leadership in small groups, peer ratings of effectiveness among officer candidates, rejection of loose sexual morals, not being criticized by parents for morals of companions, having suffered a bereavement, having acquired early social responsibilities, not incurring parental criticism for type of companions of opposite sex, being married rather than unmarried in the twenties, being an active member of a church, working long hours as a student and needing few hours of sleep, being a moderate or nondrinker, not being a college dropout, and evaluation as a spontaneous leader in small face-to-face groups.

In the home background, G is related to more years of education of parents, particularly the father ($r = 0.3$), to great warmth of the parental relationship, to the use of reasoning rather than punishment, to less strictness over detailed regulations, and to little use of coaxing with obvious rewards and praise (Barton, Dielman, and Cattell, 1973) to get good behavior. In marriage high G relates significantly to more devotion to the home.

Occupational and School Associations. The superego factor shows the most consistent positive correlations of any factor after intelligence to measured achievement (Barton, Dielman, and Cattell, 1972; Cattell and Butcher, 1968; Rothman and Flowers, 1970); it correlates also with interest in school subjects. This trait is high in accountants, airline pilots (but not military airmen), airline hostesses, mechanics, priests, musicians (who differ from artists here and elsewhere), time-study engineers, wholesale business executives. It is low in artists, young professors, social workers and some social scientists (including general psychologists), competitive athletes, employment directors, writers, journalists.

Clinical Associations. The superego remains at a moderately low level in most diagnostic groups including neurotics (except hysterics), attempted suicides, and acute schizophrenics (but not manic depressives). This trait is notably low in homosexuals, psychopaths, criminals, and gang delinquents.

Specification Equation. Positive loading in freedom from accidents; in success as a therapist or psychiatric technician; in volume of sales among salesmen; and in teaching success. There is substantial loading in school achievement. This trait has, apart from intelligence, the highest loading in success in school and other examinations.

Change with Events. Businessmen who are given more responsibilities increase in *G* compared with those who are not; there is also an increase at a lower significance in those who marry.

Eminent Illustrations. High superego is found in biblical prophets, prophets, religious leaders and saints (John Knox, Savonarola), and Browning, Tennyson, Kipling, Washington, Lincoln, Nelson, Kant, Leonidas, Florence Nightingale. Those low in superego include many notorious historical characters, Marquis de Reys, Casanova, Cellini, Cagliostro.

Theory. In view of the anomalously low score of contemporary journalists and many academics the question is frequently raised whether this factor is truly the superego since these individuals show the perseverance and self-control associated with *G* even if not the moral values. The paradox has several aspects, beginning with the fact (see Chapter Eight) that Q-data on *G* are particularly liable to motivational distortion. But criminals show subnormal *G* as do journalists and young professors; moreover the *G* scores in general correlate with such criteria as school achievement even in the sense of persistence. The explanation is probably that in these exceptions we deal with the special subculture of fashionable revolt against established ethical values which from Aristophanes to Shelley has characterized mainly the verbal behavior (but occasionally the actual behavior, as in Nero, the Borgias, Shelley, Wilde, Nietzsche, Rousseau) of those who recognize themselves as brighter than most and thus reject the *G* values. I have discussed the origins and extent of this secession of intellectuals elsewhere (Cattell, 1972b) but it is statistically unclear how far secession affects prediction from the *G* pattern in the general population.

If we set aside anomalies from special subcultures the measures of *G* show that it behaves indubitably as the superego should and that no other demonstrated factor does so (see, however, *O* and Q_3 below). There is no need at present to modify the main psychoanalytic theory of its origin and structure (Freud, 1920) except to recognize that our findings parallel Mowrer's in showing *G* to be negatively related to anxiety. The Freudian view that *G* adds to anxiety is presumably due to the mistake of sampling from the sick only. Our evidence is clear: in the normal range and especially in younger children (see Tables 19 and 20, Chapter Four) a strong superego does not generate anxiety (as it apparently may in patients of weak ego, *C*(—)) but reduces anxiety (Cattell and Gorsuch, 1965); the correlation is negative at developmental if not at adult levels. The superego *G* must therefore be assigned an integrating action, directing id impulses to the social outlets least likely to accumulate frustration and anxiety. The positive correlation of *G* with some *C* and Q_3 in the second order moral upbringing or integration factor VIII shows an integrated action of these three primaries.

H: Parmia-Threctia. *History.* Like surgency this factor has been mistaken for exvia, which probably accounts for many of the physiological associations found with the exvia conglomerate. It has been isolated in L- and Q-data clearly since the late 1940s. Parmia is an acronym to express the theory that it represents parasympathetic predominance—*par-mia*—at the $H+$ pole and sympathetic system predominance at the $H-$ pole. The latter amounts to high susceptibility to threat—hence threctia.

H (Heritability). About 0.40, which is lower than was once thought from the sympathetic system associations but may have to be revised upward.

Age Trend. The trait increases strongly through the middle years for males but only slightly for females.

General Associations. This factor is associated positively with demonstrative affection by parents and negatively with strict discipline (Barton, Cattell, 1972b) and maternal solicitousness, which invites dependence. In marriage it is correlated with planned role-sharing and personal independence (Barton and Cattell, 1972a). High *H* is significantly related to numerous social contacts, a rating as socially pushful and brash, having parents from the low-income range, a home that is cheerful but not peaceful, a rating as cooperative and friendly as a child but lazy and unorganized, an aggressive approach to the opposite sex (and many dates as a student), many social responsibilities, uninhibited sexual philosophy, parents strongly critical of adolescent companions, and indication of association with endomorphic or mesomorphic, pyknic build. In small groups such a person tends to be a leader but is voted an ineffective although important speaker.

Occupational and School Associations. In school parmia is unrelated to achievement in general but is slightly related positively to mathematics (also slightly positively to acceptable behavior and adjustment in school; Cattell and Butcher, 1968). In occupations parmia is high in competitive athletes, salesman, musicians, garage mechanics, psychiatric technicians, group psychotherapy leaders, and practicing psychologists. It is low in ministers and priests, editorial workers, farmers, and those seeking vocational rehabilitation.

Clinical Associations. Parmia is very high in psychopaths and moderately in young delinquents, especially in gangs and in the "wandered or run away" category. It is low in alcoholics, neurotics (especially obsessional-compulsive), attempted suicides, schizophrenics (in the withdrawal types, not in paranoid), husbands in unstable marriages, and most of the physically handicapped.

Specification Weights. Positive on success in marriage and success as a therapist (rated), salesman (measured), psychiatric technician, classroom teacher.

Change with Events. None yet found; unless contradicted suggests higher heritability.

Eminent Illustrations. Persons high in parmia include Theodore Roosevelt, Churchill, Columbus, Andrew Jackson, Richard I, Isadora Duncan. Those low in parmia include Emily Dickinson and Cavendish.

Theory. An appreciable constitutional component of low inhibitability is evidently involved, which fits evidence of association with EKG pattern and sympathetic responsiveness. (A correlation has been found between low *H* and speed and duration of pulse response to a cold pressor test.) The criterion associations suggest that the parmic person is insensitive to danger and is able to endure a series of shocks, social and physical, which reduce the threctic person to exhaustion and inhibition. The genetic contribution may include hormonal as well as autonomic aspects but centrally we define *H* by reference to the *H*(—) (threctic) direction—as a high sensitivity of the sympathetic nervous system leading to shyness and withdrawal from conflict. Parmia can be seen as a defense against such overreaction to threat through a balance in favor of parasympathetic action.

I: Premsia-Harria. *History*. The concept of a dimension of this kind is older than extraversion and goes back to the tender-versus-tough minded of William James and earlier sources traced by Roback (1927). As a demonstrably distinct Q-data factor it was replicated in the mid-1940s (Cattell, 1946b, 1948) and soon thereafter as a pattern in attitudes by Eysenck (1952). Although placed alphabetically as *I* in adults, that is, as a source trait of middling variance, its variance has proved consistently larger in children so that it might have been given the symbol *A* had investigation begun with children.

H (Heritability). About 0.60.

Age Trend. Steep decrease into adolescence followed by a slight continuous rise throughout life.

General Associations. Premsia has significant positive relations to lax discipline in the home background, inadequate behavioral control, warmth in permitting free aggression, more control by reasoning than by punishment, and parental preference for younger children. It is also associated with poor health, having operations as a child, chronic illness, hypochondria, effort intolerance, low athletic interest and performance. The high premsic individual was hesitant and lacked confidence as a child; he recalls dissatisfaction with the family and was seldom in trouble because of temper and aggression in school or with siblings; there is an association with the middle and upper classes and with a protected home life. Premsia also distinguishes those who go to college, take up social responsibilities, get married rather than stay single in their twenties, move away from home, and are active in church. Higher premsic persons drink less. Finally, women score higher than men in premsia.

Occupational and School Associations. Premsia is significantly associated with better than average performance in language (Cattell and Butcher, 1968) and less than average performance in mathematics (Barton, Dielman, and Cattell, 1972). Occupationally it is high in artists, clergymen, professors, administrators, biologists, social scientists, social workers, and editorial workers. It is low in physical scientists, engineers, airline pilots, military airmen, electricians, mechanics, foremen in industry, sales managers, time-study engineers, and policemen.

Clinical Associations. No clinical group has been found significantly low in premsia but it is significantly higher than average in neurotics, manic depressives, attempted suicides, criminals, antisocial deviants, and homosexuals.

Specific Equations. This source trait has a rather strong influence negatively on counselor effectiveness and teaching success.

Change with Events. Higher after an unhappy love affair, it also increases more in those who marry than in those who do not. There are increases in those who go to college compared with those who go to work.

Eminent Illustrations. High premsia people include Coleridge, Wordsworth, Marie Antoinette, Oscar Wilde, Bertrand Russell, Eleanor Roosevelt. Those low in premsia include Kipling, Samuel Johnson, Mark Twain, Napoleon, Burns, Lindbergh.

Theory. The original hypothesis for the *I* pattern put forward by myself and my associates was that of an overprotected versus an exposed and realistically demanding childhood. The fairly strong indications of a genetic component and some indication of a link with the A blood group (not to mention the strong sex association, which *could,* however, be culturally due to the "overprotection" of the female child) suggest some physiological predisposition to emotional sensitivity and fastidiousness. In any case the combined genetic and environmental influences produce a pattern of evasiveness of harsh realities, which is absent at the opposite harric pole. The premsic person lives by feelings and intuition; the harric by logic and fact. This distinction accounts for the neurosis proneness, in that neurotic hesitation and unrealism lead to incompatible dynamics. It also fits the tendency of premsic individuals who are intelligent to escape into occupations where there is comfort of cultural myths rather than meet the emotionless and mechanical world. In some studies the premsia-versus-harria pattern has been called masculinity-versus-femininity but this is a gross oversimplification; only a fraction of the male-female difference resides in *I* (*A, E,* and *O* also have statistically significant associations, and it is possible to name outstanding harric women, among them Napoleon's mother, Messalina, Queen Elizabeth I).

L: Protension-Alaxia. *History.* In my extensive survey of Q- and L-data factors in 1946 I found several suggestions by factorists of a dimension resembling introversion with paranoid features—even in the normal range. Further work located it in L-data only weakly by such ratings as "suspicious," "self-sufficient," and "jealous" but found it strongly in Q-data in a pattern that is defined as a general use of projection as a defense mechanism.

H (Heritability). About 0.55.

Age Trend. Declines entering the middle years but increases appreciably after age 40.

General Associations. Generally the father and mother of the protensic person are vigorous characters given to discussion and argument. As a child such a person had high confidence in himself, found school unpleasant but felt superior, and experienced mutual admiration and support within the family. He has experienced bereavement. There is a tendency to truancy and to need more sleep than most; such a person prefers to take a job rather than go to college, is a strong drinker, does not marry early, tends to be socially unpopular, and tends to have a pyknic build with small extremities. High protension in a small group significantly lowers its morale of synergy.

Occupational Associations. Protension is high in artists, editorial workers, farmers, managers, some creative scientists. It is low in accountants, administrators, pilots, airline hostesses, nuns, cooks, electricians, mechanics, biologists, physicists, musicians.

Clinical Associations. Protension is high in criminals, homosexuals, drug addicts, neurotics, and attempted suicides (see Wittenborn in Cattell, 1957). There are no low associations.

Specification Equation. This factor is loaded negatively on success as a policeman or salesman and on counselor effectiveness and rated teacher effectiveness (but not in women).

Change with Events. This pattern is increased by a life of free sexual expression and perhaps by bohemian living generally. It is reduced by marriage and by regular church activity.

Eminent Illustration. Those high in protension include Coriolanus, Benedict Arnold, Lola Montez, Alexander the Great, Stalin, Mahomet, Patton, DeGaulle. Those low in protension include Thomas a Kempis, Madame Curie, Eisenhower, Pericles.

Theory. Some behavioral resemblances are noticeable to dominance, sizothymia, and radicalism, from which, however, a clear factorial distinction must be made. Protension has a "Promethean will" character (appearing in the untamed as contrasted with disciplined and pedestrian occupations) and indeed participates with E and Q_1 in the second order QIV, independence.

Wenig's first factoring showed which defense mechanisms are unitary (Cattell and Wenig, 1952) and discovered that L is strongly associated with systematic habits of using true projection in perceptual situations. A promising hypothesis is that L is the general tendency to project inner tensions into outer situations. The term pro-tension embodies this theory but also suggests a preference for a given defense mechanism, namely, the notion of some higher inner tension. Alaxia implies that the opposite quality is a resigned relaxation, an acceptance of a socially low expression of individuality. In short the projective dynamism may be secondary—a necessary defense when an inner tension and strong individualism encounter a socially passive resistance. The psychoanalytic concept of infantile omnipotence fits the rapid decline with age from childhood, but not the rise with age after middle age. The heritability is not high enough for it to be considered wholly temperamental; one must look also for an early upbringing favoring self-will.

M: Autia-Praxernia. *History.* This source trait has no early recognition clinically but became evident through factor-analytic work in L- and Q-data, in the late 1940s.

H (Heritability). Around 0.40.

Age Trend. Increases in early life and then declines.

General Associations. Autious people are likely to have moved from their homes and home town. They choose college rather than a job, take part in church and social clubs but are dissenters, are not voted leaders in small groups, and reject and are rejected by groups although they are called significant members. There is some history of delicate health. Their parents disapprove of their sex life and companions; they lack regard for order and are untidy in dress; they report unhappy love affairs. This factor appears in scientists and writers. People with this trait are auto-accident prone; they often change jobs. Autia is reduced by experience of job promotion. Culturally the Latin countries—Italy, Brazil, Mexico—are more autious than Britain and Australia.

Occupational Associations. Autia is very high in artists, moderately high in editors, employment counselors, clinical psychologists. It is low in electricians, airline pilots, airline hostesses, miners, geologists, policemen, mechanics, and concrete, nonsubjective occupations.

Clinical Associations. Autia is very high in drug addicts, criminals, homosexuals, cycloid depressives, and the less stably married; it is low in those with psychosomatic and stress illnesses.

Specification Equations. This factor positively and appreciably loads accident proneness but also rated effectiveness in classroom teaching. It is negative on psychiatric technicians and salesmanship.

Change with Events. This trait declines in married compared with nonmarried people. It increases with certain failures (unhappy love affairs and not being promoted on the job). It increases in those who go to college instead of taking a job.

Eminent Illustrations. High autia persons include Spinoza, Flaubert, George Borrow, Lewis Carroll, Van Gogh, Marlow, Jack London, El Greco, Picasso, Swinburne, Byron, and the modern hippie. Those low in autia include Ford, Hoover, Prime Minister Baldwin, Carnegie, Coolidge.

Theory. Despite a moderate genetic component that has been hypothesized to produce a greater intensity of images and ideas relative to sensory stimuli, one sees evidence of environmental influence that favors bohemianism. In essence the behavior is one of accepting an intense inner, subjective life relative to the reality of the outer world and its demands—as the terms autia and autism connote. These characteristics show themselves in creativity and in accident proneness. One element in the environmental component may be affectionate spoiling by the mother or a sheltered life in which sharp demands have not been made (note the effect of college versus a job; of unmarried versus married life). At the same time there is a failure to cope with life (for example, lack of promotions). Such failure does not appear to act as a challenge to practicality, and increases the daydreaming, autistic outlet in a positive feedback system.

5. The Natural History of Shrewdness, Guilt Proneness, Radicalism, Self Sufficiency, Self Sentiment, and Ergic Tension

N: Shrewdness-Natural Forthrightness. *History.* This trait is not recognized in the clinical literature. It was identified hesitatingly in the late 1940s as an L- and Q-data factor and has been confirmed since then;

there are never high loadings but this factor adds to criterion variance predictions.

H (Heritability). Around 0.25.

Age Trend. Tends to show a steady, slight increase throughout life.

General Associations. Positively related to social status and to freedom from pathology. In small groups such people are positive influences in problem-solving and are rated high in keeping to the point. This trait relates to less social integration in marriage (Barton, Dielman, and Cattell, 1972).

Occupational Associations. High in airline hostesses, business executives, psychologists, time-study engineers, salesmen, and managers. It is low in artists, priests, garage mechanics, miners, janitors, cooks, and kitchen help.

Clinical Associations. Shrewdness is high in unstably married men or women and low in manic depressives and schizo-affectives.

Specification Equation. There is positive loading on clinical diagnostic skill, success in therapy, success in sales. There is negative loading on rating as a counselor or a schoolteacher and, slightly, on success in marriage.

Change with Events. This trait rises with promotion on the job (Barton and Cattell, 1972c).

Eminent Illustrations. Persons high in shrewdness include Casanova, O. Henry, Mrs. Simpson, Michael Arlen, Disraeli, Lloyd George, Rothschild, Metternich, Voltaire. Those low in shrewdness include Tolstoy, Diogenes, Dostoyevsky, Rousseau, John Bunyan, Kropotkin, Joan of Arc.

Theory. The pattern is one of shrewd competitiveness in which personal gain often plays a role and sophistication and deviousness appear as instrumentalities. At the opposite pole is an almost simple-minded sincerity, naturalness, and disregard of self. From observed childhood links a theory claims that the pattern begins with insecurity or a selfish social environment that forces the individual to selfishness as a defense. Its appearance in the second-order independence factor, which provokes also dominance, radicalism, and self-sufficiency, suggests that it is due partly to competitiveness and that it has bourgeois and commercial associations as well as personal qualities of studying the angles. Nevertheless some capacity to respond to competition is also implied, and the behavior is in the common sense adjustive.

O: Guilt Proneness. *History.* This trait has a long history as a factor in the questionnaire domain—under such titles as melancholy agitation, depressive tendency, moodiness, and even neurasthenia and cycloid tendency (see research in Cattell, 1956b). Better rotations have refined its meaning since then.

H (Heritability). Around 0.25.

Age Trend. Falls after childhood and early adolescence, and may rise slightly after middle age.

General Associations. This trait tends to be lower in only children and in those with few or no bereavements. It is high in those who select few friends and are selected by few, those in groups who neither attempt to lead nor are invited to lead, and those who are critical of group life and standards.

Such people are shy, ineffective speakers and are not voted leaders. They are loyal in friendship, take social failure or broken love affairs hard, and are more often observed to be tearful (ratings). In home background guilt proneness is associated with discipline by physical punishment, less overall behavioral guidance and control, and a patriarchal rather than matriarchal structure (Barton, Dielman, and Cattell, 1972). It is also high with more daughters in the family. In the person's own marriage guilt proneness is significantly associated with less than average sexual gratification and less than average togetherness in mutual role action (Barton and Cattell, 1972a).

Occupational and School Associations. High guilt proneness is associated with less than average school participation but not with underachievement. It is high in artists, farmers, priests, clients for vocational rehabilitation. It is low in military airmen, competitive athletes, administrators, physicists, mechanics, airline hostesses, psychologists, domestic help.

Clinical Associations. No clinical group has a below-average score in guilt proneness. High *O* is almost as universal in clinical cases as low *C*, notably in alcoholics, criminals, homosexuals, neurotics, attempted suicides, acute schizophrenics, manic depressives, schizo-affectives, and coronary and angina patients.

Specification Equation. There is positive but slight loading on accident proneness, and positive loading on counselor effectiveness (perhaps due to high compassion and understanding of difficulties). There is a slight negative loading on effectiveness in certain jobs, such as ward attendant.

Change with Events. This factor increases with chronic disability, illness, dependency, and frequent job changes. It declines with job promotion and many social contacts.

Eminent Illustrations. People of high guilt proneness include most religious leaders—Christ, Buddha, Saint John of the Cross, those who describe a dark night of the soul or its equivalent as the beginning of their insight. Other examples in a different context include Housman, Poe, Dostoyevsky, Churchill. Those low in this trait include Genghis Khan, Stalin, Robespierre, and many effective administrators.

Theory. The term guilt proneness has been long employed, yet it must be understood that it is not liability to particular pangs of guilt so much as a global sense of inadequacy, loneliness, and tears (see autobiography of Mowrer, 1966, for example). There is an appreciable genetic predisposition and evidence of physiological responsiveness to vitamin B deficiency (−) and to imipramine (+). Yet evidently it also responds to perceived success in life and to a sense of social support, affection, and group solidarity. It might also be considered as a heightened demand of the gregarious erg which leaves an insatiable loneliness when it is not met.

Q_1: Radicalism-Conservatism. *History.* This factor was discovered as a unitary factor of large variance by Thurstone and Chave (1929) and in a somewhat similar pattern by Guilford (Thoughtfulness, *T*) before confirmation by the 12 studies mentioned in Chapter Two here. It has consistently appeared in attitude studies by Eysenck (1944). However, it shows some of the worst manifestations of instability of pattern across subcultures and has altered to the detriment of item validities in the 16 PF factor over 20 years, such that the same scale can no longer be validly used for middle-aged men and young women students (Burdsal and Vaughan, 1973)

H (Heritability). In spite of expectations of entirely environmental determination, the heritability of this trait is about 0.10.

Age Trend. No clear change.

General Association. There is a positive correlation with affiliation with progressive political parties; there is an absence of strong church interest and a presence of some chronic illness. The conservative pole is related to strong family ties, to being the oldest or only child, to experience of bereavement, and to refusal to follow free sexual mores. In group dynamics radicals have a high participation count but are mainly critical of the group and are rated by observers as socially and emotionally negative. In marriage radicalism is associated with less than average male dominance.

Occupational and School Associations. This trait is moderately associated with good school achievement. It is high in artists, writers, accountants, engineers, professors, and employment counselors. It is low (conservative) in athletes, priests, farmers, mechanics, naval and military cadets, musicians, cooks and domestic workers, policemen, salesmen.

Clinical Associations. This factor is high in unstably married women and low in conversion hysterics, compulsives, and psychosomatics.

Specification Equation. Positive loadings on counselor and teacher success, and slight negative loadings on effectiveness as psychiatric technician. The trait has a curvilinear relation to marriage success.

Change with Events. Those who leave their parental home become more radical than those who stay. Paradoxically, radicalism increases (perhaps as a rationalization) among those practicing a free sex life and also those who are active in church. An increase in social responsibilities lowers Q_1.

Eminent Illustrations. Those high in radicalism include DaVinci, A. and J. Huxley, Frank L. Wright, Shaw, Ibsen, Brunel, H. G. Wells, Marx, Richard Strauss, Napoleon. Those low in radicalism include Churchill, most popes, Queen Victoria, Anatole France, Galsworthy, W. J. Bryan, Douglas Haig.

Theory. The large loadings are on items involving social, political, and religious attitudes but I am inclined to regard this factor as a blown-up specific (Chapter Eight) combined with a general tendency to try the new. If it were the former it would depend wholly on environment, such as being born in a right- or a left-wing family. But the moderate heritability and the association of conservatism with success in occupations requiring patient endurance, such as psychiatric ward attendant, suggest that it is a complexly determined toleration of the status quo contrasted with a somewhat impatient desire for what might be. Contrary to popular view this factor has little connection with age (up to 60): young children can be very conservative.

Q_2: Self-Sufficiency–Group Dependence. *History.* There was no recognition of this pattern before the factor experiments of the 1940s (Chapter Two); it was lost in the vague introversion concept.

H (Heritability). Around 0.25.

Age Trend. No age change in males; slight increase in females.

General Associations. Positive with those whose parents were maritally harmonious; those with this trait were seclusive as children and stubborn in school. They developed early, had few accidents, were considered mature, and had few friends and those older. Often such people are oldest or only children. As adults they have few social contacts and follow free sexual expression. They are active in church; tend to be passed over for promotion, and marry late. In small groups they give pessimistic judgments about group unity and future performance.

Occupational Association. This trait is high in artists, air cadets, engineers, professors, research scientists, and creative writers. It is low in air hostesses, cooks, domestic help, football players, nuns, nurses, social workers, and perhaps journalists (small sample).

Clinical Associations. This factor is high in conversion hysterics, inadequately adjusting personalities, and all classes of schizophrenics (moderately but consistently); it is low in psychosomatics and most types of chronic physical illness.

Specification Equation. There is positive loading on success as a police patrolman, individual sales success, prospects of marital stability and, substantially, on scholastic achievement. There is negative loading on effectiveness as a counselor.

Change with Events. Very little change with events has been reported —a result consistent with higher heritability.

Eminent Illustrations. Persons with high self-sufficiency include Copernicus, Lindberg, Bob Hope, Newton, Banting, Mencken, Greta Garbo, Pasteur. Those low in this trait include Alfred Austen, Jaurés, A. Schlesinger, Kosygin, Otto Rank, Marilyn Monroe, Laski, Hoffa.

Theory. Whatever the pattern becomes through environment, it starts early, consistently with a substantially genetic hypothesis. There may be a deficiency of gregariousness and a steadiness of emotion that favors dependence on the self and a lack of rewarding response by others. It seems to be a normal component predisposing (with low *C*, high *I*, and *O*) to some of the abnormal processes in schizophrenia but is otherwise an element in strength of character.

Q_3: Self-Sentiment Strength. *History.* The notion of a dynamic structure different from either the psychoanalytic ego or superego concepts is well developed in McDougall (1932). Confirmation came initially through the *R* (reflective) factor in Thurstone's questionnaire and a similar factor, No. 13, "scrupulous, analytical" by Cattell (1950a), by whose coworkers its pattern has since been well confirmed. Essentially this same factor, although not then built on a factor basis, was intensively examined in the 1950s and early 1960s in numerous self-concept studies because it consists of the dynamic structure around the self-concept.

H (Heritability). About 0.40 (low).

Age Trend. Is upset and reduced during adolescence but builds up strongly and steadily in early maturity, leveling off in middle adult years.

General Associations. Home reports show that parents controlled behavior more by reasoning than punishment and demonstrated affection readily. There is a negative relation to number of brothers in the family (Barton, Dielman, and Cattell, 1972). As a child the person of high self-sentiment was healthy; the family was harmonious. He did not get reported for temper or acting out at school; he especially liked science and mathematics. The Q_3 score is high in the only child, low in the oldest child, and low in college dropouts. People tend to score highly if as adolescents and later they accepted sexual ethics, rejected immoderate drinking, were not criticized by their parents for their companions and sexual relations. In small groups the trait is high in those with active participation in discussions, especially those who request and propose solutions to group problems; such people are rated effective speakers and receive few votes as "hinderers."

Occupational and School Associations. The loading on scholastic success is in general slightly but significantly positive (Cattell and Butcher, 1968; Rothman and Flowers, 1970). This trait is high in university administrators, airline pilots, scientists, electricians, janitors, mechanics, cooks, physicists, and small-group leaders. It is low in artists, employment counselors, priests, and vocational rehabilitation clients.

Clinical Associations. This factor is high in paranoids and low in criminals and gang delinquents, exhibitionists, neurotics, those with speech disorders, and attempted suicides.

Specification Equation. There is positive and significant loading on freedom from accidents, success on police patrol, teaching effectiveness, and scholastic performance at all levels.

Change with Events. This factor increases with college education, steady employment, added business responsibilities, experience of an unhappy love affair, parental illness, or the loss of a close friend or relative. It declines with excessive drinking.

Eminent Illustrations. High self-sentiment strength include Pericles, Woodrow Wilson, Newbolt, Kingsley, Yamamoto, Augustus Caesar, Captain Bligh, Robespierre, Kipling. Those low in this trait include Quisling, Kreugar (absconding financier), Benedict Arnold, Nero, Robin Hood, Diogenes, Beardsley, Herrick.

Theory. There is ample evidence (including the correlation of Q_3 with the self-sentiment factor in the Motivation Analysis Test (MAT)) that this factor represents the clarity with which the individual has developed a self-concept and the strength with which he adheres to it. This factor is distinguishable from the superego, which is partly unconscious and irrational, by being concerned with the social reputation and the admired self-image although some moral values *do* become become incorporated, in the integrated individual. At the negative pole of Q_3 are signs of lack of self-regard, social carelessness, untidiness, some anxiety and uncertainty, and "scatterbrained" behavior. The moderate genetic element(*H* about 0.40) may be a substrate of initially poor temperamental capacity to control, which disposes the individual not to try for higher Q_3 standards.

Q_4: Ergic Tension. *History.* This trait appeared in the late 1940s in my first Q-data analyses and, with slight rotation difference, probably in Thurstone's *S* (stability of emotion, negatively). If the following theory is correct, however, it is much older, going back to Freud's "id" (in part), McDougall's "total instinctual energy," and even Aristotle's "conation."

Heritability. Around 0.10.

Age Trend. Increases in early life, then declines through adulthood until 40.

General Associations. In home upbringing ergic tension is associated with great use of punishment, lack of demonstration of affection, and inadequate, unstructured behavioral control. It is positively related to size of family (Dielman, Barron, and Cattell, 1973a (and relative failure in school, especially in reading (S. Wright, 1954; O'Halloran, 1954). In groups such people are not accepted as leaders; they are dissatisfied with the group and do not feel (and are not) accepted. In early adult life they have suffered bereavements and unsuccessful love affairs (subjectively felt as "I've had a lot of bad luck"). This trait is associated also with high blood pressure and poor ability to perform under stress.

Occupational and School Associations. Ergic tension loads slightly but significantly negatively on school achievement. It is high in farmers, journalists, supermarket personnel, and writers. It is low in airline hostesses, airline pilots, naval cadets, geologists and other physical scientists, school counselors, and social workers. It decreases with job promotion and increases with frequent change of jobs.

Clinical Associations. No syndrome groups are low in ergic tension. This factor is high in alcoholics, homosexuals, exhibitionists, and all neurotic syndromes; slightly high in schizophrenics but significantly so among psychotics only in manic depressives and schizo-affectives; and very high in attempted suicides. It is higher in unstably than stably married persons.

Specification Equation. There is positive loading on accident proneness. A difference between husband and wife in this trait (wife lower than husband) contributes to marital stability. Loadings are negative on school achievement and success as a psychiatric technician, salesman, or counselor (female).

Change with Events. This trait is increased by an unhappy love affair, by not being promoted in one's job, and by chronic invalidism. It is decreased by participation in church activities.

Eminent Illustrations. Persons high in ergic tension include Macbeth, Edward VIII, H. G. Wells, Oppenheimer, Marat, Hitler, Dylan Thomas, Paracelsus. Those low in this trait include Matthew Arnold, Cardinal Newman, Gautama Buddha, Chiang Kai-shek, Epicurus, Somerset Maugham.

Theory. Excessive regard for subjective items of worry and irascibility has deflected attention from my early hypothesis (1957) that this factor is basically ergic tension—the amount of undischarged instinctual energy. But virtually all criterion evidence now supports this theory. Frustrations and deprivations of all kinds increase this factor: low rank in school and job, unhappy love affairs, bereavements. Such outlets as church activities reduce it, as does confinement. High stimulation—supermarket jobs, urgent journalistic work, the uncertainties of farming and weather—increases it.

The low heritability suggests that ergic tension is not related to high natural drive, that is, to id energy per se, but that it constitutes the difference between energy endowment plus stimulation and ergic discharge. The magnitude of the first term probably depends on high drive stimulation especially in situations that simultaneously stimulate conflicting drives. Obviously there is as much state as trait in Q_4. It seems immaterial what erg is involved; that is, it is not restricted to Freud's libido and is therefore best named ergic tension.

6. The Previously Missing Normal Primaries and the Pathological Dimensions

The factor-pattern matrices reproduced in Table 5 (Chapter Two) leave no doubt that seven more normal primary source traits exist than were originally taken into the 16 PF (they are now incorporated in the 16 PF Supplement). One knew that the "missing factors" were somewhere in the domain, for even before the markers for the 16 PF supplement became available, factorings of 16 PF material regularly added less defined extra factors, and a verdict of 19 to 22 in all was common. Cattell and Vaughan (1973b, 1973c) checked this verdict by adding the maximum-likelihood test to the scree test and confirmed that more than 20 factors are needed in the domain. The "seven missing factors" (Chapter Two, Section 7) are no longer missing, but the scales for them are so recent that the absence of criterion relations forces the interpretations which now follow to be brief and tentative. However, *D* and *J*, which belong with the seven missing factors at the adult level, have been known long enough at the child level to have yielded criterion relations, permitting *D* to be given the more extended treatment of the last section.

Description of the New Normal Primaries *J*, *K*, *P*, Q_5, Q_6, and Q_7. *J: Coasthenia-Zeppia*. This factor has distinct resemblances in meaning to Q_2, self-sufficiency, from which it nevertheless separates factor-analytically. It is both a subtle and an important factor; its importance is indicated by its association with reflective withdrawal, low interest in schoolwork and group activities, certain varieties of delinquency, low popularity with peers, and subaverage school activity interest. However, the coasthenic child does somewhat better than average in mathematics (Barton, Dielman, and Cattell, 1972) and in English (Cattell and Butcher, 1968), and gets some ratings for independent creativity.

From clinical descriptions of high *J* (coasthenic) children the factor seems to enter all three asthenia syndromes (hence coasthenia)—psychasthenia, neurasthenia, and obsessional schizoid asthenia. We hypothesize that the autistic child as defined by Rimland (1964) will have high scores on the coasthenia scale. Coasthenia is part of the second-order invia factor (see loading in Table 20, Chapter Four), just as its opposite, zeppia, is part of exvia. Zeppia has the vigorous but less thoughtful group identification expression "Let's go!" $J+$, coasthenia, has been well described as the Hamlet factor. The ratings show that the high J individual is cagey and wary of people and careful not to involve himself with them. His home background shows more than average behavioral control by the mother and less than average by the father (Barton, Dielman, and Cattell, 1972). At the same time, in spite of "laziness" and nonparticipation he has confidence in his own thinking and is willing to stand by his decisions. This trait might represent the combined effect on an initial self-will and subsequent punishing experience of the reaction of others to it.

K: Mature Socialization-Boorishness. The pattern comes out in ratings with emphasis on polished, self-disciplined, superior, and cultured, but the mental interior of the questionnaire shows more sensitive concern for humanity and unassuming, "gentlemanly," kindly qualities. The first theory entertained was that it simply represented years of education, but preliminary criterion relations point to something more specific—either temperamental or through generations of home background—representing the core of the classical ideal of a gentleman. At the opposite pole is a brutish boorishness.

Conceptually there may be difficulty in separating this from the self-sentiment, Q_3, except that the latter is a broader, dynamic, and ambitious involvement with the self concept. The high K individual according to the items likes school, is interested in social service and community affairs, and believes in training his mind and supporting ethical values. He is analytical, thoughtful, and open-minded and concerned that the feelings and aspirations of individuals be respected and defended against trespass.

P: Sanguine Casualness. The high P person enjoys discussion, feels happy, is unambitious, self-assured, not very well organized for efficiency and practical goals, modest and reasonable, casual, speculative, optimistic, and able to cope. He busies himself with varied interests but is at times hypomanic and sometimes anxious through dilemmas reached through impracticality of life style. The newly discovered loading of this primary on the second-order Independence (IV) trait fits, and brings out, the fundamental sense of personal independence here.

Q_5: Group Dedication with Sensed Inadequacy. This—and Q_6 and Q_7 below—continue the questionnaire factors of which no trace has yet been found in observer behavior ratings: hence Q. The high Q_5 individual has a wholehearted devotion to the life of groups, along with some haunting sense that people feel he is not doing as well as he should. The fact that its chief second-order loading is in the good upbringing factor VIII, along with superego, G, and self-sentiment, Q_3, suggests that it may be a more specific direction of upbringing in responsibility regarding community activity.

Q_6: Social Panache. This trait presents a consistent pattern but not one about whose causes one can presently theorize. A clinician might call

it paranoid and class it generically with the L factor of protension, since the individual believes he is being unfairly treated by society and made a whipping boy for the faults of others. There are, however, also signs of a general insecurity amounting to panic in relation to society. A search must be made with more items to see whether it has a pattern of wider meaning.

Q_7: *Explicit Self-Expression.* As suggested in Chapter Two, this most weakly defined independent factor could be peculiar to our times in that the values expressed tend to be avante garde. However, the passion for self-expression, dramatic entertainment, and garrulity with cronies is at least as old as Falstaff and Marlowe and the Emperor Nero. In general the high Q_7 individual is somewhat bohemian in his ways, with interests in drama, and given to exciting conversation. Until nature-nurture evidence is available one may suspect that most of the pattern comes from environment.

Pathological Primaries. The accounts of the pathological primaries must be kept brief because of the need for condensation. The following twelve source traits are involved.

D_1: *Hypochondriasis.* Although this trait was first located as one of the D (depression) factors it is now clear that hypochondriasis—preoccupation with bodily disabilities, ill health, or even ordinary function—is central. Indeed it correlates strongly with MMPI hypochondriasis. This trait is at its highest in psychotic depressives but is also high in simple schizophrenics (Cattell and Schmidt, 1972).

D_2: *Suicidal Disgust.* It is probably incorrect to associate suicidal tendencies exclusively with any one depression factor. However, this D_2 pattern expresses strong suicidal thoughts with general disgust with life and aggression against the self and others. Depressives and schizophrenics score significantly higher than other psychotic groups.

D_3: *Brooding Discontent or Ennui.* There seem to be fewer items in this pattern with straight depression in them than in the other Ds. The central theme is ennui—wanting something exciting to happen. The individual is phlegmatic and unworrying, yet restless and in love with risk and novelty. This trait is unusually high in psychopaths and those with personality disorders. Its difference from the generality of depression factors is also shown by its aligning only weakly with them in the second orders.

D_4: *Anxious Depression.* This combination of depression and anxiety has in some factorings simply been considered as anxiety. The individual is tense, easily upset, on edge, and clumsy in handling things; he is prey to disturbing dreams and is irritable and lacking in self-confidence. This trait suggests the syndrome of agitated depression. Its relation to the pure anxiety factor QII, however, is strangely not marked, and this finding of the distinctness of anxious depression from anxiety deserves intensive investigation. A high score on D_4 distinguishes neurotic depressives and alcoholics.

D_5: *Low Energy, Fatigued Depression.* This trait distinguishes itself readily from the other depressions by the predominance of weariness—of feeling too tired to cope. As in D_4, however, there is also worrying and dread, but centrally there is insufficient sleep and constant weariness. One theory is that this factor expresses the cumulative effect of conflict, anxiety, and overwork. (Neurasthenia is a term traditionally applied to similar expressions.) This trait is unusually high in the personality disorder category and significantly below normal in manic diagnosis (Cattell and Schmidt, 1972).

D_6: *Guilt and Resentment with Depression.* Here a tendency to self-blame, self-criticism, and groundless guilt is central to the depression. As in D_4 there is sleeplessness and agitation, susceptibility to nightmares, and some somatic upsets; but "having done something horribly wrong" and being rejected by mankind is the main pattern. This traits shows its highest clinical deviation in alcoholics and neurotic depressives.

D_7: *Bored Depression.* Withdrawal from people (most of whom one does not enjoy) and a feeling of pointlessness in life are central here. (Hamlet: "I take no pleasure in man, nor woman, either"; "fie on't oh fie, 'tis an unweeded garden that grows to seed.") One might theorize that there are schizoid components in this depression rather than any association with the manic-depressive pattern. Wishing to be alone is more salient than in other *D*s. Nevertheless the clinical scores show it to be unusually high in manics although it is also high in schizophrenics (relative to normal controls).

It should be noted in attempts to interpret the *D* factors by evidence other than questionnaires that the four second-order factors among them discussed in the last chapter have been hypothesized to coincide with UI 22, pathemia; UI 23, regression; UI 28, asthenia; and perhaps UI 33 in T-data (Cattell and Schmidt, 1972). From the pathological factors that first appeared broadly in the depression area we now turn to the five that originally appeared in the MMPI factor space (beyond the 16 PF).

Pa: Paranoid Tendency. This is the typical psychiatric paranoid tendency, expressed here, however, as a discrete component in various syndromes rather than literally shaped on a paranoid schizophrenic syndrome. It loads beliefs that one is being persecuted, poisoned, controlled, spied on, mistreated, and that no one is to be trusted. Highest scores are found in paranoid schizophrenics.

Pp: Psychopathic Deviation. The high scorer is immune to criticism, likes crowds, and is complacent about antisocial, immoral action by himself or others. He enjoys conflict, needs little sleep, and does not mind being considered deviant. Again the factor pattern coincides closely with the actual syndrome. The highest scores, apart from those of psychopaths, have been found in drug addicts, a fact which separates them from alcoholics.

Sc: Schizophrenia. The high scorer feels misunderstood, disliked, maltreated. He is beset by irrational impulses, fancies, and hallucinations; he has difficulty expressing himself and forgets familiar things and where he is. Again factor and syndrome are close—except for paranoid schizophrenia, which combines *Pa* and *Sc* dimensions. As expected the highest scores are found in most types of schizophrenia.

As: Psychasthenia. The high scorer is compulsive and worries about trifling rituals. He has nevertheless compulsive ideas—seldom or never expressed—toward disorderliness. Repetitive checkings and countings are symptomatic. Again factor and syndrome are close; the highest scale scores have been found in alcoholics.

Ps: General Psychosis and Maladapted Disintegration. This factor, although it is probably the most general in distinguishing all kinds of psychotics from normals, seems to have little of the poor reality-contact and emotional irrationality hypothesized to constitute general psychosis. It loads largely a sense of inability to cope with life, unworthiness, and especially inferiority. This person considers himself no good at all. The scale scores are highest on the personality disorders and schizophrenia; the most extreme scores appear in the schizophrenic subgroup.

If, as hypothesized in Chapter Four, the second-order factor running through at least five pathological scales has a good claim to being general psychosis, the present factor dimension has to be reexamined. Its strong presence in the personality disorders and in schizophrenia suggests that it represents some general maladaptation and disintegration distinct from mood disorders and rooted in inappropriate dynamic habit systems.

7. The Secondaries: Exvia, Anxiety, Cortertia, Independence, Discreetness, Subjectivity, Intelligence, and Good Upbringing

Research on associations of the second-order factors is not as advanced as for the primaries so a briefer format will be adopted in bringing out their psychological meaning. However, many real-life criteria have been calculated for them, including occupational and clinical averages, specification equation weights, and changes under influences. Calculation of these values is accurately achieved by combining the values for the primaries according to the appropriate weights (Chapter Four). Such a presentation would be disproportionate for this book but is available in the second-order survey by Cattell and Nichols (1972) and in the CTS Kit Handbook by Barton and Cattell (1973a). Without detailed reference its findings underlie the following conclusions.

QI: Exvia-Invia. This concept is commonly and correctly traced to Jung, although, as Roback (1927) shows, the English characterologists described it in rough style a century or two earlier. With the popular terms extraversion-introversion, however, it has unfortunately come in the last 30 years to mean almost anything. Thus we have attempted to salvage the scientific core of meaning—as soon as its uniqueness was established by the second-order QI and the psychometrically defined UI 32 in objective tests—by adopting the terms exvia-invia (living outward or inward; from Latin *vita*). We can thus speak of exviant and inviant traits and people.

By averaging 10 second-order studies we find that exvia accounts for about one-third of the variance of the first three primaries (*A, F,* and *H*) and about one-half of Q_2. What is the nature of such a general influence? Could it be a single genetic component in all of them, variously developed by specific environmental additions in the different primaries? One way to check this is to compare the loading on the second-stratum factor—as to ranks on Q_2 *F, H, A*—with the heritabilities, which according to approximations in Table 25, rank *F,* Q_2, *H,* and *A*. The hypothesis is not unpromising but exact work on the heritabilities, correlating them with already well-estimated loadings on primaries, alone can answer this.

Although the best definition for a second order is that it is something that acts on several primaries, the exactness of present work is not such as to rule out for exvia the alternative interactional emergence or spiral-feedback theory (that certain sets of primaries mutually stimulate growth). Psychologically one can understand such mechanisms and the theory also fits the factual indications that second order loadings may increase over the developmental period (compare, for example, HSPQ and 16 PF tables in Chapter Four). This learning theory explanation would suppose, for example, that a child born with high surgency (F having high heritability), quick in the skills which make him "the life and soul of the party," will become more dominant (*E*) from social reward. His attracting of more friends and acquaintances will also increase affectia (*A*), since he will respond to warmth with warmth.

As primary scales of higher validity enter experiment, and larger samples determine secondaries more exactly, choice between the theory of secondaries as distinct influence and as spiral-feedback products can be made, as well as extension of choice to a third now to be mentioned. (Such experiment would begin by comparing loadings over development.) The third theory rests on the empirical indication that *E,* dominance, loads higher in the child secondary and on new information from the nature of the objective tests that load the factor UI 32 which aligns exactly (Chapter Seven) with questionnaire exvia (Q_1). These behavioral measures show high exvia with willingness to risk decisions on vague data, quicker social and other judgments, higher optimism, more disregard of rules, and freedom from depressive inhibition over mistakes. The theory may be called that of *susceptibility to social inhibition* and supposes that the exviant individual, by a summation of genetic endowment and life experience low in social punishment, responds less strongly to social inhibition.

This social inhibitability theory must not be confused with Eysenck's reactive inhibition theory (Eysenck, 1970) based on a reflexological concept from Hull and Pavlov. The latter is operationally recognized by declining response with repeated unrewarded stimulation (exvia); the former by genetically greater autonomic and other threat response among inviants, which by experience has become relatively strongly conditioned to social stimuli. By this theory the genetic component is shared by *F, H,* and perhaps *A,* while the rest, including Q_2(—), comes from a social environment marked by little inhibition.

The family, school, occupational, and clinical associations of exvia-invia have not been so precisely worked out as have those of primaries. However, Eysenck has documented that neurotics tend to be highly anxious and inviant; the analysis of Cattell, Eber, and Tatsuoka (1970, p. 265) fully agrees. This latter analysis extends to other secondaries and shows, in accord with Cattell and Scheier (1961), that neurotics are as deviant on the third factor—III—, pathemia-cortertia—as on invia. In short, invia (I—), anxiety (II) (Eysenck's "neuroticism"), and pathemia (III—) are all necessary to account for neuroticism. Our findings also show that drug addicts, children referred to clinics, and a variety of other clinical groups (except psychopaths) deviate in the inviant direction. In the life of normal families the work of Barton shows that, as might well be expected, couples that average low on exvia participate less in community affairs, and, less explicably, that male dominance (patriarchalism) in the family is correlated with introversion.

QII: Anxiety. Although there are disagreements between Comrey, Eysenck, and myself about the technical factorial basis that objectively and uniquely defines these concepts, general agreement exists on anxiety and exvia. The problem is that the discoveries in the Illinois laboratory uniquely define eight to nine second orders, whereas Comrey and Eysenck have constructed scales aligning well only with two (possibly more in Comrey's case). Explicit disagreement remains even on the two first regarding terminology, for *Q*II is called "neuroticism" by Eysenck whereas Comrey calls its opposite "emotional stability," implying that he is referring to (low) ego strength (*C* factor).

In this area the recent vice of depending wholly on automatic computer rotation solutions, yielding patterns of low factor-trueness, has combined with casual popular naming practices, neglecting years of scholarship in the field, to produce substantial confusion. Unnecessary contributions to such confusion are the naming of anxiety as "emotional instability" or "neurosis," and exvia as "sociability." Instability, as actual behavior, is multiply determined mainly by ego weakness ($C(-)$) and ergic tension (Q_4), but anxiety also includes $H(-)$, L, and $Q_3(-)$, which can scarcely be called instability. Similarly the concept of exvia or extraversion is far more rich and precise in meaning than Howarth and Browne's description as "sociability." As for the confusion from calling anxiety "neuroticism" in the Eysenck EPI it must be pointed out that extensive studies from 1955 to 1968 (including Cattell and Scheier, 1961; Karson, 1960, 1961; Karson and Haupt, 1968; Kear-Colwell, 1965; Rickels and Cattell, 1965) show that neurotics differ significantly on several other factors besides anxiety, *Q*II. From a strictly psychometric standpoint Nunnally (1961, 1967) has also cogently made this point.

From the above identification as a unique second-stratum factor one can proceed to the associated definition in physiological terms (see the two experimentally oriented volumes of Spielberger, 1966, 1972). Anxiety at the physiological level is definable as a state of high general automatic factor activity (not just sympathetic system; see factor analysis of autonomic manifestations in Cattell, 1950a). The combined psychophysiological response can be quantitatively expressed in a mathematical model (Spielberger, 1972, p. 150) as a final function and outcome of general drive-strength level, degree of drive denial, cognitive uncertainty, instability of ego control, integration, guilt proneness, and sympathetic reactivity to threat. These are in fact (except for cognitive uncertainty, which is situational) the primary factor terms in the second-order pattern discovered above—respectively appearing as Q_4 (strength and denial), $C-$, Q_3-, O, and $H-$ (with L as a side expression). Thus as with exvia the second order is in this case considered as a product of mutually interacting primaries.

There is another problem here: that psychologists have long recognized as a general level a distinction between anxiety as a state and as a characterological trait. Until we reach in Chapter Five the technical means for separating the state from the trait the present evidence should perhaps be said to concern the trait. However, we can point out that loadings on the questionnaire primaries are the same for state and trait except for a tendency of *C, O,* and Q_4 to loom larger in the state. Indeed this superposition of state on trait correlations produces such high intercorrelations of *C*—, *O,* and Q_4 (in certain situations) that researchers with rough analyses have sometimes concluded that they are not separable primaries (Rican and others, 1970).

A parallel problem of separating the state pattern (PUI 9 in the state list) from the trait pattern (UI 24 in the trait factor index) exists in objective (T-data) and physiological measures, and the recent work of Barton, Bartlett, Nesselroade and Scheier (summarized in Cattell, 1972a) has shown the consistency of state and trait concepts in Q- and T-data. In Q-data the Barton and Cattell (1973a) CTS Kit illustrates the nature of the questionnaire items which best separate them. The practical problem of separation is incompletely solved (see Chapter Six) but conceptually the techniques are now clear.

Concerning the enormous number of physiological, social, educational, familial, and other associations that have been documented for anxiety, the reader must be referred to such basic sources as Barton, Dielman and Cattell (1972), Cattell and Butcher (1968), Eysenck and Eysenck (1969), Lazarus and Opton (1966), Rickels and others (1965), Cattell and Scheier (1961), Sarason (1966), and Spielberger (1966, 1972). A new domain of relationships has recently opened up in family and community life, where Barton and Cattell (1972a) show that high anxiety is related to less marital sex gratification, less effective marital role-sharing, less participation in community affairs, less patriarchal structure, and less social and intellectual equality of the couple's parental backgrounds. Cattell and Stice (196) have shown the demoralizing effect of anxiety in small groups and Lynn (1971) has brought out important relations to national culture pattern features. The strong associations with most neurotic (but not psychotic) conditions and with relatively poor scholastic performance have long been documented.

QIII: Cortertia-Pathemia. The antithesis of trait-poles here is more subtle than between exvia-invia or high and low anxiety. It is helpful to consider the pattern from both poles, beginning with the negative pathemia. Every primary pole in pathemia—affectia *A,* premsia *I,* autia *M* (and some guilt proneness and ego weakness)—points to a relaxed and even indulgent life of feeling. The individual is warm, sentimental, and daydreaming, likes art and drama, and lives in his sensitive emotions but particularly melancholy ones. This trait has been called pathemia (from Greek *pathos,* feeling) and it has been called speculatively "living at the hypothalamic level." At the contrasting pole the individual is alert and realistic, with feelings cool and under control, and with practical effectiveness as the main concern. This has been called cortertia, a shortening of the earlier title "cortical alertness," indicating a functional predominance of cerebral cortical action.

Part of the understanding of this dimension has come from the indication, still awaiting confirmation, that it is the Q-data equivalent of the personality dimension measured in T-data by UI 22. The latter is also called cortertia-pathemia and includes at the cortertia pole rapid reaction time, ideomotor speed, endurance of difficulty, less fluency on emotional than unemotional themes, and fewer aggressive (frustrated?) interpretations of pictures. This again fits the cortical rather than the emotional level of response, and associated criteria add evidence that pathemia arises partly from frustration and discouragement.

Presently known criterion associations include a strong relation of pathemia to neuroticism and a moderate one to depression. In life (Barton and R. B. Cattell, 1972b, 1972c) pathemia relates to having had an unhappy love affair, to having moved from the parental home, to having left the home town, and to residence in college. Pathemia as measured by objective tests, in UI 22(—), is at least as associated as invia and almost as much as anxiety, with neurotic conditions (Cattell and Scheier, 1961), and it tends to be associated with chronic illness of any kind. Its opposite (cortertia) is associated with success as a military pilot and in all other occupational performances that have been tested. Cortertia also seems to be associated with heavy use of alcohol (perhaps as a temporary relief in decortication). Cortertia increases in married people relative to unmarried, and pathemia increases in those who drink heavily. High cortertia scores of couples are associated with stability of marriage (Barton and Cattell, 1972a) and with the maintenance of individual independence by the partners. Although criterion data are only a decade old it is evident that corteria-pathemia is going to play an important role in psychometric diagnosis and prediction.

QIV: Independence-Subduedness. This pattern, which loads E strongly, F, and H strongly, and L, M, and Q_2 slightly, overlaps in three of its primaries with exvia. Although researchers repeatedly announce a second extraversion factor, close scrutiny usually reveals it to be this *Q*IV pattern or the *Q*III cortertia factor. The resemblance of I to IV in Q-data is admittedly appreciable but nothing is gained by calling *Q*IV a variety of exvia. Exvia, as *Q*I, undoubtedly aligns excellently with T-data factor UI 32 but *Q*IV has indications of aligning, if anywhere, with UI 19, independence. UI 19 includes perceptual field independence, much studied by Witkin (1962), as well as few erroneous reactions under complex instructions, high severity of judgment, and logical consistency of attitudes (Hundleby, Pawlik, and Cattell, 1965). *Q*IV is also associated with needing little sleep, with drinking and nonconformity in youth, with making many social contacts, with criticism by parents in adolescence, with rejection of sexual restraint. Higher scores on *Q*IV are associated significantly with little devotion to the home but with high ratings of sexual gratification in marriage.

The opposite pole, subduedness, is high in those who have suffered loss of close relatives and friends. Significant increments in independence are recorded in those who go to college and in those who gain many social contacts. It moves significantly in the subdued direction among those who frequently change jobs (Barton and Cattell, 1972c). It decreases with age. Its general nature is clearly a prestine self-will as opposed to a general taming by experience and deprivation.

QV: Discreetness-Naturalness. This factor is largely shrewdness *N*, socialization *A*, and explicit self-expression Q_7; it contributes little to most primaries. So far its criterion relations are practically unexplored. However, it is initially high in those who have a great number of social contacts and it increases more rapidly in those who keep many contacts than in those who do not. Its general meaning seems to be a set of acquired skills and attachments in social activities with some indications of pose rather than naturalness, and possibly an exploitative use of social skills.

QVI: Prodigal Subjective Idealism–Detached Realism. This factor is principally autia and radicalism and some self-sufficiency. It is thus an imaginative interest in idealistic change in relation to subjective goals as opposed to a practical accepance of existing realities. It could have considerable criterion importance in social psychology. Present evidence indicates that it is initially higher in entering college students than in those who do not start college and that it increases more rapidly in the 18–22 year range among those in college than among those with jobs.

QVII: Intelligence. There is no evidence that this trait is factorily different at the second-order analysis of the 16 PF than at the first order. It is really a second-stratum factor scale artificially inserted (in the 16 PF, HSPQ, CPQ) among first-stratum factors for the convenience of those who need a general ability measure among personality measures. Theoretically one might expect it as a higher order to have more of the character of fluid intelligence than of crystallized intelligence (with the primaries) but nothing of this kind has been demonstrated.

QVIII: Good Upbringing. This factor has such a substantial variance contribution to primaries that with more evidence one would have placed it earlier in the series at QV rather than at rank QVIII where the first research indications seemed to place it. The simultaneous loading centrally of superego strength and then of self-sentiment, desurgency, and low dominance clearly gives it the character of the impress of a good upbringing in morals and manners. In exercising control to build superego values and the social values of the self-sentiment, the good upbringing has necessarily also increased general restraint and thus reduced surgency and dominance. The theory of good moral upbringing and personal discipline leads one to expect little genetic correlation but considerable social and psychological associations with family, social class, church affiliation, and low delinquency, although these relations have not been explored. Cross-culturally this factor has smaller variance in Venezuela and Brazil than in Germany, New Zealand, and the United States, which suggests a Catholic-Protestant cultural difference.

Among criteria it is associated with being chosen a leader in face-to-face groups, with experience of bereavement and unsuccessful love affairs, with rejection of immoderate drinking, with staying at college rather than dropping out, with absence of criticism by parents in adolescence, and with church activity. It increases with getting married, with having fewer social contacts, and with taking on increased job responsibilities.

No criterion relations, genetic, or age data have been accumulated regarding the five tertiary factors defined in Chapter Four, so that no interpretive theoretical developments can be made here.

8. Summary

(1) Research leading to accurate recognition of trait and state structures and to the development of valid measurement instruments for them is merely the prologue to the real concerns of personality theory. Producing structured personality-scales as distinct from making questionnaire tests, for testing sake, is a vital part of the scientific enterprise of sharpening theoretical concepts. Furthermore, beyond offering increase in precision and testability of theories, the bringing of structured tests to finished, standard form provides the chief means for reaching developmental laws. The present chapter has thereby offered substantial information about the "natural history" of primary and secondary traits—their genetic components, age curves, family and social background associations, and manner of growth by learning.

(2) Two main methods—the twin and the MAVA method—have been applied to measure the heritability of primary and secondary traits. Although this work has initially been on small samples the larger samples of Klein and Cattell (1973) now give reasonably consistent results placing primaries approximately in the following declining order of heritability *B, F, J, I, A, L, C, H, G, M,* Q_3, *D, E, O, N,* Q_2, Q_4, and Q_1. For secondaries this is *Q*I (Exvia), *Q*III (Cortertia), *Q*II (Anxiety) and *Q*IV (Independence) while the complex of primaries constituting neuroticism is about as high as exvia. The central tendency in the H values is about fifty-fifty heredity and environment, ranging from about 80 percent to 10 percent hereditary.

This information on heritabilities mainly fits but also extends the theoretical concepts about the source traits. For instance, the autonomic and body build associations found for *F* and *H* agree with their higher genetic determination, while the conceptions of Q_4 as situational frustration and Q_1 as exposure to radical or conservative atmospheres fit their high environmental determination. It looks as if the heritability of the secondaries is essentially an average of that of the constituent primaries, yielding less diverse and distinctive H values than for primaries and supporting the theory that these secondaries, at least, are interactional derivatives of primaries rather than distinct new influences upon primaries.

(3) Empirically obtained plots of trait change with age can be analyzed into endogenous and exogenous components and each of these into ecogenic and epogenic components. Computing relations of longitudinal,

cursive, and cross-sectional measurements will separate these; but present evidence regarding personality source traits rests on cross-sectional data only. To permit comparisons among different source traits, the vertical scale has to be one of stens within a single year group although more sophisticated developments of this approach (such as pan-normalization) are possible. By building in tandem the curves from the ESPQ, CPQ, HSPQ, and 16 PF it is possible to present plots for the first time on 17 primary and 6 secondary source traits for males and females from 6 to 60 years of age.

(4) The primaries show highly idiosyncratic patterns, but they have moderate family resemblances according to the secondaries in which they cohere. However, it is clear even theoretically that such coherence must be limited because any primary is likely to appear in more than one secondary. In fact Q_2 in exvia-invia sometimes behaves differently from *A, F,* and *H,* whereas ego strength and ergic tension behave quite differently in the anxiety contributors from *H, L, O,* and Q_3. The chief differences in the forms of the curves are in the 6–20 year range. Although a few trends after age 20 are linear, most require a quadratic equation for a best fit.

(5) There is a general tendency to sharp changes in the curves around adolescence, followed by a gentle maximum or minimum in adult life, and therefore only slight change. The nature of the changes—for example, upset of the self-sentiment Q_3 in adolescence, steep fall of premsia *I* from childhood, steady increase of ego strength *C* into maturity—almost without exception fits the concepts developing about these source traits.

(6) A substantial array of evidence has been organized over the past 20 years on physical, occupational, educational, clinical, social, and family associations with score levels on the primaries and to some extent on the secondaries. Recently a five-year cursive longitudinal study relating personality change in 800 individuals to events in their lives has added to interpretive possibilities. On the basis of this evidence theories of the nature and origin of the various primaries are here examined and modified to more precise forms.

(7) A similar examination of theories about the secondaries reveals that exvia-invia and anxiety probably do not conform to the usual model of second orders as influences on primaries but are mutual interaction or spiral feedback products of a developmentally interacting group of primaries. In terms of significant criterion associations cortertia *Q*III and independence *Q*IV may be as important as anxiety *Q*II and exvia *Q*I. These four secondaries appear to measure the same personality factors in Q-data as UI 22, 19, 24, and 32 measure in T-data. The concepts concerning the secondaries are thus becoming clear, at any rate for six of them: exvia, anxiety, good upbringing, cortertia, intelligence, and independence.

(8) Certain generalizations possible from data in this chapter must be considered contingent on the evidence in the next chapter that what are now measured as traits may prove to be mixtures of traits and states. Thus this is incomplete in that some inferences have to be left in the air pending introduction of new technical concepts. On the other hand the presentation

is highly comprehensive and up-to-date in including both primaries and secondaries, as well as the seven primaries missing until two years ago, and the twelve newer pathological primaries.

(9) Although the first 7 of the 12 pathological primaries were initially called depression factors, they have broader pathological meanings. Indeed the first stands out as strictly pathological hypochondria. These primaries nevertheless tend to correlate mutually to a degree which shows some common generic character and which, indeed renders their separation difficult in some groups. Despite the general psychometric model which says that surface traits (syndromes) need not correspond to single source traits it would seem that most of the last five pathological source traits correspond to recognized pathological syndromes. Thus paranoia *Pa* corresponds closely to what is seen in paranoia and paranoid schizophrenia, psychopathia *Pp* to the psychopathic personality, and schizophrenia *Sc* to some underlying result of processes that we recognize in what is common to the schizophrenias. However, a clear second-order general psychoticism factor participates in all six psychotic primaries (including hypochondriasis) and a general depression factor covers most of the depressions.

VI

Moods and Source States: Methods and Findings

That *moods, states* and temporary *roles* may be as important as trait structures in understanding and predicting behavior was recognized in Chapter One, where the general conception of representing particular moods by scores on a limited number of dimensions called *source states* was introduced. Each such dimension stretches from low to high on a particular *state-response pattern,* that is, the response is a pattern of many elements. Thus a source state such as anxiety defines a whole pattern of manifestations—a more rapid pulse, a feeling of restlessness, a fall in electrical skin resistance, a sense of foreboding and inadequacy—arising from a single *internal response* that can be evoked in varying degrees.

1. Discovering States as Unitary Response Patterns by P- and dR-Techniques

To isolate and describe these unitary primary state patterns we need two devices: a method of experiment and calculation capable of recognizing and isolating the distinct patterns of response, the parts of which rise and fall together with stimulation; and a way of separating in any observed behavior the part due to traits from that due to states. Both of these goals can be achieved by forms of multivariate experiment called P-technique and dR-technique, but these techniques must be used strategically with the familiar individual-difference factoring we have so far used, R-technique.

In P-technique—so named (Cattell, Cattell, and Rhymer, 1947) because it is factor analysis of the single *person*—some *n* variables believed to be responsive to mood are measured on one person over N (perhaps 100) occasions. Figure 2 (Chapter One) shows how the scores of variables, each subset due largely to a different state, are likely to covary over time. Instead of attempting to separate the states visually we take this as a score matrix for correlation. Thus each variable has its scores—over, say 100 days—correlated with the corresponding daily scores on all other variables, producing the usual square-correlation matrix. This is then factored to find how many independent influences are necessary to account for the observed covariation. These are the independent state-response dimensions. To locate them uniquely we use simple structure as with traits since the same arguments hold here for expecting simple structure, namely, that one state is unlikely to affect all conceivable variables.

The second method—differential R-technique or dR for short—measures N people on *n* variables on two occasions sufficiently far apart for everyone to have changed his mood somewhat. The score matrix is N people assigned *n* chance (difference) scores. (Scaling problems about these difference scores are discussed in Chapter Eight.) The factor analysis yields *K* dimensions of unitary state change that are capable of accounting for the manifold changes observed between the two occasions.

These two methods, applied in programatic work with coordinated sets of variables, have revealed since the first study (Cattell, Cattell, and Rhymer, 1947) nine or ten state dimensions. As elsewhere in this book, although my central concern is with the nature and validity of the *questionnaire* measures I recognize that full support for the meaning of these factors rests on integration with general personality theory and on alignment of these Q-data patterns with observations through other media. There is every reason to expect that the mental interiors revealed by questionnaires should correspond with patterns of physiological change, especially in such states as anxiety, arousal, effort stress, depression, regression, exvia, and fatigue. Consequently in setting out the questionnaire evidence on these nine or ten states I shall also look at T-data, that is, at evidence of their existence in objective tests, especially physiological and biochemical measures.

Certain methodological and conceptual problems are best dealt with immediately, even though in some abstraction, since without these concepts the evidence that follows lacks the full richness of its meaning. The problems to be faced are with one exception not peculiar to Q-data; they belong to the general methodology of state recognition in all observation media (Harris, 1963, 1967; Nesselroade, 1966; Cattell, 1957, 1971b; Cattell and Barton, 1973). Since two methods have been proposed for discovering state concepts the following question arises: How similar is a state pattern found by P-technique to one found by dR-technique? Each has its peculiar limitations of evidence. P-technique takes one person and measures the patterns of his responses to the emotional stimuli that life presents over, say, 100 days. These patterns might be idiosyncratic in that one person has more happiness and another more sorrow and stress in his life. But this is not what the investigator is worried about; his only concern is to find the distinctive *patterns* of emotional expression. What he wants to check is whether the patterns of expression for, say, anxiety or elation in Dick are different from those in Joe. Thus the restriction of P-technique is that without further comparisons we cannot assume we have the correct loading pattern of any state in question.

The second approach—dR-technique (*differential R-Technique*)—takes a good sample of people on Monday and retests them with the same state variables on Tuesday (or next month). If there are *n* variables it then takes *n* difference scores. These scores must represent state changes due to the different emotional stimuli that people meet between Monday and Tuesday. Factoring these scores reveals the independent dimensions required to account for mood change (traits cannot enter a difference score). They are common dimensions because they describe change for all people. But unlike the P-technique they do not rest on a good sample of days. If a stock-exchange crash occurred on Tuesday morning it could be argued that the anxiety pattern is peculiar to that one incident. Thus P- and dR-techniques have reciprocal strengths: P is strong on sampling occasions and dR on sampling people. The dR-technique may take, say, 50 questionnaire items or other (such as physiological state) variables and measure them on 20 occasions on each of 10 people. The 10 people are then put in a series, yielding a total of 200 occasions of measurement. (The means—and the sigmas too if the experimenter wishes—will first be equalized for the several subjects, before joining up their score matrices in a chain. In this way no interindividual (personality) difference is confounded with the intraindividual (state) change variance.)

This chain P-technique calculation gives the state patterns as common unitary states defined across people and occasions. (It is technically called a grid design; Cattell, 1966a, pp. 99–104.) That is, the two kinds of factor (from P- and dR-techniques) are now bound to be the same because the two sources of variance and covariance are brought together for a common-factor analysis. Such experiments are rare (Barton and Cattell, in preparation (b); Cattell and Bolz, 1973) because gathering the experimental data is onerous and exacting. But the evidence accumulates that the state-response patterns—as *source states*—do not seem to change with different people and stimuli. This is not true of surface-state patterns. The mixture of anxiety, annoyance, and depression from missing a plane connection may be different from that due to losing a hundred dollars. Each of these mixtures is a surface-state pattern peculiar to the situation in view of the combination of source-state constituent scores. This observation is often mistaken for a refutation of the invariance of source-state patterns per se.

The psychologist who does research on states by P- and dR-techniques must handle a number of technical questions. At least four of these must be mentioned to ensure conceptual clarity. First, what is the psychometric and psychological effect of making repeated measures of the same variables? Briefly the learning or boredom created by repeated measures can probably be factored out (partialed out) from the true state part of the measurement.

Questionnaires in any case reduce such effects by using graphic scales to avoid repeating the same verbal answers and by employing a spread of four or more point answers to make it difficult to remember earlier answers. Second, will the pattern of a state be the same during the time it waxes in response to a stimulus as over the period when it wanes in response to homeostatic mechanisms? We do not know whether rising and falling state patterns are precisely the same but they are reasonably similar. Perhaps the conscious awareness rises early and the physiology slowly, and so on, which may account for difficulties in getting clear unity of a common Q- and T-data pattern in recent experiments (Cattell and Bartlett, 1971). Third, are such states as elation and depression to be considered opposite poles on a single dimension or distinct source states? State dimensions may be distinct yet highly correlated since high obliquities are more common than with traits. The fact that anxiety and depression factors tend to be positively correlated does not deny their distinctness as source states. The question remains whether apparent polar opposites are extremes of one dimension or two axes and patterns highly negatively correlated. Thus there has been debate as to whether (a) arousal and fatigue and (b) elation and depression are pairs of distinct states negatively correlated or one bipolar dimension. A tentative answer is that arousal and fatigue are not just opposites on the same axis nor is elation exactly a reversal of depression; precise factor analysis is necessary to achieve separation. Fourth and last, are the relations of manifestations to state response linear and additive or are they curvilinear and interactive? For example, if fatigue and excitement occur together, are levels on variables expressing them predicted by simple addition of the two influences? The answer is that we do not know for sure but that in using models we must walk before we run. The linear-additive model works well enough for initial recognition and measurement of states. Later work can add the second-power term in the equation if it is needed.

In the statistical realm, as distinct from what is strictly the mathematical model just discussed, other questions arise. (1) Since a difference score has error of measurement at both ends and therefore twice as much error variance as an absolute score, what can be done to reduce the blurring of patterns likely to result? (2) Should we score individuals so that the changes of group mean (from occasion 1 and 2) are included in dR-analysis? (3) Must P-technique measures be uniformly spaced in time? Over how many occasions (say, with 40 item variables) must we take measures to get sufficient degrees of freedom for a stable factor-analytic result?

These may seem recondite questions to the uninitiated reader but they cannot be evaded if the psychological conceptions are to be clear.[1] One

[1] The procedure sometimes followed in dR-technique from force of habit in other realms, is to put the scores for the first occasion into standard scores and similarly for the second occasion and then subtract one from the other to get individual change scores. However, if the group as a whole has shifted on, say, anxiety level, because of something causing moderate consternation to all (an imminent exam, a stock-exchange crash) this effect will not register by that procedure since zero is the standard score mean on both occasions. My argument (in Harris, 1963) is that the dimensions of change are

issue that concerns more than statistical sampling deserves comment here. We are all aware that there are moods which change in a flash and others which seem to change very slowly, with their trains of attendant physiological associations. Theoretically it can be shown that all moods should be caught by P-technique or dR-technique having an interval between testing occasions greater than is needed to produce a discernible difference in the slowest of the phase cycles involved. But in practice problems of sampling occasions do appear and there is no doubt that we now need studies at different frequencies, some recording once or twice a day over months, for example, and others recording every half-minute over a few hours.

The basic behavioral specification equation in Chapter One has an initial form (1.1) in which an act is predicted from the behavioral situational indexes (*b*s) and the trait scores, and a second form (1.2) in which both trait and state scores are included to give a more complete and statistically improved estimate. The object of this chapter is to give substance to that general equation by showing what research has revealed about recognizing and scoring particular source states and by demonstrating how to add such scores into the criteria prediction calculation.

2. A First Harvest of State Patterns from P- and dR-Techniques and the Personality Sphere

Before turning to subtle issues regarding state definition and mode of action, it seems best to illustrate present concepts with initial findings. As with traits, so with states: a concept parallel to the *personality sphere* becomes indispensable. The sphere is based not only on words for mood

---

psychologically the same for the shift in mean as for the individual changes. Consequently the practice of putting both first and second-occasion raw scores into a single standardized (and often normalized) distribution (perhaps equating the sigmas of groups on occasions 1 and 2 before doing so) is better because it utilizes all the covariance instead of making a possibly distorting selection and losing information.

The practice clarified by Lord (1963) and others (see Cattell, 1966a) of partialing first out of second score in an attempt to reduce the role of error of measurement is scarcely to be recommended. As Cronbach (1960) recognizes, once the error of measurement is entangled in a difference measurement there is no way of getting it out without doing other damage to the scaling properties. In Lord's alternative we are forcing the scores to be such that no correlation can exist between the initial and the final or the gain score. Psychological laws may require that such a connection exists. However, this does not justify Cronbach's advice to those about to use difference scores. Like Punch's famous advice to those about to marry ("Don't"), it only evades the problem. The treatment required here is one aimed at reducing error of measurement in dR-technique more thoroughly than is usually done in R-technique. Even more important than reducing random error of measurement is ensuring that the best approach to equal interval scaling is made in the measures on the two occasions (Cattell, 1966a, p. 367). An exemplary treatment of these issues is available in Nesselroade and Cable (1972) and Bartsch and Nesselroade (1973).

The reduction of degrees of freedom in P-technique (due to serial correlation), although argued by Holtzmann (in Harris, 1963) to be dangerous, may be relatively trivial. However, P-technique should never be based on less than 50 occasions; and hopefully not less than 100 (depending on the number of variables).

states but on much that has been explored by pyschologists in the physiological and T-data investigation of emotions—a popular field since James and Lange. Such variables are well represented in the work of Darrow (1942), Gellhorn (1937), Seward (1946), Lindsley (1951), Freeman (1948), Luria (1932), Masserman (1943), Young (1943), Wenger (1940), and Uhr and Miller (1960). Initial blocking-in studies thus combined Q-, L-, and T-data in P-technique theses guided by myself (Rhymer, 1946; Baldwin, 1946) or carried out on a larger scale (Cattell, Cattell, and Rhymer, 1947; Cattell and Luborsky, 1950; Haverland, 1954; H. V. Williams, 1950, 1954). Although these studies did much to define distinct response patterns they were connected with questionnaire patterns in only limited segments and cannot be directly incorporated in this discussion of Q-data.

The present treatment will also exclude, except for tangential references, all that has been done on dynamic states of ergic tension, such as the work of J. R. Williams (1958) and of Cattell and DeYoung (1973b, 1973c). This exclusion of motivation and interest fluctuations is consistent with omitting the Edwards, the Jackson, and similar questionnaires from the trait discussion on the grounds that the questionnaire is not a dependable instrument for revealing need strengths. Since there are more promising and valid devices and principles in objective test approaches I relegate the measurement of ergic tension levels to those instruments. Although the general mood states and the specific drive states must eventually be related (see Cattell and Child, 1973) it is convenient in terms of present methodology to separate them. The division between *general* states—depression, fatigue, arousal, anxiety, stress—and *specific motivational* states—hunger, thirst, sex—can in fact be as readily drawn as in the corresponding general trait and interest fixation strength domain. Although the general states may be qualities that can be abstracted from the whole set of specific dynamic states, that still leaves them essentially different.[2]

The first adequate demonstration of state patterns in a sufficient

[2] A surprising amount of research labelled as done on states is actually evidence only about traits. The authors have actually done R-technique analyses and guessed that factors may be state dimensions. So, despite the energy lavished on them one cannot integrate even the best of these, for example, Borgatta (1962), Nowlis and Greene (1957), Thayer (1970), and certain parts of the otherwise true state work of Wessman and Ricks (1966) into dependable state psychology. As Curran (1968) rightly points out, the conceptual-methodological flaw in this work—as in the adjective checklist (Lorr and others, 1962) when used for states—is that R-technique rather than P- or dR-techniques was used as if it were capable of locating pure states. This confusion is all the more surprising since both theory and examples of the proper separation of traits and states were available a decade before these undertakings. There is in fact, from the single-occasion factorings used, no proof that the patterns these investigators found are not traits. However, Borgatta's fatigue, anxiety, affectia state, and depression patterns look like states and in view of the full R-technique equation could be states. Wessman and Ricks fully recognize the default from P-technique but perhaps through experimental difficulties do not rest their main conclusions on the latter and merely suggest the likelihood that several individual P-techniques would converge upon a common pattern. At that time the research of Cattell, Haverland, Karvonen, Luborsky, Rhymer, Scheier, and Williams had already shown such convergence in objective tests (Cattell, 1957).

sample of questionnaire items rests not on P-technique (which was then felt to offer technical difficulties to satisfactorily repeated application of Q-data) but in a dR-technique design by Cattell and Scheier (1961; indexed there as study CQ2) on the 16 PF. This study took 95 men and women on 187 form A 16 PF items and retested them nine months later. Six second-order factors were found but they manifested a lower standard of simple structure (51 percent in ±10) than was customary for traits. Such reduction is now realized to be unavoidable due to the double error of difference scores. The two largest patterns (see first columns of Table 26) revealed that essentially the same patterns appear for exvia and anxiety as states as in their earlier appearance as traits. This unexpected finding is examined below as a possible artifact. The results in this case hold up, however, and we have gradually been forced to recognize as a general law, over 30 or 40 comparisons of R- and dR-technique factor patterns, that all traits have corresponding states.

Although it makes sense that anxiety should appear as both a state and a trait, apparently no one had ever regarded extraversion-introversion as a state; it had always been considered a fixed temperamental trait. Yet the secondaries best defined at that time—exvia, anxiety, cortertia, and independence—appeared as states. What revision of psychological concepts does this require? Since states should appear alongside traits in R-technique we could simply abandon the idea that anything confidently described as a trait by R-technique research is a trait. This sweeping iconoclasm scarcely recommends itself; two generations of researchers on individual differences in the trait of intelligence are unlikely to believe that there is nothing but a state of intelligence. Or we might introduce a new concept—a third term between trait and state called a trait-change factor. This concept supposes that traits are not entirely fixed and permits us with dR-technique to see a pattern of variance smaller than for states and taking the pattern of traits established by R-technique. But before we seriously consider either this new concept of trait fluctuation patterns or the statistically possible but psychologically incredible solution of saying that all traits are nothing but states we should investigate the suspicion that images of traits appear in dR-technique by some kind of statistical artifact.

The two main ways in which factors paralleling traits in pattern and stimulating states in place of occurrence could be created artificially in dR-technique—that is by statistical or computational artifact—are through differences of (a) reliability and (b) variance on the two occasions of measurement. They have been thoroughly examined elsewhere (Cattell, 1966a, pp. 366–388; Harris, 1963, p. 366; Nesselroade and Cable, 1972; Nesselroade and Bartsch, 1973) and shown not to be adequate to account for the results.[3]

[3] The argument for a necessary resemblance of change factor patterns to original factors is sometimes presented as follows, where $T_{xi(1)}$ and $T_{xi(2)}$ are person i's scores on factor T_x on occasions 1 and 2. A score a_{ij} on the first occasion can be represented as:

$$a_{ij(1)} = b_{j1}\, T_{1i(1)} + \ldots + b_{jk}\, T_{ki(1)}$$

and that on the second as

Having recognized these possible sources of artifacts my colleagues and I took good care to control for them in our dR-studies. Despite such control, however, some change factors in essentially the same form as the trait patterns still appeared. Support for their reality came next from P-technique research. By the nature of the statistical operations in P-technique these artifacts could not be created—but the trait-change patterns still appeared. An additional argument for the functional unity of a trait is that it waxes and wanes in the same pattern as that found for it in R-technique. We have further assurance of the potency of simple structure from the fact that it locates the same patterns in the two kinds of experiment.

If we accept these P- and dR-operations as yielding an operational description of independent dimensions of mood state change (along with some trait-change patterns), we find that the primary factors A through Q_4 behave as states and that the second-order factors among them behave likewise. At this point let us dismiss the hypothesis that traits are nothing but states. To do so requires familiarity with statistical principles but it has been shown that in the instantaneous snapshot of an R-technique analysis we pick up states as well as traits. Moreover the variance of a state in dR-technique is twice that in R-technique. Consequently any pattern that is a state should appear in both R- and dR-technique, doubled in variance in the latter. But a simple trait appears in R- and not in dR-technique results. Applying this check we find that many factors in R-technique are indeed traits and not states in disguise. Once the patterns in R-technique are recognized and have scales built for them the trait-state distinction becomes simple. Application of the stability coefficient between two testings, say, a week apart should thus yield near unity for traits and near zero for states.[4] At least three studies by dR-technique with two markers per primary

---

$$a_{ij(2)} = b_{j1}\, T_{1i(2)} + \ldots + b_{jk}\, T_{ki(2)}$$

It might seem to follow algebraically that

$$a_{ij(2)} - a_{ij(1)} = b_{j1}\,(T_{1i(2)} - T_{1i(1)}) + \ldots + b_{jk}\,(T_{ki(2)} - T_{ki(1)})$$

where the bs are the same on the difference factor as on the trait factor, that is, the patterns are necessarily the same. However, an actual factoring consistent with this reliably emerges only if we enter i as two different persons on the first and second occasion into the same score matrix. In this case the factor has the same loadings—in fact it is one and the same factor. If we factor occasions 1 and 2 separately (or 1 and 2 and the difference scores separately) some change in the behavioral index is likely. The solution in which difference factors come out at the same rotational pattern position by simple structure as the traits is thus certainly possible. But there are countless other possible solutions if the restrictions present in this way of handling the factor analysis are removed. In short the factoring of difference scores can resolve precisely into the same factors present in the two absolute scores; but if simple structure or confactor rotation is applied to give unique factors in differences then any agreement is due to the fact that differences need the same structures to account for them psychologically.

[4] Only near-zero for states because there is the standard error of a zero correlation to consider; and only near-unity for traits because traits oscillate slightly due to trait change factors so that a person's measurements should be taken, say, six times and averaged to define the real trait value, for instance, to get an IQ level.

show that state- or trait-change factors exist corresponding to the primaries. The chief reason for the work having concentrated on the secondaries is that the secondaries correspond to the popular categories of such broad states as anxiety, arousal, and fatigue. Therefore the seven depression factors found as traits are not directly represented in current batteries as depression states although with sufficient care and use of odd-even item parcels they probably could be. We have seen (Table 22, Chapter Four) that in the trait domain one can recognize an almost general second-order depression factor, plus two or three other second orders with a couple of primary depression loadings on each; much the same holds true for state (dR- and P-) analyses. But on the Curran state scales the depression factor measured is the *general* secondary factor. On the other hand the stress state measure may be first order, relative to anxiety, fatigue, and depression as second orders. Since definitive P- and dR-studies have become available this question of strata in the organization of states deserves expert research.

I shall set out the evidence for states in Q-data—conceived as second orders—in two stages. First this section will confine itself to dR-method factors found on the familiar basis of the 16 PF primaries. After that it will shift to the broader basis of state items used to explore the state domain per se. The outcome of the first dR-study on the 16 PF (details in Cattell and Scheier, 1961) is shown in Table 26 in the first column in each box. Beside each dR-pattern is shown to exist simultaneously with the trait the same subjects examined by R-technique. The state patterns are revealed to be highly congruent with the trait patterns in Tables 18 and 19 (Chapter Four).

Table 26

State Patterns at Second Order

First-Order Factor	*Second-Order Factor I: Extraversion-Introversion or Exvia-Invia*		*First-Order Factor*	*Second-Order Factor II: Anxiety*		*First-Order Factor*	*Second-Order Factor III: Cortertia*		*First-Order Factor*	*Second-Order Factor IV: Independence*	
	State	*Trait*		*State*	*Trait*		*State*	*Trait*		*State*	*Trait*
A	38	42	Q_4	44	67	*I*	−50	−44	*N*	21	32
F	22	40	*O*	20	60	*N*	50	37	*E*	52	28
H	12	35	Q_3	−51	−53	*A*	−18	−28	Q_1	12	27
Q_2	−39	−32	*C*	−53	−49	Q_3	04	21	*F*	17	14
M	−36	−26	*L*	08	45	*C*	08	17	Q_3	−07	−01
Q_1	−20	−19	*H*	−06	−32	*O*	(13)	−17	*C*	(02)	−15
L	−12	−14	*M*	18	30						

Note: These loadings (decimals omitted) give the form of differential R-technique (dR) factors on the basis of 16 PF primaries (Adult). N = 95 normal male and female students retested after nine months.

This pioneer state search, which showed as good simple structure and other required properties for the factor analysis per se as in trait data, demonstrated (Cattell and Scheier, 1961) that change factors had the same general structure as the familiar traits. Later studies with the 16 PF confirmed this. However, one might ask what happens to the array of recognizable states when the basis of primaries is extended. No study exists on the 16 PF and supplement covering 23 factors; but data exist on what is perhaps of even more importance: the states that appear in combined 16 PF normal and the 12 pathological factors presented in the CAQ. The findings (based on psychiatric tests for which we owe a debt of gratitude to Dr. Weckowicz) on 188 mixed normal and clinical bases retested after three months are shown in Table 27.

Table 27

Second-Order Change Structures on a Broader Basis of Normal and Pathological Primaries

	I	*II*	*III*	*VI*	*VIII*	*Depression*	*Psychoticism*	*(9)*
A	54		−32					
C		−55		32				
E	57			36	(08)	28		−59
F	95			06	(−09)			
G	24				69			
H	49	(−02)	−47	29	−23			−28
I			−72					
L		(−03)		62	−33			
M			−44	(−15)				
O	34	38	−33					
Q_1				86	−27			
Q_2	−40		−37	41				−38
Q_3	−44	−54			62			
Q_4		96						
D_1	21					55		
D_2				29		55		−28
D_3				−37	−28	35		−25
D_4				−49		54		59
D_5		23				51		
D_6	32	30				54		
D_7						83		
Pa			36				66	
Pp	−20			−24			(10)	−59
Sc			27				61	
Ag				−35			45	
Ps							74	

Note: Decimal points omitted as in all factor-loading tables. Intelligence *B* and shrewdness *N* have been omitted as variables since they define no factor. Second-order factors V, VI, and VII are not recorded; two are not present and VI has no loading on the pathological factor except 0.32 on *Pp* psychopathic. The label "untamedness" given to VI is fully supported by this new association. The anxiety factor has only a trivial association with depression items (the factors, however, correlate 0.3); superego loads anxious depression; except for D_3 brooding discontent the depression primaries all load roughly to an equal degree on the general depression factor. The existence of the general psychosis state—loading highest on the general psychosis primary *Ps* and omitting the psychopathic primary—is a new discovery.

Here the scree test indicated no more than nine factors despite the extra primaries. Among these one can at once recognize the same second-order state factors from the normal primaries as were initially found in Table 26. Because the parcels were cut to six items each and because of the inherently greater error in dR-technique mentioned above, I shall not pursue the meaning of the two additional second-order depression factors except to note that as before the depressions yield three or four second orders. Instead I shall stop with the two main additions to the previous roster of states—the general depression factor and the general psychoticism factor. As with the corresponding traits these may not be entirely general but may have low or negligible loadings on one potential ingredient; this is a matter for a follow-up study with larger samples. It may be significant that the general psychoticism second order here loads above all other second orders that primary factor in the psychotic domain to which we have been unable to attach any one psychiatric syndrome expression.

The upshot of a search for states based on the standard first-order traits covering both normal and abnormal scales is therefore a confirmation of at least four of the trait-mimicking states: anxiety, exvia-invia, cortertia-pathemia, and independence-subduedness. Less systematic findings leave little doubt that such states also exist for the remaining four arousal patterns: discreetness, subjectivity, intelligence, and good upbringing. Another result of the search was the discovery of the two new states—general depression-elation and general psychoticism. Since these states are found in mixed normal and clinical groups the inference must be drawn that even normal individuals fluctuate from day to day along the reality-contact and emotional rationality dimension that separates psychotics from normals.

3. Systematic Discrimination of States, Trait-Change Patterns, and Trait Patterns and Their Use in the Trait-State Behavioral Equation

With the preceding instances of states to guide us we can begin to classify the emerging distinctions of trait, trait change, and state patterns.

In science definition can never be from an armchair but must be made in real contact with the natural history of the data. The discovery of state patterns by P- and dR-techniques is so recent that there has been little time for criterion associations to accumulate. With regard to three questions in particular we grasp at straws of information. Over what periods of time and in what manner do these states appear and disappear? What are the major stimuli in our culture for each of the defined state-response patterns? Do individuals differ significantly in their average state level over time or does everyone oscillate about the same zero defined by the absence of any state stimulation?

The first question involves us in the trait-state distinction, for surely a state that lasts long enough—some years—qualifies as a trait. Does reversible fluctuation define a state where steady trend (say, growth) signals a trait? Are there cycles in states? Before we can define what is fluctuant (minutes or days?) and what is a steady trend we need norms from nature and do not yet have them.

Common observation suggests that there can be states of very short duration, such as those of the startle reflex or sudden wonder, and others that may endure for months and even years, such as grief or the prolonged fatigue associated with UI 23, yet both are properly described as states. As far as the operations of measurement are concerned it has been pointed out that the time interval between retestings has not proved very important; much the same patterns come from one-day and three-month intervals. The limiting condition is that the interval must be long enough to catch the longer waves, in which case we theoretically pick up the movement of the ripples too. The technical experimental fact must be kept in mind that the methods of measurement we are now dealing with—questionnaires, ratings, and most T-data except such measures as the EEG, breathing, records, and the EKG—employ a single-measurement operation which itself is of appreciable duration, spread over say half an hour's testing. This causes us to miss the short period ripples and pick up only the long waves. Even with the best technical attention a questionnaire, to have a generally acceptable reliability, must be 15 to 25 items long and from 5 to 10 minutes' duration. This means that we are dealing with states likely to last from 10 minutes to months and that we may be missing fleeting responses lasting a few seconds or a couple of minutes.

So much for restriction of the class of states per se but what of the problem of separating a *trait-change* factor from a state factor? First we should be fully aware that a P-or dR-analysis produces both patterns without indicating which is which. If between test 1 and test 2 a certain trait increases significantly by maturation or learning then the set of manifestations of that trait will change together and yield a unitary factor—an apparent source state. A striking illustration of this is Horn's finding (1966b) that the two general intelligence factors, fluid intelligence g_f and crystallized intelligence a_g, show independent unitary fluctuations in their change scores so that a person is brighter on one or the other factor independently from day to day. Common sense may suggest that the differentiation is simple: that the trend in the state is upward or downward *continuously* and spreads over a long interval, not oscillating. The trend could also be characterized by starting from a different level in different people. Regarding the last characteristic, for example, some psychologists convey implicitly the notion that if we average an individual's scores on a pattern over, say, 10 occasions and this average departs significantly from zero we are dealing with a trait. The implied corollary is that if scores on many occasions average to zero (the same mean value for everyone) the thing measured is a state.

We may make tentative definitions but it remains to be seen whether nature will oblige by fitting into them. The essential model I offer as best fitting the available facts is this: (1) that all traits change in level from occasion to occasion, both through growth and decline and through temporary fluctuations; (2) that if we measure what we define as traits several times over a few days or months and over a typical population sample, the between-person variance is larger—several times larger—than the between-occasion variance; and (3) that states similarly measured have a larger variance—

several times larger—between occasions than between persons. Within this model it remains for research to show whether there is a complete separation of states from traits when the *between-person to between-occasion variance ratio* implied above is plotted as a distribution or whether it is bimodal or simply normal; and whether all people have the same mean on states or whether, despite states varying greatly with occasion, there remains some between-person difference of means.

Granted this general model open to examination and refinement, let us scrutinize the possible nature of trait-change factors. Insofar as they are conceived as representing growth in an existing structural unity, it seems reasonable to suppose that the change pattern of each growth factor will closely resemble that of the corresponding trait. However, I hypothesize that trait change over a long period can take two forms. It can be either (1) *uniform growth* (or decline) with a pattern T_{cu} or (2) *phased growth* with a pattern T_{cp}, where cu = change uniform and cp = change phase. The first is illustrated by the growth of, say, a fish or a fir tree over most of the growth period. The proportions remain the same and therefore the measures of absolute growth from any time, t_1 to t_2 are in the same proportion and bear the same mutual relations as the individual difference measures of adult fish or fir trees, just as they stand, having ceased growth at different sizes. It follows that the trait-change factor pattern (dR) is similar to the individual difference trait (R) factor pattern. On the other hand phased growth, represented by a butterfly that goes through a chrysalid state or the building of a house in which the roof follows the walls, reaches the final form through a sequence of phases in each of which the growth pattern is different (just as the growth rate of the human head changes relative to that of the body).

We do not know how much personality growth is uniform and how much is phased but it seems reasonable to begin with the simpler uniform type at least for primary traits. On that basis we can reach a first touchstone for separating the state- and trait-change patterns as they emerge from P- and dR-analyses. Trait-change patterns can now be recognized by their close resemblance to trait patterns, whereas the state pattern can be quite different and commonly shows no resemblance to any trait pattern in the R-technique series. It has been pointed out that although P- and dR-techniques yield only state- and trait-change factors, R-technique yields both traits (as psychometrists have long supposed) and states (which fact they have been inclined to overlook). The idea that R-technique finds state patterns too may be illuminated by the analogy that if a photograph (like a single testing) is taken of great waves near a mountainous coast, a person who has never seen the sea might conclude that the waves are also mountains, not realizing that they are moving forms arrested in time. The separation thus hinges on the fact that some factors in R-technique find their matches (the states) in P- and R-technique and some (the traits) do not.

Unfortunately for the complete simplicity of this rule there remain the traits-change factors. If these patterns appearing in P- and dR-techniques are of the T_{cu} type, that is, having the same form as the traits, they at first glance appear in R-technique. The only way to separate them and recognize that they are not merely states in R-technique data is not by pattern but by magnitude. They are small in variance relative to states in P- and dR-technique and large relative to states in R-technique. As another consequence of the relative variance the estimate (or scale-measured) factor scores corresponding to the trait and identical trait-change pattern show high stability coefficients from occasion to occasion whereas the true states do not. Insofar as psychologists have noticed these conceptual issues they seem to suppose that R-technique yields only traits or (correctly) that it yields both traits and states, and that the number of factors on the latter assumpion should be decidedly more in R- than dR-analyses of the same variables. Our concept of the third term, trait-change factors, supposes that the same number should be found in both although with systematic changes of variance—and this is what results (using good checks on number of factors, as in the scree or maximum likelihood) increasingly show. The question of just what the expected differences of variance would be will be taken up below (and in Table 32).

A whole chapter would be needed to handle thoroughly the conceptual problem of separating scoring states, traits, and trait-change factors (see Cattell, 1966b; Nesselroade, 1966) but let us review the operational basis we have reached.

First, trait (R-technique) and trait change (dR-) tend to give similar patterns; states (R-, dR-, and P-) need have no resemblance to traits (although in anxiety, state and trait do show a resemblance).

Second, traits appear only in R-technique; state patterns appear in R, dR, and P-; trait change of the uniform type appears only in dR- and P-technique.

Third, slow change over time and the existence of a definite time trend in successive measures is characteristic of a trait-change pattern, whereas a state is expected to fluctuate reversibly and irregularly.

Fourth, researchers should be able to establish a causal connection between state response changes and the appearance of particular inner or outer stimulus situations in our culture, thus connecting states to causes.

Fifth, the ratio of between-occasion and between-person variance is much higher for states than traits (the between-occasion variance for traits is the trait-change factor variance). This has implications for stability coefficients (reliabilities of a special kind), which should be virtually zero for states and good for traits, and for the associated relative variance of these factors in R-, dR-, and P-techniques.

Sixth and last, some significant correlation across individuals may exist—because of inherent laws of growth—between a trait score and a trait-change score over a fixed interval, whereas no such correlation need exist for trait score and some state-change score that might resemble it.

The third and fourth points should not be taken too seriously until more research has been done on the natural history of these patterns. For example, a trait learned through some reinforcement schedule might advance for a week or two while rewarded and then fall back when the rewards vanish.

Thus the outcome of dR- and P-techniques is essentially the same but both contrast with R-technique in terms of relative variances for different patterns. It is now time to set this out in more formal equations, except for the variation being respectively across people and across occasions. As far as the possible difference between P- and dR-methods is concerned we note that they both use the same two kinds of predictor factors: trait change and state. Thus from dR-technique one predicts the magnitude of the change on a variable from time t_1 to t_2 as

$$a_{ijt2} - a_{ijt1} = b_{jc1}T_{c1i} + \ldots + b_{jck}T_{cqi} + b_{jsc1}S_{c1i} + \ldots + b_{jscm}S_{cmi} \quad (6.1)$$

where T_c has the form of a trait-change factor (q of them) and S_c has the form of a state factor (m of them) but is a change in state. Hence both S and T as change scores must have a subscript c. The factors are both measured here as change scores from t_1 to t_2 and could have $(t_2 - t_1)$ as a subscript instead of c, like the value on the left. The P-technique prediction also has only state and trait-change pattern factors but now the identifying subscript i can be dropped because the identity of the person is consistently the same; however, a subscript k must now be added for each occasion in time:

$$a_{jk} = b_{jc1}T_{c1k} + \ldots + b_{jc1}T_{cqk} + b_{js1}S_{1k} + \ldots + b_{jsm}S_{mk} \quad (6.2)$$

where T_c is one of the person's unique q trait-change factors and S is one of his unique m state patterns, both scored at their particular level at occasion k. The bs are behavioral indexes (loadings) indicating how much the given trait change or state factor affects the response behavior j.

If Equations (6.1) and (6.2) are compared with the familiar R-technique specification equation for individual differences as in Equation (1.1), it will be seen that they have these two extra kinds of structure. But when we adopted the more complete equation it was anticipated that a state term ought to be brought into the instantaneous one-occasion individual difference picture. In an equation such as (1.3) it is unnecessary to introduce any *uniform trait-change* factor since its form is so uniform with the trait that it is part of the individual difference trait; that is, on a single R-technique measure, trait and trait change are inseparable. But with a *phased change* T_{cp} the last stage of growth may be so different in pattern from the earlier that it starts as a distinct factor. In that case we must write

$$a_{ijk} = b_{j1}T_{1i} + \ldots + b_{jq}T_{qi} + b_{jc1}T_{cpk1i} + \ldots + b_{jcm}T_{cpkmi} + b_{jsi}S_{1ki} + \ldots + b_{jsn}S_{nki} \quad (6.3)$$

In this expansion of Equation (1.1) the T terms are still timeless but the m trait change terms T_{cp} and the n states S have a subscript k as in Equation (6.2) to show they are measured at the given occasion of growth and moment of fluctuation k. Thus this equation embodies the trait growths and the states, both frozen like the wave forms we took as analogs above. The neglect of all trait change and state terms that traditional psychometry has perpetuated in Equation (1.1)—sometimes falsely interpreting the state factors as traits—becomes nearly acceptable if the variables (items) are measured for the given persons over many occasions and averaged before factoring and if we are predicting an average response over many occasions. Then the positive and negative deviations of the T_c and S scores about the mean tend to cancel and these factors shrink to small variance leaving only the trait factors prominent. But few experiments in the ability trait field have observed this exacting requirement of repeated measurement.

I shall not complicate matters by assuming phase-growth as well as uniform-growth factors; thus Equation (6.3) will not be used—R-technique will be represented by Equation (1.2) With this basis of a precise model we are ready to return to the experimental findings.

4. A Dozen or More Source States Emerging from Comprehensive Research

A preliminary view has been given of what emerges by dR-technique applied to the variables in the *personality sphere as that sphere has been defined for traits.* The outcome is a set of primary trait-change (or possibly state) factors corresponding to those known in primary traits. We also discover a set of second-stratum change factors—exvia, anxiety, cortertia, and others—corresponding to the second-stratum traits. Whether these are to be regarded as trait-change or state factors remains to be decided but one is inclined to suspect the latter because the variance on the anxiety factor and exvia patterns, for example, is considerable. One wonders indeed whether some at least of the supposed second-stratum traits in R-technique, long taken to be traits, might not be states, that is, state contributions to the primaries as traits.

To this picture of eight to ten second-order states I now bring evidence from a new angle in which variables are set up from the beginning to cover all kinds of states instead of just the trait personality sphere. The first change-score factor analysis in this state domain in which explicit attention was given to representing questionnaire state variables as distinct from trait variables was the original P-technique (Cattell, Cattel, and Rhymer, 1947) research onto which were built 18 questionnaire items, in addition to observer ratings and many objective and physiological tests that were measured each day for 55 days. This analysis revealed that change factors seemingly identical with Q-data primaries appear (A, C, F, G, and H were clearest) with P-technique and showed two Q-data factors at the second order. These factors had patterns quite close to what were soon confirmed by dR-technique (Tables 26 and 27) and interpreted as exvia and anxiety states. These patterns also seemed to appear simultaneously in Q-data and L-data. There was also a second order of general fatigue. However, although variances of *Q*-, *L*-, and *T*-data variables overlapped in these factors, the alignment of all those in each state was not as simple as had been hoped.

The ensuing P-technique studies (Cattell and Luborsky, 1950; Cattell and Williams, 1953) were thinner than the pioneer study itself in their Q-items and concentrated on T-data. However, grasping what happened in T-data is part of understanding the Q-data structure to a much greater extent (for various measures) in states than traits. In Luborsky and Williams' research the Q-data gave evidence of a fatigue factor and of states corresponding to primaries *A, C, F, H,* and *E* in self-ratings and observer ratings. Second-order exvia and anxiety were not so clear.

A fourth and more ambitious P-technique analysis followed in a study by Grinker with Cattell and Scheier (1961) in which eight depressive neurotics were organized in the first use of a chain P-technique (Figure 15) design (equalized means and sigmas) offering together 40 occasions (five on

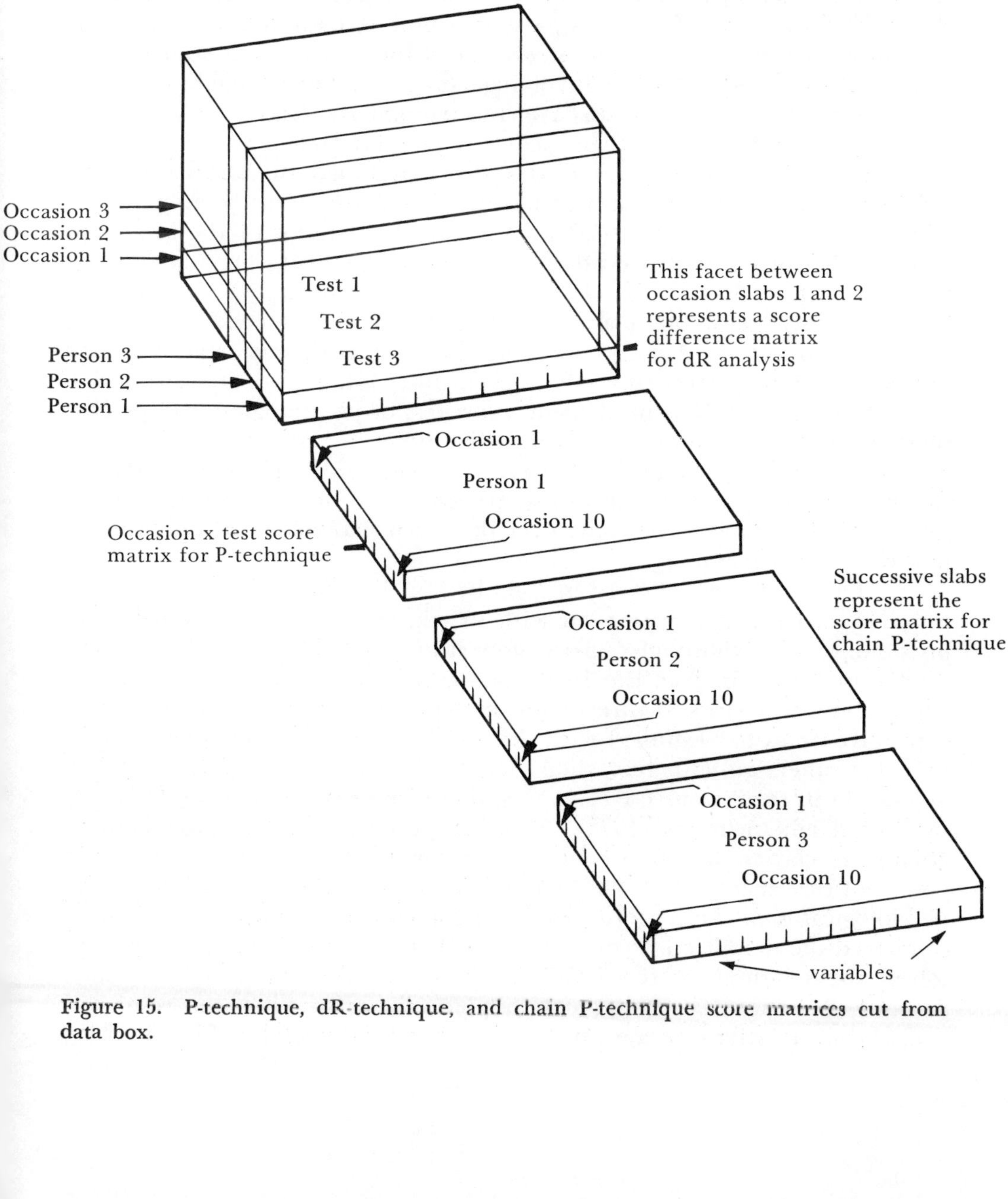

Figure 15. P-technique, dR-technique, and chain P-technique score matrices cut from data box.

each person). This was also the first manipulated (stimulus-controlled) P-technique in that Grinker gave stress interviews on about half the occasions; the rest were controls. From the 34 physiological and questionnaire variables eight factors appeared; the five that could be defined were anxiety, pathemia, effort stress, adrenergic system responses, and a new factor of raised pulse rate and raised serum cholesterol level (Cattell and Scheier, 1961, p. 206). It was concluded that because these factors were in T-data most of them should initially be considered to stand at the second order in the questionnaire realm—as was certainly the case with the anxiety and cortertia-pathemia patterns in physiological and behavioral measures.

From the medical standpoint this last research demonstrated the valuable distinction between effort stress and anxiety (although restrospectively the distinctive effort stress pattern is now recognizable earlier in the literature; Cattell, 1957). Effort stress shares the impact of a second-order factor with the new primary involving cholesterol, which embraces both primaries. It was shown by this P-technique analysis (and later in Cattell and Scheier, 1961) that the then medically popular view that anxiety raises serum cholesterol is incorrect. It was also found that the stress interview did not increase anxiety but significantly raised the effort stress response and also increased pathemia (UI 22—; *Q*III—). In terms of the associated Q-data the results were provocative. The Q-data second-stratum anxiety scale (items from $C-$, $H-$, L, O, Q_3-, Q_4-) came out strongly on the physiological anxiety factor but many Q-data items commonly considered to be anxiety by content loaded also on effort stress and pathemia as an objective test pattern. Effort stress especially picked up questionnaire items of irritation and anger as well as unpleasant awareness of physiological and psychosomatic anxiety symptoms. At the same time it was noted that some depressive items by content (for validity) went with the general anxiety factor; this has been observed consistently since. (In other words, depression items spread themselves not only over the seven depression factors but also into the anxiety factors.)

This study was followed in 1963 by Van Egeren's research by P-technique on anxiety and depression with its central emphasis on T-data and physiology. This thorough, 78-occasion study included no less than 180 questionnaire items from the 16 PF and from the newly discovered seven depression trait factors. It threw light on depression states and showed some depressive items to be linked with the anxiety factor but revealed in addition that others go with regression (UI 23—). This new finding of Q-data depression in regression (UI 23—) was soon confirmed by Tatro (1967) and by Cattell and Schmidt (1972). Although it is not my purpose here to attempt to clarify the often complex relations of Q- and T-data I should point out that at least they are separately clear. In objective behavioral and physiological data these coordinated, programatic P-technique studies have confirmed the definition of nine states in T-data. They have not, however, solved the relations of the insufficiently represented questionnaire state patterns. But the nine T-data state-response patterns, when the results of a set of manipulative (therapy and drug) studies by Rickels and his coworkers

(Rickels and Cattell, 1965) were added, were well confirmed as independent factorial dimensions. Furthermore the average pattern over several studies of distinct anxiety, effort stress, regression, pathemic depression, and other factors (see Figure 11, Chapter Five) showed substantial stability.

Although the alignment of these T-data factors with Q-data factors has been pursued with precision only for two factors, exvia and anxiety, the questionnaire data on anxiety second order, *Q*II, correlated close to unity with T-data anxiety state indexed SUI 9 (or trait-change factor CUI 24) and *Q*I, exvia-invia, matched trait-change factor UI 32 (Cattell and Rickels, 1968),[5] but other alignments were poor, for example in the Cattell and Bartlett study (1971). This research also suggested, but with significance suitable only for hypothesis, that second-order Q-data depression factors are associated with pathemia (UI 22—), regression (UI 23—), and asthenia (UI 28); such a connection is also indicated by the work of Cattell and Schmidt (1972, p. 53). The definition of emotional state response dimensions as such in T-data, constituting a firm reference system for Q-data research, would require for any complete study due reference also to the important work of Connor (psychophysiological P-technique) and of Barton (see Barton, Cattell, and Connor, 1972; Cattell and Barton, 1973).

At this point it is necessary to turn from this developing reference system in T-data, indicating Q-data factors in the six studies with too sparse a representation for complete clarity, to the direct attack on states per se in Q-data. Five investigators with major studies—Barton, Bolz, Curran, Nesselroade, and Shrader (with assistance from Bartsch, Cable, Cattell, and others)—started with various samplings of state concepts in the literature, and, exchanging marker variables, pursued the structure of Q-data states with P- and dR-techniques. Some persistent technical problems had to be faced. For example, the administration of the same question 50 to 100 times is unlikely to produce much variance in P-technique when the subject can readily remember what he answered on the previous occasion (usually a day earlier). This problem was substantially overcome (in six P-technique studies earlier and in Bolz's and Barton's studies) by using a graphic scale which in the absence of words makes recollection of the last position difficult. With dR-technique—especially beyond a week—recall effects constitute no problem. However, the dR-studies had to escape another difficulty—sticking in the rut of the middle multiple-choice answer of three or five alternatives—which they did by using a four- or six-response choice.

Although Curran's work (1968, 1972; Curran and Cattell, in press) culminated with a dR-technique, he first bridged to earlier studies by a chain P-technique in which 20 married women (mean age 24.1 years) were placed in series (common means and sigmas) for a total run of 180 (20×9) days; the measures were taken at all hours of the day in order to

[5] A word on indexing would help here. The indexing of Q-data traits at three strata by *A, B, C,* and so on; I, II, III, and so on; and α, β, γ, and so on is clear. Objective T-data factors are preceded by T or are simply given UI (universal index) numbers. To contrast state with trait patterns a prefix S is added. Thus Q(S)II is the anxiety state in Q-data, as SUI 24 (or TSUI 24) is anxiety in the objective test factor series.

get fatigue variance. A broad spectrum of variables was used: Q-data covering anxiety (28 Q-items) and depression (14 items for 7 factors); T-data for markers for SUI factors 1 through 9; markers for the principal dynamic tension factors in the MAT. By building markers on the emerging patterns of the earlier P-techniques and expanding the questionnaire data, Curran's study (1968) produced the best alignment between Q- and T-data patterns. A careful rotation (76.6 in ± 10 hyperplane) of 23 factors (indications were 19 to 23) yielded a series in which the largest were readily interpretable as well-known SUI patterns (first-order T, second-order Q).

Curran's clear separation of eight Q-data state factors , simultaneously caught in one comparative study, included anxiety (especially on Q primaries Q_4, C, and O); fatigue (with some low arousal or torpor and a few hypochondria items included); a large general depression factor (with some narcissism and self-concept involvement) presumably identical with that in Table 27; a second, narrower depression marked by low energy; a third depression marked by agitation, anxiety, brooding, and poor sleep; a familiar effort stress pattern; a regression or overwroughtness (UI 23—); and a pathemia (UI 22—, SUI 2) state. I hypothesize that these P-technique depression factors are actually second-stratum factors. From these eight general states the dynamic state factors—ergic tension patterns of sex, fear, and so forth, and of superego and self-sentiment strengths—stood out clearly in different space, supporting the general hypothesis that these specific dynamic interest states are, in any immediate measurement, essentially independent of the general mood states.

The increasing evidence that a pattern indistinguishable from exvia-invia has the large variance to be expected of a state rather than a trait-change factor thus suggests that we must henceforth recognize Q(S)I (see Table 30) as a state of exvia-invia existing over and above the trait. Similarly Nesselroade's finding (1964) of the high stability coefficients over six weeks for UI 22, cortertia-pathemia, argues that any state-change factor is of trivial variance and that the similar pattern SUI 2 (Cattell, 1957) aligning with Q(S)III is a true state involving some depression and emotional sensitivity items in Q-data. Consequently the summary hypothesis (representing patterns checked several times) reached at this point was that there are eight distinct factors at the questionnaire second stratum: anxiety, pathemic depression, low-energy depression, anxious depression, effort stress, regression (called overwroughtness UI 23— in T-data), fatigue, and arousal-torpor. However, Curran's study threw doubt on the clean separability of the fatigue and low arousal (torpor); nor has previous work in Q-data given clear evidence of separation of high energy-fatigue from high arousal-low activation. Curran found no good questionnaire items, as hypothesized in the Q(S)III set, for his eighth factor, pathemia-cortertia, although it emerged clearly marked by T-variables.

Studies to confirm the Q-data definition of some of these source states were carried out by Nesselroade, who used dR-technique on the assumption that what is found with P-technique should appear with dR-technique. First he took 160 undergraduates and exposed them to a two-month retest on 140 carefully chosen marker items for four of the main indicated factors: anxiety, depression, stress, and fatigue. Even though he encompassed markers for four states his emphasis was on broadening the valid available item markers for anxiety as a state. Here, incidentally, he wished to settle a debate as to whether the Spielberger STAI state and trait battery (1972) was correct in its item validities as far as anxiety is concerned, since some items by inspection suggested depression or stress and whether the supposed state and trait scale measures for anxiety are indeed distinct. Spielberger's criterion is to take "face valid" anxiety items and separate them into those that change much with time (low stability coefficients) and those that as traits change little. The argument of Nesselroade (and my own) is that the tendency of an item to be answered differently on occasions is a necessary but not sufficient condition to make it a valid measure of the anxiety state. The fact that high variability in an item may be partly due to low reliability—through ambiguity, and so on—means that any pool of items merely selected for variability could simply be an unreliable *trait* measure. And when they are, furthermore, picked only by face validity, the question remains unanswered: are one, two, or more unitary factors involved—or, indeed, is any of them anxiety at all?

Taking markers from the now repeatedly overdetermined anxiety factor and from Curran's largest depression factor as well as from Spielberger's STAI markers, Nesselroade proceeded to a dR-factoring on 160 undergraduates. The 105 items were grouped by marker source in 14 parcels (each parcel consisting of two or more item variables); 45 items were left as single items, the total constituting 59 variables. The scree test showed 18 factors and it soon became evident by examination of content that the first 15 were indeed the primaries of the 16 PF. Thus we have a second check that these appear as states and that the personality-sphere approach to states and the approach through concepts of states themselves are not so different. Finally, three factors appeared *beyond* the recognizable 16 PF primaries; these were considered by Nesselroade from the markers to be depression, stress, and fatigue.

Research with the fifteen 16 PF personality factors, depression, stress, and fatigue now promised to shed light on the strata problem when Nesselroade's analysis was taken to the second and third orders. The structure on the second and third strata matched quite well (Cattell and Nesselroade, in preparation) with that usually obtained. The familiar anxiety, exvia, and cortertia patterns appeared from the 16 PF markers and these and the depression, stress, and fatigue dimensions continued to be independent. However, much of the depression item variance aligned with pathemia (*Q*III−) and the stress and fatigue patterns behaved as first orders. At the second order a substantial part of their variance was accounted for by an increase in the superego (good upbringing) second order. Very provocatively for the Spielberger STAI use, the supposed trait and state measures therein now appeared as *two states* (or conceivably a trait change and a state). Thus the results confirm (see Table 28) Spielberger's supposition that the STAI contains two distinct scales but identify them by a majority of markers as being different from anxiety trait and anxiety state. The change on the trait is a solid measure of stress and the supposed anxiety state measure is an equally solid measure of depression. Since there are three or four distinct factors in this area it may see largely a matter of pure semantics as to which is to be called anxiety. But in this case the anxiety factors Q(S)II, SUI 9, and UI 24 have long been anchored to the term anxiety by every known association and criterion (including *r*s of about 0.8 with Eysenck's *N* and the manifest anxiety scale). If this is anxiety then it seems best to recognize depression and stress as the two main STAI scale scores (the anxiety factor per se is not repeated in the data analysis in Table 28).

Table 28

Definition of Depression, Stress, and Fatigue States by dR-Technique

	Depression	*Stress*	*Fatigue*
Depression, Parcel 1	44	22	26
Depression, Parcel 2	43	18	34
Stress, Parcel 1	32	40	14
Stress, Parcel 2	18	40	04
Fatigue, Parcel 1	15	01	53
Fatigue, Parcel 2	15	00	23
Spielberger State, Parcel 1	94	−01	−36
Spielberger State, Parcel 2	67	02	−05
Spielberger State, Parcel 3	72	08	−02
Spielberger State, Parcel 4	72	10	19
Spielberger Trait, Parcel 1	08	75	−19
Spielberger Trait, Parcel 2	−30	69	05
Spielberger Trait, Parcel 3	05	59	−31
Spielberger Trait, Parcel 4	−03	59	−01
Hyperplane percentage on V_{fp}	65	61	65
Hyperplane percentage on V_{rs}	68	70	73

Note: The ±0.10 hyperplane count is given for the whole factor analysis, since the subset consists of variables more highly loaded. The hyperplane percentage has in the majority of past research been given in the reference vector structure V_{rs} where the ±0.10 count is usually higher than in the V_{fp}. The latter seems more correct but the V_{rs} is also given for wider comparisons. In either case it demonstrates a very high simple structure. Note also that the loadings on the Spielberger scale parcels are higher than the other six parcels because they average five items per parcel as against less than three for the others. Corrected for scale length (parcel size) the loadings for the markers in the indicated blocks above are essentially the same.

The reader interested largely in general conclusions may find the precise accounting carried out here more detailed than he wishes. For this I feel properly apologetic; however, science is concerned with contending hypotheses, and some readers may favor hypotheses other than those I consider best. The availability of specific evidence pro and con is therefore essential. My condensation has inevitably required technical parlance, but one may hope that the nonprofessional reader will grow into this.

With the location of the unitary state dimensions goes the obligation to create dependable scales to represent the concepts in general research. Barton, Bartsch, Curran, Nesselroade and Nichols, Scheier, Shrader, and Spielberger stand out among those who have dedicated work to this objective in the domain of states. The construction of a scale subtending all eight states in correct mutual relations has been completed for adults by Curran and is being standardized. To proceed to this scale two parallel studies were coordinated, one by dR-technique by Curran (290 students retested with a one-month interval) and one by P-technique by Barton (eight students tested on 35 successive days). Barton's study constitutes the longest P-technique study to date—290 occasions.

Both studies used the same set of 24 variables; each was a short questionnaire scale of about six items. Those items are the substance of the Eight State Battery (Curran and Cattell, 1974) covering state factors found for exvia, anxiety, depression, arousal, fatigue, stress regression, and guilt-depression. (Barton used form A, dropping guilt-depression; Curran used form B.) On five states the factor-marking items were segregated into two or three marker-variable parcels for each but on arousal and fatigue six were used since previous research (Curran, 1968; Barton, Cattell, and Connor, 1972) had revealed special difficulty in separating these factors and Curran had to consider arousal and fatigue as possibly opposite poles on one factor.

The outcome of these two approaches, planned as a check by different methods, was a substantial agreement (by a test for number of factors) that seven or eight dimensions are needed. As Table 29 shows, there is virtually complete agreement between these independent studies also in regard to the same scales having corresponding, significant loadings on the same factors. Only two scales—one an arousal and one a depression variable—misfired, in the Curran analysis. Yet certain difficulties remain. First, there is a comparative failure—though not as bad as in the previous research—to separate low arousal from high fatigue; secondly, the regression factor spreads beyond the markers intended for it; and thirdly, in the dR-technique result, the guilt-depression pattern runs appreciably into loadings on anxiety, invia, and depression variables. One problem in getting separation could be that in this new state domain we are wrestling with the phenomenon of factor intercorrelations among states naturally being larger than we are accustomed to find in traits. A rise in permitted factor correlations might reduce the spread of the regression factor, and—in the dR-technique—of anxiety, invia, and depression. But the confounding of fatigue and low arousal may clear up only by more incisive choice of variables. However, enough success was achieved in mutual separation of states, and in cross validation, supporting the existing hypotheses to guide the investigators in selecting better items for converging on the true factors.

The probability must also be investigated, as soon as these scales are shaped to the concepts now indicated, that the factor model is not fully met by those data and that state interaction exists. In particular the contamination of arousal-torpor and energy-fatigue can probably be explained by high arousal being virtually impossible with high fatigue, although an unfatigued

Table 29

Definitive Statement on Eight State Factors by Combined P- and dR-Technique

Marker by Hypothesis	Barton Chain P-Technique								Curran dR-Technique							
	Exvia	*Anxiety*	*Depres-sion*	*Arousal*	*Fatigue*	*Stress*	*Regres-sion*	*Random*	*Exvia*	*Anxiety*	*Depres-sion*	*Arousal*	*Fatigue*	*Stress*	*Regres-sion*	*Guilt*
Exvia																
1	80		−25						14							−39
2	80			27					28						−30	−39
3									15							−50
Anxiety																
1		29	−42		−52			59	−27	36						48
2		32	46							35					29	50
3	−48	61								22						52
Depression																
1			77						−49		03					52
2	−57	32	51	49			41		−27		18					48
3			32	−29			38			47	17		30			32
Arousal																
1				1.12			33					−07	−51		−58	
2				42			−61				29	02	−67		−34	
3				93							50	36	−25			
4			40	92		33						20	−70			
5		−36		88	−27							88				
6				1.10								73				
Fatigue																
1				−58	41		44						89		52	
2				−65	35		37					−44	42		47	
3			47	−39	69		36						75			
4				−29	61		30			37			19			
5				−54	68		38		−26	32			24			25
6		−31		−88	1.13		−26			42	31		41			

Stress														
1			42		59	56						72		
2				30		60			37	26	29	31		27
3												63		41
Regression														
1	—49		44		35		37						15	40
2		52			59		44	—29	41				16	
3									28	39	26		34	
Guilt														
1								64						84
2										30				37
3								—34		38			25	17

Note: Decimal points omitted as in all factor loading tables. In the chain P-technique the items so far used, although they indicate the nature of the factor structure, are in two cases inescapably composite: (1) fatigue and low arousal items are mutually loaded and also loaded on regression, and (2) regression has greater breadth than the items assigned to it. It loads also some items for depression and fatigue and its items have contributions from anxiety, depression, and fatigue. The possibility is that regression is a higher-order factor contributing to both fatigue and depression.

person can be either aroused or torpid. Moreover one may well hypothesize that fatigue aids regression, UI 23(−). Some forty years ago convincing evidence was found—apparently not checked yet by independent research—that perceptual-motor rigidity, a central measure in UI 23, shows regular increase with diurnal fatigue (Cattell, 1935a, 1935b).

An up-to-date view of Q-data state patterns is not complete without a note on Bartlett's combined Q- and T-data P-technique experiment (Cattell and Bartlett, 1971) and the intensive studies of Shrader, Barton, and Nesselroade on bringing anxiety state scales to higher validity and more complete distinction from anxiety trait scales. Bartlett confirmed that stress is independent of anxiety and that fear is distinct from both, although the fear pattern resulted in reduction of anxiety objective test variable scores. He did not confirm the objective test anxiety markers (UI 24) as belonging with state anxiety (although this has been confirmed for the anxiety trait), which suggests that trait and state may differ more in T- than in Q-data.

Difference scores inevitably involve more error and therefore require larger samples and longer tests to give state finds dependability equal to those of trait research; thus factor resolution, initial replication, and staking out of state concepts requires refined factor-analytic techniques. Making the present factors available in the best possible scales is an important beginning, started by Nesselroade (in Barton and Cattell, 1973a) with the intensification of the IPAT 40-item adult scales A and B and by Shrader (Shrader and Cattell, 1973) with the 40-item high school scales A and B. As soon as these scales are available manipulative experiments can sharpen the item validities. In this connection a demonstration that the anxiety state factor behaves as would be expected from what is commonly considered anxiety stimulation (as well as a valuable, incisive demonstration of method) is found in Bartsch and Nesselroade (1973). Findings at the high school level by Barton, Shrader, and Cattell (1973) support the anxiety identification as does Tsushima's finding (1957) that anxiety increases with announcements of poor school grades. These findings relate well to corresponding manipulative studies with anxiety on T-data by Rickels and Cattell (1965); Rickels and others (1966); and DiMascio and Barrett (1965). The manipulative studies by Sarason (1966), Lazarus and Opton (1966), Epstein (1973), and others are not with factored scales but with scales that nevertheless correlate sufficiently with factor-oriented scales to make useful comparisons possible.

A study of great significance for this whole domain is that of Nesselroade and Cable (1972), who demonstrated that an R-technique analysis of Q-data yielded both a trait and a state anxiety factor of substatnial independence, whereas the dR-analysis yielded only a state anxiety factor easily identified by congruence coefficients. Nesselroade made these distinct trait and state measures available in Barton's Central Trait and State (CTS) Kit. With this survey of P- and dR-evidence on state patterns—from the use of normal and abnormal trait markers to the special studies on anxiety and other states in psychophysiological contexts—I can present the checked questionnaire state patterns shown in Table 30.

One problem remains: whether the second-order depression factors

Table 30

Summary of Second-Stratum Q-Data Source States

Regular Index in Second-Order Q Patterns [a]	*Hypothetically Corresponding UI Pattern*	*Index in T-Data States* [b]	*Title*
1. Q(S)II	UI 24	SUI 9	Anxiety
2. Q(S)I	UI 32	SUI 11	Exvia-invia
3. Q(S)IX			Depression-elation 1: pathemic, general depression
4. Q(S)XI			Depression-elation 2: low energy, depression [c]
5. Q(S)XII		SUI 1	Depression-elation 3: anxious-guilty depression
6. Q(S)XIII	UI 23	SUI 8	Regression (overwroughtness)
7. Q(S)X			Arousal (activation)
8. Q(S)XIV		SUI 3	Fatigue [d]
9. Q(S)XV		SUI 4	Effort stress [e]
10. Q(S)III	UI 22	SUI 2	Cortertia-pathemia [f]
11. Q(S)IV	UI 19	SUI 10	Independence-subduedness [f]
12. Q(S)VIII	*Q*VIII		Strong superego-weak superego [f]
13. Q(S)XVI			General psychoticism or pathology

[a] The roman numerals are the same for state or trait change as for the original traits.

[b] These SUI numbers have been kept identical for clarity since the first publication of the T-data state patterns (Cattell, 1957). Five states in the *Q* series are not given SUI numbers in the T series because objective test patterns have not yet been found.

[c] It remains to be seen whether this factor is really the same as cortertia-pathemia Q(S)III.

[d] As stated in the text most researchers to date have been unable to get a clear separation of low arousal (torpor) from fatigue. But my hypothesis is that activation and fatigue are distinct source-state patterns although highly negatively correlated in most life situations and therefore difficult to separate.

[e] There is some evidence that fatigue and effort stress (along with cholesterol and high pulse, not in Q-data) are first-order factors. The former is surely improbable since the effects of fatigue are broad; it is more likely to condition the appearance of other factors: a tired man does not easily show certain ergic patterns. But effort stress may indeed be narrower and dependent in part on second-order contributions: a person in a general anxiety state fight be likely to take action generating high stress.

[f] These three change patterns are more likely than the others to be simply trait-change patterns rather than sheer states.

*Q*XI and *Q*XII, either as states or traits, can be identified with cortertia-pathemia (UI 22—, *Q*III— as pathemia) and independence-subduedness (UI 19—, *Q*IV— as subduedness). That assumption is not made here but several studies (notably Tatro, 1967; Cattell and Schmidt, 1972) show questionnaire depression items to be associated with these and with regression. Research may evaluate the meaning of these overlaps and strata problems when scales better validated against the Q-data concepts appear. More tentative is the structure of states at the third order. The magnitude and degree of agreement of research from which tentative hypotheses can now be generated are evaluated in Table 31.

Table 31

Third Stratum of State Q-Data Dimensions

	Curran dR-Technique						*Barton P-Technique*				
	Variables	α	β	γ	δ		*Variables*	α	β	γ	δ
I	Exvia	−66	−04	−12	47	I	Exvia	−41	−03	−61	48
II	Anxiety	87	−02	−03	07	II	Anxiety	79	02	04	03
III	Depression	09	−82	26	−13	III	Depression	−04	−75	−10	02
IV	Arousal	−10	35	08	84	IV	Arousal	−08	53	−07	06
V	Fatigue	42	54	11	−08	V	Fatigue	04	35	01	−95
VI	Stress	06	12	73	−07	VI	Stress	03	08	69	−01
VII	Regression	−05	−04	46	−56	VII	Regression	−02	−02	42	26
VIII	Guilt	−08	−47	−19	−15	VIII	Random	36	−01	41	−55

Note: Decimal points omitted as in all factor-loading tables.

In view of the concern in Chapter Seven with comparing states and traits across different observational media, it is of interest at this point to compare the findings with objective measures of states. Eight state dimensions have been checked, which, as we are reminded by Table 30, should stand at the second order in Q-data. The higher-order structure among them is shown in Figure 16. Although not all variables are conceptually the same in the Q- and T-patterns (there is no adrenergic pattern in Q-data) some comparisons are suggestive.

As Table 31 shows, the cross validation of third stratum state factors is quite good regarding factors α, β, and γ, though failing on δ. The possibility has to be considered, as mooted before, that in states even more than in traits the third stratum moves out of inherent psychological structures into environmental situations. Could α be some situation that simultaneously increases the states of introversion and anxiety? The contemplating of difficult social situations could be such. And β could represent battling one's way to a successful execution of duty, which reduces depression and guilt but increases fatigue and arousal. Until more relations of these tertiary state factors to situational criteria and manipulative experiment have been recorded it would be premature to theorize, but at least we have gained tolerably supported knowledge of the third-order structures as empirical constructs.

The upshot of this section is that we are well on the way to completing the primary, secondary, and tertiary state dimensional framework by which any complex mood can be measured and represented. A physiologist has claimed that biochemistry can now create any mood—and bottle it. To check this claim the psychologist must have dimensions and scales to identify and measure whatever moods may be so created.

5. State Theories: Modulating Stimuli, Process Successions, Relations to Traits

Equipped now with some concepts of what states naturally exist and with practical capacities—still much to be improved—for measuring them in Q-data, we can return to integrating the growing knowledge and experience with these state measures into theory. The problems of conceptualization and calculation that await us can be indicated by such questions as the following. What do we know about the stimuli that characteristically trigger each state and by what index can their relative potencies be expressed? Are there laws that govern typical successions of states in processes, as seem to be indicated by the unusually high correlations among state factors? What is the relation between states and traits, particularly the relative variance contributions to actual behavior? What is the relation, perhaps in terms of lead and lag, between the conscious states recorded in Q-data and the neural and physiological substrata of emotion? How can state scale raw scores be made meaningful in applied psychology, as traits are, by standardizations?

Regarding the first question, that of organizing knowledge about emotional stimuli in terms of the classification of emotional state components, a practical challenge presents itself to the psychometrist. If emotional states are important in the behavioral specification equation (1.2) and if it is impracticable to measure a person's state immediately before behavior is to be predicted, of what use is our knowledge about states? A person's state score cannot be taken out of a file drawer as can the record of traits, such as intelligence, ego strength, and premsia. Yet if the psychologist wants to estimate how well Jim will do in an examination on Monday morning, he must consider Jim's level on such states as arousal and anxiety as well as his intelligence as in Equation (6.3), despite the fact that these states will not show their levels until the actual experience.

The answer to this question has appeared in a development of state psychology called modulation theory. This theory assumes that each individual is endowed (genetically and by previous experience) with a proneness or liability L_x to react readily with a particular emotion x. At the same time we investigate which situations provoke emotion x for most people in our culture. Any given situation k is then given a modulating value s_{kx} which says how much k stimulates x for the person of average x liability. That situation could be taking an examination, meeting a pretty girl, finding oneself in a house on fire, and so on. Modulation theory then takes the model

$$S_{kxi} = s_{kx}L_{xi} \tag{6.4}$$

where S_{kxi} is i's score on state x under situation k; s_{kx} is the general modulation for everyone of state x by situation k; and L_{xi} is i's liability (proneness, sensitivity) to state x. The susceptibility or liability L_x then becomes a trait that can be measured for the individual (Cattell, 1963a, 1973o) and preserved.

The provoker of a state can be external or internal. Externally it could be an examination room; internally an unhappy recollection or a glass of vodka. Some of our powerful moods are certainly triggered by internal reminiscences and unconscious associations as well as by states of the liver and frustrations of the colon. Once experimentation on state measurement has become sufficiently advanced, a general econetics (Sells, 1963, p. 71)—a science of the stimuli that set off recognized source states—can be built up. Development of this econetic taxonomy covering inner and environmental stimuli of the various states is undoubtedly indispensable but its comparative infancy need not deter us from exploring first the nature, measurement, and use of state responses as such.

The values L_x and s_{kx} are derived from experiment (for details see Cattell, 1971b, 1972a). The s_{kx} has to be combined with b_{jx}. Equation (6.3) reminds us that a behavioral index (or loading) b_{jx} can be calculated from a factorial experiment, which estimates how much a unit increment in a given trait—in this case a given state x—affects the performance of anyone on a given behavior response j (with trait and performance both in standard scores). Accordingly any term—such as $b_{jx}S_{xki}$ in Equation (6.3), where S_{xki} is the state level in i at the given moment k—can now be written, allowing for modulation, as

$$b_{jx}S_{xki} = b_{jx}s_{xk}L_{xi} \tag{6.5}$$

Thus we are back with trait scores that can be assigned to a person ahead of time since L_{xi} is a trait endowment—i's proneness to state x. The modulator s_{xk} is a constant found in general personality-environment theory indicating (as a datum of econetics) what the potency of situation k (say, a house on fire) is for state x. For example, if x were fear it would be large and positive. The psychometrist must note that in putting Equation (6.5) into Equation (6.3) the analysis has to be a covariance factor analysis, not ordinary factor analysis. L can also be the degree of a person's learning some particular role since formally this behaves the same: a given role cue provokes some (specifically, educated) people into assuming a role more than others who are unaware of its appropriateness.

Although L_x is technically a trait, confusion can perhaps be avoided by calling it a state-trait since it is measured by the set of items we have found to be markers for (that is, highly loaded on) the given state (dR or P) factor. L_x is the state measure when the modulator index s_x stands at unity; a state score is only a measure of L_x multiplied by some arithmetical value: its equality is state.

It is also worth focusing on the meaning of k. Every situation is defined as a *focal stimulus* j to which the person is consciously responding and an *ambient stimulus* k that constitutes the background conditions—the creators of mood, the room temperature, the general test instructions. The ambient stimulus k modifies the person's states and the focal stimulus j fixes through the behavioral indexes how the states and traits combine in producing the response to j. However, questionnaire work on states has not advanced to the point where it can yield an array of s_k modulator values for states (except for the pioneer work of Krug, 1971, and of DeYoung, 1973). Nor has the questionnaire as an instrument been used to locate, in addition to states, the role-proneness patterns, which should act similarly. Thus the preceding paragraphs present a theory to guide research.

Concerning the question of natural successions and interactions of states—such as would be visible in higher-order structure (above the second order, in which we typically operate in states)—one can only answer that sound state measurement is altogether too recent for firm answers to be available. In process study by P-technique, if two states tend to rise together or sequentially but with appreciable overlap, as in the suggestions in γ (Table 31) that stress is closely followed by regression, this is indicated at the next (third) stratum. Any characteristic overlap in rise and fall tends to produce a significant correlation of states such as we have observed in P-technique and this in turn shows itself, although with loss of some information, in third-order structures (see, however, Yule, 1926).

There is an expectation among psychologists that certain laws connect the state measurements. To study these we need to note correlations over time among them that reveal superordinate process structures (see process structure in the *Handbook of Multivariate Experimental Psychology*, Cattell, 1966a). The correlations indicating relations in time sequence sometimes arise from internal conditions (the tendency of fatigue to follow anxiety or for arousal to occur more readily with low fatigue) and from orderly sequences inherent in environmental events. An instance of the latter, of highest generality, is found in *adaptation process analysis* (Cattell and Scheier, 1961; Cattell, 1965a; Cartwright and Cartwright, 1971): a frustrating situation arouses anger, which is likely to produce attack, which is likely to produce retaliation, which is likely to produce anxiety, which in most cases without solution is likely to end in depression. These adaptation path analysis regularities should be carefully studied in connection with this chapter in Cartwright and Cartwright (1971). The widespread association of depression with anxiety can almost certainly be attributed to the adaptation path law that a certain dynamic crossroads (β in the α to δ series: Cattell and Scheier, 1961) produces situations that systematically tend to provoke both of them in close succession.

A constructive attitude to theory suggests that we reduce mere speculation by assembling evidence, however meager, on sequences and on the third-order state structure.[6] Evidence regarding the latter has been available

[6] An important proposition for research so far untried concerns the analysis of the state process by what has been called staggered P-technique (Harris, 1963; Cattell, 1957). When the state factor pattern has been determined a state score can be estimated for any moment in time t. Staggered P-technique correlates this score across many occasions of estimate $t - 3$, $t - 2$, $t - 1$, t, $t + 1$, and so on with the scores on loading variables (items) but matching an S_t score with a variable score at $t + 1$ minute, $t - 1$ minute, and so on to $t + 1$ hour and $t - 1$ hour. That is, the two series to be correlated are staggered relative to one another in time. This may reveal that an item loads the state factor better if it is scored, say, at the response 15 minutes later that the state score. Such a finding might be due to that response being typically a belated expression of the state. This is a means of throwing light on a regular process sequence in states and

for some time in T-data, where it has been shown (see Figure 16) that two third-order factors operate. My hypothesis is that F2 represents the effect of a general frustration situation (after the β crossroads in the adaptation process analysis chart). Frustration then accounts for the appearance of adrenergic response, cholesterol-pulse effort response, and especially depression in close sequence as shown to the right of Figure 16. The other factor, F1, which reverts adrenergic response and effort stress in opposition to anxiety, suggests a possible personality structure (ego strength or dominance) determiner that favors a positive response of grappling with problems (producing psychosomatic stress, SUI 4 and SUI 5) and a negative response of neurotic retreat that favors anxiety and torpid dissatisfaction (SUI 9 and SUI 1). That is, the individual grapples with the frustration and becomes stressed or retreats from a solution and becomes dissatisfied and anxious.

The questions of relations states to traits and of the new technical problems in state standardization require a refinement of the model tentatively discussed above. These questions are related; if results show that each person oscillates in his state scores about a significantly different mean from another person then we have to introduce yet a fourth concept—the trait in a state, akin to liability—and our standard score concepts regarding states must change. Until research indicates which is correct we must entertain two different models: the common-zero mode and the personal mode. Both assume a homeostatic tendency to return from high state levels to an equilibrium point but in the former that point is supposed to lie at an absolute zero of state expression whereas, in the latter the mode is supposed to be some habitual level, perhaps not far above zero, to which the person most frequently resorts when not stimulated at all. Rather than a zero, this latter is a resting point or a mode on his distribution of state scores across many randomly sampled occasions. The translation from models to statistical consequences requires space for detail, and I shall not pursue it thoroughly here. In neither model is the average state score the same as the resting level (zero in one case; a nonzero value in the other) but is proportional to the individual's liability trait score. With the possible exception of a bipolar state dimension such as elation-depression, it makes better sense to consider a model in which state responses are in one direction only from a true zero.[7] Note that the personal mode is formally the same as a trait when one accepts trait-change factors, but the existence of a mode in the case of the state model makes no assumption that such a mode has any trait-like properties. The

also on cycles. The same approach offers a defense against the blind spot in correlation created by Yule's paradox (Yule, 1926)—that if two variables in cycles of identical frequency (and therefore assumed to belong to the same process) are half a phase out of step no correlation is found between them if measured at the same instants (occasions). Truly cyclic effects in the states here studied have fortunately been so rare as to present no "Yule problem."

[7] The obtaining of this true, absolute zero has been set out elsewhere (Cattell, 1972a). Nesselroade has pointed out that the only area of measurement in which we can readily aspire to absolute scores is with difference scores. However, modulation theory presents a principle whereby absolute zeros for state scores can be inferred in the usual sense and not just the difference sense.

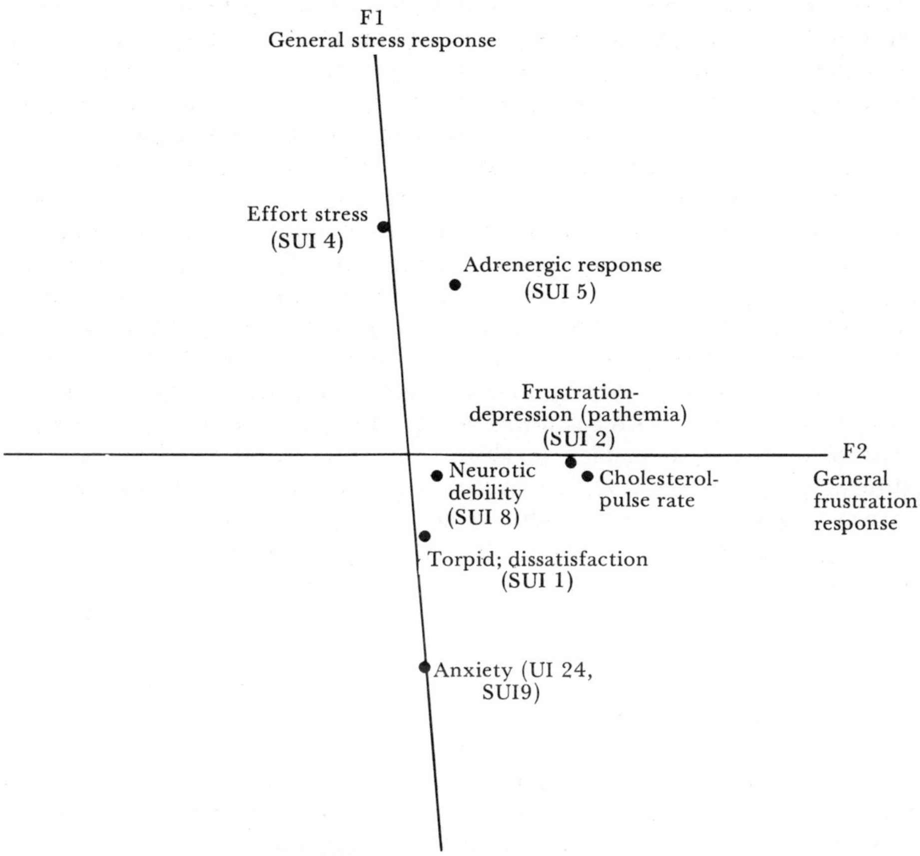

Figure 16. Evidence for third-stratum state structure for T-data measures of states (third stratum in Q-data, second stratum in T-data).

vital difference of trait and state is that in the former the differences among means of individuals are large relative to the fluctuation, while for the state the reverse is true.

By neither the common zero nor the personal mode model is it necessary for a person's level on a trait to correlate with his mean level on the corresponding state. These models suppose them to be different things. For example, if anxiety as a characterological trait and as a state can be proved to be different, no correlation of the trait with the mean of the state across occasions is necessarily expected. However, the distinction of the concepts is one thing and the possibility of keeping their estimated scale scores uncorrelated is another. If Nesselroade and Cable's (1972) experiment is confirmed, showing that anxiety as a state is a different pattern from anxiety as a trait, these two patterns still have sufficient variables loaded in common to produce marked, positive correlation between scores estimated from the two batteries. If we believe that state and trait are truly uncorrelated (across people, using a state average score, or a score on any one occasion) then the device of mutual partialing shown in Figure 17 can be invoked. In Figure 17 the items by which trait and state are scored are shown in the ovals. Although they have been selected so that each set is less involved with the other than are the typical items shown as points between them, they are still not capable of yielding orthogonal scores as required by the true state and trait factors at *S* and *T*, because one cannot find items with that degree of mutual separation. Nevertheless, by subtracting part of the scale 2 scores from scale 1, and vice versa (mutual partialing), scores can be obtained that are orthogonal as at *S* and *T*. In the absence of any reliable evidence as to just how the trait and the state (mean or one occasion) are naturally correlated (possibly slightly positively, for instance) it is safest and most convenient to assume they should be uncorrelated and in that case our aim would be to separate the scales mutually to orthogonality. This partialing is best achieved by taking out first and second centroids. Rotating through 45 degrees we find the transformation necessary to shift test scores to these new axes. It is assumed that suppressor action by finding items positive on the trait and negative on the state and vice versa is not possible in this case.

Finally we come to the seldom explored problems of standardizing

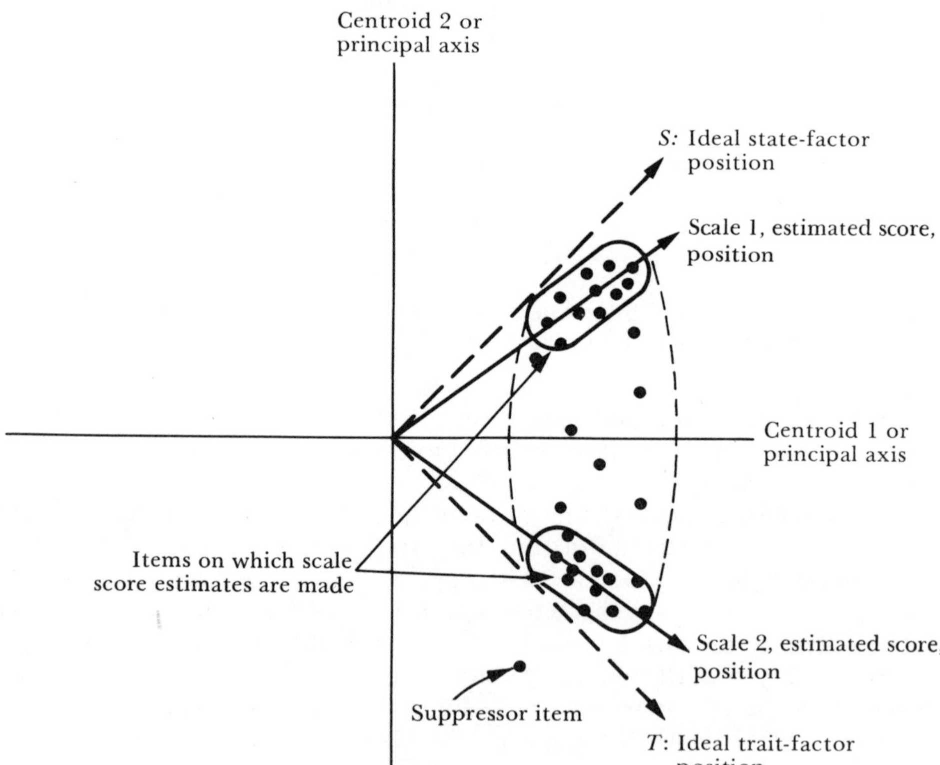

Figure 17. Mutual partialing to produce independence of estimated scale scores otherwise correlated. The correlation of estimates is due to the available items for the state having some loading on the trait and vice versa. The correction is shown here grossly for the scales, but it could be applied to each item.

questionnaire scales for states. If we accept the modulation model this problem becomes one of standardizing state liability traits since in any situation we know what the actual state level is if we know the individual's liability value L_{xi}. And each L_x is an average across a standard set of occasions, the s_{kx} values of which average unity. The standard scores, such as stens, of states in ambient situation k are then the L_x standard scores multiplied by s_k. If liabilities are to be standarized the possibility is also to be considered that as traits they can be functions of other known personality traits and their standardizations.[8]

The awkward problems of standardizing state scales arise from the requirement that two standardizations are ideally required: (1) within each individual across the ocasions of his life; and (2) among individuals pinning down any state score with respect to a distribution that is a sum of all individual distributions.

If the personal mode model holds true or if our scales are such that (unlike the outcome of Figure 17) they represent sums of trait and state scores, the sigma of state scores made on a single occasion equals the square root of a variance which is the sum of the between-individual and within-individual variances. Even if we make the assumption that the variance for all individuals is the same we still cannot take a state score on a given person at a given moment and assign it a standard score meaningful for the given individual. By repeating state measures many times across a group we can estimate the relative part in the total variance due to within-and between-individual variance. But unless we know also the mean score of the individual we cannnot translate his score at a given moment into a meaningful standard score, on the given state within *his* standardization scheme. The solution may lie in the discovery of some extraneous test that will reveal an individual's mean state score directly without having to test him repeatedly.

Even so this solution assumes that all people have the same variability; the concept of liability definitely assumes that they do not. With this latter model the only way to give a meaningful standard score to an individual is to determine both his raw score mean and variance by repeatedly testing him. On the other hand if we are not concerned that a certain level of anxiety means nothing to Brown but is terrifying to Smith, the simple procedure of standardizing on a single-occasion measure of a large group will suffice. Nevertheless this fails as a state standardization if our items to any degree confound trait with state. When the confounding is great each state measure has a standard error equal to the sigma of the trait and the state variance appears much larger than it is.

[8] The reference here is to the possibility that a general tendency to fluctuate—not a liability on some particular emotion—exists as a personality trait. This possibility has been systematically examined by Spearman (1927), Flugel (1928), Cattell (1943, 1957), Das (1955), and Wessman and Ricks (1966). Das and I both find low general variability with high ego strength *C* and superego *G*. To this Wessman and Ricks add evidence of a stronger association with the second-order exvia factor. This variability could be a second order among the L_x, L_y scores and be standardized as part of their standardization.

The standardization of state scales obviously awaits a breakthrough in terms of a discovery for measuring state modes and trait levels in clean independence of the immediate state level. Meanwhile, since we must be aware of the magnitudes of error of estimate that enter when we accept a single administration across a group as a basis of a standardization, it behoves us to take stock, by a definitive statement of the relative variance of states and traits, in the settings of P-, dR-, and R-techniques.

What we are really asking here is this: If a certain variable has an equal loading on a trait and on a state in R-technique, what are the ratios of those loadings in dR- and P-technique? We can alternatively talk about the relative variance size of *factors* in these R-, dR-, and P-alternatives but this involves complex discussions. Ordinary factor analysis artificially makes all factors the same size. And if we turn to real-base (covariance) factor analysis (Cattell, 1972a) it is still possible to give meaning to factor size comparisons only if we agree on a standard stratified sample of variables. Accordingly, taking the question in the first form above and simply comparing fractions of the variance of the sample particular set of variables accounted for under different analyses we reach the conclusions shown in Table 32.

The conclusions are examined under two assumptions but the essential conclusion is that the absolute (real-base) variance of a state is twice as great in dR- as in R- or P-technique. Regarding the relative sizes of states and traits in the R-technique analysis (the extent to which behavior is determined relatively by states and by traits) the answer depends entirely on the choice of variables. Psychology still awaits the meaningful verdict that could be given by taking an agreed stratified set of variables from the personality sphere.

These conclusions are important because when corresponding states and traits have patterns hard to distinguish, their different variance sizes in R-technique relative to the dR- and P-technique variances help us pick them out, and because the contributions are important to understanding the standardization of states.

6. Summary

(1) Unitary source states (the dimensions by means of which mood states may be precisely specified) are not located by introspection alone or by selecting items showing high variability and fluctuation (which may indicate mere item unreliability) but by coordinated use of P- and dR-techniques and by comparisons with grid analysis and R-technique.

(2) The discovery of the number and nature of such response patterns (common and unique), *as such,* must precede location and listing of the internal and external stimuli that trigger them. There can be no order in the latter until there is order in the former. Present research indicates that such operationally located change patterns are of two kinds: states on which people differ from occasion to occasion with a variance that is great relative to the differences of the means of people averaged over occasions;

Table 32

Relative Variance of States, Traits, and Trait-Change Factors

in P.-, dR-, and R-Techniques

(a) Assumption: All people have the same state mean and sigma. There is only one trait and one state involved so that the variance of the variable is wholly accounted for by them. State factor sigma equals trait sigma equals unity in the R-technique case. With both assumptions (a, and b below) the basic treatment is by covariance factor analysis. Thus in (a) dR- we have the alternative of saying the loading is $2b_{js}$ or of keeping it on b_{js} as in R allowing the factor to be twice as big. The variance of the variable is the same for R- and dR-, if $b_{jt} = b_{js}$, but the state change variable is twice as big as the state variable in R. With these conditions the variance of the variable should be half as big in P- as in R- and dR-.

R-Technique:

$$\sigma_{ij(\mathbf{k})}{}^2 = b_{jt}{}^2\ \sigma_{t\mathbf{i}}{}^2 + b_{js}{}^2\ \sigma_{s\mathbf{k}}{}^2 = b_{jt}{}^2 + b_{js}{}^2$$

dR-Technique:

$$\sigma_{\mathbf{i}j(\mathbf{k}2\ -\ \mathbf{k}1)}{}^2 = b_{js}{}^2\ \sigma_{s\mathbf{k}}{}^2 + b_{js}{}^2\ \sigma_{s\mathbf{k}}{}^2 = 2b_{js}{}^2$$

P-Technique

$$\sigma_{ijk(i)} = b_{js(i)}\ \sigma_{sk}{}^2 = b_{js}{}^2$$

Note: Subscripts in parentheses indicate what is constant for all measures: *i* in P-, *k* in R-. *j* is the specific variable, *k* the occasion. By contrast a boldface letter shows over what the variance is measured. b_j is the loading for variable *j*. ***k*** is boldface in R- and dR- because, although it is the same occasion in time, the condition is different for each person in regard to his state provocation

(b) Assumption: People have different means and sigmas for their states, which are positively correlated over people.

R-Technique:

$$\sigma_{ij(k)}{}^2 = b_{jt}{}^2\ \sigma_t{}^2 + b_{js}{}^2\ \ \sigma_{sm\mathbf{i}}{}^2 + \sigma_{s\mathbf{ki}}{}^2 + 2r_{mki}\ \sigma_{sm\mathbf{i}}\ \sigma_{s\mathbf{ki}}$$

Note: $\sigma_{sm\mathbf{i}}$ is the variance of state means across people; $\sigma_{s\mathbf{ki}}$ is the variance of individuals from their means where both occasions (***k*s**) and the sigma of individuals (***i*s**) vary. This sigma across two sources is considered approximately the mean of the sigmas of all individuals.

dR-Technique:

$$\sigma_{\mathbf{i}j(k_2\ -\ k_1)}{}^2 = 2bjs^2\ \sigma_{ski}{}^2$$

P-Technique:

$$\sigma_{jk(i)}{}^2 = b_{js(i)}{}^2\ \sigma_{sk(i)}{}^2 = b_{jis}$$

Note: This P-technique differs from that in (a) only because $\sigma_{sk}{}^2$ is peculiar to the individual whereas in (a) it was assumed the same for all individuals. Otherwise the variance of factors and variables is the same for dR- and P- in (b) as in (a). But in R- the variance of the variable will be greater and the variance of the state factor will be considerably greater (using raw scores and covariance factors). Such experimental comparisons are the means of deciding between models (a) and (b).

and trait-change factors each of which closely resembles a particular trait in pattern and in which the ratio of within-individual to between-individual variance is much lower. Methods for discriminating states, trait-change factors, and traits have been set out and the general behavioral specification equation is expanded to require terms for states as well as traits (S's and T's) and sometimes all three structures. (T's, T_c's and S's).

(3) When these techniques are applied to questionnaire and objective test observations covering the trait personality sphere one discovers a close parallel between trait and change patterns. For every known trait—primary or secondary—a corresponding change pattern is revealed that may be either a state or a trait-change structure. The possibility that this similarity could be an artifact is rejected. Accordingly one must recognize that states corresponding, for example, to the traits long known as anxiety, exvia-invia, and even intelligence, exist as fluctuating entities. The justification for considering that some of these are states rather than trait-change factors resides in their large variance and in the findings of such studies as those of Nesselroade and Cable (1972) and Rickels and Cattell (1965) that in R-technique two factors of anxiety can be found. One apparently corresponds to that found in dR- or P-techniques alone and is a state; the other is a trait. They have slight differences of pattern. For example, anxiety as a state has more emphasis on primaries Q_4, C, Q_3, and O than does the trait secondary.

(4) The search for items to ensure coverage of the principal human state factors has been made on two bases: (a) the original personality sphere represented in the 23 normal and 12 pathological factors; and (b) on what have long been considered state phenomena, particularly in terms of items found associated with research on the physiology of states classically pursued by investigators of emotion. On the first basis 10 states have been located, among them anxiety, exvia-invia, cortertia-pathemia, independence-subduedness, general depression, and general psychoticism. On the second basis extensive overlap has been shown with the first but states of stress, fatigue, arousal, and regression have been added, as well as one or two lesser second-order depression factors.

(5) Although state factors can be demonstrated at the primary level, corresponding to the primary traits in, say, the 16 PF, it seems that most of the trait terminology of psychologists and the general public pertains to dimensions demonstrable at the second stratum level. Thus of some 15 state factors which it has seemed convenient to put into scales, only two—stress and fatigue—are apparently at the first stratum level.

The investigations summarized here deal with general states, not more specific dynamic mood or interest states corresponding to ergs. The latter are known, as in the work of Horn (1966) and of Williams (1958), but through objective tests rather than questionnaires. In accordance with the criteria which caused us (Chapter Two) to set aside Edwards' and Jackson's scales of needs as traits, we have rejected specific motivational states as too fakable and unreliable for questionnaires. However, researches of a mixed questionnaire and objective test nature, covering simultaneously such dynamic states as hunger, fear, and sex, and general states, are included to help demonstrate the distinctness of general and specific dynamic states. For example, Cattell and Bartlett (1971) support the mixed conclusion that fear (specific) and anxiety (general state) are distinct states.

(6) There is evidence—ample in the case of anxiety, exvia, and

regression—that these second-order states correspond with first-order states in T-data factors, thus paralleling the rule found in traits. However, as Barton's and Bartlett's research shows, the relation of Q-data to physiological state factors has additional complications not yet understood.

(7) Research on states involves more attention to factor-analytic technicalities than does research on traits. For this reason certain ambiguities remain to be cleared up. For example, P-technique studies clearly show only one second-order depression factor whereas dR-technique studies typically show three. Also it is comparatively difficult in a few source states to get items acting relatively purely on one factor. This difficulty is so acute in the case of fatigue and low arousal that even with careful attention to item choice and rotation they are not clearly separated. Overlap also exists in fatigue and regression, anxiety and regression, and especially anxiety and depression. Indeed Spielberger's STAI, in the framework of the factor-analytic studies mentioned, measures stress as the anxiety trait and depression as the anxiety state. However, the initial alignment of the eight-state questionnaire scales with such T-data primaries as UI 21, 22, 23, 24, 28, and 32 is encouraging.

(8) As part of this advance in methodology researchers need to employ more explicit models. The modulation model is proposed here as best fitting existing knowledge. It involves the notion of individual differences in a *state liability* trait L_x corresponding to each particular state x. The liability value is transformed by a modula*tor* s_{kx}, which expresses the average stimulation for most people of the ambient stimulus k for state S_x. Modulation theory in effect introduces a fourth concept—the state-trait—beyond trait, state, and trait-change entities.

(9) Further refinement of the model extends to the alternatives of the common-zero and the personal modes. These models show that standardizing questionnaire state scales is a complex procedure. An explicit analysis here of the relative variance of states and traits in R-, P-, and dR-experiments helps clarify the standardization principles.

VII

Perspective on Personality Structure Through the Eyes of Three Media: Q-, L-, and T-Data

The behavior through which personality structure is inferred can be observed through three media, Q-data, L-data, and T-data, whose properties are stated in Chapter One. Their effects are like those we should meet if we looked at the same scenery through three different colored glasses. The analogy holds not only in that each gives more vivid emphasis to some features but also in that some variables are blocked out altogether by one or another. This creates problems now to be discussed.

1. Distortions of Pattern and Level in "Mental Interiors": The Theorem of "Indifference of Medium" and Instrument-Free Pure Trait Patterns

Well-planned scientific work is obviously designed to get the greatest possible increase of knowledge from these three perspectives, permitting us to see personality in the round. Unfortunately, however, substantial work has been invested in well-known questionnaire developments—those of

Edwards, Jackson, Howarth, and Comrey, to name a few—without the least attention to the guidance necessary from other media or broader concepts that embrace all three. By contrast the work of Eysenck and by implication that on the MMPI has systematically built theory on two or all three media, a design that has existed in the programatic work of my associates from the beginning. Indeed it has been my basic and explicit principle since 1940 in personality theory and research strategy (1946b, 1957, 1965a) that the same broad trait structures are found with understandable modifications across L-, Q-, and T-media.

The theory that the same structures will be found despite differences in medium of observation has been made explicit in the principle of *indifference of indicator* (or of medium) and the concept of the *instrument-free trait pattern.* Two rather distinct conceptual systems have developed for understanding and formulating the perturbations. First Digman and I (Cattell and Digman, 1964; Cattell, 1957, 1968) proposed a broad but precise theory of perturbation that involves the concept of instrument factors and instrument-free trait factors. Second Campbell and Fiske (1959) proposed the notions of convergent and discriminant validity. There have been doubts about what these terms really mean (D. N. Jackson, 1971; Conger, 1971), and I shall hope to show that if they are given precise definitions they actually fit into general perturbation theory and the instrument factor concepts.

The expression "the principle of indifference of medium (or indicator)" is perhaps not the best for final use since it has a negative emphasis—on the fog to be dispersed rather than on the object to be found. Or, as some would say, it appears to concentrate on the hole in the doughnut rather than the doughnut. The later term—the principle of instrument-free pure trait patterns—suggests more positive concentration on what has to be unearthed. As we shall see, the important reorientation it introduces to the present book is that the structure of traits in questionnaires cannot be understood from research in questionnaires alone.

In criticizing many questionnaire constructors for neglecting the concepts in general personality theory generated by more global approaches as set out in Bischof (1964), Cattell (1957), Eysenck (1969), Freud (1920), Horne (1950), Murray (1960), Pervin (1970), and others. I am not denying the importance of precise, careful, programatic work in factor analysis and item analysis in questionnaires themselves. The questionnaire domain needs such work in great abundance but it should be informed from the beginning of its strategy by respect for the rating (L-data) and objective test (T-data) findings as exemplified, for example, in the research of Goldberg (1968, 1972b), Wiggins (1973), Stricker (1973), and others.

A more positive statement of the indifference of medium principle is that a trait can be recognized and defined which is independent of any one instrumentality of observation. As instrument-factor concepts are defined by exemplification in this chapter in the light of comprehensive categories of perturbation theory (Figure 19) the meaning of *instrument-free patterns* becomes clearer. My theory is that after instrument factors are extracted and set aside, a pattern remains that can be called the trait itself. This instrument-free trait-behavior pattern can be *located and defined* but it can never be *measured* without contamination by the instrumentality of observation. The best we can do in measurement is to get an instrument-balanced set of measurement expressions, thus attenuating the effect of any one instrument.

In perturbation theory I have drawn a distinction between ordinary instrument factors—(d)A and (d)C in Figure 19—and *situation factors*—(d)B in Figure 19. It might be the case that a source trait of dominance *E* shows itself in some people in the home and in others on the job. If so, a well-planned factor analysis should yield domestic and job subfactors (or possibly a bipolar factor) that represent substantive but situational psychological adjuncts in the expression of the dominance factor, not instrument factors. Indeed it becomes a question of whether they are better studied under II(i) or II(ii) in Figure 19. Let it be clear, therefore, that the theory of *instrument-free* traits as higher-level abstractions from observed behavior across several instrumentalities is quite different from the indefensible concept that a real trait shows no alteration from subculture to subculture or that ancillary situation factors are not necessary to account for relatively strong expressions in particular life areas.

This chapter, in which the effect of instrumentalities and media of observation is clarified, is also the appropriate place to consider perturbation theory, particularly the effects of motivational distortion in the test-taking situation—a skeleton in the closet of questionnaire practitioners that often rattles its bones—since all these phenomena are clarified by perturbation theory. In regard to present treatments of distortion I must warn the reader that the most popular approaches, such as social desirability, suffer from the usual tendency of specialists, especially in applied work, to busy themselves with purely local solutions. Indeed in coining the term itemetrics I felt it desirable to warn the student of questionnaire designers who neglect even the wider requirements of psychometrics, let alone those of general personality theory.

The devotee of itemetrics typically shovels questionnaire items into computers and comes out with endless files of item correlations, "validated" against his favorite clusters for homogeneity or against arbitrary and changing job criteria, or against orthogonal and sometimes even completely unrotated "factors." He is, in a special sense, the slave of the machine—and of inattention to broader personality theory. The disagreements between, on the one hand, Thurstone, Eysenck, Barton, Comrey, Coan, Guilford, Horn, Nesselroade, Nuttall, Dielman, Dreger, Eber, Schaie, Shrader, Sells, Tatsuoka, and myself, and on the other, a more numerous army of busy practical questionnaire constructors lie along this axis, and become clarified if one keeps it in mind.

In any consideration of distortion in a certain medium from some inferred true trait or process there are two distinct issues: that the scores, although directed to correct concepts, are in error; and that the concepts to which the scales are directed are in error, that is, they correspond to no stable, functionally unitary theoretical concept. Without implying that the former is trivial—it certainly is not for the applied psychologist—I defer its consideration to "trait view" and "motivational distortion" concepts in Chapter Nine on psychometrics. Here I begin by asking what perturbations of the observation process could produce distortion in the trait concepts themselves.

Personality theorists—Freud, Jung, McDougall—have always by implication accepted the principle of indifference of media, freely intermixing evidence from the consulting room (Q-data), life observation (L-data), and laboratory tests (T-data). But as techniques of observation and statistical analysis advanced, psychologists appeared who were disposed to work within one technique. Now we see that positive construction of principles and methods is required to build bridges and integrate across media. The elements of such integration methodology have appeared in factor-matching techniques (congruence and salient variable similarity indexes) and in rotation to set aside instrument factors.

Before focusing on these and other techniques, however, it will help if we look at the problem of distortion and perturbation by media of observation in the broadest conceptual framework. This amounts to considering a principle of relativity in psychology. Figure 18 reminds us of the totality of possible psychological observation in terms of the basic data relation matrix (Cattell, 1946b, 1966a) or data box with respect to behavioral events.

As is well recognized, the five coordinates of the data box are stimuli, responses, subjects, background conditions (occasions), and observers. Of these five series of ids our concern is mainly with the fifth dimension—the observer—and its relation to the others. In depicting five dimensions in two, Figure 18 puts three in a box and brings observers and responses out to the front.

The chief difference between Q- and L-data is that in questionnaires the observer evaluates his own behavior whereas in L-data other observers do so. The comparison of questionnaire and rating results has to take into account both the systematic differences that arise from this and other aspects of the two media, and the probability that the individual differences in the observers' personalities will result in different distortion in the two cases. (For example, high dominance E might cause a person to overrate self-sufficiency Q_2 in the questionnaire medium but to mark down other people on Q_2 in the observer situation.)

The effects of observers can be attacked in the most general way by correlating observers over their evaluations of any one response over n subjects, as shown in the score matrix in the plane (subjects by observers) at the front of Figure 18. Alternatively analysis of variance can seek significant differences of observers in this score matrix or others. But this is not the only source of possible distortion in affixing a score for response r to a score for focal stimulus j. Variations due to sources outside r and j can come also from different ambient situations (occasions in Figure 18) as when an observer does not allow for the difference between the subject being observed alone or in company.

Although the comprehensive problems of psychological relativity can

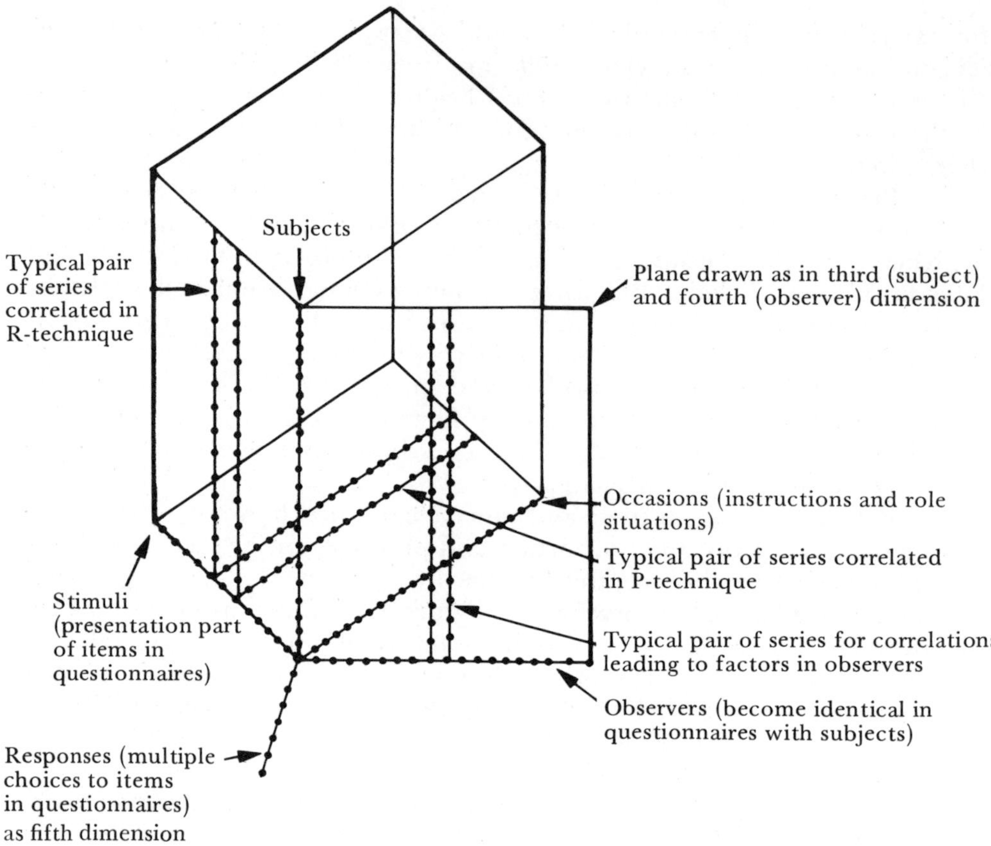

Figure 18. Observer as source of variance in the data box. The data box, or BDRM (Basic Data Relation Matrix), although five-dimensional, is typically used in three-dimensional form. The two dimensions not usually reproduced are given here as coordinates outside the main box. The series of responses in questionnaires and other tests is tied to respective stimuli; no extra dimension is needed. The indispensable fourth dimension, shown here outside the perspective of a three-dimensional box by a dotted line, is that representing a series of possible observers of the act. Regard for this fourth dimension is required for the relations of Q-data to L-data trait concepts.

best be perceived and systematically investigated in the five-coordinate data box, the typical questionnaire user would probably prefer to come quickly to the problems specific to the questionnaire realm. One certainly sees many instances of the power of the ambient situation, as when a child slapped on the head by another responds by hitting back if on the playground but probably not if with parents or in the classroom. In the case of the questionnaire there is a double ambient situation around the focal one, namely, the background defined in the item itself and the testing background in which the questionnaire is given ("Will my parents see what I write here?").

Over and above the systematic distortions in questionnaire responses due to the particular personality of the responder and the ambient situation and role effects of the test-taking situation, there are sheerly random cognitive effects due to the person's not knowing himself well enough, by which I mean largely his unawareness of different standards between himself and others. If asked "Do you experience fear of the dark? Much, average or little?" how is a child to know, from experience of his own consciousness of fear only, whether his inner emotion is average or not? Related to this are effects of sheer differences of standard, as when one person uses a point well above average in scales as if it were the average. Finally in the Q- and L-media it is possible that preconceived connections—say, that people who are shy are also secretive—are sufficiently widespread clichés or stereotypes to produce correlations where none would exist in an objective, T-data approach.

It is easy to suggest specific devices to reduce some of these distortions. For example, the subjectivity of personal standards in "fear of the dark" questions may be reduced by shifting to specific behavior in which comparisons can be made with others: "At public meetings do you get up and speak (a) as often as most people, (b) more often, (c) less often?" Likewise raters in L-data may be trained to discount certain prejudice effects. For example, low *H* in the mental interior factor obtained from Q-data shows up as shyness and unwillingness to speak. In L(BR) (observer rating) data the same behavior tends to be interpreted so that such items as "stuck-up" and "critical of others" begin to load the pattern.

The preceding statement of some typical problems regarding the intrusive effect of modes of observing responses reminds us of the complexity of this problem. Unfortunately the attempts in the literature to handle these problems have been almost without exception the construction of local and temporary remedies. There has been a plugging of leaks here and there rather than an examining of the whole fabric. The result is a patchwork of insubstantial conceptions in lie scales, acquiescence measures, social desirability definitions, and others. The results of such approaches have given scope for those who do not grasp the foundations of common-trait structures to claim, as Becker (1960), Mischel (1968), and others have done, that no true structures manifest themselves across media and that the indifference of medium principle is a myth since all is media effect. But in the last decade a more systematic approach of recognizing the true sources of relative observation in the data box and of developing a *general perturbation theory* for all kinds of observation has brought a more constructive view. This is the topic of the next section.

2. Perturbation Theory and Effect of Instrument Factors

Although space precludes my presenting here the total perspective of what has become known as perturbation theory, Figure 19 may help to remind the student with some reading elsewhere of its main features and categories. Perturbation theory attempts to define the nature and action of the influences associated with mere instrumentality of measurement and observation, modes of data processing, and ordinary measurement and sampling error.

Throughout the analysis of perturbation, that is, the modification

Figure 19. Sources of structural misinterpretation focused by perturbation theory. For adequate accounts of the breadth and nature of these influences the reader must refer to Cattell (1961), Cattell and Digman (1964), and Cattell (1968). Note that a systematic relation is possible between certain categories here and those of the five dimensions in the data box in Figure 18. Thus, II(ii)(b) deals with sampling on the subject coordinate; II(ii)(c) with the observer coordinate; II(ii)(d)A and B with stimulus-response coordinates; and II(ii)(d)B and C with selections on the occasions coordinate.

Experimental results brought to the point of uniquely rotated factors from a given experiment

- I. Error factors defined as matrix peculiar
  - Influences in data
    - Due to poor experimental control
    - Due to error of observation (systematic intrusions)
  - Influences in calculations
    - Due to scoring
    - Due to computing
      - Machine errors
      - Accidentally poor rotations
- II. Real factors defined as replicable across experiments and matrices
  - (i) *Substantive factors*
    Psychologically general, theoretically valuable "true" personality, state, learning process factors
  - (ii) *Perturbation factors*
    Inescapable in method, irrelevant to the most general theory
    - (a) *Data-treatment factors*
      Statistical-metrical tool and measurement artifacts (scaling, correlation, factor-extraction-method-related, including systematic rotation-principle error)
    - (b) *Subject-sampling factors*
      Substantive but may be so narrow and peculiar to a subsample as to be perturbation factors as far as general interests of investigator are concerned
    - (c) *Observer-view factors*
      Appearing only when observations proceed via human mind
      - A. Role-relation factors
      - B. Cognitive apperception (cultural cliché projection factors
    - (d) *Instrument factors*
      Factors associated with selections on tests (stimulus-response units) and in life situations (conditions)
      - A. *Test-form factors*
        Substantive but subordinate to those required and due to interaction of personality, motivation, and proficiency with form of test only
      - B. *Situation-of-variables factors*
        Produced by odd samplings of variables to cover life behavior in time or place not test form or test condition; include density-of-variable effects, making specifics into broad factors.
      - C. *Test-administration situation factors*
        Produced by odd samplings of situations of test-taking; include modulator effect distortions, subject roles, social desirability effects.

of general personality and process concepts by local situations and observers, two kinds of effects need to be considered: those that produce wrong values on particular measure and those that produce distorted concepts—patterns, factors, and correlation clusters. The former is less upsetting of a science of personality than the latter. Indeed I shall largely bypass the question of random error (blurring) and concentrate on the influences likely to produce false structures over and above those inherent in the subjects' actual behavior.

Regarding these false structures, perturbation theory begins (top Figure 19) by distinguishing factors that replicate across experiments from those that are accidental in the sense of being peculiar to one experiment and matrix. Whatever cannot achieve some invariance across experiments is obviously in some sense random or local error. Figure 19 next divides the former into substantive factors that correspond to the *objective* influences in personality with which psychological theory is concerned, and into *perturbation* factors that can be explained as incidental to the manner of investigation. The latter are recognized as coming from four major sources: data-treatment factors (artifacts due to analysis); subject-sampling factors; observer-view factors; and instrument of measurement factors. The two first are theoretically trivial and can be read about elsewhere (Cattell and Digman, 1964). Our present concern regarding questionnaires lies only with the two last, instrument factors and observer factors.

Instrument factors were apparently first noted by Cattell and Gruen (1955), who traced a unique simple-structure factor found in personality T-data to diurnal variations of sensitivity in a brass instrument affecting all personality measures involving the *GSR* (galvanic skin reflex). Confirmation of such factorial intrusions has since appeared in Holtzmann and Bitterman (1956) and in the work of Damarin, Campbell, and others, as well as (in a slightly different sense) from the difficulty factors of Wherry and Gaylord (1944) and of Dingman (1958). A striking instance appeared: a study of the IPAT Music Preference Test of Personality (Cattell and Anderson, 1953) by Mayeske (1962) showed an instrument factor separating all items based on a superior method of recording from those using an older method. In all these studies the effect is simple enough for the designation "instrument factor" to be recognized as entirely appropriate. The vehicle factors in measuring motivation (see Horn, 1966a) are another much-investigated example. But the term instrument, although it originates in physical instrumentalities, can be generalized to broader and more subtle effects.

Often the investigator is looking for general, substantive personality and ability factors and finds among them certain simple-structure factors evidently due (from their content and boundaries) to what he has regarded as relatively trivial features of measurement procedure—the properties of certain brass instruments, the number and difficulty of multiple-choice answers, the training of the observer, the device by which motivational strength is measured, and so on. However, unlike the error factors just set aside they are not trivial and transient but show constancy from experiment to experiment. Indeed, although I continue to call them instrument factors

(Cattell, 1965a, 1968, 1971a) they may nevertheless correspond to real psychological structures that are, however, irrelevant and unwanted. For example, if we measured arithmetic ability by some examples with words and some without we might find that differences in speed of reading intruded as an instrument factor into half of the arithmetic ability battery. In short we have to recognize that the definition is relative to a domain not only because the performance on instrument factors (such as speed of putting check marks or the general goodness of memory when using memory for pictures to assess interest) has to be something in the subject but also because there could be some arbitrariness in the experimenter's judgment of what is irrelevant. Just as dirt is arbitrarily defined as "matter out of place" so instrument-factor variance is often merely variance that the investigator prefers to do without.

Thus in the Myeske (1962) experiment a scratchy needle used in recording a subset of items on a test primarily concerned with emotional reaction to music produces a rejection factor among subjects with respect to that subset regardless of the music itself. In the objective measure of human motivational strength (Cattell, Horn, Sweney, and Radcliffe, 1964; Cattell, DeYoung, and Burdsal, in preparation) the vehicles through which the motivational strength expresses itself and is observed—memory, autism, word association—produce appreciable factors of their own—sex, fear, superego strength—outside the motivation structures themselves. The arbitrariness of stigmatizing a factor as an instrument factor is seen nowhere so clearly as in objective personality tests where, among some 15 to 20 personality factors (from tests that necessarily also involve some intelligence), a general intelligence factor commonly appears. Yet among personality factors Spearman's *g* is an interloper that is commonly thrown out. This is an extreme instance; most instrument factors are decidedly narrow, unimportant types of ability which, because they happen to be involved in the responses to the mode of construction covering several tests or observations, emerge as a broad factor across several personality factors. Although recognized as having real psychological meaning they are often specific factors that has been broadened by repetition across many tests as a feature of their instruction or even printing.

A taxonomy of the principal types of instrument factors remains to be written. But it is already quite clear with respect to our present problem of media that one must not expect simply one instrument factor for each of the three media. Rather there is likely to be a special family of such instrument factors that haunts each medium. Thus in ratings (L-data) there are apparently instrument factors that correspond to the personality factors in observers that project into the perception of others; to the particular role relation—peer, parent, teacher—of rater to ratee; and to the area in which behavior is observed—in class, at home, on the playground, at camp. In questionnaires one can imagine an instrument factor that corresponds to ability to read. The cycling of items and the balancing of yes and no answers in producing a higher score in most questionnaires prevents differences in, say, speed of reading from altering the score across the personality factors.

But Dielman and I found in six-to-eight-year olds some tendency of low intelligence to reduce all personality scores, presumably occurring only when items are such that average scores are above random scores. Probably the personality factors of the subject that intrude into his manner of self-perception play as large a role as instrument factors in questionnaires as in observer ratings. Other classes of instrument factor are peculiar to the questionnaire, such as the style of vocabulary, the design of multiple choices introducing acquiescence sets (where items for a scale are not balanced for yes and no answers), the effect of a tendency to extreme response when a fairly wide range of multiple-choice answers is allowed, general care and accuracy in answering, the role (confidential or open to later public discussion) in which the questionnaire is answered, and, in young children, the ability to understand abstract trait terms and generalized symbolic situations that often enter into questionnaire items.

Granted that instrument factors are suspected to exist, or even that they have already shown themselves as extra, previously unhypothesized factors, the methodological problem arises of effectively segregating and identifying them. As is stressed wherever I contrast the instrument-factor concept with the multimethod-multitrait formulation, the latter turns its back on what the former considers a matter for investigation—namely, the possibility that a single method is actually more than one instrument factor. The disqualifying weakness of the so-called convergent and discriminant validity concept is the assumption that one method, that is, mode of measurement, is bound to yield a single instrument factor. Yet there are many known instances where some seemingly uniform device such as memory or manipulative skill has factored to two or more distinct "instruments." Balancing for what looks like one instrumental influence is just not good enough.

To sort out such factors when they have only the low variance of instrument factors requires, moreover, an unusual degree of sophistication and care in factor analysis. Accordingly the next few paragraphs, with the aid of tables, address themselves to the technical factor-analytic problems involved.

A typical instance of instrument factors is shown in Table 33(a). It concerns the attempt to measure three dynamic structure factors—fear, self-sentiment, and parental sentiment—by two vehicles frequently employed in objective motivation measurement, namely, information on the topic and autism (bending belief and perception to the interest). A careful factor rotation has given not only the three psychological factors expected but also two factors corresponding to the extent of one of the instrumentalities. If only three factors had been taken out, ignoring the instrument factors, the result would have been a chaotic mixture of true and instrument factors with an unsatisfactory simple structure.

Consider some special types of false solution that appear when the method in Table 33(a) or (b) is not used. First suppose the wrong number of factors is taken out, say, six rather than five. A likely outcome, especially with an analytic rotation program, is that each substantive factor (any type of real psychological trait) will split into two. One will be a fusion of sub-

Table 33

True Resolution of Substantives and Instruments Versus S-I Hybrids

(a) Example from Dynamic Structure Trait Experiment
(Cattell and Digman, 1964)

	Psychological Factors			*Instrument Factors*	
	Escape Erg	*Parental Sentiment*	*Self-Sentiment*	*Information Device*	*Autism Device*
Information Measures					
1. Desire for good self-control	00	—02	[26]	[54]	03
2. Wish to know oneself	03	—05	[31]	[27]	19
3. Wish never to become insane	—06	12	[22]	[43]	04
4. Readiness to turn to parents for help	—02	[35]	09	[28]	—01
5. Feeling proud of one's parents	—06	[28]	—01	[24]	01
6. Desire to avoid fatal disease and accidents	[16]	04	13	[65]	—05
7. Wish to get protection from A-bomb	[14]	—08	03	[14]	—05
Autism Measures					
8. Desire for good self-control	01	—04	[30]	02	[22]
9. Wish to know oneself	—08	07	[37]	—01	[31]
10. Wish never to become insane	00	—01	[16]	00	[25]
11. Readiness to turn to parents for help	—08	[18]	09	—08	[42]
12. Feeling proud of one's parents	—03	[14]	01	06	[14]
13. Desire to avoid fatal disease and accidents	[26]	20	01	04	[17]
14. Wish to get protection from A-bomb	[23]	13	09	15	[10]

Note: The theoretically required salients to define the factors are boxed. Except for two values at the bottom of the parental sentiment column, the salients are high (above 0.09) where and only where they are theoretically required to be. Attitudes 13 and 14 are the same as 6 and 7 but in a different medium, and similarly for the other cross-media personality factors. Decimal points omitted as in other factor matrices.

(b) Plasmode with L-Data Variables Cut from Multi-Instrument Matrix
(Cattell, 1964)

	1	*2*	*3'*	*L*
1	53	13	17	—03
2	—37	—01	01	57
3	38	—28	01	39
4	—02	65	01	13
5	—13	34	72	—08
6	14	05	—57	56
7	—06	04	67	08

	1	*2*	*3'*	*L*
1	100			
2	32	100		
3'	08	—22	100	
L	—09	11	—06	100

Mean correlation among factors = 0.02.

Note: Factor analysis with allowance for fourth (instrument) factor. Clear, correct outcome except for some unevenness of instrument factor.

(c) Plasmode with Variables from Table (b) Factor-Analyzed One Factor Short
(no L instrument factor)

Table 33 (cont.)

	1	*2*	*3'*
1	53	18	−12
2	−45	36	−23
3	27	−01	−57
4	00	57	18
5	−03	82	50
6	−01	−11	−63
7	00	64	22

	1	2	3'
1	100		
2	38	100	
3'	11	−19	100

Mean correlation among factors = 0.10.

Note: Results in blurred hybrids (only one clear) and higher-factor correlations. Variables from Table (b) analysis without separation or extraction of instrument factor. Only one factor interpretable; instrument variance blurs solution. (Decimal points omitted.)

(d) Handling of Instrument Factors in Dynamic Domain: Alternatives of Separation and Hybrid Refraction Factors

(i) Clean Separation with Five Factors

	Factors					
	Dynamic Traits			*Instruments*		
Variable	*Esc.*	*Par.*	*S.S.*	*Inf.*	*Aut.*	*Specific*
Attitude 1	.4			.7		.6
Attitude 2		.4		.7		.6
Attitude 3			.4	.7		.6
Attitude 4	.4			.7		.6
Attitude 5		.4		.7		.6
Attitude 6			.4	.7		.6
Attitude 7	.4				.7	.6
Attitude 8		.4			.7	.6
Attitude 9			.4		.7	.6
Attitude 10	.4				.7	.6
Attitude 11		.4			.7	.6
Attitude 12			.4		.7	.6

(ii) Refraction Factors with Six Factors

Variable	*Esc. Inf.*	*Esc. Aut.*	*Par. Inf.*	*Par. Aut.*	*S.S. Inf.*	*S.S. Aut.*	*Specific*
Attitude 1	.8						.6
Attitude 2			.8				.6
Attitude 3					.8		.6
Attitude 4	.8						.6
Attitude 5			.8				.6
Attitude 6					.8		.6
Attitude 7		.8					.6
Attitude 8				.8			.6
Attitude 9						.8	.6
Attitude 10		.8					.6
Attitude 11				.8			.6
Attitude 12						.8	.6

Note: Among the best worked out examples of instrument factors are those in dynamic traits measured by objective motivation tests. The above is a simplified ideal stantive variance with instrument 1, and the other a substantive fusion with instrument 2. Thus there appears an escape erg in information (variables 1 and 4) and an escape erg couched in autism (variables 7 and 10) (contrast Table 33(d)(i) with (d)(ii)) and after the six factors so generated there are no instrument factors left.

The outcome of underfactoring is also a mixture, as shown in the contrast of Table 33(c) with Table 33(b). These mixed factors have been called (Cattell, 1965a) refraction or substantive-instrument (S-I) hybrids, the former because they are like seeing the same object as double by looking through two sides of a glass prism at once. The simple structure (c) is poorer than the true solution but acceptable, and this solution has led many investigators, among them Becker (1960), to conclude that questionnaire factors and rating factors are distinct and unmatchable so that no real trait can be said to exist outside the media. Because such refraction factors are nearly always positively correlated in pairs (33(d)), some investigators conclude that Q- and L-data versions of the same factor correlated about 0.5 are by no means identical. The answer is that an identity exists but that the estimates of the same factor in the different media, which essentially amount to the S-I hybrids, may correlate only modestly. With underfactoring the mean correlations are higher; compare Table 33(c) with (b).

The second possibility of going wrong is not in the rotation but in the choice of variables. Suppose we suspect two or three instrument factors but choose to work on the variables of only one. If we are sophisticated we expect to find a general factor over and above our main substantives as shown in Table 33. This general factor is a plasmode, a numerical example made to fit a model—the factor model—with four factors. The correlations due to the known structure are worked out and presented to an analyst who proceeds to find what he considers the natural structure to be. A correct decision on four factors does yield the true solution but an investigator who (perhaps because of conviction about the three factors he is interested in) takes out only three factors finishes with what is shown in Table 33(c). The simple structure is poor and the spurious correlations among factors average higher, but unless he uses sensitive standards he will not know that he is dealing with hybrid factors.

Such an error is probably common because tests for number of factors may easily err by one or two, and the broad instrument factor or factors will then spread a distorting variance as shown. It also means that these factors as scales or estimates do not correlate as well as they should (an indifference of medium principle) with scales for the same factors which, unknown to us, share a different instrument factor. However, even when

---

example based on a series of real data instances. On the left in (i) the extraction of five factors has pulled out the three dynamic structure factors—the escape erg, the parental-protection erg, and the self-sentiment—and the two vehicle instrument factors—information and autism. However, especially with an incorrect number of factors, the rotation easily slips into hybrid refraction factors, each dynamic factor having a double, each confounded with one of the instrument factors. This gives inflated correlations among the factors, in a specifiable fashion compared to (i).

we separate the general instrument factor carefully we have difficulties in rotating it because it has no hyperplane. Nevertheless it is good to know how much variance is from this source.

In all this study of the effect of media and different techniques and situations within media, there exist both a theoretical problem and a practical problem. The theoretical problem is to understand what is going on, and here I have continued the theory (Cattell, 1961) of instrument factors, to which the multimethod-multitrait formulation is a crude, largely actuarial approach. In its present context the theory of instrument-factor perturbations leads to the concept of the IFP trait—the instrument-free pure trait—which can be taken out either as a collateral or second-order factor and represents the trait structure in the individual stripped of effects from its particular mode of expression or observation, which latter are separable as instrument factors.

The practical problem that remains is one of estimating an individual's score on this trait; here of course it must be recognized that although conceptually we can separate the IFP trait as a real organic entity we can never measure it directly but only estimate it. Even so we can estimate it more correctly than by the multitrait-multimethod approach, which is blind sampling guided only by a priori concepts of the boundaries. The IFP trait theory calls for information on the magnitudes and boundaries of the instrument factors and guides its statistical practice accordingly.

In practice we seem to have two main possibilities. The first is *neutralization*—the principle long used in intelligence test construction of combining subtests with different specifics in such a way as to attenuate the effect of any one specific. Such *counterbalancing* should not be confused with the *elimination* which takes place in suppressor action. The IFP concept enables this to be done insightfully, if necessary with the refinement of giving different weights to the different devices added. The second is *partialing out*. Whenever a measure of the instrument-factor performance per se can be obtained, one can partial out the individual's score from his component scores provided that one has the insight possible from a proper analysis of the boundaries of the instrument factors.

It should be noted—to avoid confusing past with present positions—that before the instrument factor advances, the attempts to get unitary traits running across media were disappointing. Thus the early attempts of Saunders and myself (Cattell and Saunders, 1950) to factor Q-, L-, and T-factor markers together produced chaotic results; recent publications have reported the same. As pointed out elsewhere a null result in factor analysis should never be considered to argue against a theory; the existence of even one positive result (Cattell, 1955a) is a far more powerful argument. There are hundreds of ways in which factor analyses can go wrong and only one way in which they can hit the true target. The early experiments failed for the obvious reasons that the markers for the distinct factors in Q-, L-, and T-domains were in 1948 much too poorly defined and that the demonstration of perturbations by instrument factors had not yet been made. As results later in this chapter show, if the marker variables (well-validated scales are now available) are good enough and the factoring is competently done it is usually possible to demonstrate agreement across media even without setting aside instrument factors.

With this brief survey of perturbation theory and the instrument-factor concept, let us review sporadic attacks on the problem in the 1950s and 1960s. Light on the problem is shed by the motivation field in the magnified display of these effects in the objective measurement of motivation components (Cattell, Radcliffe, and Sweney, 1963), by the multimethod-multitrait approach of Campbell and Fiske (1959) and Fiske (1966, 1971), and by the Cattell-Digman theories on perturbation and instrument factors just discussed. As indicated, Campbell and Fiske implicitly accepted a true-trait factor criterion and required that several methods be balanced in measuring it, that is, in measuring several traits the same method and same trait should not be paired twice. As a principle of convergent and discriminant validity the measures of the same trait by different methods should intercorrelate more than for the same method with different traits, and the pattern of correlations for the same trait expressions should be similar (constant) across different methods. The resemblance of the last to Tryon's (1939) cluster search methods reminds one that this could hold for clusters (surface traits) and would not discriminate from factors (see Humphreys, 1960).

The absence of referral in this pragmatic approach to such general principles as simple structure, source traits, and distinct nonarbitrary instrument factors makes this multimethod-multitrait concept simple to grasp for the student uninitiated in factor analysis. It applies the general and largely statistical principle stated by Humphreys that a good test for any trait of broad psychological importance should be of low homogeneity. But the "mono-trait, hetero-method" (Fiske) design, while going one step beyond this, still does not invite the student to make the leap from familiar ideas to the radical reconstruction of concepts in instrument factors and the broad vista of perturbation theory. It remains close to familiar limited operations and avoids broad theoretical perspectives, a character shown by using method instead of device, vehicle, or instrument. Method should be retained in science for more general design concepts than the techniques in a particular test.[1]

[1] Although the general intentions of attenuation of instruments and MMMT procedures are in accord, it is not only the theoretical background but associated psychometric procedures that need to be recognized as different. Principally the difference is that perturbation theory requires that the perturbing instrument factors be located, recognized as to their nature, and evaluated for results other than the immediate ones (as the astronomical study of perturbations led to the location of Neptune). On this basis the measurement of a personality factor is planned to exercise both balance among known instrument factors and suppressor action within each scale. Thus it would be logical to argue from convergent and discriminant validity that the only safe way to measure a personality factor is simply to use Q-, L-, and T-data devices simultaneously and then average. But an instrument-factor investigation might indicate enough diverse instrument factors in questionnaires—perhaps of greater or lesser variance than those, say, in L-data—to ensure a more valid measure of the substantive personality factors from Q-data alone or that Q- and L-data measures should be combined in special weightings.

In confining this discussion to instrument factors, I do not mean to imply that the other three types ((a), (b) and (d)) of disturbance in questionaire or other media set out in perturbation theory in Figure 19 are unimportant. Nor should one pass over, except for reasons of space, the three main varieties within instrument factors themselves. For example the situation of variables, Class (d)B, and the test-administration factors in Figure 19 are probably just as important as the test form instances so far used. The situation-of-variables factors are just as real as any others and represent psychological influence patterns; but in terms of conceiving and estimating the total trait it is as necessary to plan their representation as instrument factors. Patterns and estimates of, say, the dominance source trait *E* in children taken from home and from school might show that a certain factor uniformly inhibits dominance over all school variables relative to home expressions (or vice versa). This situation-condition factor is of different strength for different children and explains why, of two children with equal total dominance scores, one may express it more in school and another more at home. As with ordinary test-instrument factor effects some psychologists have taken the position, in opposition to Campbell, Fiske and myself, that such findings deny (though for reason (d)B rather than (a), (b), (c), and so on) the existence of any truly general source trait (in this case, of dominance). However, this tendency of two people to express an essential trait differently is adequately explained, as the higher homogeneities and communalities in the subsets show, by recognizing the existence of subfactors. For special purposes these may be real and important but when broad personality factors are aimed at they are best set aside—but respected—as instrument factors.

3. Four Main Types of Instrument Factors Likely to Upset Q- and L-Alignment

Equipped with some concepts and methods about perturbation effects in general and instrument factors in particular, let us face the cross-media issues. The question we want to ask is this: Can personality factors be matched across media? Granted that the instrument factors can be separated this still leaves us asking how one matches factors. So far I have simply given instances of use of the congruence coefficient r_c or the salient variable similarity index *s*, which compare the patterns of factor loadings—adequate

When the methods have their boundaries chosen arbitrarily and blindly this degree of insight is not possible.

An alternative approach appeals to applied statisticians—canonical correlations. If the test media—Q- and T-data—are combined with L-data (which under special conditions may be considered the criterion), it might be argued that the common variance, or alternatively that part of Q- and T- which predicts L-data, corresponds to an IFP trait domain. Although I recognize canonical correlation as a rough substitute for the excision of known instrument factors, I nevertheless regard it with some suspicion. Is the simple structure of the canonical factors to be sought simultaneously in all media? And must we not recognize that factors which are nevertheless definitely instrument factors could yet extend across all three domains and thus be included, as variance common to all media, in the concept and measurement of an IFP, supra factor?

within one medium. But there are other ways and we must now attack the whole problem comprehensively if the cross-media issues are to be settled. Systematic study of the problem elsewhere (Cattell, 1969; Kaiser, Hunka, and Bianchini, 1971; Harman, 1967 shows that the matching of factors can rest on any one of four different experimental data bases: (1) same subjects, same variables; (2) same subjects, different variables; (3) different subjects, same variables; (4) different subjects, different variables. The last is a connoisseur's curiosity; only the first three are commonly possible. By bases 1, 2, and 3 there are two ways of assessing the hypothesis that factor x in one study is identical with factor y in another, namely:

(a) by examining the similarity of the loading patterns for cases (1) and (3); and

(b) by examining the correlations of the factor scores, which is applicable only when one has the same subjects—that is, with cases (1) and (2)—but does not require the same variables as in case (1). Actually there are two ways of using (b): (i) with estimated factor scores and (ii) by rotating in a common-factor matrix to see if the variables fall on the same factor, or, if separately rotated, to see what the cosine of the angle is between the vectors.

Ancillary minor aids such as agreement of second-order factor patterns are discussed elsewhere (Cattell, 1960).

Explicitness on factor matching is necessary because inaccurate—not to say nonsensical—statements about cross-media matches prevail in the literature. For example, many people can see that a factor in T-data is, say, the same extraversion pattern as in Q-data, and so on, whereas Becker, who wishes to see factors as different, concludes that factors cannot be identical because the correlations between the alleged equivalents are poor. This is true but since estimated scores at the stage of research he worked at had validities of only about 0.4, no better correlation than 0.16 would be expected even if the true factors were perfectly correlated.

Rotation in a common-factor matrix, method (b)(ii) above, using the same subjects, is the preferred method for answering the matching question comparatively early in research because it need not wait on development of scales of high validity. As long as one can fix the hyperplanes the angles (correlations) between the reference vectors can be determined. But as the discussion of instrument factors makes clear it is a vulnerable method if the wrong number of factors is extracted or instrument factor variance is not set aside. For example, refraction factors present distinct L- and Q-data traits perhaps only trivially correlated unless good techniques have set aside two instrument factors.

The operation of the three methods just discussed—comparing factor patterns (on different groups), correlating factor test scores (with the same group), and rotating factors together from two different media (measured on the same group)—is discussed below. But first let us develop theory as to what the perturbing influence or influences might be within any one medium that could upset such matching operations across media.

Within the questionnaire medium itself it can be said that only relatively small effects have been demonstrated from such test-form influences as number of alternative answers or extremity (difficulty) factors. Nor has anything been shown from data treatment, such as use of different correlation coefficients (with, of course, proper factor analysis) or centroid or principal axis extractions. As for subject sampling peculiarities, although these obviously affect the size and even the appearance of factors they theoretically affect the Q- and L-analyses on the same subjects in the same manner, producing no discrepancy. The three real suspects as sources of serious perturbation with which we are left to contend are: situation-condition influences ((d)B), observer-view influences, and test-administration factors.

Situation-condition influences have largely to do with differences in the areas of life from which what are conceived to be similar variables are taken in different media. For example, we have discussed dominance behavior rated in school and rated at home. Seldom have important influences in an area of science been so casually dismissed as the question of differences of Q- and L-observations in respect to this category. My first hypothesis to account for differences in Q- and L-observations is that there exists a powerful influence of this situational selection kind in ratings that is largely absent from questionnaires. Whereas most rating studies have used teachers, parents, or business and military supervisors who see the subject's behavior only in a specialized role situation—and if by peers only over part of the day—the person answering a questionnaire is free to see himself in public and private for 24 hours a day if we include his dreams and experience of sleep. It is true that because he alone observes himself the superiority of domain may be offset by inferiority of observer objectivity. But we are not yet discussing the observer effects; parents, teachers, and others are cited here only to indicate a restricted, observer-associated area of behavior, not observation distorted by a role relation. Of course questionnaire items can be unskillfully chosen, for example, to deal with behavior only in the office but this is easily avoided. Thus in respect to the situation-condition perturbation the questionnaire should theoretically be superior because it is free of perhaps two or three instrument factors of areas or particular stimulus conditions expected in L-data.

Within this situation-condition domain we must consider a different source of nonalignment of Q- and L-factors, namely, the effect of breadth and density of the variables themselves. To understand these terms let us note first that although both L- and Q-variables are taken from everyday life (unlike T-data) the questionnaire items are apt to involve more specific behavior—such as "Do you sometimes feel as if you are being followed on the street?" "Do you get annoyed when someone takes your pencil in class?" —whereas the rater is asked to abstract from several such observed types of behavior a score on some broad trait or subtrait such as suspiciousness or insecurity. Although one *can* ask trait questions of the checklist type or others that amount to direct self-rating on abstractions ("Are you a confident person?" or "I am considered a good social mixer."), using trait terms and nonconcrete, abstract behavior is poor design. It may also be poor design in rating but at present this is the kind of L-data with which questionnaires are being matched.

The difference may be succinctly described as one of high versus low *density* or particularity versus abstraction. In terms of the personality sphere the more specifically restricted the bits of behavior are the closer they are together and the more numerous they are. The abstractions from many particulars such as sociable or unstable behavior are fewer and may be described as necessarily less dense. If we accept that behavior items in the questionnaire—at least in such as the G-Z, 16 PF, HSPQ, and CPQ—are chosen more for behavioral precision and are denser and more numerous (200 to 400) than traits (20 to 30) used in ratings a reasonable expectation is that the L-data factors begin at a higher order compared to the primaries in Q-data. Certainly this happens in Q-data if instead of using items we bunch the scores of several questionnaire items with the same general meaning, such as all having to do with sociability, as Comrey does in his FHID variables. His factors are clearly at the second order relative to Guilford's or the 16 PF. However, across media when the personality sphere is used to guide choice of both ratings and items, the Q- and L-data factors come out as primaries *at the same order,* by any standards of order so far applied.

The most likely explanation is one that is consistent with the semantics of rating. When people are given words such as sociable, aggressive, and honest to rate such terms are loose enough to vary over a fairly broad area, especially with different raters. If there are in fact 16 to 24 primaries and if as many as 30 to 40 behavioral terms are given to be rated, so that it is factor-analytically and mathematically possible to extract 16 factors or so, then the spread of meaning of the rating terms is sufficient to cover the primaries that emerge from the particularities of 100 to 200 questionnaire items. Only if the questionnaire items are multiplied in specific areas, such as the classroom or a football game, not in the general rating traits, can we expect additional factors in the Q-data.

If in spite of the present evidence of much the same primaries turning up in Q- and L-data one wishes to investigate the few extra factors that undoubtedly turn up in Q-data to see whether they are instruments then a refinement beyond present rating, L-data procedures must be introduced. This means ensuring identity of L- and Q-variables by having the rater rate the subject on the Q-items, answering them as he believes the subject would. As yet no one has jointly factored such Q- and L-data.

Apart from a general acquiescence factor (tendency to answer yes rather than no) that is avoided in good questionnaire construction by balancing positive contributions to a factor from yes and no answers and a slight extremity factor that similarly tends to cancel, no test-form factor has been clearly demonstrated. Nor has any instrument factor of type dB in Figure 19 been found connected with the life area covered by the items, although in an ill-designed questionnaire they will undoubtedly be found. Consequently we turn to instrument factors of type (d)C in Figure 19. These are factors associated with test administration, constituting the last source of perturbations.

Substantial effects are claimed to appear here, and they have been conceptualized principally by Edwards (1957a), Messick and Ross (1962), Wiggins (1962a, 1973), and others under the notion of social desirability. That is, if the questionnaire is answered first anonymously and then with one's name, knowing that the results will affect one, then the second result shows a demonstrable shift from the first in the good direction on all items that may be judged as having a good and a bad alternative. Incidentally, it is not possible to avoid this effect by questionnaire design as such, as one avoids acquiescence effects. For it simply is not feasible to balance the desirability of alternatives since some alternatives in multiple choice items, for example, the neurotic or delinquent, are patently socially unattractive. Any alleged balance sought in these domains is bound to fail.

As pointed out in the introductory conceptualization one must distinguish between spurious effects on score averages and on patterns of structure. The effect of desirability qualities on average is unquestionable, as shown in Tables 56 and 57 (Chapter Nine). But the effects widely assumed to occur in structure, notably by the intrusion of a single "social desirability factor," are quite dubious. Indeed we shall question that what is sometimes described as a single social desirability factor is a single factor at all. Both from general theory and from more sensitive factor analysis I would affirm the alternative hypothesis that there are several desirabilities—not one desirability. The intruding patterns of desirability vary according to the social role in which a test is taken. Consequently, a more realistic, although subtle, way of representing the distortion effects is to consider them as complex patterns of addition to scores dependent on (a) the role interests possessed by the individual, and (b) the role situation defined in the test administration. Precisely how this works out is shown in the systematic treatment of trait-view theory in Chapter Nine. Here we must simply note that no well-conducted R-technique factor analysis has shown a single general desirability instrument factor (dR- is different). The extensive examination of second-order analyses in the last chapter, which might be expected to reveal them if any existed, shows eight or more secondaries none of which comes near being either general or identifiable simply as a desirability factor. The nearest to such a pattern is the second-order anxiety factor, which has supplied the major part of the variance for any approach to a general undesirability factor that people may have claimed to find. When they throw this desirability-undesirability variance away they indeed throw away the baby with the bath water, because anxiety has powerful and useful criterion predictions.

In saying that no single general instrument factor has appeared in questionnaires (because no general factor of any kind has) I am stopping short of the complete demonstration, which could be supplied if Q- and L-data were factored together. As Table 33 (a) and (d) shows, this is the only way of conclusively showing whether a hidden general factor exists, for if one medium alone is taken, the variance of any general factor is usually rotated out into the separate simple structure factors. Moreover, subject and observer should have different desirability patterns, visible separately in the

Q and L part, if such existed. But on existing evidence it seems unlikely that there is a general Q-data instrument factor. Instead what might appear to be desirability and kindred instrument phenomena are patchy with respect to primary factors. Indeed, they are better interpreted (Chapter Nine) as (a) projections of the observing person's own personality into the assessment process and (b) what we shall call cognitive figments—using a distinction of figments (personal or subjective) from stereotypes (universal and objective).

In this chapter, since our concern is with the effects of media, we shall not pursue further the special kind of distortion dealt with more extensively in Chapter Nine under trait-view theory. Instead we shall return to instrument factors as they associate with media. However, although the essence of trait-view theory is that each personality trait of the observer distorts in some way his perception of a trait in others, it enters into the differences among media because in L(BR)-data the observer is another person while in Q-data he is the same person. It follows that in Q-data the distortions will correlate with the real factors in the person since the subject is his own observer, whereas in L-data they enter as a set of new, uncorrelated factors. If one averages, say, 12 observers' ratings in L-data most of this instrument effect cancels; but since so broad an observer basis is rarely achieved L-factors in general fail to align with Q-factors partly because of this projected observer distortion in the L-data. Similarly there are distortions in Q-data that cannot be eliminated by averaging observers (Wiggins, 1964). In short, Q- and L-data estimates of the same factor fail to correlate well unless these two different sources of distortion are factored out first in each. The technical question of how these trait-view effects are factored out is treated in Chapter Nine; here we note only that extra, instrument variance of a rather complex nature is undoubtedly expected in Q-data. The possibility should be considered that the second-order factors V and VI, which are much more changeable in pattern than the remaining six, are expressions of this self-observation instrument effect. The corresponding distortion from the observer source is less in L-data if several observers are averaged but probably more if single raters are involved. In any case, good alignment of Q- and L-factors seems unlikely unless instrument factors from the administration or situation of observation are first set aside.

Considering conditions of administration or observation (source of instrument factors (d)C in Figure 19) has carried us into a new category of perturbation—observer-view factors. The theory just summarized is that these factors are partly projections of the individual personality and partly cultural apperceptive or stereotype effects. These latter effects being common, and indeed uniform to Q- and L-data, may cause little disturbance of Q-L media alignments, but they still need study, as in the remainder of this section.

Three terms must be defined before proceeding: stereotype, cliché, and figment. Attempts to tie down influences in this area have long been made by psychometrists, beginning with the alleged halo effect. Indeed, in L-data the halo—the tendency to rate all desirable traits higher in a person one likes—has unfortunately dazzled the eye, diverting research from finding the more probable structure of instrument factors. All three terms concern beliefs, implicit or explicit, about the way things go together—that a parsimonious man like Scrooge will also be unkind or that "Taffy was a Welshman: Taffy was a thief." I define *figments* and *clichés* as the erroneous part of such beliefs and *stereotypes* as the true part, that is, expectations that fit the true correlations. The distinction proposed between a figment and a cliché is that the former is an individual error (for example, my belief that sallow-faced men cheat you because I was once cheated by one) and that the latter is a universal error (for example, that logical men are ruthless). A stereotype, being true, is the same for an individual and a group.

Sociologists have largely been responsible (by subordinating science to the political objective of removing intergroup prejudice) for the widespread belief that all stereotypes are wrong, that is, are clichés. Much of our realistic, true adjustment to the world is economically accomplished by stereotypes. We assume that water is wet and fire will burn and that a person who is stupid on two tests will probably be so on a third. These quick Herbartian apperception masses fill in the world for us with only a certain amount of rounding error—except for the highly deviant special case and the conjuring trick.

Stereotypes are thus time-saving cognitive maps that mimic the real, average experience of life. The reason for this general convergence of our cognitive maps upon the real is obvious: we are constantly rewarded and punished in proportion to the agreement or disagreement of our stereotypes with the real world. Such beliefs as that colds are contagious, that a person in love overestimates the beauty of the beloved, or that a person who has cheated you is also likely to cheat someone else, belong to what Kipling called the Gods of the Copy Book Headings, and the life-educated person counts on them.

The effect of stereotypes in psychological rating has been shown to be strong in L-data (Naylor and Wherry, 1965) and seems likely to be so in Q-data. The interesting experiment of Passini and Norman (1966) shows that the same correlation structures arise when raters rate people they barely know (or do not know) as when they rate people they know well. The scores assigned to individuals are worthless in the first case (as shown by no agreement among raters) but the correlations among traits for any one rater are much the same in the two cases.

Logically the question must be posed whether the L and L or L and Q structures not only agree but are also true, but this question of the truth of rating procedures cannot be answered on psychological data because there is no independent way of knowing the true structure. (Q-, L-, and T-data are independent but none has a sole claim to truth; and extracting truth from a composite is complex.) Accordingly Dickman and I (1962) designed an experiment where human rating methods could be evaluated as to the structure reached by a case where the true structure could be determined, namely, with physical data. A sample of 80 balls was put through 32 kinds of behavior, such as rolling and bouncing, of which 12 are instanced in

Table 34. Here the behavior could be objectively measured as well as rated, and separate factorings were done on the physical behavior measures and on ratings by sophisticated raters. As any physicist would expect, the objective measures issued in four factors—weight, size, elasticity, and length of pendulum cord—from which a specification equation would estimate each of the 32 kinds of behavior. The striking result was found, however, as Table 34 shows, that the ratings by observers also yielded four factors of identical pattern within the usual limits of experimental and rotational error in these fields.

However, such findings do not permit us to dismiss the possibility that in other data clichés and figments distort the central tendency of stereotypes. Insofar as clichés exist they are unlikely to produce disparities in L- and Q-structures because such *common* cultural personality views are presumably shared by the man who rates others and who rates himself. This does not make L- and Q-data distortion-free but only more similar. One possible departure from the true stereotype is simply in the direction of a cliché of oversimplification. Perhaps all human maps are in varying degrees blurred and oversimplified relative to reality. One could assess this by looking for differences in refinement of factor concepts between the more perceptive, experienced, and sophisticated observers and the younger or less intelligent. Osgood, who factored word meanings in the semantic differential, has so far denied the existence of any differences of dimensionality associated with degrees of sophistication or intelligence. But one must remember that the semantic differential is not a sound device for evaluating personality. In the first place it concerns dimensions of feeling reaction to things and not the essential properties of objects per se. Moreover it deals with reactions to objects in general and is not shaped to the dimensions of behavior.

When we talk about a cognitive map for personality it is a map largely in public and verbal terms—apart from some private inexpressible intuitions—and we are therefore undoubtedly implying that personality structure exists in the structure of that part of language which deals with personality. Bertrand Russell has complained about the generation of philosophers who followed him at Oxford that by armchair research they tried to extract truth about the world from language. As students know, this is a very old vice of philosophy. And yet there is an element of method in its madness. If we take the distance in a personality factor space (by multidimensional scaling), separating any two trait terms describing personality, their distance apart or the angle between them from the proper origin should correspond to the extent to which one can predict one kind of behavior from the other. It would not be surprising, therefore, if by scaling words without rating people we got much the same dimensions as by actually rating people. However, such an approach would be only as wise and discriminating as the people asked to use the rating terms. One would expect the observed dimensionality of personality, when abstract verbal terms are used, to be more complex for a group of clinicians than for a group of six-year olds. The fact that Osgood denies this effect for the

Table 34

Agreement of Raters' Stereotypes with Real Structure of Behavior in Physical Case

		Factors Found											
		Real Physical Measures				Raters: 30-Year-Old Raters				Raters: 3 High School Raters			
Variable	*Index Number*	*S*	*W*	*E*	*L*	*S*	*W*	*E*	*L*	*S*	*W*	*E*	*L*
Rotations down inclined plane	(5)	−87	−08	00	−01	−88	−05	00	01	−85	−07	01	05
Squares blotted out by ball	(9)	93	−03	06	07	88	04	13	08	95	00	04	08
Effect on hitting paddle	(12)	24	75	05	−03	−03	99	−05	−01	−12	101	03	02
Effect on springboard	(13)	20	85	−04	01	19	85	11	02	14	86	−09	−04
Number of bounces	(15)	00	−14	78	−03	11	−24	79	00	18	−28	82	00
Communicated motion	(17)	−58	−29	63	−07	−47	−05	67	−01	−50	−29	57	−16
Amount of threading	(21)	−09	00	02	97	05	−04	07	99	−08	−04	−01	97
Swing time	(24)	−10	−07	04	−95	06	−16	13	−84	−08	−09	01	−95
Roll over carpet	(25)	17	35	56	−09	−26	54	69	−07	−02	49	57	−10
Water splashed out	(27)	67	37	−10	06	67	41	−07	02	65	38	09	05
Rebounds on string	(29)	00	12	85	10	05	−08	82	15	−04	13	91	24
Dislodging object struck (pendulum)	(32)	21	76	17	31	39	61	09	32	13	80	12	21

Note: For economy of presentation only 12 variables are taken from the Dickman (1960) study. *S, W, E,* and *L* stand for factors interpreted as size, weight, elasticity, and string lengths for a sample of 80 balls. The numbers in parentheses are those in Dickman's thesis giving a full description of the behavior variable. (Decimals omitted.)

semantic differential is no refutation; as we have seen, this use of semantics is concerned with dimensions of feeling reaction to objects not with their intrinsic, interactive natures. Nor is it refuted by our ball experiment; for although we found the same dimensions for six-year olds as adults we are talking about an area of experience—the physical world of bouncing balls—overlearned in the nursery.

In the social world too there may be so much overlearning that the perspicacity of the observer is little affected by the limits of his intelligence, so that age and intelligence differences in observers' dimensionalities would be hard to demonstrate. The issue of whether the observer is as able as a good novelist to express these differences of perception is as irrelevant as whether a person can tell you what he has learned when he learns to ride a bicycle. The fact that the dimensionality of the CPQ, HSPQ, and 16 PF is much the same is not, however, a disproof of the theory that dimensionalities differ in ratings using single terms. One reason for putting good questionnaire items into questions about behavior rather than trait abstractions and for reforming rating procecures from checklists to specific behavior is that the dependence on the cognitive map of stereotypes is reduced. The computer can then be wiser than the observer and extract dimensions from faithfully observed behavior that do not exist in the individual's cognitive map. ("There are more things in heaven and earth, Horatio, than are dreamt of in your philosophy.")

Provided that we avoid general trait terms and investigate personality structure in both L- and Q-data on a foundation of behavior recording, there is little to fear in the way of instrument factors. The stereotypes in the cognitive map no more lead a man astray than a good map of a familiar town prevents his heeding the turnings his eyes indicate to him. It is not the stereotype of what a man is but what he ought to be that haunts questionnaire work particularly and has given rise to so much research, begun by Edwards (1957a, 1957b), on the supposed social desirability factor. So far we have questioned whether this is a single factor, saying that conscious of unconscious faking is motivated by *several different kinds* of desirability, as illustrated in trait-view theory by the experiment on presenting an image that will get a job, attract a mate, or allow one to malinger in a clinic. Desirability is a function of the person's personality and the role he is trying to play. Nevertheless, if there is not a common factor there is a common cluster, and we can say that a certain pattern of primaries (see Table 57, Chapter Nine) appears when a person answers a questionnaire that will be seen by others compared to what he indicates when anonymous and strictly honest. In general, simply partialing out what changes in these circumstances eliminates much of the variance of the anxiety and some of the exvia-invia factor. Correcting Q- and L-data factoring to reveal the true alignment of undistorted factors from each is more complex than partialing out overestimates of personal desirability in the one and the projection of observer personality traits in the other. Space precludes pursuing this matter further (see Chapter Nine) but at least we see where the main source of instrument-factor perturbation lies in Q-data. Now we shall fit this together with what is known about the sources in L-data, to examine their alignment.

4. Primary L(BR)-Medium Traits and the Criteria of their True Alignment with the Primary Q-Medium Traits

Although one major source of instrument perturbation exists in Q-data one must insist, if perspective is to be maintained, that the chief cause of the poor alignment of Q- and L-data personality factors admitted in the literature is the execrable nature (no lesser expression is due) of the rating procedures in nine-tenths of L-data studies. Subjects have been rated by only one rater, sometimes with terms from a dictionary listed for the rater with no behavioral examples, and sometimes with no more experience of the subject as a person than a half-hour interview (see Hollander, 1957). In the majority of cases the subsequent factoring has applied no test for number of factors, underfactoring down to four and five, and there has been virtually no attempt to isolate media instrument factors by combining Q- and L-data in the same matrix. A review of studies in factor terms, showing possible consistencies on 12 factors, was given by Cattell (1957); and a very good (but lenient) review of the field brought up to the present date can be obtained in Wiggins (1973).

The background of the more careful and programatic studies of which there are at most 10 in the literature is as follows. Allport and Odbert (1936) combed the dictionary and obtained 4500 terms suitable for rating. By putting together indistinguishable synonyms these were reduced to 160 (171, including abilities) available in a standard list (Cattell, 1946b). These variables were rated by raters using intimately known people and brought by correlation consistency to 35 empirical clusters. This set of standard personality-rating variables (Cattell, 1957) has been used, with slight improvements, consistently in the studies of Norman, Tupes, Pierson, and several others, with the substantial advantage that findings have been kept in interlocking relations.

It would be still better if a longer list of more particular behaviors of the type used in time sampling could be set up. Indeed, one must draw a distinction in L-data (life observation *in situ*) between L(BR), which is behavior rating by a judge, and true L-data which is time-sampling, recording frequencies and intensities of particular, concrete (culture-embedded) behavior. An instance of researching for structure in the latter is Cattell and Peterson's analysis (1958) of recorded playground behavior of young children. It recorded stopwatch times of playing with others, number of quarrels, acts of assistance to others, and so on. This study resulted in clear personality factors on items of known reliability, but such time sampling with adults is difficult to get. Indeed this study has not been repeated even with children on the playground and the badly needed growth of structural evidence, joining study to study with the same variables, has not taken place. Yet it is important to obtain the meaning of the 35 to 40 terms in the standard rating set (Cattell, 1957) expressed in a set of specific cultural behaviors suitable for time-sampling records.

Meanwhile we must take what is available and see whether—short of the instrument-factor separation methodology just discussed—reasonably good alignment appears between L- and Q-factors. The desiderata for this comparison are as follows.

I. In the Questionnaire:

(1) That the items must be taken from the general personality sphere and bunched in parcels or scales constituting variables categorically corresponding to the rating variables.

(2) That administration must be anonymous to reduce the desirability factor.

II. In the Ratings:

(1) That a set of personality variables, not left as words but defined on instruction sheets in behavioral illustrations must be derived by even sampling from the personality sphere and used as markers in the standard list numerous enough to cover 20 or more factors. This list of 35 to 50 markers is provided (Cattell, 1957, p. 813).

(2) That a set of not less than 200 subjects must be obtained who can be observed in diverse situations over most of the waking day by all judges for months. This involves an implicit time-sampling procedure and could advantageously be made explicit. This condition rules out most ratings by teachers and supervisors and emphatically ratings in an interview.

(3) The raters should not be in special role relations or emotional relations to the subjects. A peer group is best. The most consistent results I know of have been from ratings by peers in sororities and fraternities and in a tank battalion and air force units in World War II. These settings ensured that diverse, nontrivial situations would be sampled in making judgments.

(4) That the subjects be broken down into groups of about 10 to 20 people (considered a limit of size for good mutual familiarity), every member of that group being rated by the others. Reliabilities of pooled 10 against 10 judges in these conditions reach 0.8 to 0.9, and projection of individual judges' personalities is minimized. Rather than extend raters to more subjects than they know it is best to obtain the necessary sample size by repeating with several groups of 10 to 20 people. At this size the scores can be combined with assumption of equal mean and sigma for all groups. Ratings should be on one subtrait variable at each evaluation session (to avoid halo, not all traits per person at one session). The process is best aimed at placing persons in a rank by paired comparisons. Ratings of children by their own parents must be avoided. Parents tend to rate against the mean of experience in their own families; half the real variance among the subjects when made up of 200 children from different families may easily be lost.

(5) The above data should be treated as normally distributed when converted from rank to point scores and correlation and factoring should meet the tenets set out earlier.

The few rating studies that make a reasonable approach to these conditions have been reviewed (Cattell, 1957; Wiggins, 1973), and three have appeared since. Only five or so rating studies—virtually all in the studies of 1946, 1947, and 1948 (see Cattell, 1957)—approach these requirements. Especially the vital, conditions (1), (3) and (4) are almost invariably absent outside this set of researches. Consequently it is on these mutually consistent studies that the main weight of the conclusions in Table 35 must rest. The studies of Tupes (1957), Norman (1963), Wittenborn (1955), Lorr (1966), Hammond (1965), Huffman (in Cattell, 1957), Degan (1952), Thurstone (1938), Kelley and Fiske (1951), Digman (1972), Cattell, Pierson, Finkbeiner, and others (1973) support the primary patterns listed in Table 35, although no study subtends all factors. The descriptive terms given to the raters and appearing in the list of well-loaded variables per factor in Table 35 combine as completely as possible the rating terms used in the research; the core is from the 1945, 1947, and 1948 studies. Several L(BR)-medium studies have stopped at five or six factors and claimed that there are no more. As Child,

Table 35

12 Established and 6 Weak Source-Trait Patterns in L(BR)-Data

(a) Factor *A* (UIL 1)

Sizia *A*— *(Reserved, Detached, Critical, Aloof, Stiff)* [a]	Affectia *A*+ *(Warmhearted, Outgoing, Easygoing, Participating)* [a]
Critical	Good-natured, easygoing
Stands by own ideas	Ready to cooperate, likes to participate
Cool, aloof	Attentive to people
Precise, objective	Softhearted, casual
Distrustful, skeptical	Trustful
Rigid	Adaptable, Careless, goes along
Cold	Warmhearted
Prone to sulk	Laughs readily

(b) Factor *B* (UIL 2)

Low Intelligence *B*— *(Crystallized, Power Measure, Dull)* [a]	High Intelligence *B*+ *(Crystallized, Power Measure, Bright)* [a]
Low mental capacity	High mental capacity
Unable to handle abstract problems	Insightful, fast-learning, intellectually adaptable
Not intelligently organized [b]	Intellectual interests [a]
Poor judgment [b]	Good judgment [a]
Low morale [b]	High morale [a]
Quitting [b]	Persevering [a]

(i) Factor *I* (UIL 9)

Harria *I*— *(Tough-Minded, Rejects Illusions)* [a]	Premsia *I*+ *(Tender-Minded, Sensitive, Dependent, Overprotected)* [a]

Table 35 (Cont.)

Unsentimental, expects little	Fidgety, expects affection and attention
Self-reliant, takes responsibility	Clinging, insecure, seeks help and sympathy
Hard (to point of cynicism)	Gentle, indulgent to self and others
Few artistic responses (but not lacking in taste)	Artistically fastidious, affected, theatrical
Unaffected by fancies	Imaginative inner life and conversation
Acts on practical evidence	Acts on sensitive intuition
Keeps to the point	Seeks attention, flighty
Does not dwell on physical disabilities	Hypochondriacal, anxious about self

(j) Factor *J* (UIL 10)

Zeppia *J*— *(Zestful, Liking Group Action)* [a]	Coasthenia *J*+ *(Circumspect Individualism, Reflective, Internally Restrained)* [a]
Likes to go with group	Individualistic
Likes attention	Guarded, wrapped in self
Sinks personality into group	Fastidiously obstructive
Vigorous	Neurasthenically fatigued
Accepts common enthusiasms	Evaluates coldly

(c) Factor *C* (UIL 3)

Low Ego, Strength *C*— *(Affected by Feelings, Emotionally Less Stable, Easily Upset, Changeable)* [a]	High Ego Strength *C*+ *(Emotionally Stable, Mature, Faces Reality, Calm)* [a]
Emotional when frustrated	Emotionally mature
Changeable attitudes, interests	Stable, constant in interests
Easily perturbed	Calm
Evades responsibilities, tends to give up	Does not let emotional needs obscure realities of a situation, adjusts to facts
Worrying	Unruffled
Gets into fights and problem situations	Shows restraint by avoiding difficulties

(d) Factor *D* (UIL 4)

Phlegmatic Temperament *D*— *(Undemonstrative, Deliberate, Inactive, Stodgy)* [a]	Excitability *D*+ *(Excitable, Impatient, Demanding, Overactive, Unrestrained)* [a]
Stoic	Demanding, impatient
Complacent	Attention-getting, shows off
Deliberate	Excitable, overactive
Not easily jealous	Prone to jealousy
Self-effacing	Self-assertive, egotistic
Constant	Distractible
Not restless	Many nervous symptoms

(e) Factor *E* (UIL 5)

Submissiveness *E*— *(Obedient, Mild, Easily Led, Docile, Accommodating)* [a]	Dominance or Ascendance *E*+ *(Assertive, Aggressive, Competitive, Stubborn)* [a]

Table 35 (Cont.)

Submissive	Assertive
Dependent	Independent-minded
Considerate, diplomatic	Stern, hostile
Expressive	Solemn
Conventional, conforming	Unconventional, rebellious
Easily upset by authority	Headstrong
Humble	Demands admiration

(f) Factor *F* (UIL 6)

Desurgency *F*— *(Sober, Taciturn, Serious)*[a]	Surgency *F*+ *(Enthusiastic, Heedless, Happy-Go-Lucky)*[a]
Silent, introspective	Talkative
Full of cares	Cheerful
Concerned, reflective	Happy-go-lucky
Incommunicative, relies on inner values	Frank, expressive, reflects group
Slow, cautious	Quick, alert

(g) Factor *G* (UIL 7)

Low Superego Strength *G*— *(Disregards Rules and Group Moral Standards, Expedient)*[a]	High Superego Strength *G*+ *(Conscientious, Persistent, Moralistic, Staid)*[a]
Quitting, fickle	Persevering, determined
Frivolous	Responsible
Self-indulgent	Emotionally disciplined
Slack, indolent	Consistently ordered
Undependable	Conscientious, motivated by duty
Ignores obligations to people	Concerned about moral standards, rules

(h) Factor *H* (UIL 8)

Threctia *H*— *(Shy, Timid, Restrained, Threat-Sensitive)*[a]	Parmia *H*+ *(Adventurous, "Thick-Skinned," Socially Bold)*[a]
Shy, withdrawn	Adventurous, likes meeting people
Retires in face of opposite sex	Active, overt interest in opposite sex
Emotionally cautious	Responsive, genial
Sometimes embittered	Friendly
Restrained, rule-bound	Impulsive
Restricted interests	Emotional and artistic interests
Considerate, quick to see dangers	Carefree, does not see dangers

(k) Factor *L* (UIL 12)

Alaxia *L*— *(Trusting, Accepting Conditions)*[a]	Protension *L*+ *(Suspecting, Jealous)*[a]
Accepts personal unimportance	Jealous
Pliant to changes	Dogmatic
Unsuspecting of hostility	Suspicious of interference

Table 35 (Cont.)

Ready to forget difficulties	Dwells on frustrations
Understanding, tolerant	Tyrannical
Lax about correcting people	Demands people accept responsibility for errors
Conciliatory	Irritable

(l) Factor *M* (UIL 13)

Praxernia *M*— *(Practical, Has "Down to Earth" Concerns)*[a]	Autia *M*+ *(Imaginative, Bohemian, Absent-Minded)*[a]
Conventional, alert to practical needs	Unconventional, absorbed in ideas
Concerned with immediate interests	Interested in art, theory, basic beliefs
Prosaic, avoids far-fetched ideas	Enthralled by inner creations
Guided by objective reality, dependable practical judgment	Fanciful, easily seduced from practical judgment
Earnest or worried but steady	Enthused but occasional hysterical swings of giving up

(m) Factor *N* (UIL 14)

Naïveté *N*— *(Forthright, Unpretentious)*[a]	Shrewdness *N*+ *(Astute, Worldly)*[a]
Genuine but socially clumsy	Polished, socially aware
Vague, injudicious mind	Exact, calculating mind
Gregarious, warmly involved	Emotionally detached, disciplined
Spontaneous, natural	Artful, devious
Simple tastes	Esthetically fastidious
Lacks self-insight	Has self-insight
Unskilled in analyzing motives	Insightful regarding others
Content with status quo	Ambitious, possibly insecure
Blind trust in human nature	Smart, cuts corners

(n) Factor *O* (UIL 15)

Untroubled Adequacy *O*— *(Self-Assured, Placid, Secure, Complacent)*[a]	Guilt Proneness *O*+ *(Apprehensive, Self-Reproaching, Insecure, Worrying, Troubled)*[a]
Self-confident	Worrying, anxious
Cheerful, resilient	Depressed, cries easily
Impenitent, placid	Easily touched, overcome by moods
Expedient, insensitive to approval or disapproval	Strong sense of obligation, sensitive to approval and disapproval
Does not care	Scrupulous, fussy
Rudely Vigorous	Hypochondriacal, inadequate
No fears	Phobic symptoms
Given to simple action	Lonely, brooding

(o) Factor Q_1 (UIL 16)

Conservatism *Q*—	Radicalism Q_1+
(Conservative, Respects Established Ideas, Tolerant of Traditional Difficulties)[a]	*(Experimenting, Liberal, Analytic, Free-Thinking)*[a]

Table 35 (Cont.)

(p) Factor Q_2 (UIL 17)

Group Dependency Q_2-	Self-Sufficiency Q_2+
(Sociably Group-Dependent, A "Joiner" and Sound Follower) [a]	*(Self-Sufficient, Resourceful, Prefers Own Decisions)* [a]

(q) Factor Q_3 (UIL 18)

Low Self-Sentiment Q_3-	High Self-Sentiment Q_3+
(Uncontrolled, Lax, Follows Own Urges, Unintegrated, Careless of Social Rules) [a]	*(Controlled, Exacting Will Power, Socially Precise, Compulsive, Follows Self-Image)* [a]

(r) Factor Q_4 (UIL 19)

Low Ergic Tension Q_4-	High Ergic Tension Q_4+
(Relaxed, Tranquil, Torpid, Unfrustrated, Composed) [a]	*(Tense, Frustrated, Driven, Overwrought, Fretful)* [a]

Note: The technical terms for source traits and their index numbers are those in standard use in both L- and Q-data (see also Table 4, Chapter Two). There is a double system: the familiar use of alphabetical identification from A through P, and the more formal universal index (UI) with Q-data numbers, such as UIL 19 immediately above. The high pole in scoring is always the name on the right. If one is prepared to base rating-factor identification on a single research then the recent research of Cattell, Pierson, Finkbeiner, Brim, and Robertson (1973) points to more rating factors than here, extending closer to the 23 found in normal Q-data.

[a] These subtitles are an attempt by the psychologist to define in about four words the essence of the given pole of the trait. The list of terms below, on the other hand, is constituted by ratings used in actual researches, from standard rating variables (Cattell, 1957), and found to have significant loadings, higher for those higher in the list.

[b] The measurement of intelligence has been shown to carry with it, as a factor in the personality realm, some of these ratings; the correlations, however, are quite low.

author of a standard text, *The Essentials of Factor Analysis* (1970), has pointed out, the five-factor solution begs every question of technique; yet articles with such faulty conclusions continue to be accepted without scrutiny by certain journals. To check this question of number of factors in rating data my colleagues and I returned to the data demonstrably based on the most thorough procedures, for which one has to go back to 1948. Reexamined by modern checks on number of factors (the scree and the maximum likelihood) the outcome exceeded the 11 to 12 of the earlier factoring and showed 12 to 14 factors.

Because of the central importance of the demonstration that questionnaire factors are not just factors in questionnaires but factors in everyday life behavior as seen by observers, it is necessary to scrutinize the methods by which alignment can be tested as follows:

(1) Most obviously through looking at the psychological similarity of the meaning of supposedly identical traits in the two media. This is not highly dependable.

(2) By the similarity of the criterion relations of the supposedly equivalent Q- and L-factors to concrete criteria (see Indirect Validity in Chapter Nine).

(3) By the faithfulness with which the markers for the same factor in Q- and L-data fall on the same simple-structure factor when the variables are factored together on one sample of people with attention to instrument factors.

(4) By examining the similarity of the loadings of what are considered to be the same primary in Q- and L-data when a second-order factoring is carried out in each medium—in other words the similarity of the Q- and L-data second orders when derived from what are considered to be the same primaries. (In Table 37 this goes further: primaries in Q-data are shown to correlate according to the correct pattern with secondaries in observer ratings.)

(5) By calculating the correlations over the same people, of the score series for putatively the same factor estimated respectively from Q- and L-data (matching L and Q traits, methods).

Regarding the verdict of the first there can be no question. Admittedly experience warns us that the mere visual matching of patterns by psychologists is not to be trusted when they want to believe that two factors have the same meaning. But in this case, through the deliberate inclusion of the representative 45 rating variables in questionnaire items in the formation of the 16 PF, categorically similar variables exist in both and we can see what happens in the factor patterns. Table 35 shows that (as far as psychological interpretation can show) the *A, B, C, D, E,* and other factors emerging in the questionnaires correspond closely in meaning with those first found in the preceding ratings.

In regard to the second source of evidence although the criterion relations for rated factors by Kelly and Fiske (1951), Digman (1972), Tupes (1957) and others agree well with those for Q-data factors (for example by the superego factor, *G,* loading school achievement and leadership criteria and *C* being low in all clinical cases), the scantiness of studies compels us to turn to a less precise and more pragmatic source. It happens that the 16 PF and HSPQ measures of primary Q-data factors have been enough in use—15 to 20 years—for considerable clinical and counseling experience to have accumulated. From this it is now abundantly seen that clinicians obtain such an exact sense of the meaning of these factors that they are able also to recognize them readily in the L-data. That is, they can make dependable predictions, after knowing a patient for a few days, as to just what his 16 PF score profile will be.

However, the most basic evidence on factor alignment must come from the third matching source; only by this joint factoring can instrument-factor intrusions be reliably located and insightfully set aside. Although the complete and definitive work in this area remains to be done, Table 36(a)—an experiment with 145 seven- and eight-year-old boys and girls (Cattell and Coan, 1957a, 1957b, 1958; and Cattell, 1961)—shows the kind of agreement reached in cross-media factoring with respect to four important source traits,

C, D, F, and *H,* each scored by two ratings and two questionnaire scores on the same individuals. In this experiment (1958) a number of instrument factors, largely in L-data, have been set aside. In the case of surgency-desurgency *F,* the loadings are not quite so good on the questionnaire as on the rating markers; such effects are expected from results prior to the refinement of the questionnaire scales achieved by programatic work.

Table 36

Agreement of Q- and L-Data Markers on Ego Strength *C*, Excitability *D*, Surgency *F*, Parmia *H*

	Cross-Media Factors			
L-Data [a]	*C*	*D*	*F*	*H* [b]
A	+20	−03	+05	+06
C	**+45**	−13	−15	−03
D	+07	**+45**	+00	−12
E	+13	−31	−08	+30
F	+39	−05	**+50**	−09
G	−19	−09	+01	+08
H	+10	−03	−07	**+48**
I	−14	+10	−01	+05
J	−04	+31	−20	+09
L	+00	+19	+00	+14
M	+10	−08	−07	−17
O	−19	−09	+07	−44
A	+03	−28	+15	+53
C	**+49**	−12	+19	+19
D	+00	**+20**	+00	−14
E	+00	+05	+01	+48
F	−13	+03	**+46**	+27
G	+12	+12	+07	+25
H	−07	−09	+04	**+55**
I	+32	−01	−07	+09
J	−06	+12	−04	−41
L	+10	+06	−11	+00
M	+12	+01	−07	+44
O	−03	−22	+07	−48

Q-Data [c]	*C*	*D*	*F*	*H*
A	−03	+06	−19	+06
C	**+36**	+28	+07	+20
D	+01	**+65**	+00	+20
E	−27	+14	+00	−03
F	+00	+10	**+49**	−03
G	−16	−01	−05	+03
H	−10	−06	−09	**+36**
I	−17	−13	−07	+02
J	−12	+10	−05	+05
N	+19	−09	−27	−17

Table 36 (Cont.)

O	−04	+04	+03	+09
Q_4	−29	+06	−01	+09
A	+14	+06	−35	−08
C	[+55]	+06	−01	−05
D	+12	[+60]	+04	−05
E	+04	+40	−04	−14
F	−07	+15	[+39]	−25
G	+09	+17	−03	−11
H	−06	+08	+11	[+69]
I	−06	−01	+01	+06
J	+12	+09	+01	+05
N	+13	+04	+07	+06
O	−17	+03	−08	+03
Q_4	−06	+00	+04	+03

Note: Decimal points omitted before loadings as usual.

[a] Two markers for each factor.

[b] Simple structure on *H* poorer than for other traits (see Figure 20).

[c] Two markers for each factor.

Since much depends on the rotational structure it is important to reproduce at this point a typical plot (see Figure 20) taking surgency and parmia from Table 36. The hyperplane (interrupted line) for surgency is unmistakable; and the four highest loadings are two questionnaire scales for *F* and two behavior ratings for *F* (each pooling half the rated variables marking *F*).

Since neglect of experiment on Q-L alignment has left us, however, with no direct attack upon it with the improved methods of the last 15 years it was decided to undertake a substantial study for the present book, jointly with Pierson, Finkbeiner, Brim, and Robertson. Therein young adults were tested on both forms of the 16 PF and, in study groups of nine, each was rated on the standard 35 variables (Cattell, 1957) by eight peers. Table 37 presents factor analytic results for the pooled first 10 groups; but the analysis on 18 groups (N = 144) is due to appear (Cattell, Pierson, Finkbeiner, Brim, and Robertson, 1973). The scree yielded 20–21 factors from the 32 L and 32 Q variables together. As Table 37 shows, taking 10 of the largest variance factors, each factor is well loaded in the four markers (2L 2Q), and this extends to all 16 PF factors. The simple structure count is good (63 percent), but as Table 37 shows, there are some off-zero loadings other than for the chosen markers.

One may conclude that if the proper conditions for rating are observed, instrument factors are not systematic enough to upset the alignment. A valuable contribution of this research has been to show that the source traits hitherto indexed Q_1, Q_2, Q_3, and Q_4 cautiously to indicate that they may be only in Q-data, actually fit into the general law of indifference of indicator, appearing with both L and Q markers.

The cross-media generality of the normal personality primaries is thus well supported, but now a more extended frontier appears for investi-

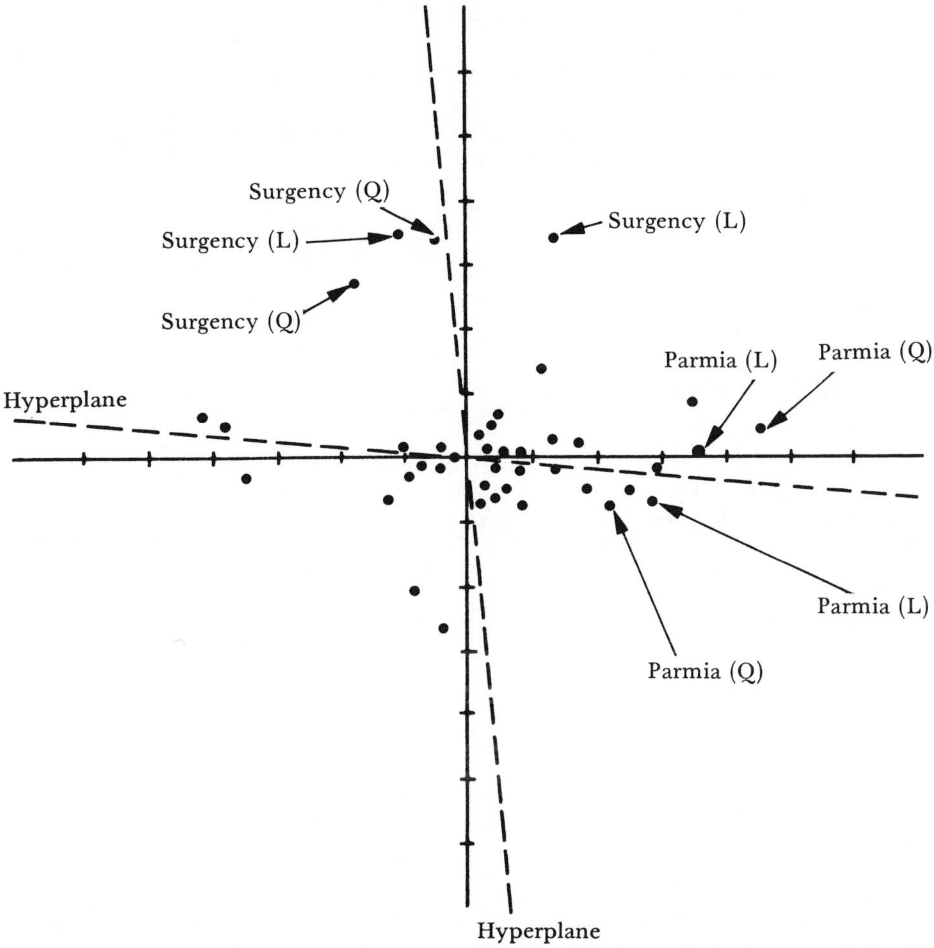

Figure 20. Agreement of Q-data with L-data factors. From a factor analysis of combined Q-data and L-data on 181 boys and girls from 7 to 8 years of age (Coan's data, 1958). The study was undertaken to answer this question: Can one personality dimension be found simultaneously loading, in a combined simple-structure plot, the variables chosen to mark what one hypothesized to be factors of the same meaning in the separate media simple-structure resolutions? These and at least two other factors confirmed the reality of such common structures (48 variables, 24 factors, 181 subjects). The obliquity of the factors is small ($r = 0.05$; angle $= 87.5$), but the H hyperplane is not unambiguous and could yield more positive correlation of F and H. Each point is a variable from Table 28 in Chapter Six.

gation through the more recent discoveries of the pathological primaries of Chapter Three. Research is as yet scanty and lacking systematic matching, though systematic findings on L-data alone in the pathological domain have existed for some time in the work of Cattell (1945), Degan (1952), Eysenck (1944), Huffman (Cattell, 1957), Kiloh and Garside (1963), Wittenborn (1955), and especially Lorr, Klett, McNair and Lasky (1962). A refactoring of Kiloh and Garside's psychiatric ratings in the depression area shows there are 12 to 13 factors (Cattell, 1973), a number that is suggestive in view of the 12 abnormal factors found in Q-data in the CAQ beyond the 16 normal.

Table 37

Alignment of L- and Q-Data at Primary and Secondary Levels

(a) Primaries: Structure from Combined Factoring of Q-Data and L-Data
(Cattell, Pierson, Finkbeiner, Brim and Robertson, 1973)

	Loadings of Primary Source Traits									
Ratings and Scales	*A*	*B*	*F*	*G*	*H*	*I*	*N*	*O*	Q_1	Q_4
Good-natured (Rating)	34						–53			
Cool, reserved (Rating)	–35				–25		36			–26
16 PF Scale, Trait *A* Form A	74		36							
16 PF Scale, Trait *A* Form B	76			–26				25		
Intelligent (Rating)		65								
Learns fast (Rating)		–59								
16 PF Scale, Trait *B* Form A		92								
16 PF Scale, Trait *B* Form B		46								
Gay (Rating)			26						–35	
Prudent (Rating)			–16	45						
16 PF Scale, Trait *F* Form A			82							
16 PF Scale, Trait *F* Form B			83							
Conscientious (Rating)				74			–27			
Persevering (Rating)				–37						
16 PF Scale, Trait *G* Form A				62						
16 PF Scale, Trait *G* Form B				50						
Frank (Rating)				40	45					35
Cautious (Rating)					–07					
16 PF Scale, Trait *H* Form A		29			62					
16 PF Scale, Trait *H* Form B		30			70					
Tender-minded (Rating)						41				
Independent (Rating)		33		40		–12				
16 PF Scale, Trait *I* Form A						98				
16 PF Scale, Trait *I* Form B						74				
Astute (Rating)							64		24	
Naive (Rating)							–28			
16 PF Scale, Trait *N* Form A	27						17			
16 PF Scale, Trait *N* Form B			–27				29			
Worrying (Rating)								47		
Self Assured								–23		–31
16 PF Scale, Trait *O* Form A						43		52		25
16 PF Scale, Trait *O* Form B					–74			19		
Experimenting							–34		45	
Conservative	27								–39	
16 PF Scale, Trait Q_1 Form A									42	
16 PF Scale, Trait Q_1 Form B	33								98	
Tense								34		80
Phlegmatic						–30				–74

Table 37 (Cont.)

16 PF Scale, Trait Q_4 Form A	30		34	39
16 PF Scale, Trait Q_4 Form B		−35		47

Note: The hyperplane width in this study is such that loadings below ±0.25 are left blank, that is, regarded as in hyperplane. However, any values below this are shown in the boxes. If the trait hypothesis is correct the second of the four loadings in each box should be negative, because ratings ranked subjects from opposite poles, to reduce halo. The sprinkling of loadings outside the boxes is about the same for each factor and makes sense psychologically in most cases in terms of possible misunderstandings of rating definitions. For example, prudent and independent-minded load the superego, *G*; absense of worrying and of tenseness load *H*, parmia (boldness); not good-natured and not conscientious load shrewdness, *N*. The loadings on markers average higher for Q scales than L ratings, as would be expected from higher reliabilities, and hypothesize lower instrument-factor variance in the former. Noteworthy here is that some of the strongest evidence for cross-media persistence of pattern is shown for what were considered weaker factors—*N* and *O*—or factors confined to Q-data—Q_1 and Q_4.

(b) Secondaries: Loading of L-Data Secondaries as Pattern of Q-Data Primaries [a]

Q-Data Primaries	*I Exvia*	*II Anxiety*	*III Cortertia*	*IV Independence*	*VIII Moral Upbringing*
A	[10]	13	[−27]	−13	−12
B			−19		−19
C		[−26]	[12]	13	
E			−35	[30]	
F	[11]			[52]	[−02]
G				−15	[46]
H	[28]	[−15]	[−10]	[04]	[−19]
I			[−22]		−30
L		[11]	−15		
M		[−41]	[−07]	[33]	−29
N			−12		
O		[45]			16
Q_1	−14		−18	[17]	−24
Q_2	[−39]	−14	15	[35]	13
Q_3		[−16]		−12	[10]
Q_4		[28]			13

[a] Data from Goldberg, Norman, and Schwartz (1972), rotating pseudo-secondaries to higher simple structure. The factors are called by these authors: I extroversion, II neuroticism, III agreeableness, IV low dependability, and V culture. All loadings below 0.10 are dropped, as lying in hyperplane. Values where significant loadings would be expected are in boxes. All signs of boxed values agree with expectation. Although the values are attenuated by rating and scale unreliability the congruence coefficients (text) show that these are essentially the second-order patterns.

Agreement of meaning of seven of these with depressions D_1 to D_7 in the CAQ (Chapter Three) was excellent, but here, as in the abnormal dimensions in ratings by the above writers, positive cross-identification experiments await research.

As to the verdict of the fifth method—the correlation of factor separately from Q- and L-media scores—dependable evidence is still rare. The studies of Hammond on adults used only low-reliability interview ratings for L-data and those of Schaie on children used teacher ratings and are not yet brought to accurate estimates. The only data meeting the rating requirements set out here are still in process of analysis (Cattell, Pierson, Finkbeiner, Brim, and Robertson, 1973) but tentatively correlations of 0.4 to 0.8 are being obtained between L- and Q-scores on the same factor.

A recent contribution which, although only on 82 subjects, is helpful in this sparsely represented approach is that of Goldberg, Norman, and Schwartz (1972). They took peer ratings under good conditions on five factors which, being the sole factors from a larger number of ratings, are undoubtedly what we have called pseudo-second orders, but close to true second orders. The subjects' scores on these were correlated with the 16 PF scores. The 16 $\times$ 5 matrix may be considered a factor structure matrix, and was converted into a factor pattern and then rotated slightly for better simple structure. The result is shown in Table 37(b) where there is no mistaking the patterns for the five largest second-order patterns as known in the questionnaire domain. The simple structure is rather poor on III and VIII but the congruences are significant at 0.76 (exvia), 0.77 (anxiety), 0.48 (cortertia), 0.60 (independence), and 0.57 (moral upbringing). The loadings are, of course, attenuated by rating and test unreliability and the actual correlation of estimates would be, in, say, anxiety, only about 0.5. But this contribution shows both significant correlation and, perhaps more importantly, that the second-order ratings projected into questionnaire data produce the well-known patterns of the Q-data secondaries. Apart from a very few such studies the L-Q relationships are unstudied, due to shoddy behavior-rating procedures in the past constituting a veritable "disaster area" in psychology.

Having familiarized ourselves with some examples, let us now scrutinize the model itself, concerning the correlations that would be expected in experiment on the basis of the theory of instrument factors. Equation (7.1a) presents the instrument-factor model, stating that the observed score on the Q-scale form A for factor X, which we write S_{AXQ}, is the function of some true-trait score T_X common to all forms and both media, plus an instrument-factor score Q_X and L_X, as well as some specifics and unwanted factors U_{AQ}, U_{BQ}, U_{AL}, and U_{BL}, plus error E:

$$S_{AXQ} = b_{ATQ}T_X + b_{AQ}Q_{AX} + b_{AUQ}U_{AQ} + bE_1 \tag{7.1a}$$

$$S_{BXQ} = b_{BTQ}T_X + b_{BQ}Q_{BX} + b_{BUQ}U_{BQ} + bE_2 \tag{7.1b}$$

$$S_{AXL} = b_{ATL}T_X + b_{AL}L_{AX} + b_{AUL}U_{AL} + bE_3 \tag{7.1c}$$

$$S_{BXL} = b_{BTL}T_X + b_{BL}L_{BX} + b_{BUL}U_{BL} + bE_4 \tag{7.1d}$$

If we assume that the U factor is in each case unique, like error, and that the bs are normalized to be factor loadings than the correlation of form A with form B in the questionnaire medium is:

$$r_{QAB} = b_{ATQ}b_{BTQ} + b_{AQ}b_{BQ} \tag{7.2}$$

and correspondingly for the two rating medium forms. The correlation of one questionnaire with one rating is:

$$r_{QLA} = b_{ATQ}b_{ATL} \tag{7.3}$$

This merely tells us that the cross-media correlation will be less than within media, for equally valid measures, but other inferences are also useful. When two measures of a factor have nothing in common but the factor, the rest being *U* and *E,* the (geometric) mean validity of such scales can be obtained simply by taking the square root of their (mutual) equivalence coefficient. This amounts to the same thing as saying that if the correlation of two such scales is "corrected for attenuation," by dividing by $\sqrt{r_{ab}r_{ab}}$, r_{ab} being the reliability in the sense of the equivalence coefficient (that is, *U* and *E* are the specific), unity will be reached. But scales with instrument factors will yield neither a true validity nor limit of unity for a corrected intercorrelation by these means, so long as we stay within one medium. On the other hand, the root of r_{QLA} (7.3) will give the mean real validity of these scales, and a comparison of this with (7.2) will give the mean size of instrument factor. The third ingredient—the error of measurement, *E*—can then be estimated from the dependability (repeat reliability), again only as a mean. Incidentally, as far as the dependability coefficients can be estimated in the Goldberg, Norman, and Schwartz (1972) data the values in Table 37(b) would be raised by about 50 percent thereby.

Although one can thus take some useful steps with as few as four scales, two in each medium, the fact that one deals with mean loadings rather than specific weights for each scale makes the estimate of the supra factor (the cross-medium structure) relatively inefficient. This weakness is in fact that of the MTMM or convergent and discriminant validity conception compared with that of perturbation theory and the instrument-factor concept. However, to handle the above measures by precise instrument-factor weights requires a factor analysis, for which perhaps nine scales and three media (four factors) would be a just acceptable minimum.

The practical conclusions from this are four: that we are doing as well as can ever be expected in measuring the same factor from two media if we get correlations of 0.5 to 0.7 (speaking of Q- and L-media). Second, that for the best measurement of a trait it is desirable to use and average all three media. Since ratings have no norms, this generally means in practice Q- and T-data. An important instance of this is the possibility of combining the 16 PF and the MAT measures of self-sentiment and superego strength.[2] Third, that although in general principle, as Fiske (1971) recognizes, the multimethod and the instrument-factor approach agree on the desirability of combining tests spread across media for the same trait, the

[2] Factors G and Q_3, superego and self-sentiment, in the 16 PF are conceptually identical with those measured under the same name by the objective motivation measures (T-tests) in the MAT. This is shown by common factoring (Cattell, 1957) and by their mutual correlations being impressive if appreciable instrument factors are recognized. These two traits and four measures offer a good field for exploring the relationships discussed here.

instrument-factor approach gives more precise guidance in reaching the proper combination weights. For example, our general conclusion from data so far available—admittedly scanty—is that the total instrument-factor variance is larger in L- than Q-data. And fourth, that because of the preceding conclusion we should be wary of any approach that considers rating (not true time-sampling) of behavior performance in situ as the prescribed and respected criterion against which tests are to be validated. Where concept validity is concerned the common structure—the supra-medium trait—in L-, Q-, and T-data may actually be more strongly represented in Q- and T-data than L-data.

Before concluding this section a fifth and last angle of evidence on the Q-L primary-factor identities must be considered. The evidence needed lies in the answer to this question: Do the higher-order structures for the primary questionnaire factors take the same form as those in L-data? That is, when the Q- and L-data primaries are given their cross-identities according to content and mutual correlation, do independent factorings give matchable second orders from the intercorrelations in each (using the accepted primary identities)? The only second-order analysis on L(BR)-data (prior to that in press by Cattell, Pierson, Finkbeiner, Brim, and Roberston) goes back to 1957 but was done on what is still the best experimental rating basis available (three studies on groups of 100 to 300 young adults using the averaged interprimary correlations from the three groups). The results in Table 38 show essentially the same patterns as in Q-data (see Chapter Four, Table 16), although the absence of rated primaries for Q_3 and Q_4 naturally prevents the full roster for the anxiety factor from emerging in L-data. On the original list of factors common to L- and Q-data these factors are unmistakably the same in every term in their meanings.

Table 38

Second-Order Factors in L(BR)-Data Compared with Q-Data

(a) L(BR)I: Exvia

A	Affectothymia	0.38
F	Surgency	0.70
E	Dominance	0.54
H	Parmia	0.17
M	Autia	0.54

Note: Q_2 not available in rating.

(b) L(BR)II: Anxiety

C—	Low ego strength	—0.50
E—	Submissiveness	—0.32
F	Surgency	0.17
H—	Threctia	0.20
L	Protension	0.47

Note: F has appeared in adolescents as here; Q_3 and Q_4 not available in ratings.

(c) L(BR)III: Cortertia

A—	Sizothymia	—0.43
I—	Harria	—0.68
L	Protension	0.72
N—	Naïveté	—0.34

(d) L(BR)IV: Independence

E	Dominance	0.33
F	Surgency	0.27
G—	Low superego	—0.46
N	Shrewdness	0.46

Note: This misses *L* and *M* in *Q*; Q_1 and Q_2 not available in *L* series.

Two rather common illusions must be abandoned here. The first is that studies failing to find alignment of L- and T-factors prove nonalignment. Technical discussions here have made it clear that in any complex scientific procedure with, say, eight necessary steps (as in factor analysis), each with a fifty-fifty chance of going wrong, there are $2^8 = 256$ ways of going wrong and only one of going right. (The rotation process alone vastly increases these chances of error above 50/50.) So when Howarth denies or Goldberg, Norman, and Schwartz (1972) fail to find alignment of factors from two media when other studies have found alignment, the most likely conclusion is that one or both of the component media studies has misfired on one or more necessary steps. Table 46, Chapter Eight, shows that many studies miss out about one-half of the eight steps. If two men receive complex directions to meet at a certain point it requires only one to fail for the alignment to fail. As we have seen, the ratings nearly always fail. It requires only a couple of studies following legitimate procedures and reaching a statistically positive conclusion to nullify the evidence of any number of failures. This should be borne in mind not only about cross-media matching but about any statistically significant matching of factor patterns from different studies. For example, Eysenck's theory, and apparent finding, of only two or three secondaries, wherein he fails to find the 20 or so primaries, has been interpreted by some as evidence that the primaries do not exist. (But not by Eysenck himself, whose familiarity with scientific method and history has caused him to avoid this conclusion.)

A second illusion, perhaps implicit in an article by Goldberg, Norman, and Schwartz (1972) and certainly in many others, is that the rating data are the criterion against which Q- and T-data must justify themselves. These investigators examine the relative predictive power of T-data (the O-A battery) and Q-data (the 16 PF) against ratings and conclude that "the results show no clear superiority of the O-A battery measures over 16 PF scores in predicting broad peer rating criteria." This is a useful contribution to knowledge but should not be considered a conclusion about the relative IFP (instrument-free pure) trait-factor *validity* of T- and Q-data, for validity is measured against the suprafactor. Although little is known about the relative magnitudes of the instrument-factor variances in the raw scores in L-, T-, and Q-data the indications are that they are probably largest in behavior-rating measures. If this seems to contradict the classic doctrine that life behavior (L-data) is the criterion it must be remembered that L(BR)-data are not L-data (actual behavior records) but a cheap substitute within the same domain which pays for its cheapness by being heavily instrument-contaminated except under rare conditions. The real criterion is the IFP trait or suprafactor common to Q-, T-, L(BR)-, and L-data.

In summary we thus have agreement that Q- and L- data yield the same primaries separately and in joint factorings; agreement separately on the patterns that emerge as secondaries in the two media; and agreement of the loadings of Q primaries on L secondaries with those for the secondaries found directly in L-data.

5. Alignment of Primary T-Medium Traits in the O-A Battery with Secondary Q-Medium Traits

It remains to consider the other frontier of the Q-data realm: the agreement of its patterns with personality traits found through T-data, that is, objective, laboratory tests. For a full description of the nearly 500 different types of objective personality tests (underlying the programatic studies on T-data personality factors generally) the reader must be referred to the compendium by Cattell and Warburton (1967). For the orderly collation of the outcome of 20 years' experimental work on factor structures the reader is referred to Hundleby, Pawlik, and Cattell for adults (1965) and to Bolz and Cattell for children (1973); for psychological theories of the factors he is referred to Cattell (1957, 1965a) and Cattell and Schmidt (1972). Twenty dimensions have now received reasonable replication of patterns, each through 5 to 15 independent studies. No one should be misled by the fact that a few studies fail to find these patterns—as in the T-data part of Goldberg's study, which is based on only 82 subjects and an inadequate search for simple structure (60 percent in ± 0.10 and only 35 percent in ± 0.05).

Since in the exploration of so many test devices the 10 hours of testing per subject commonly required in these studies compels each test to be kept unduly short, the phase of producing batteries of more highly reliable tests for practice has only begun since the late 1960s. The O-A (objective-analytic) personality test batteries have been virtually completed for children by Schuerger and Cattell (1973) and standardized through the surveys of Klein, Cattell, and Schuerger (1973) and Cattell and Klein (1973); Hundleby (1973a, b) has worked on the adult O-A battery. The presence of considerable concrete criterion validity for the factors has been shown in education by Dielman, Schuerger, and Cattell (1970) and Schuerger, Dielman and Cattell (1970) and in clinical work by Cohen (1966), Schmidt (Cattell and Schmidt, 1972), Tatro (1967), Dubin (Cattell, Dubin, and Saunders, 1954), Scheier (Cattell and Scheier, 1961), Killian (1965), Knapp (1961, 1962), and others.

Early attempts to factor these T-data markers with L- and Q-markers (Cattell and Saunders, 1950) gave ineffective (resolution; but with the great strides made in these objective test batteries and in questionnaire scales it is probable that joint factoring of Q- and L-data markers will now yield reasonably extensive matching. However, even in that early darkness we did not have to wait long for a shaft of light. In 1955 an unexpected breakthrough was made with the discovery that the alignment sought at the first order holds between second-stratum factors in Q-scales and first-stratum traits in T-data. Probably four or five objective test factors show this alignment but in only two—UI 24 anxiety and UI 31 exvia—has the relation become clear and been thoroughly checked. The results of joint factoring in Q- and T-data in these cases are shown in Table 39.

In this research the blind search for maximum and unique simple structure was carried out essentially in the 61 objective tests (11 laboratory,

Table 39

Second-Stratum Q-Data Matching
First-Stratum T-Data

(a) *Q*I: Exvia-Invia

Objective Tests	*N* = *500*	*N* = *250*
Low accuracy of perceptual closure	−0.14	−0.32
High self-confidence on untried performance	0.13	0.30
High fluency on dreams relative to total fluency	0.13	0.21
Questionnaire Scales		
A: Affectothymia	0.39	
E: Dominance	0.46	
F: Surgency	0.46	
H: Parmia	0.43	
Q_2−: Group dependence	0.25	

(b) *Q*II: Anxiety

Objective Tests	*N* = *500*	*N* = *250*
Total annoyability score	0.52	0.39
Tendency to agree	0.24	0.63
Confession of frailties	0.42	0.19
High emotionality of comment	0.35	0.18
Questionnaire Scales		
C−: Ego weakness	−0.56	
H−: Threctia	−0.33	
L: Protension	0.54	
M: Autia	0.46	
O: Guilt proneness	0.66	
Q_3−: Low self-sentiment	−0.60	
Q_4: High ergic tension	0.74	

Note: Subjects are two groups of military airmen (500 and 250) separately factored. Smaller group did not do questionnaire; their results included only to show concurrence on objective tests (not all reproduced here). Some variables (with signs and adjectives) reversed from original (Cattell, 1955a) to fit customary scoring.

50 group-administered) so that the precision with which the second-order patterns appeared in the Q-data is all the more remarkable (compare Table 39 with Table 16 in Chapter Four). The objective test loadings are relatively small here although 15 years of further work on the pioneer tests has confirmed and raised their loadings (Rickels and Cattell, 1965; Hundleby, Pawlik, and Cattell, 1965; Bolz and Cattell, 1973) on these UI 24 and UI 32 patterns. In the same study there were indications that cortertia *Q*III might correspond to objective test cortertia UI 22 and independence *Q*IV to independence UI 19. Except for some work by colleagues of Witkin (1962) on independence (Ohnmacht, 1968; Johnson, Neville, and Workman, 1969), however, no one followed up these leads thoroughly until the work on Q-data/T-data matching by Vaughan and Cattell (1973), Nesselroade, and Cattell (1966).

Their work took a tactically different approach from the others. They began by generating questionnaire scales valid for each of 12 objective test data factors and item-analyzing a comprehensive set of items directly against these factors. This was done in three stages: (1) items against the HSOA by Cattell and Meredith, (2) more items against the scales generated in (1) on a new sample, and (3) items again against the improved HSOA itself by Vaughan. It was proposed next to find the relations of these scales to the usual questionnaire primaries and secondaries in a fourth study.

It is worth examining the assumptions of this plan of research. The general indications before it began were unmistakably that only six T-data factors might be covered by Q-data secondaries. This was puzzling since the Q-factors are based on systematic use of the personality sphere and are added to by such special searches as that for the seven missing factors. Yet all the T-data factors seem to have predictive value on life criteria in school, occupation, and clinic. Is it possible that some T-data dimensions emerge in behavior of which the subject cannot easily become aware? Or have we not asked the right questions? The parallel suggests itself that although conditions markedly affecting behavior, such as hyperthyroidism or diabetes, emerge in objective and physiological measures, the physician might not pick them up on a psychological behavior questionnaire.

Our response to the situation was simply to see what new questionnaire items corresponded to the T-data factors, and gradually to explore and build new scales. In view of its positive outcome the four-stage study mentioned above must be described with more experimental detail. The opening research by Cattell and Meredith in 1964 took 300 high school children; each child was given a 12-factor O-A battery (essentially the same battery as in Schuerger and Cattell, 1973). Correlation of items with the factors successfully picked out about six items of about 0.35 validity for each of 12 factors (Cattell, Nesselroade, and Meredith, 1966). On a sample of 220 high school students the 12-scale factor structure was checked in questionnaire analysis with the addition of new items. Finally a larger-scale study with a 14-factor O-A battery on a 300 12-to-18-year sample was carried out by Vaughan, who checked the original items and succeeded in building a 14-factor OAQ test (objective-analytic personality factors in Q-data) with 12 good items for each T-data factor. The correlations of these scales with the high school O-A battery factors, both immediate and corrected for attenuation, are shown in Table 40(a). Over most instances there is reasonably good one-to-one alignment, demonstrating that Q-data scales are obtainable for 12 T-data primary factors. In a few cases, as a discrepancy of actual and attenuation-corrected correlations shows, more work is necessary, and justified, to produce sufficiently valid scales.

For identification, Vaughan's unique battery of Q-scales correlating directly with HSOA T-data factors has been called the HSOAQ. It follows that if the general principle from the alignments of UI 1 (intelligence) with *Q*VII, of UI 32 with *Q*I, of UI 24 with *Q*II, and the less definite alignments of UI 19 with *Q*IV and of UI 22 with *Q*III is correct we would expect the HSOAQ scales to appear as second-order Q-data measures when factored with the ordinary Q primaries. This theory was tested by Vaughan, who obtained the results shown in Table 40, part (b). Like any other factor-analytic finding it requires repetition, and a larger sample to evaluate the "stray" loadings, but with exceptions the verdict is that each T-data-factor derived scale behaves like a second-order scale. These properties are being tested against the second-order CTS scales of Barton and Nichols. A small contribution to the same principle is made by the discovery of Cattell and Schmidt (1972, p. 53) that three UI factors—22, 23, and 28—are essentially second order to the questionnaire primary depression factors. The obstacle to the theory—that there are more primary T-data than secondary Q-data dimensions—may vanish when the full role of secondaries from 23 normal and 12 pathological primaries is exhaustively studied.

6. Summary and Discussion

(1) The theory of IFP or suprafactors is that there are inherent personality structures, derived from general learning experiences and from specific genetic maturations, that exist independently of the mode of observation. This position is formally stated in the principle of indifference of observational medium. Consequently the exploration of personality structure by questionnaires must be conducted as part of the total possible research approach to personality. Thus it needs to be intelligently illuminated by constant cross-reference to findings in the rating (L(BR)-data) and the objective experimental measurement (T-data) approaches.

(2) Nevertheless the alignment of trait patterns and correlation of trait scores across media should not appear in simple perfection. Systematic distortions are theoretically expected and special technical developments are necessary to discover and evaluate them. These distortions have received "local" explanations by the halo and desirability notions but a comprehensive attack is possible through the general theory of perturbation. Discovery of what the distortion effects are on structure is a necessary precondition for understanding mere quantitative score changes. The parts most relevant to this problem concern the intrusive effects of instrument factors from four sources: observer projection effects, which vary with the relation of observer to subject; situation (or conditions) of variables, which mainly concerns the fractional area of expression of a trait observed in daily life; instrument factors from the test form of individual variables; desirability stereotypes and figments. Other sources, such as test-administration conditions, subject sampling, and data-scoring treatments, must be considered relatively trivial in well-designed questionnaires. It can be shown by factoring of physical data that popular stereotypes do not distort ordinary observations although they may fill them in. Definite instrument factors, however, arise in Q-data from the subject's tendency to idealize his responses according to a desirability stereotype; this is the most substantial distortion with which we have to contend.

(3) Pending precise quantitative treatment of distortion by trait-view theory (see Chapter Nine), available evidence suggests that observer effects

Table 40

Correlations of OAQ Scales with the Objective Analytic Battery Factors and Q-Data Secondaries

(a)(i) Correlation of OAQ Scales with T-Data Factors

T-Data Factor in O-A Battery		OAQ *Scales Indexed According to T data Factors at Which Aimed*											
		16	*17*	*19*	*20*	*21*	*23*	*24*	*25*	*26*	*28*	*32*	*33*
Ego Strength	UI 16	.49			.22								
Inhibition	UI 17		.55	−.31				.27					
Independence	UI 19			.66					.38		−.21		
Comention	UI 20				.61								
Exuberance	UI 21			−.30		.58			−.27				
Regression	UI 23						.80						
Anxiety	UI 24			−.30			−.31	.77	−.31		.23		
Realism	UI 25			.37	.23			.21	.71				
Narcism	UI 26									.56			
Asthenia	UI 28			.23				.23			.82		
Exvia	UI 32									.31	−.21	.63	
Dismay	UI 33												.69

(*Note:* Nonsignificant, P>.01 values omitted.)

(a)(ii) OAQ–T-data Correlations Cross-Validated on New Sample

OAQ *Scales Indexed According to T data Factors at Which Aimed*

	16	*17*	*19*	*20*	*21*	*23*	*24*	*25*	*26*	*28*	*32*	*33*
Correlation with Corresponding UI (T-data) Factor	.31	.24	.42	.47	.38	.45	.51	.53	.31	.52	.47	.33

[a] In the cross-validation shrinkage has occurred but in every case the correlation of the OAQ scale with the UI target is the highest in the row and column concerned.

Original Sample N = 158 children

New Sample N = 158 children

(b) Relation of T-data-determined OAQ Scales to Q-data Secondaries
Eleven Secondaries Found in HSPQ plus OAQ
(Indexed by usual Q numbers)
Q Secondaries

I. OAQ Scales		*I*	*II*	*III*	*IV*	*V*	*VI(−)*	*VII*	*VIII*	*UI 17*	*UI 21*	*UI 25*	*UI 26*
Inhibition	UI 17									78			
Independence	UI 19		−43		54	31					80		
Exuberance	UI 21										80		
Regression	UI 23					48						32	
Anxiety	UI 24		47	.26								−32	
Realism	UI 25											80	
Narcism	UI 26												68
Exvia	UI 32	37			−45		26				−27		
II. HPSQ Primaries													
Affectia	*A*	67		−17		01							
Intelligence	*B*							62					
Ego Strength	*C*		−1.00			−55							
Excitability	*D*		73										
Dominance	*E*			52	32	15							
Surgency	*F*	60			24				−56				
Superego	*G*		−60					43	55				
Parmia	*H*	33	−73			−10							
Premsia	*I*			−79	−35		−04						
Coasthenia	*J*				01								
Guilt Proneness	*O*		62				−43						
Self Sufficient	Q_2	−25			05								
Self Sentiment	Q_3		−52		11		35		61				
Ergic Tension	Q_4		93			13							

Note: The usual markers for the secondaries are in boxes. The agreement of this simple structure with that usually found is excellent (high congruence of coefficients) except for V and VI. Note these latter are marked as in the HSPQ not the 16 P.F. Handbook, since they apparently change with age. The long-hypothesized (Cattell, 1955; Cattell, Hundelby, and Pawlik, 1965) alignment of I, II, and IV with U.I. 32, 24, and 19 is supported (that of III with U.I. 22 cannot be checked in the absence of U.I. 22). The new hypothesis started here is that U.I. 23, Regression -vs- Mobilization is the same as HSPQ *Q*V. Q VI is ill defined and has no U.I. associate, A VII is expected to have none since intelligence was not in the U.I. series, Q VIII is very well defined but evidently we have not yet found its objective test associate (U.I. 29 has been hypothesized but was not used). The four remaining OAQ UI's confirm their independence and scale validities but show no pattern on primaries previously seen in HSPQ second order studies; hence indexed by their UI temporarily here. Data from Cattell and Vaughan (1973a).

are more powerful in behavior ratings than other media, representing projections of the judge's own personality, his relation to the subject, his figments, and the special area of the subject's daily behavior he observes. Provided that precautions are taken against these limitations—notably by peer rating, total life observation, averaging of 6 to 12 judges, and so on (see five conditions)—it should be possible to align the corresponding Q- and L-personality factors with relatively little distortion.

(4) Even when not all of these conditions are met it should be possible to reveal the underlying cross-media matches by factoring to set aside instrument factors before seeking matching or alignment of the decontaminated substantive factors. Through experiments with plasmodes (artificial numerical models) an understanding has been gained of what happens when one factors data with instrument factors present. (1) They are ignored; no extra factors are taken out for them, which results in poor simple structure and abnormally large correlations among the blurred factors. (2) They produce hybrid or refraction factors in which each substantive trait appears in as many forms as there are instruments, positively correlated and somewhat blurred. (3) The instrument factors are carefully factored out as pure instruments thus leaving a true picture of the pure common substantive structure patterns.

(5) Most of the scattered research on which judgments about alignment of Q- and L-traits have been based suffers not only from lack of technique but also from extreme crudity of rating procedures. Rating factorization has indeed been a disaster area in personality; studies in the interim have lost the technical finish of those made 20 years ago. In the three or four studies where these three conditions have been met, however, there is substantial agreement on about 12 to 18 primary personality factors now indexed *A* through *P* corresponding to the Q-data factors. These factors, when examined by the matching conditions—factor pattern similarity, similar criterion relations, evidence of loading the same factors in joint experiment, similarity of higher-order derivatives, and correlation of estimated Q- and L-factor scores—give every evidence (except in the last-mentioned) of good alignment with the corresponding Q-data primaries. The comparatively poor support from this last condition is due partly to the poor bases of factor estimation, which contemporary work can overcome, and partly to the inescapable attenuation by instrument-factor variance. Ideal source-trait measurement requires a combination of Q-, L-, and T-data scores with precise allowance for the size of instrument factors in each.

(6) As to the frontier between Q- and T-data the confused results of early efforts to align questionnaires with factor structures in objective tests were finally resolved by the discovery of clear-cut alignments in three cases —exvia, anxiety, and intelligence—between first-order objective test factors UI 32, 24, and 1 and second-order questionnaire factors *Q*I, *Q*II, and *Q*VII. There are also indications of UI 19 and 22 aligning with *Q*III and *Q*IV. The construction of questionnaire scales (the HSOAQ) directly to measure in Q-data the UI factors in the O-A battery has proved possible for 10 to 12 UI factors, and it has been shown that the HSOAQ scales thus produced tend

to align, as hypothesized with second-order Q-data factors. Provided that factors from higher-order analyses are correctly assigned to strata it seems that second-stratum traits in Q-data are first-stratum traits in T-data. Note, however, that this requires intelligence to be registered (as with Spearman) as a first-order T-factor, so that Thurstone's primary abilities stand at the same level as Q-primaries.

Two questions arise at this point: Why has the personality sphere, when translated from the L(BR)-domain to the Q-domain, failed to be broad enough to yield (at the second order) all the dimensions found directly from the more than 400 objective tests of Cattell and Warburton (1967)? And why do questionnaire and rating items pick up factors at a lower stratum than objective tests? Possible answers to the first question are that there are more dimensions of behavior than the subjects are aware of. This idea requires no dependence on a Freudian unconscious. It simply means that perception depends on language, and that there are more facets than the social usage of language over the past two thousand years has seen fit to bring into public discussion and into the dictionary. Moreover the right questions have not been asked in extending the personality sphere, which is still too socially oriented. However, work showing 23 normal plus 12 pathological primaries makes it possible than enough Q-data second orders will be defined to extend to the 20 T-data primaries now known. Possible answers to the second question are than there is a difference of density of representation (power of the microscope) between the specific Q- and L-data items on the one hand and the general temperamental measures in T-data on the other. The Q- and L-bits of behavior are smaller, more local and numerous than general behavior conceived in laboratory, T-data tests.

Novakowska (1971) says that the "indifference of medium" principle still awaits "complete verification" and that it accepts the need for perturbation theory and the probability that traits have more variance in some media than others. If my presentation seems to minimize L-data in defining the basic cross-media source traits it is only because the technical quality of those data has been poor in this generation. For, on the other hand, only life observation in situ can do credit to the full expression of the individual personality in the stream of history, whereas the Q- and L-test behavior is only a brief cross-sectional snip from that behavior. In the other hand the life stream has too many uncontrolled specifics. What would have been the the evaluation of Napoleon's military skill had the French Revolution not occurred, or Shakespeare's genius as a playwright if he had been born in Patagonia instead of in the ferment of Elizabethan England? Ways will undoubtedly be found of encompassing L-data evaluations despite these vagaries; meanwhile the meaning of source-trait structures rests with more psychometric rigor in Q- and T-data.

(7) Although the historical flux of the L-data world means that a more precise, replicable factor structure exists in Q- and T-data, the psychometric meaning of the IFP trait—the *instrument-free pure trait*—implies that no medium is the sole criterion. The best estimation of the IFP trait, by neutralization or partialing of instrument factors specific to media, re-

quires that all media be involved. In the fullest sense of *concept validity*, therefore, a questionnaire cannot be validated against a factor demonstrated and measured only in Q-data. However, since there are indications that the Q-medium bias (when trait-view theory is used) is slight such validation probably puts scales in general in their correct validity order.

VIII

The Extent of Variation of Concepts with Methods, Populations, and Cultures

To this point the aim has been to integrate a large volume of findings into a unified, coherent theory. Whenever such a stage is reached in science the central coherence out of chaos provides an anvil on which more specific developments can be hammered out.

Although this degree of integration is now possible, discordant claims continue to be made which might give a newcomer to the literature the impression that we are still at a cruder stage of development. One reason for these discords, it will be shown, is that to large a fraction of publication in this area in fact still is at a poorer technical level than is needed and possible in view of the sophistication of factor methods available in such books as those of Child (1970), Gorsuch (1973), Cattell (1966, 1972), Harman (1970), Pawlik (1968), Rummel (1970), Uberla (1968), and others. The second reason for unnecessary conceptual confusion is the failure to grasp principles governing statistical modification with changes of sample, and, more importantly, changes of population, age, and culture. Differences of conclusion merely about the validity, standardization, and so on, of particular scales are examined in Chapters Nine and Ten, since our concern here is the more fundamental one of first correctly conceiving the trait and state structure itself.

1. The Eight Basic Requirements for Effective Factorial Investigation

The kinds of differences we need to examine can spring from very different sources, as follows:

(1) *Unanchored Semantic Concepts.* Differences in views about traits that are either meaningless or purely verbal arise when concepts from the earlier "clinical" phase of Allport, Freud, Murray, and others, tied poorly or not at all to mathematical models, are treated as if they had exact models. Chapter One, here, should free us from the type of chaos.

(2) *Misunderstood Techniques.* Differences of conclusion, even with adoption of the same model, will arise if techniques are poorly applied, or if the effects of some differences of method are not understood.

(3) *Inadequacy of Logic and Meta-Theory.* Real differences of structure will arise even with correct method when different ages, cultures, and so on, are studied. To reconcile these something more than statistics, namely, a framework of developing logical constructs, is needed.

My concern here is mainly with (2) and (3), although inasmuch as general personality theories enter into the debate (1) will intrude. Here let us not forget the lesson that Renaissance science grasped and classical philosophy did not: that knowledge advances by answering limited and precise questions, not by constructing vast and cloudy theories. Between vague, pretentious theorizing and unimaginative, pragmatic data-gathering lies a middle path of daring but hard-headed theory linked to constant experiment. This path which we shall follow relates to richer personality theories than the average itemetric, purely statistically interested psychometrist takes into his reasoning and to more precise and complex psychometric methods than all too many personality theorists seem able to acquire.

To reach a constructive statement of a unified theory embracing trait and state, strata, developmental and pathological relations, and the effect of different media the clearing in the jungle made in the preceding chapters has had to begin at some practical point. I have concentrated on the hundreds of researches that have achieved methodological coherence over 20 to 30 years of planned, programatic work. Some reviewer will undoubtedly deplore that hundreds of other studies in the same period were not surveyed in equal detail. But my aim is not to compile a mere catalog of questionnaire scale constructions, variously carried out by methods good, bad, and execrable. It is to examine carefully any important alternative methods or positions in relation to the unified theory.

The only limitation to the present integration which could be at all serious is the restriction of investigations—except for a few in Germany, France, and Japan—to English-speaking cultures. Yet when examined more closely this involves very little selection of available data, for nine-tenths of the research on questionnaires is in English, and questionnaires in other countries have largely derived from these.

A reviewer from the ranks of classical bivariate experiment might add a second objection that more evidence rests on multivariate experimental (factor-analytic) than on bivariate designs. To this the answer is that bivariate designs alone would have made negligible progress in this area in the time and that good practice calls for the two-handed approach we have made.

At any rate, our purpose here is to view apparently divergent results —those from laboratories with different methods and from populations with possible real differences of pattern. But the first—the differences from diversities of methods, standards, and, occasionally, models—is the more fundamental. If we cannot get constant conclusions within our own culture how can we expect to reach them across cultures? It is only in the past few years that serious discord over conclusions has arisen. As an illustration of Hogben's (1937) "economic determination of scientific history" I must point out that the sudden increase in availability of computers, the nearness of large, captive undergraduate classes, and the appeal to the undergraduate teacher of being able to fix his own name to a printed questionnaire have combined to produce an eruption of publication with standards and goals very different from those of long-established scholarship in basic personality research. Much of this industry claims to be producing scales of higher psychometric properties than the factor scales based on systematic personality structure theory, but the buyer should not be deceived by the face value of these figures. The better psychometric properties prove to be merely higher homogeneity (intercorrelation of items), which is easy to get if one wants it but quite undesirable. As Ashton and Goldberg (1972) have shown, even nonpsychologists are easily capable of developing highly valid items for arbitrary, narrow scales, whereas it may take 20 years of progressive rectification (this chapter) to accumulate enough moderately valid items for a truly broad, subtly expressed personality source trait shown by programatic factoring to be a natural, functionally unitary structure.

The numerous ad hoc questionnaire scales for subjectively defined qualities are proud castles in the sands of itemetrics that can be left to the tide of improved technical examination. What are perhaps more misleading than these ad hoc scales are the statements on source traits from studies that go through the motions of objective investigation and factor analysis but fail to perform its real services. Nowadays it should surely be unnecessary to reject the unrotated principal components as an acceptable alternative model, nor does the reader need to be asked to preoccupy himself with red herrings in the form of alternatives in factor extraction such as the centroid, the powered vector, and other ingenious variants by Comrey, Demaree, Overall, and others. As Gorsuch (1973) rightly says, these variations are trivial but might distract the incautious from the main issues. The main issues lie within such alternative models as factoring with communalities preserved versus alpha factoring, underfactoring versus overfactoring, orthogonal versus oblique rotation, and claiming results simply on R-technique versus the broader involvement in theory advocated here through combined use of R-, P-, and dR-techniques in strategic counterchecks.

This chapter is inevitably technical: in science major alternatives in theory may hinge on a small, recondite technical observation or analysis. The justification for the basic technical positions taken here must be left to such writings on factor analysis as the *Handbook of Multivariate Experimental Psychology* (Cattell, 1966a), Harman (1967), Child (1970), Comrey (1973), Gorsuch (1973), Guertin and Bailey (1970), Rummel (1970), and other texts. In any factoring of questionnaire items one must make careful tests for the number of factors, estimate communalities rather than use unities, and rotate to a unique position (by simple structure or confactor rotation) that corresponds with the action of a source-trait influence. There should also be a test for significance of simple structure, a check for significance of pattern resemblance to previous research (possible only if markers were included in the original choice of variables), and a search to see if higher-strata structures agree with those found among the alleged primaries. Without these conditions no research is adequate. Yet claims for alternative conceptual resolutions to those integrated in the last seven chapters are constantly made on the basis of one or two studies that omit one or more of these requirements. For reference the standards for evaluating factorial findings are set out as eight points in Table 41.

Table 41

Eight Required Conditions in a Factor Analytic Experiment to Define Unitary Traits

1. *Strategic Choice of Variables.* Personality sphere for discovery; marker variables for hypothesis testing.
2. *Sampling of People.* At least three times the number of variables and preferably over 250, beyond which little is gained. Sample should be from a population due to exhibit traits concerned.
3. *Decision on Number of Factors by an Objective Test.* Maximum-likelihood and scree test are best.
4. *Fixing of Communalities.* By iterative analysis from condition 3.
5. *Unique Oblique Rotational Resolution.* Based on properties not predilections; by confactor or by simple structure demonstrably pursued to a maximum. This means proceeding beyond the first approximation by an automatic analytical program. (An automatic topological program may suffice.)
6. *Test of Significance of Simple Structure* (Bargmann, 1953).
7. *Check on Degree of Invariance of Pattern Across Research.* By congruence (Burt, 1940) or salient-variable similarity index (Cattell, Barcar, Horn, and Nesselroade, 1969).
8. *Check on Invariance of the Higher Order Structure.* This rests on the factor intercorrelations in condition 7.

These eight conditions are necessary in a single-factor analysis; but in research a strategic relation among separate factor analyses is also necessary, as insisted on above in programatic work and developed specifically below in the concept of progressive rectification. A single factoring, no matter how large the sample, proves nothing.[1] In every one-shot factoring there are a few degrees of rotational uncertainty in the simple structure and accidents of sample, as well as general errors in scoring, card-punching, and so on. Only the massive verdice of consistency over experiments, populations, age groups, and so forth is good enough for conclusions on personality structure.

Regarding departures from the standards of Table 41, one must expect to meet arguments that are quixotic or at least esoteric. After it was demonstrated that no analytic program reaches the best simple structure and that two or three months of hand rotation by rotoplot may be necessary to carry the history of the hyperplane plot to a true maximum, one researcher replied that "life is too short for that kind of thing." Others less frank shown that this is their philosophy also. It is a philosophy with which, fortunately, Koch, Kepler, the Curies, and the designers of the gaseous diffusion process for nuclear energy were not tainted. The fact remains that until some such superior method of rotation as confactor is perfected (see Cattell and DeYoung, 1973a), science has no way of reaching unique resolution in factor analysis except by prolonged trial-and-error rotation after the analytic programs or even topological automatic programs such as maxplane have carried one by machine as far as they can go.

Even more quixotic than this button-pushing—after this approach has been shown not to work—is the whimsical choice of a number of factors

[1] The reader must judge for himself at what points these criticisms apply to certain recent research by Comrey (1973), Eysenck and Eysenck (1969), and Howarth and Browne (1971a, 1971b). They do not apply to the careful studies of D. N. Jackson (1966), Sells, Demaree, and Wills (1970), Nesselroade and Friel (1973), Nesselroade and Bartsch (1973), Dielman (1973), Harman and French (1972), and others. Howarth and Browne (1971a, 1971b) eventually apply a test for the number of factors but, apparently disliking the conclusion, complete the analysis with their own subjective choice. It is typical of the disagreement among these technically inadequate solutions that Howarth (communication to Professor Kulhavy) asserts that "the Eysenck Personality Inventory [actually] has 15 factors and claims to measure two, whereas the 16 PF claims to measure 16 and measures 10." Regarding the second statement the reader is referred to Figure 5 (Chapter Two). Howarth's plot of eigenvalues (1971b, Figure 1) should have 187 entries but is not carried beyond 18, thus making the application of the scree test for number of factors impossible.

Regarding the effectiveness of the search for oblique simple structure, some studies just referred to have not even begun to look for oblique structure but have used varimax. Varimax and other orthogonal rotations such as quartimax have the characteristic vice of not spreading sufficiently, that is, not getting unanchored, from the large first principal component and to some degree the second. There is little doubt that promax, starting to go oblique from varimax, does the same (Dielman and Cattell, 1973; Cattell 1973a). Varimax and promax are thus appreciably affected by the experimenter's choice of initial variables and less likely to be invariant across researches. Because of its high loadings the first factor is apt deceptively to look the same (as the principal component with the same variables is necessarily the same) across studies, as when Eysenck takes out extraversion as the first factor. But subsequent factors depart increasingly from their more true oblique counterparts until by the third or fourth the distortion from the true pattern brings complete obscurity.

different from that indicated by any statistical test. Howarth is undoubtedly right in maintaining that Eysenck's scale items have *decidedly* more factor dimensions than the three—*N, E,* and *P*—that he has for two decades defended as the ideal scales. Peterson (1960) has carried this simplification-for-the-user to the ultimate expression in extracting just two factors—well-behaved versus delinquent and sociably extravert versus introvert. (The first may be a rough approach to second-order *Q*VIII, moral upbringing, as Eysenck's *N* is to *Q*II, anxiety.) Digman (Western APA, 1969) has said what needs to be said, from the standpoint of serious research, about Peterson's "solution."

These and other solutions that have led to misleading concepts through neglecting requirements 3, 4, and 5 in Table 41 are easier for the alert student to catch than are certain vaguely philosophical deviations. For example, Harris (1971) expresses the view behind the practice of many when he suggests that the patterns which receive common names despite differences of rotation and nonrotation, and many and few factors, must be correct. This begs the question by assuming that in these apparent instances any true consistency does emerge. I have said that a crude approximation to three or four of the second orders is the last state of many poorly planned studies—those getting anywhere at all. But as soon as a precise evaluation of similarity of results is applied, the mangled nature of the outcome, compared to the good matching from careful techniques, is obvious. It is illogical to expect the same results from different procedures—for example, from trying to dissolve a mixture in alcohol and in water or calculating angles by plane and spherical trigonometry—although consistent results can be obtained up to a point by several people using the same wrong method, as in the tolerable agreement of Peterson, Eysenck, and to some extent Comrey on the nature of the first two or three large secondary factors. However, anyone who compares the congruence coefficients in Table 15 (Chapter Four) of Nichols' careful studies with the congruence claimed in the technically unchecked studies just mentioned will see a great difference. Even if a dozen studies pointed to three rough second orders while three studies reaching high congruence pointed to eight, the latter would have to be accepted. In this case even the "vote"—the majority verdict of studies—is the other way: for Nichols' studies are not only more exactly matched but more numerous. This has not prevented Comrey (1970) from asking us to explain our "error" in diverging from his result.

This last case brings us to another example of dubious philosophy of science. Comrey states that he gets his results by following simple structure only up to a point. The rotation, he insists, must also be adjusted to give proper meaning to the factor. One need not labor the point that every psychologist could have his own idea of the best meaning and that this is nothing more than introducing subjectivity. But Comrey's instance is at least that of one having the courage to espouse openly what many do surreptitiously. But it may still be an error; and indeed there is no such thing as being slightly subjective any more than one can be slightly pregnant. Once one departs from objectivity in deciding rotation, number of factors, or any other issue a slippery slope leads back to subjectivity as great as in those who described types, traits, and personality theory with the abandon of a century ago.

2. Points at Issue Among Investigators

With this general introduction to the technical points at issue, let us get to particular conceptual differences among the chief investigators. I have tried to draw a distinction between an explicit determination of two investigators to choose different models, applying the different techniques appropriate to them, and the failure—through accident, compromise with limited resources, or predilection for an arbitrary concept—to apply admittedly necessary techniques. A survey of the literature (see, for example, Vaughan, 1973) must surely convince one that the second is far more prevalent; anyone with experience in the field is also likely to notice that some apparent instances of the first actually develop as afterthoughts compelled by the second. (For example, a researcher who cannot get significant simple structure may decide that is an unnecessary principle anyway.) Again the availability of nothing but the orthogonal varimax solution in computer centers in Australia, Europe (until quite recently in Britain and Germany), and most American universities has resulted in nine-tenths of studies being published, with apologies, as orthogonal resolutions.

In a few cases, as in the Guilford-Zimmerman scales, leaving the resolution orthogonal represents the explicit adoption of a model—as in the first alternative above—and this difference can be logically debated. But in the vast majority, the founding of questionnaire scale concepts on attempts at orthogonal simple structure (a contradiction in nature) has no such respectable origin. The investigators have simply failed to consider and construct such programs as maxplane, the H-K, oblimax, promax, and rotoplot to obtain maximum simple structure or, in rushing to completion, they have failed to give the two or three months of patient space-search required by daily rotoplots. Yet as Thurstone argued powerfully on theoretical grounds and as Cattell and Dickman (1962), Cattell and Jaspars (1967), and Gorsuch (1973) have also shown in practice with natural data of known structure, both simple structure and maximum invariance from study to study are better achieved, jointly, with obliqueness. Moreover although the difference may somethimes seem mathematically slight between the orthogonal and oblique solution, or between the mass-produced automatic program output and the finished rotoplot result, the difference in psychological meaning can be fatal to the purpose of checking a precise theory.

As Figure 21 shows, for two different Q-data studies each examined separately by items and by parcels, the typical research for maximum simple structure is a long one, gradually advancing over perhaps 20 rotations to a position essentially unimprovable over the next half-dozen trials. In both experiences, both analyses and both widths of hyperplane the initial analytical programs (oblimax and promax), reaching 60 to 75 percent in the ± 0.10 hyperplane, were decidedly improved upon, especially in the ± 0.05, which is probably the apt width for larger samples. The change from the automatic to the rotoplot substantially altered factor interpretations. Of course some differences exist between automatic programs, which are either analytic, maximizing some function, like the H-K or promax, or they are topological like maxplane and rotoplot; reasons are given elsewhere why the topological solution is definitely superior: see Cattell (1973d).

Since the basic model for questionnaire traits and states has been sufficiently stated in Chapters One, Five, and elsewhere and since the form of factor-analytic procedures to fit and test that model have been thoroughly set out (Bartsch and Nesselroade, 1973; Cattell, 1966a; Gorsuch, 1973; Harman, 1967) and are generally agreed upon, I shall spend no more time on the choice of model. But there is no escape from an inquest regarding the differences of view regarding conceptions of specific questionnaire traits and states which arise from inadequacies and confusions in the use of the procedures. For these account for nine-tenths of the debated conclusions. Some limit, fortunately, can be set to this cleaning of the Augean stables, if, using the equivalent of Hercules' river Alpheus, we wash aside at once all trivial and one-shot studies with defects obvious to a tyro and concentrate on serious and relatively programatic positions.

Among these more substantial positions we find that of Comrey (1970, 1973), who claims eight primaries that he believes differ from the 16 PF-HSPQ primaries and that of Eysenck and Eysenck (1963, 1969), who develop theories around three factors, but with O. White's techniques have to report 11. We must examine also some interpretive emphases of Fiske (1971); the adoption of other than factored scales by Goldberg (1972b); the attempts of Howarth and Browne (1971a, 1971b) and Rorer (1965) to demolish the structures concluded here to be basic; the belief in the real existence of a large and disabling social desirability factor by Edwards (1957a) and Wiggins (1962a); the willingness of Adcock (1965) to accept his one orthogonal second-order study structure when it departs (only moderately, it is true) from the dozen oblique solutions shown to have excellent mutual fit by Gorsuch and by Nichols; the similar criticism of the second-order structure by Becker (1960) and by Timm (1968), each on the basis of one poor simple structure; the criticism of factor-analytic solutions as a whole by Lykken (1971); and the doubts of those who mistakenly assume that the present solutions should align with the Guilford-Zimmerman, the Jackson, and the Edwards scales (although the first is orthogonal and the two last start in a different modality of variables—the motivation variables of Murray's needs).

In addition to these main debates over structure and interpretation we find some psychometric issues when Eysenck (1971), Howarth and Browne (1971b), Comrey and Duffy (1968), and Levonian (1961) assume that the highest possible homogeneity should be sought in any scale. Here they disagree with the 16 PF, HSPQ, and CPQ, which do not accept this restriction, and with Humphreys (1951, 1952), Cattell and Tsujioka (1964), Nunnally (1959), and other psychometrists who hold that maximum homogeneity is undesirable. Another subissue—although a major one in any true perspective—lies in the debate on the number of personality factors in observer ratings, where Norman (1963) and Tupes (1957) have settled for only six dimensions and Howarth for only five (1972), against the finding in Chapter Seven that there are at least 12 and probably 16 to 21 matching the main Q-series. Similar doubts, now partially answered (Cattell and Vaughan, 1973), concern the lineup of Q-, L-, and T-data personality factors claimed as partially established in Chapter Seven. Finally there are the careful findings of Sells, Demaree, and Will based on an exemplary coverage of variables, but flawed in the factoring process which, according to their matching, represent in our concepts a mixture of first orders and some second orders appearing together at the first order.

There has been a tendency to view these alternative possible conclusions as an attack on the establishment, and when that occurs positions which are themselves mutually incompatible are often mistakenly seen as in alliance. The attacks of Comrey (1973), Howarth (1971a), Eysenck and Eysenck (1971), and Rorer (1972) have explicitly claimed this position, but in fact they have severe mutual incompatibilities compared with the essential agreement in the established programatic work here gathered from Barton (1973b), Coan and Cattell (1958, 1959), DeYoung (1927), Digman (1963, 1972), Cattell and Gruen (1954), Friel 1971), Guilford (with obliquity handled as in Gibbons, 1966), Schaie (1973), Shrader and Cattell (1973), Saville (1972), Kear-Colwell (1965, 1969), Nichols (1973a, 1973b), Dielman and Cattell (1973), Nesselroade (1966), Wilde (1973), and many others. Actually not a single congruence coefficient has yet been presented among the factor systems of Comrey, Eysenck, Howarth, Jackson or Rorer, and whatever indications of agreement exist are no more than for two or three pseudo-second orders as described below.

Any assertion of dependable agreement among discovered factors is possible only if identical marker variables are used, and if the populations are reasonably similar in age and origin. The most broadly derived set of markers from the personality sphere in both ratings and questionnaire searches over 30 years exists in the items and scales of the 23 normal dimensions in the family of questionnaires constituted by the 16 PF, HSPQ, CPQ, ESPQ, and so on, and the 12 pathological dimensions of the CAQ. Fortunately for firm progress these are the markers chosen in common by the otherwise diversely planned researches of Eysenck and Eysenck, Howarth and Browne, Levonian, and Sells, Demaree and Will.

There is some question here of whether items or scales should be markers, and this we shall discuss. But the critics have chosen items and the 184 items of Form A of the 16 PF (omitting the two buffer items) have become the most representative reference set these past ten years for the contending personality structure theories of Eysenck, Howarth, Becker, Sells, Demaree, Will, Levonian, Timm, and others. Theories differ first as to the number of factors required, ranging from 3 for Eysenck to 18 or more for the present writer, and second as to the identities of the traits, which means the rotational position regarded as uniquely indicated.

I have contended for some time that number of factors and rotation reached are not independent, and this has been clearly shown recently by

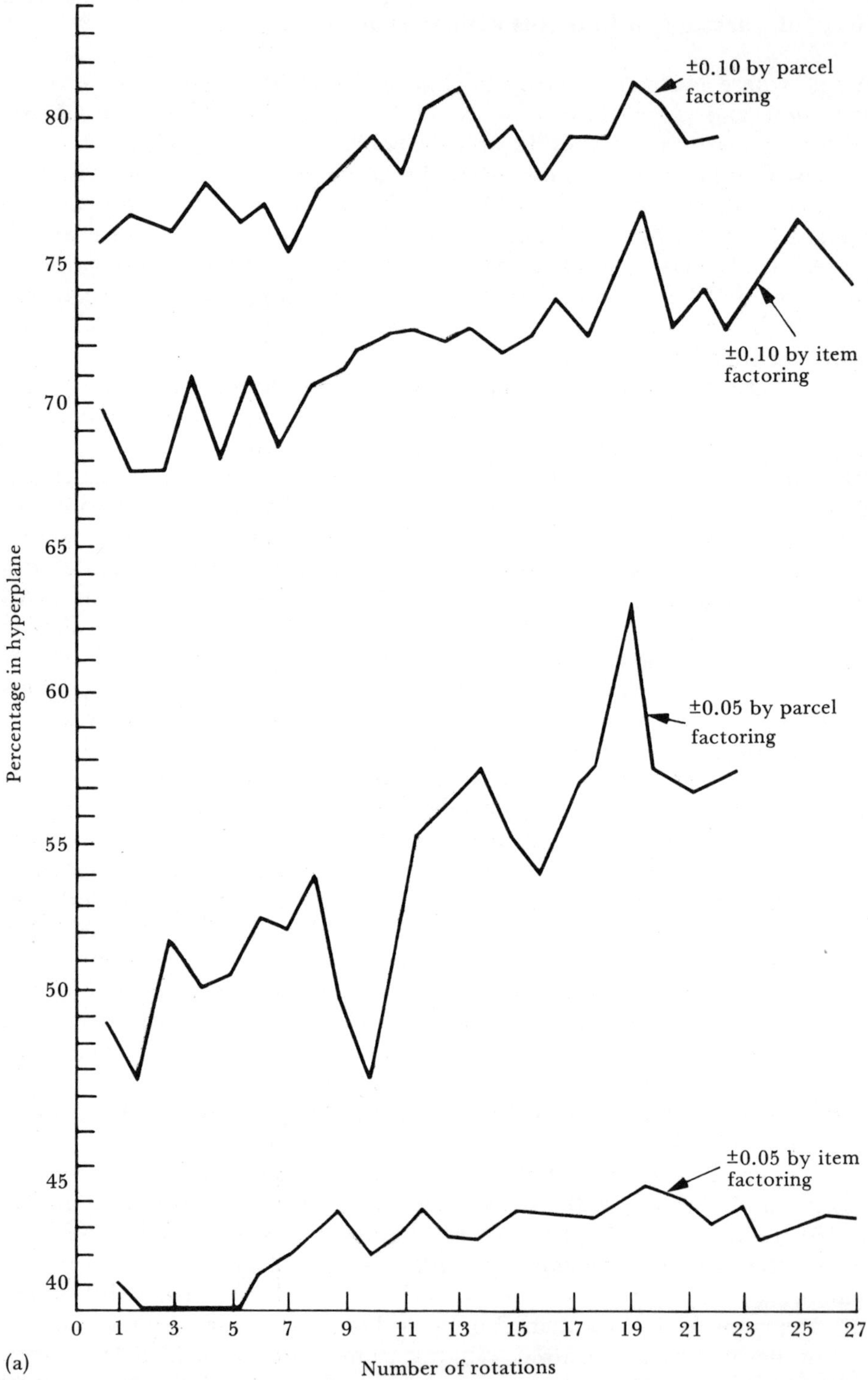

Figure 21. Approaches to maximum goodness of simple structure recorded in four studies: (a) adult group of 780 on 16 PF by items and parcels, (b) student group of 250 by items and parcels. Hyperplane counts are given for two widths, ±0.10 and ±0.05. In the larger sample, ±0.05 is the more sensitive index.

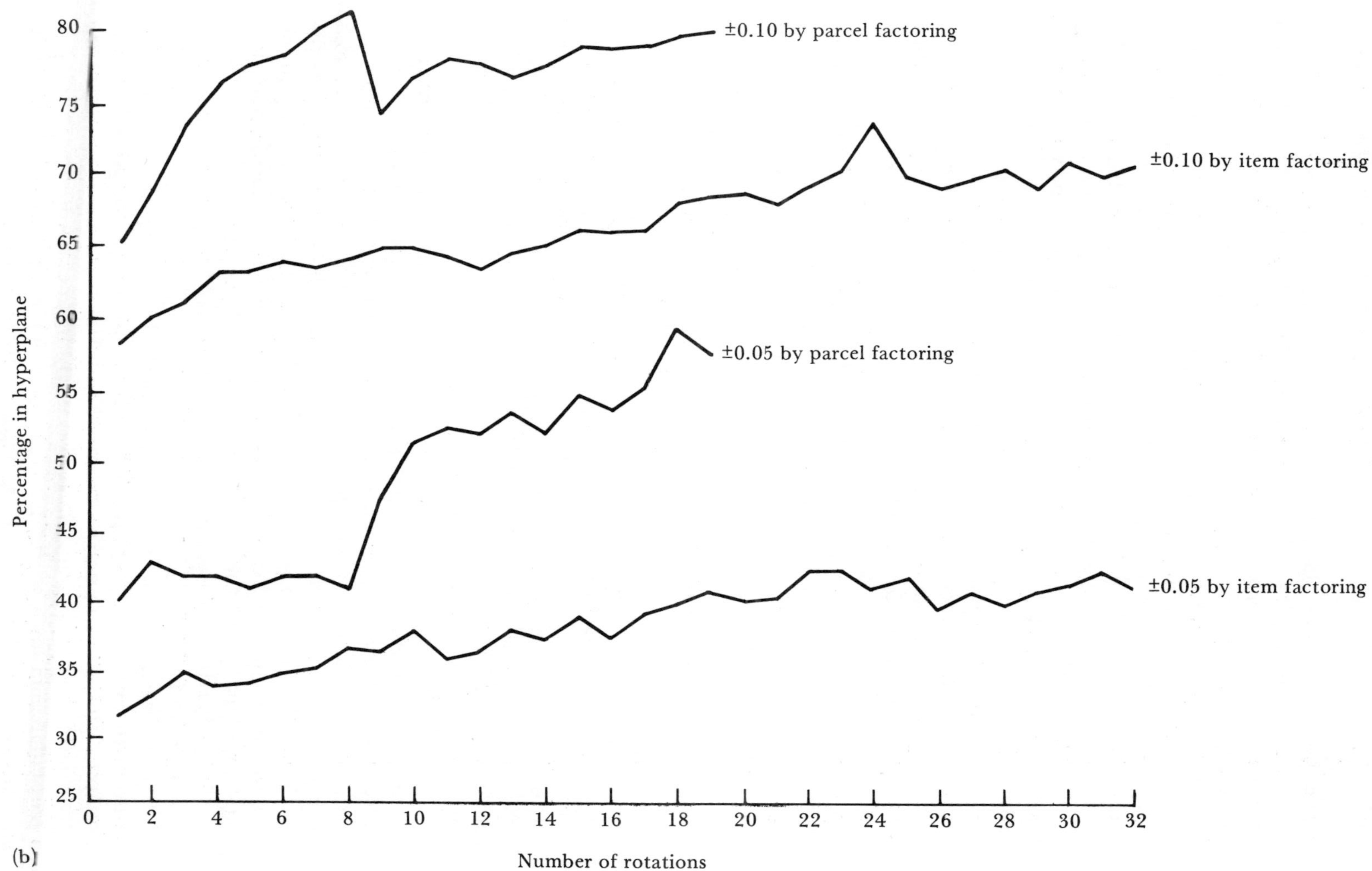

±0.10 by parcel factoring
±0.10 by item factoring
±0.05 by parcel factoring
±0.05 by item factoring
Percentage in hyperplane
Number of rotations

(b)

DeYoung, finding that the factors become increasingly second orders as one increasingly underfactors (DeYoung and Cattell, 1973) (see Table 42). Some operational definitions are needed here. We shall call a second-order factor obtained by underfactoring, that is, taking p instead of k factors out of items, where there are really k primaries and p secondaries from the k primaries, a pseudo-second-order factor. In order to identify it, since it is a pattern on items, one must project the true secondaries on items, using the Cattell-White formula (Chapter Four) in what can be called a grounded secondary, since it is not expressed in primaries but on the ground of items.

When these grounded patterns are worked out it becomes evident that Eysenck's EPI is operating with the first two or three of our nine second orders; Sells, Demaree and Will with 10 or 11 factors some of which are clearly grounded secondaries and other primaries, and Howarth (10 factors) the same. Comrey's factors are largely second orders approached by a different method from the others, namely by starting with parcels (his FHIDS) which are homogeneous and offer variables which are approaches to first-order factors from the beginning. These conclusions are supported below, but on the rotational issue we would add that any factoring of items, even with correct number of factors, offers alternative simple structures of primaries or grounded secondaries and that underfactoring merely forces the second alternative.

3. Item versus Parcel Factoring and the Theory of Progressive Rectification

The questions of what the true primaries are has got caught up in a prior debate over factoring items versus factoring homogeneous parcels or short scales as variables. Doubtless many psychologists would support one side or the other, but they have become represented on one side by Eysenck (1971), and Howarth and Browne (1971b) denying the validity of any factoring not based on items, and Comrey (1970) (and by inference, Nunnally, 1967) denying that items can be a suitable basis.

My own conclusion is that both are legitimate and, properly conducted, give the same answer, but that parcels can give a cleaner answer. Indeed, I have argued for, and adopted in the past twenty-five years of 16 PF, HSPQ, and so on, construction, a planned sequence of the alternative methods in relation to stages of development. Let us study the pros and cons of the two, in the light of both psychometric principles and experience, beginning —since the argument for items has recently been more rashly and dogmatically stated—with the objections to items. They are:

(1) that items show low reliability (dependability coefficients) from occasion to occasion.

(2) that they show low transferability; that is, they are so specific in nature that their factor loadings change from subculture to subculture. For example, "Do you go to movies often?" has different meanings in New York City, Alaska, and an Indian village. Even within one culture the validity of a particular item for a particular factor (say, for radicalism-conservatism in students and in 40-year olds) changes drastically over time.

Table 42

Effect of Underfactoring, Causing Emergence of Secondaries Instead of Primaries

(a) Data from 184-variable 16 PF Adult Item Factoring and from Sells, Demaree, and Will (1968): 19 true primaries and 10 true secondaries

Extent of Underfactoring: Number Taken Out	*Matches with True Primaries* [a]	*Matches with True (grounded) Secondaries* [a]
3 factors (promax)	0	3
8 factors (promax)	$3\frac{1}{2}$	$4\frac{1}{2}$
11 factors (Sells and others)	$5\frac{1}{2}$	$4\frac{1}{2}$

[a] $\frac{1}{2}$ factors indicate that a factor matched a true primary and a true secondary factor equally: it could not reach a unique high simple structure without variance.

(b) Data from DeYoung's Plasmodes: 3 Primaries and 1 Secondary: Oblimax and Rotoplot with 2 Factors Extracted

Extent of Underfactoring	*Matches with True Primaries*	*Matches with True Secondaries*
Plasmode 1	1	1
Plasmode 2	1	1
Plasmode 3	$1\frac{1}{2}$	$\frac{1}{2}$

(c) Data from Plasmode 30-10-5-2 (Cattell and Jaspars, 1967): 10 true primaries and 5 true secondaries analysis in (DeYoung and Cattell 1973).

Extent of Underfactoring	*Matches with True Primaries*	*Matches with True Secondaries*
2 factors (promax)	0	2
2 factors (oblimax)	0	2
5 factors (promax)	2	3
5 factors (oblimax)	2	3
7 factors (promax)	4	3
7 factors (oblimax)	5	2

(3) that items are liable to have different meanings for different subjects. It might be answered that this merely makes the item a useful projection test. But if the stimulus situation has different meanings the factors involved in responding to it become different for different subjects. Factor-analytic results then suffer an apparent loss of communality.

(4) that, if properly constructed to deal with specific actual behavior (rather than self-rating on traits), items will tend to have little common factor and much specific factor compared to parcel of items. The central tendency in correlation of items as usually constructed with a factor is 0.3, thus leaving possibly nine-tenths of the variance belonging to a specific. This makes any one item a poor representative of a factor but the situation is actually a little worse than this simple analysis indicates, for an appreciable part of the useless variance belongs to other common factors.

The nature of these instabilities demands scrutiny for psychometric stereotypes of reliability might mislead us. Undependability, or fluctuation from occasion to occasion, may be due partly to its wording permitting a change of meaning for him as the subject meets the item again. This does not prevent simple structure from being obtained each time: it is merely a different trait structure on the two occasions. On the other hand—and this is perhaps the major criticism of the item—it is so short in duration, the decision being in a second or so, that a moment's inattention to meaning, a distracting stimulus, or a moody toss-up between alternatives can introduce substantial random-measurement error. Cartwright has suggested that one reason for item undependability is the possibility of shift of attention from stimulus to response, at random. Wundt showed in simple reaction times a systematic difference of speed between attention to stimulus and to response. In the similarly brief event of an item this could be one of the several accidental circumstances affecting meaning and dependability. If this intrusion of several sources of sheer random error in a brief decision is the cause of the low dependability coefficient, then the effect is not only to decrease communality but to blur the common-factor hyperplane. That is to say, a variable that should truly have zero loading on a certain factor will have, say, 95 percent of its distribution on successive factorings spread as widely as from +0.15 to −0.15, or more. It is this blurring of the hyperplane when using items which creates problems and disputes in finding simple structure by item factoring.

The effect of the second weakness—low transferability—is merely to make the recognition of a given factor difficult and uncertain from one investigator's work to another because of the inherently low invariance of even the larger loadings of items. Sources (3) and (4) above act differently; they increase the rotation problem because they imply that test vectors are shortened relative to those of the usual subtest or parcel variables. The effect, to be explained below, is that the points which represent the variables become, in a case of items, a tight swarm around the origin. This makes rotation of large numbers of items difficult (as encountered in Eber and Fuller's attempt to factor all the items in the MMPI). Difficulty here means uncertainty and disagreement as to the unique position, as shown in the substantial number of factors that cannot be identified across research in, for example, the item-factor analyses of Eysenck and Eysenck (1969), Howarth and Browne (1971b), the varimax rotations of Sells, Demaree, and Will (1970), and countless others.

Thus the two main problems in factoring by item are the difficulty of reaching an unambiguous simple structure and the likelihood that even when correct rotational resolutions have somehow been divined the factor pattern of item loadings is unstable from subculture to subculture, making identification and scoring by the same key unreliable.

It was to overcome these difficulties that in 1956 I introduced factoring by homogeneous parcels of four to eight items each, which may be considered homogeneous scales but are not necessarily factor-homogeneous (see Figure 33, Chapter Nine). The purpose of this new design was apparently misunderstood to be mere economy, making possible, say, the factoring of 600 items as 100 parcel variables of six items each. This economy was of course important with early computers; it still is important inasmuch as many psychologists are compelled to omit the necessary factor procedures (notably iteration of communalities and rotoplot) when the n becomes too large, as when Sells, Demaree, and Will omit iteration to get the proper communalities (Table 46) because of cost. But the major support for the parcel procedure comes from the clarification of rotation. As Tsujioka and I (Cattell and Tsujioka, 1964) have pointed out, the loadings of a parcel as a variable are related to those of the constituent items as illustrated in the case of two items:

$$a_j = b_{j1}T_1 + b_{j2}T_2 + \ldots + b_{jk}T_k + b_jT_j \tag{8.1}$$

$$a_h = b_{h1}T_1 + b_{h2}T_2 + \ldots + b_{hk}T_k + b_hT_h$$

Here j and h are two items and there are k common traits—the Ts—and two specifics T_j and T_h.

To obtain the new loading $b_{(aj+ah)}$—which we write b_{p1} for loading of the whole parcel a_p on factor T_1—we must find the contribution of factor T_1 to the variance of a_p. Assuming orthogonal factors for simplicity, unit length factors, and unit standard deviation single items,

$$\sigma_{p1}^2 = b_{j1}^2 + b_{h1}^2 + 2r_{j1h1}\, b_{j1}\, b_{h1} \tag{8.2a}$$

(σ_{p1}^2 is the contribution of factor T to the variance of a_p). Since $r_{j1h1} = 1$ and because both contributions from T_1 are perfectly correlated,

$$\sigma_{p1}^2 = b_{j1}^2 + b_{h1}^2 + 2b_{j1}\, b_{h1} \tag{8.2b}$$

But the total variance of a_p now exceeds unity, and if similar extended contributions from other factors are similarly written,

$$\sigma_p^2 = \sum_{x=1}^{x=k} (b_{jx}^2 + b_{hx}^2 + 2b_{jx}\, b_{hx}) + b_j^2 + b_h^2 \tag{8.3}$$

The loading we desire for parcel a_p, expressed for any factor T_x, is

$$b_{px} = \sqrt{\frac{b_{jx}^2 + b_{hx}^2 + 2b_{jx}\, b_{hx}}{\sigma_p^2}} \tag{8.4}$$

If the loadings of j and h are of similar sign —if j and h have positive homogeneity—a_p has (compared with the items composing it) increased loadings on the common factors and reduced loading on the specific factor because the loadings for the specifics sum simply whereas those for the common factors have products added.[2] The parcel thus has greater communality than its items, and the parcel variables stand out farther from the origin (Figure 22), assisting recognition of simple structure. The geometrical result is that the

[2] The general basis for the increased factor loading and communality is given by Cattell and Tsujioka (1964):

$$r_{fp} = \frac{\Sigma_j^{N} b_j\sigma_j r_{jf}}{\sqrt{\Sigma_j^{N} b_j^2\sigma_j^2 + 2\Sigma_{jk}^{N(N-1)/2}\, b_j b_k \sigma_j \sigma_k r_{jk}}} \tag{1}$$

parcel variables are projected from the origin of the set of items that are parceled further than for items. This greater definiteness greatly aids rotation.

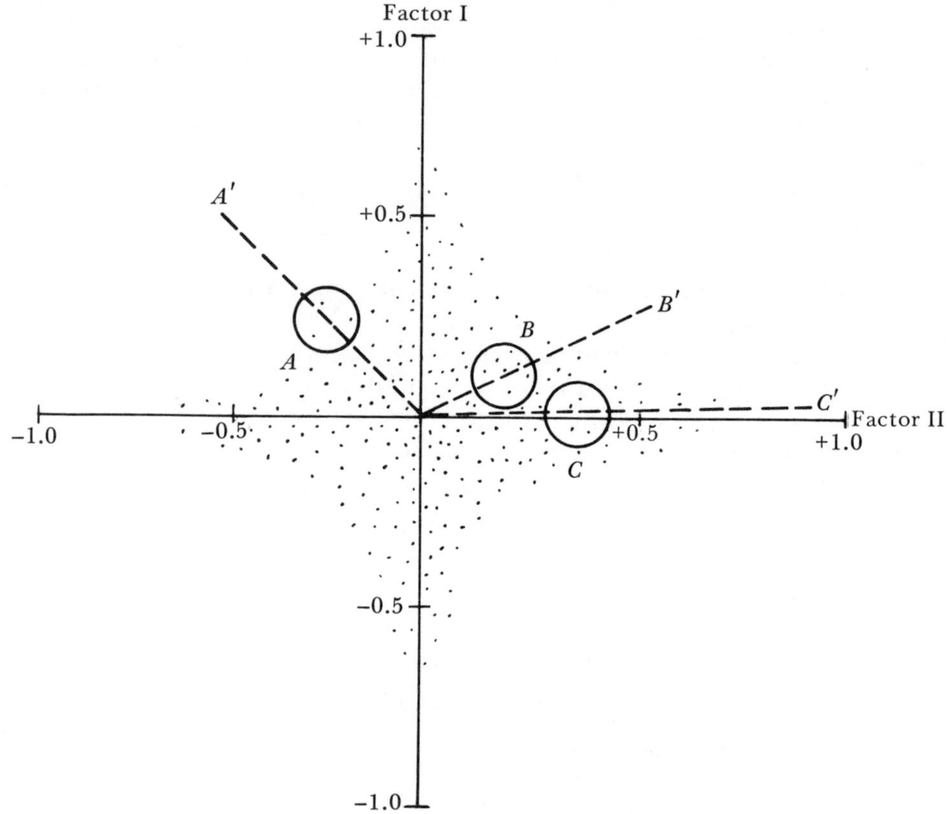

Figure 22. Typical factor plot of item loadings showing effect of switch to parcels. Items in clusters *A, B, C,* when added for each parcel as a single score and factored in with items, move in loading pattern out to *A′, B′, C′* (see data in Chapter Seven), increasing the communality.

A common misapprehension seems to be that parceling reduces the dimensionality present in the items. But except in the quite extreme case (1) where insufficient parcels (less than $2k$, ideally $3k$) are used to define the factor space and (2) where items are put together deliberately to make primary scales as in Comrey's work, this is incorrect.

The implications of Equations (8.1) and (8.2) are threefold: (1) that the same number of factors—indeed the same factors—are found from parcels as from items; (2) that the parcels have higher loadings on the common traits than do the items; and (3) that they consequently give cleaner hyperplanes. After the location of factors, the loadings for items can be obtained by undoing the parcels and using the Dwyer extension (1937) with Guilford's (1954) correction for the inflation of the item correlation due to the item having its specific already in the parcel.

An empirical demonstration of the first principle is given in Figure 23. In this study the 184 items in form A of the 16 PF were factored as items and as 46 parcels. The scree test shows the number of factors to be essentially the same although there is a slight increase in the parceled data. This result is not unusual since the summation effect in the parcels magnifies minor common factors enough for them to become visible.

Evidence is presented for two instances, a group of 606 adults and a group of 250 students. The data show the felicity of the scree test in giving essentially the same number for the independent studies and methods. The original factoring by scales (Cattell, Eber, and Delhees, 1968) also gave 19 factors. Again, the slight increase in number of factors with decrease in sample size is a usual phenomenon in our experiment and is a consequence of the larger change of common-error factors in a smaller sample.

Proceedings with the pros and cons we next recognize that parcels have their disadvantages. In the first place, different psychologists make them up in different ways, some of them undesirable. In what he calls factor-homogeneous parcels (FHIDS) Comrey claims to make up not only homogeneous but factor-homogeneous parcels (see contrast of these concepts in Figure 33, Chapter Nine). One has to ask how this can be done before one has factored and rotated the items to the best simple structure. Comrey's reply seems to be that he depends on my primaries and those of Guilford and others. If the goal of constructing, by face validity, scales for existing primaries were reliably achieved he would be factoring scales for primaries and his ultimate factors would be second orders. One can demonstrate (by Comrey's own results and Barton's factoring of Comrey's scales with the 16 PF) that this is what has happened. However, since it is impossible to construct truly factor-homogeneous scales (FHIDS) by human judgment of items, the second or higher orders that derive from correlating them are to that extent rough, as Barton shows.

A survey of the literature shows, as stated above, that parcels (FHIDS, subscales, homogeneous packages) mean different things to different investigators and have widely different legitimacy. Indeed only one of the four types of parceling provides a variable truly dependable for factor analysis. The first type is *subjectively judged factor (face-valid) homogeneity*. Except for swollen specifics made by repeating virtually the same item, such homogeneities are worthless. One psychologist or psychiatrist in twenty can use face validity *for personality factors* scale construction with success; even then it is a poor success—a mixed scale—compared to a simple-structure-derived primary. The second type of parceling is the fixed-minimum correlation cluster where items are put together, for example, by the *Taxonome* program or other objective *cluster search method*. The result is a set of items all of which intercorrelate above some fixed minimum, say, 0.3, across all items. The third type of parceling is the same except that one only insists on the same number of items in all parcels. The fourth type of parceling—equal size, radial parceling—works on a principle different from correlation and is the only satisfactory basis for factoring. The second type is widely used but has a seldom recognized Achilles heel that disqualifies it for simple-structure resolution.

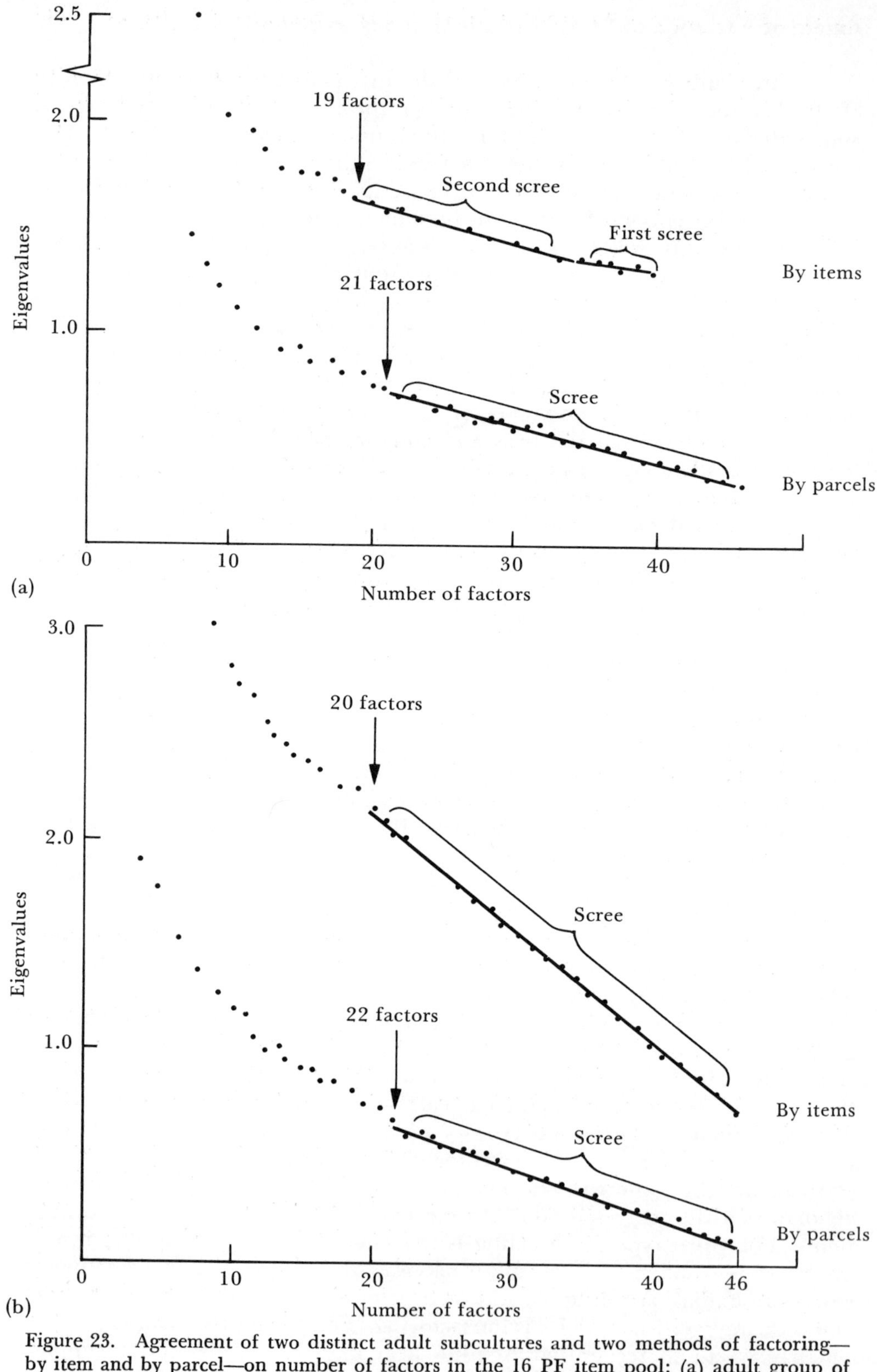

Figure 23. Agreement of two distinct adult subcultures and two methods of factoring—by item and by parcel—on number of factors in the 16 PF item pool: (a) adult group of 780 (Cattell, 1972, 1973), (b) student group of 250 (Burdsal and Vaughan, 1973).

Since this last affects a lot of studies it is illustrated in two dimensions by Figure 24. A fixed minimum means that the variables considered to be in the same parcel must all be within an area of a certain size; if the pattern-similarity coefficient r_p rather than r is used, its shape is essentially a circle as in Figure 24. For each set of points falling within that circle we substitute

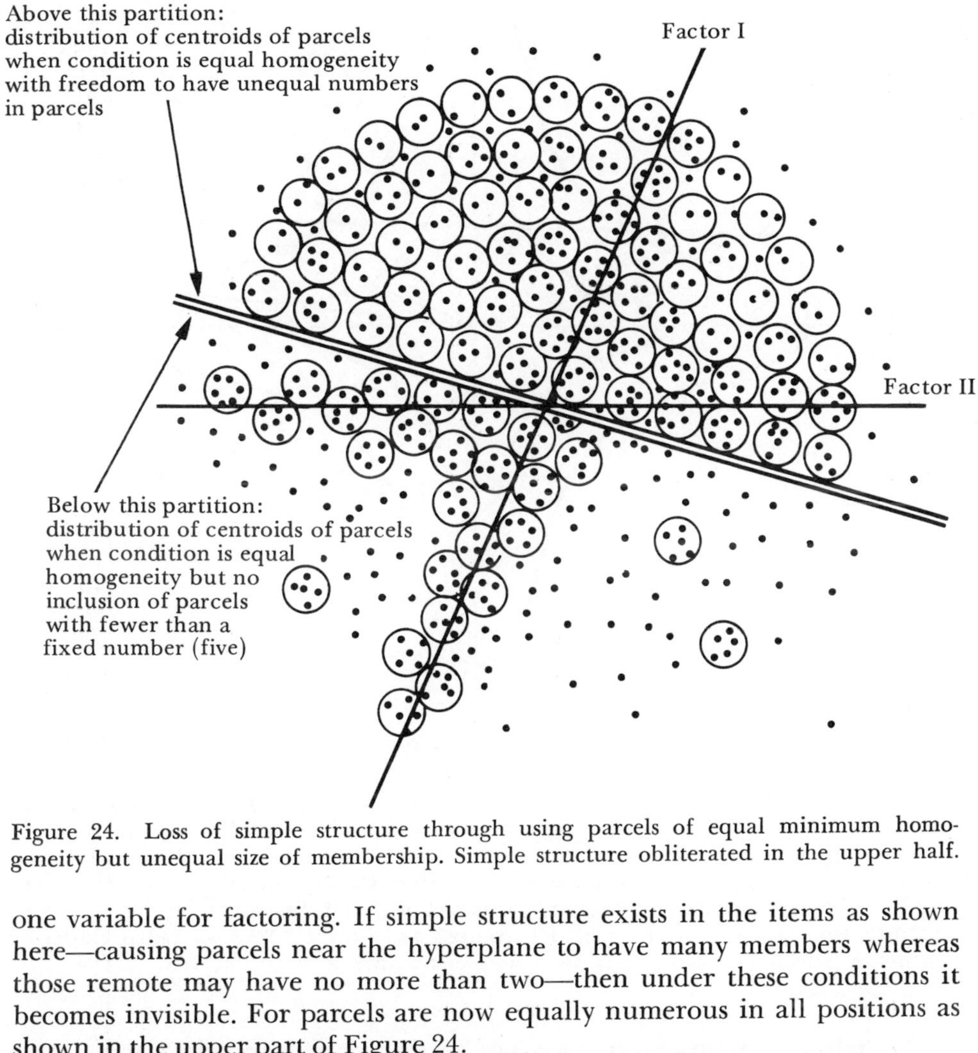

Figure 24. Loss of simple structure through using parcels of equal minimum homogeneity but unequal size of membership. Simple structure obliterated in the upper half.

one variable for factoring. If simple structure exists in the items as shown here—causing parcels near the hyperplane to have many members whereas those remote may have no more than two—then under these conditions it becomes invisible. For parcels are now equally numerous in all positions as shown in the upper part of Figure 24.

By contrast, if we switch to parcels of the third type and admit as variables only those that exceed some average number of items in them, the simple structure is still visible, as shown in the lower part of Figure 24. However, this supposes use of r_p. If we use r, as is commonly done, we encounter a new problem, shown in Figure 25. If the communalities are high enough, two items at a large angle (as at a and d) correlate as highly as two at a small angle (as at a' and d'). Putting such variables as a, b, c, and d together in a parcel destroys simple structure as surely as unequal parcel membership but parceling a', b', c', and d' does not.

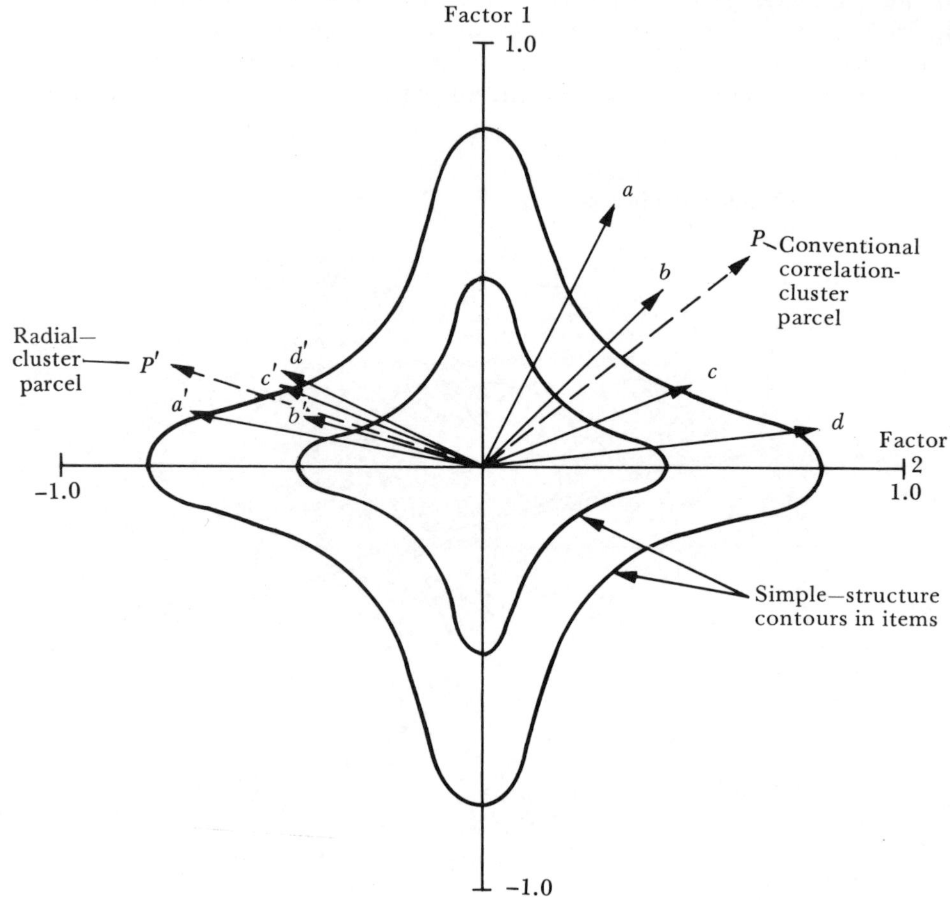

Figure 25. Contrasting effect of parceling by conventional homogeneous cluster and by radial cluster. Correlation of two items (such as *a* and *b*) equals $h_a h_b$ cos *ab*, where *h* is the root of the communality. All mutual correlations among items *a, b, c,* and *d,* and among *a′, b′, c′,* and *d′* exceed 0.3 and justify putting the four items in a cluster in each case. But the conventional process puts the parcel at *P* and distorts perception of simple structure, whereas the special calculation (Cattell and Burdsal, 1973) of radial clustering distributes parcels essentially as in item simple structure.

Selecting items to go together by this procedure called *radial parceling,* (see Cattell and Burdsal, 1973), which restricts to items like *a′* and *b′* in a parcel, but adds restriction to parcels of equal size of membership, retains the simple structure most completely and indeed emphasizes it. The third parceling method works, as in our own earlier use, but by no means as efficiently. But the second method, which allows unequal size and leaves blank structure in Figure 24 (upper) only if items are totally absent from an area, normally does not work at all. This was shown by Ford (1965) in taking the Sells, Demaree, and Will (1970) 16 PF and the Guilford-Zimmerman 600-item case and putting items in simple homogeneous parcels, in each of which all correlations among items were better than 0.3, whereupon no significant or unambiguous simple structure could be found.

Accordingly the structures (Chapter Two) defining the main primaries (but not the secondaries, where the item problem does not arise) were approached *initially* through item factoring; the refining was done through parcel and scale factoring. Psychologists who accept that this approach gives our primaries greater dependability of rotation and meaning than conflicting findings based on items have nevertheless justifiably raised a haunting suspicion: that once a structure is represented by a set of scales like those of, say, the Guilford-Zimmerman or the 16 PF, later checks on simple structure are prejudiced by this initial structure.

It is easy to see that this imprisonment within the initial choice is likely to be serious if only two dimensions with, say, just four scales are involved and when the scale communalities are very high. But when 64 scale variables and 16 dimensions are involved and many obliquities are permitted the original structure ceases to be commanding. The number of possible hyperplanes among 64 variables taken 60 at a time is enormous (635,376) and only 16 of these will be chosen. It is likely that if the 16 first chosen do not in fact represent the best simple structure obtainable in the system, new choices will soon be made that do. The scale variables marking factor *X* are located only by being out of a hyperplane; thus they are free, as fresh items are put into the cluster to move through appreciable angles in successive factorings. And as they move they are, as part of the hyperplanes of other factors, likely to shift the reference vectors of those factors. In short, granted many tentative scales and, say, 10 or more dimensions, the scale system is far freer than one might at first suppose to migrate to a better position of simple structure than the initial one if such exists.

So far the argument is only for freedom. But if research to improve scales is made by progressive factor analyses—substituting new items in the scales to give higher loadings *(not just picking new items that correlate better with the existing scales)*—there is not only freedom but also movement systematically toward the truer simple structure.

To clarify this principle of *progressive rectification* consider the assumption, consistent with our beginning at factor rotations with items, that there *is* simple structure in the item loading distribution, although it appears in coarse hyperplanes in a swarm of variable points on such short vectors (communality) that the investigator's gropings can emerge only with considerable uncertainty of angle. Figure 26 shows in two dimensions a contour outline (inner contours omitted for simplicity) of this rough simple structure in the items, in which we suppose that the true hyperplane for factor *B*, and therefore the true position for factor *A*, is at *A*.

From the first factor analysis by items the researcher might reach a hyperplane at A_1 and set up a promising group of items to form a scale as shown in Figure 26 by the points enclosed in the lowest circle (its centroid on the A_1 vector). If this is scored as a scale it will have greater communality than any constituent items and its vector projects outward and takes the position A_1. Normally, however, this experimental scale does not define the true position for factor *A* or the true hyperplane for *B* very well. In the next

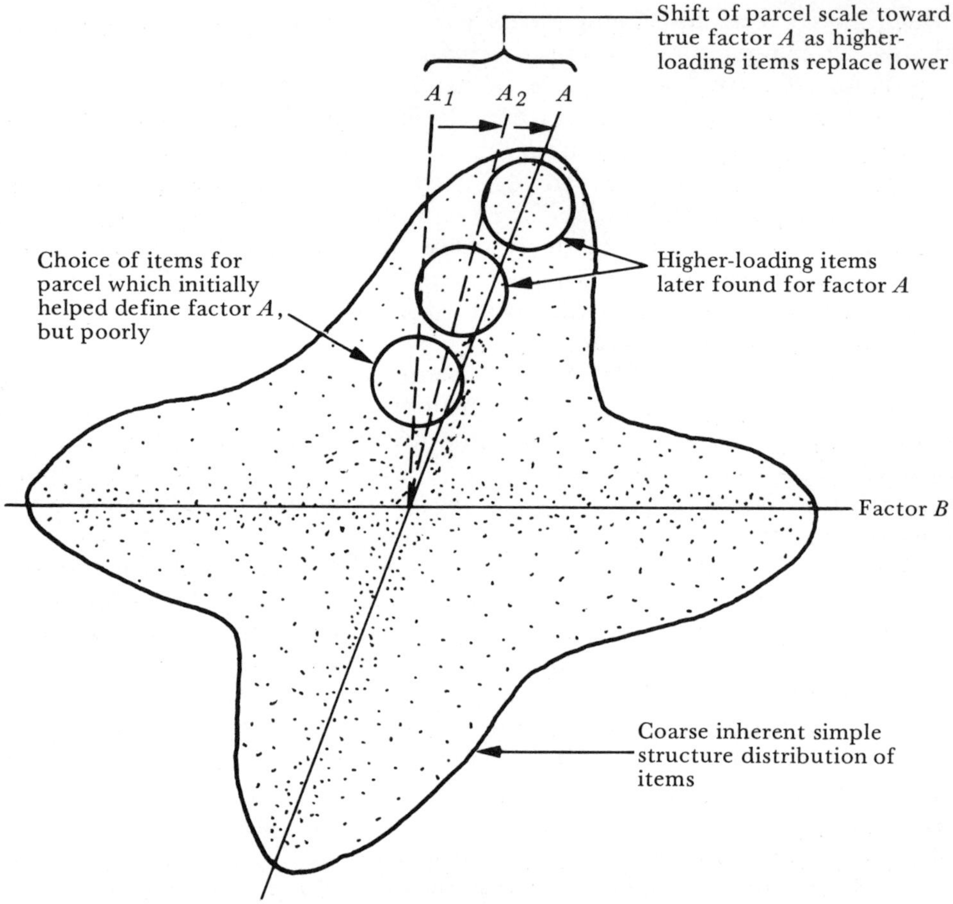

Figure 26. Progressive rectification. This diagram shows migration of parcel toward simple structure axis with each substitution of higher loaded items for those in the existing scale parcel.

factor analysis—probably by parcel—in the programatic series of factor analyses, if the researcher is able to find higher-loaded new items (as shown by the second circle up, projecting to parcel A_2) they are likely to form a scale that is not only more valid but also more factor-true, that is, closer to the true position *A*. This happens because by the simple-structure item distribution, the higher items are mainly found in that direction. Thus on a third factor analysis by parcel the next parcel is likely to move in toward the ideal consummation illustrated in Figure 26, directly to the true *A* position.

If instead of choosing items from a likely set of extension questionnaire items each time by their having *higher-factor loadings* than the items already in the parcel one tried to get by *without* the labor of a series of factor analyses and merely chose items correlating highly *with the experimental scale itself,* this *progressive rectification* would proceed much less efficiently. However, psychometric logic suggests that it would proceed, although slowly, because the choice of high-correlating items would tend to be taken from the nearest hyperplane region. If one demanded high homogeneity it would be even slower because a high-loaded and true item far from A_1 would be rejected for one closer to the A_1 axis.

Thus the unreliability and instability of items and especially their inability to guide simple-structure search efficiently make it desirable to supersede the first explorations of structure by item by refined work with parcels as soon as a rough structure has emerged. Even so this zeroing-in on the correct structure provided by progressive rectification is likely to be a long procedure. But no one-shot construction of a scale, no matter how large a sample it boasts, is a substitute. The reasons for the slowness are that the best items change with population (sex, age, subculture, range, item cut) and that when new items are found by the Dwyer extension (since factoring large numbers of items is impractical) the estimate of the factor against which items are evaluated changes with the item pools used even though the factor does not change. Regarding the last, Guttman (1950) has pointed out that for any fixed validity of estimate there is an infinite possible series of different estimated factor scores. (At 0.7 validity, for example, there is an infinite series of pairs of such estimates that are mutually correlated about zero.) The selection of improved items by correlating new extension items merely with the existing target scale is therefore an inefficient procedure, like Marco Polo's zigzag journey to the court of the Grand Khan, continually readjusted by new rumors about its direction.

Despite effective principles—such as progressive rectification—for approaching the functionally unitary factor concepts in questionnaire scales, reaching high factor validity is a task of a totally different level of difficulty and aspiration from that of constructing item-homogeneous scales valid against arbitrary criteria. To evaluate the size of item correlations or rate of progress toward a good scale by the same mechanically applied values as are used for arbitrary scales—as is done by some reviewers in Buros (1972)—is to display an ignorance costly to the progress of research. Incidentally, even when the goal of factored scales is accepted, one should note that the inherent character of the psychological structures in different domains is such that higher loadings and homogeneities are more readily obtained in ability and dynamic modalities. In the latter—as in Edwards' or Jackson's pursuit of Murray's needs, or in Cattell and Horn's pursuit of the ergs of fear, sex, and pugnacity, for example, in the MAT—high validity with homogeneity is more quickly gained than when broad personality factors such as ego strength, affectia, and surgency, for example, are the concepts for which measures are sought. Such broader, qualifying considerations help us reach firmer conclusions in the disputes about the identity of factor-trait scales discussed in the next section.

4. Reexamination of 16 PF Structure by Item and by Parcel Factoring

In the light of the more refined concepts and methods in the above three sections one may profitably attack the issue of the various alternative concepts of structure, for example in Comrey, Eysenck, Howarth, Sells, Demaree, and Will, to the primaries as concluded in Chapters Two and Three. It is no minor argument that the given primaries and secondaries rest on the programatic work of some 50 investigators over 25 years, whereas the mutual unaligned findings by various critics are largely one-shot studies. But the major argument will come from new experiments, addressed to such issues as that only three to ten factors suffice, or that certain second orders should be considered first orders.

Two main experiments, called A and B, will each examine the same pool of 184 items treated by the critics. First, the studies will meet those on their own ground who argue for items only Eysenck, Howarth) by item factoring and those who request parcels (Comrey) by parcel factoring—incidentally showing both to be the same. Second, to answer the possible criticism that the scale structure approached by progressive rectification holds the rotation in a vice, the items and parcels will be taken randomly and without knowledge of content and blind rotations will be performed as done in the early stages 20 years ago. Experiment A (Cattell, 1972, 1973) is on a sample of 780 adults (the 606 in Cattell, Eber, and Delhees, 1968, plus 174 more) comprehensive in social range, sex, and age (17 to 65 years). Experiment B (Burdsal and Vaughan, 1973, Vaughan, 1973) rests on a sample of 250 male and female undergraduate students and is typical of the favorably homogeneous groups on which most test constructors base their conclusions. Form A of the latest edition of the 16 PF was used. Incidentally, it should be noted that studies by Eysenck (1971), Howarth and Browne (1971a, 1971b), Karson and O'Dell (1973), and Sells, Demaree, and Will (1970) are based on obsolete experimental forms from a stage of progressive rectification more than 10 years old, though they could be compared by abstracting items that have not changed.

On this basis factor analysis was conducted strictly to meet the eight requirements in Table 41. As to the number of factors, my theoretical position is that the 16 PF items are set up to measure the largest 16 factors but that its items also contain some of the 7 missing factors. Study A was analyzed by 184 items (AI) and by 46 parcels (AII). The test for number of factors by the scree test on items is shown in Figures 6a and 6b (Chapter Two); but it is reproduced, with some reduction, in Figure 23 to permit a comparison of both samples and both kinds of variables to be seen at a glance. There is good agreement on the narrow range of 19-22 factors, which is supported also by 19 from the different experiment on scale factoring (Cattell, Eber, and Delhees, 1968). Vaughan has checked this with the maximum-likelihood method (Joreskog's program), which supports the scree at 20 factors. Common-error factors are large with small samples so that BI and BII—items and parcels—go about one factor more than AI and AII; and parcels, for reasons above, should give slightly more common factors than items. The agreement with the number hypothesized (from Chapter Two) is thus close for all five analyses. One may ask how this can be reconciled with the very large sample study of Sells, Demaree, and Will (1970)—which as a landmark in large-item matrix factoring has been quoted as disagreeing with our 16 by declaring 10. By kind permission of these investigators, who stopped at 10 "because all the variance seemed used up," we have applied the scree to their data. As shown in Figure 27 the number of factors indicated appears to be 22.

In view of the consistency of these results one may surely venture to suspect that if data could be obtained from the other investigators, as from Sells, Demaree and Will, their equally arbitrary stopping points—10 for Howarth, 8 for Comrey, 3 or 10 for Eysenck and Eysenck—might yield by the scree or the maximum-likelihood the 20 or more which these researches show to be in the 184 to 300 items representing the personality sphere.

And now what agreement is found among these recent A and B and other researches in regard to rotation and the identities of the emerging factors? First, higher simple structure was reached here than in any published result by the dissident studies. In all four studies the rotoplot simple structure climbed beyond the analytic program levels at which the latter were left, reaching in AI, AII, BI, and BII percentages of 75 (by items), 80 (by parcels), 71 (by items), and 80 (by parcels) at the $\pm.10$ width in plateaus shown in Figures 4 and 21. The statistical significance of these simple structures reaches entirely adequate values for the researches as a whole but is weak for certain factors, notably radicalism-conservatism Q_1 and autia M. But as the reader may check for himself the significances of experiments claiming alternative simple structures are decidedly lower and in no case higher. Since the two most deviant studies (Howarth and Browne, 1971a, 1971b; Eysenck and Eysenck, 1969) publish neither significances nor the tables from which they could be calculated one can only doubt that such plateau levels as in Figure 21 have been reached. The Howarth study (1971b) fails to locate by rotation even such a well-checked pattern as the general intelligence factor.

Finally, what is the consistency of the factor patterns found in independent rotations in four analyses (step 7 in Table 41)? We have calculated invariance of patterns first among the four analyses themselves, by congruences and salient-variable similarity indexes, and secondly, as to agreement with our theory about the nature of the primary factors, as set out in Chapter Two and operationalized in the scoring key in the 16 PF Handbook.

To calculate the invariance of patterns (Table 43) in the case of the parcel analyses it is necessary to project from parcels to get loadings on items. This check between the item and the parcel analysis is particularly significant for two reasons. First, this agreement dispels the argument that item analyses are superior to parcel analyses (Eysenck, Howarth); indeed they are not different. Second, since the nature of the individual parcels (unlike that of items, which is easily known) is meaningless in rotation to the rotator we have a guarantee that this recent outcome is unaffected by the long familiar meanings of the 16 PF factors and is indeed a recent independent confirmation.

However, though the structure as a whole is confirmed by these two independent researches and four independent types of analysis, certain individual factors proved to be weakly defined in one or the other of the samples,

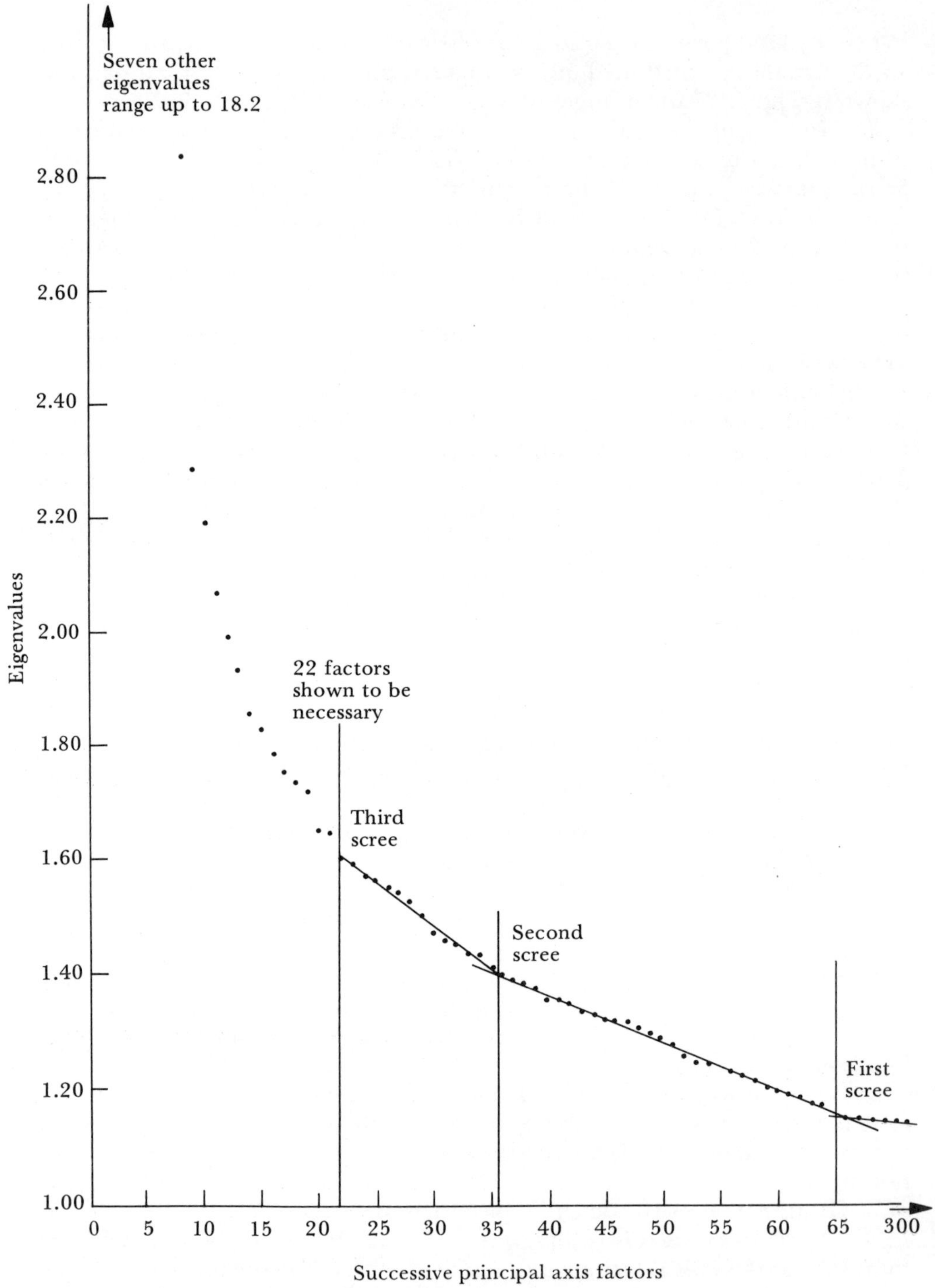

Figure 27. Scree test for number of factors based on Sells, Demaree, Will (1970) 300-item principal components. The original research took out only 11 factors, resulting in the mixture of primary and secondary that Table 42 shows to result from underfactoring. Up to 30 or even 36 factors could be taken out here according to various indicators. The Kaiser-Guttman indicates over 65.

Table 43

Agreement of Resolutions by Items and Parcels in Relation to Ideal Structure

(a) Mutual Congruences for Five Representative Factors by Salient-Variable Similarity Index

Factor B (intelligence)	*Sample A Item Factoring*	*Sample A Parcel Factoring*	*Sample B Item Factoring*	*Sample B Parcel Factoring*
Sample A item factoring				
Sample A parcel factoring	63			
Sample B item factoring	39	41		
Sample B parcel factoring	33	30	43	
Ideal pattern	23	20	37	29

Factor G (superego)	*Sample A Item Factoring*	*Sample A Parcel Factoring*	*Sample B Item Factoring*	*Sample B Parcel Factoring*
Sample A item factoring				
Sample A parcel factoring	58			
Sample B item factoring	19	14		
Sample B parcel factoring	09	06	27	
Ideal pattern	24	31	21	26

Factor I (premsia)	*Sample A Item Factoring*	*Sample A Parcel Factoring*	*Sample B Item Factoring*	*Sample B Parcel Factoring*
Sample A item factoring				
Sample A parcel factoring	51			
Sample B item factoring	37	42		
Sample B parcel factoring	19	31	55	
Ideal pattern	49	30	30	21

Factor Q_1 (radicalism)	*Sample A Item Factoring*	*Sample A Parcel Factoring*	*Sample B Item Factoring*	*Sample B Parcel Factoring*
Sample A item factoring				
Sample A parcel factoring	09			
Sample B item factoring	04	−06		
Sample B parcel factoring	13	30	11	
Ideal pattern	20	17	12	16

Factor Q_4 (ergic tension)	*Sample A Item Factoring*	*Sample A Parcel Factoring*	*Sample B Item Factoring*	*Sample B Parcel Factoring*
Sample A item factoring				
Sample A parcel factoring	32			
Sample B item factoring	12	33		
Sample B parcel factoring	15	55	35	
Ideal pattern	28	40	43	35

Table 43 (Cont.)

(b) Mutual Congruences: Mean of All 16 Factors

	Sample A Item Factoring	*Sample A Parcel Factoring*	*Sample B Item Factoring*	*Sample B Parcel Factoring*
Sample A item factoring				
Sample A parcel factoring	27			
Sample B item factoring	17	21		
Sample B parcel factoring	19	25	33	
Ideal pattern	29	26	28	24

Note: This table uses a cutoff point for salients/nonsalients at a loading of 0.19. N for A = 780; N for B = 246 (250 on some).

A salient-variable similarity index *s* is significant beyond the $P<0.01$ level above 0.12. One good, three middling, and one weak case of item-parcel matching are taken from Cattell (1973j) and Cattell and Vaughan (1973). The weak cases are Q_1 and *N*, which are being improved. The problem with radicalism Q_1 is that its expression has altered rapidly during the decade of test construction. In regard to superego *G*, although there is good agreement of pattern in items and parcels within the older adult group and within the student group, the adult and student patterns show poor agreement. Both, however, converge on the ideal score pattern. The ideal is the mean pattern of salients from all research prior to these four studies. Agreement between item and parcel factoring is thus as good as between two item or two parcel studies. A table for different factors shows all *s* values close to zero and insignificant.

and the factors that have been of rather low variance do not reach as high validity *as scales* as is sometimes reached in arbitrary scales of the same 10-item length. However, this has nothing to do with low homogeneity, considered a defect by tyros but here recognized as a psychometric virtue. Setting a cutoff level of 0.10 (consistent with the usual hyperplane standard) to set aside items that do not load on the factor (see Table 3 in Cattell, 1973c) and applying it to the complete factor-pattern matrix of 184 variables at the unique rotation position just defined we ask: How many salients supposed by theory (the scoring key in the 16 PF Handbook) to load actually do so? As the chi-squared values in the first column of Table 44 show, the trait-pattern concepts are supported with high significance for all except the radicalism-conservatism factor Q_1. The same is true of our reanalysis of the 300-item Sells, Demaree, and Will data (1970). When 22 factors as shown in Figure 27 are taken out instead of the 10 used by Demaree, the second orders which appeared through that underfactoring straighten out and appear as recognizable primaries.

Column 2 of Table 44 brings us to the heart of the debate that began with Levonian (1961) and Comrey (1970) and persists in many circles today. It shows that the conventional homogeneity measures in a true-factor scale, such as the 16 PF scales, are as the critics correctly observe very low. However, when we come to principles of test construction, in Chapter Nine, it is evident that low homogeneity is a desirable feature of sophisticated design.

Table 44

Statistical and Psychometric Properties of Simple-Structure Item Factoring of 16 PF

Scale	*Significance with which Hypothetically Expected Salients Are Located by Blind Resolution* χ^2 *value* (*df*=1)	*P value*	*Mean Intercorrelation of 10 or 13 Items Keyed for Factor*	*Validity: Multiple Correlation of Scale (of 10-13 item length) with Pure Factor* *Raw*	*Reduced*	*Validity: Multiple Correlation When All 16 PF Items Are Used for Estimating Factors* *Raw*	*Reduced*
A	10.27	$P < 0.01$	0.044	0.63	0.62	0.92	0.90
B	17.24	$P < 0.001$	0.048	0.61	0.60	0.92	0.90
C	13.12	$P < 0.001$	0.064	0.55	0.54	0.87	0.83
E	7.97	$P < 0.01$	0.076	0.54	0.53	0.86	0.81
F	10.13	$P < 0.01$	0.096	0.77	0.76	0.90	0.87
G	11.14	$P < 0.001$	0.082	0.69	0.69	0.89	0.85
H	19.65	$P < 0.001$	0.143	0.79	0.79	0.92	0.90
I	29.88	$P < 0.001$	0.079	0.74	0.73	0.87	0.83
L	8.89	$P < 0.01$	0.067	0.45	0.44	0.83	0.77
M	10.63	$P < 0.01$	0.011	0.52	0.51	0.82	0.76
N	6.81	$P < 0.01$	0.014	0.41	0.40	0.87	0.82
O	26.12	$P < 0.001$	0.069	0.66	0.65	0.88	0.84
Q_1	1.96	($P < 0.2$)	0.022	0.48	0.47	0.85	0.79
Q_2	12.66	$P < 0.001$	0.051	0.57	0.57	0.91	0.88
Q_3	20.30	$P < 0.001$	0.115	0.64	0.64	0.89	0.85
Q_4	22.90	$P < 0.001$	0.113	0.73	0.73	0.92	0.89

As Figures 30 and 31 (Chapter Nine) show, it is desirable for suppressor action, particularly for retaining a grip on a truly broad personality factor and in a scale that must be transferable across a diversity of subcultures.

Accordingly the concepts of bloated specifics and instrument factors have been discussed as dangers from items selected for too high homogeneity. However, one does desire as high a factor concept validity (loading) for individual items as is compatible with avoiding these two dangers. Ten items of 0.3 validity each is as many as one can use (even in a nine space of unwanted factors) without some degree of homogeneity appearing in the scale. The scales in the preceding research (Tables 43 and 44; Figures 23, 27, and 28) are 10 to 13 items in length; as the full factor-pattern matrix (Table 3, Cattell, 1972e) shows, many item validities fall below this ideal value in one sample or another. The authors of the 16 PF, HSPQ, CPQ, and ESPQ have located the correct factors but there is no doubt that they still have years of work to reach by progressive rectification the ideal upper limit of item validities for a suitably broad, behaviorally concrete, low-homogeneity set of scales.

However, in looking at the low-loading values for items supposed to score on one scale—items that load from 0 to 0.6 (Table 3, Cattell, 1972e)—

the critical psychologist may easily overlook that an appreciable validity can be obtained for a 10-to-13-item scale as shown in columns 3 and 4 of Table 44.[3] This validity changes from appreciable to highly satisfactory if we go beyond this little set either by calling in equivalent forms B, C, and D or by using all 184 items in form A in computer synthesis scoring as shown in columns 5 and 6 of Table 44. The critic may also forget that the validities assigned to each item are not to be taken as seriously as the validity (columns 5 and 6) of the scale as a whole. The instability of items has been sufficiently discussed and much of this is due to low transferability. That is, as we shift from students to airline pilots to soldiers to housewifes, individual items change their validities. It is easy to obtain a set of uniformly high validity items for one population, say, freshmen students in Australian universities. But the present 16 PF is constructed on the basis of average loadings across diverse adult groups; what might be a uniform 0.3 loading across 10 items for one group is likely to range from 0 to 0.6 in another (Table 3, Cattell, 1972e). Psychometrically, one should note this is as true for established factors like intelligence (*B* in Table 44) as for new personality factors.

Only occasionally does the whole factor pattern break down; this occurred between our student and middle-age groups, conspicuously for the radicalism-conservatism factor (Table 44, column 1). There is no doubt that this factor in the 16 PF can be definitely located since its first clear demonstration by Thurstone (1937) and Eysenck (1944). My theory is that this factor is not just a sociopolitical fashion but a general intellectual independence of the individual that may show itself at different ages in different

[3] The typical cause of inflated communalities in these questionnaire studies is putting unities into the diagonal of the *R* matrix for the component analysis and stopping at *k* factors without bothering to iterate communalities to *k*. The residuals of the unities at *k* factors are bigger than the communalities all along the line. This happened in Howarth and Browne, in Sells, Demaree, and Will (because of expense of iteration), and in many other studies, and accounts for some of their failure to find the primaries.

The effect of the relative sizes of the true primaries and true secondaries is of considerable importance; if the latter are large—and they are large in personality where they account for at least 60 percent of the first-order variance—second orders are liable to break through as pseudos in the direct factoring of items. This happened, for the same reason, for 30 years in abilities and left long unrecognized what Thurstone later isolated as primaries.

The basis of this effect can be seen in the model, condensed in matrix terms, if we consider how the variance-covariance in the correlation matrix of variables is accounted for:

$$R_v = V_{fp1} R_{f1} V'_{fp1} + U_i^2 \tag{2}$$

where U_1^2 is the uniqueness of the variables. But if we write into this how the second orders produce the correlations among the primaries, then

$$R_v = V_{fp1} (V_{fp2} R_{f2} V'_{fp2} + U_2^2) V'_{fp1} + U_1^2 \tag{3}$$

where U_2^2 is the uniqueness variance in the primaries.

From this one can see that the part of the correlation matrix that is reproduced by the factors consisting of the second orders projected on the primaries, namely, $V_{fp1} V_{fp2} R_{f2} V'_{fp2} V'_{fp1}$, is substantial if U_2^2 is small. If U_2^2 is small these factors are likely to predominate in determining the simple structure.

beliefs. (Mark Twain said that when he left home as a teenager his father was so ignorant and backward he could scarcely bear to be around him, but on returning years later he found him marvelously improved.) This is a clear example of what happens with all source traits. In time the 16 PF, HSPQ, and others will need special forms for males and females, old and young, West Coast and East Coast, and so on.

5. Technical Resolution of Deviant Findings

From the preceding survey the student reading the literature of this decade could get an impression of turmoil. He finds theoretical structure checked in some places by solid evidence and in others by inadequate evidence. With improved methods, however, one may hope that future conclusions will be simpler and less fraught with ifs and buts.

Even the technically alert reader who has never had illusions about a three-factor view of personality faces a problem akin to that of the earliest navigators. When maps developed they were at first consistent in separated areas of exploration: the coast of China, the Mediterranean basin, the triangle of islands known to the Polynesians. Similarly here there are only a few areas where programatic work has established a globally coherent picture; our task has been to put out feelers from the largest area of consolidation, attempting at times to form a theory embracing the other areas that must rest a while on tenuous links. Some possibilities I have had to mention in the name of open-mindedness may become disproved guesses.

Once order was established in the 16 PF-HSPQ area my colleagues and I moved as quickly as possible to explore links with other questionnaires, links which the authors of those questionnaires seemed insufficiently concerned to make. A useful solution of the 16 PF-MMPI common space was reached by Bolton (Cattell and Bolton, 1969) and by Delhees (in preparation); a reasonably clear answer about the 16 PF and the Guilford-Zimmerman was given by Gibbons (1966) and Cattell and Gibbons (1968). Barton (1973b) has done a thorough job of checking that the Comrey and Eysenck scales are the second orders of the 16 PF with some deviations of angles; Hundal, Sudhakar, and Sidhu (1972) have obtained consistent pictures at this same second order.

Two major bridging studies to check these conclusions have been launched by Sells, Demaree, and Will (1970) and by Harman and French (1972). The former has cut a wide swathe among many published questionnaires, the majority of them never before factored, which should at least bring some translations. From a somewhat different angle than that of finding personality structure, the work of Goldberg (1972b) attempts to integrate large numbers of questionnaire items.

The previous section has shown that certain deviant researches by no means disprove the central theory of rather more than 20 primaries and 9 secondaries. The present section asks, further, what the constructive interpretation of various extra findings may be. This is a large task needing more space, and several years, but I shall attempt what order is possible to this point. If the aim were only that of finding translations as Goldberg (1972b) has efficiently done and Cattell and Bolton (1969) have attempted with the MMPI, by discovering multiple regressions or transformation matrices from one set of arbitrary questionnaire scales (even obliquely and orthogonally factored) to another, the job calls merely for careful accountancy. But the task is rather that of making structural sense, and possible integration, of extensive but methodologically weak deviant findings.

To do this the concepts of pseudo-secondaries and grounded secondaries must be sharpened. If one takes out, say, four factors where programatic research indicates, say, 18 primaries and 7 secondaries, these four are likely to find their best simple structure close to that which four of the real secondaries would have if projected on items (by the Cattell-White formula $V_{IIv} = V_I V_{II}$). However, they cannot be the correct grounded secondaries, as these latter are called, because parts of their variance needing to be rotated into them has been left behind in the factors not taken out. For this reason the EPI factors and their like are strictly pseudo-second orders.

This tendency of pseudo-second orders to approach in rotation to true (grounded) second orders, however, requires an interesting but debatable new assumption: that if factors corresponding in number to second orders are taken out at the item level there will exist a real simple structure position for them. An examination on statistical grounds (Cattell, 1965e) of the probability of a second-order simple structure on primaries yielding a simple structure on items suggested there is no automatic reason for this to occur. It must therefore be psychologically determined and it agrees with the Schmid-Leiman model—accepted as a scientific model of actual influence discussed in Chapter Four. It should be noted, however, that by this model the third order will not yield item simple structure. The empirical evidence, meanwhile, fully supports the conclusion that both first- and second-order grounded factors will give simple structure on items and that in every rotation there are two, not one, series of slots into which rotation to simple structure can fall.

The rotations of Eysenck, Howarth and Sells, Demaree, and Will are not "new primaries" as they have been inclined to believe, but, from the matching evidence below, are instances of falling into the slots for the grounded second orders—but a little clumsily due to being pseudo-second orders. (Comrey's second orders, as we have seen, arise from a different cause —parceling items so that parcels represent true primaries.)

What decides whether a rotation drops down one side of the roof into the primary slots or the other into the secondary? First, as shown in DeYoung's table above, underfactoring predisposes to secondaries, finishing completely with pseudo-secondary positions when the extraction of primaries does not go beyond the number of secondaries. But secondly, there is some evidence from the research of Finkbeiner (1973), uncompleted but summarized at this stage in Table 45, that the exactingness of the hyperplane width—say, 0.05 or 0.15—accepted for simple structure has an influence too. As Table 45(a) shows, the hyperplane width when maximum simple structure is pursued varies with item and parcel data, and so on, and the width for secondaries and grounded secondaries tends to be different from that for primaries. Some of the explanation for deviant findings therefore seems to lie in using different rotational programs and accepting different standards of hyperplane width.

Guided by these newer methodological considerations, as well as by an examination of the thoroughness with which the eight conditions of good factor analysis are observed in the contending solutions, one finds much understandable in what was previously confused. Several of the deviant findings are either pseudo-second orders or underfactored series mixing some secondaries with some primaries. Since there is virtually no disagreement nowadays—at least as to the eight points—among the leading exponents of factor analyses in the psychological model such as Child (1970), Cattell (1966a), Gorsuch (1973), Guertin and Bailey (1970), Harman (1967), Rummel (1970), and Uberla (1968), what is frankly needed is a better application of these principles by some of those working in the questionnaire domain.

To determine how real this need is Vaughan (1973) has surveyed typical and quite recent studies for their care in relation to vital conditions, as shown in Table 46.

There can be no mistaking the startling verdict that more than three-fourths of recently published questionnaire studies—studies asserting very definite theoretical conclusions—lack more than one vital technical condition for dependable conclusions. Five of them lack as many as four—if restriction to a known inadequate orthogonal rotation is counted as one—though even lack of one can alter meaning radically or throw doubt on concerning oneself seriously with the result.

With this retrospect I shall now attempt to put into perspective, as constructively as possible, the more important conceptions of traits dissident from the organized position stated here.

First, the Guilford factors have remained orthogonal and have therefore, as the hyperplane count shows, not reached simple structure. Some factors, although orthogonal, are close to the true primaries (Cattell and Gibbons, 1968); others are linear combinations of primaries.

Second, the three factors in the Eysenck scales (*P, E, N*) are essentially the second-order exvia, anxiety, and psychoticism factors of Table 14, 16, and 22 (Chapter Four). How valid they are in precise construct-validity coefficients, through being reached as pseudo-secondaries, remains to be seen. The comparisons of the *N* scale with the IPAT anxiety second order by Hundal, Sudhakar, and Sidhu (1972), however, shows it to be of distinctly lower validity; Barton's results (1973b) confirm this and show contamination with other second-order factors.

Third, Table 47 shows that Comrey's first two factors have the essential primary markers for the exvia and anxiety factors (Comrey, 1970); there are indications in his work, as well as definite proof in Barton's (1973b) research, that most of the rest are second orders. Comrey confines himself to stating that there is "certainly substantial overlap." Probably he has one new factor, in the esthetic interests area. This is possible because interests are excluded from Tables 14, 16, and 22 (Chapter Four) and from the 16

Table 45

The Hyperplane Test for Distinguishing True Primaries and Secondaries from Pseudosecondaries

(a) Values found at maximum simple structure of true secondaries on primaries; variables are primaries

Study data based on	*Number of factors*	*% within ±05*	*% within ±10*	*% within ±15*
HSPQ, scales	7	27.7	52.9	62.2
16 PF parcels	8	33.8	50.0	64.4
16 PF items	8	25.8	51.6	65.8
Plasmode variables	5	42.4	57.6	65.2
HSOA subtests	7	32.8	53.8	71.4
Mean	7.0	32.5	53.2	65.8

(b) Values found at maximum simple structure of pseudosecondaries (underfactoring of primaries) on variables; variables are items

Study data based on	*Number[a] of factors*	*< ±05*	*< ±10*	*< ±15*
HSPQ scales	7	29.6	50.5	64.5
16 PF parcels	8	29.5	56.8	67.3
16 PF items	8	33.0	56.2	73.6
Plasmode variables	5	28.0	48.5	70.4
HSOA subtests	7	34.4	62.0	74.7
Mean	7.0	30.9	54.8	70.1

(c) Values at maximum simple structure of true primaries on variables; variables are items

Study data based on	*Number of factors*	*< ±05*	*< ±10*	*< ±15*
HSPQ scales	17	43.5	73.6	85.8
16 PF parcels	21	52.1	79.4	88.4
16 PF items	19	43.2	75.0	87.4
Plasmode variables	10	45.8	60.6	67.9
HSOA subtests	17	41.6	77.2	84.1
Mean	16.8	45.2	73.16	82.72

[a] Note that the underfactoring here in (b) is down to the true number of secondaries as fixed in (a) above.

Note: A maximum sampling of media and style of variable has been made over six studies. The verdict is that secondaries on primaries and the same number of factors taken out and rotated directly on variables finish with about the same counts. Compared to the true primaries maximally rotated on variables, however, the pseudosecondaries (which might by derivation also be called pseudoprimaries and are sometimes so mistaken) have noticably poorer simple structure, by which they can be detected.

Sources: HSPQ: Cattell, Wagner, and Cattell, 1970; 16 PF parcels: Cattell, 1973g: 16 PF items: Cattell, 1972; Plasmode: Cattell and Jaspars, 1967; HSOA: Cattell and Klein, 1974.

PF and HSPQ owing to their position in the dynamic motivation modality.

Fourth and last, since more than eight second orders are taken out one would expect the Sells and the Howarth and Browne factors to mix first- and second-order factors although the latter with proper rotation and communalities should have had enough factors to go clearly to primaries. Since these studies are on items and not scale-factor markers the identities cannot be established in a brief table, but the 16 PF items in Howarth's sociability and emotionality (Table 47) are entirely consistent with their being secondaries. Since Howarth indicates that other of his factors are matched with 16 PF primaries one must conclude that his scales mix first and second orders. The Sells, Demaree, and Will (1970) underfactoring, according to matching congruences by Finkbeiner, similarly leads to mixtures of first and second orders in the same output, but Sells has been sufficiently aware of this not to follow Howarth in constructing scales on that basis.

In retrospect over the past 30 years of factored questionnaire research it is now obvious that relatively crude methods have sufficed to approach the pseudo-secondaries underlying what we now know as 8 to 14 true secondaries. But to identify and replicate the 20 to 30 primaries greater technical care has been necessary—in estimating the number of factors, in using the advantage of parcel factoring, in estimating communalities, and especially in pursuing the maximum oblique simple structure beyond blunt automatic computer instruments. It is one more reproach to psychology as a progressing science that recent easy access to large computers has brought into this field investigators less trained in multivariate personality theory. Either they have not asked themselves the crucial questions about number of factors, soundness of rotation, and bases of invariance or else they do not realize that effective tools for handling these decisions were given in the literature before they entered the field. Consequently advance to the subtle questions that must be considered in reaching precision is hampered by out-of-date misunderstandings. The secondary factors are too broad for anyone to miss but the advance in personality theory hinges on recognizing that dynamics of personality development depends on the interactions of the primaries, in terms of which, according to our interactive spiral theory, at least two of the secondaries are alone to be understood.

A recurring problem caused by new investigators from outside the area, and due to the easy access to computers and the availability of large undergraduate groups in class for questionnaire research, is a naïve renaming of factors arising not from fresh insight into their nature but merely from ignorance of existing knowledge. Fortunately the vitality of sophisticated technical work is such that the domain need fear no general dark age repeating on a small scale the overwhelming of classical civilization. Fortunately also, there are models and precedents in established sciences that show how the indexing of findings can proceed by orderly growth and how naming can retain essential continuity with gradual advance in interpretation. As the elements were confirmed in chemistry it was usual to adopt a new term for a new precision of identification (except for long-known sub-

Table 46

Survey of Factor-Analytic Procedures and Standards

Study	*Structure Checked*	*Variables*	*Subjects*	*Test for Number of Factors?*	*Communality or Unity*	*Number Rotated*	*Rotation Method*	*Hyperplane Count*	*Simple-Structure Significance Tested?*	*Congruence Coefficient Applied?*
Sells, Demaree, and Will (1970)	16 PF primaries	300 (16 PF items)	2011 Air Force recruits	No	Communality	11	Varimax and promax	69% 76%	No	No
Cattell (1972e)	16 PF primaries	184 (16 PF items)	780 general adults	Scree	Communality iterated	19	Maxplane and hand rotoplot	73%	Yes	Yes
Burdsal and Vaughan (1973)	16 PF primaries	184 (16 PF items)	246 undergrads	Scree	Communality iterated	20	Maxplane and hand rotoplot	70%	Yes	Yes
Comrey, Jamison, and King (1968)	Comrey FHIDS	80	252 undergrads	Indirectly	No	10, 15, 24, 28	Varimax and high homogeneity	Not given exactly, but low	No	No
Comrey and Duffy (1968)	Comrey FHIDS and Cattell and Eysenck scales	70	272 undergrads	Indirectly	No	8, 15, 23	High homogeneity	Not given exactly, but low	No	No
Howarth and Browne (1971a)	Obsolete edition of 16 PF	187	567 undergrads	Yes (but ignored)	Unities	10, 18	Varimax and hand	No level claimed	No	No
Howarth and Browne (1971b)	Sells, Cattell, and Eysenck markers	77	329 undergrads	K-G	Unities	15	Varimax	No level claimed	No	No
Eysenck and Eysenck (1969)	16 PF without intelligence	99	1200 general adults	Arbitrary	Unities	20	Varimax and promax	No level claimed	No	No

Eysenck and Eysenck (1969)	G-Z inventory		1200 general adults	Arbitrary	Unities	20	Varimax	No level claimed	No	No
Timm (1968)	16 PF second order	15	80 Volkschule students	No	Communalities	4, 6	Varimax	32% and 40%	No	No

Note: Correlation coefficients and computational methods of extracting unrotated factors are not included since all were Pearson r and principal components. Comrey and Sells, Demaree and Will, used modified methods that do not affect essential conclusions. Only two studies meet all the checks discussed in the text. Four or five are left at orthogonal positions. Five do not use communalities. Seven fail to report hyperplane counts by which simple structure could be evaluated. Eight provide no test of simple-structure significance and do not examine congruence (invariance) with respect to other research.

Table 47

Approaches to Second-Order Factors in Alleged Primary Personality Factor Scales

(a) *Q*I: Exvia-Invia

Factor found by Comrey's analysis (1970)			*Loading*
16 PF markers (3 of 4) for exvia	*F*	Surgency-desurgency	0.60
	H	Parmia-threctia	0.60
	$Q_2(-)$	Group-involvement	0.30
Comrey parcels		Opposite of seclusiveness	0.69
		Opposite of lack of social poise	0.69
		Low social activities	0.64
		Eysenck *E* scale	0.59
Factor 3 found by Howarth and Browne (1971b) "sociability"			
Item markers for 16 PF exvia	*H*	I am always glad to join a large gathering, for example, a party, dance, or public meeting.	0.61
	Q_2	I like to take an active part in social affairs, committee work, and so on.	0.57
	H	On social occasions I readily come forward (vs. quietly stay in the background).	0.51
	A	I would prefer the life of an artist (vs. a secretary running a social club).	—0.52
	F	I would hate to be where there wouldn't be at lot of people to talk to.	0.48

(b) *Q*II: Anxiety

Factor found by Comrey's analysis (1970)			*Loading*
16 PF markers for anxiety	*C*—	Ego weakness	0.39
	L	Protension	0.35
	O	Guilt proneness	0.61
	Q_4	Ergic Tension	0.57
Comrey parcels		Inadequacy	0.74
		Pessimism	0.65
		Paranoia	0.39
		Eysenck's *N*	0.71
Factor 1 found by Howarth and Browne (1971b) "emotionality"			
Item markers for 16 PF anxiety	Q_3	I have periods when it is hard to stop a mood of self-pity.	—0.54
	Q_1[a]	I feel a strong need for someone to lean on in times of sadness.	—0.49
	O	When I am called in by my boss (or teacher), I see a chance to put in a good word for things I am concerned about (vs. fear something has gone wrong).	0.48
	Q_4	Small things sometimes get "on my nerves" unbearably though I realize them to be trivial.	—0.39
	C	An alternative resolution offered by the authors includes: I sometimes cannot get to sleep because an idea keeps running through my mind.	—0.39

[a] The item listed Q_1 actually loads on *O*.

stances like gold or carbon) or to follow the term given by the discoverer. Most psychologists now prominent in this area such as Barton, Bartsch, Coan, Dielman, Delhees, DeYoung, and so down the alphabet to Schaie, Scheier, Tatsuoka and Vaughan accept this approach. Thus intelligence T_1 and anxiety *Q*II are instances akin to gold in the history of chemistry and retain a popular label; but exvia *Q*I is a meaningful adaptation akin to oxygen, and superego, affectia, and cortertia are instances of new psychological terms for new, uniquely operationally defined concepts (in one case first clinical and then factor-analytic). Writers have named "factors" that can be shown not to exist as replicable factors. This does little harm that time cannot cure. More frequently they have not carried out the congruence checks that would enable them to recognize that they have replicated a factor already replicated. Their net contribution is thus to have helped create a Tower of Babel. Renaming *Q*I "sociability" (long recognized as extraversion and shortened to exvia) invites, like any popular term, all the inexactitude of the diverse popular connotations of the term.

As stated in general theory in Chapter Five there is no inherent contradiction in using both primary and secondary factors, provided that their strata are distinguished and that they are not confused by shifting terminologies. If the technical level can be reached of setting up scales for the primaries as stubs and truly independent scales for the secondaries, then primaries and secondaries can be used together in the comprehensive specification equation (4.2), where there are k first-order and p second-order factors (the latter in boldface):

$$a_{ij} = b_{j1} F_{1i} + \ . \ . \ . + b_{jk} F_{ki} + \mathbf{b}_{j21} \boldsymbol{F}_{21i} + \ . \ . \ . + \boldsymbol{b}_{j2p} \boldsymbol{F}_{2pi} \qquad (4.5)$$

and it could be continued to third and higher orders.

However, this equation cannot legitimately be derived directly from factoring items—even though we believe secondaries to have simple structure on the items—because a test for number of factore gives k, not $(k + p + \ . \ . \ .)$. Trying to get primaries and secondaries simultaneously from taking k factors necessarily misses out factors and is neither practically nor theoretically defensible. But a proper progression to higher orders, which are projected later on items by the Schmid-Leiman formula, is a constructive way to reach equation (4.5).

In summary, much tidying and cross-checking remains to be done before it can be established beyond cavil that various scales published today correspond validly to the 20 or so primaries and the 8 to 10 secondaries set out. An improvement in factoring and matching practices, to meet modern technical standards, is going to be needed, as well as programatic procedures such as progressive rectification. Finally, the field needs careful, cataloging of the pattern changes over diverse cultural subgroups, if this central core is to become precisely defined and perhaps extended in a reasonable time.

6. Variation of Trait Patterns by Subpopulation, Notably by Social Class, Age, and Sex

The preceding analysis may suggest designs for further research to demonstrate to the satisfaction of all that any remaining divergences of conclusion among laboratories are not irreconcilable. For if purely procedural differences between laboratories cannot be resolved how can we hope to estimate the magnitude of the real structural differences that almost certainly exist between subcultures, races, and nations?

If we can recognize that when technical solecisms are avoided the agreement on basic trait patterns in one culture is good, as the tables of Chapters Two, Three, Four, and Six suggest, then it is time to investigate across cultures. Cross-cultural comparison of factor patterns introduces a notion which it is now timely for us to study, namely that it would be a mistake to expect absolute identity. For when the same source trait is operating, its pattern of expression *should* alter from population to population and the sooner we learn how to allow for the nature of this change in our calculations the better. Consequently we shall now examine evidence on constancy and variation of trait patterns across cultures, proceeding from primaries to secondaries and from subcultural variations (in this section) to international changes later.

First let us define a position on theory and on method. In regard to theory the position has already been taken that the observed trait patterns are the result of distinct maturational (genetic) or structured-learning influences (Cattell, 1968, 1970a) or more commonly both. Genetic differences of pattern, rather than level, are probably smaller than differences of pattern due to cultures, and it is in the latter that we first looked for them. The hypotheses that really gross differences of pattern might arise—so great as to frustrate recognition by matching—is unlikely, for the common features constituted by such institutions as the family, the school, the church, and the peer group should produce similar structured learning. At least this is true of the countries from which we first obtained data: the U.S.A., Britain, British Commonwealth countries, and European countries. After that differences might be expected for, say, India, Japan, China, and Tanzania, but of course this questionnaire has not been tested still further afield in Stone Age or preliterate cultures. As Spengler (1962) points out, history is not linear, and radically new patterns appear. But my hypothesis in beginning this cross-cultural work was that the primary personality traits, unlike interests and dynamic sentiments, are universal, that is, that human nature is basically the same anywhere.

As to technical matters it is necessary to point out that although ordinary factor analysis has so far sufficed for comparisons it is not good enough for refined comparisons of levels on the same traits. Ultimately the studies I report here must be redone in covariance factor analysis. This approach permits factors to be of different sizes (Cattell, 1972a) whereas in ordinary factor analysis this reality is ignored in the interests of the statistical convenience of giving all factors the same size—unit variance—and not allowing that size to alter from population to population.

If in one population the variance of a source trait is larger than in another—as, for example, that of intelligence in the general population compared to an intelligence-selected undergraduate population—the loadings for intelligence as a factor are larger relative to those of other factors than they are in the student group. And in ordinary factor analysis it is important to notice that even if none of the other factors changes, the patterns of all these other factors are altered by changes in size on just one factor in the set. Since the rule is that the variance of a variable must remain at unity, the other factors have to accommodate the change in the size of the intelligence factor; in short their loadings are reduced.

Psychometry has worked out these mutual effects. As Thurstone (1938), Thomson (1939), and others have shown, the effect of such univariate or unifactorial selection can be accommodated by recognizing that in the ordinary factor-analytic layout it can be absorbed by allowing it to affect the correlations among the primary factors instead of the patterns themselves. That is, the pattern for a factor changes proportionately whereas its correlation with other factors alters and the simple-structure description of each factor remains the same, that is, it can still be located. However, there is little doubt that researchers would do better in studying degrees of factor constancy to use covariance factoring and real-base treatment (Cattell, 1972a), preserving the correct primary correlations for a true picture of the second order. In real-base factoring the essential relations can be stated in matrix formulations as follows:

$$R_{vc} = V_{fpc} \, R_f \, V'_{fpc} \tag{8.6}$$

where R_{vc} is the covariance matrix among variables n; R_f is the correlation among factors, and V_{fpc} is the covariance-factor-pattern matrix.

In any experiment a simple transition can be made from the ordinary to the covariance factor pattern V_{fpc}:

$$V_{fpc} = V_{fp} \, D_v \tag{8.7}$$

Here one sees that V_{fpc} is V_{fp} in that experiment with the rows boosted by the raw-score sigmas in the diagonal matrix of variable sigmas D_v. If we go to another experiment t in which the factors are at different variances—as shown by the diagonal matrix of tensors in D_{ft} that stretch or contract factors relative to Equation (8.6), the initial experiment—the new variable-covariance matrix R_{vct} can be obtained from the values in Equation (8.6) by

$$R_{vct} = V_{fpc} \, D_{ft} \, R_f \, D_{ft} \, V'_{fpc} \tag{8.8}$$

Thus Equation (8.8) shows that the covariance-factor-pattern matrices obtainable from R_{vct} are the same in form of item loadings as those from R_{vc} (the first occasion) but stretched. The constancy is in the proportionality.

However, one should watch the trap of assuming that $V_{fpt} = V_{fp} D_{ft}$. That is, with ordinary factoring the relation of loadings to size is not clear and simple because adjustment is needed to keep the standard size of unity.

Even though this real-base factoring theoretically preserves the pattern of the same factor when it is the same, there are other than statistical influences likely to change it. Consequently those who identify traits across cultures only in terms of seeking precise matching of patterns proceed on an oversimplified basis. There is more to identifying traits than "a pattern is a pattern is a pattern" (to transpose Gertrude Stein). The pattern is only the superficial expression of an influence; although it is all we have to go by, the source-trait influence itself is what we really want to match. The correct procedure calls for two steps in comparison of a hypothetical match: first calculate how the covariance factor pattern changes for purely statistical reasons (for example, how a population variance changes) and then explore the range of disagreement of the corrected patterns that can be tolerated in terms of cultural modification of the same influence.

Handling the first—the statistical changes—follows from the preceding. As to the possible cultural modifications, the simplest and most familiar field in which to illustrate them is that of the general intelligence factor (either as g_f or a_g; Cattell, 1971a). Here we note that the loadings of such tests as the Séguin formboard or the Manikin are good with four-year olds but negligible with 14-year olds, whereas other performances change loading with intelligence level of the population sample regardless of age. The formboard exercises the intelligence of four-year olds, whereas in adults it is solved almost by spatial habit skills alone. Equally clear are the experiments of Fleishman (1957), Tucker (1966), and others in the field of learning where the same performance by the same groups of people at different states of learning loads the same factors differently at each stage. Again, the same attitudes in the same people have been shown (Cattell and Hendricks, 1972) to load the same ergic factors differently after individuals have had more experience in the field.

As to broad cross-cultural comparisons one suspects that the general relation-perceiving capacity which is intelligence may show itself in some races through visual and in others through auditory capacities. Similarly, in regard to gross age differences between populations, one suspects that the *D* factor of excitability shows itself more in six-year olds in hyperkinesis and in 60-year olds more in sleeplessness. On the learning side it is evident that whereas intelligence loads successful solutions of quadratics among beginners in algebra, the manipulations become habitual and later lose their *g* loadings; dominance *E* shows itself in confrontations in the young, but in tactful ways of dominance by an older, skilled administrator. In short the *psychological* sources of differences in loading patterns among groups of different heredity, age, and experience have to be accounted for by the whole gamut of psychological laws. This allowance for the operation of psychological laws of maturation and learning raises epistemic questions about the meaning of identity. These I answer later in terms of establishing identity of two patterns through developmental continuity and both belonging to one discrete species type pattern. The meaning of developmental continuity is obvious; it is illustrated by the sense in which we speak of the intelligence factors g_f and g_c being the same across wide age ranges, permitting comparisons by mental age units. In all such comparisons, however, there are technical matters (discussed below and in Cattell, 1965b, 1966a, 1970a; Harman, 1960; Royce, 1963; Tucker, 1966) to work out. The meaning of belonging to a discrete type involves recognition that the loading patterns may belong to some type in a Platonic sense. Patriotic sentiment in Japan and in France may have attitude loading patterns that are not statistically mutually translatable over all behavior markers; but the historian and the psychologist feel justified in using the same term for them.

Matching by demonstrated continuity and demonstrated belonging to a discrete set of patterns (forming a species type: Chapter One) must begin in statistical-experimental evidence. Such comparison has been shown to reduce to matching evidence from four theoretically possible bases of evidence only three of which are practical: same subjects, same variables; same subjects, different variables; and different subjects, same variables. In the questionnaire world we have used the second method to establish identity of source traits by the continuity principle across age in boundary studies linking the ESPQ, CPQ, HSPQ, and 16 PF factor scales. Seeking to establish the identity of factor patterns across two groups such as the sexes, we can use (in addition to common-group factoring) the third method with pattern similarity and congruence coefficients. It is on this method that we have to lean in cross-cultural identification, where subjects obviously cannot be the same.

In all trait comparisons we are interested first in asking if we can claim identity in the species sense; if the answer is yes we are interested next in examining any intriguing minor differences of expression. Thus in regard to the genetic-cultural differences of the two sexes there has never been any doubt about the answer to the first question—the identification of affectia, ego strength, dominance, and so forth across the two; in Chapters Two, Three, and Four I have treated them as the same. But now we are interested in possible systematic differences. The data of Table 48 present possible clues and hypotheses for those who would pursue such research.

Since the statistical question of significance of differences of factor loadings has not been solved to everyone's satisfaction I draw no firm conclusions. The outstanding fact is that their great similarity at this second-order level permits no doubt about matching. The obvious conclusion is that differences of structure with age are greater than with sex.

Comparisons across cultures and subcultures always have two steps. First we establish identity of the trait. When and only when the first step is successful can we, secondly, compare the mean scores on the trait. Countless crosscultural studies have been made without taking the first step. Problems arise, as will be seen later, in comparing scores when the loading patterns are similar enough to justify a conclusion of identity but yet have statistical differences. Meanwhile, in the case of the sexes the results of Table 48 suggest that we may proceed to Table 49—comparison of score levels—without complications.

Table 48

Agreement of Patterns of Secondaries
Between Males and Females
at Two Age Levels

(a) I: Exvia

	16 PF		HSPQ	
	M	*F*	*M*	*F*
A	61	61	71	78
F	63	61	54	57
H	54	48	48	55
J	(Not in)		32	41
Q_2	−78	−78	74	77

(b) II: Anxiety

	16 PF		HSPQ	
	M	*F*	*M*	*F*
A			−22	−19
C	−80	−80	−74	−67
D	(Not in)		80	76
G			−15	−19
H	−40	−41	−60	−57
L	51	52	(Not in)	
O	87	88	72	62
Q_3	−46	−46	−39	−37
Q_4	84	84	74	79

(c) III: Cortertia

	16 PF		HSPQ	
	M	*F*	*M*	*F*
A	−32	−22	−26	−28
I	−74	−62	−57	−61
J	(Not in)		−16	−17
M	−46	−32		

(d) IV: Independence

	16 PF		HSPQ	
	M	*F*	*M*	*F*
E	60	63	41	48
F	28	29	31	32
H	39	46	32	32
L	43	43	(Not in)	

(e) VIII: Upbringing

	16 PF		HSPQ	
	M	*F*	*M*	*F*
F	−21	−32	−50	−51
G	77	68	63	62
Q_3	58	62	57	61

Note: Only factors with loadings greater than 0.15 included. Decimals omitted.

Table 49 presents the levels on primaries since these are fundamental (see Cattell, Eber, and Tatsuoka, 1970 for secondaries). Highly significant differences in the mean level (not the pattern) on both primaries and secondaries were first discovered and clearly recorded on the 16 PF in the 1961 edition and on the HSPQ a couple of years later. It has since been shown that the sex differences continue with considerable consistency throughout the age range as illustrated in Table 49. We can no longer, as in Terman's time, speak of a single sex difference dimension—a masculinity-femininity factor. For differences are significant beyond the $P < 0.001$ level on 10 to 12 primaries and on the same proportion of secondaries. If one sets out to make a masculinity-femininity scale today it will differ from Terman's in being multidimensional (as the IPAT neuroticism scale differs from Eysenck's neuroticism scale in being multidimensional). The psychologist is thus not speaking of a single dimension of sex but of a pattern of differences of two types, which naturally requires description in terms of many factors.

The striking point about the results summarized for large samples, for British and American, and for young and old in Table 49 is the pervasive consistency of the pattern of significant differences.

The differences that are highly significant and also large and maintained at all age levels are these: males are more dominant *E*, parmic *H*, and protensic *L;* females are more affectic *A*, premsic *I*, guilt prone *O*, conservative Q_1—, and higher on ergic tension Q_4 (except before adolescence). This pattern results in higher anxiety and pathemia in females at the second order. With these quantitative results it should be possible for researchers to begin developmental analysis and the sorting out of genetic and cultural components. It is in any case one more important source of evidence of the concrete validity of the primaries and secondaries in Q-data that they so powerfully sort out the sexes, largely in accordance with differences noted in literature for three or four thousand years.

These studies on sex differences, like those on national differences below, throw further light on the relative value of primary and secondary trait concepts in both practice and theory. For both adults and children it will be noted that Table 49 shows females to be more affectic (*A*+) and group-involved (Q_2—), and males more surgent (*F*+) and parmic (*H*+). Yet these are the four markers for the second-order exvia factor, so that on one pair of scores the females are more extravert and on another pair the males. The supposed monolithic unity of exvia-invia is split down the middle. Similar results arise between national groups. British children (Table 53) are simultaneously more sizic (*A*—) and surgent (*F*+) than American, which again splits the extraversion concept apart. Such findings support the theoretical position I have taken here that the primary traits are the primary independent structures and that the secondaries are derivative emergents from them. This does not deny that the latter may be equally large in variance, but it does imply that they are less functionally unitary composites of the primary influences.

Equally interesting are the changes of expression with age. Unlike my handling of the sex difference, this discussion will be confined to differences in the pattern of expression, since differences in absolute level on the factors with age were thoroughly explored in Chapter Five I depend largely on the IPAT scales—the 16 PF, HSPQ, CPQ, and others—because these alone have been tried out on sufficient ranges of population to yield an answer. This fact has relevance to the claims examined earlier in this chapter to finding alternative structures; the present search reveals that these claims are frequently based on only one type of population, such as experiments with undergraduate students, or even on males only, as in a military population of young men.

A striking instance of an age differential is found in the radicalism-conservatism pattern. This was established initially in the 16 PF as a replica-

Table 49

Mean Sex Differences on Primary Personality Factors

(a) Among American Adults (16 PF)[a]

	A	*B*	*C*	*E*	*F*	*G*	*H*	*I*	*L*	*M*	*N*	*O*	Q_1	Q_2	Q_3	Q_4
Men																
Mean	18.49	13.44	32.96	24.28	26.18	28.21	28.50	17.83	16.70	22.15	21.93	19.91	20.13	20.49	23.54	22.21
SD	6.84	3.27	6.92	6.28	7.89	5.71	9.82	5.59	5.04	5.89	3.79	6.90	4.60	5.51	4.95	7.93
Women																
Mean	23.14	13.44	33.26	17.30	25.86	28.69	25.43	24.78	14.96	24.17	20.53	23.43	17.61	20.22	22.78	26.78
SD	6.12	3.27	7.87	6.54	7.75	5.01	9.90	4.58	5.04	5.67	3.98	7.30	4.32	5.10	4.92	8.30
Difference[b]	—4.65	0.00	—0.30	6.98	0.32	—0.48	3.07	—6.95	1.74	—2.02	1.40	—3.52	2.52	0.27	0.76	—4.57
t Value	15.50	0.00	0.91	24.93	0.89	2.00	6.67	28.96	7.91	7.21	8.24	11.00	12.60	1.13	3.45	12.35
P	<0.001	NS[c]	NS	<0.001	NS	<0.05	<0.001	<0.001	<0.001	<0.001	<0.001	<0.001	<0.001	NS	<0.001	<0.001

[a] Between men and women corrected to age 35 (raw scores).
[b] Positive if men higher.
[c] NS = not significant.

(b) Among British Adults[a]

	A	*B*	*C*	*E*	*F*	*G*	*H*	*I*	*L*	*M*	*N*	*O*	Q_1	Q_2	Q_3	Q_4
Men																
Mean	17.58	14.65	30.80	25.00	26.27	24.63	27.25	17.63	17.72	22.94	20.96	19.69	18.86	20.40	24.86	23.77
SD	5.85	3.47	6.99	7.30	9.23	5.90	10.30	5.76	4.95	5.63	4.80	7.79	4.97	5.76	6.00	9.20
Women																
Mean	21.72	14.16	28.07	19.09	26.42	24.79	23.48	25.01	15.89	21.75	22.34	25.35	16.49	19.68	23.13	28.78
SD	5.02	3.44	6.67	6.69	8.61	5.46	10.36	4.58	4.94	5.92	4.71	7.58	4.71	5.59	5.73	8.16
Difference[b]	—4.14	0.49	2.73	5.91	—0.15	—0.16	3.77	—7.38	1.83	1.19	—1.38	—5.66	2.37	0.72	1.73	—5.01
t Value	17.02	3.18	8.96	18.92	0.38	0.63	8.18	31.78	8.29	4.62	6.50	16.50	10.97	2.84	6.61	12.91
P	<0.001	<0.01	<0.001	<0.001	NS[c]	NS	<0.001	<0.001	<0.001	<0.001	<0.001	<0.001	<0.001	<0.11	<1.112	<2.222

[a] Courtesy of Peter Saville and the National Foundation for Educational Research.
[b] Positive if men higher.
[c] NS = not significant.

(c) Among Adolescents at age 14–16 (HSPQ)

Factor	U.S.A. First Population Sample (N = 1143 boys, 1497 girls) t Value and Significance	Higher Sex	Mean Difference Raw	Sten	U.S.A. Second Population Sample (N = 1151 boys, 1540 girls) t Value and Significance	Higher Sex	Mean Difference Raw	Sten	U.S.A. Third Population Sample (N = 1076 boys, 1460 girls) t Value and Significance	Higher Sex	Mean Difference Raw	Sten	Britain Stratified Population Sample (Saville and Finlayson, 1973) (N = 1261 boys, 1168 girls) t Value and Significance	Higher Sex	Mean Difference Raw
A	12.59***	G	1.7	0.96	10.98***	G	1.4	0.83	14.22***	G	3.3	1.07	13.15***	G	1.8
B	4.39***	G	0.3	0.32	4.91***	G	0.3	0.39	4.09***	G	0.5	0.34	NS	—	0
C	9.16***	B	1.2	0.71	6.66***	B	0.9	0.51	9.32***	B	2.2	0.73	10.91***	B	1.5
D	0.72	B	0.1	0.06	0.80	G	0.1	0.09	0.44	B	0.1	0.04	0.98 NS	B	0.1
E	15.83***	B	1.9	1.19	14.78***	B	1.7	1.11	18.78***	B	3.7	1.42	26.51***	B	3.3
F	4.58***	B	0.6	0.36	5.38***	G	0.7	0.42	0.0	—	0.0	0.00	7.18***	B	1.0
G	7.82***	G	0.9	0.60	13.13***	G	1.8	0.98	12.04***	G	2.6	0.94	1.32 NS	B	0.2
H	4.86***	B	0.7	0.37	7.30***	B	1.0	0.55	7.11***	B	1.8	0.55	10.28***	B	1.5
I	45.90***	G	5.6	2.69	28.07***	G	3.2	1.91	45.12***	G	8.8	2.70	44.21***	G	6.7
J	7.44***	B	0.9	0.58	1.81	B	0.2	0.14	5.13***	B	1.0	0.41	9.69***	B	1.2
O	7.14***	G	0.9	0.54	3.03**	G	0.4	0.23	6.79***	G	1.5	0.53	8.97***	G	1.2
Q_2	14.41***	B	1.6	1.08	8.20***	B	1.0	0.63	14.35***	B	2.8	1.09	15.71***	B	2.1
Q_3	5.04***	G	0.6	0.41	8.82***	G	1.2	0.68	8.18***	G	1.8	0.64	2.72**	B	0.4
Q_4	5.00***	G	0.7	0.43	6.35***	G	0.8	0.49	6.60***	G	1.4	0.52	5.04***	G	0.7

Note: *** = Significant at P<.001 level.
** = Significant at P<.01 level.

(d) Between Boys and Girls at Age 10.5 (CPQ)

	A	*B*	*C*	*D*	*E*	*F*	*G*	*H*	*I*	*J*	*N*	*O*	Q_3	Q_4
Girls														
Mean	13.8	13.2	12.0	8.0	7.2	7.1	14.1	10.3	11.2	9.0	5.2	8.3	14.0	7.5
SD	2.9	3.4	3.4	3.8	3.0	3.0	3.2	3.4	3.4	2.8	3.1	3.6	3.7	3.6
Boys														
Mean	12.7	12.6	11.7	8.7	10.7	11.3	12.6	10.7	6.6	8.7	7.6	7.6	12.0	8.8
SD	3.0	3.7	3.4	3.8	3.2	3.0	3.2	3.2	3.2	2.8	3.5	3.7	4.1	3.7
Difference [a]	–1.1	–0.6	–0.3	0.7	3.5	4.2	–1.5	0.4	–4.6	–0.3	2.4	–0.7	–2.0	1.3
t Value	–9.92	–4.49	–2.35	4.90	30.03	37.26	–12.47	3.22	–37.08	–2.85	19.32	–5.10	–13.63	9.48
P	<0.001	<0.001	<0.05	<0.001	<0.001	<0.001	<0.001	<0.01	<0.001	<0.01	<0.001	<0.001	<0.001	<0.001

[a] Positive if boys higher.

tion of the pattern by Thurstone (1937), also firmly established by Carlson (1934), Eysenck (1960), and Lentz (1938, 1939)—all on students. Yet consistency of the pattern has almost vanished, as the pattern of present students compared with those 20 years ago and with present adults shows (Table 44 and Cattell, 1973j).

Table 50 examines similarities and differences of expression with age at the level of secondaries. Age cultures rather than age is used in the table title because (as the discussion on ecogenic and epogenic curves in Chapter Four reminds us) each age is also a temporal subcultural division—an epogenic product.

The trends noted in Table 50 must be considered tentative at the 7-year (6 to 8) and 10-year (8 to 12) levels because the ESPQ and CPQ are still in the process of progressive rectification. However, there are definite indications that dominance is part of exvia at earlier and not later ages. The same may be true of intelligence, possibly because intelligence favors successful social interaction. Three indications are of interest regarding anxiety: the falling out of sizia *A*−, coasthenia *J*, and low superego *G*− after the early years; the last is not evident in these data but is clear enough in some findings. My tentative theory is that the withdrawal in sizia and the reduction of energy in coasthenia are initially products of anxiety but later become autonomous. High *G* presumably reduces anxiety in the early years because it brings behavior avoiding parental punishment, whereas *G* behavior in adult life tends to move beyond what is covered by criminal law.

That intelligence is affected by cortertia in the early years suggests that cortical alertness resides initially in a general physiological contribution to cortical efficiency. It is noticeable that at early ages *Q*VIII, good upbringing, does not require desurgency (general inhibition) but that inhibition spreads from the moral realm with age. My theoretical comments must be laconic; but any psychologist can see that refinement of these age changes in factor patterns would provide a goldmine of theories regarding personality development.

This examination of resemblances of trait patterns by sex and age within the English-speaking culture thus establish the existence of a high degree of constancy that leaves no doubt about identities. It also establishes significant differences in level and probably some trends in pattern. A sense of perspective about these degrees of constancy and change has been conspicuously lacking among such critics as Rorer (1972), Howarth (1972), and Lykken (1971) and has caused some confusion. Those who stress the inconstancy of factor patterns fail to consider the immense distance in terms of sequences of calculation and the practical possibility of clerical and random error between data and final factor patterns. They fail to see the minor miracle when different populations and samples still yield the easily recognizable degree of constancy shown above. On the other hand, those who claim that absolute constancy is attainable fail to recognize that there are good reasons why items change their loadings from setting to setting *as evidence of the constancy of the underlying influence itself.*

From the point of view of conceptually correct comparison of scores

Table 50

Differences of Age Cultures in Patterns of Secondary-Source-Trait Expression

(a) Exvia and Anxiety

Factor	*I: Exvia* 7 yrs.	10 yrs.	14 yrs.	Adult	*II: Anxiety* 7 yrs.	10 yrs.	14 yrs.	Adult
A	33	52	74	58	−18	−18	−21	01
B	24	37	01	−00	−18	−09	01	−02
C	09	32	05	07	−03	−52	−71	−66
D	−11	31	05		54	53	77	
E	19	25	−03	07	24	45	−10	−00
F	37	72	56	51	07	09	03	−03
G	05	−00	03	06	−03	−01	15	−03
H	36	72	51	50	−09	−21	−60	−38
I	11	−31	03	07	04	08	04	00
J	−07	−10	−40		52	21	06	
L				05				54
M				−00				03
N	02	−19		−00	63	00		−02
O	−09	−06	13	−02	84	39	69	78
Q_1				−02				−06
Q_2			−76	−65			−07	−01
Q_3		−00	−09	−05		−06	−38	−43
Q_4	63	−32	01	00	27	17	75	80

(b) Cortertia and Good Upbringing

Factor	*III: Cortertia* 7 yrs.	10 yrs.	14 yrs.	Adult	*VIII: Good Upbringing* 7 yrs.	10 yrs.	14 yrs.	Adult
A	−10	−28	−30	−25	13	10	00	−01
B	16	35	00	00	22	−01	04	−01
C	−01	−19	14	10	18	−07	15	05
D	−17	30	05		−13	−21	01	
E	54	−12	44	01	14	03	−02	−18
F	03	14	02	01	08	−01	−51	−27
G	−07	07	−09	01	59	11	64	67
H	−03	−29	03	−14	08	00	−00	−00
I	−37	−12	−62	−73	15	−13	08	02
J	−59	27	00		04	39	09	
L				06				04
M				−47				−08
N	17	37		00	08	−15		03
O	04	02	−16	−06	−09	02	−07	03
Q_1				−01				−02
Q_2			07	−04			01	01
Q_3		−79	03	01		50	60	47
Q_4	−17	62	01	−05	25	−14	−03	−02

Note: Blanks mean that factor has no scale to measure it at given age level. Boxes mean that value is considered a standard marker at upper and lower age levels.

the ideal response to these subcultural differences would be to construct distinct scales for each sex, age, and social subculture. Even in terms of basic research this is at present impractical; from the standpoint of test construction and unsubsidized publishers it is prohibitive. At present it takes no less than 42 different tables in the 16 PF Handbook, and about the same number in the supplements to set out the psychometric properties and standardization constants for a single test. One promising approach is to discover scale items with high transferability, a process which may take 20 years of progressive rectification of the scales at each age level for the HSPQ, CPQ, ESPQ, and others. Meanwhile, if an investigator need not bother about standardization but can work with raw scores he can take advantage of the solution offered in the computer synthesis programs for these IPAT scales—namely, using the same test but weighting the items differently, according to the subcultural factorization values (see Chapter Ten).

7. Constancy and Variability of Primary Source Traits Across National Cultures and Classes

Many psychologists have been heard to make the wry remark that cross-cultural research has reached epidemic proportions because it provides social psychologists with enjoyable facilities for travel. Yet serious cross-cultural research has arrived none too soon if psychology, like older sciences, is to aspire to universal laws of international verity. Until we have checked acress cultures how can we tell how universal our laws of structure and process are? Mature methodologists in the social sciences have long recognized that relative to the physical sciences their initial laws remain at a descriptive level and are more rooted in local cultural conditions and the flow of history. They also recognize that only by building on collections of proven local laws can they proceed to universal laws.

Such areas as personality and ability structure, behavior genetics, and most of the psychometrics of individual differences have, until the marked advance of Japan, been by a 10:1 ratio a contribution of the English-speaking world and Northern Europe. (Russia compensates in learning and physiological psychology.) Consequently the issue opened up above as to how far the personality and ability structures with which English-speaking psychologists deal are local or universal has invited a range of opinions. They extend from those of some sociologists that personality and ability factors are so different as to be unrecognizable with change of culture to the intuitive dictum of many psychologists that human nature is the same everywhere.

The research sequence advocated by those in programatic work on primary and secondary traits has been to stabilize in English and then translate and compare (since greater research resources have existed in America). This, fortunately, has realized itself historically, aided by the rapid growth in the number of psychometrists in other countries since World War II. The flow from America has resulted in the Guilford-Zimmerman scales, the MMPI, the IPAT 16 PF, the HSPQ, the Eysenck EPI scales, and others being translated into several languages and in some important instances actually refactored in the other culture. Skillful and thorough checks of this kind have been made in Britain by Warburton and Saville at NFER, in Australia and New Zealand by Vaughan, Adcock, ACER and NFER, in Germany by Arnold (Würzburg), Schneewind (Trier), Schröder (Cologne), Schmidt, Fahrenberg, and Schumacker (see Fahrenberg, 1967; Pawlik, 1968; Schneewind and Cattell, 1970; Cattell and Schmidt, 1972; Timm, 1968); in France by the Centre de Psychologie Appliqué; in Italy by Cusin and the Organizzazione Speciali; in India by Hundal, Jalota, and Kapoor; in Mexico by Rayek Zaga; in South America by Rimoldi (Argentina) and DeAndrade (Brazil); and in Japan by Ishikawa (1973), Yamaguchi (1973), Tsujioka (Tsujioka and Cattell, 1965a), and Tsushima (1957). If we survey the results in terms of thoroughly factored scales we are restricted largely to the 16 PF, the HSPQ, the CPQ, and the anxiety and other state scales. Either singly or as part of a coordinated set these have been translated since 1950 into French, German, Italian, Japanese, Chinese, Swedish, Spanish, Polish, Portuguese, Hindi, Urdu, Czechoslovakian, Serbo-Croatian, Hebrew, Flemish, Thai, Finnish, Hungarian, and Icelandic. If we concentrate on cultural or at least national comparisons in which translation in the ordinary sense is not involved, a closely knit plan of comparisons of profiles is possible among the United States, Britain, Australia (ACER), New Zealand (NZCER), and South Africa (NIPR).[4]

Where factor analyses of the primary structure have been made—as in France (Cattell, Pichot, and Rennes, 1961), Germany (Cattell and Nesselroade, 1965; Cattell, Schroder, and Wagner, 1969; Schneewind and Schroder, 1973). Czechoslovakia (Rican, In preparation), Italy (Meschieri and Cattell, 1960), and India (Kapoor, 1963; Hundal, Sudhakar, and Sidhu, 1972)—the

[4] I wish to express my indebtedness for data here, and for the enjoyment I have had, in the spirit of international cooperation for common scientific goals, in working with the principal architects of the conclusions in this chapter, especially Abbele (Italy), Adcock (New Zealand), Alves and DeAndrade (Brazil), Arnold (Germany), Berke, (Holland), Bhagaliwal (India), Birkin (Australia), Bjerstedt (Sweden), Brichaçek (Czechoslovakia), Calderon (Chile), Chevrier (Quebec), Choynowski (Sweden), Cleary (Peru), Cusin (Italy), Delhees (Switzerland), De Venanzi (Venezuela), Evrard (Belgium), Fahrenberg (Germany), Fernandez (Mexico), Fertilio (Chile), Fischer (Switzerland), Gonzales (Spain), Hermochova (Czechoslovakia), Hoffman (Hungary), Hundal (India), Ishikawa (Japan), Jalota (India), Julius (Yugoslavia), Kalimo (Finland), Kapoor (India), Kiedrowski (Poland), Kline (Ghana), Levy (Colombia), Liu (China), Maceira (Mexico), McQuaid (Scotland), Mehrotra (India), Meredith (Hawaii), Montag (Israel), Nichols (Canada), Novaga (Italy), Novakowska (Poland), Pelgrim (Holland), Pichot (France), Rennes (France), Rican (Czechoslovakia), Robbertse (South Africa), Schneewind, Schmidt, and Schroder (Germany), Strelau (Poland), Taylor (New Zealand), Tsujioka (Japan), Tsushima (Japan), Wichiarajate (Thailand), White (England), Yela (Spain), Schumacher (Germany), and my constant collaborator Frank Warburton in the English analyses.

Readers should be alerted to misconceptions being caused by publications of translations and research as late as 1973 with obsolete (1962 or even 1949) editions of the 16 PF. When the weak N, O, and Q_1 primaries have not come through clearly in translation there are instances (Japan, Czechoslovakia) of these being left as gaps in the primary scales instead of pursued with new items more suitable to the culture. Generally, however, cross-cultured analysis has been pursued with remarkable perseverance and success and has retained essential structures to permit cross-national comparisons.

essentials of the first-order structure have unequivocally reappeared. However, this has occurred with some modification of items and occasionally the failure to reproduce the weaker, smaller variance factors *N*, *O*, or Q_1. Table 51 presents the results of one of two German studies. (Cattell, Schroder, and Wagner, 1969) In spite of some objections by Greif (1970) and Timm (1968) that are based on defects of technique and that studied only the second order, it is noteworthy that the two main German studies show excellent agreement on the test for number of factors. These well-executed studies also attained a high level of simple structure as well as high congruence coefficients for the ultimate identification of the patterns (both mutually and between samples) and with the English data for the same scales. Only the upper left-hand corners of the factor-pattern matrix and the congruence matrix are reproduced in Table 51, although the complete congruences down the diagonal are given in Table 51(b) and the complete tables are given in the references concerned (see Cattell, Schroder, and Wagner 1969).

In Japan an equally clear agreement on primary structure (in parcel factoring) was found by Tsujioka (Tsujioka and Cattell, 1965a). In this case we have the added methodological interest of being able to compare the

Table 51

Factor Patterns and German-English Congruences in Cross-Cultural Comparison of Primaries

(a) Loading Patterns of 16 PF Scales Translated for German Sample

					Source Trait					
Variable	*A*	*B*	*C*	*E*	*F*	*G*	*H*	*I*	*L*	*M*
Scale Trait A Form A	74									14
Scale Trait A Form B	43						13	49		
Scale Trait B Form A		59								
Scale Trait B Form B		65								
Scale Trait C Form A			52		12	28		−11	−14	
Scale Trait C Form B			59					11	−19	
Scale Trait E Form A				34	16		15	−15		
Scale Trait E Form B				72						
Scale Trait F Form A					49		35			
Scale Trait F Form B			16		51		15	20		
Scale Trait G Form A						39				
Scale Trait G Form B						69	−12	13		11
Scale Trait H Form A							78			
Scale Trait H Form B							82			
Scale Trait I Form A	20				−11	−11		69		51
Scale Trait I Form B								56		
Scale Trait L Form A									51	
Scale Trait L Form B			−12						55	
Scale Trait M Form A										51
Scale Trait M Form B							18			45

Note: This is an illustration; the rest of the table is available in Cattell, Schröder, and Wagner (1969). All values of ±0.10 or less, that is, those in hyperplane, are omitted from this table. A second large-scale factoring by Schneewind is in press.

Table 51 (Cont.)

(b) Congruence of Total Source-Trait Patterns Between English-American and German Samples

English-American Sample	*German Sample*							*Remaining Congruences*								
	A	*B*	*C*	*E*	*F*	*G*	*H*	*I*	*L*	*M*	*N*	*O*	Q_1	Q_2	Q_3	Q_4
A	86						16									
B		93														
C			69			27										
E				39		−26										
F					75		37									
G						74										
H				20			82	63	68	46	65	25	68	71	44	57

Note: Insignificant congruences of 0.14 or less omitted for economy.

(c) Statistical Significance (Bargmann's test) of Blindly Reached Simple Structure in German Experiment Personality Factor Scale

A	*B*	*C*	*E*	*F*	*G*	*H*	*I*	*L*	*M*	*N*	*O*
0.001	0.001	0.100	0.001	0.010	0.001	0.010	0.001	0.001	0.050	0.001	0.001

Q_1	Q_2	Q_3	Q_4
0.001	0.001	0.001	0.010

differences among two American samples and a Japanese sample. Figure 28 uses a Mahalanobis distance function between the factor patterns expressed for convenience finally as lengths on the side of a triangle. The striking conclusion is that the Japanese pattern resembles the two sampled American patterns more than they resemble each other. Also, although the test was first constructed on factorings in English the factorial simple structure in Japan had noticeably better hyperplane count than the original.

It is clear from these detailed experimental findings that agreement across cultures on the primary factor patterns by item and especially *by parcel* (subscale), is of a high order. This degree of resemblance was noted first among Western nations but the evidence on the number and nature of primary factors surprisingly shows no less agreement when we move to remote cultures, as shown by the Japanese data and those of Kapoor, Hundal, and others in India. Larger population samples and sharper methods will undoubtedly reveal and clarify small systematic differences; at present the remarkable fact is that the agreement of American, German, and Japanese samples is indistinguishable from that between two samples from different parts of America.

Turning from resemblances to slight but possibly systematic differences my discussion must be speculative and on the basis of indications only.

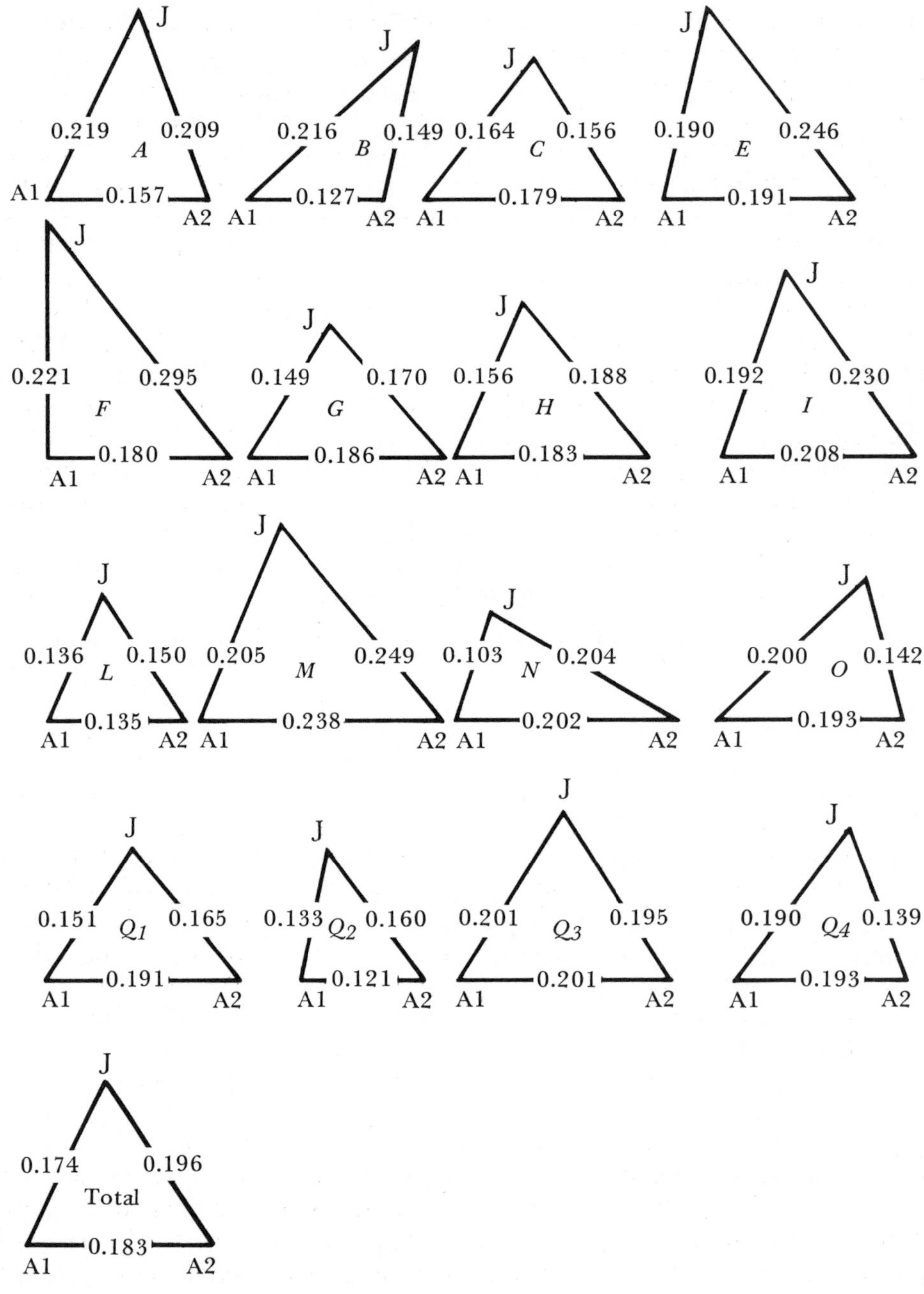

Figure 28. Comparison of international and intranational primary source-trait patterns. Sample J was 200 Japanese undergraduate males; sample A1 was 117 American undergraduate males; sample A2 was 1000 American undergraduates and other subjects (Cattell and Gorsuch, 1965). The sides of the triangles are distance functions based on summed squared differences of the interfactor correlations for each factor. Factors *A, E,* and *F* seem to be the only ones where some Japanese deviation is consistent (Tsujioka and Cattell, 1965a).

Here I would theorize that certain factors—notably dominance *E*, autia *M*, guilt proneness *O*, and self-sentiment Q_3—show real differences even among Western nations whereas ego strength *C* and superego strength *G* may change in remote cultures. Possible real differences can be seen in the low parcel congruences and in differences in the item loadings (when the primaries have been factored at the item level) as in the French (Cattell, Pichot, and Rennes, 1961) and Italian (Meschieri and Cattell, 1960) analyses. Regarding the French primary analysis (due to the help of Vidal, Pichot, and Rennes) our conclusion was that six items involved mainly in surgency *F*, dominance *E*, and radicalism Q_1 were responded to in a way that has been called "the older established radicalism and individualism in the French culture." Similarly there was a noticeable difference in the Italian data in the dominance *E* factor in loadings on existing and new 16 PF items. Items expressing interest in upper status in a hierarchy loaded *E* better in the Italian dominance pattern; items expressing free enterprise and self-direction ("I would rather run my own business than be securely paid in someone else's") loaded the factor more in America.

Much discussion on changes in source-trait expression rests on casual observation and impression. Anyone commenting on source-trait differences would do well to note the possibilities of methodology shown in Tsujioka's work. Before concluding that, say *N* is more changeable he should remember that some factors have low congruences and variances even within one culture. Thus Rican and his coworkers at Prague, as well as Tsujioka and Ishikawa at Kyoto, have noted difficulties in locating clear variance on *M* and *N* and in separating *O* from Q_4, with which it is substantially correlated. The Prague researchers, however, hypothesized that these factors, and possibly radicalism-conservatism Q_1, do not exist in their culture. But the last factors in the list—*M, N, O,* and *P*—by the *original definition of alphabetic indexing by declining variance* are of small variance in the original culture itself. (Investigators of English-language items have also failed sometimes to go beyond 12 factors; see Eysenck and Eysenck, 1969). When large samples and careful methods are used the four weak Q-data factors—*M, N, O,* and Q_1—are still indubitably found in foreign data. The problem created by the protean form of radicalism-conservatism Q_1 has been sufficiently discussed above.

Such persistence of more than 16 primary personality traits across many national cultures of diverse pattern, together with such evidence as that of Vandenberg (1965) showing a similar persistence of the primary abilities, does seem to argue that human nature is the same the world over and invites the scientist to share Longfellow's faith that "every human heart is human." As pointed out this does not compel us to accept a solely genetic explanation inherent in *homo sapiens*. For over and above genetics there is, across diverse cultures, a common core in the form of inescapable similarities of learning pattern: learning to live in a family, acquiring a self-concept, having emotional experiences, liking or disliking a peer group, acquiring varying degrees of emotional self-control, and so on. One must remember that nature/nurture ratios for the source traits in questionnaires are about 50/50.

Although the underlying source traits are thus recognized as essentially the same in number and nature in all cultures tested, the modes of expressing high spirits in surgency *F* or the inhibitions of the cultural superego *G* or the forms of expressing dominance *E* have many indications of varying among cultures. These variations are perhaps minimized by the translators' deft switches to the best equivalents in their attempts to get the best translation of an item. A more exact determination of the degree and meaning of these psychometric constants remains for social psychology to investigate.

The findings regarding cross-cultural constancy or difference of secondaries now deserve thorough inspection. It has been a central argument in the theory of personality structure that primary and secondary findings must show mutual consistency and constancy. Any global and organic theory of personality involves relating both the primary and secondary structures to developmental, genetic, physiological, and learning forces, thus testing the verity of both. Accordingly Table 52 sets out data from six countries and eight samples on second-order analyses. Wider evidence exists but I have restricted the table to experiments involving both sexes, adequate samples, and both forms (A and B) of the 16 PF. I broadened the base of methodology by taking both scale and true-factor factoring and by including two samples from one country. Although an American sample is included the main English-speaking second-order analyses to be compared with these are in Table 16 (Chapter Four). Second-order analyses throughout the childhood age range are only now beginning to be made abroad; the HSPQ result included is an early and comparatively crude contribution.

8. Methodology of Cross-Cultural Trait-Level Comparisons

Now that the same personality and ability structures can be demonstrated in different cultures, each with its characteristic loading pattern, the way is opened to comparisons of national cultures, social classes, and subcultures as to their loads on intelligence, ego strength, anxiety, numerical ability, dominance, and other traits. Proof of operational similarity of concepts is an important gain, but we still have to discuss how to put comparisons on a legitimate psychometric basis. Advance here is vital because the social scientist is eager to treat such measures as the independent variable in understanding differences in economic, sociological, and historical performances of groups and as dependent variables in discovering laws about the effects of different upbringing, national values, economic conditions, and so forth on personality.

Unfortunately the use of cross-cultural research to investigate causal connections in personality formation has rested on shaky foundations. As Humphreys and other psychometrists have somewhat unpopularly insisted, the bulk of cross-cultural research is psychometrically indefensible. Most

Table 52

Agreement of Eight Second-Order Factor Patterns
Across Six or More Diverse Cultures

(a) Adults: First Two Factors

	I: Exvia								*II: Anxiety*							
	1	*2*	*3*	*4*	*5*	*6*	*7*	*8*	*1*	*2*	*3*	*4*	*5*	*6*	*7*	*8*
A	74	67	61	53	66	37	62	51	01	−08	−02	−04	06	−02	03	−04
B	−01	−10	00	−01	−00	−01	−03	03	00	02	−01	−02	−03	−03	−02	−02
C	09	−22	05	−01	06	16	12	02	−83	−65	−73	−78	−74	−34	−60	−74
E	17	24	05	05	06	04	11	08	15	−09	−00	−01	03	02	−13	06
F	35	54	56	54	53	29	55	57	−02	−00	−03	−08	−08	−01	−00	−16
G	08	−17	01	01	09	08	15	−01	−01	−04	−03	−01	−05	−01	−16	−14
H	65	56	54	56	56	40	47	58	−32	−42	−42	−37	−37	−25	−48	−47
I	01	13	03	07	10	02	13	13	−01	−11	−02	−07	00	−02	02	09
L	03	24	−00	−01	05	−28	03	17	62	66	59	55	56	43	51	79
M	−09	−07	−17	−09	−09	−35	−18	−32	−11	11	10	17	04	06	04	−06
N	−01	−02	00	−01	04	−01	−03	00	−04	12	−01	02	−07	04	−04	04
O	−15	06	−08	−02	−06	04	10	15	82	80	83	81	84	69	68	67
Q_1	04	−32	−01	−01	03	−08	−01	−24	02	−14	−06	−03	−05	−08	−01	−04
Q_2	−75	−33	−61	−69	−70	−54	−62	−88	12	11	−03	−06	−03	00	02	−09
Q_3	−09	11	−10	−03	−08	−07	03	−10	−44	−82	−42	−38	−53	−41	−37	−42
Q_4	11	06	02	03	−01	−06	−05	00	88	83	76	76	86	78	68	87

Note: To show the simple structure the actual loadings hypothesized to be in the hyperplane are given literally here, not left blank if below ±0.20 as in the following tables. The boxes pick out the standard primary markers as in Chapter Four. For exvia and anxiety the samples are in order, American, Japanese, German lower class, German upper class, British, Brazilian, Venezuelan, and New Zealand as specified by Dr. K. E. Nichols (preliminary data in Cattell and Nichols, 1972).

Table 52 (Cont.)

(b) Adults: Remaining Secondaries

III: Cortertia-Pathemia

	Germany 1	*Germany 2*	*Venezuela*	*NZ*	*Japan*	*Chile*	*Brazil*
A	−29	−32	−35	−54	−20	−20	−23
C							31
I	−88	−83	−71	−59	−82	−63	−59
M	−45	−33	−50	−67	−67	−63	−36
O				−45			

Note: Here only nonhyperplane > ±0.20 loadings are reported.

IV: Independence-Subduedness

	Germany 1	*Germany 2*	*Venezuela*	*NZ*	*Japan*	*Chile*	*Brazil*
E	55	67		66	68	66	62
F	35	27		25	27	62	56
G					−44		
H	37	32		63		56	36
L	31	21	61	28			25
M	(18) [a]	(19)		31			(18)
O						29	

[a] Here and later when an expected marker falls below ±0.20 it is placed in parenthesis to call attention.

V: Foxiness-Secure Naturalness

	Germany 1	*Germany 2*	*Venezuela*	*NZ*	*Japan*	*Chile*	*Brazil*
A	21	(13)	(18)	54	(12)		30
H							27
L				24	28		
N	88	85	67	77	32		41
Q_1					55		26
Q_4				22			

VI: Untamedness

	Germany 1	*Germany 2*	*Venezuela*	*NZ*	*Japan*	*Chile*	*Brazil*
E				38			
F				−24			
I							32
M	23	21					
Q_1	78	75	69	35			23
Q_2				21			
Q_3							20

Table 52 (Cont.)

VII: High Intelligence-Low Intelligence

	Germany 1	*Germany 2*	*Venezuela*	*NZ*	*Japan* [b]	*Chile*	*Brazil*
B	89	88	70	67		61	46
C				32			
F				38			
L							−29
Q_1				21		27	
Q_4				22			

[b] These two factors VII and VIII were not extracted but left as specifics in these instances.

VIII: Strong Upbringing-Weak Upbringing

	Germany 1	*Germany 2*	*Venezuela*	*NZ*	*Japan*	*Chile*	*Brazil*
C				−29			
E	−20		−67	−26			
F	−26	−30	−32	−54			−25
G	86	83	39	81	(Less than ±0.20)		57
H			−36				
Q_3	38	27	45				38

(c) Early Adolescent Second Orders

	Exvia Aus	*Exvia USA*		*Anxiety Aus*	*Anxiety USA*		*Cortertia Aus*	*Cortertia USA*
A	40	37	*C*	−27	−52	*A*	(−12)	(−07)
F	45	38	*D*	45	47	*C*	12	24
H	53	15	*E*	16	34	*E*	30	30
J	−26	−39	*H*	−36	−65	*I*	−67	−58
Q_2	−39	−47	*O*	54	79			
G	−17	−37	Q_3	(−07)	−26			
			Q_4	66	65			
			G	(−11)	−27			

Note: Cattell (1965c): 296 American 12–14-year old boys and girls. Cattell (1965c): 209 Australian 12–14-year old boys and girls.

(d) Agreement by Congruence Coefficients of Second-Order Patterns: One English, One German

English Group		*I*	*II*	*III*	*IV*	*V*	*VI*	*VII*	*VIII*	*IX*
		German (Higher-Education) Group N = 1800								
Exvia	I	(99)	−18	−19	37	15	−07	−02	−09	−35
Anxiety	II	−09	(97)	−06	−04	−04	−08	04	−14	−24
Cortertia	III	−09	−01	(96)	−09	−08	−14	00	00	10
Independence	IV	28	10	−00	(94)	−00	25	−02	−21	−04
Foxiness	V	12	−04	−10	−27	(90)	−01	−05	10	10
Untamedness	VI	−06	09	−23	07	−03	(94)	−05	01	07
Intelligence	VII	−06	−12	−06	03	−09	10	(91)	−05	−10
Superego	VIII	−11	−14	11	−11	06	−06	00	(93)	56
Error Factor	IX	−18	−04	09	06	−02	17	−03	08	(10)

Note: Decimal points omitted throughout. Critical values in parentheses.

investigators have proceeded without establishing the comparability of patterns of structures or facing the necessary scaling problems in comparing levels. Since, with the exception of the American, German, Japanese comparisons on Objective-Analytic batteries (Cattell, Schmidt, and Pawlik, 1973), virtually all cross-cultural comparisons have been by questionnaires and attitude inventories we must take the inventory as the instrument in question and ask how scores on a questionnaire scale in two languages for, say, surgency, exvia, or ergic tension can be compared.

This problem runs into deep issues discussed elsewhere (Cattell, 1969, 1970a); only a note on essentials is possible here. Although the problem of identity of meaning has been tackled, the assumptions of identity and species identity briefly mentioned above must be made explicit before proceeding. As to the meaning of identity, three operational possibilities follow.

Identity with Content Adjustment to Group Uniqueness. This possibility rests on within-group factoring. Two methods are possible. The first is with two distinct groups with variables made (by translation) as identical as possible (same variables, different subjects) followed by pattern-similarity identification of the corresponding loading patterns as in Table 52. The second is with different sets of variables given to the same people (same subjects, different variables) followed by correlations of the factor scores to establish identity. This is possible only with a bicultural sample. For a group of students in Kenya who speak both English and Swahili, the items designed for, say, premsia need not even be pairs of mutual translations. If the factors estimated from the Swahili and the English items correlate +1.0 (within experimental error) we would give it the same meaning—premsia. By either method the result is a pair of scales measuring the same factor defined by a pattern of within-group covariance.

Super-Group Definition. What I call transgroup or transcultural factoring involves putting many different groups into one factor analysis. This can be done by (a) combining the within-group covariance matrices (*combined intra-group factoring*) or by (b) correlating across all groups using the mean scores of each group as a single row in the score matrix (*combined intercultural trait factoring*). In the former the measures as individual deviations from the mean of each group are polled for the groups concerned and then factored. In the latter the same items (also closely translated) are given in perhaps a hundred countries, the means are calculated in each, and a transcultural factor (Cattell, 1957) is established from the correlation of variables over all countries. The first uses only the within-group covariance and the second only the between-group covariance, but both produce a *single factor pattern that holds across all cultures.* A hybrid of (a) and (b) is possible in which within- and between-group covariances, suitably weighted, are combined.

Conceptual, Functional Equivalence. A philosophical approach in which equivalence is argued to exist from the classification of functional groups has been briefly mentioned as the Platonic *species-type* approach. Objects which in dernier cri furnishings are presented as chairs have no visible resemblance to the statistical mode of the chair pattern and may be so called only for functional reasons, namely, that most people deposit the same part of their anatomy on them. This principle of calling concepts psychometrically equivalent when they have only a broad class equivalence is open to abuse, especially by cross-cultural researchers who call concepts the same on face validity without any demonstration of typological similarity by factor measures.

Of the three preceding alternatives the transcultural factor identification is psychometrically sound but does not recognize shades of pattern difference between groups and has never been fed enough data to be used. Provided that the first and third methods are accompanied by objective use of congruence coefficients demonstrating either identity or model grouping of factor patterns across cultures (in a type for each source trait) a logic and an operation exist for recognizing two source-trait influences as identical despite modification of loading across cultures.

Granted that the logic of speaking of the same trait in different cultures is thus settled by a preference for the first and third methods we may turn to the no less difficult problem of measuring levels, as when we say that the population average on anxiety is higher in Poland than in Britain or that spatial ability declines between 18- and 60-year-old groups. The assumption at this point is that two factor patterns on the same variables are similar enough to be considered the same trait yet differ enough not to be identical numerically. They have to be transformed into factor-estimation matrices of weights and applied to the variable scores to give trait scores. The rough and most used way is to average the two weight matrices and apply them to the raw scores, but a desirable refinement is to respect the separate patterns by the equipolent or isopodic estimation method.[5]

One can illustrate the use of questionnaire measures cross-culturally by the simple method that uses the same weighting for all. Two practical

[5] For any of these procedures we get the factor-estimation matrix V_{fe} from the obtained factor pattern V_{fp} by

$$V_{fe} = R_v^{-1} V_{fp} R_f^{-1} \tag{4}$$

where R_v is the correlation among variables (items, subscales, or parcels) and R_f is the correlation matrix among factors. Note that the matrix V_{fe}—the weights to get factors from variables—differs from the reverse regression in V_{fp}—the loadings of factors in estimating variables. Both differ from the correlation of the variables with factors V_{fs}. It is possible for an item to have zero loading on a factor and yet correlate positively with it and have a useful weight in estimating the factor.

Factor scores are then obtained by this V_{fe} from the individuals' scores thus

$$S_f = S_v V_{fe} \tag{5}$$

where S_f is the $N \times k$ factor and S_v an $N \times n$ variable score matrix.

The justification for comparing these across cultures is basically that the groups are thrown into the same standard scores for variables and that a common factor analysis has been done.

The correction for equipotency takes the two sets of weights V_{fe} and corrects them so that the multiple R on the same sigmas is the same for both sets of data. The *isopodic* correction brings the variable raw scores into the same units before applying weights specific to each population corrected to equipotency (see Cattell, 1970a).

steps are, however, necessary. One is making sense of the equivalence of the questionnaire items by a single back-translation or a spiral. This involves x translating the items from language A to B and y tranlating them back until agreement is reached. The other is making sure that the samples from the two cultures are equivalent, either by taking a stratified sample in each (as used in the British-American comparisons in Tables 49 and 53) or by using an equivalent category (university students) in each.

The only extensive data on factored source-trait differences rest partly on equivalent sample categories (students) and partly on stratified samples, on the primaries of the 16 PF and HSPQ and the second-order anxiety factor (IPAT anxiety scale), as well as the IPAT neuroticism scale. Table 53 shows some of these findings. Despite their present limitations of weighting one can recognize at once that the differences found are highly significant and consistent with sociology, history, and quantitative cultural anthropology see Gorsuch, 1973; Rummel, 1970; and others).

A book could be written on these differences, their causes, and their consequences; present space forbids more than superficial comment. Definite differences not tabulated here (but see Cattell, 1946b; Cattell, Eber, and Tatsuoka, 1970) have been found for social class and occupational sub groups. A stimulating beginning in relating these cultural differences, notably on anxiety, to the total culture pattern has been made by Lynn (1971). Allowance for sex difference is necessary in the data from Table 53 before further comparisons are made; moreover the college or high school versus general population needs to be considered (see supplement to 16 PF Handbook for constants). When such comparabilities are reached, the differences are still highly significant on several factors. For example, the Latin countries seem high on protension L; the Chinese are low on ego strength C and high on self-sentiment Q_3; the Australians are high on exvia; the Germans are high on cortertia; and so on. An interesting check, of course, would be to see how far these differences are persistent and consistent at the 16 PF and HSPQ age levels.

9. Summary

(1) The psychologist who would proceed to the next field of questionnaire use—cross-cultural comparison of structure—is arrested by apparently chaotic findings about structure in our own culture. Accordingly I have first focused attention on differences of findings among laboratories, exponents of methods and theories, and constructors of questionnaire scales.

(2) Current debates concern largely the correct number of primary factors (since 1950 I have stood by 22 or 23; 3 to 10 are taken out by other studies; up-to-date methods confirm 23); the concepts generated by unique rotational resolution; and the capacity of the items in published scales to measure validly the source traits thus defined. The attainment of clear and negotiable findings capable of settling these issues calls for attention to eight points in the design and execution of factor-analytic experiments. Most

questions of method, either neglected or raised as if new by recent inconsistent results, were discussed and clarified 20 years ago.

(3) A great majority of the alternative solutions fail in mutual congruence and in congruence with the core of programatic work by some 40 investigators exhaustively examined here. A systematic check on their experimental formulations (Table 45) shows that they have failed to meet not only one but usually several of the eight requirements. The technical omissions are mainly: failing to apply an objective test for number of factors; using unities instead of communalities; using orthogonal automatic rotation programs or failing to demonstrate pursuit of simple structure to a maximum (and significant) hyperplane count; and failing to apply coefficients for congruence (invariance of the asserted source-trait pattern) across experiments. Rotation is the crux of all decisions on the nature of factors; it is this which most frequently goes wrong. Moreover pseudo-second orders achieved by underfactoring can never uniquely and invariantly define a factor by rotation. The concepts of extraversion and anxiety were first uniquely defined by Cattell and Scheier in 1959 and 1961 and previous to that time were only semantically defined, even in psychological measurement.

(4) To see what common conclusions might be possible, I have examined the distortions that arise from variations in procedure. My conclusions are fourfold. First, that contrary to the notions of Howarth and Eysenck, factoring the same data by parcel is as good as or better than by item. It leads to the same solutions. Radial parceling, however, is almost essential. Second, that except in oversimplified plasmodes no automatic analytical program and possibly only one automatic topological program reaches maximum, significant simple structure without further aid by rotoplot. Third, that factoring parcels (scales) developed from previous item-factoring does not compel all later simple-structure resolutions to conform to the first, but that with 50 or more scales the alternatives for simple structures are so great that better simple structures can continue to emerge unprejudiced. Fourth and last, that a major cause of disagreement on source-trait concepts is underfactoring, since this prejudices the resolution in favor of appearance of pseudo-secondaries. If we call secondaries projected on variables *grounded secondaries* then underfactoring *strictly produces pseudo-grounded secondaries.*

(5) Since first and second orders have simple structure on items, although with different distributions, rotation can give a mixture of primaries and secondaries. The proportion of the latter has been shown to be largely a function of the degree of underfactoring and slightly of the rotation program. Eysenck's three factors, *P, E,* and *N,* obtained by gross underfactoring, are pseudo-grounded secondaries. Comrey's are an approach to true second orders, being based on FHIDS (his notation) which, as subjectively set-up primaries, cannot give such true second orders as simple-structure primaries. Furthermore, as Gorsuch points out, the absence of any referral to a personality-sphere concept of sampling of variables leaves doubt as to the relative breadth and completeness of Comrey's factors. Howarth's reso-

Table 53

1. National Culture Differences: National Levels of Primary and Secondary Traits

	Sex	N	Primaries A	C	E	F	G	H	I	L	M	N	O	Q_1	Q_2	Q_3	Q_4	Secondaries I	II	III	IV
Australia	M	694	5.1	5.6	5.2	5.6	5.1	4.5	5.7	6.1	5.3	6.1	5.9	5.6	6.6	5.4	5.5	7.61	6.42	5.28	6.80
Brazil	M	1406	5.6	4.7	4.8	3.7	5.6	5.3	6.4	7.6	7.2	5.0	6.5	6.1	6.1	5.5	6.0	3.06	6.63	5.12	7.23
China	M	425	5.4	3.9	3.9	3.8	5.1	4.8	6.1	7.0	6.5	4.6	5.5	6.0	6.2	6.7	4.8	3.92	9.45	4.61	6.63
Germany	M	1000	5.7	6.1	4.9	5.5	5.5	5.4	3.6	5.7	4.9	6.6	5.7	6.5	5.3	7.1	4.4	4.84	5.04	7.60	6.61
India	M	100	4.6	2.6	3.4	3.5	5.0	4.8	2.4	5.5	5.0	4.2	4.6	5.3	4.7	4.6	3.9	3.96	6.44	4.91	4.63
Japan	M	300	4.2	3.3	5.3	3.2	4.5	3.8	6.0	5.9	7.2	5.7	6.7	7.3	6.8	4.6	6.6	3.05	7.38	6.94	7.92

Note: The above results are in stens on American norms so that comparisons are immediate with the U.S.A. mean (5.5). Thus, for example, all countries but Germany are higher than the U.S.A. on anxiety *Q*II. Details and further examples are available in Cattell, Eber, and Tatsuoka (1970).

2. Social Status Differences

	Primaries A	B	C	E	F	G	H	I	L	M	N	O	Q_1	Q_2	Q_3	Q_4	Secondaries I Exvia	II Anxiety
Upper Class																		
Mean	9.32	7.50	15.25	11.27	13.13	13.96	12.00	7.45	9.18	10.82	10.89	10.40	9.35	11.31	11.13	12.90	4.66	6.30
Sigma	3.12	2.11	3.48	3.91	3.94	2.97	4.81	2.99	3.33	2.97	2.40	3.63	2.66	3.24	3.05	4.49		
(N = 199)																		
Lower Class																		
Mean	8.92	6.88	14.93	11.15	12.10	12.88	10.70	7.89	9.53	11.48	10.28	11.15	8.56	12.59	10.82	13.20	4.02	6.68
Sigma	2.73	1.81	3.17	3.33	3.85	3.39	4.41	2.77	3.11	2.77	2.57	3.47	2.48	3.05	2.91	4.22		
(N = 130)																		
Class Higher[a] (U or L)		U			U	U	U			L	U		U	L				

Note: Data from F. J. Ryan (1973) on nonstudent men under sixty years of age. Similar data at the child level by C. W. Jackson (1973) support difference on *B* and *F* (on HSPQ) and add significant U gain on *E*, which has been found before but misses significance in Ryan.

[a] Recorded only if significant at $P < .05$.

British-American Differences in Adults by 16 PF

	A	*B*	*C*	*E*	*F*	*G*	*H*	*I*	*L*	*M*	*N*	*O*	Q_1	Q_2	Q_3	Q_4
British																
Adjusted mean	19.29	14.65	34.19	27.38	28.48	25.38	30.75	16.87	16.11	24.98	19.98	15.04	18.86	20.40	25.96	20.20
SD	5.85	3.47	6.99	7.30	9.23	5.90	10.30	5.76	4.95	5.63	4.80	7.79	4.97	5.76	6.00	9.20
American																
Mean	20.36	14.08	34.69	26.71	28.40	26.88	30.30	18.25	14.78	25.86	19.76	17.60	18.20	18.25	25.24	20.61
SD	6.32	3.72	8.18	6.37	7.45	5.78	10.26	5.75	5.48	6.36	4.37	8.49	4.88	5.78	6.01	9.41
Difference [b]	—1.07	0.57	—0.50	0.67	0.08	—1.50	0.45	—1.38	1.33	—0.88	0.22	—2.56	0.66	2.15	0.72	—0.41
t Value	4.16	3.75	1.56	2.29	0.22	6.04	1.03	5.65								
Significance of									6.03	3.48	1.12	7.44	3.15	8.78	2.83	1.04
Difference P	P<0.001	P<0.001	NS [c]	P<0.05	NS	P<0.001	NS	P<0.001	P<0.001	P<0.001	NS	P<0.001	P<0.001	P<0.001	P<0.01	NS

[b] Positive if British is higher.

[c] NS = not significant.

Note: This comparison of British and American adults, corrected to 30 years of age, gives results in raw scores. The sample sizes are 2118 men and women for British (Saville, 1972) and approximately 9000 for U.S.A.

British-American Differences in Children by the HSPQ

		A	*B*	*C*	*D*	*E*	*F*	*G*	*H*	*I*	*J*	*O*	Q_2	Q_3	Q_4
British	Mean	10.72	7.08	9.12	10.58	9.48	10.28	10.95	9.53	9.31	8.49	8.92	9.41	10.00	11.00
(Mean Age 14.3 yrs.)	SD	3.57	2.01	3.49	3.52	3.51	3.60	3.36	3,65	5.02	3.11	3.35	3.47	3.26	3.49
American	Mean	10.94	6.78	8.76	10.57	8.72	9.67	11.08	9.90	10.37	8.56	9.36	8.79	10.16	10.38
(Mean Age 14.5 yrs.)	SD	3.50	1.96	3.47	3.52	3.28	3.52	3.33	3.55	5.00	3.10	3.37	3.41	3.21	3.46
Difference in Means [d]		—.22	.30	.36	.01	.76	.61	—.13	—.37	—1.06	—.07	—.44	.62	—.16	.62
t Value		2.65	6.43	4.43	0.12	9.45	7.30	1.66	4.37	9.06	0.97	5.62	7.69	2.11	7.63
Significance of Difference	P	<.01	<.001	<.001	NS	<.001	<.001	NS	<.001	<.001	NS	<.001	<.001	<.05	<.001

[d] Sample 1168 girls from Saville and Finlayson (1973) British data and approximately 3500 from latest U.S.A. standardization.

lution and the careful (but underfactored) solution of Sells, Demaree, and Will are a series mixing primary and secondary factors ($k + p$ instead of k factors would need to be extracted to yield a series complete in both). Two decades of research show that secondaries are comparatively easy to discover, and survive poor method of instrumentation although with some distortion. It is the sharp definition of primaries that requires refined technical work and good research designs.

(6) On the basis of these investigations of methodology I conclude that adherence to the indicated standards (especially that of adequate rotation to a plateau on the hyperplane count) is vital and that the best general approach to factored questionnaire scales is by progressive rectification, in which radial parcels or scales are factored repeatedly over different population samples, with progression replacement by extension material at each step of low-loaded by high-loaded items. Even scales aimed at one trait, such as ego strength, can reach their goal only if rotated with markers (hyperplane stuff) for several other factors; thus progressive rectification is a principle of wide utility.

(7) The mutually inconsistent conclusions are due not only to methodological but also to conceptual confusions. Chief among these is that of applying the same itemetric desiderata to arbitrary, homogeneous item scales to scales for broad personality factors as have traditionally applied to arbitrary, homogeneous item scales for concrete criteria. In the former low homogeneity is desirable; and high correlations (above 0.5) with the factor concept are not expected because the concept is broad and because concrete item behavior is almost invariably factorially complex. It is still common to find students instructed that high homogeneity is an ideal in factor-scale construction. (D. Jackson in Buros, 1972, p. 210, refers to low homogeneity or even "moderate homogeneity" as "a serious technical inadequacy.") If a factor scale should show very high-homogeneity items the suspicion should be investigated that a bloated specific factor (Figure 31) sits on top of a true general personality factor, or that, although a single psychological factor, it is one of narrow life reference. In the next decade, as the pursuit of primaries extends beyond the present 23 normals (and 28 with abnormals) one may expect narrower factors to be picked up. At some point such factors must be set aside for taxonomic museums as insufficiently relevant to life criteria. The personality-sphere concept provides a basis for determining relevancy.

Meanwhile the scale construction needs to discover items sufficiently loaded (say, 0.3 to 0.5) on a broad personality factor and yet not too homogeneous. Even when thorough and correct techniques are used in factor-scale construction, progress toward higher-loaded items is slow (Guttman's principle) compared to progress toward scales for concrete specific criteria (or narrow surface traits) easily defined by items of high scale (not factor) homogeneity.

(8) Expectations of constancy of factor pattern need to be enlightened by several seldom discussed concepts. First, factor invariance is to be sought in the factor pattern and not in the correlations of items with the

factors, which vary with factor intercorrelations. Second, constancy of the underlying factor influence calls for a predictable difference on the factor pattern from one population to another. Third, the instability of items, especially their low transferability, is likely to cause the pattern of individual items to oscillate appreciably from one setting to another. Only parcels or scales in which a majority—although a different majority—of the items functions validly in different situations can hope to demonstrate factor invariance.

Furthermore one must recognize the difference between statistical loading changes due to error (of measurement sampling, and selection within a population) from that due to real psychological differences of populations. To get comparable measures despite the latter we must either find items that combine high validity with high transferability (which may take decades of search) or make up a different set of items for each factor for each subculture (sex, age, social class). At this stage of research any claim that a scale has uniformly high validity per item (say 0.5 to 0.6) in diverse groups can only be regarded with skepticism. Yet because of standardization costs a new test for each group is impractical; the best solution is probably to adjust by scoring weights as in the computer-scoring service offered with the 16 PF and HSPQ. These arguments apply almost as strongly to traditional intelligence tests as to personality factors in questionnaires. The belief that intelligence tests are of a higher order of validity than personality tests is obsolete: if experimenters use both forms of the 16 PF (A and B, with 20 to 26 items) they can get an entirely satisfactory validity for the testing time, that is, as good on an average as for an intelligence test of the same length.

(9) Primary and secondary source traits examined by translated items in other cultures are essentially the same in number and pattern as in our own culture. Indeed present data suggest that they modify less with culture than with age or sex. This evidence for common structure of human nature does not indicate, of course, that source traits are genetic patterns; most cultures have basically similar institutions and learning situations that are likely to produce the same environmental mold traits in personality source traits (but not in interests).

This finding opens the way to relatively exact cross-cultural research and to finding universal psychological laws. The danger is not that of throwing together results from different cultures but of making crude measures of a concept in one culture. Thus it is disastrous to generalize about extraversion-introversion from all measures going by that name. The unique definition of exvia-invia and anxiety, for example, rests on exact determination of the true second-order factors concerned (not on pseudo-grounded second orders); this was achieved (Cattell and Scheier, 1961; Cattell 1950a, 1957) but has not been used in all extraversion or anxiety theorizing since.

(10) Comparisons of trait scores and profiles across cultures presupposes (a) that identity of trait is established, and (b) that score scaling is comparable. The former has three methods: (1) a one-to-one alignment of independent factorings by loading patterns or scores; (2) a joint factor de-

lineation by combining data in a common transcultural, within-group or between-group mean factoring, giving one loading pattern for all groups; and (3) a species-type logic, in which trait patterns are grouped. Comparability of scale score is a complex issue, but two approaches—the equipotent and isopodic—have been proposed (Cattell, 1970a).

(11) Cross-cultural work as yet lacks these refinements, but by "spiral translation" and fixed common-weighting systems it is possible to get roughly comparable estimates on the same primary and secondary factors across national cultural groups. When this is done it is found that highly significant differences of level exist among nations and classes on primary and secondary source traits. Indeed, questionnaires shaped on factored source traits have shown themselves unexpectedly sensitive instruments in revealing difference in age, occupation, sex, and culture (Cattell, Eber, and Tatsuoka, 1970; Angleitner and others, 1972). The results appear to be psychologically meaningful and provide a firm foundation for social-psychological and cultural-anthropological theories employing population personality scores as independent variables explaining group behavior and as dependent variables understood to be the consequences of cultural upbringing and experience.

IX

Questionnaire Psychometric Properties: Test Evaluation and Improvement

A difference of aim between personality researchers and itemetric psychometrists which shows itself constantly in current literature is that the former consider progress to be the establishing of structure, with measurement to follow. The latter concern themselves with the item properties of scales, and provided a scale has validity—and, for some reason, homogeneity—they are not interested in the theory of the structure of that against which it is valid. By contrast, my approach here has so far been that the scientific aim is structure, that preoccupation with scale properties has repeatedly led to neglect of structure, and that valid scales for established source traits will come, in applied psychology, in their own good time.

However, the stage is now reached where it is appropriate in this chapter to deal with the properties of scales and in the next and last with their effective use in applied psychology and research.

1. The Evaluation of Scale Consistency and Validity

The enterprise before us is that of defining psychometric properties to be evaluated, and also of evaluating the distortions and corrections needed in common testing situations. As far as the first is concerned the approach will be broader than that often made to questionnaires because the new concepts used embrace all three media, that is, ratings and objective tests too. These concepts, set out more fully elsewhere (Cattell, 1957, 1964; Cattell and Warburton, 1967), claim to supersede some, such as "concurrent" and "predictive" validity, now in use; to improve the operational definition of others; and to introduce new coefficients of *transferability, utility,* and *efficiency*. The reader must judge for himself whether the new features constitute a more elegant formulation, but at least he must be forewarned to expect some novelties and reconstructions. In such authors as Kleinmuntz (1967), Gorsuch (1973), Horn (1964, 1966a), Nunnally (1970), and Wiggins (1973) these concepts are already entering discussion.

Validity is, of course, the test property of first importance; without it all other virtues, such as reliability, brevity, and a foolproof administration or scoring system, are irrelevant. The generic definition of validity is: *the ability of a test to predict some behavior other than that shown in the test itself*. This other behavior is commonly called the *criterion*. There are three ways in which validity may be conceived. They may be set out as three bipolar *dimensions* (Figure 29) yielding $2^3 = 8$ combinations, each presenting a type of validity coefficient.

The first dimension—degree of abstractness of the criterion—ranges from *concrete* to *conceptual*. The correlation of a test with a score in high school Latin or a 10-year count of traffic court summonses is a concrete, particular validity. But, its prediction of rated invia or of the individual's level on a concept of anxiety is a conceptual validity (sometimes called a construct validity). The layman may ask how one gets a criterion score on so abstract an entity as a concept with which to correlate the test score. Obviously validity would be a fiction without this operation. The answer is that apart from using combinations of conditional selection (Cattell and Warburton, 1967), the concept is defined as a unique unitary factor. Thus the factors of fluid intelligence g_f or affectia *A* or exvia *QI* have to be estimated from many behavioral variables by a conceptual formula that yields a score that can be correlated with any test. Or we can put the test into a total factor analysis and get its correlation with the pure factor directly. A concrete validity is of interest only to an applied psychologist—there is, for example, no concrete performance that can be called the sole expression of intelligence. Tests for research certainly need concept validity, for example, if one is to relate initial anxiety to rate of recovery under therapy or language learning to intelligence. Indeed in many instances where people now talk about concrete validities it would be more correct and lucid to talk of concrete relevancies. No single concrete behavior is the sole criterion except in some special cases (industrial performance and special tests).

The second dimension of validity is *naturalness,* which ranges from an *artificial* to a *naturally occurring* criterion. The former might be an old intelligence test used to validate a new one. Of course even behavior outside the laboratory or test room might be called artificial if it is embedded in culture since culture is artificial. But in the sense used here it is real behavior and part of human history. Artificial thus means designed in the laboratory

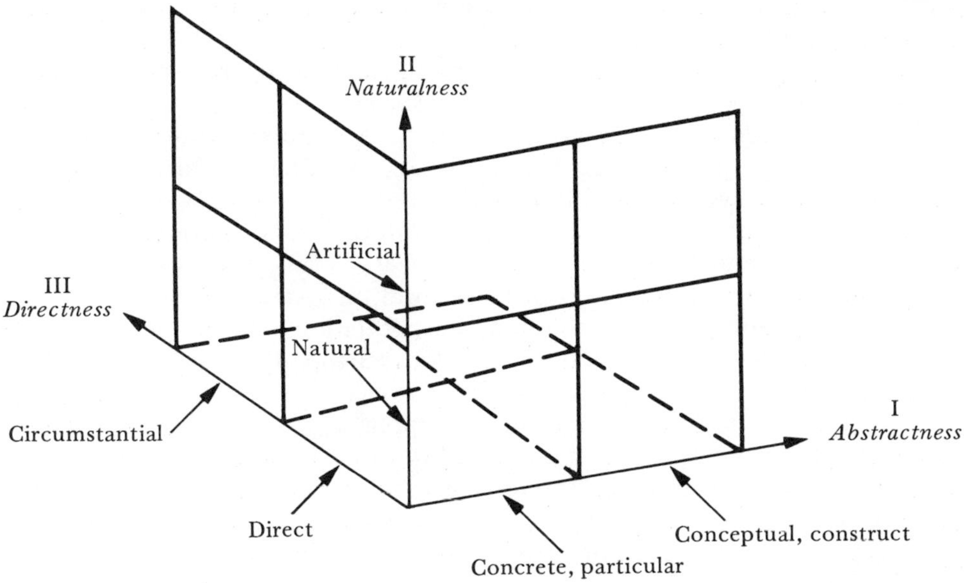

Figure 29. Three parameters of validity and eight validity coefficients. Of the eight forms of validity coefficient, represented by the smaller cubes possible in this cube, direct-conceptual combination validity is most frequently involved in questionnaire validation. The ground floor covers both natural and artificial; although questionnaires cover behavior in situ and are therefore natural, obtaining evidence through a test might be called artificial. However, the implicit criterion is the factor that resides in life behavior. In principle and in practice (Cattell, Eber, and Tatsuoka, 1970), indirect validity is involved in some questionnaires (the 16 PF and HSPQ) as much as is direct validity and hence includes right half of cube. The concrete, particular validities of questionnaires—left half of cube—are discussed in Chapter Ten. However, since no single behavior can represent a factor, they are treated as test relevances rather than as validities. Note that neither so-called content validity nor predictive validity has been included because they are not true validities and permit no coefficient to be calculated for them. Predictive validity applies to a trait (its fluctuation) as much as a test does and is not strictly the validity of a test.

or test room. There is not much use for artificial criterion validities since in correlating one test with another the choice of criterion is always arbitrary and to validate, say, a culture-fair intelligence test against the WAIS is at best the scientific equivalent of a dog chasing its tail.

The third dichotomy of validation is that between *direct* and *indirect* validity. Direct validity is the correlation of the scale or battery with the criterion. Indirect (circumstantial) validity is the degree to which the correlations of the test with a diversified set of reference performances agree with the correlations of the criterion with that same set of reference performances. Typically it is calculated as a correlation between two series of correlations. The concept is new,[1] but preliminary use (Cattell, Eber, and Tatsuoka, 1970)

[1] Fiske's (1971) concept of "extrinsic convergent validity" in the frame of multi-method-multi-trait thinking has been named as an approach to the indirect validity concept. It supposes that different "method" (instrument) components of the test should

suggests that direct and indirect validities are likely to work out at much the same values, as they should.

Consistency—the second of the two general properties of any test—is the *agreement of a test with itself.* As Table 54 reminds us it has three main varieties that are necessary because they correspond to the basic dimensions of the data box (Figure 18, Chapter Seven). That is, consistency is an agreement that can be conceived across test items—homogeneity—across *occasions*—reliability—including across *administrators,* scorers, and other conditions—dependability—and across *subjects*—transferability. This analysis is part of my general analysis of behavioral measurements and their relations in the five dimensions of the Basic Data Relations Matrix (BBRM) or data box (Cattell, 1946b, 1966a; Cattell and Warburton, 1967, p. 36). The five ultimate cartesian coordinates of possible variation are made from the four here by splitting items into stimuli and responses, a refinement unnecessary for tests, where responses are bound indissolubly to stimuli. The idea has been extensively developed in interesting ways by Cronbach, Gleser, Nanda, and Rajaratnam (1972), who use the facet concept but put the emphasis on generalizability rather than on structured factor inference as here.

Homogeneity, the first aspect of test consistency, is familiar to most psychologists in the split-half reliability coefficient and in that useful summary statistic for homogeneity of items, the alpha coefficient (Kuder and Richardson, 1937; Cronbach, 1951), and in the equivalence coefficient between two test forms. The second aspect is primarily given by the test-retest coefficient. For the third and fourth aspects there have been no popular terms. Precise terms, consistently used, become imperative here because the use of "reliability" has deteriorated into several vague and divergent popular approximations. My proposal here is to apply it strictly and only to repeat measurements across occasions (Cattell, 1957). Some people prefer to use reliability as the generic term in place of consistency. This has the disadvantage of making homogeneity a subform of reliability, which in any normal use of the term it is not.

Reliability, defined as test-retest consistency, can be broken down into a whole series of coefficients (Cartwright, 1965; Cattell, 1957) according to the number of the conditions held constant between the two test occasions—the administrator or observer, the time of day, the scorer,[2] and so on. The

---

correlate with the extrinsic criterion in a certain pattern. So far it agrees, but in indirect validity there is the notion that both test and criterion should show the same correlational relations to some third series, as the second order factors and the OAQ scales have the same pattern of correlations with primaries in Table 40. The indirect validity concept thus permits more precise statement and measurement of the validity.

[2] The term *conspection coefficient* has been suggested to apply specifically to the *scoring reliability* of a test. It is derived from *con* and *spectare,* meaning to "look together," and asks what agreement is to be expected between two scorers presented with the same record of subject response. The conspection coefficient is obviously important in bringing to our notice certain diverse test properties. An essay examination or an interview have low conspect reliability, whereas a multiple-choice test might average 0.95 with a typical pair of human scorers and 0.98 with machine scoring (even machines blink).

usage suggested here is to specialize *administrative dependability* for the consistency with maximum change of context. Only the test stays the same, and conditions of time of day, administrator, and so on change, so that one is measuring the dependability of the test over the various conditions it is supposed to meet. Simple dependability is by contrast a reliability when administrator and circumstances are the same. Intrinsic reliability assumes changes in details of the test itself, so that it is evaluating the intrinsic reliability of that type of test.

The varieties of reliability coefficient that could be developed by a logical taxonomy are as numerous as the possible combinations of the four or more sources of possible retest error. At this point we should perhaps pause to head off a few common misunderstandings. First, three of the reliability coefficients—conspect, dependability, and intrinsic reliability—suppose an immediate retest, since if time elapses the trait or state itself may alter. It is best to call the retest after a substantial interval a stability coefficient. A stability coefficient, like the so-called predictive-validity coefficient, cannot be called a characteristic of a test. In such coefficients the value is determined as much by the character of the trait as that of the test. It is important to separate the trait fluctuation from the test unreliability and since we are interested in the latter (Chapters Five and Six handled the former) we must pause to show psychometrically how this can be done.

The habit of thought that the fraction of the variance of y predictable from x is the *square* of the correlation coefficient needs to be watched when we are asking what fraction of the variance is *common* to two forms of a test as inferred from the reliability or equivalence coefficient r_{xx}. In that case r_{xx} unsquared literally states the magnitude of variance common to the two forms. Thus if we let σ_e^2 equal the error of measurement, σ_t^2 equal the true variance of the trait, and σ_f^2 equal the fluctuation or modulability (Cattell, 1971b) of the trait itself, then:

$$r_s = \frac{\sigma_t^2}{\sigma_t^2 + \sigma_f^2 + \sigma_e^2} = 1 - \frac{\sigma_f^2 + \sigma_e^2}{\sigma_t^2 + \sigma_f^2 + \sigma_e^2} \tag{9.1a}$$

which, when all values are in standard scores, that is, the sigma of the scale is unity (s),

$$= 1 - \sigma_{f(s)}{}^2 - \sigma_{e(s)}{}^2 \tag{9.1b}$$

This assumes, as seems reasonable, that stable trait scores t do not for any reason covary with the function fluctuation score component.

The dependability coefficient representing an immediate retest is affected only by error of measurement, so, as just seen above for r_{xx},

$$r_d = \frac{\sigma_t^2 + \sigma_f^2}{\sigma_t^2 + \sigma_f^2 + \sigma_e^2} = 1 - \frac{\sigma_e^2}{\sigma_x^2} \tag{9.2a}$$

If the error of measurement is given as in 9.1b) in units of standard score of the scale itself, then

$$r_d = 1 - \sigma_{e(s)}{}^2 \tag{9.2b}$$

Table 54

Varieties of Consistency Coefficients

Property of Test Examined			*1. Reliability*		*2. Homogeneity*		*3. Transferability*
Name of Coefficient	Dependability Reliability	Conspect Reliability	Intrinsic Reliability	Stability	Scale Homogeneity	Form Equivalence	Transferability over standard populations
Data coordinate over which there is variation	Occasions (ambient stimulus)	Observers (administrators and scorers)	Superficial form (not content) of items	State of subjects	Items or variables within a scale	Two forms of same scale	People (type of subject)
Mode of examining variation in testing operations	Correlation of two occasions with same administrator and scoring	Correlation with different scorers (Administrative dependability when administrators change)	Correlation with same items but different writing style, form of response system, etc.	Long-term retest permitting change of trait and state	Correlation among items, subtests, forms	Correlation of two forms	Pattern-similarity coefficient applied to behavioral-index vectors in factor specification equations
Symbol for specific coefficient	r_{rd}	r_{rc}	r_{ri}	r_{rs} or r_s	r_h	r_e	r_{pt}
Symbol for Corresponding index	d_{rd}	d_{rc}	d_{ri}	d_{rs}	d_h	d_e	d_t

Note: Conspect reliability coefficient is so called from *con* and *spectare,* to look together. It defines agreement between two administrators scoring same test performance. This r_{rc} is unity in selective (multiple-choice) tests, distinctly below unity in an inventive (open-ended) questionnaire, and far from unity in evaluating by interview.

If from these two coefficients—dependability and stability—gathered on the test we wish to ascertain the constancy *of the trait itself,* which has nothing to do with the test, we should seek a coefficient of trait constancy or freedom from fluctuation, r_{tc}, comparing the common and total variance as follows.

$$r_{tc} = \frac{\sigma_t^2}{\sigma_t^2 + \sigma_f^2} = 1 - \frac{\sigma_f^2}{\sigma_x^2} \quad (9.3a)$$

$$= 1 - \sigma_{f(s)}^2 \quad (9.3b)$$

It should be noted one cannot get (9.3b) from (9.1b) and (9.2b) by subtraction, that is, $r_{tc} \neq 1 - (r_d - r_s)$ because the standard score in the case of t is smaller than in the scale s since the former covers only the trait variance. "Unity" does not mean the same unit in (9.1b) and (9.2b) as in (9.3b). Instead of deriving r_{tc} from the observables (9.1a) and (9.2a) by subtraction, we can, however, derive it thus:

$$r_{tc} = \frac{r_s}{r_d} \quad (9.4)$$

Transferability, the third aspect of consistency, is evaluated by a coefficient of transferability that cannot be directly computed. It is a statement of how much the test tests the same things in two different populations. If we want to compare the soundness of two tests in this respect the magnitude of the difference of the populations concerned must be defined in terms of some taxonomy of populations. Reduced to purely statistical terms we might say a given difference is equal to half a standard deviation in a distribution of a population of populations. Transferability is to be calculated by correlating the vector of the *b*s (loadings) from the factorings in typical samples from the two populations. The *b*s may differ thus

$$\begin{aligned} a_{j(1)} &= b_{1(1)}T_1 + b_{2(1)}T_2 + \ldots + b_{k(1)}T_k \\ a_{j(2)} &= b_{1(2)}T_1 + b_{2(2)}T_2 + \ldots + b_{k(2)}T_k \end{aligned} \quad (9.5a)$$

It will be noted that (9.5a) deals only with the k common factors. The degree of similarity of their loadings—the transferability coefficient—can be given quickly as the correlation of their series of loadings, thus

$$r_t = r_{b(1)b(2)} \quad (9.5b)$$

where the *b*s are a series of loadings. However, a decided improvement in calculating r_t would be to use the pattern similarity coefficient r_p instead of r since the former takes account of the *absolute* level of loadings and therefore of the size of the specific.

Instead of comparing just two populations one could advantageously use a broader, but harder-to-get measure by taking the inverse of the variance of the concept-validity coefficient across a standard set of populations (Cattell and Warburton, 1967, p. 49). Whichever form of coefficient or calculation is used there are at present gaps in the technique of evaluating the transferability coefficient (as also in the circumstantial validity coefficient below) in defining the distribution properties on which rigorous statistical inference is to be based, and these gaps await work by mathematical statisticians. The transferability coefficient is a form of test consistency only recently defined and as yet scarcely ever calculated. Yet the degree to which a test continues to test the same thing psychologically in different groups is an extremely important property. The ways to augment its magnitude are insufficiently understood, but in the discussion in the last chapter on use of the same test across the sexes and across cultures I give reasons to expect that a broad spread of behavior in items having a low homogeneity results in higher transferability.

From the aspects of consistency just defined as *homogeneity* and *transferability* above let us turn to the third and last subdivision of consistency, namely *reliability*. As Table 54 reminds us, this is "retest" consistency, and it subdivides into the dependability coefficient, the conspect reliability coefficient, the stability coefficient, and so on according to the conditions that are allowed to alter between the two testings. In the *dependability* coefficient there is an immediate retest (so that the subject cannot alter) with no change of administrator or scorer. But less restricted (and lower) reliability coefficients permit the intrusion of a whole series of sources of possible error (analyzing further the $\sigma_{e(s)}{}^2$ in Equation 9.1b) as shown for the more important of them in

$$1 - r_r = e_p{}^2 + e_a{}^2 + e_b{}^2 + e_s{}^2 + e_r{}^2 \tag{9.6}$$

This equation considers the error to be due to experimental error in the sense of psychological accidents and inattention $e_p{}^2$, error due to the effect of the individual administrator and scorer $e_a{}^2$, error due to the style of item presentation $e_s{}^2$, and error due to poor definition of available responses $e_d{}^2$. (What we have called intrinsic reliability in Table 54 proposes to evaluate $e_s{}^2$ and $e_d{}^2$ for a given item form.) A conceptual analysis of other error sources is given by Cartwright (1965) and Horn (1963, 1971). Cronbach, Gleser, Nanda, and Rajaratman (1972) split what is essentially the unreliability aspect of test inconsistency into still more sources than these, but these five are perhaps the most important. The reliability coefficients which these five errors respectively reduce might usefully be called dependability-reliability (all unchanged but occasion background; hence $e_p{}^2$ and $e_b{}^2$ as error), conspect-reliability (administrators and scorers also changed; hence $e_p{}^2$, $e_a{}^2$, and $e_b{}^2$ as error), and intrinsic-reliability (across administrators), which could be subdivided according to stimulus and response form changes.

Inconsistency (that is, the most generic "unreliability") needs to be evaluated not only by correlations but also by a measure of the shift of mean from occasion to occasion if all effects are to be watched. This can be done by an index (*d* for difference in Table 54) for relative shift of means. Alternatively one could use the intraclass correlation or the pattern-similarity coefficient (see Cattell and Warburton, 1967), each of which gives a single figure expressing the combined effect of shift of mean and of rank (correlation).

2. Validity in Relation to Homogeneity, Reliability, and Test Length

No matter how clearly the distinctive natures of the validity and the consistency coefficients are set out, reports show that it is not possible to avoid their occasional confusion or misuse in applied psychology or in theory. In this section I propose to ward off misunderstandings by illustrating the use of these coefficients with questionnaires. This exposition is aided by the introduction of some refined and widely relevant derivatives of these basic psychometric parameters, called secondary or derived parameters, which have sometimes been mistaken for primary test parameters.

The most common misuses of test consistency are: (a) to confound reliability—for example, as dependability—with homogeneity, (b) to forget that what is *sometimes* called a reliability (dependability) coefficient is truly only a stability coefficient (it is not a dependability coefficient unless the retest is made *soon enough to avoid function fluctuation*), and (c) to employ the wrong form of consistency coefficient in various ensuing calculations; for example, in correcting a validity for attenuation or evaluating the reliability of a test in a test review (D. N. Jackson, 1972).

In regard to the first—homogeneity and its relation to reliability and transferability—the point was made in the last chapter that a questionnaire scale of low homogeneity is likely to have a high validity, assuming that item validity remains constant. It has also been argued that because a test of lower homogeneity tends to sample behavior more widely, it is more likely to maintain its validity across different subcultures and cultures, that is, to reach a high *transferability coefficient*. The reason for wider sampling helping transferability as well as other properties is that a particular behavior described in an item may have different meanings in different cultures, and if all items are alike and from the same narrow life behavior area, instead of attentuating specific distortions, they will accumulate the same intercultural displacement. Consequently, although a high *reliability coefficient* is very desirable for a test, a high *homogeneity coefficient* is not. Indeed, advance in the use of the best test designs is delayed as long as writers continue to confuse these two terms and concepts as in recent reviews by Rorer (1972) and others in Buros (1972). Instead of maximizing homogeneity as, for example, Jackson and Lay (1968) aim to do, test designers need to pursue the more sophisticated concept and harder practical research ideal of an *optimum* value for the homogeneity coefficient.

In regard to scales used as conceptual anchors in this book homogeneity needs to be scrutinized in relation to supposed criticisms of the 16 PF by Howarth and Browne (1971a and 1971b), Levonian (1961), and possibly some less emphatic critics. The misconceptions involved are clarified in Figure 30. Two items *a* and *b* are shown out of many items in a scale for a wanted factor *W*. Each has a validity of 0.7; that is, both are correlated 0.7 with the wanted factor (the criterion) *W* as is shown by the 0.7 projection of the vector for the item on the vertical factor axis. On the second factor *U* (the unwanted, intrusive common factor) each is also loaded 0.7, but now the two items correlate with *U* in opposite directions, so that +0.7 and —0.7 wipe out any loadings of the summed two-item scale thereon. This example illustrates the ideal use of suppressor action upon unwanted factors, which is invoked if not always achieved in the construction of the 16 PF, HSPQ, and other unitractic scales (see below), for example, the CAQ. By adding scores on such items as *a* and *b* we accumulate the contributions to the wanted factor *W* while canceling them on the unwanted factor *U*.

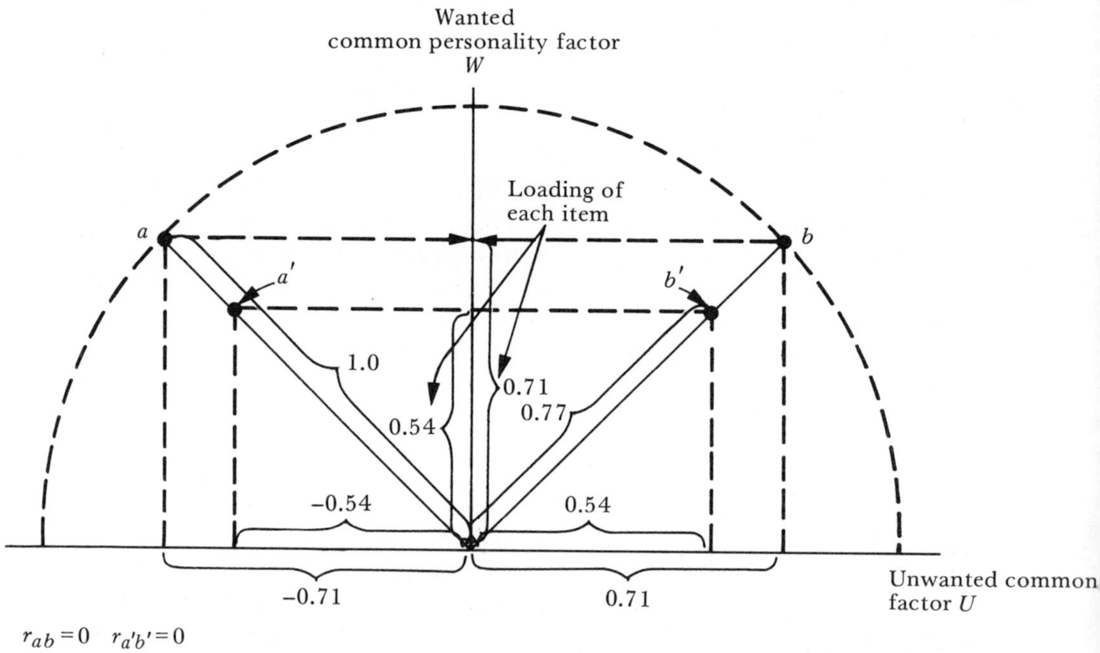

Figure 30. Demonstration of high validity with zero homogeneity. Loadings are as shown. Validity of two-item scale is 1.0 if only two broad factors are involved. If a specific is involved, taking 40 percent of variance and reducing length of item vectors as shown at *a′* and *b′*, then their joint validity is reduced to 0.77, but their correlation remains zero.

The simplification for didactic purposes by taking just two items in Figure 30 in no way upsets the generality of the argument. The first and main simplification in this example is considering that only two common factors account for all the variance in the two items. But if we want to allow for specific factor variance, all we have to do is shorten the test vectors, as shown at points *a′* and *b′*, representing two items with appreciable specific factors in them. In this case the two-item scale maintains suppression of the unwanted factor and zero homogeneity of items but no longer gives full validity on *W*. Next, we show that these arguments are not restricted to this simple illustration of two factors but apply generally to inferences about item homogeneity and validity in any dimensionality. (See also Horn, Wanberg, and Appel, 1973.)

The general principle brought out by Figure 30 is that high scale homogeneity is not necessary for high scale validity. Since the items available for a scale—those showing the best item-factor correlation we can find—virtually always share some other common (unwanted) personality factor besides the wanted common factor, it is necessary to invoke suppressor action. This requires about half the items to load the opposite direction from the other half on each unwanted common factor. In practice (see Table 55) the random tendency to opposite loadings on these other factors will reduce the item homogeneity virtually to zero, and there is no harm if they do. If these items cross-validate well—and as pointed out above under transferability they will tend to produce scales which do so because they are less likely to share a common distortion than highly similar items do—such low homogeneity has many advantages. Moreover, as shown in Figure 31, avoidance of high homogeneity has other advantages. This evaluation of homogeneity runs directly contrary to beliefs descending from classical itemetric scaling as expressed, for example, by well known writers like Loevinger (1959), Jackson (1972), and many routine writers of test reviews. Even without the structured personality test theory propounded here, however, astute practical psychologists, such as Humphreys (1973) regarding World War II test makeup, Horn (1965), Dubois (1970), and Nunnally (1965), have long recognized that test items should "have something but not too much in common." The ideal of low homogeneity also derives directly from the formula for multiple correlation, showing that for the same correlation of items with the criteria a higher R results from lower mutual correlation of items.

A second argument for low homogeneity in a scale for a personality source trait is a purely psychological one: that items should cover a high diversity of situations. Only in this way can one be "fair" to different individuals whose areas of self-expression are somewhat different and also ensure transferability when the test is used with different social groups. Incidentally, this point should not be mistaken for an argument for so-called "indirect" or "associated" measurement—for example, including female sex in a measure of anxiety because women average higher on anxiety. This latter practice generally implies including a measure of factor Y in factor X because factor Y itself happens to correlate with X. In contrast to such mistaken attempts at "validity by association" the "behavioral dispersion" principle simply states that the behaviors of factor X should be sampled widely across the life expressions of X.

Third, since low homogeneity means different specific factors and suppressor action by opposite loadings on unwanted common factors, a connoisseur of tests is wisely suspicious that a test which (misguidedly) advertises high homogeneity is contaminated either with a bloated specific or by items sharing a common unwanted factor. Incidentally, a statistician as such may ask how two variables can share a specific. The limits that define a specific factor, since Spearman's definition, have been simply that no two tests in one matrix share it. But since the introduction of the personality-sphere concept (Cattell, 1946b), the specific factor has acquired an operational basis in keeping with the psychological concept of something that is behaviorally very narrow.

For example, affectia A and threctia $H(-)$ are broad primary factors respectively of emotionally expressive sociability and generalized timidity; but being fond of Eskimos or being nervous when alone in a particular house can well have specific factors—for example, conditionings—that derive from added specific experiences not themselves an intrinsic part of the broad temperamental primary. However, let us suppose a test constructor takes an item that loads the broad factor but has a specific like the above and then writes it in his questionnaire several times with minor modifications. Thus he might write: "I feel nervous when other people leave me alone in my house," "I feel nervous in my home at the weekend," and so on. He readily obtains that high homogeneity of items for his scale which, by classical itemetric thinking, he is commended for reaching. But he does so by making the items share what is psychologically—and was initially statistically—a specific. Figure 31 shows how the correlations among such items become higher than among those that are uncontaminated by sharing the original specific, now bloated.[3] Stratified sampling from the personality sphere is our initial guard against this sort of thing, but the final verdict comes from sensitive factor analysis revealing the creation of a spurious common factor—a bloated specific—sitting on top of the true general factor.

Considering these comments on homogeneity, the constructor may well ask, "If I get items so highly loaded with the wanted factor that they also correlate mutually to an unduly high degree, should I drop one of them?" Provided the constructor is sure he has eliminated bloated specifics and unwanted common factors, the question becomes a reasonable one. But it still belongs to a never-never land, for, in the hard world of test construction, psychologically acceptable items which load so highly on the wanted factor that they are forced to high mutual correlation are rare. For example, if two items loaded the wanted common factor 0.7 and otherwise loaded only specifics, their homogeneity would be 0.5, which we would consider high. There would nevertheless be no reason to drop one, though it would be better if they loaded oppositely, say 0.7 and —0.7 as in Figure 30, on an unwanted common factor and had zero homogeneity since this would mean that the behaviors are more unlike. Thus, if the wanted factor is superego strength, it would be a good idea to sample it in both social (high F factor) and nonsocial (low F factor) expressions. Real-life behaviors are generally psychologically complex, that is, multifactorial in their determination. Consequently, even with the clearest conceptions of the factor before him, the constructor who makes his items behaviorally concrete (rather than semantically dependent because of a mere stereotype) is likely to get items

[3] The objection in the last chapter to the procedures of Howarth and Browne and Comrey is clarified by this principle. The former, having allowed themselves severely to censure the 16 PF for its low homogeneity set out to compile items of high homogeneity. In Comrey's research, the search for high homogeneity is initially only a piece of scaffolding to produce parcel variables more reliable than individual items. This means that for a given number of items and testing time much less of the personality sphere is covered. One may suspect from the rotational results that it leaves insufficient sampling of the personality sphere to give good rotation. Moreover Comrey does not sufficiently remove the scaffolding. The high homogeneity in the FHIDs is carried over with the second-order factor scales, leaving them excessively homogeneous.

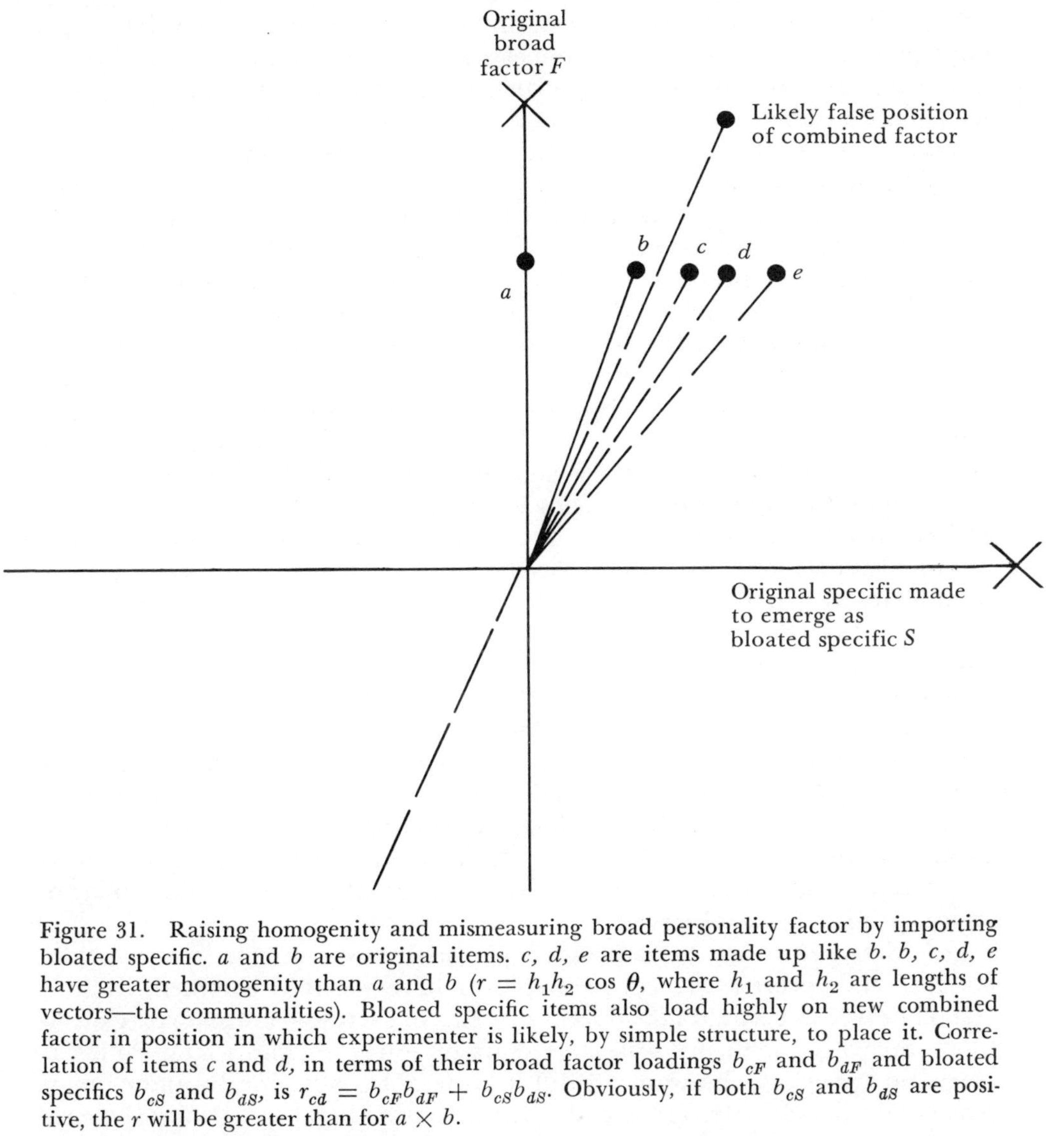

Figure 31. Raising homogenity and mismeasuring broad personality factor by importing bloated specific. *a* and *b* are original items. *c, d, e* are items made up like *b*. *b, c, d, e* have greater homogenity than *a* and *b* ($r = h_1 h_2 \cos \theta$, where h_1 and h_2 are lengths of vectors—the communalities). Bloated specific items also load highly on new combined factor in position in which experimenter is likely, by simple structure, to place it. Correlation of items *c* and *d*, in terms of their broad factor loadings b_{cF} and b_{dF} and bloated specifics b_{cS} and b_{dS}, is $r_{cd} = b_{cF}b_{dF} + b_{cS}b_{dS}$. Obviously, if both b_{cS} and b_{dS} are positive, the r will be greater than for $a \times b$.

that give only moderate (0.3 to 0.4) loadings on the factor and low (0.1 to 0.2) homogeneities. For example, if he asks, "Do you ever examine the coins in your purse to see if any are counterfeit?" instead of "Are you of a suspicious nature?"—he is likely to find that other suspicious behaviors correlate quite lowly with the first item. But high homogeneities can always be easily and spuriously obtained by asking virtually the same question twice or by cashing in on the cultural, semantic, trait framework which sometimes merely imprisons in the errors of folklore. ("Are you anxious on the train?" "Are you anxious in the rain?"). This introduction of what we may call the semantic concept instrument factor, usually a stereotype (see below), is most dangerous in careless observers of self or others.

Returning to statistical consequences of avoiding homogeneity, I must point out a difference of emphasis in experimental aims between the initial factoring to determine the structure of a domain and the subsequent selection of items to produce scales for the structures found. The former should rest on a stratified personality sphere of items, for if one takes the items ultimately built into a scale, explicitly following a policy of maintaining low homogeneity (and other special properties), and factors such an item pool, the selection is likely to make the hyperplanes hard to find. This may be the reason some investigators—for example, Howarth and Browne (1971), Sells, Demaree, and Will (1970)—have not located all the primaries in 16 PF items, though, as I have shown in Chapter Eight, with sufficient care and sensitive methods there is still no difficulty in confirming the structure even after this comparative dispersal of clusters in the original personality sphere pool of items.

The question of exactly what should be considered acceptable item validities and proper homogeneities for a scale of a given number of items and required scale validity in a given field is far more complex than is commonly considered in classical itemetrics or current texts on testing. The complexity is generated on one side by the requirements of what I may call the natural history of the domain (ranging from sociology to genetics, effects of age and sex differences, rate of social change, conventional degrees of self-awareness, and so on) and on the other by the unusual complexity of the purely statistical psychometric laws involved. As to the psychological and sociological realities it cannot be too strongly stressed that progressive rectification (Chapter Eight) of main factor scales by research carried on since after World War II has produced items with loadings that have crept up only gradually to about 0.4 to 0.5. At least this is true of averages across populations and on general source traits when the above sound psychological principles are observed.

Many who wish to construct a personality test in a few months lose patience and revert to poorer principles. I have received comment such as "Good heavens, it would take dozens of items of such low mutual correlation to get anywhere with my scale and years of search to find them!" This is true, and test users who want a valid, transferable, behaviorally rather than sematically based scale, for a truly broad personality factor, must be prepared to take the testing time to apply "dozens" (three dozen at any rate) of items for one scale. Similarly test constructors will need to sift by factor analysis hundreds of items to get those having validity despite high diversity. Perhaps the distinction has not sufficiently sunk into the minds of psychometric students between *conceptual* validity against a broad temperamental trait concept and the more familiar *concrete* validities in the applied field against some relatively specific performance. Interitem correlations (homogeneities) of 0.7 to 0.9 can doubtless be readily obtained against such concrete external criteria as in "Would you consider yourself in the upper income bracket?" or "Do you play tennis a lot?" with corresponding high validities. But if investigators make such claims for important broad factors in personality then almost invariably they have allowed the above artifacts and bloated specifics to aid the appearance of their tests. If one approaches even so well-founded a factor as general intelligence—by questionnaire self-evaluative items, not tests—the item validities are only around 0.2 to 0.4 just as for a broad personality source trait. Moreover, as we shall see, even the 0.4 item validities well established for use in one population virtually disappear for certain individual items (but not for the whole scale) when used on a population differing somewhat socially or in age or sex. What can normally be expected in a well-researched personality test is shown in Table 55, which covers both general adults (Cattell, 1972e) and student populations (Burdsal and Vaughan, 1973).

Table 55

Homogeneity and Validity Levels Illustrated in 10- and 13-Item Primary Factor Scales from Student and Adult Groups

(a) 240 Students Aged 18–22

Dominance E												*Item*	*Correlation with Factor*
												1	37
17												2	41
08	10											3	33
15	05	16										4	21
05	16	03	04									5	13
16	09	05	02	−02								6	04
14	14	09	15	02	03							7	22
13	06	05	04	13	20	08						8	53
09	08	−00	−00	07	−03	02	−00					9	11
−00	06	−03	00	−02	18	02	13	06				10	31
−00	06	−03	02	24	−03	−01	14	13	06			11	08
02	01	01	10	13	10	00	16	07	31	15		12	32
09	10	05	11	07	05	14	19	00	10	09	13	13	31

R scale validity by weighting = 0.84. Mean item validity = 0.26. r_{sw} scale validity by Formula (9-11) = 0.67.

Ego Strength C												*Item*	*Correlation with Factor*
												1	19
−02													
11	−06												
24	07	−02											
17	07	05	11										
10	16	−08	17	34									
28	15	−15	22	30	36								
07	00	05	04	05	04	19							
06	11	−02	00	04	05	08	07						
15	05	09	15	17	23	24	04	09					
13	03	02	01	08	02	13	21	41	05				
25	−02	15	00	07	03	05	−07	05	11	11			
23	−06	03	11	12	08	13	16	13	08	22	13		

R scale validity by weighting = 0.96. Mean item validity = 0.15. r_{sw} scale validity by Formula (9.11) = 0.41.

Table 55 (Cont.)

Self-Sentiment Q_3									*Item*	*Correlation with Factor*
									1	24
03									2	16
–01	16								3	15
–05	03	05							4	11
–06	–07	–01	09						5	22
06	13	12	16	06					6	49
–00	01	01	00	08	–02				7	02
06	09	19	02	–01	18	09			8	51
–10	01	18	10	12	11	00	14		9	25
01	–00	12	07	–01	18	–05	08	08	10	28

R scale validity by weighting = 0.76 (for 13 items R would be 0.78). Mean item validity = 0.24. r_{sw} scale validity by Formula (9-11) = 0.63.

(b) 780 Adults Aged 18–60

Parmia H												*Item*	*Correlation with Factor*
												1	45
29												2	53
26	10											3	26
09	16	–00										4	15
17	26	10	15									5	37
16	21	12	06	22								6	25
18	11	14	19	19	17							7	23
34	28	30	–01	13	10	07						8	52
22	23	18	05	14	03	03	28					9	42
20	15	29	08	15	10	10	31	21				10	36
19	16	10	08	02	–10	–00	17	18	14			11	29
13	26	17	06	23	19	08	23	14	22	08		12	42
10	10	15	–09	05	06	01	18	20	14	11	10	13	23

R scale validity by weighting = 0.79. Mean item validity = 0.34. r_{sw} scale validity by Formula (9-11) = 0.75.

Ego Strength C												*Item*	*Correlation with Factor*
												1	48
11												2	16
–03	03											3	10
15	13	04										4	18
15	11	02	19									5	26
12	04	08	10	14								6	17
06	05	01	–02	10	22							7	18
06	04	00	01	04	04	07						8	34
–08	–13	05	–09	–04	01	05	05					9	04
17	13	–11	00	08	08	16	09	–02				10	16
06	00	–05	09	–02	01	06	08	25	10			11	12
23	12	03	09	07	14	17	17	–09	27	08		12	27
02	07	16	03	10	07	03	06	13	01	14	01	13	21

R scale validity by weighting = 0.56. Mean item validity = 0.21. r_{sw} scale validity by Formula (9-11) = 0.55.

Table 55 (Cont.)

Self-Sentiment Q_3									*Item*	*Correlation with Factor*
									1	13
05									2	22
09	09								3	38
08	11	06							4	27
07	20	15	28						5	40
12	04	10	22	14					6	28
12	18	03	35	23	31				7	34
03	08	10	13	13	06	12			8	25
04	15	10	20	19	08	29	15		9	25
00	11	10	02	10	05	02	−03	−00	10	23

R scale validity by weighting = 0.61 (for 13 items R would be 0.67). Mean item validity = 0.28. r_{sw} scale validity by Formula (9-11) = 0.61.

Note: When factor C is compared for adults and students, item by item the validities alter appreciably: two even swing into the negative. But the scale as a whole retains acceptable validity—for a 13-item scale.

As to the purely psychometric and statistical interrelations of validity and homogeneity, classical itemetrics has hitherto not grappled very effectively with the real complexity of the problem. Particularly it has not embraced the full variety of conditions—test structure conditions—that have to be specified before lawful regulations can be stated among such parameters as scale validity, item validity, homogeneity, size of common and specific factors, degree of suppression of unwanted common factors, and relative numbers of factors and items involved in the scales. I propose here to scan the roster and the relations of these essentials, but illustratively rather than comprehensively since what I call *structured test psychometrics* would require a book.

Psychometrists are often primarily concerned to relate the validity and reliability of a scale to the properties of the items in it. But the interdependencies of variables and the practical aims of construction are such that prediction of other properties than validity and reliability as dependent variables may sometimes be required. In any case, the following are the "characters in the play"; among them, relations are sought.

Properties of the Scale as Such

- r_{sw}: the validity of the given scale s against the given factor w
- R_{sw}: the validity of the given scale s against the given factor w when weighted item scores are used in a multiple R
- r_d: the dependability reliability of the scale
- n: the number of items
- k: the number of common factors spanned by the items
- p: the effectiveness of suppression of unwanted common factors in the scale as a whole (not by single items or single factors); a simple index for this can be suggested here:

$$p = \frac{n(k-1) - \sum^{k\text{-}1} (\Sigma^n r_{ju})^2}{n(k-1)} \tag{9.7}$$

where r_{ju} is the correlation of item; with some unwanted factor u. Since complete suppression gives $(\Sigma^n r_{ju})^2 = 0$, it then yields $p = 1$ (compare Chandler, 1961). But this suppression coefficient (p) cannot descend to zero. $h_{sw}{}^2$, $h_{su}{}^2$, and $s_s{}^2$ have the meanings for the scale s corresponding to those of the item j below.

Properties Related to Items

r_{jw}: the validity of an item (its correlation with factor w)

r_{jm}: the correlation of any item j with any other item m

$h_{jw}{}^2$: the wanted factor variance on an item ($r_{jw}{}^2$)

$h_{ju}{}^2$: the variance of an item on unwanted factors (note that h is the symbol used here since this is communality as far as the unwanted factors are concerned, and for uniformity h is also used with wanted factor so that $h_j^2 = h_{jw}{}^2 + h_{ju}{}^2$)

s_j^2: the specific and error factor variance on item j

In structured psychometrics, as contrasted with itemetrics, something more than or different from the simple assumption of equal validity of items and uniform homogeneity of items is commonly required to specify the full structural quality of the scale. Two main structural models are important here, although a third is necessary for comprehensive coverage: (I) the Exclusively Common Factor Model (ECF), in which items have no specifics, so that for any item j:

$$h_{jw}{}^2 + h_{ju}{}^2 = 1 = \sigma_j^2 \tag{9.8}$$

(II) the General Model (so called because it is most widely applicable and can include I as a special case), where specific factors are also admitted, thus:

$$\sigma_j^2 = h_{jw}{}^2 + h_{ju}{}^2 + s_j^2 = 1 \tag{9.9}$$

This model does not permit complete suppression since loading on the specific, which is also "unwanted," occurs once only and cannot be neutralized.

A model III, which may also be considered a special case of II, is another logical possibility in which $\sigma_j^2 = h_w{}^2 + s_j^2$. This corresponds to a set of items constituting what I define (Section 3 below) as a unique univocal (in contrast to a unitractic) scale. However, this model is essentially unattainable in practice in personality measurement for reasons given below. Model II deals with what can be realistically achieved in well-designed scales and therefore receives our main attention, though the comparative simplicity of I justifies discussing it as an exercise—especially in understanding suppressor action—before we approach II. Incidentally, the argument that all specifics are as yet undiscovered broad factors, which would seem to justify staying with I, does not in fact justify using I since suppression is impossible as long as they remain specifics. Similarly the argument is that a situation where complete suppression of unwanted factors is achieved justifies the simplicity of III is incorrect since suppression of unwanted factors on the scale as a whole does not remove their variance from items but only from scales.

In the present discussion of II, as of I, I set aside r_d from the formulations and therewith in the main approach omit the discussion of accidental error of measurement σ_e^2 as distinct from the specific variance σ_s^2. For appropriate modifications of the equations I reach, such as a correction for attenuation, can always be made subsequently when the dependability coefficient is determined, which is easily done. Even so, the formulations are complicated enough. Indeed, the main fact one needs to keep in mind in seeking the relations of the above dramatis personae of item and scale properties is that *equations of complete mutual determination are possible only if the properties of every individual item are taken into account.* Only limited statements can be made from average values, though, as we shall see, if it can be arranged that there is no dispersion, that is, if all stand at the average, more complete solutions are possible. Thus, in general the only complete statements are in matrix algebra, not ordinary algebra, the former taking account of the property of every item. A specific consequence is that the matrix formulation can also include the assigning of special individual score weights to items whereas the ordinary algebraic formula must assume equal or unit or average weights for all items. The assignment of unequal, specific weights permits scale scores with special properties unattainable by equal weights. Although classical psychometrics—for example in the Spearman-Brown formula and several valuable algebraic formulas in Guilford, Gulliksen, and others—often yields adequate calculations for most simple itemetric uses of tests, the use of factorially structured tests in structural psychometrics, requiring statements about factor validities and so forth, is less easily handled in that way and forces us increasingly to resort to matrix algebra. In short, structured scale psychometrics has to deal with *patterns* among items, and although, as we shall see, the addition of sigma or other distribution values to the mean value may enable somewhat more to be predicted by simple algebra, the only *complete* item-to-scale predictions require the full matrices of item information.

Provided we know V_{fp}, the factor pattern matrix, and R_f, the correlations among the factors, we can estimate almost all scale parameters, and if we add the item score matrix S_v, all scale score parameters (over and above the relational properties above) can also be obtained. For instance, if r_{sw} (scale with wanted factor) is the required value, we calculate R_{vo} (the "reduced" correlation matrix among item variables) as $V_{fp}\ R_f\ V_{fp}'$. Converting R_{vo} to R_v by substituting unities in the diagonal, we can then calculate V_{fe}, the $n \times k$ factor estimation matrix, giving the weights to apply to items to get the best factor score estimate, thus: $V_{fe} = R_v^{-1}\ V_{fp}\ R_f$. Then we calculate $V_{fs}'\ V_{fe}$ (where V_{fs} is the factor structure matrix equal to $V_{fp}\ R_f$—that is the correlations of the factors with items), the diagonals of which are the R_{sw}^2s, that is, the square of the multiple Rs which are the validities of the weighted scale scores. These Rs are the validities reached for each wanted factor in turn (as one goes down the diagonal) when the correct weights are applied.

The other values in this $V'_{fs}V_{fe}$ matrix are, as one for instance goes down the column for factor 1 (dropping from the corner diagonal), the correlations (squared) which the weighting for factor 1 gives with the other, unwanted factors. Each value is the inner product of the vector of correlations of the items with the given unwanted factor multiplied by the weights which the wanted factor assigns to them and is thus the extent to which the unwanted factor is included in the score for the wanted factor. If we call these misweighted contributions to the score S_{u1}, S_{u2}, and so forth, then the obtained score for S_w can be considered to be made up of S_w and S_{u1} and S_{u2} and . . . The corresponding variance contributions are R_{wt}^2 and R_{wu1}^2 and R_{wu2}^2 and . . . ., where the subscript *wu* means the weights of the wanted factor applied to the unwanted factor. These off-diagonal values offer, therefore, another avenue to calculating p, the index of suppression in equation (9.7). There the items are unweighted, so it would require only that we substitute a V_{fe} with score key values of 1 and 0 to get an equivalent to it in terms of the present approach through the magnitudes of the multiple *R*s with the unwanted factors.

Matrix calculations thus give all required properties—validity, suppression, and so forth—precisely determined for any particular scale in a nutshell; but although they also give a sense of general principles to those who think in matrix terms, they still leave most psychologists hankering for the insightful generalizations that we grasp more readily in ordinary algebraic equations: namely, the statistical laws relating *average* values of item parameters and scale parameters. For example, one would like to know how fast scale validity increases with average item validity at each size of scale (n) when homogeneity is held constant. Or at a fixed validity and number of items, how does average homogeneity change as average item-factor correlation is increased? Since, as we shall see below, these generalizations can be made only to a limited degree and with special assumptions it would be useful to practicing psychometrists—though perhaps not as edifying as theoretical statisticians would like—if some researcher would generate curves and functions from the above matrix methods for the domain of most naturally occurring values by Monte Carlo methods. That is to say, he would use matrix algebra processes on plasmodes made up to represent the typical means and ranges of item validities, homogeneities, scale factor structures, suppressor actions, communalities, numbers of items, and so forth in common use and set out tables or approximate functions giving empirical guidance to test constructors.

Meanwhile I proceed further algebraically here. One important generalization—that in equation 9.11 below—can be made with few assumptions, but to get still further one must adopt certain simplifying assumptions, principally that all items in the scale stand at the same r_{jw} value (have the same validity: the mean) at the same homogeneity with every other item r_{jm} and with complete suppressor action on unwanted common factors—that is, $p = 1$. To have these properties, however, scales must have quite special structural properties, which can nevertheless be sufficiently approximated in practice to make the formulations useful. Chief among these structural properties which we have to recognize is that for all items to have equal correlation with the wanted factor, equal correlation with each other (homogeneity) and complete suppressor action, a necessary (but not sufficient) condition is that there must be *at least as many common factors as items.* Space is not taken for a formal proof here because the illustrations suffice to convey it for those familiar with matrix factor theorems. That the condition is not impracticable is shown by such questionnaires as the 16 PF HSPQ, G-Z, and CAQ, where in one form there are usually 10 to 12 items for one factor scale, but as many as 12 to 18 common factors on which most of these items have some projection. Usually the loading is quite small on any one of the unwanted factors, but it is enough to offer the possibility of the balancing, and so forth, required.

Illustration will now be pursued by the small numerical examples in Figure 32(a). Since the reader has hitherto seen the suppression effect only geometrically, let us start with a simple case of four items in which there are equal and opposite loadings on each unwanted factor, as in Figure 30. In order to introduce this case in matrix form so as also to illustrate zero correlation of items, we are compelled to take seven factors in Figure 32(i) and (ii), and of course one cannot in calculation take seven factors from four item variables so this must be considered an artificial case or fragment from a larger matrix. On squaring the (orthogonal) loadings along each row ($0.5^2 + 0.5^2 + 0.5^2 + 0.5^2 = 1.0$) we have communality of unity for any item, so that we are in Model I (Exclusive Common Factor). The inner products of each pair of rows, yielding the item correlations, all are zero—for example, $r_{12} = 0.5 \times 0.5 + 0.5 \times -0.5 + 0.5 \times 0 - 0.5 \times 0 = 0$. On taking the validity as correlation with the factor as r_{sw}^2 equal to predicted variance/total variance, we have $r_{sw}^2 = \dfrac{(4 \times 0.5^2)}{1} = 1$. The example thus illustrates that four items with zero homogenity, each correlating 0.5 with the factor, can give a scale of perfect suppression and perfect validity by Model I.

Before returning to Model I in a more ordinary example, less contrived for simplification, note in (ii) what happens when we switch to Model II, as represented in general form in (9.9), where the scale on any item a_j breaks down into commons and a specific:

$$a_j = b_{jw} F_w + b_{ju1} F_{u1} + \ldots + b_{j\,(k-1)} F_{u(k-1)} + b_{jk} F_k \qquad (9.10)$$

taking in this case a loading of 0.7 on the specific factor in each case. The common factor variance must then shrink to a communality of $h^2 = 0.5$, and we shall let the shrinkage from (i) to (ii) be proportional on all values. Then the homogeneity of the scale is still 0, but the correlation of each item with F_w is 0.35. Consequently the square of the validity coefficient is $4 \times 0.35^2/1$, which equals 0.5, giving a validity of 0.71. Thus even perfect suppression does not bring perfect validity when specific factors are present.

For simplicity of illustration the suppressor action in (i) and (ii) has used the immediately obvious balance of unwanted loadings ($+0.5 \times -0.5$

(i) Total suppression: Simplified by more dimensions: Model I

Item	F_w	F_{u1}	F_{u2}	F_{u3}	F_{u4}	F_{u5}	F_{u6}	h^2
1	0.5	−0.5	0.5	−0.5				1.0
2	0.5	0.5			−0.5	0.5		1.0
3	0.5		−0.5		0.5		−0.5	1.0
4	0.5			0.5		−0.5	0.5	1.0

$r_{sw} = 1 \quad r_{jm} = 0$

(ii) Total suppression: Simplified by more dimensions: Model II with specifics

Item	F_w	F_{u1}	F_{u2}	F_{u3}	F_{u4}	F_{u5}	F_{u6}	h^2	$S1$	$S2$	$S3$	$S4$
1	0.35	−0.35	0.35	−0.35				0.5	0.7			
2	0.35	0.35			−0.35	0.35		0.5		0.7		
3	0.35		−0.35		0.35		−0.35	0.5			0.7	
4	0.35			0.35		−0.35	0.35	0.5				0.7

$r_{sw} = 0.7 \quad r_{jm} = 0$

(iii) Total suppression: Appropriate scale dimensionality: Model I (three items)

Item	F_w	F_{u1}	F_{u2}	h^2
1	0.8	0.6		1.0
2	0.8	−0.3	0.52	1.0
3	0.8	−0.3	−0.52	1.0

$r_{sw} = 1 \quad r_{jm} = 0.46$

(iv) Total suppression: Appropriate scale dimensionality: Model I (four items)

Item	F_w	F_{u1}	F_{u2}	F_{u3}	h^2
1	0.5	0.82	−0.29	0	1.0
2	0.5	−0.41	−0.29	0.7	1.0
3	0.5	−0.41	−0.29	−0.7	1.0
4	0.5	0	0.87	0	1.0

$r_{sw} = 1 \quad r_{jm} = 0$

(v) Total suppression: Model II with specifics

Item	F_w	F_{u1}	F_{u2}	F_{u3}	$S1$	$S2$	$S3$	$S4$	h^2
1	0.4	0.66	−0.23	0	0.6				0.64
2	0.4	−0.33	−0.23	0.56		0.6			0.64
3	0.4	−0.33	−0.23	0.56			0.6		0.64
4	0.4	0	0.69	0				0.6	0.64

$r_{sw} = 0.8 \quad r_{jm} = 0$

Figure 32 (A).

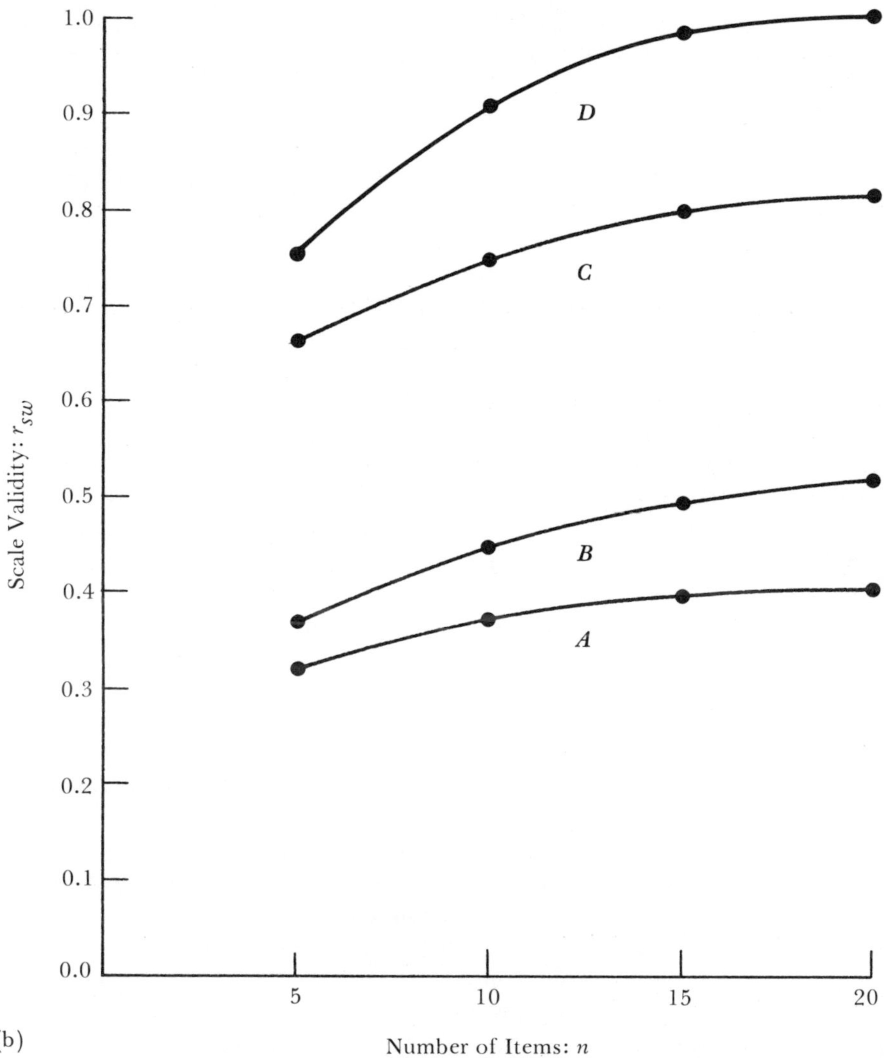

Figure 32. Relations of item and scale parameters: (a) Illustrations; (b) plot of relations of r_{jw}, r_{jm}, and n under special assumptions. Curve A: $r_{jw} = 0.2$, $r_{jm} = 0.2$. Curve B: $r_{jw} = 0.2$, $r_{jm} = 0.1$. Curve C: $r_{jw} = 0.4$, $r_{jm} = 0.2$. Curve D: $r_{jw} = 0.4$, $r_{jm} = 0.1$.

or $+.35 \times -0.35$) as in Figure 30, but with the idea clarified we can now turn to the more general, less obvious case which requires only that the loadings in each column of an unwanted factor (for perfect suppression) sum to zero, not necessarily with equal, balanced values throughout. In this case we do not need the artificiality of a fragment matrix with more factors than items, as in (i) and (ii), but need only to meet the limiting condition defined by our principle above of having as many factors as variables. Thus in (iii) we have built for illustration a three-item and in (iv) a four-item scale. By summing columns the reader will find that there is perfect suppression, and by multiplying rows he will find that the homogeneity is respectively $r = .46$ and $r = 0$. In both cases the validity is perfect, and to show the alternative basis of calculation by covariance/product of standard deviations, we set it out:

$$\text{(iii)}\ r = \frac{3 \times 0.8}{1 \times \sqrt{3 + 3 \times 2 \times 0.46}} = 1.0$$

$$\text{(iv)}\ r = \frac{4 \times .5}{1 \times \sqrt{4 + 4 \times 3 \times 0}} = 1.0$$

(The calculation of the scale sigma in the denominator is as $\sqrt{n + n\ (n - 1)\ r_{jm}}$—that is, it is the root of the variance of n unit variance items plus their covariance, the latter depending on their intercorrelation r_{jm}.)

The reduction of this validity when specific factors are introduced, as was done in (iii), can be seen by adding specifics of any value (same for all) and reducing the common loadings proportionately. Incidentally, a deceptive line of reasoning sometimes encountered suggests that even with specifics a perfect validity can be reached. Let us consider two items like a' and b' in Figure 30, but loading 0.316 (instead of 0.54 as in the figure), the square of which is 0.10. Then ten such vectors can be set up which correlate zero in 10 space, and the simple sum of their variance will be 1.0, accounting for all variance of the criterion. This "solution," however, belongs to the class of visual illusions, for in order to retain this projection on the wanted factor, with zero correlation, in 10 dimensions the vectors would have been extended, with each new dimension added, ultimately to unit length—that is, having no longer a specific.

Looking at the symmetrical and nonsymmetrical loadings in unwanted factors in Figure 32, one may wonder what range and variety is possible while the conditions for complete suppression are still met. If one originally has balance—complete suppression—in the unwanted factor space, one can cut off that space from the wanted—that is, take all columns to the right of the first, and spin these axes in any way without losing the balance of loadings on each. (This might be called a special case of the principle in Harman, 1967, p. 354.)

A comparison of the calculation above for (iii), which has a homogeneity of 0.46, and (iv) of zero (when the same weight is given in each to specifics) brings out clearly that for the same constituent item correlation with the factor r_{jw}, the scale with the lower homogeneity has a better validity because the denominator increases more rapidly when there is positive correlation among the items.

Cattell and Tsujioka (1964) put this in general terms, using average homogeneities $\overline{r}_{jm}$ and average factor-item correlations $\overline{r}_{jw}$, dropping the restriction here that all items must be at the *same* r_{jm} and r_{jw} value (with as many factors as items).

$$r_{sw} = \frac{n\bar{r}_{jw}}{\sqrt{n\left[1 + (n-1)\,\bar{r}_{jm}\right]}} \tag{9.11}$$

Since this general itemetric scale-validity-item property formula, as we may call it, turns out to be just the same as the structured scale validity formula explained in our arithmetical examples above (and, incidentally, is consistent with Guilford's formula for the effect on validity of extending a scale), one may well wonder what the importance and specific effect of the structural restrictions above: k = n, symmetry of suppression, and zero sigma of r_{jw} and r_{jm} are. (The Cattell-Tsujioka weighted version of the above (1963) is also consistent with the matrix algebra solution. The unweighted (9-11) calculation in general underestimates validities as obtained by the full matrix solution, as can be seen from comparison of values for the six factor scales in Table 55.)

The answer is relatively subtle. Equation 9-11 does not get us into trouble when the conditions of no variance of r_{jm} and r_{jw} values (all values at mean), of symmetry of suppression, and of equal communality of items are maintained, as in our special model above, possible when $k = n$. It is also true independently of what the communality magnitudes may be. (For it can be derived in such a way as to pass through the expression

$$\frac{\Sigma h_j r_{jw}}{\sqrt{\Sigma h_j^2 + 2\Sigma\Sigma h_j h_m r_{jm}}}$$

at which point one sees the communality canceling out—no matter what its size.) But without these restrictions—that is, when (9-11) is applied to Models I, II, or III without these structural requirements being added—r_{jm}, r_{jw}, and n are not truly independent variables. If one has values obtained in an empirical case, they can safely be inserted. But if one plays with insertion of quite independently chosen r_{jm}, r_{jw}, and n values, one is likely to run into absurdities because other functions connect r_{jm}, r_{jw}, and n—functions which depend on the relation of k, the number of factors to n, the number of variables, and the distribution of the r_{jw} and r_{jm} values around their means. In fact, Hunter (1973) has rightly pointed out that the attempt to treat r_{jw} and r_{jm} as truly independent values, followed in classical itemetric theory, using the unstructured version here, results in absurdity.

Elsewhere (Cattell and Tsujioka, 1963) curves have been set out relating n, r_{jw} and r_{jm} at the point where complete validity exists (and, therefore, specifics vanish) in a formula as follows derived from (9.11).

$$n = \frac{1 - \bar{r}_{jm}}{r_{jw} - \bar{r}_{jm}} \tag{9.12}$$

However, as Hunter points out, this formula is subject to the restriction that

$$\bar{r}_{jm} = r_{jw}^2 - \frac{\Sigma^k \ \sigma_{r_{jw}}^{\ 2}}{n-1} \tag{9.13}$$

that is, the distribution of r_{jw} must also enter into the calculation from (9-12).

The curves set out in Figure 32(b) illustrate the same truth—that if one uses the general scale item property relations, one may get into unreal domains, or, at last, into unstated changes of the model. In this case there appears to be only one such because the values of r_{jw}, r_{jm}, and n are deliberately chosen to apply to what are known to be obtainable and commonly obtained values in practical factor scale construction today. (In fact they span the central empirical ranges of Table 55.) However, at 15 items, with an r_{jw} of 0.4 and an r_{jm} of 0.1, one already reaches perfect validity, which can be possible only if our values have forced the structure to change from Model II (with specifics) to Model I (exclusively common factors). Since we know this change is unattainable in practice, that part of the curve is imaginary. Incidentally, however, the remaining curves show that with the presently attained r_{jw} and r_{jm} values in many 16 PF and HSPQ scales, 20 to 30 items (as with Forms A and B together) are capable of approaching very high validities, even without weighting.

The mutual dependence of the entries in equation (9-11) discussed above can be seen in general terms from our introductory discussion, for once the two conditions break down and k becomes less than n, an increase in n crowds more items into the factor space. It is no longer possible, with the same r_{jw} value, to keep the value of r_{jm} (the homogeneity) down, nor can one maintain all items at the same mutual correlation magnitude—that is, no random r_{jm} any longer normally equals r_{jm}. Or, in another relation, if n is held constant and r_{jw} is increased (again with fixed inadequate k), then r_{jm} tends to increase. Thus although (9.11) is a true statement of the relations that exist between scale validity and item properties in any empirical data, we are not free to construct hypothetical cases by entering into it any combinations of $\overline{r}_{jw}$, $\overline{r}_{jm}$, n, and so forth, that we choose.

In certain contexts the issue of the relation of communality (or specificity) to validity comes to the fore. For example, how valid are test scales likely to be when we have to take items from factor matrices with communalities down to 0.4? The size of the specific factor interests the test constructor in other ways—namely, concerning the psychological role that he is giving in source trait estimation to particular idiosyncratic conditionings, to biographical incidents in childhood (as in Freudian trauma), and to culture-geographical backgrounds. ("Do you remember an inn in the High Pyrenees, Miranda?").

As pointed out, our root equation 9.11 holds regardless of the level of h. The effect of increased specificity—increased h^2 (see Figure 30)—is to reduce r_{jw}^2 and r_{jm}^2 while maintaining their fixed ratio. If it seems surprising —since h^2 *does* affect the scale validity—that neither the magnitudes of specifics nor the unwanted common factor magnitudes enter into (9.11) and so forth, one should reflect that what they do is already expressed in the sizes of r_{jw} and r_{jm}. The correlations, on the one hand, and the factor structure figures (including h^2), on the other, are, largely, alternate ways of saying the same thing. They are not exhaustively equivalent because the factor structure says something more than the correlations do—for example, it describes the rotation. As usual, one can best initially observe the effect of a parameter by taking a restricted or simplified case—for example, that of $r_{jm} = 0$ with maximum suppression of unwanted factor. Then

$$r_{sw} = \frac{n\bar{r}_{jw}}{\sqrt{n^2\bar{r}_{jw} + \bar{n}s^2}} \qquad (9.14)$$

which shows that for a given r_{jw} a larger specificity reduces scale validity. It also shows that by continuing to add items with different specifics—and the same wanted factor loading—we at best only *attenuate* the effect of specifics and prevent any one from giving a major "prejudice" to our factor scale. The indefinite increase of n, at a fixed degree of specificity in each item, can never yield a perfectly valid scale, but asymptotally approaches a limit—less than 1.0—as n becomes infinite.

It is of interest also to work out the relations in the subworld of r_{jw}, r_{jm}, and h values. This problem proves to be difficult since it depends on the dimensionality of the scale, but we have worked out expressions for what we have above defined as the structural symmetrical scale, for two and three dimensions, as follows. For two dimensions,

$$\bar{r}_{jm} = 2\bar{r}_{jw} - h_j^2 \qquad (9.15a)$$

and for three dimensions,

$$\bar{r}_{jm} = h^2 \ (1 - h^2 - r_{jw}^2) - r_{jw}^2 \qquad (9.15b)$$

It would be interesting to see whether any formula with k for the number of dimensions would permit a generalization of (9.15a) and (9.15b) to any dimensionality.

Having glanced at the main relations of item properties to scale validity I now test the extent to which the questionnaire scales studied in this book fit one or another of the models—in a brief, rough, and simple fashion—by asking how the values calculated from the algebraic statements above agree with those calculated from the exact matrix computations. Parenthetically, in considering these approximations the reader should again be reminded that Equation (9.11) deals with unweighted scoring, whereas Cattell and Tsujioka (1963) have geared even the algebraic mean statement to express summed weighting effects, so that the discrepancies from the matrix calculation need not be quite as much as here.

In connection with this comparison of the validity estimated by equation (9.11) and that reached by "computer synthesis" (Chapter Ten, where the matrix process is focused), we should glance also at the effect on suppressor action. In a structured symmetric scale, the loadings on an unwanted factor are set to add to zero with equal weights for items, but they no longer do so when unequal weights are assigned—unless the latter are very special. The weights in a V_{fe}—those corresponding to a multiple R maximized for the wanted factor—are also such as should tend to produce minimal (but not zero) contribution of the unwanted factors on the wanted factor estimate. (That is, if wanted and unwanted are originally uncorrelated.) But even on the equal item weight system one would expect that with a sufficiently long test (and with the 16 PF and HSPQ, and so forth, run to 150 to 200 items that can be used for suppression), the likelihood of any randomly weighted sum of them departing markedly from zero is small.

As is seen from Table 55 (lower left of each of the six scales) the values by Equation (9.11) are always, as expected, somewhat lower than those from the weighted *R;* but for five cases the underestimates center on a loss of only .07. The exception is *C* factor, ego strength, on the student group only, where the negativeness of two items has been compensated by negative weights in the *R* but not in the r_{sw}, so that *R* is much better. Also perhaps *C* departs more from the structured symmetrical model.

As stated at the outset so brief a treatment as this cannot hope to set out comprehensive solutions and detailed algebraic derivations systematically but only to alert the reader to the complexities of the problem and to illustrate with solutions at particular points. At the least the analysis shows that the pursuit of homogeneity for its own sake by certain classical itemetrists is an incorrect goal. It springs from an oversimplified view lacking appreciation of the many parameters with which one needs to be concerned in structured psychometric test construction.

Although interitem homogeneity needs to be kept at an optimal low value in proper relation to other parameters notably item-factor correlations, in one test construction situation what can be thought of as a form of homogeneity should be high—namely, in the correlation between two alleged equivalent forms of a factor scale. Yet even here—if it is a factor scale and not a scale against an external criterion—there are reasons why the equivalence coefficient should not reach unity or, indeed, exceed a certain definable value. Since no test scale can be perfectly valid, the agreement of one form with another should not exceed that value due to and to be expected from the validity of each with respect to the wanted factor (Equation 9.17). At least, it should not do so unless for some special reason it is appropriate to go in for what is defined below as "herringbone" construction of equivalent scales.

The innovations which have appeared in construction principles for structured as contrasted with itemetric formulations can be brought out in this connection. In the latter, where the constructor has set up two equivalent forms to predict some external criterion, such as success as a salesman or voting behavior, he is entitled to hope for and aim at the goal of raising their equivalence coefficients to their mean reliability (dependability)—that is, they should overlap in everything but experimental error of measurement coefficients. But in a structured scale, oriented to a pure, conceptual factor criterion, there would in practice be something wrong if equivalence equaled dependability. Typically each *n*-item form will have the construction:

$$\begin{aligned}\text{Form A score} &= \sum^{n} b_{aw}F_w + \sum^{n} b_{au1}F_{u1} + \ldots + \sum^{n} b_{au(k-1)}F_{u(k-1)} + \sum^{j=n} b_{aj}F_j \\ &\quad b_{aw}F_w + b_{au1}F_{u1} + \ldots + b_{au(k-1)}F_{u(k-1)} + b_{aj}F_j\end{aligned}$$

where F_j is any specific and *n* such specifics as are added in. The inner product of two such specification equations exceeds the value due to the wanted factor, namely,

$$r_{AB} = \sum^{n} b_{aw} b_{bw} \tag{9.17}$$

(omitting any term due to correlation of factors) if they have any similar loadings on the unwanted factors or if the supposed specifics of any item in one scale (summing into F_s) happen to be the same as any items in the second. Commonly, therefore, $\sqrt{r_{AB}}$ overestimates validity.

Conceivably in some circumstances, even in the factorially structured questionnaire, it is a legitimate goal to raise the equivalence coefficient by incorporating equivalence on factors other than the main one wanted. But it is important at any rate to distinguish between the ordinary factor scale equivalence and such a specially structured equivalence, which I have called *herringbone equivalence* (Cattell and Warburton, 1967). The latter is most quickly described by imagining a test of general scholastic achievement which contains English, arithmetic, geography, and history; we would not expect history necessarily to correlate with arithmetic. It is necessary in such a "general education" scale, where no common factor underlies all parts, to stipulate that the proportions (or weights) given to the various parts in one equivalent form of a general scholastic battery be the same as in the other (hence symmetrical, or herringbone, equivalence). This is an extreme case, for more often we deal with an array of specifics on top of a common factor.

Although a herringbone design for a test aimed only at F_w would give a spuriously high value for the equivalence to its forms as measures of the *factor,* in a sense such a descriptive statistic is sometimes defensible. Let us suppose that research has established a deirable optimum stratified sample of areas in which a source trait should be tapped by the scale items in the interest of attenuating instrument factors. Then the second form could not fall short of the same optimal sampling, and some rise in equivalence ensues from these specific area factors other than F_w necessarily appearing in both. A slight effect of this kind can be shown in the 16 PF, where the equivalence coefficient between forms is a little greater than would be expected from the split-half homogeneity (corrected to double length) for the single forms. One should note in this connection that the alpha coefficient (Cronbach, 1951; Cronbach and others, 1972) of internal homogeneity is based both on unwanted and wanted common factor covariance and does not escape the criticism leveled at this kind of equivalence coefficient—namely, that unwanted specific or common factors inflate one's estimate of the goodness of equivalence in the test. By the Spearman-Brown formula the equivalence coefficient of two forms should equal $\frac{2\sqrt{r_{11}r_{22}}}{(1+\sqrt{r_{11}r_{22}})}$ calculated from their split halves r_{11} and r_{22} and if this value is higher than the obtained equivalence, then common specifics (the herringbone structure) can be inferred to exist over the two forms. Equivalence coefficients can also be spuriously high—relative to equivalence as applied to the true factor score—through shared unwanted common factors. From comparisons of the empirical r_{AB} and the r_{AB} values and those estimated from r_{11} and r_{22} as well as r_{sw} we can determine proportions of common wanted, common unwanted, and repeated stratified choice of specifics (herringbone equivalents) in a scale.

Finally, in relating equivalence to other properties we should beware of saying that where there is no equivalence there can be no validity (associated with the usual generalization that validity cannot exceed the square root of the equivalence). One form can have high validity, but if the other has none, equivalence can be zero.

Among practical inferences from the above is that in an omnibus test averaging 10 to 12 items per factor the present stage of factor scale intensification has not reached a level where one form—assuming it to be 8 to 12 items only for each factor—can be used with confidence in important decisions, as Cronbach points out (1960). In spite of IPAT having provided equivalent A, B, C, and D forms for the 16 PF, HSPQ, and so forth, and its strongly advocating in the Handbooks that at least two be used, many users prefer the lower equivalences and validities of single forms. The user is free to do as he wishes, but even when all four forms are used only 15 to 20 minutes are being assigned to measuring each primary. This is not much when one remembers that such a major aspect of personality needs to be sampled across a wide range of behavioral expression and that decisions affecting the life and adjustment of the subject are being made thereon.

At the outset of this discussion on r_{sw}, r_{jm}, r_{jw}, and n relations I said that except where mentioned the experimental error term would for simplicity be left outside. This term is defined by the dependability form of the reliability coefficient—the immediate test/retest. Unfortunately there is a continual recrudescence in the literature of confusion of dependability—and also of other forms of the reliability coefficient—with homogeneity. A word on perspective regarding dependability seems necessary, therefore, in conclusion. Inasmuch as we follow Polonius, that "to thine own self be true" is necessary in order not to "be false to any man," we recognize that dependability is vital and also that validity cannot normally equal (because of specifics) and certainly cannot exceed the square root of the reliability as measured by dependability. (Equivalence is another matter, as above.) Also, one must note the word *immediate* in dependability. For two measures on a state factor (Chapter Five) an hour apart can show zero reliability, and in such cases they retain high validity and good equivalence between even and odd half-forms. Indeed, if a state measure shows high reliability (as a stability coefficient), we are compelled on general principles to argue that it has poor validity.

Since a test can be perfectly reliable yet of no validity against any important concepts that it is intended to measure—as alas is well illustrated by many nonfactorial questionnaires—reliability *in itself* is of small interest. It becomes important only insofar as it affects validity, equivalence, and other coefficients affecting test interpretation. On such connection concerns the effect of lengthening a test upon its reliability and therefore its validity. The ordinary Spearman-Brown formula for the effect on reliability of adding new items simply says that they must be of the same composition as the existing items—or, at least, intercorrelate with themselves and the old items in the way the old items did. However, in structured tests this can mean three distinct things: that they are identical in factor composition but have the same amount of error of measurement, that they are identical on common factors but not in specifics, or that they are identical only on the wanted common factor. New formulas for these structured conditions have been set out by Cattell and Radcliffe (1962). However, taking the simplest assumption as in the classical Spearman-Brown, we see that validity increases with scale length as follows:

$$r_{nac} = \frac{r_{ac}}{\sqrt{\frac{1 - r_{aa}}{n} + r_{aa}}} \tag{9.18}$$

where n is the ratio by which the length of the test is increased, a is the given scale, and c is the factor criterion. The highest possible validity for an infinite-length test—a value of interest for comparing "kinds" of tests—is

$$r_{\infty ac} = \frac{r_{ac}}{\sqrt{r_{aa}}} \tag{9.19}$$

The important feature to note is that validity increases with length less rapidly than does reliability. No amount of increase of length makes a non-valid test (for a defined criterion) valid. As seen above, while what are widely considered to be tolerable validities are reached in the 16 PF by using form A alone (with 10 to 13 items per scale), there is still appreciable gain from extension—for example, using at least forms A and B and thus going to 20 to 26 items per source-trait scale.

3. Unitractic Scales, Scale Units, Item Balance, and Standardization

What do other standard psychometric concepts—beyond consistency and validity—mean for the personality questionnaire domain? To answer this question, we proceed in Section 4 to new domains definitely beyond common psychometric concepts. But here we need first to sharpen a number of concepts and definitions in common use covering factor validity and factor trueness, factor-homogeneous item sets and test-homogeneous item sets, unitractic and univocal scales, and other expressions often applied to questionnaire problems. Their nature and distinction can be quickly grasped by considering Figure 33. Parenthetically Figure 33 obviously cannot as a whole be supposed to represent the usual distribution of items in simple structure. It assumes that factors have been found by simple structure but that we are now dealing with groups of items artificially put together for scale purposes. Also the figure represents homogeneity as the inverse of distance of items apart, whereas usually we do so by some other index, such as a correlation, a pattern similarity coefficient, an angular distance as in

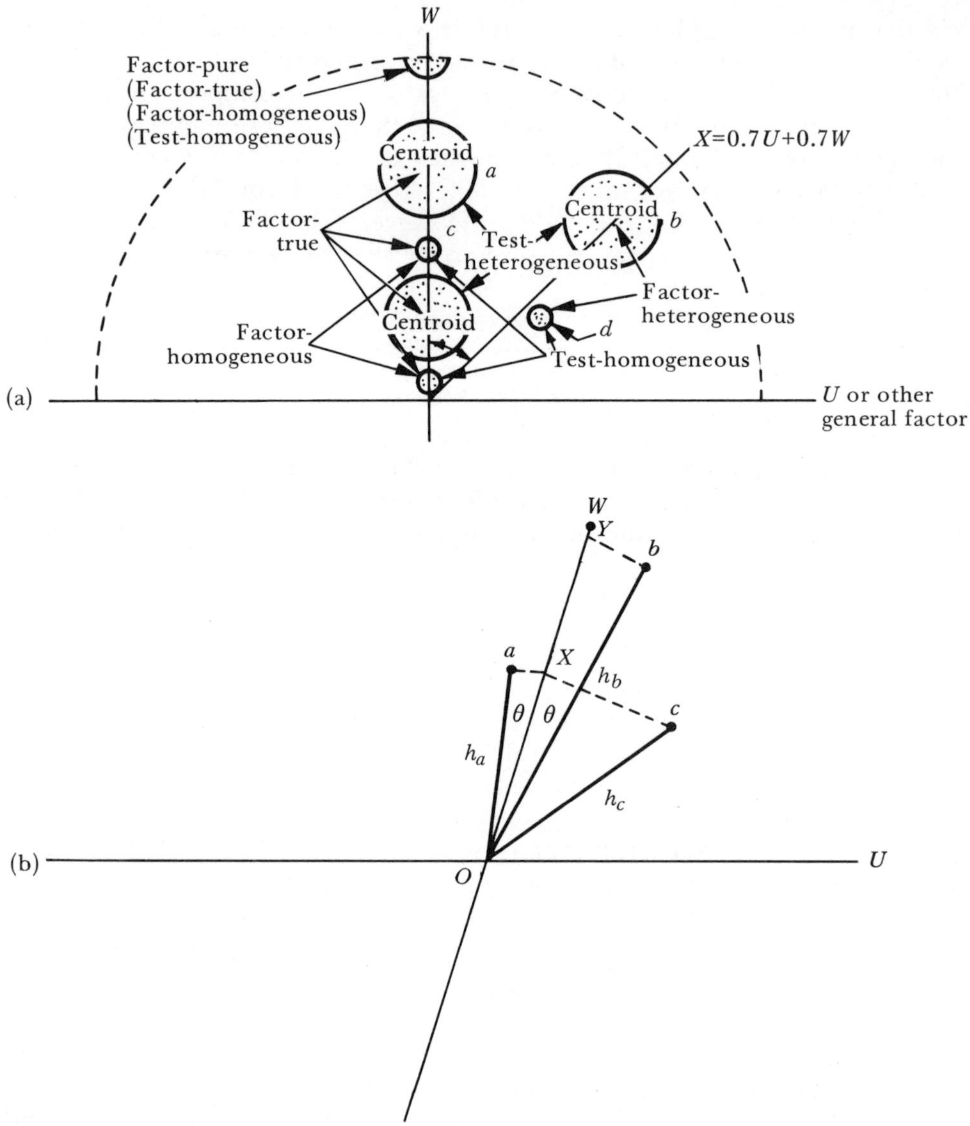

Figure 33. Special meanings of homogeneous, valid, unitractic, and univocal: (a) types of homogeneity, (b) factor trueness and factor validity.

radial parceling (Cattell and Burdsal, 1973). But this way of drawing is clearest for conveying essentials.

Difference Between Factor-Homogeneous and Test-Homogeneous Item Sets. If axes in Figure 33—*W* and *U*— represent true, simple-structure, psychologically meaningful factors—wanted and unwanted, respectively—then the clusters of items at points *a* and *b* represent fairly low homogenity scales, that is relatively widely separated points. But the scale set at *a*, although therefore relatively test-heterogeneous, has all items clustering around the true-factor axis *W*, whereas *b* does not. Thus *b* cannot be factor-homogeneous—its items are all mixed *W* and *U,* whereas *a* approaches factor homogeneity. If each scale is made up of virtually test-homogeneous items as shown by the relatively tight circles at *c* and *d,* then *d,* although now test-homogeneous, is still factor-heterogeneous; even if it were a point it would still represent a mixture of factors *W* and *U,* whereas *c* items are almost pure *W* factor except for specifics.

Difference Between Factor-True and Factor-Valid Tests. A test may have high factor trueness, in the sense of being little contaminated with any other factor except a specific. Thus it may have zero correlation, for example, with the other factor scales in an omnibus battery—or indeed with any other known primary trait—but still not have high validity by the test of correlating highly with the factor it represents. Geometrically a correlation is a cosine multiplied by the length of the two vectors (in this case of one since the factor is unit length). Consequently in Figure 33(b) the trueness of test *a* is represented by the angle θ and its validity by the correlation with the factor, that is by $h_a \cos \theta$, which equals OX. The difference between validity and trueness is visible in that although test *b* is as factor-true (the angle θ being the same) for *W* as is test *a,* test *b* is decidedly more valid since OY is greater than OX. Test *c* has the same validity as test *a,* namely, OX, but is decidedly less true. In particular, test *c* would be far more correlated with the undesired factor *U* than would test *a* and would thus be more unrepresentative of *W*'s correlation with other variables.

In most research and practice we are concerned with validity, but trueness is a better, more correct concept to use in special instances. In developing a correct understanding of second-order factor structure, high trueness of the primary scales is more important than high validity without trueness (as at *c*). Factor trueness is illustrated for sets of different homogeneity and validity in Figure 33(a). Incidentally, when a scale is highly factor-true, it may still correlate with another factor. Indeed if it is perfectly factor true for factor *W,* it will correlate with another factor and exactly as factor *W* does (but reduced in proportion to its reduced length).

Difference Between Unitractic and Univocal Scales. A univocal scale appears to be defined by Guilford as one in which all items measure nothing but one and the same common factor and specifics.

By others it is unclear, as in Eysenck (1971), whether univocal is being used in this sense or for items which measure only one common dimension plus error of measurement. In the latter sense it is superfluous since such items do not exist. Indeed, to go further, it is extremely doubtful that anyone can produce in practice items which measure only specifics beyond the single factor they have in common. The condition is sometimes approached in collections of subtests, rather than items, as in the ability field in Spearman's hierarchical correlation matrix, from which anything that upsets the tetrad difference criterion has been combed out.

However, as Thurstone points out, Spearman's procedure does not guarantee that this common unitary dimension lies along a *meaningful* simple-structure factor position since no hyperplane has ever existed to define such a unique position. In other words, to show that a given matrix is rank one is not to prove that the items are measuring a pure unitary trait factor in common: it may be a mixture of unitary traits. Consequently in defining a univocal scale as one the items of which are concerned with only one vector and specifics, we must recognize that component factor analysis, which does not rotate, means that the axis concerned need not be a unitary trait when considered in the larger context of known unitary primaries. Thus if in Figure 33(a) W and U are meaningful primaries, a univocal set of items can lie along the axis X at b, representing a mixed W and U vector ($0.7W + 0.7U$). Incidentally, even had Guilford's G-Z questionnaire scales been univocal, according to his ideal, their departure from simple-structure positions (necessitated by fixing them as orthogonal scales) means that they would not represent real unitary source traits.

The important distinction must therefore be made between univocal and *unitractic,* meaning, by the latter, measuring a single unitary trait (Latin *tractus* from which our word *trait* is derived). The concept of unitractic has more reference to real data for it defines a scale as one in which all items have their largest loading on the same uniquely rotated source trait and some of which share low but opposite suppressing loadings on other common factors, while all items have loadings on specifics.

The value of the unitractic scale is one that it succeeds (experimental error aside) in measuring by the summed scores of its items one factorial source trait only. However it necessarily does so by exerting *suppressor action* between items loading in opposite directions on the other, unwanted common factors, though allowing specifics to remain. The scale, but not its items, is then factor-true. Thus in the 16 PF (see Cattell, 1972e, Table 1) suppression is seen where the items loading a factor positively as salients have loadings (and, more importantly, item weights) that are about equally positive and negative on other factors.

Discussion of scale structure and the notions of univocal and unitractic forms would not be complete without reference to the Guttman scale (or what for historical correctness should perhaps be called the Walker-Guttman scale [4]). When items are arranged by the rank-ordering operation in such scales, one might suppose that a univocal (but not necessarily unitractic) scale is being constructed. However, the resulting correlation matrix does not have unit rank but typically has many common factors, coinciding with the correlation matrix shaping itself as a simplex (high values close to the diagonal). The relation of any item to the scale score as a whole is nonlinear and often discontinuous. Consequently the properties do not come into the same realm of discourse as here.

In summary, both univocal and unitractic concepts require a rank one matrix but the unitractic requires in addition evidence of a unique unitary trait from simple structure in a personality-sphere-sampled domain. If one plots the scale items in a set of items covering two or more common fac-

[4] As Nunnally (1967, p. 528 points out, the Guttman scale "is unrealistic for the measurement of most human traits" since psychologists who seek items that fit that model always find themselves with "only a handful of items" left. Moreover the specifics in such scales can be called specifics only by ignoring the fact that each probably represents (in, say, a ten-item P-G scale) one of several different broad factors.

tors, both vectors lie along a straight line from the origin (falling short of unit length according to their specificities), but the unitractic vector falls additionally at a position fixed by simple structure and other evidence of functional trait unity. If anyone doubts that it is possible to be "fooled" by a collection of variables having the uncommon quality of combining two meaningful factors in just the same proportions, so that a rank one matrix occurs at a false, nonunitractic position, he should consider the Cattell-Dickman ball problem (1962), where "behavior" that depend on the *density* of the balls tend to lie along the 45° vector between the unitractic vectors for the true traits of weight and size. The pursuit purely of univocal (rank one) scales among items, as by Jackson and others, without regard to the wider psychological theory of unitractic scales, puts technical fixations above science. Moreover, in a broader context even when the greater part of the common variance of a set of scale items is well directed toward a unitractic target, the statistical technical model that items should consist solely of specifics and a common factor is almost certainly a conceptual mirage diverting researchers from better technical goals in practical test construction. So-called univocal scales and unitractic scales that have not made efforts to balance and suppress unwanted common factors always have other common (if only instrument) factors covering their items and enteering the final score. By a fully unitractic scale—which is the nearly practical and proper ideal of test construction—I mean one which has unwanted common factors but succeeds in suppressing them in the final score. Thus it is in two important respects different from the univocal scale above.

Formulas for estimating reliabilities and validities of unitractic scales—that is scales in which there is necessarily suppressor action—have been worked out by Cattell and Radcliffe (1962). The Spearman-Brown formula for calculating the effect of lengthening the number of items in a questionnaire scale is there matched by the Cattell-Radcliffe formula for doing so with the different assumptions of a unitractic scale as defined here, and the effects of item weighting and buffering are considered.

From the internal construction of scales in relation to their evaluative psychometric parameters, we must now turn briefly to scaling problems. Although most of the hunting in the tangled jungle of scaling problems has been done by highly competent psychologists the most desired trophies—an equal-interval unit and a true zero—have never been brought home. To avoid solecisms and for general enlightenment the reader may turn to the works of Gulliksen (1950), Torgerson (1958), Cronbach and Gleser, Nanda, and Rajartanam (1972), Harris (1963), Lord (1963), Lord and Novick (1960), Tucker (1966), Cliff (1960), Jöreskog (1970), and many other incisive writers. Here I shall briefly indicate new principles which, even though unfinished, at least have hope of leading to the scaling properties necessary for most of the adding, averaging, and other calculating we now do on faith.

The chief hope of passing from raw scores based simply on counting the number of items correct to units that are in some deeper psychological sense equal lies in two directions: the pan-normalization principle and the relational simplex principle.

Pan-normalization is less fundamental in principle but more attainable in practice. It assumes that human traits are influenced by a relatively large number of independent genetic and environmental factors, so that in any large population sample the distribution of true scores approaches normality. One has therefore only to plot the distribution of raw scores in the course of standardization and find the transformation of raw scores that converts the distribution to normality. This is done, in connection also with standardization, by creating n-stens (normalized stens) and has certainly proved effective in bringing out research relationships with the 16 PF, HSPQ, CAQ, and other scales. *Pan-normalization* adds to this simple normalization only the concept that one does not stop with applying the normalization criterion to a simple, single group. Instead a collection of groups—of social or age groups or of different means—is put in overlapping raw-score distributions and the scaling transformation used that simultaneously gives the best fit to a normal curve on every group—that is, evaluated over the whole range of overlapping groups (Cattell, 1970a).

The *relational simplex* principle is more fundamental. It requires that intercorrelating scales for different traits have a series of experimental transformations of raw scores to scaled scores tried out on each. The aim is to discover the combination of transformations that maximizes the numerical value of the mean correlation coefficient in the matrix of correlations among them (Cattell, 1962a, 1970a, 1972a). The argument is that departures of the raw scores from the true scale intervals act like error and thus tend to attenuate a given scale's correlations with other variables. The particular stretching and contracting that by trial and error increases the intercorrelations thus constitutes a rescaling that moves toward equal intervals.

It may be objected that if a true equal-interval scaling existed and if two measures deviated from it in exactly the same way (say, both being stretched at the top end) no indication of this would be given by a decline in correlation. This is true, and it is the reason for putting in one matrix a diversity of variables that make such common distortion improbable. It can also be argued that such a distortion would be revealed by the effect of the common change of range on the correlation coefficient taken at different sections of the variable score ranges.

Practical application of the relational simplex is in its infancy, but its trial has been aided by a computer program by Lingoes (1965) that in effect puts the raw scores through a systematic sampling of the chief possible deformations. Thus it gives system to the trial-and-error discovery of the transformation that maximizes the correlations. An application by DeYoung of Lingoes' program to the 16 PF scales shows (DeYoung and Cattell, in preparation) that the n-stens come close to an ideal relational simplex scaling. Since the *n*-sten scaling is based on the pan-normalization principle one should expect convergence to much the same result as the relational simplex because the two principles can be regarded as theoretically congruent.

Even a rough approximation to equal scale units is acceptable for most operations with questionnaires. But when *differences* of scores are concerned, as Figure 34 shows, departure from equal units in the absolute scores (the scale on which differences are measured) produces a greater departure from equality in the ensuing difference score units. (This is akin to the error variance—which wrong scaling amounts to—being twice as great in the difference scores.) And when age curves are involved the departure can make the difference between concluding that a linear or a curvilinear growth function is involved.

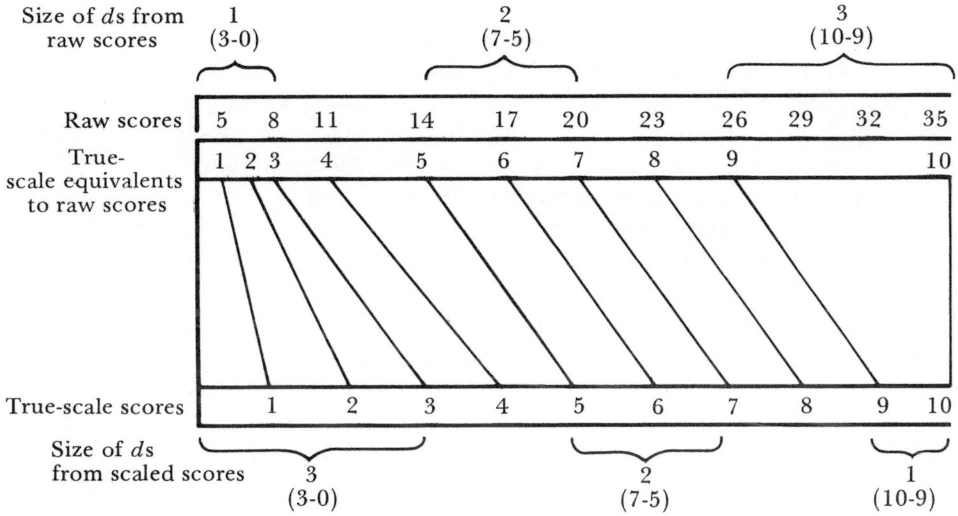

Figure 34. Magnified effect of inadequate scaling on difference and summation scores. This diagram shows transformation between raw-score values in upper row in what are known to be true-scale scores in lower row. (A slight difference in lower raw scores means a lot; equivalent differences at top do not correspond to much real increase.) Rank order of three people in difference scores given in raw scores is exactly the opposite of that from scaled scores. Such complete reversal is, of course, an extreme instance. The effect is most noticeable in difference scores but is also evident in summing scores of different people. A difference in means of two groups summing individuals in 26–35 raw-score range, compared with two groups summed in 5–8 raw-score range, would give a misleading impression. From Cattell (1966a).

In dismissing the ideal of a true zero from current practical consideration, I should point out that in states the assignment of true zeros is theoretically quite promising (Cattell, 1972a). It has in fact been incorporated in the state model (Chapter 5) and in standardization schemes for states in the next chapter. What steps may nevertheless be taken for approaching true zeros (absolute scales) in questionnaire *trait* scales can be studied in the same monograph (Cattell, 1972a), but it is in regard to states that we may expect the model for true-zero scales first to be tried experimentally.

From scaling one can proceed to standardization, although admittedly with little more foundation than a pan-normalization scaling. There are few special problems in questionnaire standardization beyond those related to psychological measurement by any instrument. Perhaps the only one worth mention is that arising from the desirability of applying different weighting patterns (V_{fe}) to the items in the same questionnaire for the same trait in different populations by computer synthesis scoring. This approach produces a different standardization table with each weighting, but if one is willing to take one population as standard the other linear combinations can be scored in regard to its distribution.

Turning next to a common consideration in all standardizations—the size of sample—one notes that the novice is apt to evaluate a standardization mainly by its magnitude. It is "good" if it runs from two to thirty thousand or more, as does the Stanford-Binet. Yet aptness in a small sample can give better results than a large sample. Twenty thousand students would be a superfluously large and also in apt standardization for a general adult questionnaire. Indeed it is far more important to build the standardization on about 2500 obtained as a stratified sample (for social class, race, age, sex, and so on) than on some astronomical sample of which all members are of the same special class, such as students or military groups. Nor is it satisfactory to base a clinical questionnaire only on clinical cases; a cutoff point for clinical treatment must be made on a general sample. By these standards the only satisfactory questionnaires in the 20 or more surveyed here are the established questionnaires—the Guilford-Zimmerman and the IPAT questionnaires. It is surprising to find that the MMPI, although developed at about the same time as the G-Z and the IPAT questionnaires, is based on only 700 normal adults and 250 precollege and college students (Hathaway and McKinley, 1951, 1967, p. 8). At the school level a proper sampling is altogether easier to get; not only the HSPQ but also the CPQ, the Junior EPI, and the ESPQ promise to be on adequate standardizations. The HSPQ has a basis of close to 10,000 (4450 boys, 5000 girls) and the CPQ close to 3000 (1420 girls, 1484 boys). The 16 PF provides a general population standardization, separate for men and women, and one for students, and has kept a correct balance for such minority groups as Negroes and Mexican-Americans in the United States. This separation of norm groups gives the psychologist full resources for comparison but also requires him to think about what is needed in relation to his predictions.

A model standardization has been set out for the 16 PF form C for American women on the basis of the National Family Opinion survey, cross-stratifying with correct proportions by state, by rural-urban proportion, by age, and by family income. The percentages are close—within 1 percent—to those in the American population as a whole (Cattell and Greene, 1961). However, the British standardization of the 16 PF forms A and B carried out by Saville and others for the National Foundation for Educational Research in London is easily the largest stratified sample and the best approach to an ideal standardization. Both this and Saville's HSPQ standardization exceed the basis of the other important questionnaires, such as the MMPI, Guilford-Zimmerman, Eysenck, Jackson, Comrey, and Edwards. The British 16 PF covered 2227 adults sampled from 10 demographic regions, both sexes, four social classes, five marital classes, nine educational levels, and five age groups from 15 to 69, in the correct stratified proportions for the general population. This standardization is likely to be a goldmine of social analysis data for researchers concerned with distribution of traits by region, sex, age, and social status. In fact, to the psychologist with imagination there is far more theoretical interest to a standardization than just good statistical accountancy. There is a contribution to history in that personality trait standardizations undoubtedly change with time, and the records of questionnaire standardizations will thus provide the social historian of the future with a firm basis for generalizations about trends in human nature in its social adjustments. For example, there are strong indications that between 1955 and 1970 the young become more surgent *F*, extravert *Q*I, and autious *M*, although the data are not yet suitable for publication.

The aim of standardization is of course to permit translation of raw scores to centiles or some other measure more directly meaningful than raw scores. The two basic alternatives are *centiles,* which can be cut from the raw-score distribution, and some form of *standard score,* which can be derived either from the raw-score distribution as it stands or from raw scores transformed to redistribute to a perfect normal curve.

If standard scores are used, a choice of unit size has to be made since ordinary sigma units are inconvenient: +1 and −1 are too coarse, negative scores are awkward, and ordinary scores carried to several decimals are cumbersome. Guilford, working in military psychometry, therefore proposed stanines—units of half a sigma with the central value, 5, centered at the mean. Bowing to the universal acceptability of the decimal system, I proposed the contrasting system of *stens* ("standard tens"). These were first introduced, and the values and limits of the central tendency for each sten set out, in the first edition of the 16 PF (1949). Canfield (1951) examining the sten concept usefully from an independent angle supported it, but proposed no essential changes.

Another reason for settling at 10 rather than at stanines or even staves (fives) is that in correlation of scores with this less coarse grouping, Sheppard's correction for grouping ceases to be important. (It ceases to be generally significant at 12 points, so that with staves or even stanines one might still be uneasy.) A number greater than 10 or 12 would be awkward. Indeed the range of raw scores with, say, 12 items each giving 0, 1, or 2 if items are well chosen (from, say, 1 to 23) does not permit translation into 12 without distortion. Relatively minor advantages of stens over stanines are that the scale does not leave the extreme categories—1 and 9 in stanines; 1 and 10 in stens—covering quite so wide and skewed an array of final raw scores and that it makes both 5 and 6 sten values essentially average scores. The latter arrangement means that the psychometrically defined average—the cases falling at both 5 and 6—includes more cases and corresponds better with the popular use of average than does 5.0 in stanines. (The exact average in n-stens is 5.5 and the percentage in the broad 5 and 6 "average people" category is 38 percent.)

It is necessary to describe the difference between n-stens (normalized stens) and s-stens (standard-score stens). In n-stens, centile sections are cut off on the raw-score distribution corresponding to half-sigma intervals on the normal curve, and the standardization goes from raw scores to stens on this basis. The stens obtained are thus inherently normally distributed. In s-stens the half-sigmas are taken from the raw-score sigma; if the raw scores are skewed downward there may therefore be no cases occurring, for example, at sten 10. The essential relations are shown in Figure 35.

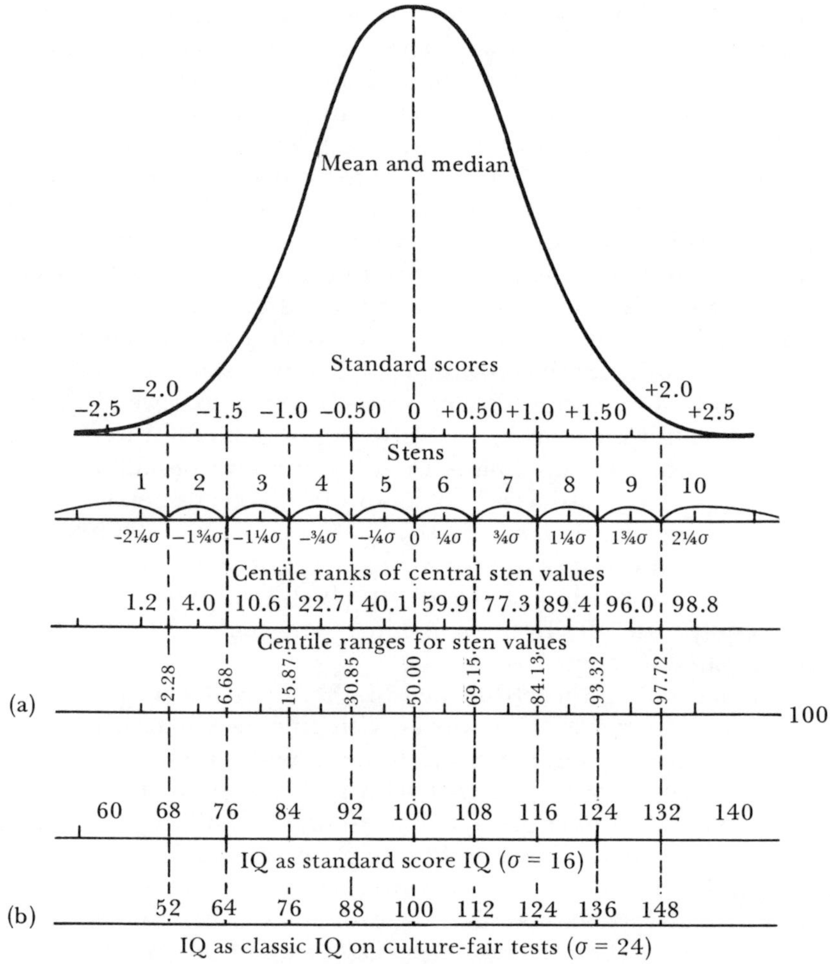

Figure 35. Standard scores, stens, and centiles: (a) general translations, (b) translation to IQ. The term *percentile* is unfortunately in more common use than *centile*. That the latter is the more logical word should be clear when it is recognized that we are referring to a concept analogous to decile, quartile, and tertile. To speak of percentile is just as awkward as to say perquartile for quartile. From the *Handbook for the 16 Personality Factor Questionnaire* (16 PF) © 1970, Institute for Personality and Ability Testing, Champaign, Illinois, U.S.A. Reproduced by permission.

When the raw scores have a small range (say, only over 10 points) as occurs, for example, if one cuts to one form only of the CPQ or ESPQ, I suggest staves of five equal intervals as more appropriate to remind one of the true accuracy. By contrast a 16 PF scale of 13 items in one form for one factor has a raw-score range from 0 to 26 and is thus basically suitable for stens, and even more so when forms B, C, and D bring this range to 0 to 64 raw-score points for each factor in the shorter and 0 to 76 in the longer scales in the 16 PF (84 for the intelligence scale).

Regarding abilities psychologists talk of the difficulty of an item, defined as the percentage of a population that answers it correctly. Regarding personality the corresponding term is extremity or eccentricity. Psychometric texts offer simple calculations for proceeding from the percentage of yes-no cuts—for example, 70/30, 24/76—on a collection of items to the mean and sigma of the scale formed from the total scale score. In theory this is a test construction choice analogous to that on homogeneity of items in that a scale has a higher sigma (a better spread of the population) as the fraction of items with 50/50 cut increases. This advantage of middle cuts is true of the main population although even there it can meet its nemesis in which everyone above average gets the extreme top score and everyone below the extreme bottom score. If items are perfectly correlated they "flop over" together. But when one uses the test for extreme groups there is poor discrimination within them unless there are enough items with extreme cuts (for the general population) catering for the extreme group. Correspondingly if the difficulty of items in an intelligence test is right for discriminating five- from six-year olds the test is unlikely to contain items discriminating well between two- and three-year olds or eleven- and twelve-year olds.

The problem of ideal extremity of yes-no cuts in questionnaires illustrates the general principle that the purely statistical, psychometric decision, correct for an ideal population, is seldom the full answer in the practical world. Theoretically, with positively intercorrelated items the biggest spread (sigma) for a number of items is when every item has a 50/50 incidence of yes and no. But in practice, since there is not one population but several and since discrimination in extreme ranges is often of signal importance, one needs items that distribute more broadly on extremity of cut from the middle 50/50 to 80/20 and even 90/10. Nevertheless the construction problem is generally that of finding as many items as one needs at the 50/50 cut. The researcher on structure and instrument factors should be aware that factor analysis of sets of items differing widely in difficulty seems to produce, in addition to the personality factors, what are called difficulty factors or extremity factors (Smith, 1950; Dingman, 1958; Cattell, 1957). These factors, positively and negatively loaded on extreme high and low cut items on one factor, emerge clearly only with the ordinary correlation coefficient (when distorted by operating with only two or three categories of range) but not with the tetrachoric. One would therefore like to avoid extremity of this degree.

Another problem of test design in relation to score distribution is that of discovering items to provide a balance of items on each factor on which the positively contributing answer is yes (to the right) and on which it is no (to the left). Such an equal number of yes and no contributors, extremity being correct, can eliminate the acquiescence factor, which is an instrument factor due to some subjects having a mental set to answer yes. Attention was called to this response set in questionnaires by Cronbach (1946), although I had already investigated the set and employed it in the construction of objective tests (Adjutant General's Office, Personnel Research, objective test of personality) because it showed personality associations. Here was an instance of "one man's meat . . .," since I conceived response sets as important expressions of personality to be measured by objective tests whereas in questionnaires they were viewed by Cronbach as contamination to be eliminated. The tendency to respond yes rather than no is so significantly loaded on T-data factor UI 21 and 24 that it is now in use as a valuable subtest for anxiety (Cattell and Scheier, 1961; Schuerger and Cattell, 1973). Because of this possible distortion in questionnaires, however, the whole series of IPAT questionnaires has its items carefully balanced factor by factor; this is now done in perhaps one-half of all published questionnaires. When the combined needs for optimum homogeneity, optimum extremity of cut, suppressor action, and balancing for mental sets are considered, it is seen that questionnaire scale construction requires expertise and research beyond the basic definition of factors. When all has been done that can be done in regard to eliminating shortcomings in the test design, further limitations can be removed by improvements in scoring. These points are taken up in the next chapter. Meanwhile we must examine a major distortion at the heart of all questionnaire usage.

4. Motivational Distortion and Sabotage

Most psychological tests, like most medical tests, require in practice and in ethics a voluntary participation and a cooperative attitude on the part of the subject. Nevertheless in many situations the subject either consciously or unconsciously presents a misleading set of responses. Indeed the vulnerability of the questionnaire in this respect has always been notorious, and it was partly for this reason that I began to develop T-data measures after encountering this Achilles heel in Q-data (1936). The argument for using T-data rather than Q-data personality tests is that they are definitely less susceptible to distortion (although equally susceptible to sabotage). But in practice the advice to use T-data, as in the O-A (objective-Analytic) batteries, is not often followed because these batteries require more psychological training and time. Meanwhile, ever since Guilford (1959) summarized the realities of situational effects on questionnaire scores, alert users have begun to face up to some awkward problems. Many patchwork remedies such as lie scales and social-desirability corrections were made in response, but there are ways—resting on more complex personality theory—whereby much of the systematic error can be taken out of the questionnaire approach.

Systematic error in questionnaires come from two sources: *sabotage* and *motivational* distortion. The latter includes role effects (such as responding differently when one is anonymous) and the general human tendency to "fake good" (social desirability), as well as the effects of sheer ignorance of one's personality. Sabotage—by which I mean refusal to cooperate, which leads to attempts to wreck the test and give false information—is rare. Naturally there is no correction for it; one can merely detect it. When detected, the individual's results can only be thrown away; this is a small gain to the practicing psychologist but is often a considerable gain in research work.

One simple way of looking for sabotage is to inspect the answer sheet for some regular but psychologically meaningless (say, geometrical) pattern. A rough and ready regular response is easiest and many saboteurs choose it. This is often spotted simply by inspection of the answer sheet for patterns of checkmarks or omissions. Another way of detecting sabotage is to use quality control methods with the scores taken from the answer sheet locating an excess of factor scores out of the normal distribution. With a single scale such as an anxiety scale this alone is not worth putting much weight on. But in omnibus scales with 12 or more factors it is extremely unlikely that a person would be $2\frac{1}{2}$ sigmas or more (5+ stens) from the mean simultaneously on several factors; it is also unlikely that his sigma about the mean would be less than a certain value. O'Dell (1971) has applied this quality control to extremity of item response. Although this application is a little more time-consuming if extremities are compared with average frequencies of *all* items, his results show that it is an efficient method for separating a cooperative group from a group acting under sabotage instructions.

A subtle method (which, as O'Dell's results seem to show, does not always work) is that of checking the *factor consistency*. This method is based on the fact that in a genuinely executed test it is possible to predict with a standard error of estimate the form B score from the form A, or vice versa, or even between odd and even item totals on one form. Normally one would take the equivalence coefficient r_e and assume that S_A, the score on form A, should be predicted from the form B score by $S_B = S_A\ r_e$. The chances are only 1 in 20 that the score will lie outside $\pm 2\sqrt{1 - r_e^2}$ of this value. It would be interesting to apply this not to the regressed value of A from B but on the assumption that A and B scores are equal. When the individual has deliberately answered items in a random fashion without realizing their built-in consistencies, this limit is likely to be exceeded; if it shows on several factors, then the calculated probability of sabotage is high. Moreover the scores on second-order factors will be abnormally low because random relations of primaries will have destroyed the normal summation.

There are formal resemblances between guessing—as part of a genuine instruction to guess, instead of omitting an answer—and indifferent sabotage that results in random scores. In many tests subjects are instructed to guess when they are in doubt rather than omit an item. If one knew how much of this essential randomness had occurred, the models of correcting for guessing discussed by Nunnally (1967, pp. 576–588; but not translated from ability to personality tests) might be applied. In principle the extent can be calculated from the decline in reliability or equivalence coefficients; we might thus pass from the conception of outright sabotage to a conception of degrees of carelessness in performing the test. This is a matter for future research.

Systematic, nonrandom *motivational distortion*—in contrast to sabotage, which is rare—is a pervasive condition of questionnaire use but is fortunately subject to certain corrections. It is obvious to the man in the street that questionnaires are likely to be vulnerable to idealizing and he is justifiably suspicious of their results. Psychoanalysis has defined the defense mechanisms that might distort even a pious intention to respond truly. An old French adage has it that "language is given us to hide our motives." Trait view theory, which I introduce here, states that such distortion can be subsumed under three headings: role intrusion, stereotype injection, and relative ignorance of oneself. Both the mean of the group and the relative position of the individual in the group will be affected by the two first, and position also by the last.

Let us deal with stereotypes first, since role intrusion is subtle. Every person undoubtedly carries some cognitive image (in addition to that map of the usual personality correlations discussed earlier) of what society holds up as the *ideal personality* and also a personal image of his own self-ideal. The latter is a compromise between the abstract ideal and what he has learned by experience to be his limitations. Much research has been done on these concepts with elaborate models that prove to be little related to the realities. Poets and practical men have long recognized distinctions as subtle as any in this literature. Judge Wendell Holmes spoke of John's ideal John, the real John (or John's real John), and Thomas's (the world's) idea of what the ideal John should be. Another poet has continued:

There were three men went down the road
As down the road went he
The man he was, the man they saw,
And the man he wished to be.

Meredith (1968) has shown, by comparison of primary source-trait scores under different mental sets, that the effects of such stereotypes can be quite powerful. Table 56 (a) shows the effects of four instructional sets. In virtually every trait the ideal deviates significantly from the general population average and in all but three source traits the perceived *generally* socially desirable ideal and the average person's *self*-ideal deviate in the same way. The exceptions are that premsia I, autia M, and self-sufficiency Q_2 are valued more by individuals than they believe they are valued by society. This exception is due possibly to Meredith's group being largely young adults and students, among whom these bohemian qualities might be valued more than among older adults.

The effect of assured anonymity in DeVoogd's study with students is shown in Table 56(b). It seems that the difference between the anonymous role and the normal student role is not as great as that between either of these and the "fake ideal" instruction, although the directions are essentially the same: higher A, C, G, and H and lower Q_4. However (and this is perhaps a tribute to the conscientiousness of students) not a single difference is significant in the anonymous-normal comparison.

Attempts have been made, notably by Edwards (1957a, 1957b), Wiggins (1962a, 1962b, 1973), Jackson and Messick (1962) to demonstrate that social desirability is a single perturbing factor in questionnaires. Although one factor has been extracted in some studies, sensitive statistical checks on number of factors (Block, 1965) and psychological analysis show that this factor does not correspond to the complete mechanisms that are in operation. In applied psychology it may be permissible as a rough correction to assume

Table 56

Mean Desirability Shifts on Personality Factors Due to Stereotypes and Lack of Anonymity

(a) Effects of Instructions to Pursue Stereotypes [a]

	Source Trait															
Set	*A*	*B*	*C*	*E*	*F*	*G*	*H*	*I*	*L*	*M*	*N*	*O*	Q_1	Q_2	Q_3	Q_4
Normal	5.5	5.5	5.5	5.5	5.5	5.5	5.5	5.5	5.5	5.5	5.5	5.5	5.5	5.5	5.5	5.5
Desirable	7.1	6.0	7.7	5.6	6.5	6.9	7.9	4.9	4.2	4.9	6.8	3.4	6.6	4.1	7.7	2.5
Undesirable	3.7	1.2	1.7	7.4	2.9	1.8	3.0	5.0	8.6	7.8	4.0	8.8	5.2	7.1	2.5	8.5
Most ideal self	6.2	6.5	8.0	7.1	6.8	6.3	8.3	5.7	4.1	5.5	6.2	3.1	6.9	6.0	6.8	2.9
Least ideal self	4.2	1.3	1.6	4.8	2.6	2.5	2.8	4.9	8.2	6.5	3.5	9.5	5.4	5.6	3.8	8.3

[a] From Meredith (1968): N = 163 (80 males, 83 females). Mean scores in stens of subjects under normal and deliberate faking sets four instructional sets.

(b) Effects of Anonymous and Role Conditions [a]

	Source Trait															
Condition	*A*	*B*	*C*	*E*	*F*	*G*	*H*	*I*	*L*	*M*	*N*	*O*	Q_1	Q_2	Q_3	Q_4
Normal	9.5	9.2	14.2	13.1	16.0	11.6	12.3	11.5	8.8	12.9	9.1	12.1	9.6	9.8	10.8	14.8
Anonymous	9.6	9.1	15.0	13.3	16.0	11.3	12.7	11.4	8.9	13.2	9.2	12.1	9.7	9.7	10.8	14.5
Ideal	12.8	8.1	20.2	12.9	14.7	15.5	20.0	9.4	6.4	12.5	10.8	6.4	9.5	7.1	15.4	5.4

[a] From Cattell and DeVoogd (1973). Note that Meredith's and DeVoogd's findings agree. Furthermore the latter's results show little difference—at least among students—between normal and anonymous conditions. Results of Krug (1968), not added here, are also closely in accord on the factors affected by faking in aproval-seeking roles. Results in (b) in raw scores.

(c) Statistical Significance of Role Differences

	Source Trait															
Condition	*A*	*B*	*C*	*E*	*F*	*G*	*H*	*I*	*L*	*M*	*N*	*O*	Q_1	Q_2	Q_3	Q_4
Normal-anonymous	1.2	0.8	1.5	0.9	0.2	1.2	1.2	0.8	0.5	1.3	0.8	0.3	0.6	0.6	0.9	1.2
P	NS [a]	NS	NS	NS	NS	NS	NS	NS	NS	NS	NS	NS	NS	NS	NS	NS
Ideal-anonymous	9.5	5.1	12.0	1.2	2.9	11.1	12.7	5.3	8.0	3.1	5.4	11.4	1.4	7.2	13.3	16.8
P	<0.01	<0.01	<0.01	NS	<0.01	<0.01	<0.01	<0.01	<0.01	<0.01	<0.01	<0.01	<0.01	NS	<0.01	<0.01
Ideal-normal	10.3	5.4	13.1	1.0	3.1	11.0	13.7	5.4	7.5	3.8	5.9	11.9	1.6	7.9	13.1	17.9
P	<0.01	<0.01	<0.01	NS	<0.01	<0.01	<0.01	<0.01	<0.01	<0.01	<0.01	<0.01	NS	<0.01	<0.01	<0.01

[a] NS = not significant. Values in (c) are *t*'s for mean differences.

that there is, in different degrees in different test situations, one direction of motivational distortion—toward a stereotype of social desirability (the ideal personality). But the theory that there is one common direction of distortion, and that one need only find how much each individual is distorting (as a sum of conscious and unconscious intentions) and correct by a single vector of subtractions consistent with the pattern in Table 56 does not suffice. If one simplifies discussion to the second stratum it is obvious from Table 56 that, when "faking desirable," people tend to make themselves more extravert (*Q*I), less anxious (*Q*II), and more moral in upbringing (*Q*VIII). Different persons and even the same person in different situations distort these factors in different ways. Sensitive factor analysis shows that there is not one desirability factor but distinct dimensions of change.

The conventional social-desirability approach not only assumed a single direction of change, but in its special corrective scales it assumed that the absolute level on a set of explicitly socially desirable items (included to detect distortion in the MMPI F scale and the EPI distortion scale) is a measure of distortion. Yet such items as "I never say anything bad about anyone" could be checked correct by a saint without his being guilty of distortion—and some people are less saintlike than others. We are not entitled to conclude, therefore, as the MMPI and EPI do, that the absolute score on such a scale is the extent of his lying. The measure needed to indicate conscious or unconscious intention to fake superior is the difference between his score a on a motivational distortion scale when he is not falsifying (as when he takes the test anonymously) and the score b when he is faking; that is, we need $(b - a)$ not b.

If the motivational distortion (MD) scale is used—and when in haste it alone may be practical—the last-mentioned principle must be observed. It connotes three steps. The first is not deciding a priori what constitutes a lie, but administering a test once anonymously and again under motivation and finding which items change and how much. The second is finding the correlation of shift on this MD scale with shift on each personality primary. The third is taking not the absolute score on the MD but the difference of the individual's score from the general mean (since his own is not obtainable) and estimating by the regression in the second step how much to correct each primary scale score. These conditions are observed in the 16 PF MD scale construction but not in the MMPI and others. Even so the method has the remaining weakness that the estimate should be made from the shift on the MD from the individual's own true (mean) position, whereas we have to make it on the shift from the *group's* "anonymous" position, that is, from $(b - \bar{a})$ instead of $(b - a)$, where a is the unmotivated score for individual a (unknown) or group $\bar{a}$.

However, greater weaknesses than this one derive from the MD scale based on the theory of a single social desirability. They are, first, that there are desirabilities rather than one desirability and, second, that, besides the regression of X correction properly being on $(b - \bar{a})$ rather than just b, the regression rate itself changes with different situations and roles.

Desirability is by no means the only instrument factor that has been suspected and investigated in the style responses to questionnaires. Others include acquiescence (the tendency to make yes or positive answers); response bias as defined by Wiggins (1962); defensiveness (CPI score *Wb* and *Gi;* MMPI score *L*); and the tendency to make extreme responses. Most of these tendencies correlate with actual first- and second-order personality factors, principally in anxiety *Q*II correlating largely with low social desirability and slightly with acquiescence; exvia *Q*I slightly with low desirability and more than *Q*II with acquiescence; and superego *G* with desirability and extremity (Couch and Keniston, 1960; Wiggins, 1968). A well-planned check on these tendencies has been given by Stricker (1973), who shows that the theory of response styles appearing as single factors at higher orders does not hold even if pursued to the third order.

When, as in Stricker's study, the possibility of the correlations of acquiescence with scales through response set is ruled out, because the 16 PF primaries are balanced in score regarding yes and no (right and left) answers, one is forced to recognize my alternative to the theories that are behind most of the activity on response style. The alternative is that response styles do not affect personality scores as much as personality traits affect response-style scores.

There are two ways in which this happens. First, there is no doubt that anxious (partly neurotic) answers and (in the main cultures investigated) introvert answers are intrinsically in the class of culturally undesirable directions of response, while high *G* and Q_3 (superego and self-sentiment) have a socially desirable quality everywhere. High responses are nevertheless made by the average honest person if they describe him, although with some tempering of the wind to the shorn lamb. In short if a single desirability factor is found it is almost certainly crude factor analysis. Consequently if scores are corrected for it a lot of true description of anxiety and exvia is thrown away with it.

Second, the correlation of personality scores with styles arises from the latter being real expressions of personality (which is different from saying that in describing oneself one has to say desirable things). Here we encounter one of those phenomena in the history of psychology that disciplined scientists view with amusement or dismay. The workers with questionnaires in the 1950s and 1960s—the heyday of conceiving behavior in terms of response styles—seem to have been so narrow in psychometric interest that they were unaware of the objective test (miniature situation) personality structuring of the preceding decades available in the O-A batteries. Among the 500 tests and over 1000 behavioral-response measures eventually reviewed by Cattell and Warburton (1967) the diverse principles of design included a due proportion of some 20 response-style measures.

The personality factors found among them loaded an expected percentage of these. For example, UI 24 anxiety loaded acquiescence (Cattell, 1955a; Cattell and Scheier, 1961) and UI 31— dissofrustance (a factor in psychoticism) loaded extremity of choice in three- and five-point answers. If instead of creeping up on objective tests via bits of style obvious in questionnaires and intelligence tests these psychometrists had followed more boldly the imaginative approach of deliberately designed objective miniature situations, it would have been clear that stylistic behavior in Q-data is largely the expression of well-known personality factors in T-data. And since the predominance in the latter of general behavioral tests having nothing to do with response style forbad the conclusion that correlation is primarily due to these styles affecting the personality scales, the inevitable conclusion is that the styles are the effect of the personality factors. The issue also relates to the difference in objective test research itself between those who, like Hundleby, Warburton, Schuerger, and myself, see the UI factors as developing entirely new theories about personality structure and those who, like Gardner and the response-style researchers, start with traditional or intuitive theories. The latter have restricted themselves to styles in conventional questionnaires or existing ability tests instead of launching into the broad new domain of objective test design associated with the UI concepts. This antithesis is best summaried by G. S. Kline (1970). My contention is that response styles and cognitive styles are best understood (as Berg, 1967, also argues) as expressions of the concepts in objective personality measurement—that is, of the UI source traits from O-A batteries—and that it is a timid and poor strategy to merely sidle into the objective, miniature situational domain by styles rather than by a major reorientation to the UI theories.

The well-designed questionnaire eliminates acquiescence directly by balancing, as in the 16 P.F. and HSPQ, the agree-disagree responses separately on each factor. It can also eliminate the extremity effect, but only with extra calculation to bring all people to the same sigma on alternatives. (The extremity effect is substantially eliminated by balancing for acquiescence.) And it can eliminate desirability distortions by the trait-view theory. In these circumstances the correlations of response-style measures with personality factors that remain, as in the summary research of Stricker (1973), are most economically interpreted as expressions of the personality factors themselves. Thus none of these personality factors, at the first or higher orders, is likely to account wholly for these complex factors; we should expect, as Stricker found, that no response style corresponds to a personality factor (although with suitable repetition in other tests each style might produce a single instrument factor).

5. Trait-View and Scale-Vulnerability Theories of Distortion and Their Associated Correction

The concepts and associated corrections that have grown up as a patchwork of ad hoc devices for handling distortion—such as the halo in L-data, and general desirability, lie scales, and MD scales in Q-data—are being replaced by more general theories and corrective solutions. The defects of the ad hoc solution are sufficiently illustrated by social desirability: at best it gives a correction crudely unresponsive to the situation; at worst the partialing out throws away a substantial and disproportionate fraction of the general anxiety factor *Q*II.

Even if one considered that a social-desirability factor is indicated by the evidence, a good way to eliminate it would be at the item level. The complexity of handling it this way (notably by forced-choice) is shown by incisive research by Jackson and Buss and Burghill in their adjective lists. In the first place one must recognize that in forced-choice some types of behavior simply cannot be balanced. It is easy to produce equally unattractive alternatives in a trait running from "spendthrift" to "stingy" or "overinhibited" to "reckless," but scarcely in "kind" to "unkind" or "intelligent" to "stupid." Furthermore there is a strong tendency, in forced choice, as shown by D. N. Jackson and Voyce (1972) for desirable alternatives to be answered with such disproportionate frequency that itemetric problems associated with uneven cuts arise. Clearly, because of this popularity of response effect, gross differences of desirability must be avoided at the item level; but the motivational distortion effect can by no means be removed simply by item design.

The alternative propounded here is to understand the structure of effects in terms of perturbation theory, and to correct by factor allowances in scale scores. But this does not mean simply assuming a large social-desirability instrument factor. One reason for doubting social desirability as a uniform factor—despite the clear evidence in Table 56 that all scales change when people attempt to appear attractive—is that no well-conducted factor analysis has produced such a factor either as a new primary or as a secondary or tertiary in which all the lower strata factors involved havein common—and only in common—socially desirable. Such a factor should appear as a general factor, in R-technique; it should appear with larger variance in dR-technique, when people are compared as each shifts to a situation with greater need to fake. A general factor at the second order might for a time escape notice, but the domain has been thoroughly explored (Table 20) and none has appeared. The third order has not been so well explored (Table 24) except for Stricker's negative finding (1973), and there is a faint possibility that one might be found with the required character. But what we see in psychology generally fits another model better.

This model says that the first-, second-, and higher-order personality factors retain their identities and true forms in all situations, and that the situational desirability distortion acts on them as unitary entities, increasing or decreasing their reported levels. In discussing instrument factors and perturbation theory in Chapter Six I introduced trait-view theory—which says that every distortion of perception and evaluation in Q- or L-data is to be understood as a product of the personality of the observer and his situation. Misperception is thus behavior, like any other, to be predicted from the behavioral specification equation. Anxiety might lead a man to underestimate his intelligence (the underestimation would be a function of *C-*, *O*, and Q_4 and of the job-seeking situation); dominance and desire might lead him to overestimate his natural surgency when describing himself to a prospective fiancée.

Stripped to essentials distortion is mainly illustrated here in terms of the effects of primary personality factors. But the full effect can be predicted only if (a) ability and dynamic-trait modalities are also included—

what distorts more than interest and prejudice? (b) Specific role factors relevant to the testing situation must be measured, and (c) certain cognitive concepts in the mind of the (self) evaluator are included (Mulaik 1964). In common-trait specification equations these stereotypes or clichés of what is attractive in personality must also be common traits—though cognitive. However, there are several of them—what is attractive to an employer, to the general public, to a person of the opposite sex, and so on.

At this point role theory must be defined. A role is most quickly illustrated by the special attitudes and skills of a father, a manager, a servant, a teacher, or a person taking a questionnaire examination to get a job. Every behavioral response is made within an ambient-stimulus situation (Cattell, 1963a, 1971b), something surrounding the focal stimulus. This gives one a clue as to which role one should adopt, that is, what restrictions or injunctions should modify one's response to the focal stimulus. Structurally roles are dynamic traits. They fall in the class of relatively "narrow" sentiments, built by learning, as aggregates of attitudes. Like any other common dynamic trait, roles are possessed or assumed (for they are both permanent and temporary) more easily by some people than others. One man knows how to take the role of, say, a classroom teacher; another does not and so on. To the sociologist role traits seem more important than personality traits—the limit of what a person will do when he stands up to teach a class, or sits in a theater, or meets an amber traffic light is decided more by the extent to which he has learned the role requirements suitable for everyone than by his individual personality. In highly culturally determined situations the sociologist is right; but in other and wider contexts the psychologist gets along quite well by measuring personality factors, letting the extent to which a person can adopt a particular role be handled by minor error variance. In any case *the variations of behavior within the role*—which is not entirely a straitjacket—are decided by personality differences.

When people agree to assume a test-taking role, however, roles are important enough for us to add role factors. Let us distinguish them by writing *R*s in addition to the *T*s (traits). It has been pointed out in introducing the effect of modulation of state levels by ambient stimuli that roles probably also modulate (Chapter Five) like states. That is, the set of dynamic attitudes constituting *role-readiness* in the individual is excited, as a state is excited, to a new level by the cues in the ambient situation. This change occurs before the role or state comes into play in reacting to the focal stimulus. The extent to which the role, when excited for action, *affects* behavior is shown by the behavioral index *b*, a value specific to that role trait in that situation.

In the complete analysis of role action roles must be considered as "readinesses" (pronenesses or liabilities) which, as described in Chapter Six, are *modulated* by an index s_k expressing the provocation of the ambient situation *k*, before *b*, the behavioral index operates. Thus we have $b_{jx}\ s_{kx}\ R_x$ where *j* is the focal and *k* the ambient role-provoking stimulus. However, in factor analysis the loading which is obtained directly by calculation, and which we shall write below as $\boldsymbol{b}_{jkx}$ cover $b_{jk}\ s_{kx}$. So for simplicity here we shall keep to b_{jkx} in a first exposition. Note also in the following equation that the effect of cognitive clichés is represented by a single instance, though normally there would be several.

$$d_{jki} = b_{jk1} T_{1i} + \ldots + b_{jkj} T_{ji} + \ldots + b_{jkp} T_{pi} + b_{jkR1} R_{1i} + b_{jkC1} C_{1i} \tag{9.20}$$

Here the distortion d_{jki} on scale j by individual i in test-taking situation k is considered, like any other behavior, to be predictable from the p personality factor endowments (T_i through T_p) of his total personality, each multiplied by the appropriate weights for the situation. In addition one role factor R_1 and one cliché C_1 are brought in, although in practice two or three might be simultaneously involved, as when the subject is taking the test in his role as an applicant for a research assistantship but also as a rival to his peers.

The score that a psychologist would record from the questionnaire for j is not d_{jki} but O_{jki}—the final observed score for trait T_j in person i in situation k. That is, O_{jki}, where k is the test-taking situation, is considered a sum of the distortion and the person's true score on that trait T_{ji} thus:

$$O_{jki} = T_{ji} + d_{jki} \tag{9.21}$$

If we add T_{ji} to both sides of Equation (9.20) we get

$$O_{jki} = b_{jk1} T_{1i} + \ldots + (b_{jkj} + 1) T_{ji} \text{ and so forth} \tag{9.22}$$

We can get O_{jki} values for a whole series of equations such as (9.22) by administering a multitrait scale like the 16 PF—covering 14 to 16 traits like j—to a lot of subjects. We can get more equations if each scale is administered in several different test-taking roles. For example, if the 14 factors of the HSPQ are scored from the same subjects in four different test-taking situations, there are four observed scores, O_{jk1}, O_{jk2}, O_{jk3}, and O_{jk4}, for each trait T_j and thus 56 (4 × 14) variables and equations in all. From the factoring of these 56 variables (to which some interest measures to mark the individual's development of role attitudes could be added) all 14 true-factor scores would be obtained as factors and each could be estimated, as well as the individual's scores on the role factors (including his endowment in the cognitive clichés). The true personality factors, as the real influences in the situation, should factor out as different from the observed scale scores O_{jk}, O_{pk}, and so on, which are the actual variables. Furthermore the b (behavioral index or factor pattern) and w (factor estimation) weights so obtained could be filed for reference in future single testings. Thus, as a matter of practical convenience, whenever a subject takes a test in that situation we should not have to factor again. Instead of taking the observed scale score O_{jki} on trait j as the best approximate score for him on that trait as we now do, we should calculate the true T_{ji} score as a weighted composite of the observed O_{jki} score and his other factor scores (O_p and so on).

This is the theoretical essence of trait-view theory, and although experiments with it are recent it works quite well (Krug, 1970). In practice one should find that the questionnaire scale for the trait in question O_j has the largest weight in determining the estimate of the true trait T_j. But on general psychological grounds one might expect the role factor to play perhaps the next largest part and virtually all traits to play some part. And we must not forget that each cognitive cliché about desirability also plays its part, according to the b (loading) weights that factor analysis finds for it in that situation. An important, germinal research by Krug (1970; see condensation in Krug and Cattell, 1971) examines this question by giving the 16 PF in four situations: anonymity, job-seeking, presenting an esthetically ideal self, and seeking a date in a dating bureau. In addition to the 16 PF variables two role trait scores, by objective attitude and motivational-strength measurements, were made—the strength of interest in getting a job and in meeting an attractive member of the opposite sex. Thus when an earlier worker in distortion and social desirability said that distortion must be treated as "an interaction of self-knowledge and self-esteem" rather than simple social desirability, he was approaching the idea of trait-view correction, in which, however, not only self-esteem but also the whole personality enters the transaction.

Krug's results showed a clear role factor in both situations (job and date) and that it weighted the estimation of the true score for every factor evaluated. However, contrary to our initial expectation the weights for the role factors are no more than the average for the general personality factors. Krug showed that the trait-view correction, by these weights, gives psychologists a significant gain in obtaining the true score free of motivational distortion. Across all traits and all four instructional situations allowance for the perceptual effects of other traits on the recording of the trait significantly raised the validity. The addition of the role weights raised them somewhat more. Table 57(a) shows the magnitude and significance of the gains. They are not spectacular, but in every case they show an increase in trueness of measurement—that is, in validity—significant at the $P < 0.01$ level. Table 57 also shows the degree of specificity of the desirability clichés—the Cs in equations such as (9.16), for when we set out the average score change as here the principal effect is due to the common R and the common C.

It should be evident that TV (trait-view) theory works and in fact supplies a more reliable and sensitive model for correcting motivational distortion (including social desirability) than the ad hoc patching of results by a single distortion or lie scale or indiscriminate general desirability allowance. Increasing practical use of the TV correction requires research to establish the mean shift and the weights for each trait by factoring for situations in which questionnaires are used in applied psychology. Both the (a) and the (b) values are required in order to return an individual's observed score to a corresponding true score. Regarding the mean difference for all persons in the role and nonrole situations, Tables 56(b) and 57(b) show appreciable consistency in the idealizing pattern and suggest agreement on a general desirability. Thus people wish to be, and to be thought by others to be, high on affectia A, ego strength C, superego G, parmia H, and self-sentiment Q_3. (We can confidently add intelligence B. The absence of difference for B

Table 57

Correction of Motivational Distortion by Applied Trait-View Theory

(a) Gain in Validity (Evaluated on multiple R) over Usual Scale Scoring

Test Situation	*Effect of Correcting for Influence* *Personality Traits*	*Personality and Role Traits*
Job-seeking	+0.08	+0.10
Date-seeking	+0.06	+0.07

Note: Values are multiple R (shrinkage corrected) for trait-view validity minus validity for simple scale scoring. All differences significant at $P < 0.01$ level.

(b) Variations in Social Desirability Cliché as Shown by Change in Mean Score from Anonymous Administration to Three Role Situations

Factor	*Job-Seeking*	*Socially Ideal Self*	*Date-Seeking*	*General Desirability* [a] *(Meredith)*
Affectothymia	1.2	1.6	1.0	1.4
Intelligence	−0.1	−0.3	0.0	−0.7
Ego strength	1.9	2.9	1.7	2.3
Dominance	−0.2	−0.6	0.0	−0.3
Surgency	−0.7	−0.1	0.0	0.3
Superego	2.1	2.5	0.6	1.7
Parmia	1.9	2.3	1.7	2.4
Premsia	0.2	−0.2	−0.4	−1.1
Protension	−1.6	−2.1	−1.5	−1.4
Autia	−0.5	−1.1	−0.7	−1.4
Shrewdness	1.1	1.4	0.8	1.5
Guilt proneness	−2.3	−3.0	−1.9	−2.5
Radicalism	0.9	1.0	0.7	0.6
Self-sufficiency	−0.8	−1.3	−0.9	−1.5
Self-sentiment	2.5	2.9	1.4	2.5
Ergic tension	−2.8	−3.6	−2.2	−3.2

[a] These four patterns of desirability are presented as a difference similarly calculated for the three roles as from Meredith's and DeVoogd's results in Tables 15 and 56, with which they should be compared. Virtually all differences, except those for intelligence, surgency, and premsia, are significant at $P < 0.01$ level. Data from Krug and Cattell (1971). Positive sign means desirable.

in Tables 56 and 57 is a tribute to the objective test as opposed to the questionnaire: B was not rated but objectively measured.) People similarly wish to be low on protension L, guilt proneness O, and ergic tension Q_4 and, less definitely, in this culture on self-sufficiency Q_2 and autia M. (As pointed out earlier, this combination indicates a high summation on avoiding the second-order QII anxiety factors—C-, H-, L, O, Q_3-, Q_4—as well as favoring exvia QI—A, F, H, and Q_2—in all but surgency F. Thus, in spite of appreciable agreement on general desirability (which is not to say it appears as a general desirability factor) the specific desirabilities that distinguish impressing an employer from impressing a girl friend are quite evident.

As we pass from the TV correction the reader should note two important points. First, the form and calculation of the weighting correction are similar to multiscale synthesis in *computer-scale synthesis* or variance allocation (see below). The difference is that in trait-view correction the combining weights are peculiar to a test-taking situation, whereas in computer-scale synthesis one uses averaged values obtained across all situations. In the latter the weights on other scales are considered simply as indications of missing and misplaced variance from the scale in question rather than as situational perception effects. Second, the use of TV correction in questionnaires is consistent with and an integral part of trait-view theory as it affects ratings by observers—L(BR)-data. Although L(BR)-data are not in the scope of this book, this broad application gives TV theory an elegance and practical value in making a global correction in a joint use of Q-data and L(BR)-data. This is not the place to pursue the observer-rating analysis, but it may be said that TV theory in the rating area doubles the length of Equations (9.20) and (9.22) by requiring one set of weights for the effect of traits other than T_j in the *person observed* since they confuse the observer's perception of T_j, and another set for the same traits in the *observer* as they affect (by projection) his perception of trait T_j in another. In the questionnaire, where one individual is both the observer and the observed, TV theory supposes that both effects operate as in L-data; but mathematical statistics permits us to combine the two weights into a single value since they operate on the same T-score (Cattell, 1968, 1964).

A second approach is being developed to correct for motivational distortion, one that is consistent with the general trait-view theory but uses assumptions that simplify it in practice. This approach is the *vulnerability-coefficient* (VC) method. It is simpler in practice because one needs only two measures (on one occasion) for trait T_j instead of measures for all of a person's traits. These two measures, however, must be on two special scales of known and unequal *vulnerability*. From a comparison of the vulnerability coefficients of these two scales and the two scores one can infer the true score for the limiting case of a scale that by definition would be invulnerable to motivational distortion.

The VC model collapses all the influences assumed to be at work in Equation (9.20) into a single *distortion force* D_{xki}—the sum of all terms on the right of Equation (9.20). As the subscripts show, this distortion force needs a value specific to the trait T_j, to the situation k, and to the individual i. However, unlike the TV method it does not have to examine the common personality influences one by one—the b_js in Equation (9.20)—or know individual i's endowments of other personality traits. Instead it wraps the total effect of the general bs—applicable to everyone in that situation—and the individual's traits into a single parcel D_{jki}—the total distortion—where k is the ambient test-taking situation. The VC model introduces a new term, however, with which we did not concern ourselves in TV, namely v_{ja}, which is the vulnerability of a particular scale a for measuring trait T_j, defined as the effect when one unit of distorting force is applied. It takes the form

$$T_{jaki} = b_{kja} T_{ji} + v_{ja} D_{jki} \tag{9.23}$$

Here we have a simple linear equation but the terms have the meanings and the ranges of values of factor-analytic specification equation terms. The observed score on scale a for trait j for person i on occasion k is i's true score on scale a for j, namely, T_{ji}, given weight b_{kja} to be defined plus a component due to distortion that is a product of the vulnerability of the scale a for trait T_j, namely, v_{ja}, as affected by i's strength of need for motivational distortion of trait T_j in situation k.

Since b_{kja} is merely the weight necessary to make T_{ji} bring T_{jaki} to unit variance—that is, $b_{kja} = \sqrt{1 - v_{ja}^2}$, there being no specific factor left over—it is necessary only to know the observed score T_{jaki}, vulnerability v_{ja}, and D_{jki} in order to solve for the true score T_{jai}. Vulnerability v_{ja} is a fixed characteristic of the scale. It may be obtained by a prior factor analysis of a minimum of eight or nine scores—for example, those of scales S_{ja} and S_{jb} in four different testing situations k_1, k_2, k_3, k_4—which should yield five factors: T_j, D_{kj1}, D_{jk2}, D_{jk3}, and D_{jk4}; the last four are loaded on only two measures. The loading values at the correct rotation position constitute v_{ja} and v_{jb} and the b values. If we prefer a model that allows unique factor variance it can be accommodated in these equations, but for simplicity it is omitted here since it does not affect the general argument.

Now we cannot obtain the true score T_{ji} from a single measure T_{jaki} in a single ambient situation k, even if we know b_{kja} and v_{ja}. We can take a great number of alternative scales for it and estimate it as a factor from that number of equations, as in TV theory in (9.23). Or we can take *two* scale scores a and b in situation k. If we have already calculated v_js and b_js from enough situations, as the practical psychologist will have done for his files, we can proceed to solve as follows:

$$T_{ji} = \frac{v_{jb} T_{jak} - v_{ja} T_{jbk}}{v_{jb} b_{kja} - v_{ja} b_{kjb}} \tag{9.24}$$

where T_{jak} and T_{jbk}, the two scale scores in the situation, are all we need.

Indeed we may not need to know the bs. If the error uniqueness is known from test reliability, then $b_{kja} = \sqrt{1 - v_{ja}^2 - e_{kja}^2}$. A detailed statement of these derivations is available elsewhere (Cattell, 1973b); Cattell and DeVoogd (1973) have explored the soundness of the VC model and the accompanying calculation on real data (16 PF scores on college students). The results suggest that the vulnerability coefficient of a scale may vary with the situation and that specifics must be added, complicating but not halting solution.

In conclusion the difference between the VC and trait-view correction is one of emphasis: each is adapted to different practices. There is no difference in regard to the underlying, *generic* model from which both are derived. Whereas the TV model splits the distortion force D_{jk1} into detailed origins but has no index for the scale's vulnerability, the VC model extracts reciprocally the vulnerability of the scale from the shift in mean and the bs in which it is hidden in the TV model, but takes the personality, dynamic influences as a composite. Consequently it is ultimately possible to bring the notation into a single generic model.

What "vulnerability to distortion" means in terms of scale construction and item content we cannot know until more research has been done to relate measured vulnerability coefficients of scales to hypothetical causes in item content and form; but some hypotheses are found in the study of item form in the next section. And although the VC and TV theories (especially with role measures) offer prospects of real control of distortion, it is perhaps unlikely, in view of the values in Table 57, that they will succeed in raising questionnaire validity to the levels of such objective personality batteries as the O-A battery (Schuerger and Cattell, 1973).

To complete this survey of sabotage and motivational distortion through personality, role motivation, and cognitive clichés, we must examine one more source—sheer ignorance. "Know thyself" is a maxim of philosophers that not even they can achieve. The possibility suggests itself that this might be handled under trait-view theory, inasmuch as some people are more naïve about themselves than others: this might be a function of low intelligence $B-$, low self-sentiment Q_3-, and naïveté $N-$. But TV theory assumes that each observer trait produces a distortion in a particular direction in the evaluated trait, whereas now we suppose a curvilinear relationship in which ignorance can cause a greater deviation in either direction.

Self-ignorance may operate more in some traits than others, but its general nature is that of random error and its effect on questionnaire scores is much the same as guessing (Nunnally 1967, 1970; Wiggins, 1973). Its effect on most questionnaire constructions is to bring the individual nearer the mean than he should be. Consequently if we had some independently derivable "index of self-ignorance"—and this may someday be possible—we could increase the deviations appropriately, as one does a group parameter (say, a correlation) by correcting for attenuation by unrealibility.

Such approaches are at present speculative and since the matter cannot be handled in scoring it must be attacked by test construction itself. An unintelligent or thoughtless man may not be able to evaluate himself in terms of traits, which are abstractions, but he can respond as reliably as anyone else on what he does. However, couching the questionnaire items in defined situations and responses reduces homogeneity to about 0.1 and is not so immediately rewarding in giving fat correlations with the factor as do such items as "Are you an extravert?" It demands that many more items be used, sampling behavior broadly, to get the same validities, and it underlines the need to insist that two to four forms of a test be used rather than one. As Humphreys (1973) has said, "there is rarely any good excuse for making inferences affecting the lives of individuals on the basis of very short tests, or shortened forms of standard tests."

6. Over-All Test Design in Relation to Common Testing Conditions

My aim in this section is to discuss the psychometrics of questionnaires in relation to features of design and administration more qualitative than those handled in the discussion of basic statistical parameters. Moreover I do so in relation to issues less basic than consistency or validity, namely, in regard to the convenience and acceptability of the procedures to the subject, the psychologist, and the community.

The more detailed technical issues involve both design and administration. Considerable attention has been given to the itemetrics of design by Goldberg (1972b), Neil and Jackson (1970); Tryon (1968), Rimm (1963), and others. The length of a test is one issue that involves both administration and design. The typical test user cannot demand all the time he needs from the subject in one block—nor would good testing requirements, such as the avoidance of fatigue or rejection, permit it. Moreover he will want to retest subjects on the same traits—especially in experiments on intermediate treatments—sometimes after so short an interval that the subject would remember and repeat mechanically his earlier answers. (The shortest safe period in my experience is one or two weeks, judging by the subject's ability to recognize repeated items.) Consequently all tests must have *equivalent forms*. Most IPAT personality questionnaires have no fewer than four, A, B, C, and D. As far as the labor of the designer and publisher are concerned, this production is a labor of love, inasmuch as later forms are not bought one-tenth as much as the first in the present climate of demanding brief, indeed instant, measurement.

The design of providing extensions into equivalent forms—the telescopic principle—is necessary for reasons other than experimental repetition or the avoidance of fatiguing sessions. Reliable and valid measures of personality factors designed with the life-spread principle—concreteness of behavior with breadth of life region covered—demand that we work with 35 to 55 items per factor. Unfortunately it is an endemic illusion of applied psychologists that it is appropriate to test 10 to 20 personality factors in 40 minutes—about 12 items per factor. Yet in intelligence testing they are accustomed to giving this time begrudged to 20 dimensions to just one dimension, Spearman's *g*. The reliabilities and validities for a 10-to-13-item personality scale, such as affectia (A) or parmia (H), are *as good as or better than the intelligence test of the same length in the same scale*. Personality tests, in other words, intrinsically demand no more time than any other test modality. Indeed in some scales of the same length—see the 16 PF Handbook—they exceed intelligence tests, offering a reliability of about 0.8 as against 0.6 for intelligence and a validity of 0.7 as against 0.5 for the same length. Nevertheless no important personality prediction should be based on form A only; in most research the simultaneous use of three or four forms is recommended. The telescopic principle of having forms A and B of one length and forms C and D of another permits, by their possible combinations, a telescoping of the battery to almost any desired length. The parallel form and telescoping principles are devices for adjusting test length and for convenience of retesting, not for permitting the unconscionably short testing that many single-form tests on the market encourage.

Any discussion of test length ultimately encounters the need to distinguish between sessions and equivalent forms. With young children the appropriate time for sustained attention defines a session. It is then found that such a single sitting is insufficient for the required reliability length of an "equivalent form," so the form must be cut again into separate printed sessions 1 and 2. Regarding time and the questionnaire, note that since a questionnaire is untimed and yet must be completed by all, the administrative trick of pacing becomes necessary. A rate of two to six items per minute is a reasonable average, depending on length of item and reading capacity. Experience shows the distribution of finishing times to be badly skewed upward—most subjects finish promptly but some go on forever. Therefore the subject should be given some pacing by being told how far along he needs to be. Thus it is usual in the 16 PF or HSPQ to say after 10 or 12 minutes, "You should now be one-third of the way through, at about item 50." Moreover there is some consensus among psychologists—but no adequate research—indicating that the instruction "Respond as quickly as you can, giving your immediate answer" is sound not only in increasing the information per minute of testing, but in yielding more honest responses.

Questionnaire instructions normally require the subject neither to leave the test before he gets to the end nor to omit any items. Sporadic omissions or failure to complete the test present a difficult scoring problem. Proportionality will not do because items vary considerably in extremity. The instruction to "answer everything, regardless of doubts" is like that in ability tests to "guess when uncertain." But the effect on the score is different in that random response in an ability test tends to bring some gain (25 percent when one answer in four choices is correct), whereas in the ordinary balanced questionnaire it moves him toward the trait mean. The question of whether more information per minute comes from fewer or more multiple choices per item has scarcely been attacked except for the work of Barton (in press), but it is considered as a special design problem below.

The format of a questionnaire as well as the item structure must naturally be adapted to the age and education of the subject. As to format the IPAT series—which is the only one with the same factor traits measured (in five stages) continuously from four years through seventy or more—makes the time of a single *session* shorter relative to age. A conflict of design arises in that, as far as research indicates, young children need more items than older ones to get the same scale reliability and validity, yet their attention and fatigue spans are shorter. To cope with this impasse the IPAT designs distinguish, as above, between sessions (A1 and A2 in the ESPQ), which are cut to *the length a child may be expected to attend,* and forms which, as with the high school and adult scales, are acceptable minimum lengths of equivalent scales, for validity, reliability, and standardization scatter. With enough sessions the required form length can be provided.

Age adaptation in content is also a planned part of measuring the same factor at different age levels—in the expanding vocabulary, in the form of presenting the item, and in the form of the response required. In the 16 PF, HSPQ, and CPQ (above age eight) the item is read by the subject, the word count reducing as eight years is approached. From six to eight years in the ESPQ the question is read by the psychologist. At that age, too, the child does not respond on an ordinary complex-looking machine answer sheet but by marking under small pictures. From four to eight years in the PSPQ (Pre-School Personality Questionnaire) not only are the questions oral, as in the ESPQ, but since young children respond more to cues than to words (to the innuendos of intonation) they are presented in a standard voice from a tape-recorder. At the same time the testing shifts from classroom administration to individual testing and the responses are oral; the psychologist himself records the responses on an answer sheet.

Little is known about the effect—in regard to possible increase of errors—of the use of machine answer sheets in older groups. Whereas not completely understanding and not finishing on time are normal characteristics of ability and achievement examinations and are recognized as part of the expression of low ability, the aim of a personality questionnaire is to make the cognitive comprehension and the manner of response as clear, easy, and equal as possible. Consequently there is no objection to reading out items or to explaining word meanings, provided that it can be done without suggestion, even with older subjects. Nor is the danger of suggestion an objection to giving tests in an individual situation provided that the subject can give his *response* in privacy on an answer sheet without personal oversight by the examiner. Objections do arise if the examiner reads and explains the question because he inevitably introduces personal interpretation and suggestion. Moreover there is a psychological difference between responding, privately on paper and giving one's answers before the critical eye of a stranger. This is one more case, over and above the other deficiencies of the interview demonstrated by Eysenck (1971), in which the questionnaire is superior to the interview. Of course the subject knows that his replies to individual items could be seen by someone, but with machine scoring the likelihood seems remote. Consequently in comparing the technique and results of the interview with those reached impersonally in a questionnaire one should bear in mind that one is dealing with different things. A better solution for adult illiterates or near-illiterates is Eber's 16 PF form E (and equivalent F), which is printed but requires only a small vocabulary. As for reading and writing problems, Eber has brought further improvement by his use of headphones and microphone tape-recording of questions and answers in a private booth setup.

This discussion of the conditions of testing and the manner of adaptation to age and education also defines the desiderata of instructions. In machine scoring the assurance of privacy can go as far as a promise to the subject that no one will see the individual item response; and since we know that distortion drops markedly in the anonymous situation this assurance is valuable. An important item in most questionnaire instructions is a statement that it is not an ability test so that the subject can be assured that there are no right and wrong answers. The subject is in fact stating his tastes or temperament traits, and if testing has its usual objectives he can be promised that such statements could help him personally. For example, testing will help him clinically or prevent his becoming a "misfit" educationally or occupationally.

Leaving discussion of items to the next section we still need to consider total test construction. Does the sequence of items matter? The fact that item-factor validities have not been shown to alter, beyond chance expectation, with different item orders suggests that there is no major effect. But research may show effects of propinquity on validity and on extremity (cuts). Suspecting that if several items for the same factor follow in close contiguity there is a risk of the person's perceiving the intent and being better able to fake and a risk of response-inhibiting effects modifying the true cuts, the IPAT series cycles the order of items by repeating the factor series—A through Q_4 in this case—an item from each at a time.

A question that occurs to those familiar with the criteria of psychophysical methods concerns the questionnaire's use of absolute judgments instead of paired comparisons. The subject gives an absolute judgment separately for each item instead of getting ultimately to a more dependable ranking through paired comparison. The implicit or real paired-comparisons method was given a trial in the Q-sort of Stephenson (1953) used by Rogers, but for other reasons was as fallacious in theory as it was costly in practice.[5] (Paired comparisons among 200 items is a day's work.) Refinements of scoring can be introduced that help scaling but they are too costly to be adopted. For example, different people use extreme scores with different frequencies. (This itself is a personality trait: Hundleby, Pawlik, and Cattell, 1965.) Since so wide an array of questions samples virtually all behavior, the extreme answers could be given the individual weights for each person that are indicated by his distributions of central and extreme answers. More practical is the recording of the frequency of use for all people together of central and extreme categories and the relative weighting of item responses according to their average frequency. However, this has never offered enough gain relative to the labor involved to recommend itself to the practicing psychologist (see Chapter Ten). In the event that one uses computer synthesis by item the relative use of extremes is taken care of by the assigned special weight to each item.

7. The Main Parameters of Item Content and Form

Principles for the design of items in relation to test conditions and purposes are more discussed than experimented on (but see Hase and Goldberg, 1967). In the mathematical statistics of that branch of psychometry that deals with item relations, which is a kingdom vast enough to deserve its own name, itemetrics, there is seemingly endless publication on scaling effects, forced-choice, number of responses, weighting, and incomplete

[5] There were three major flaws in Q-sort: inability to tie down the dimension with respect to which the items were ranked within the person ("importance to him" being vague); the fact that in later use of such data to determine resemblance of people the correlation was completely unstable, changing with each new sample of items (there was no *personality sphere*); and the use of the correlation coefficient for such profiles instead of the new pattern-similarity coefficient r_p is statistically faulty. The two last points do not concern us here, but the first does. What one really seeks is the extremity score of the item in the makeup of the person after each of his responses is normatively scored across people. To attempt to get this by asking the person how important the item is to him could be very different indeed from the extremity of his normative score.

responses but almost all studies refer to statistical rather than psychological properties and concepts. As far as statistics is concerned the central emergents, beginning with the Spearman-Brown formula, have been vital. But the reader must be familiar with the central formulas from testing courses, including the inference (see Guilford, 1954) from the Spearman-Brown formula for the relation of length to validity and the adaptation to factored scales in the Cattell-Radcliffe formula (1963). Thus I shall deal with psychological issues in construction.

It goes without saying that items should operate with the minimum effective vocabulary and should avoid what is socially objectionable or an unacceptable invasion of privacy. It is useful in practice to make a distinction for this reason between normal and abnormal population scales, since those intended for clinical use must obviously ask questions about pathology impertinent to the normal person. The IPAT 16 PF has been used in government organizations where the Congressional Inquiry into Invasion of Privacy (see Congressional Record and the *American Psychologist,* January 1963) caused withdrawal of the MMPI. But the IPAT Clinical Analysis Questionnaire (CAQ) is like the MMPI in asking questions about "crazy behavior" to which people in a nonclinical group might raise objections.

In the name of common sense one must comment that in some psychological circles it is the fashion to outdo one another in displays of alleged ethical sensitivity, demanding restrictions which, had they been applied to psychological experiment historically, would have deprived us of half of present scientific knowledge. In the applied field this tendency threatens to invalidate the diagnostic capacities of the practicing psychologist. Emotionally and socially the antitest movement has unmistakable resemblance to antivivisectionism in physiology and that which denied Vesalius access to human anatomy. The real values in this situation have been well stated in *Psychological Tests and Constitutional Rights* (1966). If a patient comes for help to a physician he expects to take his clothes off; by the same token if he is averse to "invasion of privacy" in questionnaires he should not come to a psychologist. And in regard to meeting the effectiveness requirements of jobs the wisely designed questionnaire asks nothing that has not been asked in interviews. The individual who seeks help medically or psychologically should be prepared for some sacrifices not only for his own sake but also as repayment for advantages from therapeutic knowledge gained by the previous sacrifices of others to experiment.

In turning now from general structure and instructions to a taxonomy of items it is convenient to divide considerations into two aspects: *psychological parameters* and *parameters of form.* The first concerns the best sampling of the behavioral field, the handling of instrument-factor effects, and the maintenance of reference as far as possible to behavior, on which the person can hope to compare himself with others objectively. The main principles behind these aspects of test design have been discussed. Regarding breadth of items I have pointed out that in early questionnaires the psychiatric interview and clinical observations first biased the field, but that the *personality-sphere* concept led out of this canyon into the uplands where at first 18 and then 23 normal primaries were found (with 12 abnormal dimensions appearing). The discussion of instrument factors has brought sophisticated choice of items to produce a balance of known instrument areas. Psychologists sometimes refer to these in rough metaphor as splinter factors. Nunnally (1967), for example, views the matter in terms of broad, primary personality factors somehow splintering into areas that must be represented—see Table 33d for structure of such splinters. From Chapter Seven we recognize that there are observer-view instrument factors which arise from role relations and areas of observation; since they cannot be excluded the next best thing is to sample them evenly. In questionnaires this means sampling behavior with respect to such areas as home, occupation, and hobbies and to a good division between behavior with the physical world and with people.

As pointed out in Chapter Seven, although these subareas bring instrument factors one type of splinter pattern—that concerning areas of expression—has subfactors that are psychologically quite real. They arise from some persons exercising their trait more in one field than another, such as one man expressing his dominance (*E* factor) in business, another in the family, and another in sports. However, regardless of whether these subdomains are considered strictly instrument factors or substantive trait subpatterns, the constructor of tests has to have them in mind and create items to span and sample them evenly. The effect of good spanning is to reduce scale homogeneity almost to zero (see Table 55). It removes the risk of entering a fool's paradise of high homogeneities and pseudo-validities based on bloated specifics. There is every reason to believe, too, that it increases the retention of validity across groups as shown by the transferability coefficient. In test construction this balancing of instruments by broad and deliberate sampling results in a valid estimation of the factor score against which the test items are selected. Any unitractic factor scale should therefore come from a systematic plan of sampling with due proportion from home, school, business, recreation, and so forth.

It is important in questionnaire research occasionally to step outside the thinking of ordinary psychometry and remember that an item falls into the broad psychological framework of a stimulus-response event. An item can be redesigned and perhaps improved at both ends: stimulus and response. Essentially I have discussed the stimulus aspect that calls for good sampling of situations as part of the personality-sphere concept in its *culture-sampling* aspect (Cattell, 1946, 1957; Cattell and Warburton, 1967). Before leaving that stimulus aspect of the item let us consider the degree of *concreteness versus semantic generality* in the item. We may write an item in this way: "On a quiet suburban street after midnight I look around nervously. Often, Seldom, Never." Or we may write it in this way: "I easily become fearful. True, False." Still more general and abstract is the form in many inventories or checklists in which the item is simply given to the subject as if it were a trait rating: "Which fits you better? Greedy or Lazy?" (forced-choice) or "Are you lazy? True, False."

It is evident from my personality theory and experimental work that the use in questionnaires of such a simple checklist of abstract trait items—"Are you sociable? Honest? Impatient?"—is a poor procedure. Nevertheless it takes sophisticated procedures to show this; the first effect of asking "Are you a sociable person?" in six different semantic forms is to yield high homogeneity coefficients, good reliability, and apparently acceptable validities—in a shallow sense. The objections to the general rather than the specific behavioral question are threefold. First, that the homogeneity of the general is spurious—purely semantic—and as such is a bloated specific instrument factor. Second, that it is vulnerable to faking because the subject is more ready to fool himself and the tester about a vague generality than about a specific action he recalls concretely and because the desirability distortion is tied more to a trait than to a specific act from which the inference that the tester will make is not obvious. Third, the general trait probably shows poor transferability across cultures because figments are partly peculiar to a culture—"honest" in the Mafia does not mean the same as in the middle class. One must indeed suspect that the superficially good psychometric properties of the trait self-checklist and the general item are like those clear and convincing maps that Schiaparelli drew of the canal systems of Mars before sophisticated instruments showed craters and fault systems.

Yet it must be recognized that specific behavioral questions are difficult to make as precise and concrete as the ideal laboratory stimulus-response situation. Faced with "Would you rather go to a party or read a book?" Jane will tell you "If George called I would go to the party, but if Douglas, then I'd naturally stay home and read." When one considers such typical items—different in meaning for the sexes, and modified by the quality of the caller and the author of the book—it is not surprising that item-factor analysis is under suspicion and that even when factors are defined by parcels and scales the discovered item loadings vary with samples.

However, the solution is not to swing back to trait questions but to search more diligently—as has been done in trying more than 10,000 items for reasonable stability of factor validity in the 16 PF—for better behavioral items. They must be better in the sense that although relatively concrete they can be shown by factoring to reflect much the same trait expression in different cultures. Finally it must be recognized that this approach is likely to yield items that not only have distinctly lower homogeneity than semantically overlapping trait reference items but also have lower individual correlations with the factor. The latter means that a short scale (say, 12 items) made from types of behavior does not have the same factor validity as one of the same length made from trait words. This is why users are urged always to use forms A and B, not A alone, in the 16 PF, HSPQ, and other tests on this principle.

One fact that psychometrists should face squarely is that one cannot get a valid measure (beyond, say, 0.6) of a broad human personality source trait from 10 items and $2\frac{1}{2}$ minutes of testing (as a physicist recognizes that he cannot, at present, photograph accurately below certain light intensity and time of exposure). The questionable practice in Buros' *Mental Measurement Yearbook* of allowing test authors to review rival tests—without explicit confession of interest and without reciprocal opportunities—has permitted highly misleading advice to test users on this easily distortable question. A claim to validities of 0.9 on 10 item scales, or the statement that 10 item-scale validities below this are evidence of poor construction for validity, means that the nature of validity is not understood. Higher apparent validities and homogeneities on 10-to-12-item scales are almost certainly being spuriously obtained by substituting a bloated specific (as an instrument factor or a situational or semantic specific) for much of the general personality factor that one claims to measure.

The problem of concrete and particular versus abstract and general items has been exacerbated in state measurement over anything encountered in trait questionnaires. Such true-false items as "I am happy," "I feel good," and "I feel cheerful" have proved in Spielberger's state-trait anxiety scale to show high homogeneities and high apparent validities against the factor. But is the factor what it seems to be? Does it include the physiological and behavioral measures belonging to T-data factor UI 24 (in the multi-instrument concept of the anxiety factor) as Scheier's, Curran's, Barton's, and Nesselroade's behavioral state questionnaires have been shown to do? The risk of retreating into an Osgoodian semantic domain where verbal relations correctly represent, as stereotypes, the apparent factor relations in nature but where the scores of individuals are quite false (Passini and Norman, 1966) is especially great in state measurement. Moreover, the use of whole trait or state checklist terms brings in the solipsistic standardization error. Since feeling is by nature introspective and subjective the individual can have little idea where the level of his feeling falls relative to that of another person. The only tangible basis of comparison we have is behavior. Is he so timid that he avoids, more than his friends do, a visit to the dentist? Is he so depressed that he weeps or refuses to talk? Formally the solipsism problem is like that of comparing parents' ratings of their children with those by peers or teachers. The between-family variance is lost, as the between-person variance threatens to be lost when feelings are not referred in state measurement to outside behavior.

In pursuing this discussion I have often crossed the not too sharp boundary between parameters that are psychological and those only concerned with item form. Matters not yet discussed regarding the parameters of item form concern (1) should items begin "Do you do so and so?" or "I do so and so"? (2) Should one permit items that deliberately depend slyly on projection rather than on true self-opinion? (3) Is it effective to use items such as "People say I am lazy" rather than "I am lazy"? (4) Is it desirable to make the opposite poles in the answer *equihedonic*—that is, equally attractive—as in one kind of forced-choice, selective-answer design? And (5) should one ask about obviously *dynamic* traits, such as *interests* and *values,* as an avenue to assessing general personality and temperament?

As to the first, nothing is known. I adopt the "I do" form mainly for simplicity. The second question requires a digression. It has been clearly shown that the defense mechanisms (Wenig, 1952; Cattell and Wenig, 1952) are as factorially unitary as Freud described them to be and operate as hypothesized. Consequently projection and other defenses can be effectively used as truly objective tests in measuring the strengths of interests, sentiments, and other dynamic traits (Murray, 1938; Cattell, 1936; Cattell, Horn, Sweney, and Radcliffe, 1964). Since the first designs of projective tests, simultaneously by Murray in the United States and myself in Britain, nearly 40 years ago, evidence has accumulated extensively—by McClelland and Atkinson (McClelland and others, 1953; Cattell, Horn, Sweney, and Radcliffe, 1964)—that the approach is valid for dynamic traits. The issue therefore reduces to whether we want to use dynamic traits to get at traits of a temperament modality as well as at dynamic traits themselves. (Personality covers temperament and dynamic but not cognitive modalities.)

Before proceeding to answer question (2) above let me remind the reader that projective behavior has been shown (Cattell and Wenig, 1952) to spring from two distinct projective mechanisms: *true projection* (dynamic in nature, as just discussed) and *naïve projection* (Anderson and Anderson, 1950; Cattell and Wenig, 1952). The latter is nothing more than distorting the perception of others or of some inanimate object through the limitations of one's experience. Naïve projection—as when a teetotaler assumes that another person who declines a drink is a teetotaler—is perfectly acceptable as an objective test device, but it proves to be neither powerful nor dependable. True projection (or any dynamic defense) has appreciable validity, although only for the dynamic, interest-strength trait. The real problem, therefore, does not reside in the validity of questionnaire items of a projective character—"Most people are obsessed with sex"—as measures of interest and attitudes, and values; it resides in getting at general personality-temperament through specific interests and values.

That some variance in attitudes and values is contributed by basic personality traits was recognized long ago when William James said that the systems of individual philosophers are best understood as a function of their temperaments. This has received precise experimental support in the work of Eysenck (1960), myself (1957; with Warburton, 1967), and others showing that substantial variance in values and beliefs, notably in the "toughminded-versus-tenderminded" domain of social attitudes, is contributed by premsia (sensitivity in Eysenck's list). Consequently such projective statements as "People are usually hostile" or such value statements as "Capital punishment should be abolished" are appropriate forms of true-false personality items. The distinction between such use and relying on questionnaires simply to measure the strength of a particular interest (learning a foreign language, attending meetings of a society) or an *ergic drive tension* (sex, gregariousness) is nevertheless considerable. But provided that we can produce empirical evidence and have a clear theory about the abstraction of temperament from interest variance through the operation of personality as a hidden premise, good use can be made of projective questions, especially for such general dynamic traits as the ego and superego strengths. This does not contradict my earlier position that the ordinary (nonprojective) questionnaire item is unsuitable for measuring interest strength and dynamic traits.

These paragraphs answer questions (1), (2), and (5) about form above. As for (4) I reject the forced choice design because, as stated earlier, it is not possible to balance for desirability across all fields, because it involves abstract trait list items rather than behavior, and because experience shows that it begets a resentment—perhaps hard to demonstrate experimentally—in the subject. As to (3), "people say I am" instead of "I think I am," though there is no evidence, one may hypothesize that the former would be more objective.

In summary, with present knowledge it seems best to use item forms of the most varied kinds—likes, dislikes, preference (values); statements about life generally ("A long life is not better than a well-lived short one"); what my friends think of me; occupational preferences; facts about the work of my own mind ("I find it hard to get my ideas into words"); statements about other people ("Judges are inclined to be sadistic"); what I want people to think of me; and the standard behavioral "What I actually do." Such variety reduces homogeneity coefficients relative to those from uniform items. But this is the usual price of avoiding instrument factors. At the present stage of research we must get breadth of trait expression by whatever ingenuity in creation of stimulus situations we can bring to bear. Maintaining breadth of both life area and item form should certainly be a conscious aim in all personality questionnaires. In this connection it is conceivable that sensitive factorial research will show that some instrument factor corresponds to each formal type of question. Thus my emphasis on the need for a variety of item styles must not be interpreted as calling for casualness of construction, but rather for deliberate sampling of known instrument factors.[6]

[6] As pointed out earlier in this chapter, instrument factors can be contamination in one place and information in another. Nunnally may be taken as representative of a common position among psychometrists who have not worked in objective personality tests (T-data). He simultaneously overestimates the difficulty of reducing the intrusion of response styles—desirability, acquiescence, extreme deviancy—in Q-data and underestimates the wealth of knowledge about the personality meaning of response styles available in T-data by saying that "research on response styles has mainly built on false hopes and methodological flaws" (1967, p. 115). This is true of those who have treated response styles only as a side-effect in traditional questionnaire fields and whose sole aim has been to keep response-style effects out of questionnaires (or to use observations on ability tests to elicit information about personality). Such writers as Rorer (1965) have merely castigated the uselessness of this response-style research; but some like Husek (1961) have glimpsed constructively its relation to true objective personality measurement. Those who have boldly entered personality structure and measurement wholly in objective tests, as did Bolz, Damarin, Dielman, Hundleby, Klein, Schuerger, Pawlik, and others in personality research, had the chief response styles later discussed by questionnaire constructors already located and understood as personality factor expressions before the questionnaire constructors reached the stage merely of recognizing them as a nuisance.

Unfortunately, limited reading by the questionnaire and cognitive-style researchers resulted in a failure to utilize these basic T-data findings. It was demonstrated by 1950 that acquiescence is an expression primarily of the personality factors indexed as UI 20 and 24, group dependence and anxiety. Indeed Scheier and I (Cattell and Scheier, 1961) found acquiescence sufficiently valid to be used as a regular subtest in the IPAT O-A anxiety battery (1963). Social desirability also, is heavily loaded (negatively) on anxiety,

Finally we must return to the stimulus aspect of item design and consider the relative vagueness and ambiguity. Some investigators, on the theory that every questionnaire item is a projection test, have presented evidence which seems to show that relatively unstructured items can be as valid and precise in properties as those sharpened to concrete situations. What they have not shown is that such items have normal transferability. From theory one would expect the factor composition of such items to change significantly across groups. Nunnally (1967) voices the opinion of experienced test designers when he says that he is appalled by the prevalent ambiguities of meaning or uncertainty in indicating the type of required response. One encounters such items as "I like school but I disagree with some teachers." Does a strong endorsement mean strong disagreement with teachers or strong liking for school? Getting precision of stimulus and category of response in reasonably short items is an art.

A special case requiring comment arises when items found valid scored by "yes" have to be reworded and reversed, as frequently happens in the attempt to get a balance of yes and no answers. There is no guarantee that reversing the wording ("I do" to "I do not"; "I like" to "I dislike") algebraically reverses the sign and retains the same loading, as McQuitty (1961) has shown and Rorer (1965) has discussed. A useful list of common opposites in items has been provided by Neil (1972). This problem occurs particularly in constructing items for those factors in abnormal behavior defined in Chapter Three. The opposite behavior to depression may be elation, that to excessive suspicion may be excessive trust, and so on. But how can one get a positive symptom check that is the real opposite to anxious forebodings or having hallucinations? This problem continues to present extra difficulties in the way of balancing for set and suppressor action (with retention of good validity) when constructing pathological factor scales.

Moving now to the response end of the stimulus-response item we encounter an immense bibliography of research on varied questions. Is forced-choice better than true-false? (Forced-choice is commonly understood, in the form raised by Edwards' work on social desirability, as a choice

---

whereby acquiescence and (low) desirability distortions must be significantly related. Tendency to extreme response, as investigated by Berg (1961), is found consistently negatively loaded in four studies (survey in Hundleby, Pawlik, and Cattell, 1965) on UI 23, mobilization-regression; that is, it goes with the neurotic end of this factor (using Scheier's and Eysenck's finding of marked association of UI 23 with neurotic groups). Extreme response set may also be partly determined by cortertia, UI 22. In short the names which style investigators attached to concepts of specific response behaviors do not express *single* personality factors. They are composite expressions, but their variance still derives mainly from broad personality traits rather than some trivial instrument factor.

Naturally, with this knowledge about response sets, some thought has been given to utilizing the contamination as an aid in practical work with questionnaires—indeed as an adjunct score instead of something to be eliminated. This would require that an acquiescence measure be added to the second-order anxiety *Q*II score and that an extremity score from all items be added to cortertia *Q*III. However, the labor of additional scoring is usually out of proportion to the gain. There is also a certain inelegance about this mixture of types of score. Consequently in the IPAT series the aim of design has been to minimize all such response-style effects.

between two traits that are planned to have equal social desirability or undesirability; but in some contexts it means two alternatives with no intermediate.) As to this issue in contrast to true-false (which brings in acquiescence) we have already given the opinion that it is not effective and that it probably builds up unwillingness to cooperate attentively. A good study in this area is that of D. N. Jackson, Neill, and Brown (1971) which after reviewing the work of Izard and Rosenberg, Krug, Norman (1963), Scott, Waters and Wherry, and others, comes to the conclusion that "neither nonforced nor forced-choice items have a clear advantage." And although their survey of other research suggests that forced-choice items may have high reliabilities, their own experiment came to the opposite conclusion. The answer to this is evidently not a general one. In any case the trait view theory approach makes it unnecessary to avoid desirability effects by this means.

As to the response issue of whether many or few response alternatives are desirable the answer seems to depend partly on the age and motivation of the subjects. The answer given by Guilford some years ago (1954) that more than two is an improvement continues to stand up well, but it is not the whole answer. Psychometrically it can be shown that slight improvement of reliability and validity occurs, as he points out, even up to a 20-point scale, although he shows it to be uncertain and negligible after six or seven multiple choices. Guilford's and others' work shows that the effect is one in which both error and true variance increase as one goes from two to seven, but the latter more rapidly. However, the argument on these grounds for a scale of six or seven points in multiple-choice meets three counterarguments. First, that it takes the subject longer to read and probably also to decide on such items, especially the man with an obsessional temperament. Second, that whereas two or three alternatives can be anchored in absolute meaning by brief verbal descriptions, it is not possible either psychologically or in printers' space to give descriptions for seven. Third, that subjects are likely to get both fatigued and irritated (and therefore careless) when too much hair-splitting is required.

Evaluating these influences experimentally has so far defied the ingenuity of psychometrists, but I am inclined to agree with Eysenck and Crowne that there is little to be said for multiplying alternatives beyond three or four. This question is taken up again in Chapter Ten in connection with the efficiency coefficient of a test—its validity per minute. In relation to all these generalizations, the 12 or so questionnaires—normal and abnormal, primary-factor and second-order factor, single-purpose and omnibus—designed by psychologists for IPAT have aimed at a judicious interpretation of psychometric and other rules together, in relation to the circumstances likely in each kind of test. Thus the maximum of six alternatives is used with adults and with state measurements but four are used with children. With trait measurements, on the other hand, since adult time is important the 16 PF uses three answers. Passing from adulthood to early childhood or from more to less educated subjects (as in the 16 PF form E) the multiple-choice is reduced to two opposites but these are fully spelled out; that is, they are anchored in relatively full behavior definitions. The reason for the even number in states is that it tends to prevent subjects from lazily accepting a middle alternative. The reason for four or six rather than two in states is that state measures are frequently used with brief retest intervals, and it is desirable to prevent subjects from remembering the previous response.

The number of alternatives raises again the scaling question of size of interval. Especially when difference scores are involved, the question of whether a shift from point 2 to 3 is equal to 3 to 4 (on a four-point alternative) could be important. Analysis of frequency of responses, when examined by a normal tester, could permit refinement of values given to the alternatives. But this complicates scoring and one is usually satisfied if choices can be reasonably assumed to be on a true continuum and, best of all, on an evenly spaced continuum. In practice one is generally confined to behaviorally defining the extremes and using a variety of adjectives in between—partly true, partly false, always, sometimes, hardly ever, never, very little, intensely, and so on. In general there are two ways of verbally expressing extremity in behavior: by intensity and by frequency. As pointed out (in Chapter Six on states) in commenting on Endler and Hunt's argument that in measuring anxiety these scores should be regarded as independent, the evidence is that they are not independent. Indeed the modulation theory (Cattell, 1972a) is that the frequency of just noticeable anxiety (a threshold anxious response) and the level of mean intensities of anxiety must be highly correlated in individual difference terms.

Finally it must be noted that there is some conflict between the ideal of making both stimulus and response specific and concrete in behavioral meaning and the need to construct items in simple newspaper English and short in reading time. The authors of the 16 PF, for example, have sometimes been criticized for couching the 16 PF forms A and B in somewhat too elegant English. The reply is that precision of stimulus and response is of paramount importance as in any psychological experiment, and that the semiliterate person gets more meaning than the observer supposes—provided that meaning is already in the item. However, the practical solution is to design a series of equivalent forms graded for demand on language; in the 16 PF this is provided in a reduction from the A and B equivalent forms through the C and D smaller-vocabulary forms to the E and F equivalent forms designed by Eber for the semiliterate.

8. Summary

(1) Test *consistency* can be evaluated in four directions corresponding to the primary coordinates of the data box (Cattell, 1956c, 1966a). This approach issues in four coefficients: *reliability* across time (observers plus conditions); *homogeneity* across test parts (stimuli); *transferability* across subpopulations (people); and *conspection* (across observers and scores alone).

Test validity has three parameters according to the nature of the criterion: (i) concrete to conceptual (construct); (ii) artificial to natural;

and (iii) direct to indirect. Such conceptions as content (or face) validity and predictive validity, although unfortunately much quoted, are misleading since they confound in the first case real criteria with subjective concepts of the observer and in the second case natural historical properties of the trait with true validity. They also fail operationally by providing no precise, test-general coefficient for calculation. The interactions of consistency and validity are psychometrically well known, although the use of the wrong form of consistency coefficient (as in correcting validity for attenuation) leads to difficulties (see analysis in Cattell and Radcliffe, 1962).

(2) High test consistency in the first three forms—reliability, dependability, and transferability coefficients—is desirable but homogeneity coefficients should reach only a low and optimum, not an indefinitely high, value. The requirement of a low, optimum value arises from the need (a) to sample a personality trait widely in its domains of expression, (b) to invoke suppressor action for unwanted factors, and (c) to avoid confounding the personality source trait with a bloated specific (this disaster is commonly the outcome of seeking high homogeneity). Because of the way in which personality structures express themselves a little in each of many acts, and the statistical requirements of high multiple correlation a broad span low homogeneity scale is the best. Incidentally, the counter argument that in ability and dynamic traits high item validity and homogeneity are simultaneously obtained overlooks (a) that figures quoted are commonly for subtests not items, (b) that the nature of temperament traits is broader than interests or special abilities, and (c) that items here are not objective.[7]

(3) A single equation relating scale validity to all parameters of items and scale—item validity, scale homogeneity as item correlation, item difficulty, degree of suppressor action, size of specifics, number of factors and number of items—is not possible because pattern as well as mean values enters. Moreover, although these are thought of as independent variables they are not, and separate equations among the rest must be set up for various fixed values of n, k, r_{jw} and so on. Nevertheless, using simplified conditions, notably that $k \geqq n$, and there are no specifics, several useful relations can be derived between item validity, homogeneity, number of items and scale validity. This suggests that with obtainable item validities of about 0.3 homogeneity is best kept around 0.1 or less. The higher homogeneity obtained by bloated specifics or semantic similarity is false and almost certainly in practice means low transferability and susceptibility to distortion. However, planned low homogeneity (by sampling diverse instrument factors systematically) within one form does not mean that there should be low equivalence between forms. Herringbone construction can yield a higher equivalence coefficient than the within-form split-half Spear-

[7] If instead of actual intelligence test problem items we ask "How well do you solve arithmetic problems?" or "Are you as quick as most to understand a joke?", such specific items correlate about 0.2 with the intelligence factor and have almost zero homogeneity; that is, they behave statistically like general personality factor items, although slightly poorer because of the relative unfitness of the questionnaire for ability measurement.

man-Brown corrected for doubling length, but that construction may not be desirable.

(4) An intensive examination of the psychometric parameters and concepts necessary for describing and evaluating questionnaire scales requires recognition of the precise meanings and distinctions of *factor* validity and *factor trueness, factor homogeneity* and *test homogeneity,* and *univocal* and *unitractic scales.* It also requires consideration of coefficients more broadly conceived than the validity coefficient—efficiency and utility coefficients. A univocal scale (contrast Guttman scale) requires only one factor and specifics to define the items (a rank-one matrix). A unitractic scale requires that the major factor measured by the items be centered on a uniquely rotated meaningful trait, so that the summed scores of items contribute to that factor far more than to any other; but a unitractic scale normally has other common factors in the items although reduced by suppressor action to zero in the ideal unitractic scale score. As Nunnally points out, a unitractic scale that is also univocal may be ideal, but it is simply impractical if more than a few items are required. And a univocal scale that is not unitractic would be useless for measuring meaningful source traits.

(5) Personality measurement aspires to progress from ordinal to equal-interval and even to absolute-zero (ratio) scale properties. The last is still a remote ideal, although it may be realized sooner in state than in trait measures. Several scaling procedures have been suggested for approaching equal intervals. Rejecting those that depend on judges' evaluations of distances and degrees of similarity, I propound *pan-normalization* and the *relational simplex*. Practical programs exist for approaching these criteria, and it has been shown that 16 PF scale scores do approach equal intervals by the relational simplex criterion. For most questionnaire uses an ordinal scale, monotonically relating to other ordinal scales generally has to suffice. The lack of equal-interval properties is likely to be more disturbing in state than trait scores since difference scores are particularly affected.

(6) Little is said here about standardization procedures since they are well set out in many textbooks. However, the nature of stens, stanines, and staves is mentioned and the difference between s-stens (standard-score stens) and n-stens (normalized stens) in relation to centiles is described. The relation of *extremity* of cut in component items to the effective range of the resulting scale is discussed. Standardization should be on stratified sampling, which is more important than gross size of sample. Although this is achieved in the child range, several adult questionnaires, especially those for clinical use, have so far failed to achieve this broad stratified population as a standardization basis. An illustration of its attainment is given by the 16 PF, which has been placed on a completely stratified sampling basis in the United States for women (form C), and in Britain for both men and women (forms A and B), and elsewhere has used larger samples than, for example, the MMPI.

(7) Departure from defined true-trait scores arises in questionnaires through motivational distortion, sabotage, and the subject's self-ignorance.

Sabotage can be recognized and evaluated but not corrected for. Self-ignorance similarly cannot be adequately corrected for, but because its random effect is to alternate and reduce deviations it could be corrected for if an independent measure of it was available. However, all that is definable as motivational distortion is the largest source of error; several approaches now exist for systematic correction of consciously or unconsciously introduced error due to "faking good" or wishing to appear fit for a particular role. The attempt to conceive and handle motivational distortion by such concepts as a single social-desirability factor or by such response sets as "tendency to acquiesce" have failed to fit theory; and the theoretically associated correction by a motivational distortion or lie scale has severe limitations. Although a rough common stereotype of social desirability may be said to exist there are several social desirabilities, each peculiar to a role and a testing situation. After defining a role factor as distinct from a personality factor I propose a new and distinct theory for correcting questionnaire distortion. It is derived from the general setting *perturbation theory* and a wider use of the instrument-factor concept. My approach takes two mutually consistent practical forms with different emphases in the model—*trait-view* theory and *scale-vulnerability* theory

(8) Trait-view theory, which has the scientific attractiveness of encompassing both self-rating (Q-data) and ratings by others (L-data), treats distortion as something to be estimated, like any other behavior, from personality, role, and cognitive cliché factors scored for the subject and behavioral indices calculated specifically for the situation. Since there is every indication that interests play a large part in distortion it is essential to include a measure of the person's dynamic role factor for the role that is most involved in performance in the test-taking situation. Experiment with trait-view theory shows that it is entirely practical and yields consistent results, and that personality factors are about as important statistically as the roles.

Vulnerability-coefficient (VC) theory calculates a coefficient of susceptibility to distortion for each scale and a distortion force for the individual in that situation. In practice it is simpler than the trait-view (TV) correction and requires only that two scales of differing vulnerability be administered on the same testing occasion. These two theories are supplementary: TV analyzes the motivation in detail and VC the test vulnerability in detail, so that they can, if required, be combined in a single extensive formula. Any proposed correction for motivational distortion, including these, involves calculation of a shift of group mean and of the individual's shift as a deviation therefrom.

(9) The overall design of questionnaires requires the telescopic principle of parallel equivalent forms to permit longer or shorter testing according to need. Public demand pushes the designer to make a single form so brief as to reach a lower limit for acceptable reliability and validity—perhaps 8 to 10 items per factor. Consequently the use of single forms in research is to be deprecated; four equivalent forms have been standardized for the IPAT scales but very rarely indeed for others. However, in practice an array

of concrete criteria is better predicted from 20 scales deficient in validity because of brevity than from the same testing time used on one scale of high validity.

Session length and form length are two different things; the former is set by the child's capacity to attend to a task, the latter by the number of items necessary to reach acceptable validity and reliability. For young children a single form is printed in the IPAT scales in two sessions (such as A1 and A2 for form A) but for adults session and form are one. Continuous modification is also designed across the five age ranges in language, number of response alternatives, oral versus reading presentation, and oral response.

(10) There is an enormous literature on effects of item design but not much of it is conclusive; some of the most psychologically important (as distinct from psychometrically relevant) have not been touched. Apart from the social-psychological considerations—such as educational suitability of reading (word-count) level; acceptability in terms of "invasion of privacy"; avoidance of abnormal behavior references in normal questionnaires—the main issues can be considered in terms of optimal parameters of the stimulus and the response form. Questionnaire design is illuminated by being considered under general psychological stimulus-response principles as well as psychometric requirements.

(11) The chief considerations regarding the stimulus form of items are these: broad choice of topics to cover the life space and to balance and attenuate instrument factors; presentations that do not ask the subject directly to estimate his traits (as by checklists) but request a report on concrete behavior; avoidance of solipsistic judgments, notably in states; freedom from ambiguities; providing a variety of stimulus form (requesting response on behavior, beliefs, response of others to one's behavior, tastes, activities, reactions to both personal and impersonal environment, and so on).

The parameters of the *response* aspect of item design are these: forced-choice between equally attractive alternatives versus true-false; elimination of acquiescence sets by balancing numbers of yes and no items for each factor; achieving interval equality in a series of responses (or at least more accurate definition of points) by anchoring the answer sheet alternatives to verbal definitions of extremity; presenting the best number of response alternatives for the subjects. Theoretically validity rises up to seven alternatives or more, but broader considerations suggest four or six for states and fewer for traits (as few as two for quite young children). Although there is an enormous itemetric literature on the effects of specific modifications of form for specific situations and subjects, the field is far from achieving generally valid principles possessing psychological meaning.

X

Use of Questionnaire Measures in Research and Practice

Considerable contact with psychologists using questionnaires in clinical, industrial and educational areas convinces me that except by a minority the full potentiality of these instruments is not being brought to bear. In this chapter therefore I propose to discuss the sophisticated use of questionnaires, which begins with a wise choice of test and continues into a practice which goes beyond a competence in psychometry into applying our broader knowledge of personality psychology.

1. Perspective on Choosing Tests by Psychometric Indices

Psychometric statistics are a necessary but not a sufficient basis for test choice and use. Discussions in this area have been plagued too long by a difference of interest and practice between the general psychological scientist and the psychometrist whose primary interests are in mathematical statistics. The latter pursues his mathematical statistics perhaps faultlessly, but so long as he can get a prediction—say a multiple correlation—of a certain significance and process it on a computer he is all too frequently not interested in why it works or in the conceptions and underlying models of the psychologist. Yet it would be hard to say whether psychology has been retarded more by the narrowness of mere psychometric accountancy or by that all too common variety of clinical and counseling practice by a crystal ball, which is ignorant of the powers of psychometric prediction.

The hard-headed accountant type, who is prepared to throw measurement instruments together in any way provided that they give him a significant multiple *R* with the criterion, or effective canonical factors, or practical separation by some obscure multiple-discriminant function, usually says that the psychological laws we talk about do not yet exist. One must comment that they are unlikely to exist, in any useful degree, as long as no more interest than this is shown in developing them. Moreover the ad hoc construction of questionnaires before 1950 was such that no psychological laws could be applied. But with the construction of instruments based on substantial structural research on personality traits and states, the situation is now entirely different. The primary and secondary source traits and states have now had their heredity, their origins from learning influences, their growth curves, their physiological associations, and their relations to job success, school achievement, cultural anthropology, and the social psychology of groups extensively explored, as Chapter Five has shown. If this much can be accomplished in little more than a decade, putting us firmly on the threshold of psychological understanding of our psychometric measures, the promise of a rapid beneficial augmentation of blind statistical prediction by powerful mathematical prediction from psychological laws themselves becomes very real.

Nevertheless for a long time to come—and in a refined sense always—the psychologist's calculations will have to be combined with less explicit hunches from intuition born of experience. Especially is this true as he enters a new area where we do not yet possess criterion weights from previous experiment, so that the psychologist has to take his stand on the general understanding he has gained of the meaning of the trait in question. For example, we may expect from the physiology of the anxiety factor (Cattell and Scheier, 1961; Grinker and others, 1961) that several hours spent at a high anxiety level induce more fatigue than the same time spent at a low anxiety level; but as yet there is no experimental proof of this. Or one might suspect that a neurotic higher than usual on *C* factor but otherwise meeting the neurotic profile diagnosis would have a better chance of responding well to therapy. Or one might intuit from the nature of premsia that it is likely to rise in the cultural trend of the immediate future, following increases in social welfare. To use a current phrase the "surplus meaning" that comes from the psychological grasp of a trait means that predictions will become more dynamic—and in the end even statistically more significant—than from the static, purely mathematical-statistical use of psychometrics.

If I am right in supposing that diagnosis, the guidance of treatment, and the use of prediction in education and other applied fields are going to be rapidly transformed by such incorporation of psychological laws, now made possible by structurally based measurement, then the features by which tests are chosen will also alter considerably. The psychometric notions of consistency and validity are bound to become more clearly conceived and given meaning in a wider context. In particular the psychologist will need precise concepts of the traits that questionnaires measure and to make a distinction between properties of a test as a test and properties that involve wider concepts and assumptions about traits. This difference between the scientific, quantitative psychologist of tomorrow and the narrow test psychometrist often dominating the field today will show itself both in their choice of diagnostic and predictive formulas and in their choice of tests. The test psychometrist is at present too concerned with an immediate concrete criterion and often does not stop to ask the conceptual validity in terms of general structural theory. Or he may be preoccupied with the relative scaling properties of two tests originally worked out on students when he is choosing one for use with middle-aged men, forgetting that *test properties are not simply properties of tests, but of tests-cum-populations.* This same psychometric accountant may use linear regressions to three decimal places when every psychological indication is that the relation to the criterion must be curvilinear. Frequently he uses a strictly mathematical model with no psychological meaning, for example canonical factors, when a scientific model admittedly more complex is strongly indicated. A familiar instance of this is the use of orthogonal factors as predictors (Guilford, 1954; Howarth and Browne, 1971b) or even unrotated principal-axis factors despite the fact that the known psychological properties—the laws of change with age and situation—apply only to the unique oblique simple-structure source-trait factors.

Without pursuing this lack of perspective in choice of formula and test into the statistical fastnesses where it is most rampant, I can illustrate it clearly enough by the simple case of reliability and validity of short and long tests. Some writers—Cronbach and trained psychometrists among them—advising teachers on tests have suggested that the reliabilities and form equivalences of the 16 PF forms are low for *individual* casework. These values, centering (for form A) on 0.74 and 0.50 (Cattell, Eber, and Tatsuoka, 1970), are of course low for those accustomed to intelligence tests of at least three quarters of an hour's duration where 0.90 and 0.80 would be usual. But it must not be overlooked that the 0.74 reliabilities come from scales of only 10 to 13 items and two to three minutes in length and that enough parallel, equivalent forms are available if the psychologist gives the testing time. That it is not in the nature of the 16 PF personality scales to be weak is shown by the fact that the reliabilities for the corresponding *B* (intelligence) scales, also 13 items long, are no different from those of the personality scales! In other words with the Spearman-Brown correction these low values come up to those for ability tests with which the educational psychologist is familiar. The 16 PF user is supplied with enough parallel forms (A, B, C, D, E) to bring each scale for one trait to about 45 items in length, offering the exemplary observed reliabilities that go with that length. Moreover he is constantly urged to use them.

If despite the pundits (and the appeals of the test constructors themselves) the psychologist decides under pressure of circumstances to use form

A only because, say, the job application conditions allow him only 30 to 40 minutes of testing time, he still has reason on his side. Both information theory and the multiple R tell us that the average criterion prediction is higher from measuring 10 things roughly than from measuring one with great exactness in the same time. To give substance to this consider the 16 PF where a psychologist has 40 minutes of testing time and chooses between using all the time on one scale, thus getting a reliability (by the Spearman correction) of 0.98, versus staying with 16 scales with a mean reliability of 0.74 each.

The choice can be handled in terms of information theory or psychometrics. In the former we ask whether it is better to have one bit of information of high probability of truth or many bits of lower probability. Over most ranges the answer is indubitably the latter. In psychometrics we must make a calculation on the case of 16 factors and one criterion, where for fairness in the comparison we must assume that all scales have the same criterion relevance. Then we ask whether the correlation with the criterion is better for one scale or for 16 scales each one-sixteenth as long. The general formula for change of validity with length is:

$$r_{cns} = \frac{r_{cs}}{\sqrt{\dfrac{l - r_{ss}}{n} + r_{ss}}} \tag{10.1}$$

where r_{cs} is the observed correlation of the short scale s with the criterion c; r_{ss} is the short reliability; and r_{cns} is the validity when s is increased n times. Thus if we suppose a validity of 0.2 for one scale (a length of one-sixteenth) and a reliability of 0.74, the corresponding criterion validities for 40 minutes on one scale versus the same on all 16 together (assuming independence of the 16 scales) are 0.23 versus 0.80. There is surely no doubt then that the psychologist does better to work with several short, low-reliability 16 PF scales in the typical case where all scales contribute by a low but roughly equal correlation with the criterion. The researcher's equivalent to the practitioner's gain is that he explores the theoretically significant relations of the whole gamut of personality factors instead of letting his research stand or fall (usually fall) by examining a single hypothesized trait relation to the criterion.

This is but one of many possible illustrations of the emphasis in testing philosophy propounded in this chapter. It is a difference between mechanically choosing tests by reported test validities and reliabilities in test handbooks or such surveys as Buros (1972) versus taking into account many broad considerations in the basic research on the test. It is the difference between applying equations as blind statistical estimation procedures and applying them when informed by psychological knowledge of the natural history of the traits and states involved.

Two common instances of treating a psychometric coefficient as if it belonged to a test rather than a trait have been mentioned—the use of the term reliability for a stability coefficient and the use of the bastard term predictive validity for a future-referent prediction which confounds the psychological properties of the trait and the test and is not a real validity coefficient for the test. The latter has been sufficiently illustrated in Chapter Three (imagine the test validity one would get from predicting performance five years hence from a perfect measure of surgency *F* today). The former deserves to be given concrete illustration here from data by Baltes and Nesselroade (1972). In Table 58 we see the dependability (reliability) coefficient—the immediate retest correlation for 14 factors (one being intelligence) of the HSPQ on 292 eleventh-grade children. The next four columns show the stability and constancy coefficients for 12- and 15-year olds. From the arguments leading to Equation (9.4) we see that dividing the stability by the dependability coefficient yields a coefficient of constancy—the complement of fluctuation in the trait itself. Column 3 gives the constancy for 12 year olds, column 5 for 15 year olds, and column 6 a mean value.

As theory requires the dependabilities are uniformly higher than stabilities which also warns us against the practice of some reviewers of treating stability coefficients as properties intrinsically of the test. Although the differences among traits from one study are not to be taken too seriously, it is noteworthy that except for intelligence the traits that have had wide predictive validity—utility in the sense of Chapter Nine—namely ego strength, dominance, superego, and premsia, are most constant, and guilt proneness and coasthenia the least. A rough positive relation of ranking to heritability can also be seen.

On the other hand some weight can be given to the observation that trait constancy is higher from 15 to 16 than 12 to 13, since the r_{tc} value in the latter is higher in every case. Perhaps one can relate this to the markedly greater imprinting occurring in the earlier period and certainly to the greater inertia of older more integrated trait structures. Meanwhile the results show that we should be prepared for appreciable change in rank order of trait scores of preadult subjects over one year. Psychologists who realize this are unlikely to make the mistake of considering a low stability coefficient to be a sign of test unreliability.

2. The Psychological Significance of the Derived Test Property Parameters: Utility, Efficiency, and Universality

For setting down the properties of a questionnaire scale the reader is already familiar with the central concepts of test consistency and test validity from Chapter Nine. The former covers coefficients of reliability, homogeneity, and transferability, as well as corresponding indices showing how far the mean score has stayed constant, since the latter is overlooked in the correlation coefficient.

Validity is covered by three dichotomous dimensions (and therefore eight possible types of coefficient)—from conceptual to concrete, from natural to artificial, and from direct to indirect (or circumstantial). Little has been said here about the mutual interrelations of these primary properties, such as validity and reliability, since the mechanics of the calculations

Table 58

Dependability (r_d), Stability (r_s), and Trait Constancy (r_{tc}) Coefficients for Scales and Traits in a Personality Questionnaire

	12-Year Olds			15-Year Olds		
Trait	*Dependability Coefficient, r_d (Immediate retest) N = 292*	*Stability Coefficient: 1 Year, r_s N = 294*	*Coefficient of Trait Constancy, r_{tc}*	*Stability Coefficient: 1 Year, r_s N = 394*	*Coefficient of Trait Constancy, r_{tc}*	*Mean Trait Constancy Coefficient, r_{tc}*
Affectia *A*	86	47	55	64	74	65
Intelligence *B*	85	48	56	54	64	60
Ego strength *C*	79	49	62	58	73	68
Excitability *D*	81	44	54	54	67	61
Dominance *E*	76	53	70	59	78	74
Surgency *F*	82	47	57	58	71	64
Superego *G*	74	48	65	57	77	71
Parmia *H*	89	43	48	61	68	58
Premsia *I*	90	76	84	81	90	87
Coasthenia *J*	82	40	49	44	54	52
Guilt proneness *O*	84	41	49	47	56	53
Self-sufficiency Q_2	85	46	54	62	73	64
Self-sentiment Q_3	80	35	44	44	55	50
Ergic tension Q_4	91	48	53	60	66	60
Mean	83	48	57	57	69	63

Note: Stability coefficients are from Baltes and Nesselroade (1973). Dependabilities from Handbooks.

is fully handled in textbooks. However, the thesis may be stated in regard to the newer concept of transferability that high homogeneity, by sharing a swollen specific over and above the wanted factor, is likely to reduce transferability. Relatively specific patterns of clustering of behavior are likely to be peculiar to one group among groups, as they are in terms of local factors among items in the areas of variables. A broad factor commonly survives as a factor across groups when a narrow, culture-bound cluster or factor does not.

The familiar validity and consistency hallmarks of a test are fundamental properties of a defined test, in relation to a defined population. With these restrictions on the meaning of the numerical values the latter should be allowed to enter only as elements into a broadly based judgment of test suitability. The values themselves should not automatically give the judgment. Although the practice of choosing tests by looking up these values in published handbooks or in such a compendium as Buros (1972) and accepting them as arbiters is better than ignorance it still presents a relatively unsophisticated level of evaluation. Handbook values are not very dependable because usually no quantitative statement is given about the range of the population sample on which they are based—and a wide range can readily boost values. Nor are we usually given in the published values the results of several studies—but possibly only one that by chance reached a high value. After a test has been in use for 10 or 20 years we can be sure that different investigators will have reported across a suitable testing experience, but new tests like new discoveries usually appear with correlations that repetition reduces. However, more important than misleading valuations from this source are errors of judgment that arise from the psychologist, as user, himself ignoring the modifications and allowances that should be made from alertness to conditions. He should ask when comparing tests if he has made appropriate allowance for test length and administration time, transferability (rarely recorded), the soundness of factor estimation in getting the concept validities, and the breadth of stratification of the standardization.

The last is not coordinate with the other concepts and can be briefly handled almost in an aside before we plunge into certain new concepts about consistency and validity. Few psychologists lack familiarity with the important features of a good standardization. What is sometimes overlooked, however, is that encompasssing 2000 or 3000 in a correctly stratified sample is better than 10,000 not so representatively sampled. What is more often overlooked is that in most psychological tests norms change with time. This is also an argument against disproportionate investment of time and interest in large standardizations—say, 30,000 rather than 3000—because too heavy an investment in a large sample disinclines the publishing organization—whether private or governmental—to make the necessary periodic restandardizations. A classic instance is the astronomical sample gathered in the standardization of the Stanford-Binet (1936) compared to the IPAT culture-fair intelligence tests, which used a decidedly smaller (but stratified) sample. Yet we know from such studies as those of Tuddenham (1948) and Thomson (1939) that traditional intelligence tests have shifted their norms upward by about one-half sigma in the last generation; the trend on the level of crystallized intelligence g_c is substantial. A traditional, crystallized-intelligence, intelligence test therefore has a standardization that is obsolete from the moment it is completed. Culture-fair tests do not show this trend (Cattell, 1971a). But there is reason to suspect that there may be a "cultural creep"—either drift or trend—on personality tests too. Indeed I hypothesize that there is a small upward movement on *E* and *F* and possibly a fall in *G* in this generation.

The question arises also as to how often standardizations need to be changed as better-loaded items are substituted through progressive rectification. Progressive rectification might indeed be brought to a standstill if the improvement of scales by this means required that they be totally restandardized every two to four years. Fortunately small percentages of item change can be handled by changing the mean and sigma of the scales by comparison of the mean, sigma, and covariance obtained on large samples, for the new items only, with those of the replaced items; but this can be trusted only up to a point, and restandardizations inevitably become periodically required. Thus as a matter of practical economics there is a tendency for tests with the most extensive standardizations to be less frequently revised and improved. In this connection factored tests based on extensive preconstruction research on personality structure have an intrinsic advantage in regard to criterion relations if not to standardizations. All the accumulation of criterion relations, occupational group means, and so on around a questionnaire the scales of which are subjectively defined and embedded in the interests of one generation—the Allport-Vernon Study of Values, the California Personality Inventory, the Strong Interest Blank—are largely lost when the test is improved and modified. But in the domain of factor concepts the correlations that the 16 PF primaries or the Eysenck or Comrey secondaries accumulate with clinical or achievement criteria, however, are essentially statements not merely about a scale but about how a natural source trait correlates with the criterion. And as such a test improves its concept validity—the correlation of the scale with the factor—nothing is needed to make the old values still useful other than a new correction for attenuation appropriate for the change in validity (and perhaps some allowance for a known specific). By using tests in the stream of scientific structural knowledge the useful criterion information of the applied field is not lost.

Although we have no certain knowledge that any powerful epogenic (Chapter Five) trend occurs in personality factors, it is well known that questionnaire personality factor scores have an impressive sensitivity to differences of culture and subculture, as shown in Table 52 in Chapter Eight. Consequently in the standardization of these scales one must pay attention to proper representation by proportional sampling of groups by religion, social class, and of course age and sex. As of 1973 (as a glance at Buros' *Yearbook* shows) few of the frequently used questionnaires meet this requirement. The standardization of form C of the 16 PF by Greene and myself (Cattell and Greene, 1961) used the National Family Opinion Poll list to sample by geographical location (state), social class, and age (for women separately) in the precise proportions existing in the total population. Similarly, the well-planned stratified sampling done by Saville on the English standardization of the 16 PF and HSPQ presents a true basis for the general population and one from which future cultural trends can be accurately estimated and allowed for in criterion relations.

Granted that the standardization is sound along these lines and that primary consistency and validity coefficients have been set out, we have what is commonly considered an adequate statement of the psychometric properties of a test. However, these parameters are only the first floor in the showhouse of psychometric properties. A whole series of second-floor *derived parameters* must be considered. Of these the most important is the *efficiency coefficient,* which might be more fully designated as *efficiency of validity* since the essential virtue of test reliability ultimately emerges in its validity. For the psychologist the efficiency of validity of a test—its efficiency—can be evaluated in terms of information provided by it, that is, predictive information on criteria per unit of testing time. The Spearman-Brown or Cattell-Radcliffe extension calculations are usually set to deal with change of test length in terms of number of items rather than in minutes. But since test length simply multiplies proportionally in items done and minutes required we can use the usual formulas for bringing to a standard length just as readily for minutes as for items.

The aim of the efficiency coefficient is to bring the validities for diverse tests to a *standard time length* to permit true comparisons among them. As to taking some convenient standard length as a reference base, an hour is probably too long and a minute is definitely too short for a trait scale. (An hour is not too much for a whole battery.) Probably 10 minutes is the central tendency in practice for a good questionnaire scale measurement of one factor. Consequently I suggest that the efficiency coefficient be initially the value r_{cns} in Equation (10.1) *when the observed value is corrected to 10 minutes.* Thus the standard efficiency coefficient of the average three-minute scale (validity 0.64), which users settle on when they use only form A or B of the 16 PF, assuming a reliability of 0.71, becomes 0.72 when brought to a 10-minute length. For many transactions—those in which the efficiencies of several different tests must be added to give the efficiency of a particular battery, especially with concrete validities—it would be useful to square this in an efficiency value, since such magnitudes, being the variances accounted for in the source trait, could then be simply added for independent predictors.

The second derived coefficient that is especially informative is the *utility coefficient,* which is more subtle. The well-educated psychologist brings to any purely psychometric prediction a wealth of knowledge about psychological laws or generalizations (such as those in Chapter Five) that extend his predictive power beyond the immediate situation and the immediate test figures. Of two tests with equal reliability and equal validity against a concrete criterion, one test may be far more useful to psychologists because it measures a clear-cut unitary trait concerning the natural history of which much is known and which has already been used in a great number of predictive situations. For example, a test measuring surgency *F* or anxiety *Q*II is more useful than one that measures, say, speed of perceptual closure or some questionable but fashionable factor of empathy about which little is known. There are two senses in which a utility coefficient can be defined: as *scientific utility,* which is the sense considered here, asking what amount of scientific information has accumulated in files for the trait involved through years of basic personality research; and as popular utility, asking in how many batteries and areas of applied psychology the test is currently accumulating criterion information. The latter—as an expression of fashion —does not concern us except insofar as it adds to scientific utility by ultimately contributing to information.

To bring the idea of scientific utility to a tangible coefficient psychologists must state a defined domain of total behavior with which test prediction is agreed to be concerned. This means a basis for a stratified sample of criteria and conditions under which they must be predicted—with and without the lapse of a year from the time of measurement, change with and without psychotherapy, trends for those who will go to college next year and those who will not, and so forth. To make the best predictions under such varied conditions and under such diverse impacts the psychologist needs to know the natural history of the trait the test measures. He must have psychological laws to answer questions like these: How far is change determined by heredity? How will this state change if I introduce such and such a stimulus? At what level will this trait be a year hence among people at this level who get married? Utility might then be defined as the *average validity over a standard set of situations of a remoteness and transformation from the immediate testing situation* commonly met in practice. This definition is related to the concept of predictive validity already criticized. The latter term is justly criticized by anyone who values scientific clarity because it confuses test qualities with trait qualities. We should not be guilty of saying that a test has low (predictive) validity simply because it is measuring a changeable trait or even a state. The *utility coefficient* clearly differs from any attempt at a predictive-validity coefficient because it separates what we know from psychological research about the trait from the test per se. Furthermore, it is not a value attached to any particular criterion but to all criteria of which the trait is predictive. It has to be calculated as an abstraction across a standard set of situations of change over which various criterion predictions commonly need to be made. Probably the best form in which to couch the utility coefficient is as a correlation corresponding to the mean percentage of variance accounted for in, say, 10 standard criteria, such as school achievement three years hence, release of patients from hospitalization after six months of a defined treatment, and so on.

The third derived coefficient is the concept of a *universality index* or coefficient. The intention of such a concept is to generalize the *transferability* coefficient, which covers only the consistency of validity, to consistency across groups of all major parameters of a test. As the name indicates, it asks how universally useful a test is. From the standpoint of the generalizations of science it is useful to know how transferable from subculture to subculture and age to age the validity, reliability, standardization, and other properties of a test are. For example, compared with the Stanford-Binet or the WAIS, the IPAT culture-fair intelligence test can shift from an American to a German or a Chinese population with a far higher retention of all three of these properties. A detailed expression for calculation of such a coefficient is bound to have arbitrary features into which we need not go here, such as the statistical form of agreement; the standard assortment of population samples across which the vulnerability versus "hardiness" is to be calculated; and the relative weight to be given to invulnerability of validity, reliability, and standardization to changes of subculture.

Still higher-order derivatives have been proposed elsewhere (Chapter Five, in Cattell and Warburton, 1967) although they mostly concern applied rather than pure psychology. Especially in establishing a test installation—that is, a standard battery of tests applied routinely at strategic points and periods, is in a school system or an industry—the *man-hours consumed or economic cost in getting units of information* via different tests become important. The matter may be illustrated by clinical diagnostic testing as seen in mental hospitals, where I, like other research psychologists, have encountered groups of psychologists operating probably five times as efficiently as others trained for the same profession. The poorer performances arise from clinging to obsolete tests, from failure to embrace new research concepts (such as the nature of primary and secondary source traits and of depth psychometry), and even simply from failure to utilize the psychometric computing aids now available. Among the latter are machine answer sheets and machine scoring, as well as available specification equation weights (Cattell, Eber, and Tatsuoka, 1970) and such aids to judgment as the pattern-similarity coefficient. If we consider this cost per unit of effective information in an economic efficiency index we should attend also to avoiding the use of more highly paid personnel in routine tasks. For example, much time is often spent writing case reports, where, with a good testing installation, such as the 16 PF Culture-Fair, or Clinical Analysis Questionnaire, a computer narrative printout (IPAT, 1971) could be used. The latter tells the story in a very readable form and one in which the use of adjectives tells more because they are used in a standard relationship to numerical values and probabilities.

At least within any one domain of psychological work, an index of *economic efficiency* on these lines could be worked out through a typical cost-accounting of the processes involved in relation to the information gained (as represented in the efficiency coefficient). Such improvements as Krug, Eber, Ford and Fuller, Schmidt, and others have worked out in clinical, industrial, and educational testing would have their value clearly brought out by such an index (see Rimm, 1963).

The essential points of this section are twofold. First, that for proper guidance of test selection the primary indices of consistency and validity should be brought to *standard* forms on a 10-minute length, a standard population range, and a standard set of testing situations that embrace a defined range of subcultures. Second, that in the ultimate choice of questionnaire tests it is the higher-order derived property coefficients that should most concern the psychologist.

3. Improved Conceptions in Trait and State Scale Scoring and Evaluation

The 16 PF and HSPQ series and most recent tests avoid the confounding of scores that occurs in, for example, the MMPI scales, where certain items are scored on two or more scales. One set of items contributes to one scale and no more, and each item keyed is given equal weight. This suits most users, is novice-proof, and cannot go wrong in most situations. But here we shall consider some alternatives to this simplicity and safety that hold substantial advantages if one is prepared to face a few complexities. The reader concerned more with general psychological understanding than the specifics of psychometrics or computer aids might be advised to skip the technicality of this section, at a first reading of the book, or be content to read only for general sense of the validity aids discussed.

The main issue here is whether (1) to key-score questionnaire scales simply on the main items intended for each factor, as above, giving them equal (unit) weight; (2) to give them unequal weight (requiring computer aids) to get the maximum validity as theory indicates we can; (3) to proceed to further refinement by adapting to the differences in factor expression for the same factor in the same set of items according to differences of age, social, and other subcultures. In the usual simple procedure (1) we should speak strictly of equal *nominal* (or *manifest*) weight, since when we give one point to each of 12 items in a scale they still do not contribute equally, but in an unplanned unequal fashion according to the variances they happen to have (a function of the cuts) in that population.

After the first sophisticated look at weightings 40 years ago psychologists decided that Likert's (1932) demonstration that weighted and unweighted item sums correlated 0.99 settled the issue in favor of the simpler, unweighted total. The fact that we are now estimating factors instead of merely asking for the goodness of correlation with the pool that constitutes the scale makes things a little different, but not totally so. For example, experiments on factor estimates by Baggaley and Cattell (1956) showed little validity gain from more versus less exact weighting of variables. Sophisticated evaluations of weighting and factor estimation have appeared in the theoretical mathematical-statistical literature (see Gorsuch, 1973; Guttman, 1950; Harman, 1967; Heermann, 1963; Horn, 1964; Horst, 1962). Regarding weights versus correlations, Goldberg (1968) has shown empirically that there is little to choose between estimating factor scores in the proper way by weighting according to the V_{fe} matrix, and by ignoring the correlations among items and simply using the V_{fs} (the correlations of true factors with items).

The major difference—and one needing debate—is between confining scoring in a multifactor-scale questionnaire to a limited set of nonoverlapping salients specified for each factor with or without equal weighting, and using weights on all available items (assuming that all might contribute) in which case fractional weighting may as well be used anyway. The appropriate weighting of all available items is entirely familiar as the V_{fe} in factor analysis but is best distinguished by a special term among test users and variance reallocation and computer synthesis have been suggested respectively by Eber and myself. The latter term serves to remind the user that a computer is indispensable in this use. There are three forms of computer synthesis, one weighting all item scores, one weighting only items in the keyed marker set, and another operating on the scale scores. The first costs most and gives greatest gain.

Although simple structure rules out about 70 percent of the 184 items in the 16 PF from contributing to any particular factor and although no other scale loads a factor at anywhere near the level of that of the specified scale for that factor, the substantial gains in sheer validity from either method are shown by comparisons in Tables 3, 44, and especially 59. There are, however, some awkward side effects, notably on the magnitudes of correlations among the primary factor scores.

If only the items in the marker set (the scale items) are weighted, the gains relative to the unweighted (unit item weight) totals are small, as seen in Table 59 by comparing column (7) the conventional way of scoring, in the handbook, with column (8). This finding supports the generally accepted view that such weighting of markers is scarcely worth the trouble. But the gains from the other two forms of computer synthesis are substantial, and from item synthesis more than from scale synthesis. Column (9) has fewer items per factor—roughly 60 percent as many—as column (6). The gain is particularly great for the perennially weak factors M, N, O, and Q_1 by item synthesis, agreeing with the notion that these are pervasive factors with temporally unstable markers. This consideration brings us to the second advantage of item computer synthesis (and to a lesser degree of scale computer synthesis). By fitting new V_{fe}s into the scoring program it permits an adaptation to the change of factor expression in different subcultures. Although the chi-squareds in column (1) of Table 44 (Chapter Eight) show there is no doubt about factor identification between mature adult and freshman student groups, the agreement on the patterns is not high. Table 60(a) shows the agreement in loadings and weights for adults and students on a typical factor, Q_4. In two cases there are disagreements even on the sign of weights; only the adult group agrees completely as to sign with the results from other adult research. Table 60(b) shows the salient-variable similarity indices between freshmen and adults. Although these look small to eyes accustomed to correlation coefficients, which have different distribution from r_ps, every one of the patterns but M is statistically significantly ($P < 0.01$) reproduced from one group to the other (though Q_1 not for loading pattern). However, the extent of change—see Q_4 in Table 60(a)—leaves little doubt that the comparison of, say, 18-year-old university student and 40-year-old general adult scores would gain considerably in verity if each were scored by its own weighting system, using computer synthesis by item (see

Table 59

Comparison of Validities of Four Ways of Scoring Questionnaires[a]

Trait	*Forms A + B + C + D (N = 606)* Simple Markers (1)	Computer Synthesis (2)	*Forms A + B (N = 958)* Simple Markers (3)	Computer Synthesis (4)	*Forms C + D (N = 606)* Simple Markers (5)	Computer Synthesis (6)	*Form A Only (N = 780)* Simple Markers (7)	Markers Weighted (8)	*Item* Computer Synthesis (9)
A	91	93	86	90	80	86	69	63	92
B	78	84	53	72	66	72	45	61	92
C	87	92	77	82	68	81	71	55	87
E	83	90	71	90	79	86	49	54	86
F	90	93	88	93	74	86	72	77	90
G	86	90	77	89	79	86	58	69	89
H	94	96	94	92	84	92	79	79	92
I	90	93	80	88	81	85	70	74	87
L	80	91	67	85	69	84	49	45	83
M	49	78	71	85	29	68	44	52	82
N	47	77	66	84	08	58	40	41	87
O	54	79	86	94	51	69	56	66	88
Q_1	82	89	68	84	78	85	46	48	85
Q_2	81	89	80	88	37	76	69	57	91
Q_3	82	91	80	90	78	87	63	64	89
Q_4	89	95	63	87	81	90	55	73	92
Mean	79	89	75	87	65	81	59	61	89

[a] The four methods are:

1. Simple use of keyed marker items (10 to 42 in number) in columns (1), (3), (5), (7).
2. Weighted use of keyed marker items (10 to 13 items) in column (8).
3. Scale computer synthesis in columns (2), (4), (6).
4. Item computer synthesis (from Table 44) in column (9).

Columns (7), (8), and (9) are from different samples; (1) through (6) are from the same sample. Consequently it is possible for column (7), itself a mean of the handbook sample and one other, to be larger than the best-weighted composite of the same markers in a few cases due to sampling. Averaged, (8) is better than (7) as anticipated.

Note: Figures are two decimal places with decimal points omitted.

Table 60

Loadings and Estimation Weights on Items Compared for Students and General Adults

(a) Detailed View by Items [a]

	Factor Q_4			
	Loadings		*Weights*	
Item	*S*	*A*	*S*	*A*
1	0.423	0.103	0.120	0.033
2	0.365	0.516	0.069	0.112
3	0.119	0.341	0.009	0.048
4	0.217	0.201	0.054	0.041
5	0.600	0.183	0.142	0.015
6	0.412	0.203	0.151	0.055
7	−0.047	0.169	−0.041	0.026
8	0.602	0.313	0.202	0.095
9	0.210	0.389	0.024	0.055
10	0.292	0.155	0.035	0.034
11	0.070	0.280	0.045	0.032
12	0.415	0.398	0.104	0.092
13	0.228	−0.016	−0.008	0.014

[a] S = students, A = adults.

(b) Congruences by Salient-Variable Similarity Indices Across Two Populations (Students and general adults) for All Factors

	A	*B*	*C*	*E*	*F*	*G*	*H*	*I*	*L*	*M*	*N*	*O*	Q_1	Q_2	Q_3	Q_4
Index "s" on loadings (V_{fp})	0.20	0.35	0.04	0.13	0.12	0.19	0.33	0.47	0.26	0.05	0.09	0.10	0.04	0.15	0.28	0.12
Index "s" on weights (V_{fe})	0.17	0.15	0.24	0.13	0.00	0.31	0.80	0.57	0.10	0.08	0.35	0.00	0.19	0.09	0.13	0.44

Note: With the exception noted in the text these "s" (salient variable similarity) indexes are significant. They should not be read as correlations.

the equipotent method, Cattell, 1970a). One must remind the nonfactorist again that this difference of pattern is no denial of the identity of the underlying influence or source trait.[1]

[1] Current publications by newcomers to the questionnaire field show in some cases (such as Howarth and Browne, 1971a and 1971b; Rorer, 1972) rampantly erroneous assertions based on fallacious assumptions which cannot be allowed to proliferate. They include (1) that the unique rotational position and therefore the nature of factors can be established by a couple of experiments—or even one; (2) that identities across researches can be decided by a glance at patterns, and (3) that when exact matching does exist, it will take the form of identity of loadings and perfect correlation of scales. The above discussion takes care of much of this, as Guttman's paper (1950) on factor estimation takes care of the naivete of the latter. However, to get scales the correlation of which will test hypotheses of identity, keeping to unit weight on the most frequently repeated markers in progressive rectification research is a sound beginning. For comparing criteria and other factor relations in distinct groups revised weighting and attention to isopodic and equipotent principles (Cattell, 1970a) is needed.

Scale computer synthesis, which augments the main *X* scale for factor *X* by reallocating whatever stray *X*-scale variance has been unsuppressed in other factors, thus giving some weight to all other scales in scoring *X*, is of course possible only with factors oblique to the given factor. But even factors designed to be orthogonal, as in the Guilford-Zimmerman, are oblique as measured and therefore capable of contributing to one another. For clarity it is necessary to react to what some students will doubtless notice here, namely, a formal similarity between the weighting of scales other than *X* in computer synthesis to improve an *X* score and the correction applied to the score of *X* for motivational distortion in trait-view theory (Chapter Nine). The similarity is purely in one part of the procedure. The difference is that in trait-view theory the weights are peculiar to the situation—to the effects of the individual's personality on the perception of himself in that situation—whereas in scale synthesis we are in principle taking the average weights across all situations and saying that the interscale correction still needed represents genuine contamination of one scale by others. This contamination in the scale can be removed by variance reallocation. An additional difference is that regression used in trait-view corrections includes a weight from psychological factors outside personality factors, namely, from purely dynamic measures of degree of role adoption and cliché effects that have nothing to do with computer synthesis.

It was pointed out in Chapter Four that higher-order factors can be derived either from scale correlations or from pure-factor correlations (from cosines reached at simple structure) among primaries and that the primary correlations and resultant secondary patterns agree well from the two sources. But the primary correlations among factor scale estimates from computer synthesis, by scales and especially by items (bringing in item-specific variances in common), no longer approach true values. In simple marker set scoring, using 12 to 40 items unique to each scale and present in no others, there exists unwanted specific variance in each scale-score estimate but it is not the same unwanted variance in every scale. By contrast, when the same 184 variables are used to estimate all factors—with different weights but necessarily some overlap of weights—a spurious factor correlation is introduced that blurs the true correlation which should exist among primary scales. In scale computer synthesis this added spurious correlation is considerable, but even in item computer synthesis (where there is more chance of cancellation with many variables) it is by no means negligible.

Problems arise from this spurious correlation when computer synthesis scale scores are used in two common situations—estimation of second order scores, and of criteria by primary specification equations. In both the weights would have to be modified because of the changed intercorrelations. This can be done—and here I pause to remark that my original criticisms of the MMPI scales for spurious correlations from using the same items in two scales are based on the constructors' failure to recognize and allow for the effect.

The problem can be handled by a couple of ad hoc devices—namely, by by-passing it, first, through getting second orders directly from nonover lapping sets of items and, second, by using the synthesized scales and calculating new weights appropriate to the new correlations. But these ad hoc tricks will scarcely appeal as much as a radical cure by restoring the true correlations to the scale estimates by deriving new scale estimates from them which have the old true correlations but retain some of the validity gain through synthesis. Elsewhere (in preparation) I have begun with the approaches of Kaiser and of Heermann (1963) which achieve best fitting orthogonal estimates and derived other procedures aimed at restoring the true primary correlations. This relational restoration procedure, as it may be called,[2] loses some but by no means all of the computer synthesis gain in validity, so the compromise is acceptable. The practical value of computer-synthesized and correlation-restored scale scores remains to be evaluated in actual practice as IPAT extends the scoring services on the 16 PF, HSPQ, to these new refinements.

It will be evident that the main improvements in scale scoring and use developed here have to do with the replacement of itemetric by structured psychometric concepts. Sometimes the differences affect applied psychology only in a relatively subtle way. An instance of this is that the itemetric assumptions in the Spearman-Brown prophecy formula for predicting the reliability of lengthened tests are not always appropriate for structured tests and may lead to false evaluations of their reliability.

The S-B formula assumes that the items in a lengthened scale are of the same composition (except for specific error variance) as the existing items, that is, that all items in the calculation are factorially isometric in the sense of Table 61. The items in the scale are considered homogeneous for the wanted and the unwanted factors (the latter being those subjected, as far as possible, to suppressor action). In structured psychometrics the truth is more likely to be that the items are as different as possible in everything but the wanted factor. The C-R formula (Cattell and Radcliffe, 1962) for reliability of a lengthened test proposed as more appropriate than the S-B for a structured test of this kind is

$$r_{d_n} = \frac{\sum_{j=1}^{n} r_{dj} + 2\sum_{j<k}^{n} r_{jk}}{n + 2\sum_{j<k}^{n} r_{jk}} \tag{10.2}$$

[2] To be more descriptive the title should be "relation restoration among factor estimates" (RRFE). It has already been illustrated in simplest form by the two-dimensional case in Figure 28 (Chapter Six) for mutual partialing of state and trait measures of anxiety. There, however, having no true bases for knowing the correlation of state and trait we assumed it to be zero. In the general case there are several factors and the desired relation among them is given by the ideal, true-factor intercorrelation matrix R_{ft}. The problem is to take the matrix of correlations among the factor estimates R_{fe} and (1) find the transformation from R_{fe} to R_{ft} when each factor estimated from the V_{fe} is nearest to its corresponding R_{ft} factor, and (2) to change the weight on items or scales in computer synthesis to give scores the correlations of which bear the closest relations to the R_{ft} matrix. A tentative solution is offered in Cattell (1973n).

where r_{d_n} is the dependability (reliability) coefficient for test j extended n times, r_{dj} is the dependability at the original length j, and r_{jk} is the correlation of two parts (j could, of course, be a single item length). The only assumption here is that the additional units have the same variance as the original.

Table 61

Terminology to Define Type of Item Structure in Factored Scales

	Isomorphous	*Allomorphous*
Isometric	Factorially isometric	Factorially allometric
Allometric	Factorially configurant	Factorially disparate

Note: The question of *constitution,* (what factors are present) is confused in earlier terminology with the question of *variance composition,* (the proportions in which factors are present). The first is here defined by a dichotomy of *isometric* (measuring the same factors) and allometric (having different factor ingredients). The second is defined by *isomorphous* (having factors in the same variance proportions) and allomorphous (having different quantitative contributions from the same factors). As shown, these two dimensions generate four varieties of test structure. The configurant category is somewhat artificial since it defines a set of tests that have the same structure—one general and one specific factor—but in qualitatively different traits. The Spearman-Brown formula (both reliability and validity) holds only for the *factorially isometric* condition; the Cattell-Radcliffe formula is wider in application.

The use of the same model leads to a C-R formula for the validity of an extended test as follows

$$r_{v_n} = \frac{\sum_{j}^{n} r_{vj}}{n + 2\sum_{j<k}^{n} r_{jk}} \tag{10.3}$$

where r_{vj} is the original (short form) validity, and r_{jk} is the typical homogeneity of parts.

Apart from some reduction of assumptions in the C-R formula the chief difference from the S-B is that the difference between two items is not restricted to a specific factor but involves difference on unwanted common factors too, which is much more likely to be true in most scale construction. Further discussion of the C-R formulas, notably in regard to suppression effects on unwanted factors, can be pursued elsewhere (Cattell and Radcliffe, 1962).

There are other instances in which the shift of formulations of validity and consistency (notably of transferability) in questionnaires to structural concepts requires revisions of homogeneous-scale-itemetric concepts and calculations, but this instance must suffice to alert the reader to the problem.

4. Educational Use of Questionnaires Illustrating Combined Specification with Dynamic and Ability Measures

Having sharpened necessary psychometric formulas relating to tests on the foundation of structural knowledge in earlier chapters, we are ready to turn to the practice of questionnaire measurement in the applied field. Since appropriate tests are presumed to have been chosen by the practitioner with known properties according to the preceding principles, the rest of this chapter asks how the substantive interests of a psychologist in the educational, industrial, clinical, and social fields can be aided by technical insights into the use of questionnaires.

In educational psychology the central theme is the prediction of achievement with the corollary of insightful understanding of deviation or backwardness in the individual case. Personality questionnaires have been demonstrated beyond cavil in the last decade to augment the prediction of attainment (Cattell and Butcher, 1968; Barton, Cattell, and Dielman, 1972) and understanding of individual causes of backwardness, over and above what has been traditionally achieved through the illumination of intelligence tests. Our main concern is to see how the specification equation can be carried a stage further by combining questionnaire scores with ability and motivation scale measures. The form of the specification equation probably requires no further discussion except to remind the educational psychologist or the teacher that the weights of traits are not their correlations with the criterion, that is, achievement, in whatever field is concerned. The weights are not the correlations because the personality factors are themselves mutually correlated. The weights must be derived from the correlations as in any multiple correlation—by inverting the matrix of correlations among the predicting traits and multiplying as follows:

$$W = R_f^{-1} R_c \tag{10.4}$$

where W, in the case of the HSPQ, would be a (14×1) vector of weights for each of the 14 factors in estimating the achievement criterion; R_c as usual is a column vector of the 14 correlations with the criterion; and R_f is the square matrix of correlations among the 14 primaries (from the handbook if need be, but better from the sample).

Specification equations have been worked out for estimation of examination achievement at most levels from second grade through graduate college (Barton, Cattell and Dielman 1972; Cattell, Barton, and Dielman, 1972; Birkin, 1969; Cattell and Butcher, 1968; Graffam, 1967; Lavely, 1963; O'Halloran, 1954; Russell, 1969; S. Wright, 1954; Warburton, Butcher, and Forrest, 1963). The two major generalizations that can be made are that loadings alter little with age and that it is hardly possible to find a significant difference in the pattern with different school subjects (except for some drop on the weighting for intelligence in going from mathematics and English to graphic art and athletics). Typical specifications for personality factors for different subjects and primary and secondary trait measures are shown in Table 62.

Table 62
Personality, Motivation, and Intelligence Variables Related to School Grades and Achievement Scores

(a) Correlation of Personality and Intelligence Variables with Grades

	Personality Factors														
	A	*B*	*C*	*D*	*E*	*F*	*G*	*H*	*I*	*J*	*O*	Q_2	Q_3	Q_4	CFIQ
Grade 6 (N=169)															
Subject areas															
Spelling	22[a]	32[a]	13	–08	–11	–21[a]	30[a]	24[a]	00	–07	–17	–07	20[b]	–12	36[a]
English	23[a]	43[a]	10	–09	–13	–18	34[a]	20[b]	08	–08	–16[b]	–06	25[a]	–08	45[a]
Social studies	21[a]	47[a]	10	–04	–15	–15	35[a]	15	10	–04	–18[b]	–05	22[a]	–08	47[a]
Mathematics	19[b]	40[a]	03	–04	–12	–15	28[a]	13	–05	–10	–11	–02	19[b]	–06	45[a]
Science	24[a]	41[a]	10	–01	–10	–19[b]	31[a]	16[b]	09	–05	–20[b]	–04	25[a]	–03	41[a]
Grade 7 (N=142)															
Spelling	13	28[a]	11	–11	01	05	22[a]	14	–21[a]	–22[a]	–09	–13	–02	–07	38[a]
English	10	45[a]	12	08	00	09	31[a]	20[b]	–13	–32[a]	–17[b]	–18[b]	23[a]	07	53[a]
Social studies	07	54[a]	12	12	–03	13	37[a]	13	–10	–30[a]	–17[b]	–17	22[a]	08	56[a]
Mathematics	11	40[a]	14	–08	01	03	31[a]	18[b]	–24[a]	–14	–24[a]	–10	23[a]	02	54[a]
Science	03	30[a]	09	04	–06	04	16[b]	04	–01	–20[b]	–09	–06	11	08	43[a]

[a] $P < 0.01$.
[b] $P < 0.05$.
Note: From Barton, Dielman, and Cattell (1971). Decimal points are omitted. CFIQ means Culture Fair Intelligence Test.

Table 62 (Cont.)

(b) Standard Weights from Full Model Prediction Equations (CFIQ and 10 SMAT-I Scales) for Grades 6 and 7

	Standard Weights							
	Grade 6				*Grade 7*			
Predictor	*Social Studies*	*Science*	*Arithmetic*	*English*	*Social Studies*	*Science*	*Arithmetic*	*English*
CFIQ	25	22	44	29	29	30	49	38
SMAT assertiveness (I)	12	00	04	11	15	10	20	15
SMAT sex (I)	11	15	18	11	−04	07	19	16
SMAT fear (I)	08	17	08	20	−03	08	01	04
SMAT narcissism (I)	00	02	02	11	15	−01	02	11
SMAT pugnacity (I)	20	03	14	08	09	15	08	08
SMAT protectiveness (I)	00	07	08	05	08	22	06	05
SMAT self-sentiment (I)	10	18	05	23	16	11	02	09
SMAT superego (I)	30	20	17	29	27	22	10	22
SMAT school sentiment (I)	05	11	00	10	07	10	05	14
SMAT home sentiment (I)	04	05	13	09	10	04	11	11

Note: From Dielman, Barton, and Cattell (1971). Decimals are omitted.

As usual the total contribution—the multiple R^2— to the variance is better for the primaries than the secondaries. If any change in contributory weights is worthy of comment it would be that $E-$ (submissiveness) is important early, that is, docility is more important in classroom learning than in graduate work including research or original papers.

A specification equation is as relevant to understanding the causes of individual backwardness (or, conversely, "overachievement") as in predicting typical achievement. Looking to see which substantially loaded source trait in the general specification equation is low in the given individual should supply the clue. However, the skilled psychologist will add much to his understanding here, as in business and clinical fields, by a thorough grasp of the psychology of the factors themselves (Scheier, 1968a). It is necessary to remember that correlation of personality and achievement variables, as in all correlational work, can indicate causation in either direction. Thus in the well-known instance of negative correlation of anxiety with achievement it remains for auxiliary research to show to what extent anxiety is a consequence of failure and how much it is contributory to failure.

The achievement specification equation, after all, is a summary statement of effects occurring at several different phases of a cumulative process. The personality and ability traits weighted here may have causal action on capacity to study, freedom from emotional upsets, shrewdness and calmness in the examination itself—and until further research is done on the phases in the process we cannot be sure at which phase particular traits mainly act or are acted on. Certainly it is reasonable to interpret the significant loadings invariably found on superego strength G and self-sufficiency Q_2 as representing conscientious work habits and absence of need for outside stimulation. However, one would expect the specification equation to alter with the style of teaching—formal classroom, private study, project method, computerized teaching—and as far as one can get indications it does.

In studies where Thurstone's primary abilities are added to the personality questionnaire scales on the one flank and to motivation measurements on the other, the prediction of achievement is significantly improved, as shown in Table 63. It can be demonstrated that, except in special subjects such as mathematics, the increase is only trivially due to augmenting the 16 PF or HSPQ with ability contributions (the intelligence part of the Thurstone primaries was there before in the *B* factor) but that it occurs mainly from bringing in the third, untouched modality, that of dynamic traits, as can be seen from comparing Table 63 with Table 62. This fact, together with the direct evidence of only minor correlation between the personality modality and the dynamic, motivational modality tests (only *G* and Q_3 in questionnaires are related significantly to self-sentiment in the MAT) supports the position taken at the opening of this book: that the general personality dimensionality is indeed different from the dimensions that appear as interests and needs. (Of course, investigators have attempted to measure both by the same instruments—inventories and questionnaires—but my position is that by the nature of interests and need strengths the questionnaire is less apt and less valid than objective devices for dynamic traits, as provided in the MAT and SMAT.)

Not only are objective measures of motivation substantially correlated with achievement, but interesting psychological differences are demonstrable between what are called the integrated and unintegrated components of motivation (see Horn, 1966). However, the general psychological meaning is clear: that certain ergs, such as constructiveness and gregariousness, and certain sentiments, such as self-sentiment and superego, contribute positively to scholastic achievement, whereas others such as unintegrated sex contribute negatively. For our present concern with the contribution of questionnaire personality factors, however, the important perspective lies in the generalization from the work of Barton, Butcher, Dielman, Pierson, Sweney, and others: that almost exactly one-third of the total 75 percent of the predictable variance in achievement comes from each of the three modalities—ability, personality, and specific motivation. But two-thirds of this prediction—a total of 50 percent of the observed achievement variance—can in most situations be predicted from the intelligence factor *B* and the personality primaries, all conveniently brought together in a single questionnaire format in the 16 PF, HSPQ, CPQ, and other scales.

Scholastic achievement is certainly not the sole concern of education. Attention has rightly been directed to two other criteria of development: creativity and the development of personality itself. Creativity is a weakly defined criterion. If defined as fluency or inventiveness in a test period it is predictable from abilities; but if, as I claim is more important, it is defined as *inventiveness and productivity over a certain number of years* of real-life performance, it is predicted better from personality questionnaire measures. The characteristic profiles of the scientist and artist are shown in Figure 36.

A direct *specification equation* (as distinct from a profile) for lifelong

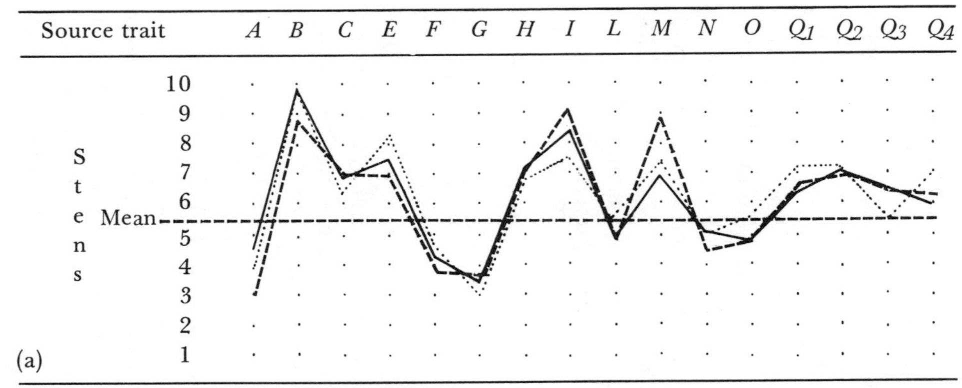

		N	A	B	C	E	F	G	H	I	L	M	N	O	Q_1	Q_2	Q_3	Q_4
General writers	31	M ——	4.4**	9.7**	6.8**	7.5**	4.3**	3.4**	7.2**	8.5**	4.8*	6.9**	5.1	4.8	6.3**	7.1**	6.5**	5.9
		σ	2.0	0.6	1.4	2.3	1.5	1.3	1.6	1.9	1.8	2.0	2.1	2.8	1.0	1.2	1.4	2.5
Artists	64	M - - -	3.1**	8.8**	7.0**	6.8**	3.9**	3.7**	7.0**	9.2**	5.0	8.9**	4.4**	4.8	6.4**	7.0**	6.3**	6.3*
		σ	1.5	0.7	3.0	2.5	1.9	2.0	1.9	1.9	2.3	2.2	1.7	3.0	1.2	1.3	1.4	2.8
Science fiction writers	58	M	3.8**	9.7**	6.4**	8.3**	4.7*	3.0**	6.7**	7.6*	5.6	7.4**	5.0	5.6	7.2**	7.2**	5.6	7.0**
		σ	2.4	0.6	1.3	2.4	2.3	2.0	1.1	1.5	2.3	2.5	2.4	2.6	1.3	1.3	1.5	2.3

Figure 36. Characteristic creativity and research profiles: (a) profiles for creative artists and writers, asterisks indicate those factors on which differences from the general population are significant at (*) the 5 percent level or (**) the 1 percent level. From the *Handbook for the 16 Personality Factor Questionnaire* (16 PF) © 1970, Institute for Personality and Ability Testing, Champaign, Illinois, U.S.A. Reproduced by permission.

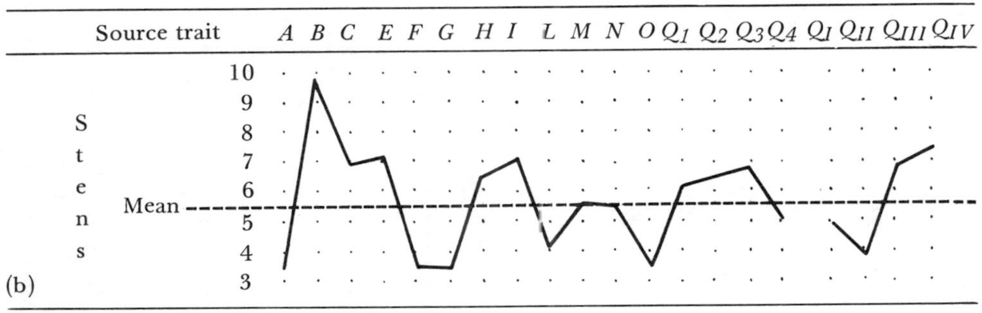

	N	Sex		A	B	C	E	F	G	H	I	L	M	N	O	Q_1	Q_2	Q_3	Q_4	QI	QII	QIII	QIV
Research scientists	144	m	M	——	3.4	9.8	6.9	7.2	3.5	3.4	5.5	7.1	4.1	5.6	5.5	3.6	6.2	6.5	6.8	5.1	4.9	3.8	6.8	7.4
			σ		2.0	0.8	1.0	1.1	2.2	2.2	1.9	1.8	1.9	2.4	1.8	2.1	1.3	1.4	1.5	1.9				
Biologists	96	m	M		3.4	9.3	6.9	6.7	3.1	3.9	6.3	7.3	4.1	5.4	5.6	3.7	6.1	6.5	7.1	5.2	4.6	3.9	6.4	7.0
			σ		2.1	0.8	1.0	2.3	2.1	2.0	1.9	1.7	1.8	1.9	1.7	2.1	1.4	1.5	1.2	2.1				
Chemists and chemical engineers	161	m	M		4.3	9.5	6.3	5.8	4.6	5.6	5.6	4.3	5.3	5.5	5.9	4.7	6.6	6.3	6.0	4.8	5.0	4.5	7.0	6.5
			σ		1.3	0.8	1.1	0.9	1.4	0.9	1.4	0.9	1.0	1.3	1.5	1.6	1.0	1.5	0.9	1.1				
Geologists (Australian)	21	m	M		4.8	8.7	6.4	5.3	5.3	5.1	5.0	4.9	4.7	4.4	5.4	4.5	6.3	6.1	6.1	4.8	5.1	4.5	6.5	6.1
			σ		2.9	2.3	2.5	2.5	2.6	2.4	2.6	2.5	1.9	2.2	2.1	2.6	2.4	2.5	2.1	2.2				
Physicists	91	m	M		2.8	9.6	7.3	6.2	3.1	3.9	6.1	6.8	3.8	4.9	5.6	3.7	5.6	6.3	7.2	5.1	4.4	3.8	7.0	6.5
			σ		1.7	0.8	1.0	2.3	2.2	2.3	2.0	1.5	1.7	2.4	1.8	2.0	1.2	1.1	1.3	1.9				
Psychologists	107	m	M		5.0	9.8	6.2	7.9	4.4	2.7	7.2	6.8	4.3	6.1	5.4	3.5	6.5	6.1	6.0	5.1	5.8	3.9	6.5	7.9
			σ		2.5	0.8	1.8	2.3	2.1	2.0	1.9	1.8	2.0	2.1	1.9	2.1	1.4	1.5	1.6	2.1				

Figure 36. Characteristic creativity and research profiles: (b) profiles for scientists. From the *Handbook for the 16 Personality Factor Questionnaire* (16 PF) © 1970, Institute for Personality and Ability Testing, Champaign, Illinois, U.S.A. Reproduced by permission.

Table 63

School Achievement Specification Equation When Primary Abilities and Dynamic, Motivational Traits Are Added

(a) Prediction from Estimated Relation of Motivational Dynamic Factors (SMAT Battery) to Achievement Factor

Dynamic Structure Factors	*Correlation with Achievement Factor*
Constructiveness	36
Curiosity	−20
Fear	−24
Pugnacity	21
Gregariousness	17
Assertion	−23
Religion	−34
Submissiveness	50
Self-sentiment	−37
Superego	44
Narcissism	−33
Sex	−15
Acquisition	−39
Protectiveness	21

Note: Decimal points omitted.

(b) Multiple Correlations Between Tests of Personality, Motivation, and Ability, and Measures of School Achievement (144 grade 7 and 8 pupils)

Test of Personality Motivation, and Ability	*Number of Predictor Variables*	*Criteria* *Standardized Achievement Test*	*Average of School Grades*
SMAT	15	52 (28)	48 (16)
HSPQ (less factor *B*)	13	52 (33)	60 (46)
HSPQ + SMAT	28	69 (37)	72 (45)
HSPQ + SMAT + IQ	29	85 (73)	81 (65)

Note: Figures in parentheses are multiple correlation coefficients corrected for shrinkage. Decimal points omitted.

creativity has never been obtained on a large enough group for reliable values, but since Figure 36 is based on large and well-evaluated groups one can use the data to derive a specification by indirect methods. Indeed what I am about to describe as the *type-gain* calculation is a useful device in many fields of applied questionnaire work where, generally, profiles are more plentifully and easily provided than are good specification equations against objectively measured criteria of success. The device consists of a formula for calculating a specification equation from a difference of means between the successful group profile and the general population profile. The sten means on the personality factors for the latter run evenly at 5.5 stens, so that by taking into account the sizes of the two groups—the general population control and the successful group—and their differences of means and sigmas on each trait we can develop a specification equation utilizing the multiple-point biserial correlation as shown in Equations (10.4) and (10.7). First one calculates the beta weight b_{fg} (f being the factor and g the occupational criterion) for each personality factor score as follows:

$$b_{fg} = \frac{(R^{-1} D_g)f}{D'_g R^{-1} D_g} \tag{10.5}$$

where the numerator is the fth element of the vector product of R^{-1} and D_g, and R is the square matrix of correlations among the source traits (16×16 for the 16 PF). D_g is a column vector (16×1) in which each entry d_{gf} is

$$d_{gf} = \frac{M_{gf} - M_{pf}}{S_{pf}} \tag{10.6}$$

where M_g is the mean of the occupationally adjusted group for occupation g on factor f; M_{pf} is the general population mean; and S_{pf} is the general population standard deviation. Assuming that all is handled in sten units instead of ordinary standard scores, a constant a must be added, calculated as

$$a = 5.5\,(1 - b_{1g} - b_{2g} - \ldots - b_{kg}) \tag{10.7}$$

where there are k factors. Thus the individual i's adjustment to occupation score Y is

$$Y_{ig} = b_{1g}\,T_{1c} + b_{2g}\,T_{2c} + \ldots + b_{kg}\,T_{kc} + a \tag{10.8}$$

(See Tatsuoka and Cattell, 1970, for particulars of assumptions and further developments.) The assumption of this type-gain calculation is that the existence of the observed differences between the given type and the general population represents a gain in performing whatever job that type has been selected to perform. For this reason the calculation may be designated the type-gain formulation.

Education for general achievement and for creativity are much discussed, but education of personality and character is surely no less important. We should be directing research to finding changes directly on the personality factors for those going to school or college compared to those who do not. The work of Behm (1967), Graffam (1967), Cattell, Barton and Dielman (1972), and R. C. Nichols (1965) has given consistent results showing (in the United States and New Zealand) significant increases in E, I-, Q_1, and Q_2 in those who spend time in college relative to those of the same age who go directly into jobs. Related to this is the evidence that significant personality questionnaire scale scores distinguish college dropouts: in effect low I, high F, and high Q_2 (Pennsylvania State University School Dropout Research, 1970).

Finally a different but important role of personality in the school has been investigated in connection with the effects of the teacher's personality, notably in correlating trait measures and teaching success. The criterion is frequently a practicable rating rather than an ideally objective evaluation of change in pupils, but the results are reasonably consistent in showing success with high affectia A, superego strength G, parmia H, self-sentiment Q_3, and sometimes ergic tension Q_4 and intelligence B (Start, 1966, 1968; Warburton, Butcher, and Forrest, 1963; Hadley, 1953; McClain, 1968; Mattsson, 1968). A specification equation can be written (Cattell, Eber, and Tatsuoka, 1970) for use with sten scores thus:

$$\text{Teaching effectiveness} = 0.15A + 0.45B - 0.15C - 0.15F + 0.45G + 0.30H - 0.30L + 0.60M + 0.30Q_3 - 3.58 \quad (10.9)$$

However, it should be pointed out that the behavioral index values alter sharply with the type of teaching and with the criterion used, as shown in Cattell, Eber, and Tatsuoka (1970), and (10.9) is only the central tendency.

In view of the demonstrated role of personality primaries and secondaries not only in understanding achievement but also in character education it seems that a well-organized education service should have a regular testing installation in schools to measure personality and adjustment. Surely this is as important as the scholastic examination. Comparable testing instruments aimed at the same primaries and secondaries, available at each age level from school entrance onward, now make this a practical possibility.

5. Use in Vocational and Industrial Psychology Illustrating Pattern Similarity, Taxonomic Methods

The issues in industrial psychology that concern organization and morale are appropriately left to the next section on the behavior of groups. Here I concentrate on the problems of job selection (sorting a set of applicants for fitness for a given job) and vocational guidance (directing the individual at graduation or later to the best job for him).

No argument is necessary for the importance of personality traits here, since the joint specification equations of abilities and personality traits for most criteria show the two modalities to be about equally important. When, furthermore, variance on abilities is minimized, as it is by preselection by the professional examination requirements in teaching, engineering, medicine, and other professions, the role of the personality trait in later success becomes even greater. What the magnitudes of the weights become in success in certain occupations for which relatively reliable criteria are available is shown in Table 64. It is often forgotten in theorizing about the demonstrated degree of importance of personality in job success that criterion of success is generally the weak term in research evaluations. It is rare indeed for a reliability coefficient to be published for a criterion, and the validity of the index in terms of being an adequate measure of total success is almost always in doubt.

The encouraging fact for personality measurement by modern tests is that whenever there is evidence of the criteria having been well estimated the loadings of personality factors in the specification equation have risen appreciably from their previously low values, showing that nowadays it is rarely the personality measures that are at fault. However, it should also be noted that correlations for individual personality factors with the criterion from 1.5 to 0.25—often dismissed as discouragingly low—are not unexpectedly or ineffectively low to the insightful psychometrist. In the usual multiply-determined behavior constituted by a complex criterion we do not expect one personality factor to predominate completely over others. And if the whole criterion behavior were completely predictable from personality, we should not expect the average loading—if there are as many as 16 independent factors—to exceed 0.25 ($16 \times 0.25^2 = 1.00$). In fact, if they were equally contributing, it is statistically impossible for any loading to exceed 0.25. A correlation of a personality factor with a criterion of 0.1 to 0.2 is therefore usually significant and useful.

At this point attention must be given to the fact that the specification equations commonly used in psychology are linear, as the title of Table 64 reminds us. Although the factor model is necessarily linear and the scores of factors to be measured must emerge as linear combinations, there is no reason whatever why the items added for a trait scale should not eventually, through further research, be put together more effectively in nonlinear fashion if that is what is required. Similarly, scale scores can be combined curvilinearly to estimate the criterion. The linear model is an initial research approximation: as factor influences are located with it their relations can be refined by other methods. In the applied field there is no need to keep the criterion specification—that is, the combining of the factor scale scores to predict the criterion—in strictly linear form. Indeed a few instances are becoming established in which curvilinear relations can be shown to exist, and several other instances are suspected. For example, an increase of intelligence *B* beyond a certain point brings diminishing returns on routine jobs; and although increases of exvia, especially on such primaries as surgency and parmia, are likely in salesmanship to bring increased success up to high average and slightly above on these traits, there are indications that at very high trait values they lose positive contributions, presumably by becoming obnoxious to the customer. A curvilinearity in the opposite direction—that is, where the *criterion* is curvilinear—is shown by low *C* (ego weakness) expressing itself in excessive hysterical behavior at one pole and anxious depression at the other, both low on an adjustment criterion.

Once the linearity restriction is set aside, specification equations can be written with freedom to set up whatever mathematical functions prove best when fitting an empirically derived curve. Such advances require that each factor in turn be plotted against the criterion to yield a curve for which a best-fitting second- or higher-power function can be calculated. Such curves have been calculated and evaluated by Tatsuoka in regard to age plots on various factors. However, no such experimental accuracy has been reached to permit this finesse to appear in higher-degree equation construction against important practical criteria. The principal workable attempt at going beyond linear usage has been in the application, initially with the 16 PF, of the qualification grid shown in Table 65.

The use of the qualification grid is simple, as shown by the instruction and example in Table 65, but its construction requires attention to interesting statistical problems in combining weights from different kinds of functions. These can be studied elsewhere (Cattell, Eber, and Tatsuoka, 1970).

Table 64

Linear Specification Equations on Job Success for Primary Personality Traits

Bakery Sales:

$$C_B = 0.44A - 0.11B + 0.11C - 0.22E + 0.11F - 0.11G + 0.22H - 0.33L - 0.11M + 0.11N + 0.110O + 0.440Q_2 + 0.22Q_3 - 0.22Q_4 + 1.87$$

Teaching Effectiveness:

$$C_T = 0.34A + 0.34B + 0.34C + 0.68M + 0.34N + 0.17Q_3 - 0.17Q_4 - 5.72$$

Psychiatric Technician:

$$C_P = 0.12A + 0.31C - 0.12E + 0.19G + 0.19H - 0.19M - 0.12O - 0.19Q_1 + 0.19Q_3 - 0.12Q_4 + 4.07$$

Freedom from Accidents (driver and other):

$$C_A = 0.12B + 0.18C - 0.12E - 0.12F + 0.30G - 0.30M - 0.18O + 0.18Q_3 - 0.18Q_4 + 6.16$$

Note: None of these equations is corrected for unreliability of criterion (which might raise loadings by one-third or more). First equation derived by Tatsuoka and Cattell (1970) method. Constant at the end is to give criterion score C in stens when personality scores are entered in stens.

Table 65

Use of Nonlinear Criterion Specification by Qualification Grid for Wholesale Salesman

(a) Conversion of Individual Sten Scores to Criterion Estimate by Weighting Grid

	Personality Factor															
	A	*B*	*C*	*E*	*F*	*G*	*H*	*I*	*L*	*M*	*N*	*O*	Q_1	Q_2	Q_3	Q_4
Stens for Individual	6	5	8	4	6	7	1	3	4	5	6	6	5	4	6	2
Sten Score	Weights															
10	4	1	1	3	3	3	0	0	0	0	5	1	0	0	6	0
9	5	2	2	3	4	4	0	1	1	1	6	1	1	1	7	1
8	7	3	[3]	4	6	5	0	1	2	2	6	1	1	2	6	2
7	6	4	4	5	7	[4]	0	1	2	3	5	1	2	3	5	3
6	[5]	3	3	4	[6]	3	1	1	3	4	[4]	[1]	2	4	[5]	4
5	4	[2]	2	3	5	2	1	1	4	[5]	3	2	[3]	5	4	5
4	3	1	2	[2]	3	2	1	1	[5]	6	2	2	3	[6]	3	6
3	2	0	1	1	2	1	1	[1]	3	7	1	2	2	7	2	7
2	1	0	1	0	1	0	0	0	1	8	0	1	1	8	1	[5]
1	0	0	0	0	0	0	[0]	0	0	8	0	0	0	8	0	4
Weight for Individual	5	2	3	2	6	4	0	1	5	5	4	1	3	6	5	5

Total Weighted Score for Individual 57
Qualification Level QL2

Note: Acknowledgment and thanks for these results are due to the late Dr. Joseph King.

Detailed steps for qualification grid are as follows:

1. Applicant's raw scores are first converted into stens and entered as in top row of figures in table.
2. Weight is encircled opposite his sten.
3. Weights are carried to bottom row.
4. These are added directly to give criterion score translated by table (b) to qualification level score.

(b) Translation of Criterion Score to Qualification Level

Total Weighted Score	*Qualification Level*	*Brief Interpretation*
0 to 29	UQ (under-qualified)	Not recommended for placement in this job area.
30 to 47	QL1 (minimum qualified)	Recommended only in a tight labor market.
48 to 69	QL2 (well qualified)	Better than average risk for this job area.
70 to 80	QL3 (best qualified)	Excellent risk for this job area.

Whenever the curvilinearity is such that an optimum value for a trait exists for an occupation and effectiveness falls off in either direction, there arises (especially with psychologists who like a pattern approach) an argument for changing from the specification equation to profile-similarity methods. If we know the ideal profile for an occupation we can in principle assess an individual's fitness for it by an expression that states how close his profile is to the ideal. Indeed not only in vocational placement but also in clinical work current applied work always overtly or implicitly uses one of two distinct practices: the effectiveness method (fitness by criterion performance) and the adjustment method (type-similarity placement by matching procedures).

Not only the statistics but also the social and psychological philosophies of these two techniques are different. The effectiveness method, as the regression or (in factor terms) the specification equation, has been with us from the beginning of this book. It supposes that a continuous score (which can be dichotomized into success and failure if necessary) exists on some criterion performance—in school, on the job, or in clinical prognosis—and that a weighted combination of continuous personality scores can estimate it.

By contrast, with the adjustment method we are asking if a person belongs more to this type than that—be it an occupation, a clinical syndrome, or the successful student type. As regards vocational guidance it is in a sense both more casual and more modest in its psychological assumptions and goals than the specification-against-success method. If a man's profile is similar to that of the typical journalist this approach assumes he will make a better journalist than someone not resembling the prevalent journalist profile. A less casual and more critical viewpoint might be that we have no certainty that the average person currently in journalism has the best makeup for a good journalist. If examined by a realistic criterion and a specification equation we might find that quite different qualities than those in which the average journalist deviates from the general population are positively related to effectiveness. The modesty in the adjustment approach is that it does not assume that any success criterion we use to get the specification equation necessarily covers all that is required for a journalist. It argues, moreover, that fitting the pattern is realistic in that it accepts the market by recognizing that if a man were too good a journalist (had qualities that overqualified him) he might soon become something else. The man who is not fired and who does not move up and out is the "model" in this approach. Statistically this approach has the property of being curvilinear; trait deviation above an optimum value is penalized as much as that below.

Profiles on primary and secondary traits for a substantial number of occupations have been provided by the work of a considerable array of able contributors (see list in the 16 PF Handbook). A brief list of profiles represented by scores on primaries is set out in Table 66. Scores on secondaries are also given for some occupations in the handbook and elsewhere (Scheier, 1968; Tatsuoka, 1968).

Statistically significant differences exist among most of these occupational mean profiles, and most psychologists who have worked in guidance are able to attest that the special levels also make sense psychologically both through the direct demands of the occupation and through selective competition from related jobs. For example, as I write these words on a TWA 707 crossing Labrador I am glad that airline pilots hit a mean of 7.8 stens on emotional stability *C* and that stewardesses are low on protension *L* and ready to give a third serving of wine without suspicion! A brief but thorough

Table 66

Personality Profiles for Varied Occupations

Occupation	*N*	*Sex*	*A*	*B*	*C*	*E*	*F*	*G*	*H*	*I*	*L*	*M*	*N*	*O*	Q_1	Q_2	Q_3	Q_4
Accountants (American)	94	m	7.1	7.9	4.9	5.5	4.9	6.4	5.6	4.5	6.3	6.1	6.6	5.7	6.3	6.2	5.8	5.1
Airline hostesses	139	f	6.6	6.1	7.5	5.9	6.8	7.1	7.7	5.0	3.8	4.3	6.8	3.6	6.4	4.1	7.7	2.8
Airline pilots	360	m	5.1	7.2	7.8	6.0	6.7	7.2	6.9	3.8	3.7	4.1	5.7	3.5	5.8	5.1	7.5	3.0
Artists	64	m, f	3.1	8.8	7.0	6.8	3.9	3.7	7.0	9.2	5.0	8.9	4.4	4.8	6.4	7.0	6.3	6.3
Business executives	178	m	7.8	7.5	5.7	5.8	5.3	5.5	6.6	5.6	5.4	5.7	6.2	5.5	6.4	5.5	5.8	5.3
Electricians	67	m	4.6	6.6	7.2	5.5	4.9	5.7	5.7	3.9	4.4	3.7	6.4	3.8	4.5	5.7	6.6	4.8
Industrial plant foremen	165	m	5.1	6.5	5.4	5.1	4.5	5.8	5.1	5.1	4.5	4.9	5.7	5.7	5.6	5.5	5.6	5.4
Military (army) cadets	1282	m	5.4	6.0	6.1	5.6	5.9	6.4	5.7	5.0	5.2	5.4	6.1	4.6	5.5	5.4	6.3	5.2
Miners (Australian)	137	m	5.2	5.8	6.1	5.6	5.9	5.5	4.8	4.6	5.0	4.4	5.9	5.6	5.7	5.3	5.9	5.3
Nursing students	176	f	5.3	6.1	6.2	4.8	5.8	5.5	4.8	4.7	6.1	6.0	6.1	5.7	5.4	4.5	5.8	5.8
Physicians	170	m	5.4	6.2	5.4	4.8	5.6	5.1	5.4	5.7	5.4	5.5	5.8	5.5	5.6	6.4	6.1	5.0
Physicists	91	m	2.8	9.6	7.3	6.2	3.1	3.9	6.1	6.8	3.8	4.9	5.6	3.7	5.6	6.3	7.2	5.1
Policemen	106	m	6.0	5.0	6.0	6.5	5.1	5.7	5.5	3.9	5.2	4.4	5.3	5.0	4.7	4.8	5.9	5.5
Teachers (elementary)	1280	f	5.6	6.5	5.0	5.5	5.5	5.7	5.6	5.9	5.0	5.4	5.8	5.1	5.5	5.7	6.0	5.3
Teachers (elementary)	88	m	5.7	6.6	5.7	5.1	5.9	5.6	5.5	5.9	5.4	5.8	5.0	5.6	5.3	4.7	5.5	5.5
Teachers (junior high)	94	f	4.3	6.9	5.4	6.7	6.0	4.1	5.8	5.2	5.3	6.7	6.1	4.8	6.7	5.2	6.0	4.8
Teachers (junior high)	132	m	3.7	6.1	5.0	5.4	5.4	5.4	5.0	5.8	5.3	6.4	5.3	5.9	5.8	5.4	5.3	5.5
Teachers (senior high)	92	f	4.5	6.8	5.5	6.2	5.8	4.4	6.3	5.5	5.4	6.6	6.2	4.7	6.6	5.4	5.8	4.3
Teachers (senior high)	177	m	4.4	6.2	5.2	5.3	5.4	5.1	5.3	5.8	5.6	6.0	5.4	5.8	5.9	5.6	5.2	5.2
Writers	89	m, f	4.1	9.7	6.6	8.1	4.6	3.2	7.0	7.9	5.3	7.3	5.1	5.4	6.9	7.2	5.9	6.7

Note: Norms used in converting these group profiles from raw scores to sten scores are those for general population, except where groups are indicated as students (in which case student norms were used). All values are in stens (population mean 5.5). Standard deviations within occupations are also given in table of 73 occupational groups from which these 15 are taken (Cattell, Eber, and Tatsuoka, 1970; p. 175).

treatment of the job relevance of various personality factors and the associated statistics has been made available by Tatsuoka (1973).

Visually comparing the profiles of person and occupation is a primitive form of matching patterns for vocational guidance; it can be done better, and by computers, using the profile-similarity coefficient r_p, calculated as follows:

$$r_p = \frac{2k - \sum_{x=k} d_x^2}{2k + \sum_{x=k} d_x^2} \qquad (10.10)$$

where k is the number of traits involved in the comparison (16 in these profiles) and d_x is the difference between one person and another on the traits in standard score units. However, one must be careful to modify Equation (10.10), which is the basic r_p between two persons, for comparison *between one person and a group* or *between one group and another* (see Appendixes 3 and 4, Cattell, Eber, and Tatsuoka, 1970). Regardless of this adaptation of sigmas to setting, the central properties of r_p are that it is $+1.0$ for complete likeness, approaches -1.0 when profiles are as unlike as possible, and is 0 when the resemblance is no better than chance.

When the resemblance of a person to the mean for people in an occupation is calculated, there is still this question: How strongly does this figure indicate recommendation for the job? When a person resembles the doctor and the physicist profile equally one needs to know whether most physicists resemble their central profile more than doctors do the doctor profile. For more discussion of these problems, which when clarified can be handled once and for all by a suitable computer program, the reader is referred to articles by Tatsuoka and Cattell (1970) and Horn (1966a) and to Appendixes 3 and 4 of the 16 PF Handbook.

Here it must suffice to point out that the adjustment method of using questionnaire score profiles, although more coarsely pragmatic, is reasonably effective. This may be because it recognizes curvilinearity by assuming that too high a score is as bad as too low, either psychologically or socioeconomically (because the person will leave the job for something better). However, an additional subtle correction has been suggested for large-scale computer use of the method. This correction supposes that in the ordinary casual gravitation of people to jobs the selection processes are not as efficient as they should be, and that the ideal target profile is more distinctive—say roughly twice as deviant from the mean as is the empirically obtained occupational profile in Table 66.

Any use—industrial, clinical, or research—of multidimensional questionnaire scales opens up the general issue of types as described and defined in Chapter One, and of the methods of finding them. It is not safe to assume that occupations constitute distinct (nonoverlapping) personality types and less so to assume that the clinical syndrome groups defined by psychiatrists constitute discrete types that can be statistically treated as such against a source-trait profile. Chapter Seven defines a type as a high (modal) frequency of people in multidimensional space. The profile-similarity coefficient r_p is high when in spatial terms two people are close together in the trait space, so that r_p is our best device to find clusters of similar people. At present the vocational psychologist intuits that the skills and personalities of people in an occupation cause them to form a distinct cluster in measurement, just as the clinical psychologist believes he observes that schizophrenics or conversion hysterics form groups of similar people. But these groupings need to be found *objectively* by r_p applied to people in all possible pairs in what is called a Q-matrix. For this one might use, say, 16 (the 16 PF for normals) or up to 28 (the CAQ for clinical cases) questionnaire trait scores.[3]

Analysis can be done by a computer program called taxonome, which works as follows. First it builds a Q-matrix (Q is contrasted with R- and P-matrices; see the data box) containing the r_ps of everyone with everyone else. Then it makes a "ramifying linkage" search among these r_ps and writes out all the groups in which each person is related to everyone else in that group above a given figure (say, $r_p = 0.5$). Then it takes these *homostats* (stats for short) and finds if they link in *segregates,* that is, sets of people in which there is a *continuity* of high resemblance even though the first and last persons need not closely resemble one another. The taxonome program has been useful in finding taxons in biology too; its principles are universal (Sokal and Sneath, 1964; McQuitty, 1961, 1963). For example, taking measures on behavioral dimensions *alone* on dogs it has classified them into terriers, sheep dogs, basenjis, and so forth (Cattell, Bolz, and Korth, 1973).

Before long, occupations may thus be objectively and functionally classified on profiles of 24 to 36 questionnaire and ability factors. The fact that they have separate names is no proof that they segregate themselves in this way. There may, for example, be one modal cluster (a type) covering teachers and another covering mechanics. Alternatively the various kinds of teachers—kindergarten, high school, and so on—may form quite distinct types. Statisticians have so far sought to get maximum distinction among groups in terms of psychological measurement by the multiple-discriminant function. What must not be overlooked is that this begs the question as to what types exist. It merely starts with the arbitrary and perhaps falsely labeled classes that we already know and sees what weights on the traits best maintain that separation. But what we need to know are the natural classes.

[3] A discrete species type of segregate, when located by taxonome is finally definable as a unique pattern of mean scores on source traits. Such a profile of scores on elements is the same as a point position in multidimensional space. Such a point has little relevance unless, as the result of certain psychological laws, a large number of people naturally congregate there in contrast to all possible positions in intervening space—as people come together for functional reasons more densely in some parts of a city than others. That is, the type must be located and demonstrated as both a homostat and a segregate as defined in Chapter One and in technical expansions of those concepts (Cattell, 1965a; Bolz, 1972; May, 1971; Sokal and Sneath, 1964). The relation of types to dimensions is thus seen as a reciprocal one. It is through measuring dimensions that the framework is given by which to recognize types, and it is through the existence of the individual demonstrating properties shared with others (in or out of types) that the substance for dimensions is provided.

The calculation from a 16 PF or HSPQ measure of a young person's probability of fitting an occupation—or of his fitting this occupation better than that—depends not only on the r_p value but also on the degree of overlap of the natural groupings. His r_p may show him to be closer to the mean profile of *A* than *B*, but if *A* has a much smaller scatter he may be a better prospect for *B*. This is handled mathematically in the sources described above (see 16 PF Handbook, Cattell, Eber, and Tatsuoka, 1970).

However, both the effectiveness (criterion performance) and the adjustment (resemblance to those who stay in the occupation) methods are only beginnings. The future will deal with complex, curvilinear functions in which relative psychological fitness for various occupations is combined with the relative economic demand in those occupations.

6. Clinical Psychology: Illustrating the Use of State Measures in Conjunction with Traits

The tasks of clinical psychology can be broadly divided into diagnosis on the one hand, and attention to prognosis and plans for therapy on the other. The questionnaire is especially suitable for clinical work since the foundations of its information blend well with that obtained by reports of symptoms and by free association in the consulting room. Moreover, in this doctor-patient relation we can be sure that the evidence (except in the case of the military malingerer) is willingly given with minimal faking. Nevertheless, the alternative approach by objective tests, as in the O-A battery, has given powerful clinical separation of patients in diagnosis (Cattell and Schmidt, 1972). Probably the best future practice, therefore, will combine introductory analysis of cases by the questionnaire, followed or accompanied by intensive study with T-data batteries (Tatro, 1967; Mahrer, 1970).

Regarding choice of questionnaires the finding has already been reported—as expected from theory—that although the normal personality dimensions in the 16 PF (and its supplement—23 factors), the HSPQ, the CPQ, and other scales tell most of the tale about separation of neurotics from normals or about delinquency and most behavioral disorders (Krug, 1971), they miss—and are unable to predict—much difference between psychotics and normals. This finding agrees with the general evidence from all directions that in psychosis a transformation of a different—largely biochemical-neurological—kind has cut across all personality expressions. Indeed the habitual underlying personality and dynamic structures tend to persist in the psychotic, as every psychiatrist recognizes, but with those twists and exaggerations that loss of functional control and cognitive damage bring to them.

Consequently it has been necessary, as Chapter Three has shown in terms of basic factor research on wide varieties of behavior, to recognize 12 new primary dimensions in abnormal behavior (which yield a general psychosis secondary and one or more general depression secondaries). The MMPI and the CAQ (Clinical Analysis Questionnaire) are the two questionnaires (apart from Eysenck's single general psychosis scale) that have gone most thoroughly into these dimensions. However, their scales are quite different in orientation: the MMPI aims at the syndrome grouping traditionally recognized by the psychiatrist (such as the hysteric, the depressive, the manic, the paranoid, the schizophrenic) and treats them psychometrically as observed empirical correlation clusters, surface traits, or types (Chapter One). The CAQ scales, which largely share the same behavioral space, are in principle aligned quite differently—they make a different conceptual analysis of the same data (Krug 1971c). The CAQ measures the individual's *dimensions,* corresponding to functionally unitary source traits, as evidenced by simple structure: the MMPI seeks to pigeon-hole the individual in syndromes, which are *types* or surface traits. From the CAQ analysis, in terms of deviation on these dimensions or functions, it is a second and distinct step by r_p to assign the individual to a syndrome category as in the MMPI.

A word is necessary on "special-purpose tests." If the general principle adhered to throughout this book is correct—that test development should follow only when structure has been amply investigated and checked—then the sporadic development of tests for particular areas of practice is probably wasteful. One must not overlook that it is the same individual, with the same basic psychological makeup, who turns up in the classroom, the clinic, and the job. The central personality structure which he possesses should be the target of structured measurement, and the same principles apply to its functioning in different settings. Although a few adaptations such as vocabulary and number of items for different scales are called for, there are many advantages in keeping to the same general-purpose trait scales. This approache possesses moreover the general advantage of accumulating knowledge and laws about the same personality source traits. The point just made about test adaptation by the separate construction of a 16 PF and supplement for normal groups and a CAQ for clinical work is no denial of the general principle. The difference in scale supplementation instead shows a recognition of the incontestable fact that in this case certain pathological dimensions do exist with large variance in clinical groups, dimensions that are of such small variance in normals as to be irrelevant. It also shows the introduction of minor adaptations in length and level to the convenience of each domain. The overlap of normal and abnormal is considerable. The CAQ is equipped with Part I (Part II is the 12 abnormal dimensions), which measures the usual 16 normal factors, although more briefly than in the 16 PF. This arrangement is necessary because the prepsychotic-personality or normal personality structure must also be known if the individual and his treatment are to be understood. The characteristic CAQ profiles of a number of abnormal groups are shown in Table 67.

Even in the range of normal personality factors there are nevertheless notable differences among syndrome groups (Cattell, Tatro, and Komlos, 1964, 1965). For example, neurotics are low in the primaries of ego strength, dominance, and surgency and high in premsia and guilt proneness. In the secondaries they are high in anxiety *Q*II, somewhat inviant *Q*I—, and also decidedly pathemic *Q*III—. Alcoholics are high in anxiety and are inviant (Fuller, 1966). Criminals combine low to moderate ego strength with low

Table 67

Characteristic Profiles of Principal Abnormal Diagnostic Syndrome Groups

(a) On Normal Primaries Only (16 PF)

	A	*B*	*C*	*E*	*F*	*G*	*H*	*I*	*L*	*M*	*N*	*O*	Q_1	Q_2	Q_3	Q_4
Neurotics (N = 272)	5.8	6.5	3.0	4.0	3.6	4.6	4.3	7.0	7.2	6.5	5.4	8.1	5.4	6.1	4.4	8.0
Alcoholics (N = 1019)	5.7	4.6	3.4	4.3	3.8	4.9	4.5	6.4	6.3	6.8	5.2	7.6	4.7	5.9	5.0	7.6
Homosexuals (N = 133)	6.6	4.2	2.6	5.0	4.8	3.6	5.3	7.6	7.3	7.7	5.3	7.9	6.1	6.6	4.8	7.4
Schizophrenics (N = 334)	5.4	4.6	4.4	4.9	4.4	5.1	4.7	5.8	5.8	5.6	5.0	6.3	5.0	6.1	5.9	5.7
Manic-Depressives (N = 53)	5.4	4.5	3.4	4.2	4.2	5.6	4.3	6.7	6.6	6.3	5.3	8.0	5.1	6.4	4.9	7.4

Table 67 (Cont.)

(b) On the 12 Pathological Primaries (CAQ)[a]

Two Groups[b] *Examined for Differences*	D_1	D_2	D_3	D_4	D_5	D_6	D_7	*Pa*	*Pp*	*As*	*Ps*	*Sc*
1–5		* −										
1–6		** −					** −				** −	
1–7	** +	** +	** +	** +	** +	** +	** +	** +	** +		** +	** +
2–5				* −		** −			** −			
2–6		** −				** −	* −		* −		* −	
2–7	** +	** +	** +	** +	** +	** +	** +	** +	** +		** +	** +
3–5									** −			
3–6											*	
3–7	** +	** +	** +	** +	** +	** +	** +	** +	** +		** +	** +
4–5		* −					* −		** −		* −	
4–6		** −					** −		* −		** −	
4–7	** +	** +	** +	** +	** +	** +	** +	** +	** +		** +	** +
5–7	** +	** +	** +	** +	** +	** +	** +	** +	** +		** +	** +
6–7	** +	** +	** +	** +	** +	** +	** +	** +	** +	* −	** +	** +

[a] Each row in Table (b) examines differences of each pathological syndrome group in turn from the normal group—7 (see paired numbers on left). A plus shows the group on the left is higher and a minus lower. The degree of significance of the difference is shown by an asterisk ($P < .05$) or two asterisks ($P < .01$) (by Tukey's HSD test). Data from May (1971).

[b] (1) paranoid schizophrenics, (2) chronic schizophrenics, (3) organic brain damage, (4) personality disorders, (5) neurotics, (6) affective disorders, (7) normal controls.

superego and low self-sentiment. Psychopaths differ in being high in ego strength, surgency, and parmia and low in superego (the sample is small, but diagnosed with intensive selection of true cases). Among psychotics, although the main trouble lies elsewhere, one can still see statistically significant differences in the normal traits, however: all are below normal on the *C* factor and less markedly so on *N*; most syndromes are high in *L* and Q_4. Above all the introvert (inviant) prepsychotic personality of the schizophrenics of all kinds (but especially the process insidious-onset type) is clearly manifested. Only the manic-depressives show extraversion.

The differences on the 12 pathological factors are emphatic; discriminant functions have been worked out by May (1971) that give considerable diagnostic separation. The six factors in the CAQ that are still not well understood are those that correspond to the depression factors first found by Cattell and Bjerstedt (1967) based on the data of the MMPI, Grinker and Spiegel (1945), and Nunnally (1959). These factors were thought to be in some cases *state* factors peculiar to depressives, but it is now evident that they are also traits and of importance in picking out deviant syndromes other than those directly recognized psychiatrically as depression. However, these six depression factors inter-correlate so highly (at least in mixed normal and hospital groups) that just the three second orders among them may be sufficiently diagnostic scores. With this proviso it is interesting to look at the discriminant-function weights for the 12 factors and to see how these functions separate the groups, as shown in Figure 37.

A discriminant function (Tatsuoka, 1970) is a set of weights applied to personality trait measures or other scores. They are derived from a procedure that maximizes the ratios of the between-group to the within-group variances and covariances. Consequently a set of scores so weighted gives the cleanest possible separation of individuals into the assigned syndrome groups (Tatsuoka, 1970). However, the groups can have such functions calculated only on as many dimensions as there are groups (less one) and provided that there are sufficient variables. Almost invariably there is little use in separating the later functions after two or three discriminant-function dimensions have been applied. Thus Figure 37 sets out only the first three. As noted beneath Figure 37, these three dimensions separate the normals from the patients very well, and separates the further membership in the different syndrome groups of patients reasonably well. Although the combinations of weights in the multiple-discriminant-function approach are not always meaningful in terms of general psychological principles but vary somewhat with the company of groups involved, they furnish some basis for further theoretical inference. In any case, with the aid of a computer they offer a rapid and objective means of assigning individuals optimally to syndrome groups if that is one's diagnostic purpose.

Unlike the taxonome procedure, the multiple-discriminant function begins by accepting the syndrome categories that psychiatrists have traditionally reached. It then finds what separates these catogories in terms of weights on meaningful source traits—in this case on a multidimensional questionnaire, the CAQ. One might surmise that the taxonome approach is not likely to alter radically but only to refine the categories that have survived the intensive scrutiny of three generations of psychiatrists and the perceptive genius of men like Freud, Janet, Kraepelin, Bleuler (1911), and Kretschmer (1921).

The conceptual problem is therefore this: Why do people cluster only in certain spaces within this framework of normal and abnormal dimensions? The problem is as old as biological structure and adjustment. Why are there no creatures half-way between men and horses, like the centaurs of mythology? One must suppose that there is a functional or necessary mutual dependence of these separate features of endowments such that extreme in-

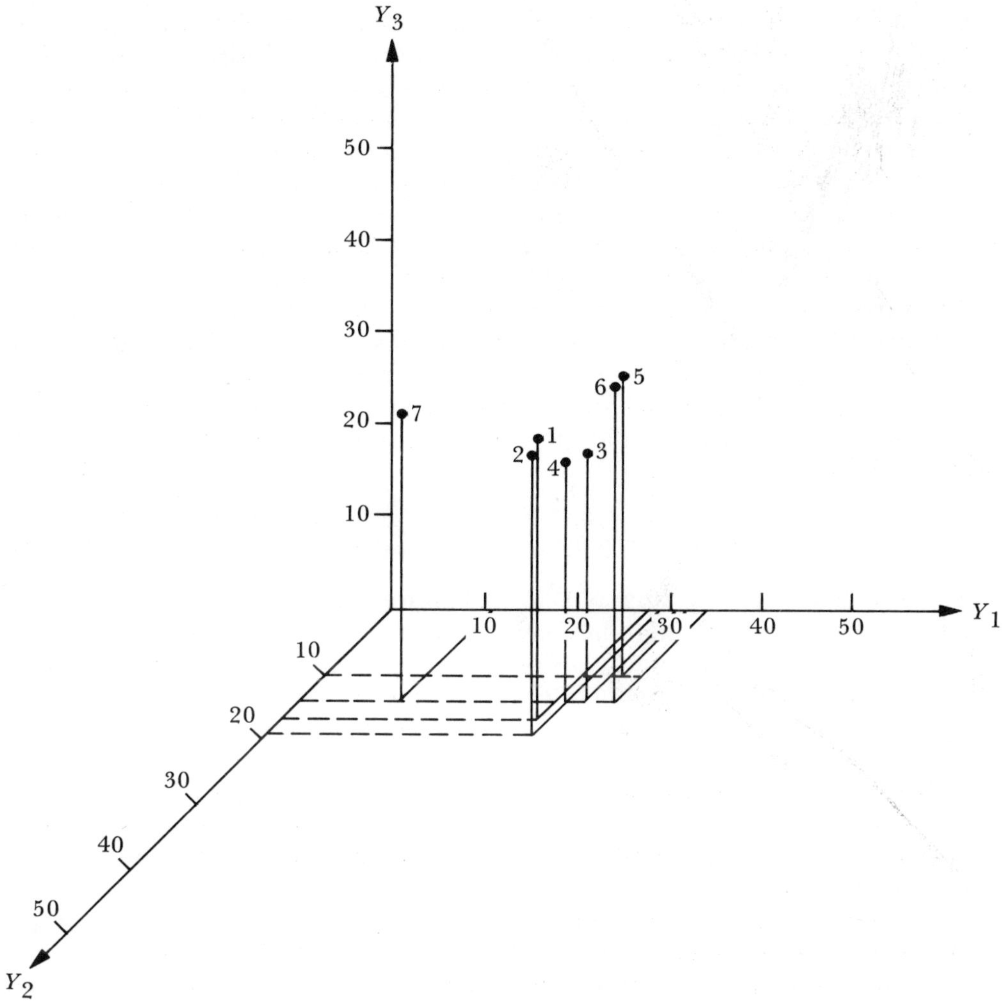

Figure 37. Separation of classic psychiatric syndrome groups using three discriminant functions from CAQ. Key to groups: (1) paranoid schizophrenic, (2) chronic schizophrenic, (3) organic brain damage, (4) personality disorders, (5) neurotics, (6) affective disorders, (7) normal controls. The first function Y_1 separates all pathological groups from normals. The second separates both types of schizophrenics at one end (high Y_2) from neurotics at the other. The third contributes to separating brain damage and personality disorders from the next by assigning them a low score on Y_3. Assignment of individuals to groups on basis of these weighted scores yielded close agreement with consensus of psychiatrists.

troversion, for example, tends to produce also hallucinations, or that a combination of high surgency and low ego strength (control) creates a tendency to manic talkativeness and impulsiveness.

Such profound issues are beyond the scope of this book but we must take note of a concept that has developed in the interaction of structured measurement with clinical psychology—*depth psychometry*. This concept has already been briefly introduced in connection with utilizing the joint information about primary- and secondary- trait scores for the same individual. It was suggested, in connection with the clinical ideas of Vidal, that knowing the extent to which a primary receives its score in an individual from his secondary factor score provides a valuable new understanding of the personality. The application of depth psychometry can now be extended from the primary-secondary relation to the contrasting of surface-trait and source-trait scores. Surface traits are syndromes, though syndromes can be at once types and surface traits, since the existence of a dense cluster of people in a given direction from the origin creates a trait correlation cluster.) The surface-trait syndromes could be scored by the MMPI, the source traits by the CAQ. The same high score on a surface-trait syndrome such as neuroticism —as on the IPAT neuroticism scale questionnaire (NSQ), a special-purpose composite—can be reached by different persons by many different source-trait score combinations. This is evident if we consider the specification equation for neuroticism N:

$$N = -0.26C - 0.17E - 0.38F - 0.10G + 0.10H + 0.22I + 0.26O + 0.35Q_4 \ (+6.27 \text{ for stens}) \qquad (10.11)$$

which includes only loadings of 0.10 and above. One can see that one person might get an unusually high neuroticism score by high source-trait scores on guilt proneness O and ergic tension Q_4, and another person by poor ego strength $C-$ and high premsia I. After finding that two people have an equally high neuroticism score by a surface-trait measure such as the NSQ it becomes clinically important to know that in one case anxiety components (O and Q_4) and in another personality structure and social upbringing features ($C-$ and I) are important. Depth psychometry is a procedure in diagnosis that is already half-way to prognosis and thus offers positive guidance to therapy.

The preceding discussion is designed partly to bring out the concept of two kinds of questionnaire or other tests—*analytical* or general-purpose tests, and *special-purpose* tests. The distinction is useful not only in clinical work but also in all applied psychology. By an analytical (or structural-analytical) test I mean the kind we have been dealing with all along, in which each scale is directed with an analytical intention to a functionally unitary personality structure—a source trait. Such a comprehensive analytical test is generally to be preferred for the psychological illumination it brings. But with several scales involved it is likely to become a relatively long test and there are undoubtedly instances where only a particular combination of factors—like a patent medicine or even a composite prescription for a particular illness—is needed. This situation occurs most often in making social surveys of the frequency of a mental illness or in some frequently repeated check on one individual with regard to the severity of a particular condition. The NSQ, which is only 10 minutes and 40 items long, is a typical illustration in that it combines the primaries of the 16 PF in the particular weights in which they fall in Equation (10.11), thus giving a measure of the severity of the total neuroticism condition itself and not just of anxiety or of premsia —to name two constituents. Similarly there may be use for a special-purpose test for a certain job or for selection of leaders and so on, in each case combining only those factors the specification equation shows to be important for the evaluation and in a brief (say, 10-minute) test.

The use of brief special-purpose tests is not to be mistaken for the previously rejected principle (or lack of principle) by which tests such as the Rorschach are developed. The results of such tests lack generalizability to personality structure as defined here, and accumulate only lore for a type of patient and testing situation. Nevertheless, in measuring the severity of neuroticism or alchoholism-proneness is useful as such, and special purpose tests have their roles and are used in both industrial and clinical surveys and diagnostic procedures. The problem is that the availability of brief special-purpose tests tempts the psychologist sometimes to forget the greater value of comprehensive, analytical questionnaires. An instance is evident as we turn from diagnosis to prognosis and therapy. Scales are proposed (a diminution of score on the NSQ would be one) for measuring a patient's therapeutic improvement as a single variable. Therapeutic change is total personality change—not change on one dimension (Cattell, 1966c)—and it is important to know what features are changing in the case. Hunt, Ewing, LaForge, and Gilbert (1959), Rickels, Cattell, McAfee, and Hesbacher (1965), and others have shown that psychotherapy with neurotic students raises ego strength, dominance, and surgency, and lowers anxiety. Other studies confirm these as typical changes; but the wisest use of this finding would not be to concoct a composite scale from these dimensions (unless terribly pressed for testing time) but rather to use such general-purpose scales as the PEN, the Comrey, the 16 PF, and the CAQ to help the therapist grasp analytically just what *pattern of changes is* taking place through his treatment (Cattell, 1966c). Only thus can he guide the next steps. Admittedly most of the principles by which such guidance would be informed are not known—partly because clinicians have not used analytical measures long enough in the therapeutic process to establish insightful generalizations relating treatment to score changes. Table 68 shows the results of collaboration of psychiatrist and psychologist using factored measures to monitor therapy, in which significant anxiety score changes were produced (Rickels and Cattell, 1965). The results have the added interest of a dynamic comparison of a questionnaire measure change with an objective (O-A battery) measure change on the same factor, as well as relating anxiety changes to changes in regression.

It is the new techniques of Q-data state measurement, however, that are about to open interesting applied possibilities in therapy. In psychoanalysis, for example, it has long been said that a rise of anxiety typically shows that the therapist is finding his way through old established defenses in the patient and is approaching the root of some aspect of the conflict. If measures of such states as anxiety and depression could be brought to the requisite sensitivity the psychotherapist could use them tactically, as the internist uses the thermometer or measures of cholesterol, in deciding the next clinical step.

The 20-to-40-item scales, such as Scheier's (1967) anxiety scale, Curran's (1973) eight-state battery, and Barton's CST Kit (1973), seem to be

Table 68

Comparison of Anxiety and Regression Change Under Therapy on Questionnaire and Objective Test Measures [a]

	Initial Score (1)	*Final Score (2)*	*Change (2) − (1)*
IPAT Verbal Anxiety			
(N = 46) Patients	46.09	43.02	−3.07 [c]
(N = 53) Controls	26.13	26.77	0.64
O-A Anxiety Battery			
Patients [b]	0.361	0.198	−0.163 [c]
Controls	−0.361	−0.472	−0.111
O-A Regression Battery			
Patients	0.440	0.114	−0.326 [d]
Controls	−0.458	−0.611	−0.153 [c]

[a] N = 46 patients, 53 normal controls.

[b] Numerical agreement of these two initial values for patients and controls is accidental. All scores are raw scores and have no comparability immediately from objective to questionnaire values, being unstandardized.

[c] Significant at $P < 0.05$.

[d] Significant at $P < 0.001$.

Note: Results from Cattell, Rickels, and others (1966).

approaching the required sensitivity. In evaluating psychoactive drugs, for example, DiMascio (DiMascio and Barrett, 1965), Cattell and Rickels (Rickels, Cattell, McAfee, and Hesbacher, 1965; Cattell and Rickels, 1968), and others have shown significant and consistent changes of the theoretically expected nature from drugs alone and from combined drugs and therapy on anxiety and regressive depression (see Table 68). The work of Barton (1973b) and Bolz and Cattell (1973) indicates also the gains of understanding that are possible through combining such measures of daily changes in anxiety, arousal, depression, and fatigue with measures of *specific ergic-tension* levels as in the MAT. Although questionnaires have been used for a long time in clinical work, the full power of their role—as *structured* questionnaires intelligently related to general personality theory—in depth psychometry and in combined use of trait and state measures is therefore only beginning.

7. Social Psychology: Group Dynamics and Cultural Analysis

The use of personality questionnaires in social psychology covers two distinct areas with as yet tenuous links between them. On the one hand we have the psychology of groups of relatively small size—sometimes called the study of group dynamics—which covers experimental work in small groups including the family and which extends in larger groups to questions of morale and management in industrial psychology and to leadership. On the other hand, we have the psychology of mass cultures—national cultures, subcultures, and classes—which blends eventually into history, economics, and cultural anthropology. In both areas the questionnaire measurement of traits and states has begun to yield important experimental findings although the latter area, because of the great cost of large-scale sampling, is likely to lag appreciably.

It has irritated many a student of the social sciences that social-psychological and sociological theories often mix no better than oil and water. The sociologist and the cultural anthropologist virtually ignore personality and seek explanations in the laws of the larger organism: the group and its culture. When they come to the molecular level—that of individual behavior—they tend to argue that differences of role and custom account for the observed patterns of behavior, whereas the psychologist sees the differences between groups in their performances and certainly the many events of history as fully explicable only by individual personalities. Performance rests for him on the same trait measures as determine behavior in school and clinic. The sociologist points to behavior in driving along a street in terms of traffic lights and car signals that virtually everyone obeys; the psychologist accounts for accidents and important differences in speed and control in terms of personality. Yet there is really no contradiction but only a little rivalry between these sciences since the sources of variance that each emphasizes are supplementary. (Alas, both often wear their textbooks like a horse's blinkers and see only the abstractions lying immediately in front of them!)

A formal model exists to bring psychologist and sociologist together, but it is not much realized outside multivariate investigators. It includes such diverse features as the use of role factors illustrated in trait-view theory, the sentiment structures, cliché and stereotype behavior, and the dimensionalizing of culture patterns (Rummel, 1970; Cattell, Breul, and Hartman, 1952) and group syntalities (Cattell and Stice, 1960) in functional group traits.

Although the measurement of role factors lies outside questionnaire methods since objective-interest measurement devices seem required (Krug, 1969), the need to combine them with qustionnaire measures of personality justifies a brief discussion of the role concept. These role-proneness factors—readiness to step into the role of a teacher, a mother, a policeman—are *formally* the same as the state-*proneness factors*. They are predispositions from past learning to respond to an *ambient-stimulus* situation (a role cue) by coming powerfully into action. Like states they are modulated by the ambient stimulus.

That the individual's main mode of action in a traditional group is determined largely by his role must be conceded to the sociologist; but within this role of leader, parent, or teacher the variations of behavior from person to person are largely expressions of the personality and dynamic-structure factors. These are, for example, good leaders and bad leaders, popular leaders and effective leaders, and so on.

The most dependable and statistically significant research on leaders has so far been in neonate groups—groups of persons never before brought together but now placed in a group to compete with other groups, the group's reward for success being split among the members. Both the performance of such groups and the nature of the individuals they choose for leaders are demonstrably affected by the population's personality source traits, as the work of Gibb (1969), Haythorn (1953), Cattell and Lawson (1962), Cattell and Stice (1960), and many others shows.

As to the performance of the group as a group on such variables as construction tasks, reaching the best decisions on skimpy data, and so on to the physical tug-of-war—Stice and I (1960) showed, in correlations across 100 groups of 10 men each, more than 50 associations significant at the $P < 0.001$, < 0.01, and < 0.05 levels between the group's performance and its average score on personality factors. We also showed the same significant connections between measured personality traits of individuals and their behavior in the group, such as speaking up freely, contradicting, and attempting leadership, some of which are shown in Table 69(a).

Table 69

Significant Relations of Primary Traits to Behavior in Small Groups

(a) Relation of Individual's Traits to Behavior in Group

	Trait and Associated Behavior from Group "Minutes"	*r*
A.	Affectia: Socioemotional positive remarks	0.29
B.	Intelligence: Rated an effective speaker	0.25
C.	Ego Strength: Satisfied with group coherence	0.21
E.	Dominance: High ratio of socioemotional to task-oriented remarks	0.23
F.	Surgency: Many votes as leader in construction	0.29
G.	Superego: High percentage of task-oriented remarks	0.26
H.	Parmia: Many votes, as an accepted personal friend	0.34
Q_4.	Ergic Tension: Dissatisfied with group conformity to rules	0.34

(b) Personality Profiles of Leaders Rated Effective in Group Action and Popular, Elected Leaders

	Primaries															
	A	*B*	*C*	*E*	*F*	*G*	*H*	*I*	*L*	*M*	*N*	*O*	Q_1	Q_2	Q_3	Q_4
Elected leaders (N = 92)	6.0	7.3	5.7	5.8	7.1	6.3	6.7	5.2	5.2	4.8	5.7	3.9	4.9	4.9	6.4	4.9
Effective leaders (N = 43)	4.7	7.8	6.2	5.9	5.5	6.1	7.0	5.0	5.0	5.1	5.9	5.0	5.6	6.2	6.5	3.8

	Secondaries			
	QI	*QII*	*QIII*	*QIV*
Elected leaders	6.8	4.6	5.9	5.6
Effective leaders	5.8	4.2	6.4	6.2

Note: Scores in stens.

Table 69 (Cont.)

(c) Factor of Purposeful Morale [a]

Group Performance Variable	*Loading on Morale Factor*
High performance on tug of war	0.68
High mean score on parmia H	0.69
High mean score on self-sentiment Q_3	0.63
High mean score on superego G	0.62
Group coherence: felt accepted by other members (mean all members)	0.43
Many leaders come forward	0.36
Members feel free to participate	0.32
Dislike long group discussions	0.65
High mean score on dominance E	0.51
Low mean score on ergic tension Q_4	0.41

[a] A dimension found from factoring 80 groups of 10 men on performance of group and population personality means.

Note: Traits at negative end of group performance dimension are largely primaries in neuroticism.

Substantial personality predictions have also been found for selection as a leader and for popularity, which, perhaps not unnaturally in a democratic society, have been confused. The effective leader and the popular person, in a group that votes in the leader, are reasonably related, as Table 69(b) shows. Nevertheless there is little doubt that further research will separate them more clearly. Popular leaders are higher in surgency and lower in guilt proneness but effective leaders (effectiveness estimated from achieving group goals) are more intelligent and more self-sufficient.

An area of important research—for which not only the 16 PF but both its normal supplement and the CAQ supplement should be included for high coverage—concerns the effect of the average population level in certain factors on the group behavior as a whole—on its syntality. Syntality has been defined as the equivalent among groups of personality in the individual: *it is that which predicts what a group will do when the circumstances in which it acts are also defined.* As such it should have, on a syntality sphere of group behavior, a set of k discernible unitary dimensions like traits in an individual such that

$$a_{ij} = \sum_{x=k} b_{jx} T_{xi} \qquad (10.12)$$

expresses the estimate of act a_j by group i when its syntality traits are represented as Ts, and bs are loadings. Groups of a defined character—e.g., a group democratically led, with a population of ten, neonate—with individual reward for group success do have uniquely definable, functionally unitary, measurable dimensions such as *purposeful morale* in Table 69(c), in which the average personality endowments of the 10 members play a substantial part. Thus high superego *G* in members is important for morale, whereas Stice and I show that a high mean neuroticism score reduces group capacity to integrate more than any other factor. Unfortunately social psychologists have been slow to check and follow up these findings, for the understandable reason that 100 groups of 10 men, each performing over three days of measurement, constitutes a circus needing considerable organization. The ultimate analysis, too, is complex.

A special kind of group—the family or married couple—has been much more intensively studied. Several dependable empirical laws have been established about the primary and secondary personality factors in relation to marital stability, premarital dating selection, and family upbringing practices. Relations have been established to child and parent personality, notably by Barton, Curran, Dielman, and Nesselroade. Some of them are set out in Table 70.

A law of congeniality by similarity and a law of self-realization by proxy have been hypothesized. The former is easy to demonstrate, as in Table 70, for virtually all traits—notice the constantly higher correlations for stably than unstably married in Table 70(a). But demonstration of the latter, which tends to produce opposite associations to the former, hinges on complex statistics (Cattell and Nesselroade, 1967, 1968; Signori, Rampel, and Pickford, 1968). Regarding the child aspect of the family the relation between questionnaire factor scores for children and manner of upbringing is clear in the work of Dielman and Rhoades (Dielman, Cattell, and Rhoades, 1972) but the *direction of causal action* is hypothetical. For example, does high self-sentiment in the child provoke more physical punishment or does more physical punishment aid self-sentiment development? Causal direction remains to be checked by sequential studies.

Turning to the third type of group—the industrial organization—it is frustrating to have to report (partly through industrial secrecy but largely through lack of coordinated effort and excessive use of special-purpose tests) that clear-cut generalizations are few. Much is available specifically about the typical personality profiles of foremen, executives, technical officers, and others, but little is known about the relation between group personality scores in an industrial organization (or those of its leaders) and morale and productivity. Specification equations for success in particular jobs, however, are beginning to appear, as in the driver and salesman equations cited in Table 64 and also in this equation:

$$\text{Wholesale sales success} = 0.21A + 0.10B + 0.10C + 0.10E + 0.21F + 0.10G - 0.10L - 0.31M + 0.21N - 0.31Q_2 + 0.21Q_3 - 0.21Q_4 + 3.80 \qquad (10.13)$$

Having surveyed questionnaire use and usefulness in the applied field it is worth considering practical problems of setting up the most suitable test installation in applied fields as well as studying the problems of recording and communicating results. Previous discussion of the efficiency and universality indices should have made it clear that in regard to the choice

Table 70

Relation of Questionnaire-Measured Personality to Marital Stability and Child-Upbringing Practices

(a) Primary Personality Factors and Marital Compatibility

	Husband-Wife Correlations in Stably Married															
	A	*B*	*C*	*E*	*F*	*G*	*H*	*I*	*L*	*M*	*N*	*O*	Q_1	Q_2	Q_3	Q_4
Cattell and Nesselroade (N = 102)	16	31	32	13	23	33	23	−15	18	22	18	11	27	15	27	16
Barton and Cattell (1972) (N = 171)	30	37	13	35	38	32	12	28	29	33	13	20	26	27	25	16
Barton (N = 138)	62	64	68	61	69	60	67	72	56	60	15	53	64	59	50	69

	Husband-Wife Correlations in Unstably Married															
	A	*B*	*C*	*E*	*F*	*G*	*H*	*I*	*L*	*M*	*N*	*O*	Q_1	Q_2	Q_3	Q_4
Cattell and Nesselroade (N = 37)	−50	21	05	31	−40	19	12	−13	−33	−01	27	36	34	−32	−02	−11

Note: Dissimilarity on affectia *A,* surgency *F,* protension *L* and self-sufficiency Q_2 is apparently most unfavorable.

(b) Marital Behavior [a]

Frequency of disagreements	Affectia *A,* +0.20
Frequency of going out together	Surgency *F,* +0.22
Frequency of sexual relations	Low self-sentiment Q_3, −0.33

[a] Husband's personality measures; Barton, Kawash, and Cattell, 1972.

(c) Children's Personalities Correlated with Style of Family Upbringing

Child-Rearing Practice Variable	*r*	P	*Child Personality Variable*
From Mother's Child Rearing Practice Measures			
High warmth, free expression of aggression	24	<0.01	with High intelligence—HSPQ(*B*)
Inadequate behavioral control	20	<0.05	with High ergic tension—HSPQ(Q_4)
High behavioral control	16	<0.01	with Sizia—HSPQ(*A*)
Demonstrative affection	16	<0.01	with Low ergic tension—HSPQ(Q_4)
From Father's Child-Rearing Practice Measures.			
Early authoritarian discipline	35	<0.01	with Low intelligence—HSPQ(*B*)
High use of physical punishment	19	<0.01	with Low superego—HSPQ(*G*)
High use of physical punishment	22	<0.01	with Self-sentiment—HSPQ(Q_3)
Demonstrative affection	23	<0.01	with Low excitability—HSPQ(*D*)

Source: Data from Barton, Dielman, and Cattell (1973).

of tests one should not usually build the testing installation from special-purpose tests. And since intelligence is only one of several about equally important factors one should aim at a design that includes an intelligence measure on a par—as far as testing time is concerned—with a wide span of personality factors. It was on this philosophy that the 16 PF (with Supplement) was designed with factor *B* (intelligence) standing among twenty-two primary personality factors and eight other secondaries.

The most effective style of recording in an installation that arranges for, say, a biennial testing of the same individuals can be called the two-file system (Cattell, 1957). By this organization the personality profiles of those in the industry or educational system who may sometime be considered for promotion, scholarships, psychological help, or job specialization are kept as records from the accumulated repetitive testings (for reliability) in one field system. Meanwhile the accumulated specification equations (the *b*s or weights) for the full range of positions in the industry or school (or treatments in a clinic) are kept in another. In an industry appropriate computer procedures (Horst, 1962) can maximize the effectiveness of disposition of personality and ability resources in that population in terms of fitting available personnel to available positions.

A systematic and scarcely solved problem in educational, industrial, and even clinical psychology is that of communicating results produced by the psychologist in technical terms and quantitative score values into familiar, more popular terms to workers and management, to parents and children, and when necessary to patients. A systematic basis from which the psychologist can begin exists in the provision of a *parallel technical and popular system of titles* for source traits (Table 4 in Chapter Two). An increasingly popular positive solution is the narrative output by Krug, Eber, Fuller, and others. In this plan a report is produced from the test scores by the computer on each individual which, in addition to giving statistical probabilities of success in various vocations or positions, expresses in *verbal, surface-trait terms* and criterion estimates the outcomes of the source-trait scores from the psychologist's technical profile. As Table 71 shows, the result is not easily distinguishable from the narrative recommendation or evaluation of a psychologist written as an ordinary case report. But it has the advantage of a standardized use of words not available in idiosyncratic evaluations by different psychologists (or the same psychologist in two moods) and it is far quicker and requires less psychological and clerical labor in its production.

To complete this survey of questionnaire use in applied and research areas a brief reference must be made to the research of social psychologists into patterns of national cultures and cross-cultural research. Here I refer the reader to Chapter Eight and Table 52 for the significant differences of questionnaire personality factor profiles found among different cultures. The necessary reservations with regard to comparability of scoring were discussed in Chapter Eight. By any checks we can apply the population personality differences seem significant and consistent with the qualitative insights of cultural anthropologists. The further pursuit of results along

Table 71

Automatically Produced Narrative Evaluation:
Specimen Computer Printout, Girl Leaving High School, Tested on HSPQ.

Primary Scores in Stens

A	*B*	*C*	*D*	*E*	*F*	*G*	*H*	*I*	*J*	*O*	Q_2	Q_3	Q_4
7	8	8	1	9	3	10	7	9	7	1	7	9	1

Note to psychologist: The following is a probabilistic statement with calculable margins of uncertainty. Confidential to qualified professionals only.

Primary Personality Characteristics of Special Interest

Capacity for abstract verbal skills is high.
Problems are approached with emotional stability and calmness.
She has a rather phlegmatic, indifferent temperament, to a very marked degree.
Interpersonal relationships are carried on in the direction of being dominating, independent, and stubborn.
Her style of expression is often sober, serious, restrained, and older than her years.
Regard for moral standards, duty, and conscientious perseverance is high, indeed, very high.
As a person, she is tenderminded and sensitively imaginative, as from a sheltered life.
She usually feels secure and self-assured, and under no need for any self-justification. This is a very decided characteristic.
A definite self-concept and determination to control oneself to fit a personal and social image characterizes this person.
At present she is relaxed, tranquil, and under no feeling of frustration. This is a very decided characteristic.

Evaluation of Second-Stratum Traits and Criteria of General Importance

This person is outgoing, socially alert, and most suited vocationally to a job which demands interpersonal contact. Her extraversion score, 6.7, is above average.
This individual's anxiety score of 1.0 is extremely low.
Her propensity toward alert and decisive responses, reflected in a score of 3.9, may be considered below average.
The tendency of this individual toward independent and self-directed behavior is expressed by a score of 4.3, which can be thought of as below average.
The degree of social responsibility and control she has achieved is reflected in a score of 10.0 that may be considered extremely high.
A score of 1.0 indicates that her accident proneness is extremely low.

Projections

The following projections about this individual's promise in the areas of academic achievement, leadership, creativity, and vocational success are made relative to her educational opportunities, her aptitudes, and the appropriate peer setting.

Her general capacity to work creatively, to transcend custom, and to generate new ideas, indicated by a score of 9.8, is extremely high.

A score of 10.0 on leadership potential suggests that the probability of her effectively accepting a role of central authority and direction in a group situation is extremely high.

From known relationships between personality and scholastic performance this individual's score of 9.1 indicates that her level of achievement in main school subjects will be very high.

The capacity of this individual to adjust to the demands of a skilled occupation and to grow into a job is expressed in a score of 10.0, which may be regarded as extremely high.

A score of 9.1 suggests that her ability to perform dependably in a job or task which is repetitive or tedious is very high.

Source: Reproduced by permission of the Institute for Personality and Ability Testing Service Department.

these lines is an interesting and enlightening area of questionnaire research. The question of causal relation between features of the culture as a whole and these average personality patterns remains open, although such theories as those of Lynn (1971), McDougall (1924), and myself (1972b) offer frameworks for design of experiments.

8. Summary

(1) Past applied work and even basic research with questionnaires has been largely psychometric and statistical, directed narrowly to obtaining significant criterion predictions from ad hoc special-purpose questionnaires and little concerned with psychological theory. As questionnaires are shaped toward structured personality measurement of traits, about which personality theory has something to say, a more fruitful integration of measurement findings with psychological theory will become possible. Added possibilities of prediction from psychological laws can now augment the limited prediction possible from statistical rules alone. Even within purely psychometric values past practice has been too mechanically aimed at augmenting such test properties as high scale homogeneities and stability coefficients. In contrast we have brought out here such tenets as (a) that homogeneity may be undesirable; (b) that in all state and some trait measures too high a stability shows a scale defect; and (c) that with limited testing time, better criterion prediction is reached using several short, moderate-reliability factor scales than one long high-reliability factor scale.

(2) To encourage thinking in broad terms even within psychometry it would be useful if psychologists evaluating tests did not stop at the first-order parameters in coefficients of consistency and validity but paid regard to a set of *derived* (second-order) coefficients. These latter include principally the concepts of efficiency (validity standardized to a standard, e.g., 10-minute test); utility, which takes into account how much the test measures traits concerning which much is known psychologically to enrich prediction across a standard field of criteria; and universality, which is a generalization of the transferability coefficient.

(3) There are four ways of scoring questionnaire scales. The simplest is the usual procedure of giving unit weight to each of a set of marker items keyed only for the scale. The other ways are weighted markers; computer synthesis by scale, and computer synthesis using all item. More sophisticated methods than these need to be considered, especially in the light of the general conclusion here that the proper item weights for estimating a factor score alter (with differences of subculture sample) more than psychometrists have previously been willing to recognize. Computer synthesis (variance reallocation) can use all items or all scales in a multiscale test to score the scales. Costs suggest that use of computer synthesis on scales is likely to be the most widely used variant. However, although the gain from validity augmentation is appreciable the primaries so scored can no longer be used with their usual established weights for scoring secondaries, nor can they use the

existing weights exactly in specification equations because the primary scale intercorrelations are altered.

(4) In regard to separating trait and state measures, mutual partialing is desirable since mutual contamination is at present the rule. An extension of this principle—the relational restoration calculation—would restore the deviant correlations among scales produced by computer synthesis back to the true intercorrelations (though there is no experience in its use).

The movement of questionnaire scale design from a basis of purely itemetric principles toward structured, source-trait concepts requires modified parallel developments for several now standard psychometric procedures and formulas. One instance is the shift from the Spearman-Brown to the Cattell-Radcliffe formula for effect of increased length. Another is a change in formulae relating homogeneity to validity. But mainly the change calls for a shift of emphasis among properties used for reviewing and evaluating tests.

(5) In the educational use of personality questionnaires, great strides have been made in predicting school achievement—and therefore in analyzing causes of backwardness—from a combination of objective ability and motivation measures with questionnaire measures of personality. Research shows the variance contribution of the three modalities to be about equal, at 25 percent. Thus a total prediction of 70 to 75 percent of school achievement variance is being approached. Creativity and simple scholastic achievement have significantly different specification equations on source traits and both are sensitive in their coefficients to the total life situation and style of schooling in which work goes on.

Questionnaire usage in education is extending beyond analysis of causes of scholastic achievement and backwardness to direct evaluation of the growth of personality and character, as goals of education. Published findings on the specific nature of personality score changes being produced in schools would help to clarify and broaden educational aims. Meanwhile findings are becoming available also on the effect of the teacher's measured personality on classroom education and for guiding selection of effective teachers by personality.

(6) Vocational guidance and selection employ two distinct principles: (i) fitness against a criterion, evaluated by the criterion specification equation; and (ii) adjustment to the occupation, as shown by the similarity of the individual's profile to that of persons found to be well-adjusted to the occupation. Data exist on certain questionnaires and occupations for both methods of guidance, and the use of r_p, the profile-similarity coefficient, is illustrated. The two approaches come together in use of the *qualification grid,* which rests essentially on a curvilinear specification equation defining optimum values. The taxonome program uses r_p to find the natural groupings for occupations or clinical groups according to profile. Knowledge of profiles can generate specification equations by the type-gain principle.

(7) Clinical psychology introduces us to the combined use of trait and state measures, the latter having use in monitoring the course of therapy.

For comprehensive clinical work it is necessary to have scores on normal and abnormal (pathological) factors, since it is useful to know the underlying personality in psychosis. However, the pattern of deviations on normal source traits alone seems capable, by contrast, of diagnosing neurotic, addictive, alcoholic, and delinquent conditions. The 12 pathological dimensions are additionally necessary, however, to diagnose psychosis. For reasons just given, it is still desirable to keep measures of the normal factors in psychosis (to have both normal and pathological scores) as is arranged in the design of the CAQ. Enough evidence on 16 PF and CAQ profiles of clinical groups has become available to provide diagnostic profiles and, in some cases, effective discriminant functions for separating syndrome groups.

A method of examining surface-trait syndromes (as in the MMPI) along with source traits (as in the CAQ) is described as *depth psychometry*. There are new possibilities of monitoring therapy by using state measurements (questionnaire and objective motivation measures) in the light of depth psychometry and of evaluating improvements with therapy as *multidimensional change*. State measures, notably of anxiety, regression, and depression, have become indispensable in research on drug therapy.

(8) The application of personality questionnaires in social psychology has been fruitful in diverse directions (even excluding value and attitude research, which is better done by objective tests). In particular, significant relations have been found by personality questionnaires to individual behavior in groups and the behavior of groups, notably in group-dynamics research. The social psychologist's most promising theoretical model for dimensional predictions is one which embraces sociological parameters by introducing role factors, which have the same structure as state liability traits and which modulate with the ambient role-cue situation. Although sheer differences of roles account for much difference in social behavior, personality factors affect both degree of *adoption* of roles and the variance of behavior *within* roles. An important role is illustrated in leadership, where the primary personality-factor scores show that leaders are powerfully selected for personality and that their personality differences account for variations of effective leadership behavior within the role.

The theoretical model for such work is thus one that distinguishes personality factors from role factors—the latter being subject to strong modulation by the role-cue situations.

(9) In the large, structured groups of industry, findings on questionnaire personality score predictions are less organized and are often kept private. However, the relations of some factors to group morale and to likelihood of promotion are becoming known. There are three important characteristics of a well-designed testing installation in industry, in educational systems, and elsewhere. First, a battery of tests with high efficiency and utility indices, one which is routinely readministered at one- or two-year intervals for reliability and for trend analysis. Second, a two-file recording system of the profiles of individuals and the profiles or specifications found for particular positions. Third, a system for communicating findings to those concerned in ways suitably modified from the technical terminology and

mathematics of psychology as a science. For use by nonpsychologists the plan of explaining score values as a computer narrative printout is now feasible. Full advantage has by no means been taken of the technical possibilities, partly because industry has been given more to expedient special-purpose tests than to comprehensive planning of a psychologically meaningful test installation devised to utilize psychological as well as statistical prediction.

(10) In the areas of social psychology that verge on cultural anthropology and political science—cross-cultural research—translated personality questionnaires have proved sensitive enough to establish significant population differences. The relation of these population differences on the one hand to the behavior of groups as such, on the other, measured on such culture pattern dimensions as affluence and cultural pressure, is now open to quantitative investigation.

References

ACKERSON, L. *Children's behavior problems: 2. Relative importance and interrelations among traits.* Chicago: University of Chicago Press, 1942.

ADAMS, D. K. & HORN, J. L. Non-overlapping keys for the MMPI scales. *Journal of Consulting Psychology,* 1965, *29,* 284.

ADCOCK, C. J. A comparison of the concepts of Cattell and Eysenck. *British Journal of Educational Psychology,* 1965, 35, 90–97.

ADCOCK, C. J., & ADCOCK, N. A check on the factor structure of the 16 P.F. in New Zealand. Wellington, New Zealand: University of Victoria, Laboratory Printing, 1972.

ALLPORT, G. W. A test for ascendance-submission. *Journal of Abnormal and Social Psychology,* 1928, 23, 118–136.

ALLPORT, G. W. *Pattern and growth in personality.* New York: Holt, Rinehart and Winston, 1961.

ALLPORT, G. W., & ODBERT, H. S. Trait-names, a psycho-lexical study. *Psychological Monographs,* 1936, 47, 171.

ALLPORT, G. W., VERNON, P. E., & LINDZEY, G. *The Allport-Vernon study of values.* Boston: Houghton Mifflin, 1951.

ANASTASI, A. *A Differential Psychology.* New York: Macmillan, 1958.

ANASTASI, A. *Psychological Testing.* New York: Macmillan, 1961.

ANDERSON, H. H., and ANDERSON, M. *Projective Techniques.* New York: Prentice-Hall, 1950.

ANDERSON, H., and HORN, J. L. "The Separation of Fluid and Crystallized Intelligence Factors Compared in Two Different Social Samples." In press.

ANGLEITNER, A., and others. Die Altershängigkeit der Persönlichkeit im Sinne von R. B. Cattell, *Act. Gerontol.,* 1971, *1,* 721–730.

ANGOFF, W. H. *The Development of Statistical Indices for Detecting Cheaters.* ETS Research Bulletin RB-72-26. Princeton Educational Testing Service, 1972.

ARDREY, R. A. *The Territorial Imperative.* New York: Atheneum, 1966.

ASHTON, S. G., and GOLDBERG, L. R. *In Response to Jackson's Challenge: The Comparative Validity of Personality Scales Constructed by the External (Empirical) Strategy and Scales Developed Intuitively by Experts, Novices, and Laymen.* Paper presented at the 1972 meeting of the Society of Multivariate Experimental Psychology. Fort Worth, November 9, 1972.

BAGGALEY, A. R., and CATTELL, R. B. "A Comparison of Exact and Approximate Linear Function Estimates of Oblique Factor Scores." *British Journal of Statistical Psychology,* 1956, *9,* 83–86.

BALDRY, A. I., and SARASON, I. G. "Test Anxiety, Preliminary Instructions, and Responses to Personality Inventories." *Journal of Clinical Psychology,* 1968, *24,* 67.

BALTES, P. B. "Longitudinal and Cross Sectional Sequences in the Study of Age and Generation Effects." *Human Development,* 1968, *11,* 145–171.

BALTES, P. B., and NESSELROADE, J. R. "Cultural Change and Adolescent Personality Development." *Developmental Psychology,* 1972, 7 (3), 244–256.

BALTES, P. B., and NESSELROADE, J. R. A Study of One Year Changes on the High School Personality Questionnaire. Report to the Office of Education, 1973a.

BALTES, P. B., and NESSELROADE, J. R. The Developmental Analysis of Individual Differences on Multiple Measures. In J. R. Nesselroade and H. W. Reese (Eds.), *Life-Span Developmental Psychology: Methodological Issues.* New York: Academic, 1973b.

BANKS, C., and BROADHURST, P. L. *Studies in Psychology.* London: University of London Press, 1965.

BARGMANN, R. *The Statistical Significance of Simple Structure in Factor Analysis.* Mimeographed. Frankfurt-Main: Hochschule für Internationale Pädagogische Forschung, 1953.

BARTLETT, H. W. *School Counselor Personality Profile as Measured by the 16 Personality Factor Test.* Personality Profile No. 1. Champaign, Ill.: Institute for Personality and Ability Testing, April, 1968.

BARTLETT, M. S. "Tests of Significance in Factor Analysis." *British Journal of Psychology,* 1948, *1,* 73–81.

BARTON, K. *The CTS, Core Trait and State Kit.* Champaign, Ill.: Institute for Personality and Ability Testing, 1973a.

BARTON, K. *The Relative Validities of the CTS, the EPI and the Comrey Scales as Measures of Second Order Personality Source Traits by Questionnaire.* Advance Publication No. 1. Boulder: Institute for Research on Morality and Adjustment, 1973b.

BARTON, K., BARTSCH, T. W., and CATTELL, R. B. *Longitudinal Relationships Among Achievement and Personality Variables.* Advance Publication No. 2. Boulder: Institute for Research on Morality and Adjustment. In preparation (a).

BARTON, K., BARTSCH, T. W., and CATTELL, R. B. *The Effects of Fatigue on Psychological States.* Advance Publication No. 3. Boulder: Institute for Research on Morality and Adjustment. In preparation (b).

BARTON, K., and CATTELL, H. "Personality Characteristics of Female Psychology, Science and Art Majors." *Psychological Reports,* 1972, *31,* 807–813.

BARTON, K., and CATTELL, R. B. "Marriage Dimensions and Personality." *Journal of Personality and Social Psychology,* 1972a, *21,* 369–375.

BARTON, K., and CATTELL, R. B. "Personality Before and After a Chronic Illness." *Journal of Clinical Psychology,* 1972b, *28* (4), 464–467.

BARTON, K., and CATTELL, R. B. "Personality Factors Related to Job Promotion and Turnover." *Journal of Counseling Psychology,* 1972c, *19* (5), 430–435.

BARTON, K., and CATTELL, R. B. "Real and Perceived Similarities in Personality Between Spouses: Test of Likeness Versus Completeness Theories." *Psychological Reports,* 1972d, *31,* 15–18.

BARTON, K., and CATTELL, R. B. "Personality Factors of Husbands and Wives as Predictors of Own and Partner's Marital Dimensions." *Canadian Journal of Behavioral Science,* 1973. In press.

BARTON, K., and CATTELL, R. B. *The Effectiveness of Attempts to Manipulate Arousal on Measures of Psychological States.* Advance Publication No. 5. Boulder, Colo.: Institute for Research on Morality and Adjustment, In preparation (a).

BARTON, K., and CATTELL, R. B. *Psychological States: Their Definition through P-Technique and Differential R- (dR)-Technique Factor Analysis.* Advance Publication No. 6. Boulder, Colo.: Institute for Research on Morality and Adjustment. In preparation (b).

BARTON, K., and CATTELL, R. B. *The Relation of the Pseudo-Second Order Questionnaire Traits in the Eysenck PEN and the Comrey Scales to Second Order Structure in the CTS Kit.* Advance Publication No. 7. Boulder, Colo.: Institute for Research on Morality and Adjustment. In prep. (c).

BARTON, K., CATTELL, R. B., and CONNOR, D. V. "The Identification of State Factors Through P-Technique Factor Analysis." *Journal of Clinical Psychology,* 1972, *28,* 459–463.

BARTON, K., CATTELL, R. B., and DIELMAN, T. E. "Personality, Motivation and IQ Measures as Predictors of School Achievement as Grades: A Non-Technical Synopsis." *Psychology in the Schools,* 1972, *9,* 47–51.

BARTON, K., CATTELL, R. B., and DIELMAN, T. E. "Prediction of School Grades from Motivation, Personality and IQ Measures." *Personality: An International Journal,* 1973.

BARTON, K., CATTELL, R. B., and SILVERMAN, W. "Personality Correlated of Verbal and Spatial Ability." *Social Behavior and Personality.* In press.

BARTON, K., DIELMAN, T. E., and CATTELL, R. B. "The Prediction of School Grades from Personality and I.Q. Measures." *Personality: An International Journal,* 1971, *2,* 325–333.

BARTON, K., DIELMAN, T. E., and CATTELL, R. B. "Personality and I.Q. Measures as Predictors of School Achievement." *Journal of Educational Psychology,* 1972a, *63,* 398–404.

BARTON, K., DIELMAN, T. E., and CATTELL, R. B. Personality, Motivation and IQ Measures as Predictors of School Achievement and Grades: A Nontechnical Synopsis. *Psychology in the Schools,* 1972b, *9,* 47–51.

BARTON, K., DIELMAN, T. E., and CATTELL, R. B. "Child Rearing Practices Related to Child Personality." *Journal of Social Psychology,* 1973.

BARTON, K., KAWASH, G., and CATTELL, R. B. "Personality, Motivation, and Marital Role Factors as Predictors of Life Data in Married Couples." *Journal of Marriage and the Family,* 1972, August, 474–480.

BARTSCH, T. W. *The Influence of Instructional Material on the Temporal Stability and Structural Invariance of Certain Measures of Trait and State Anxiety.* Unpublished doctoral dissertation. Morgantown, West Virginia University, 1972.

BARTSCH, T. W., and CATTELL, R. B. *The Child Central Trait-State Kit.* Champaign, Ill.: Institute for Personality and Ability Testing, in preparation.

BARTSCH, T. W., and NESSELROADE, J. R. "Test of the Trait-State Anxiety Distinction Using a Manipulative, Factor-Analytic Design." *Journal of Personality and Social Psychology,* 1973.

BATH, K. E., DALEY, D. L., and NESSELROADE, J. R. *Replicability of Factors Derived from Individual P-Technique Analysis.* Unpublished manuscript. Morgantown: Department of Psychology, West Virginia University, 1972.

BECK, A. J., WARD, C. H., and others. "An Inventory for Measuring Depression." *Archives of General Psychiatry,* 1961, *4,* 53–63.

BECKER, W. C. "The Matching of Behavior Rating and Questionnaire Personality Factors." *Psychological Bulletin,* 1960, *57,* 201–212.

BEHM, H. D. *Characteristics of Community College Students: Comparison of Transfers and Occupational Freshmen in Mid-Western Colleges.* Unpublished doctoral dissertation. Columbia: University of Missouri, 1967.

BELL, H. M. *The Adjustment Inventory.* Palo Alto, Calif.: Consulting Psychologists Press, 1934–1939.

BENDIG, A. W. "A Factor Analysis of Scales of Emotionality and Hostility." *Journal of Clinical Psychology,* 1961, *17,* 189–192.

BEREITER, C. "Some Persisting Dilemmas in the Measurement of Change." In C. W. Harris (Ed.), *Problems in Measuring Change.* Madison: University of Wisconsin Press, 1963.

BERG, I. A. "Measuring Deviant Behavior by Means of Deviant Response Sets." In I. A. Berg and B. M. Bass (Eds.), *Conformity and Deviation.* New York: Harper, 1961.

BERG, I. A. *Response Set in Personality Assessment.* Chicago: Aldine, 1967.

BERNREUTER, R. G. *The Personality Inventory.* Palo Alto, Calif.: Consulting Psychologists Press, 1935–1938.

BIRKIN, T. A. *Some Educational Influences on Creativity Changes.* Adelaide: Australian Association of Advanced Science, 1969.

BLEULER, E. "Dementia praecox oder Gruppe der Schizophrenien." In K. Aschaffenbrugs (Ed.), *Handbuch der Psychiatrie.* Leipzig: Thieme, 1911.

BLOCK, J. *The Challenge of Response Sets.* New York: Appleton Century, 1965.

BOLZ, C. R. "Types of Personality." In R. M. Dreger (Ed.), *Multivariate Personality Research.* Baton Rouge: Claitor's Publishing Division, 1972.

BOLZ, C. R., and CATTELL, R. B. *Personality Factors in Children in Objective Tests.* Advance Publication No. 10. Boulder, Colo.: Institute for Research on Morality and Adjustment, 1974.

BORGATTA, E. F. "A Systematic Study of Interaction Process Scores, Peer and Self Assessments, Personality and Other Variables." *Genetic Psychological Monographs,* 1962, *65,* 219–291.

BRAUN, J. R. "Forced-Choice Self-Report Devices: A Look at Some Unwarranted Claims." *Measurement and Evaluation in Guidance,* 1969, *2* (3), 153–156.

BROGDEN, H. E., and THOMAS, W. F. "The Primary Traits in Personality Items Purporting to Measure Sociability." *Journal of Psychology,* 1943, *16,* 85–97.

BRUNSWIK, E. *Perception and the Representative Design of Psychological Experiments.* Berkeley: University of California Press, 1956.

BURDSAL, C. A., and CATTELL, R. B. *Child Motivation Analysis Test.* Champaign, Ill.: Institute for Personality and Ability Testing. In press.

BURDSAL, C. A., and VAUGHAN, D. "A Check on Factor Structure of the 16 PF by Item Factoring on a Student Group." *Journal of Genetic Psychology,* 1973.

BURDSAL, C. A., and VAUGHAN, D. "A Third Check on the Factor Structure of the HSPQ." *Journal of Genetic Psychology.* In press.

BUROS, O. K. *Seventh Mental Measurement Yearbook.* Highland Park, N. J.: Gryphon Press, 1972.

BURT, C. L. *Factors of the Mind.* London: University of London Press, 1940.

BURT, C. L., and HOWARD, M. "The Multifactorial Theory of Inheritance." *British Journal of Statistical Psychology,* 1956, *9,* 115–125.

CABLE, D. G. *Separation of State and Trait Anxiety in the Context of Short-Term Change.* Unpublished doctoral dissertation. Morgantown: West Virginia University, 1972.

CAMPBELL, D. T., and FISKE, D. W. "Convergent and Discriminant Validation by the Multitrait-Multimethod Matrix." *Psychological Bulletin,* 1959, *56,* 81–105.

CANFIELD, A. A. "The Sten Scale—A Modified C-Scale." *Educational and Psychological Measurement,* 1951, *11,* 295–297.

CANTER, S. *Personality Traits in Twins.* Paper presented at the annual conference of the British Psychological Society. London, 1969.

CARLSON, H. B. "Attitudes of Undergraduate Students." *Journal of Social Psychology,* 1934, *5,* 202–213.

CARSON, R. C. *Interaction Concepts of Personality.* Chicago: Aldine, 1969.

CARTWRIGHT, D. S. *A Generalized Equation for Total-Test Variance.* Paper presented at the annual meeting of the Society of Multivariate Experimental Psychologists. Fort Worth, November 16, 1962.

CARTWRIGHT, D. S. *A Comprehensive Analysis of Sources of Variance in Psychometric Measurements.* Paper presented at the Society of Multivariate Experimental Psychologists. November, 1965.

CARTWRIGHT, D. S., and CARTWRIGHT, C. F. *Psychological Adjustment: Behavior in the Inner World.* Chicago: Rand McNally, 1971.

CATTELL, R. B. "Temperament Tests: I. Temperament." *British Journal of Psychology,* 1933a, *23,* 308–329.

CATTELL, R. B. "Temperament Tests: II. Tests." *British Journal of Psychology,* 1933b, *24,* 20–49.

CATTELL, R. B. "On the Measurement of Perseveration." *British Journal of Educational Psychology,* 1935a, *5,* 76–92.

CATTELL, R. B. "Perseveration and Personality: Some Experiments and a Hypothesis." *Journal of Mental Science,* 1935b, *61,* 151–167.

CATTELL, R. B. *A Guide to Mental Testing.* London: London University Press, 1936.

CATTELL, R. B. *The Fight for Our National Intelligence.* London: King, 1937.

CATTELL, R. B. "An Objective Test of Character Temperament: I." *Journal of Genetic Psychology,* 1941, *25,* 59–73.

CATTELL, R. B. "Fluctuation of Sentiments and Attitudes as a Measure of Character Integration and of Temperament." *American Journal of Psychology,* 1943, *56,* 195–216.

CATTELL, R. B. "The Diagnosis and Classification of Neurotic States: A Reinterpretation of Eysenck's Factors." *Journal of Nervous and Mental Disorders,* 1945, *102,* 576–589.

CATTELL, R. B. "The Riddle of Perseveration: I. 'Creative Effort' and Disposition Rigidity." *Journal of Personality,* 1946a, *14,* 229–238.

CATTELL, R. B. *The Description and Measurement of Personality.* New York: World, 1946b.

CATTELL, R. B. "Simple Structure in Relation to Some Alternative Factorizations of the Personality Sphere." *Journal of General Psychology,* 1946c, *35,* 225–238.

CATTELL, R. B. "Confirmation and Clarification of Primary Personality Factors." *Psychometrika,* 1947, *12,* 197–220.

CATTELL, R. B. "Primary Personality Factors in the Realm of Objective Tests." *Journal of Personality,* 1948, *16,* 459–487.

CATTELL, R. B. "A note on factor invariance and the identification of factors." *British Journal of Psychology,* 1949a, *2,* 134–138.

CATTELL, R. B. *The Sixteen Personality Factor Questionnaire.* (1st ed.) Champaign, Ill.: Institute for Personality and Ability Testing, 1949b.

CATTELL, R. B. *Personality, a Systematic Theoretical and Factual Study.* New York: McGraw-Hill, 1950a.

CATTELL, R. B. "The Fate of National Intelligence: Test of a Thirteen Year Prediction." *Eugenics Review,* 1950b, *42,* 136–148.

CATTELL, R. B. *Validation of New Items for the 16 P.F. in Four Factorings (Multiple Group) Centered on Four Factors in Each.* Advanced Publication No. 2, Series 1. Champaign, Ill.: Laboratory of Personality and Group Analysis, 1950c.

CATTELL, R. B. "The Main Questionnaire Factors in Questionnaire Self Estimate Material." *Journal of Social Psychology,* 1950d, *31,* 3–38.

CATTELL, R. B. *Factor Analysis.* New York: Harper, 1952.

CATTELL, R. B. "Research Designs in Psychological Genetics with Special Reference to the Multiple Variance Method." *American Journal of Human Genetics,* 1953, *5,* 76–93.

CATTELL, R. B. "The Principal Replicated Factors Discovered in Objective Personality Tests." *Journal of Abnormal and Social Psychology,* 1955a, *50,* 291–314.

CATTELL, R. B. *The Objective-Analytic (O-A) Personality Factor Batteries.* Champaign, Ill.: Institute for Personality and Ability Testing, 1955b.

CATTELL, R. B. *Psychiatric Screening of Flying Personnel: Personality Structure in Objective Tests.* Report No. 9. Randolph Field, Texas: USAF School of Aviation Medicine, 1955c.

CATTELL, R. B. "A Shortened 'Basic English' Version (Form C) of the 16 P.F. Questionnaire." *Journal of Social Psychology,* 1956a, *44,* 257–278.

CATTELL, R. B. "Validation and Intensification of the Sixteen Personality Factor Questionnaire." *Journal of Clinical Psychology,* 1956b, *12,* 205–214.

CATTELL, R. B. "New Developments of Personality Theory from Quantitative Factor Analytic Research." *Review Internationale de Philosophie,* 1956c, *35,* 1–35.

CATTELL, R. B. "Second-Order Personality Factors in the Questionnaire Realm." *Journal of Consulting Psychology,* 1956d, *20,* 411–418.

CATTELL, R. B. *Personality and Motivation Structure and Measurement.* New York: World, 1957.

CATTELL, R. B. "Extracting the Correct Number of Factors in Factor Analysis." *Educational and Psychological Measurement,* 1958, *18,* 791–838.

CATTELL, R. B. "Anxiety, Extraversion and Other Second Order Personality Factors in Children." *Journal of Personality,* 1959, *27,* 464–476.

CATTELL, R. B. "Evaluating Interaction and Non-Linear Relations by Factor Analysis." *Psychological Reports,* 1960, *7,* 69–70.

CATTELL, R. B. "Theory of Situational, Instrument, Second Order and Refraction Factors in Personality Structure Research." *Psychological Bulletin,* 1961, *58,* 160–174.

CATTELL, R. B. "The Relational Simplex Theory of Equal Interval and Absolute Scaling." *Acta Psychologica,* 1962a, *20,* 139–158.

CATTELL, R. B. "The Basis of Recognition and Interpretation of Factors." *Educational and Psychological Measurement,* 1962b, *22,* 160–174.

CATTELL, R. B. "Personality, Role, Mood, and Situation-Perception: A Unifying Theory of Modulators." *Psychological Review,* 1963a, *70,* 1–18.

CATTELL, R. B. "The Structuring of Change of P-Technique and Incremental R-Technique." In C. W. Harris (Ed.), *Problems in Measuring Change.* Madison: University of Wisconsin Press, 1963b.

CATTELL, R. B. "Validity and Reliability: A Proposed More Basic Set of Concepts." *Journal of Educational Psychology,* 1964, *55,* 1–22.

CATTELL, R. B. *The Scientific Analysis of Personality.* London: Penguin, 1965a.

CATTELL, R. B. "The Configurative Method for Surer Identification of Personality Dimensions, Notably in Child Study." *Psychological Reports,* 1965b, *16,* 269–270.

CATTELL, R. B. "A Cross-Cultural Check on Second Stratum Personality Factor Structures—Notably of Anxiety and Exvia." *Australian Journal of Personality,* 1965c, *17,* 22–23.

CATTELL, R. B. *The* IPAT *Culture Fair Intelligence Scales 1, 2 and 3.* 3rd edition. Champaign, Ill.: Institute for Personality and Ability Testing, 1965d.

CATTELL, R. B. "Higher Order Factor Structures and Reticular vs. Hierarchical Formulae for Their Interpretation." In Charlotte Banks and P. L. Broadhurst (Eds.), *Studies in Psychology.* London: University of London Press, 1965e.

CATTELL, R. B. *Handbook of Multivariate Experimental Psychology.* Chicago: Rand McNally, 1966a.

CATTELL, R. B. "The Scree Test for the Number of Factors." *Multivariate Behavioral Research,* 1966b, *1,* 140–161.

CATTELL, R. B. "Evaluating therapy as total personality change: theory and available instruments." *American Journal of Psychotherapy,* 1966c, *20,* 69–88.

CATTELL, R. B. "Trait-View Theory of Perturbations in Ratings and Self Ratings (L-, BR- and Q-Data): Its Application to Obtaining Pure Trait Score Estimates in Questionnaires." *Psychological Review,* 1968, *75,* 96–113.

CATTELL, R. B. "Comparing Factor Trait and State Scores Across Ages and Cultures." *Journal of Gerontology,* 1969, *24,* 348–360.

CATTELL, R. B. "The Isopodic and Equipotent Principles for Comparing Factor Scores Across Different Populations." *British Journal of Mathematical and Statistical Psychology,* 1970a, *23,* 23–41.

CATTELL, R. B. "Separating Endogenous, Ecogenous, Ecogenic, and Epogenic Component Curves in Developmental Data." *Developmental Psychology,* 1970b, *3,* 151–162.

CATTELL, R. B. "A Factor Analytic System for Clinicians. I. The Integration of Functional and Psychometric Requirements in a Quantitative and Computerized Diagnostic System." In A. R. Mahrer (Ed.), *New Approaches to Personality Classification.* New York: Columbia University Press, 1970c.

CATTELL, R. B. *Abilities: Their Structure, Growth and Action.* Boston: Houghton Mifflin, 1971a.

CATTELL, R. B. "Estimating Modulator Indices and State Liabilities." *Multivariate Behavioral Research,* 1971b, *6,* 7–33.

CATTELL, R. B. "Real Base True Zero Factor Analysis." *Multivariate Behavioral Research Monograph 72-1,* 1972a.

CATTELL, R. B. *A New Morality from Science: Beyondism.* Elmsford, N.Y.: Pergamon, 1972b.

CATTELL, R. B. "The Nature and Genesis of Mood States." In C. Spielberger (Ed.), *Anxiety: Current Trends in Research.* New York: Academic Press, 1972c.

CATTELL, R. B. "The Interpretation of Pavlov's Typology and the Arousal Concept, in Replicated Trait and State Factors." In V. D. Nebylitsin and J. A. Gray (Eds.), *Biological Bases of Individual Behavior.* New York: Academic, 1972d.

CATTELL, R. B. "The 16 P.F. and Basic Personality Structure: A Reply to Eysenck." *Journal of Behavioural Science,* 1972e, *1,* 169–187.

CATTELL, R. B. "The Rotational Process in Factor Analysis." In K. Enslein (Ed.), *Statistical Methods for Digital Computers.* New York: Wiley-Interscience, 1973a.

CATTELL, R. B. *The Vulnerability Coefficient Hypothesis for Correcting Motivation Distortion in Questionnaire Scales.* Advance Publication No. 11. Boulder, Colo.: Institute for Research on Morality and Adjustment, 1973b.

CATTELL, R. B. *The Second Order Structure on a Broader Basis of Twenty-Three*

Primaries. Advance Publication No. 12. Boulder, Colo.: Institute for Research on Morality and Adjustment, 1973c.

CATTELL, R. B. *A Cross-Validation of the Second Order Structure on a Basis of Twenty-Three Primaries.* Advance Publication No. 13. Boulder, Colo.: Institute for Research on Morality and Adjustment, 1973d.

CATTELL, R. B. *First Order Structure on the CAQ (a) Abnormal, (b) Normal.* Advance Publication No. 14. Boulder, Colo.: Institute for Research on Morality and Adjustment, 1973e.

CATTELL, R. B. *Definition of Chief Factors in Psychiatrically Rated Depression and Their Comparison with Q-data Source Traits.* Advance Publication No. 15. Boulder, Colo.: Institute for Research on Morality and Adjustment, 1973f.

CATTELL, R. B. *A Re-Analysis of the Sells-Demaree-Will Questionnaire Factors.* Advance Publication No. 16. Boulder, Colo.: Institute for Research on Morality and Adjustment, 1973g.

CATTELL, R. B. *Second Stratum Personality Structure on a Basis of Parceled Factoring.* Advance Publication No. 17. Boulder, Colo.: Institute for Research on Morality and Adjustment, 1973h.

CATTELL, R. B. *Second Stratum Structure on a Basis of Pathological Factors.* Advance Publication No. 18. Boulder, Colo.: Institute for Research on Morality and Adjustment, 1973i.

CATTELL, R. B. *A Check on the Structure of the 16 P.F. by Parceled Factoring, in Comparison with Item Factoring.* Advance Publication No. 19. Boulder, Colo.: Institute for Research on Morality and Adjustment, 1973j.

CATTELL, R. B. *An Analysis of State and Trait Change Factors by dR-Technique on the CAQ.* Advance Publication No. 20. Boulder, Colo.: Institute for Research on Morality and Adjustment, 1973k.

CATTELL, R. B. *A Second Order Analysis of State and Trait Change Factors by dR-Technique on the CAQ.* Advance Publication No. 21. Boulder, Colo.: Institute for Research on Morality and Adjustment, 1973l.

CATTELL, R. B. *Third Order Structure in Questionnaires.* Advance Publication No. 22. Boulder, Colo.: Institute for Research on Morality and Adjustment, 1973m.

CATTELL, R. B. *The theory of relational restorations of true correlations among estimated factors in questionnaire scales.* Advance Publication No. 64. Boulder, Colorado: Institute for Research on Morality and Adjustment, 1973n.

CATTELL, R. B. *Radial parcel factoring vs. item factoring in defining personality structure in questionnaires: theory and experimental checks.* Advance Publication No. 27. Boulder, Colo.: Institute for Research on Morality and Adjustment, 1973o.

CATTELL, R. B. *Separation of Anxiety Trait from Anxiety State Measures.* Advance Publication No. 23. Boulder, Colo.: Institute for Research on Morality and Adjustment, 1973p.

CATTELL, R. B. "A More Sophisticated Look at Structure: Perturbation, Role and Trait View Theories." In R. B. Cattell and R. M. Dreger (Eds.), *Handbook of Modern Personality Theory.* New York: Appleton Century Crofts, 1974.

CATTELL, R. B., and ANDERSON, J. C. "The Measurement of Personality and Behavior Disorders by the IPAT Music Preference Test." *Journal of Applied Psychology,* 1953, *37,* 446–454.

CATTELL, R. B., and BAGGALEY, A. R. "The Salient Variable Similarity Index for Factor Matching." *British Journal of Statistical Psychology,* 1960, *13,* 33–46.

CATTELL, R. B., BALCAR, K. R., HORN, J. L., and NESSELROADE, J. R. "Factor Matching Procedures: An Improvement of the *s* Index, with Tables." *Educational and Psychological Measurement,* 1969, *29,* 781–792.

CATTELL, R. B., and BARTLETT, H. W. "An R- dR-Technique Operational Distinction of the States of Anxiety, Stress, Fear, etc." *Australian Journal of Psychology,* 1971, *23* (2), 105–123.

CATTELL, R. B., and BARTON, K. *A Check on the Psycho-Physiological Structure of the 9 Primary Source States.* Advance Publication No. 24. Boulder, Colo.: Institute for Research on Morality and Adjustment, 1973.

CATTELL, R. B., and BARTON, K. *The Higher Stratum States. A Survey of dR- and P-Technique Factorizations.* Advance Publication No. 25. Boulder, Colo.: Institute for Research on Morality and Adjustment. In preparation.

CATTELL, R. B., BARTON, K., and DIELMAN, T. E. "Prediction of School Achievement from Motivation, Personality and Ability Measures." *Psychological Reports,* 1972, *30,* 35–43.

CATTELL, R. B., and BELOFF, H. "Research Origin and Construction of the IPAT Junior Personality Quiz." *Journal of Consulting Psychology,* 1953, *17,* 436–442.

CATTELL, R. B., and BELOFF, H. *The High School Personality Questionnaire.* Champaign, Ill.: Institute for Personality and Ability Testing, 1960.

CATTELL, R. B., and BJERSTEDT, A. "The Structure of Depression by Factoring Q-Data in Relation to General Personality Source Traits." *Scandinavian Journal of Psychology,* 1967, *8,* 17–24.

CATTELL, R. B., BLEWETT, D. B., and BELOFF, J. R. "The Inheritance of Personality: A Multiple Variance Analysis Determination of Approximate Nature-Nurture Ratios for Primary Personality Factors in Q-Data." *American Journal of Human Genetics,* 1955, *7,* 122–146.

CATTELL, R. B., and BOLTON, L. S. "What Pathological Dimensions Lie Beyond the Normal Dimensions of the 16 P.F.? A Comparison of MMPI and 16 P.F. Factor Domains." *Journal of Consulting and Clinical Psychology,* 1969, *33,* 18–29.

CATTELL, R. B., BOLZ, C. R., and KORTH, G. "Behavioral Types in Pure Bred Dogs Objectively Determined by Taxonome." *Journal of Behavioral Genetics,* 1973, *3,* 21–28.

CATTELL, R. B., and BURDSAL, C. *The radial parcel double factoring design: a solution to the item vs. parcel controversy.* Advanced Pub. No. 8. Boulder, Colo.: Institute for Research on Morality and Adjustment, 1973g.

CATTELL, R. B., and BUTCHER, J. *The Prediction of Achievement and Creativity.* Indianapolis: Bobbs Merrill, 1968.

CATTELL, R. B., CATTELL, A. K. S., and RHYMER, R. M. "P-Technique Demonstrated in Determining Psycho-Physiological Source Traits in a Normal Individual." *Psychometrika,* 1947, *12,* 267–288.

CATTELL, R. B., and CATTELL, M. D. *The High School Personality Questionnaire.* Champaign, Ill.: Institute for Personality and Ability Testing, 1966.

CATTELL, R. B., and CATTELL, M. D. *Handbook for the Jr.-Sr. High School Personality Questionnaire* (HSPQ). Champaign, Ill.: Institute for Personality and Ability Testing, 1969.

CATTELL, R. B., and CHILD, D. *Motivation and Dynamic Structure.* London: Holt, Rinehart and Winston, 1974.

CATTELL, R. B., and COAN, R. W. "Child Personality Structure as Revealed in Teachers' Behavior Ratings." *Journal of Clinical Psychology,* 1957a, *13,* 315–327.

CATTELL, R. B., and COAN, R. W. "Personality Factors in Middle Childhood as Revealed in Parents' Ratings." *Child Development,* 1957b, *28,* 439–458.

CATTELL, R. B., and COAN, R. W. "Personality Dimensions in the Questionnaire Responses of Six and Seven Year Olds." *British Journal of Educational Psychology,* 1958, *28,* 232–242.

CATTELL, R. B., COAN, R. W., and BELOFF, H. "A Re-Examination of Personality Structure in Late Childhood and Development of the High School Personality Questionnaire." *Journal of Experimental Education,* 1958, *27,* 73–88.

CATTELL, R. B., and COULTER, M. A. "Principles of Behavioral Taxonomy and the Mathematical Basis of the Taxonome Computer Program." *British Journal of Mathematical and Statistical Psychology,* 1966, *19,* 237–269.

CATTELL, R. B., COULTER, M. A., and TSUJIOKA, B. "The Taxonomic Recognition of Types and Functional Emergents." In R. B. Cattell (Ed.), *Handbook of Multivariate Experimental Psychology.* Chicago, Ill.: Rand McNally, 1966.

CATTELL, R. B., and DELHEES, K. H. "Seven Missing Normal Personality Factors in the Questionnaire Primaries." *Multivariate Behavioral Research,* 1973. *8,* 173–194.

CATTELL, R. B., DELHEES, K. H., TATRO, D. F., and NESSELROADE, J. R. "Personality Structure Checked in Primary Objective Test Factors for a Mixed Normal and Psychotic Sample." *Multivariate Behavioral Research,* 1971, *6,* 187–214.

CATTELL, R. B., and DEVOOGD, T. *A Check on the Structure of the Comprehensive Twenty-Three Personality Primaries in Q-Data.* Advance Publication No. 28. Boulder, Colo.: Institute for Research on Morality and Adjustment. In preparation (a).

CATTELL, R. B., and DEVOOGD, T. *A Test of the Vulnerability Coefficient Model for Correcting Motivational Distortion in Q-Data Personality Measurement.* Advance Publication No. 29. Boulder, Colo.: Institute for Research on Morality and Adjustment. In preparation (b).

CATTELL, R. B., and DEYOUNG, G. E. *Confactor Resolution in Factor Analysis.* Advance Publication No. 30. Boulder, Colo.: Institute for Research on Morality and Adjustment, 1973a.

CATTELL, R. B., and DEYOUNG, G. E. *A Demonstration of Motivational Components in Hunger in Humans.* Advance Publication No. 31. Boulder, Colo.: In-Colo.: Institute for Research on Morality and Adjustment, 1973c.

CATTELL, R. B., and DEYOUNG, G. E. *The Relation of Measured Ergic Tension in Sex to Some Situational Variables.* Advance Publication No. 32. Boulder, Colo.: Institute for Research on Morality and Adjustment, 1937c.

CATTELL, R. B., and DICKMAN, K. "A Dynamic Model of Physical Influences Demonstrating the Necessity of Oblique Simple Structure." *Psychological Bulletin,* 1962, *59,* 389–400.

CATTELL, R. B., and DIELMAN, T. E. *A Check on Personality Source Trait Structure at 6–8 Years of Age, in Q-Data.* Advance Publication No. 34. Boulder, Colo.: Institute for Research on Morality and Adjustment. In preparation.

CATTELL, R. B., and DIGMAN, J. M. "A Theory of the Structure of Perturbations and Observer Ratings and Questionnaire Data in Personality Research." *Behavioral Science,* 1964, *9,* 341–358.

CATTELL, R. B., and DREGER, R. M. *Handbook of Modern Personality Theory.* New York: Appleton Century Crofts, 1974.

CATTELL, R. B., and DREVDAHL, J. E. "A Comparision of the Personality Profile of Eminent Researchers with That of Eminent Teachers and Administrators." *British Journal of Psychology,* 1955, *44,* 248–267.

CATTELL, R. B., DUBIN, S. S., and SAUNDERS, D. R. "Personality Structure in Psychotics by Factorization of Objective Clinical Tests." *Journal of Mental Science,* 1954, *100,* 154–176.

CATTELL, R. B., EBER, H. W., and DELHEES, K. H. "A Large Sample Cross Validation of the Personality Trait Structure of the 16 P.F. with Some Clinical Implications." *Multivariate Behavioral Research,* Special Issue, 1968, 107–132.

CATTELL, R. B., EBER, H. W., and TATSUOKA, M. *Handbook for the Sixteen Personality Factor Questionnaire.* Champaign, Ill.: Institute for Personality and Ability Testing, 1970.

CATTELL, R. B., and FINKBEINER, C. *The Effect of Breadth of Hyperplane in Simple Structure Rotation on Primary versus Pseudo-Secondary Resolution.* Advance Publication No. 35. Boulder, Colo.: Institute for Research on Morality and Adjustment. In preparation.

CATTELL, R. B., and FOSTER, M. J. "The Rotoplot Program for Multiple, Single-Plane, Visually-Guided Rotation." *Behavioral Science,* 1963, *8,* 156–165.

CATTELL, R. B., and GIBBONS, B. D. "Personality Factor Structure of the Combined Guilford and Cattell Personality Questionnaires." *Journal of Personality and Social Psychology,* 1968, *9,* 107–120.

CATTELL, R. B., and GORSUCH, R. L. "The Uniqueness and Significance of Simple Structure Demonstrated by Contrasting Organic Natural Structure and Random Structure Data." *Psychometrika,* 1963, *28,* 55–67.

CATTELL, R. B., and GORSUCH, R. L. "The Definition and Measurement of National Morale and Morality." *Journal of Social Psychology,* 1965, *67,* 77–96.

CATTELL, R. B., and GORSUCH, R. L. "Personality and Socio-Ethical Values: The Structure of Self and Superego." In R. B. Cattell and R. M. Dreger (Eds.), *Handbook of Modern Personality Theory.* New York: Appleton Century, 1974.

CATTELL, R. B., and GREENE, R. R. "Rationale of Norms on an Adult Personality Test, the 16 P.F.– For American Women." *Journal of Educational Research,* 1961, *54,* 285–290.

CATTELL, R. B., and GRUEN, W. "The Personality Factor Structure of 11 Year Old Children in Terms of Behavior Rating Data." *Journal of Clinical Psychology,* 1953, *9,* 255–266.

CATTELL, R. B., and GRUEN, W. "Primary Personality Factors in the Questionnaire Medium for Children Eleven to Fourteen Years Old." *Educational and Psychological Measurement,* 1954, *14,* 50–76.

CATTELL, R. B., and GRUEN, W. "The Primary Personality Factors in Eleven Year Old Children by Objective Tests." *Journal of Personality,* 1955, *23,* 460–478.

CATTELL, R. B., and HENDRICKS, A. *The Sensitivity of the Dynamic Calculus to Short Term Change in Interest Structure.* Advanced Laboratory Publication No. 20. Urbana: Laboratory of Personality Analysis, University of Illinois, 1972.

CATTELL, R. B., and HORN, J. "An Integrating Study of the Factor Structure of Adult Attitude-Interests." *Genetic Psychological Monographs,* 1963, *67,* 89–149.

CATTELL, R. B., HORN, J., SWENEY, A. B., and RADCLIFFE, J. A. *The Motivation Analysis Test.* Champaign, Ill.: Institute for Personality and Ability Testing, 1964.

CATTELL, R. B., and JASPARS, J. "A General Plasmode (No. 30-10-5-2) for Factor Analytic Exercises and Researches." *Multivariate Behavioral Research Monograph 67-3,* 1967.

CATTELL, R. B., KARSON, S., and NUTTALL, R. *Handbook for the* IPAT *High School Personality Questionnaire,* Champaign, Ill.: Institute for Personality and Ability Testing, 1962.

CATTELL, R. B., KAWASH, G., and DEYOUNG, G. E. "Validation of Objective Measures of Ergic Tension: Response of the Sex Erg to Visual Stimulation." *Journal of Experimental Research in Personality,* 1972, *6,* 76–83.

CATTELL, R. B., KLEIN, T. W. and SCHUERGER, J. M. *A Definitive Factor Analysis of the High School Objective-Analytic Personality Battery on 2500 Children.* In preparation, 1974.

CATTELL, R. B., KOMLOS, E., and TATRO, D. F. "Significant Differences of Affective, Paranoid, and Non-Paranoid Schizophrenic Psychotics on Primary Source Traits in the 16 P.F." *Multivariate Behavioral Research,* Special Issue, 1968, 33–54.

CATTELL, R. B., and KRUG, S. E. "Personality Factor Profile Peculiar to the Student Smoker." *Journal of Counseling Psychology,* 1967, *14* (2), 116–121.

CATTELL, R. B., and LAWSON, E. D. "Sex Differences in Small Group Performance." *Journal of Social Psychology,* 1962, *58,* 141–145.

CATTELL, R. B., and LUBORSKY, L. B. "Personality Factors in Response to Humor." *Journal of Abnormal and Social Psychology,* 1947, *42,* 402–421.

CATTELL, R. B., and LUBORSKY, L. B. "P-Technique Demonstrated as a New Clinical Method for Determining Personality and Symptom Structure." *Journal of General Psychology,* 1950, *42,* 3–24.

CATTELL, R. B., and MUERLE, J. L. "The Maxplane Program for Rotation to Oblique Simple Structure." *Educational and Psychological Measurement,* 1960, *20,* 569–590.

CATTELL, R. B., and NESSELROADE, J. R. "Untersuchung der Interkulturellen Konstanz der Persönlichkeits Faktoren im 16 P.F. Test." *Psychologische Beiträge,* 1965, *8,* 502–512.

CATTELL, R. B., and NESSELROADE, J. R. "Likeness and Completeness Theories Examined by 16 P.F. Measures on Stably and Unstably Married Couples." *Journal of Personality and Social Psychology,* 1967, *7,* 351–361.

CATTELL, R. B., and NESSELROADE, J. R. "Note on Analyzing Personality Relations in Married Couples." *Psychological Reports,* 1968, *22,* 381–382.

CATTELL, R. B., and NESSELROADE, J. R. "The Discovery of the Anxiety State Pattern in Q-data, and its Distinction, in the LM Model, from Depression, Effort Stress, and Fatigue." *Multivariate Behavioral Research,* 1973.

CATTELL, R. B., and NESSELROADE, J. R. *Principles of Human Behavior Genetics.* In preparation.

CATTELL, R. B., and NICHOLS, K. E. "An Improved Definition from Ten Researchers of Second Order Personality Factors in Q-Data (with Cross-Cultural Checks)." *Journal of Social Psychology,* 1972, *86,* 187–203.

CATTELL, R. B., and PETERSON, D. R. "Personality Structure in 4–5 Year Olds, by Factoring Observed, Time-Sampled Behavior." *Estratto dalla Rassegna d Psicologia Generale e Clinica,* 1958, *3,* 3–21.

CATTELL, R. B., and PETERSON, D. R. "Personality Structure in Four and Five Year Olds in Terms of Objective Tests." *Journal of Clinical Psychology,* 1959, *15,* 355–369.

CATTELL, R. B., PICHOT, P., and RENNES, P. "Constance Interculturelle des Facteurs de Personnalité Mesurés par le Test 16 P.F. II. Comparison Franco-Américaine." *Revue de Psychologie Appliquée,* 1961, *11,* 165–196.

CATTELL, R. B., PIERSON, G., FINKBEINER, C., BRIM, R., and ROBERTSON, D. *Proof of Alignment of Personality Factors from Ratings and from Questionnaires.* Advance Publication No. 38. Boulder, Colo.: Institute for Research on Morality and Adjustment, 1973.

CATTELL, R. B., PORTER, R. B., and SCHAIE, K. W. *Measuring the Anxiety and Exvia Second Orders in the* CPQ. Advance Publication No. 39. Boulder, Colo.: Institute for Research on Morality and Adjustment. In preparation.

CATTELL, R. B., and RADCLIFFE, J. "Formulae and Tables for Obtaining Validities and Reliabilities of Extended Factor Scales." *Educational and Psychological Measurement,* 1957, *17,* 491–498.

CATTELL, R. B., and RADCLIFFE, J. A. "Reliabilities and Validities of Simple and Extended Weighted and Buffered Unifactor Scales." *British Journal of Statistical Psychology,* 1962, *15,* 113–128.

CATTELL, R. B., RADCLIFFE, J. A., and SWENEY, A. B. "The Nature and Measurement of Components of Motivation." *Genetic Psychological Monographs,* 1963, *68,* 49–211.

CATTELL, R. B., and RICKELS, K. "Diagnostic Power of IPAT Objective Anxiety Neuroticism Tests." *Archives of General Psychiatry,* 1964, *11,* 459–465.

CATTELL, R. B., and RICKELS, K. "The Relationship of Clinical Symptoms and IPAT-Factored Tests of Anxiety, Regression and Asthenia: A Factor Analytic Study." *Journal of Nervous and Mental Disease,* 1968, *146,* 147–160.

CATTELL, R. B., and SAUNDERS, D. R. "Inter-Relation and Matching of Personality

Factors from Behavior Rating, Questionnaire and Objective test data." *Journal of Social Psychology,* 1950, *31,* 243–260.

CATTELL, R. B., and SAUNDERS, D. R. "Beiträge zur Faktoren-Analyse der Persönlichkeit." *Zeitschrift für Experimentelle und Angewandte Psychologie,* 1955, 325–357.

CATTELL, R. B., and SCHEIER, I. H. *The Meaning and Measurement of Neuroticism and Anxiety.* New York: Ronald, 1961.

CATTELL, R. B., and SCHMIDT, L. R. "Clinical Diagnosis by the Objective-Analytic Personality Batteries." *Clinical Psychological Monographs,* 1972, *34,* 1–78.

CATTELL, R. B., SCHMIDT, L. R., and PAWLIK, K. "Cross-Cultural Comparison (U.S.A., Japan, Austria) of the Personality Factor Structures of 10–14 Years in Objective Tests." *Social Behavior and Personality.* In press.

CATTELL, R. B., SCHRODER, G., and WAGNER, A. "Verification of the Structure of the 16 P.F. Questionnaire in German." *Psychologische Forschung,* 1969, *32,* 369–386.

CATTELL, R. B., SEITZ W., and RAUSCHE, A. "Zur Konstanz der Persönlichkeitsstruktur von Kindern, gemessen durch Questionnaire- (Q-) Daten." *Zeitschrift für Experimentelle und Angewandte Psychologie,* 1971, *4,* 513–524.

CATTELL, R. B., and SELLS, S. *The Clinical Analysis Questionnaire* (CAQ). Champaign, Ill.: Institute for Personality and Ability Testing, 1974.

CATTELL, R. B., SHRADER, R. R., and BARTON, K. "The Definition and Measurement of Anxiety as a Trait and a State in the 12–17 Year Range." *British Journal of Social and Clinical Psychology,* 1973.

CATTELL, R. B., and STICE, G. F. *The Psychodynamics of Small Groups.* Final report on research project NR-172-369, Contract ZN80nr-79600. Washington, D.C.: Human Relations Branch, Office of Naval Research, 1953.

CATTELL, R. B., and STICE, G. F. "Four Formulae for Selecting Leaders on the Basis of Personality." *Human Relations,* 1954, *7,* 493–507.

CATTELL, R. B., and STICE, G. F. *The Dimensions of Groups and Their Relations to the Behavior of Members.* Champagn, Ill.: Institute for Personality and Ability Testing, 1960.

CATTELL, R. B., STICE, G. F., and EBER, H. *The 16 Personality Factor Questionnaire.* Champaign, Ill.: Institute for Personality and Ability Testing, 1949.

CATTELL, R. B., and SULLIVAN, W. "The Scientific Nature of Factors: A Demonstration by Cups of Coffee." *Behavioral Science,* 1962, *7,* 184–193.

CATTELL, R. B., and TATRO, D. F. "The Personality Factors, Objectively Measured, Which Distinguish Psychotics from Normals." *Behavioral Research Therapy,* 1966, *4,* 39–51.

CATTELL, R. B., TATRO, D. F., and KOMLOS, E. "The Diagnostic and Inferred Structure of Paranoid and Non-Paranoid Schizophrenia from the 16 P.F. Profile." *Indian Psychological Review,* 1964, *1,* 52–61.

CATTELL, R. B., TATRO, D. F., and KOMLOS, E. "The Diagnosis and Inferred Structure of Paranoid and Non-Paranoid Schizophrenia from the 16 P.F. Profile. II." *Indian Psychological Review,* 1965, *1,* 108–115.

CATTELL, R. B., and TSUJIOKA, B. "The Importance of Factor Trueness and Validity Versus Homogeneity and Orthogonality, in Test Scales." *Educational and Psychological Measurement,* 1964, *24,* 3–30.

CATTELL, R. B., and VAUGHAN, D. *Alignment of the Objective Test Factor-Derived HSOAQ Scales with Second Orders in the HSPQ.* Advance Publication No. 40. Boulder, Colo.: Institute for Research on Morality and Adjustment, 1973a.

CATTELL, R. B., and VAUGHAN, D. *A Large Sample Cross Check on the Factor Structure of the 16 P.F. by Item and by Parcel Factoring.* Advance Publication No. 41. Boulder, Colo.: Institute for Research on Morality and Adjustment, 1973b.

CATTELL, R. B. *A Comparison of Item and Parcel Factoring in Four Studies.* Advance Publication No. 42. Boulder, Colo.: Institute for Research on Morality and Adjustment, 1973r.

CATTELL, R. B., WAGNER, A., and CATTELL, M. D. "Adolescent Personality Structure in Q-Data, Checked in the High School Personality Questionnaire." *British Journal of Psychology,* 1970, *61,* 39–54.

CATTELL, R. B., and WARBURTON, F. W. "A Cross-Cultural Comparision of Patterns of Extraversion and Anxiety." *British Journal of Psychology,* 1961, *52,* 3–16.

CATTELL, R. B., and WARBURTON, F. W. *Objective Personality and Motivation Tests: A Theoretical Introduction and Practical Compendium.* Urbana: University of Illinois Press, 1967.

CATTELL, R. B., and WENIG, P. "Dynamic and Cognitive Factors Controlling Misperception." *Journal of Abnormal and Social Psychology,* 1952, *47,* 797–809.

CATTELL, R. B., and WILLIAMS, H. F. "P-Technique, a New Statistical Device for Analyzing Functional Unities in the Intact Organism." *British Journal of Preventive and Social Medicine,* 1953, *7,* 141–153.

CATTELL, R. B., YOUNG, H. B., and HUNDLEBY, J. D. "Blood Groups, and Personality Traits." *American Journal of Human Genetics,* 1964, *16,* 397–402.

CHANDLER, R. E. "Two Additional Formulae for Use with Suppressor Variables." *Educational and Psychological Measurement,* 1961, *21,* 947–950.

CHILD, D. *The Essentials of Factor Analysis.* London: Holt, 1970.

CLARIDGE, G., CANTER, S., and HUME, W. I. *Personality Differences and Biological Variations: A Study of Twins.* New York: Pergamon Press, 1973.

CLEMANS, W. V. "An Analytical and Empirical Examination of Some Properties of Ipsative Measures." *Psychometry Monographs,* 1966.

CLIFF, N. "Adverbs as Multipliers." *Psychological Review,* 1959, *66,* 27–44.

COAN, R. W. "A Comparison of Oblique and Orthogonal Factor Solutions." *Journal of Experimental Education,* 1959, *27,* 151–166.

COAN, R. W., and CATTELL, R. B. "Reproducible Personality Factors in Middle Childhood." *Journal of Clinical Psychology,* 1958, *14,* 339–345.

COAN, R. W., and CATTELL, R. B. "The Development of the Early School Personality Questionnaire." *Journal of Experimental Education,* 1959, *28,* 143–152.

COHEN, J. "The Impact of Multivariate Research in Clinical Psychology." In R. B. Cattell (Ed.), *Handbook of Multivariate Experimental Psychology.* Chicago: Rand McNally, 1966.

Committee of the Judiciary, U.S. Senate. *Psychological Tests and Constitutional Rights.* Washington, D.C.: Government Printing Office, 1966.

COMREY, A. L. *Manual for the Comrey Personality Scales.* San Diego: Educational and Industrial Testing Service, 1970.

COMREY, A. L. *A First Course in Factor Analysis.* New York: Academic, 1973.

COMREY, A. L., and DUFFY, K. E. "Cattell and Eysenck Factor Scores Related to Comrey Personality Factors." *Multivariate Behavioral Research,* 1968, *4,* 379–392.

COMREY, A. L., JAMISON, K., and KING, N. "Integration of Two Personality Factor Systems." *Multivariate Behavioral Research,* 1968, *3,* 147–160.

CONGER, A. J. "Evaluation of Multimethod Factor Analysis." *Psychological Bulletin,* 1971, *75,* 416–420.

COUCH, A., and KENISTON, K. "Yeasayers and Naysayers: Agreeing Response Set as a Personality Variable." *Journal of Abnormal and Social Psychology,* 1960, *60,* 151–174.

COURT, J. H. "Anxiety Among Acute Schizophrenics and Temporal Lobe Patients." *British Journal of Social and Clinical Psychology,* 1965, *4,* 254–258.

COWDEN, J. E., PETERSON, W. M., and COHEN, M. F. "The 16 P.F. vs. the MCI in a Group Testing Program Within a Correctional Setting." *Journal of Clinical Psychology,* 1968, *24,* 221–224.

CRONBACH, L. J. "Response Sets and Test Validity." *Educational and Psychological Measurement,* 1946, *6,* 457–494.

CRONBACH, L. J. "Coefficient Alpha and the Internal Structure of Tests." *Psychometrika,* 1951, *16,* 297–334.

CRONBACH, L. J. *Essentials of Psychological Testing.* New York: Harper, 1960.

CRONBACH, L. J., GLESER, G. C., NANDA, H., and RAJARATNAM, N. *The Dependability of Behavioral Measurements: Theory of Generalizability for Scores and Profiles.* New York: Wiley, 1972.

CRONBACH, L. J., SCHÖNEMANN, P., and MCKIE, D. "Alpha Coefficients for Stratified Parallel Tests." *Educational and Psychological Measurement,* 1965, *25,* 291–312.

CURRAN, J. P. *Dimensions of State Change, in Q-Data, and Chain P-Technique, on Twenty Women.* Unpublished masters Thesis. Urbana: University of Illinois, 1968.

CURRAN, J. P., and CATTELL, R. B. *Definition of Eight Independent Psychological State Factors in the Questionnaire Medium.* Advance Publication No. 43. Boulder, Colo.: Institute for Research on Morality and Adjustment. In press.

CURRAN, J. P., and CATTELL, R. B. *The Eight State Questionnaire Battery.* Champaign, Ill.: Institute for Personality and Ability Testing, 1974.

CUSIN, S. G., and NOVAGA, M. "L'adattamento e la Standardizzazione Italiana della Forma C del 16 P.F." *Bollettino di Psicologia Applicata,* 1962, *51–52,* 71–89.

DAHLSTROM, W. G. Commentary: "The Roles of Social Desirability and Acquiescence in Responses to the MMPI." In S. Messick and J. Ross (Eds.), *Measurement in Personality and Cognition.* New York: Wiley, 1962.

DAHLSTROM, W. G. *Personality Systematics and the Problem of Types.* Morristown, N.J.: General Learning Press, 1972.

DAHLSTROM, W. G., and WELSH, G. S. *An* MMPI *Handbook.* New York: Psychological Corporation, 1960.

DALY, D. L., BATH, K. E., and NESSELROADE, J. R. On the Confounding of Inter- and Intraindividual Variability in Examining Change Patterns. *Journal of Clinical Psychology,* 1973.

DAMARIN, F. "A Special Review of Buros' Personality Tests and Reviews." *Educational and Psychological Measurement,* 1971, *31,* 215–241.

DARROW, C. W., and HEATH, J. L. "Reaction Tendencies Relating to Personality." In R. S. Sashley (Ed.), *Studies in the Dynamics of Behavior.* Chicago: University of Chicago Press, 1932.

DAS, R. S. *An Investigation of Attitude Structure and Some Hypothesis Personality Correlates.* Unpublished doctoral dissertation. Urbana: University of Illinois, 1955.

DE ANDRADE, E. M., DE GODOY, A. D., and FORD, J. J. "A Comparison of North American and Brazilian College Students' Personality Profiles of the 16 P.F. Questionnaire." *International Journal of Psychology,* 1969, *4,* 55–58.

DEGAN, J. W. *Dimensions of Functional Psychosis.* Richmond: Byrd, 1952.

DELHEES, K. H. "Conflict Measurement by the Dynamic Calculas Model, Its Applicability in Clinical Practice." *Multivariate Behavioral Research,* 1968, *2,* 73–96.

DELHEES, K. H., and CATTELL, R. B. "The Dimensions of Pathology: Proof of Their Projection Beyond the Normal 16 P.F. Source Traits." *Personality,* 1971, *2,* 149–173.

DEYOUNG, G. E. "Standards of Decision Regarding Personality Factors in Questionnaires: A Critique of Howarth and Browne's Analysis." *Canadian Journal of Behavioral Science,* 1972, *4,* 253–255.

DEYOUNG, G. E. *A Test of the Theory of Modulator Action in Psychological States.* Advance Publication No. 44. Boulder, Colo.: Institute for Research on Morality and Adjustment, 1973.

DEYOUNG, G. E., and CATTELL, R. B. *The Effect of Underfactoring upon the Proportion of Pseudo Second Order Factors in Rotational Resolutions.* Advance Publication No. 45. Boulder, Colo.: Institute for Research on Morality and Adjustment, 1973.

DEYOUNG, G. E., and CATTELL, R. B. *Systematic Empirical Checks on Testing for Number of Factors by the Scree Test.* Advance Publication No. 46. Boulder, Colo.: Institute for Research on Morality and Adjustment. In preparation.

DICKMAN, K. W. *Factorial Validity of a Rating Instrument.* Unpublished doctoral dissertation. Urbana: University of Illinois, 1960.

DIELMAN, T. E. "A Note on Howarth and Browne's Item Factor Analysis of the 16 P.F." *Personality: An International Journal,* 1973.

DIELMAN, T. E., BARTON, K., and CATTELL, R. B. "The Prediction of Junior High School Achievement from Objective Motivation Tests." *Personality: An International Journal,* 1971, *2,* 279–287.

DIELMAN, T. E., BARTON, K., and CATTELL, R. B. "Adolescent Personality and Intelligence Scores as Related to Family Demography." *Journal of Genetic Psychology,* 1973a.

DIELMAN, T. E., BARTON, K., and CATTELL, R. B. "Prediction of Objective Motivation Test Scores in Adolescence from Family Demographic Variables." *Psychological Reports,* 1973b.

DIELMAN, T. E., and CATTELL, R. B. "Child Personality Structure by Questionnaire Data in the Early Grades: A Summary of Seven Coordinated Studies." *Child Development,* 1974 (In press).

DIELMAN, T. E., CATTELL, R. B., and RHOADES, P. "Childrearing Antecedents of Early School Child Personality Factors." *Journal of Marriage and the Family,* 1972 August, 431–436.

DIELMAN, T. E., CATTELL, R. B., and WAGNER, A. "Evidence on the Simple Structure and Factor Invariance Achieved by Five Rotational Methods on Four Types of Data." *Multivariate Behavioral Research,* 1972, *7,* 223–242.

DIELMAN, T. E., COAN, R. W., and CATTELL, R. B. *The Early School Personality Questionnaire* (ESPQ). Champaign, Ill.: Institute for Personality and Ability Testing, 1974.

DIELMAN, T. E., SCHUERGER, J. M., and CATTELL, R. B. "Prediction of Junior High School Achievement from IQ and the Objective Analytic Personality Factors U.I. 21, U.I. 23, U.I. 24 and U.I. 25." *Personality,* 1970, *1,* 145–152.

DIGMAN, J. "The Principal Dimensions of Child Personality as Inferred from Teachers' Judgments." *Child Development,* 1963, *34,* 43–60.

DIGMAN, J. *The Persistence of Factor Structure over Time.* Paper presented at the 12th annual meeting of the Society of Multivariate Experimental Psychology. Forth Worth, November 9, 1972.

DIGMAN, J. *High School Academic Achievement as Seen in the Context of a Longitudinal Study of Personality.* Proceedings of the annual convention of the American Psychological Association, 1972.

DIMASCIO, A., and BARRETT, J. "Comparative Effects of Oxazepam in high and low Anxious Student Volunteers." *Psychosomatics,* 1965, *6,* 298–302.

DIMASCIO, A., MEYER, R. E., and STIFLER, L. "Effects of Isoquinazepan on Individuals Varying in Level of Depression." *American Journal of Psychiatry,* 1968, February Supplement, *124,* 8–16.

DIMASCIO, A., SHADER, R. J., SALZMAN, E., and HARMATZ, J. S. "An Evaluation of Isoquinazepan." *Current Therapeutic Research,* 1967, *9,* 517–521.

DINGMAN, H. F. "The Relation Between Coefficients of Correlation and Difficulty Factors." *British Journal of Statistical Psychology,* 1958, *11,* 13–17.

DREGER, R. M. *Fundamentals of Personality.* Philadelphia: Lippincott, 1962.

DREGER, R. M. "Developmental Structural Change Evidenced from Child Psychology." In R. B. Cattell and R. M. DREGER (Eds.). *Handbook of Modern Personality Theory.* New York: Appleton Century Crofts, 1974.

DREGER, R. M., and CATTELL, R. B. "Personality Structure as Revealed in Questionnaire Response at the 5 Year Old Level." *Child Development,* 1974 (In press).

DREGER, R. M., and CATTELL, R. B. *Handbook for the Pre-School Personality Questionnaire.* Champaign, Ill.: Institute for Personality and Ability Testing. In press.

DREGER, R. M., CATTELL, R. B., and DIELMAN, T. E. *A Check on the Factor Basis of the Pre-School Personality Questionnaire: The PSPQ.* Advance Publication No. 49. Boulder, Colo.: Institute for Research on Morality and Adjustment. In preparation.

DREVDAHL, J. E., and CATTELL, R. B. Personality and Creativity in Artists and Writers. *Journal of Clinical Psychology,* 1958, *14,* 107–111.

DUBOIS, P. H. "Varieties of Test Homogeneity." *American Psychologist,* 1970, *25,* 523–530.

DUNNETTE, M. D. *Personal Selection and Placement.* Belmont, Calif.: Wadsworth, 1966.

DWYER, P. S. "The Determination of the Factor Loadings of a Given Test from the Known Factor Loadings of Other Tests." *Psychometrika,* 1937, *2,* 173–178.

EBER, H. W. "Toward Oblique Simple Structure: Maxplane." *Multivariate Behavioral Research,* 1966, *1,* 112–122.

EBER, H. W. Personal communication on factoring of MMPI items, 1967.

EBER, H. W., and CATTELL, R. B. "Information on the Low Literate Form E of the 16 P.F." In *Institute for Personality and Ability Testing Special Publication Interpreting the 16 P.F. profile: Some Case Studies.* Champaign, Ill.: IPAT, 1968.

EDWARDS, A. L. *Edwards' Personal Preference Schedule.* New York: Psychological Corporation, 1953.

EDWARDS, A. L. *The Social Desirability Variable in Personality Assessment and Research.* New York: Holt, 1957a.

EDWARDS, A. L. *Edwards' Personal Preference Schedule.* New York: Psychological Corporation, 1957b.

EPSTEIN, S. "Experiments on Anxiety." In C. D. Spielberger (Ed.), *Anxiety: Current Trends in Theory and Research.* Vol. II. New York: Academic, 1973.

EVANS, G. T. "Transformation of Factor Matrices to Achieve Congruence." *British Journal of Mathematical and Statistical Psychology,* 1971, *24,* 22–48.

EYSENCK, H. J. "Types of Personality—A Factorial Study of 700 Neurotics." *Journal of Mental Science,* 1944a, *90,* 851–861.

EYSENCK, H. J. "General Social Attitudes." *Journal of Social Psychology,* 1944b, *19,* 207–277.

EYSENCK, H. J. *The Scientific Study of Personality.* London: Routledge, 1952.

EYSENCK, H. J. *Manual of the Maudsley Personal Inventory.* London: University of London Press, 1959.

EYSENCK, H. J. *The Structure of Human Personality.* London: Methuen, 1960.

EYSENCK, H. J. "Principles and Methods of Personality Description, Classification and Diagnosis." *British Journal of Psychology,* 1964, *55,* 284–294.

EYSENCK, H. J. *Readings in Introversion and Extroversion. I. Theoretical and Medical Issues.* London: Staples Press, 1970.

EYSENCK, H. J. "On the Choice of Personality Tests for Research and Prediction." *Journal of Behavioral Science,* 1971, *1,* 85–90.

EYSENCK, H. J., and EYSENCK, S. B. G. *Manual for the Eysenck Personality Inventory.* San Diego: Educational and Industrial Testing Service, 1963.

EYSENCK, H. J., and EYSENCK, S. B. G. *Personality Structure and Measurement.* San Diego: Knapp, 1969.

EYSENCK, H. J., and LEVEY, A. "Conditioning, Introversion, Extraversion and the Strength of the Nervous System." In V. D. Nebylitsin and J. A. Gray (Eds.), *Biological Bases of Individual Behavior.* New York: Academic, 1972.

EYSENCK, H. J., and PRELL, D. B. "The Inheritance of Neuroticism." *Journal of Mental Science,* 1951, *97,* 441–465.

EYSENCK, H. J. Primaries or second-order factors: a critical consideration of Cattell's 16 PF battery. *The British Journal of Social and Clinical Psychology,* 1972, Volume II, Part 3, 265–269.

FAHRENBERG, J. *Psychophysiologische Persönlichkeitsforschung.* Göttingen: Hogrefe, 1967.

FALEK, A. "Differential Fertility and Intelligence: Current Status of the Problem." *Social Biology,* 1971, *18,* S50–S59.

FERTILIO, A. T., and CALDERÒN, E. T. *Factores de secundo orden: Neuroses.* Universidad de Chile, Escuela de Medicina, Departmento de Psyquiatria, 1969.

FINKBEINER, C., and VAUGHAN, D. "A Check on Cattell's Theorem of Identical Structures from Factoring Items and Parcels." In preparation.

FINNEY, J. C. "The MMPI as a Measure of Character Structure as Revealed by Factor Analysis." *Journal of Counseling Psychologists,* 1961, *25,* 327–336.

FISKE, D. W. "On the Coordination of Personality Concepts and Their Measurement." *Human Development,* 1966, *9,* 74–83.

FISKE, D. W. *Measuring the Concepts of Personality.* Chicago: Aldine, 1971.

FLANAGAN, J. C. *Factor Analysis in the Study of Personality.* Stanford: Stanford University Press, 1935.

FLEISHMAN, E. A. "A Comparative Study of Aptitude Patterns in Unskilled and Skilled Psychomotor Performances." *Journal of Applied Psychology,* 1957, *41,* 263–272.

FLEMMING, E. G. "A Factor Analysis of the Personality of High School Leaders." *Journal of Applied Psychology,* 1935, *19,* 596–605.

FLUGEL, J. C. "Practice, Fatigue and Oscillation." *British Journal of Psychology Monograph Supplement No. 13,* 1928, 1–92.

FORBES, A. R. The Validity of the 16 P.F. in the Discrimination of the Hysterical and Obsessional Personality." *British Journal of Social and Clinical Psychology,* 1969, *8,* 152–159.

FORD, J. J. *Personality Dimensions Beyond the Sixteen Personality Factor Questionnaire.* Unpublished masters Thesis. Urbana: University of Illinois, 1969.

FORREST, G. L., BORTNER, T. W., and BAKKER, C. B. The Role of Personality Variables in Response to Chlorpromazine, Dextroamphetamine and Placebo. *Journal of Psychiatric Research,* 1967, *5,* 281–288.

FREEDMAN, A. M., and KAPLAN, H. I. *Comprehensive Textbook of Psychiatry.* Baltimore: Williams & Wilkins, 1967.

FREEMAN, G. L. *The Energetics of Human Behavior.* Ithaca: Cornell University Press, 1948.

FREUD, S. *General Introduction to Psychoanalysis.* New York: Liveright, 1920.

FRIEDMAN, A. S. "Syndromes and Themes of Psychotic Depression." *Archives of General Psychiatry,* 1963, *9,* 504–509.

FRIEL, J. C. *Replication and Cross-Validation of Primary Source Traits Measured by the* HSPQ. Unpublished masters thesis. Morgantown: West Virginia University, 1972.

FRIEL, J., and NESSELROADE, J. R. "Test of the Replicability of Cattell's HSPQ Factor Structure Using Five-item Parcels." In press.

FULLER, G. B. *Research in Alcoholism with the 16 PF Test.* Information Bulletin No. 12 Champaign, Ill.: Institute for Personality and Ability Testing, 1966.

GALTON, F. *Inquiries into Human Faculty and Its Development.* London: Dent, 1883.

GALTON, F. "Family Likeness in Stature." *Proceedings of the Royal Society,* 1886, *30,* 49–53.

GELLHORN, E. "The Effect of Carbon Dioxide in Combatting the Effect of Oxygen Deficiency on Psychic Processes: The Fundamental Relation of Psychic and Physiological Reactions." *American Journal of Psychiatry,* 1937, *93,* 1413–1434.

GHISELLI, E. E. *The Validity of Occupational Aptitude Tests.* New York: Wiley, 1966.

GIBB, C. A. *Leadership.* London: Penguin, 1969.

GIBBONS, B. D. *A Study of the Relationships Between Factors Found in Cattell's 16 P.F. Questionnaire and Factors Found in the Guilford Personal Inventories.* Unpublished doctoral dissertation. Los Angeles: University of Los Angeles: University of Southern California, 1966.

GLESER, G. C., and GOTTSCHALK, L. A. "Personality Characteristics of Chronic Schizophrenics in Relationship to Sex and Current Functioning." *Journal of Clinical Psychology,* 1967, *23,* 349–354.

GOCKA, E. F., and MARKS, J. B. "Second Order Factors in the 16 P.F. Test and MMPI Inventory." *Journal of Clinical Psychology,* 1961, *17,* 32–35.

GOLDBERG, L. R. "The Interrelationships Among Item Characteristics in an Adjective Check List: The Convergence of Different Indices of Item Ambiguity." *Educational and Psychological Measurement,* 1968, *28,* 273–296.

GOLDBERG, L. R. "Parameters of Personality Inventory Construction and Utilization: A Comparison of Prediction Strategies and Tactics." *Multivariate Behavioral Research Monograph,* 1972b, *72,* 1–59.

GOLDBERG, L. R., NORMAN, W. T., and SCHWARTZ E. "The Comparative Validity of of Questionnaire Data (16 P.F. Scales) and Objective Test Data (O-A Battery) in Predicting Five Peer Rating Criteria." *ORI Research Bulletin,* 1972, *12,* 1–18.

GOODWIN, W. L., JOYCE, J., ABRAMS, A., BIAGGIO, A. B., and BAGGIO, L. I. "Note: Relationships Between Matching Scales of the Cattell 16 Personality Factor Questionnaire and the High School Personality Questionnaire." *Journal of Educational Measurement,* 1965, *2,* 220.

GORSUCH, R. L. *The Clarification of Some Superego Factors.* Unpublished doctoral dissertation. Urbana: University of Illinois, 1965.

GORSUCH, R. L. "The General Factor in the Test Anxiety Questionnaire." *Psychological Reports,* 1966, *19,* 308.

GORSUCH, R. L. Discussion on paper by A. L. Comrey at the 12th annual meeting of the Society of Multivariate Experimental Psychology. Fort Worth, November 9, 1972.

GORSUCH, R. L. *Factor Analysis.* Springfield, Ill.: Saunders, 1973.

GORSUCH, R. L., and CATTELL, R. B. "Second Stratum Personality Factors Defined in the Questionnaire Realm by the 16 P.F." *Multivariate Behavioral Research,* 1967, *2,* 211–224.

GOTTESMAN, I. "Heritability of Personality: A Demonstration." *Psychological Monographs,* 1963, *77* (9) (Whole No. 572).

GOUGH, H. G. *California Psychological Inventory.* Palo Alto, Calif.: Consulting Psychologists Press, 1957.

GRAFFAM, D. T. "Dickinson College Changes Personality." *The Dickinson Alumnus,* 1967, *44,* 2–7.

GRAY, J. A. "The Psychological Nature of Introversion Extraversion: A Modification of Eysenck's Theory." In V. D. Nebylitsin and J. A. Gray (Eds.), *Biological Bases of Individual Behavior.* New York: Academic, 1972.

GREIF, S. "Untersuchungen zur Deutschen übersetzung der 16 P.F. Fragebogen." *Psychologische Beiträge,* 1970, *12,* 186–213.

GRINKER, R. R., and SPIEGEL, J. P. *Men Under Stress.* Philadelphia: McGraw-Hill, 1945.

GRINKER, R. R., and others. *The Phenomena of Depressions.* New York: Hoeber, 1961.

GUERTIN, W. H., and BAILEY, J. P., JR. *Introduction to Modern Factor Analysis.* Ann Arbor: Edwards, 1970.

GUILFORD, J. P. *Fundamental Statistics in Psychology and Education.* New York: McGraw-Hill, 1954.

GUILFORD, J. P. *Personality.* New York: McGraw-Hill, 1959.

GUILFORD, J. P. and others. "A Factor Analysis Study of Human Interests." *Psychological Monographs,* No. 375, 1954, *68* (4).

GUILFORD, J. P., and ZIMMERMAN, W. S. *The Guilford-Zimmerman Temperament Survey: Manual of Directions and Norms.* Beverly Hills, Calif.: Sheridan Supply, 1949–1955.

GULLIKSEN, H. *Theory of Mental Tests.* New York: Wiley, 1950.

GUTTMAN, L. "The Principal Components of Scale Analysis." In S. Stouffer, and others (Eds.), *Measurement and Prediction.* Princeton: Princeton University Press, 1950.

HADLEY, S. T. "A Study of the Predictive Value of Several Variables for Student Teacher Success as Measured by Student Teaching Marks." *Research for the Teaching Profession,* 1953.

HAKSTIAN, R. "Primary Ability Structure at the 18 Year Level." In preparation.

HAMMOND, S. B. "Personality Studied by the Method of Rating in the Life Situation." In R. B. Cattell and R. M. Dreger (Eds.), *Handbook of Modern Personality Theory.* New York: Appleton Century Crofts, 1973.

HARBURG, E., JULIUS, S., MCGINN, N. F., MCLEOD, J. H., and HOOBLER, S. W. "Personality Traits and Behavior Patterns Associated with Systolic Blood Pressure Levels in College Males." *Journal of Chronic Diseases,* 1964, *17,* 405–413

HARLOW, H. F., and HARLOW M. "Social Deprivation in Monkeys." *Scientific American,* 1962, *207,* 136–146.

HARMAN, H. *Modern Factor Analysis* (2nd ed.) Chicago: University of Chicago Press, 1967.

HARMAN, H., and FRENCH, J. *Experimental Design for a Study of Self Report Personality Items.* Paper presented at the 12th annual meeting of the Society of Multivariate Experimental Psychology. Fort Worth, November 9, 1972.

HARRIS, C. W. (Ed.) *Problems in Measuring Change.* Madison: University of Wisconsin Press, 1963.

HARRIS, C. W. "On Factors and Factor Scores." *Psychometrika,* 1967, *32,* 363–379.

HARRIS, C. W. Paper presented on ability structure at the ETS Invitational Conference on Test Construction in Q-Data. Princeton, N.J., 1971.

HARTMAN, B. J. "Personality Factors of the Cattell 16 P.F. Test and Hypnotic Susceptibility." *Psychological Reports,* 1966, *19,* 1337–1338.

HASE, H. D., and GOLDBERG, L. R. "The Comparative Validity of Different Strategies of Deriving Personality Inventory Scales." *Psychological Bulletin,* 1967, *5,* 231–248.

HATHAWAY, S. R., and MCKINLEY, J. C. *The Manual of the Minnesota Multiphasic Personality Inventory (Rev.).* New York: Psychological Corporation, 1951, Revised, 1967.

HAVERLAND, E. M. *An Experimental Analysis by P-Technique of Some Functionally Unitary Varieties of Fatigue.* Unpublished masters Thesis. Urbana: University of Illinois, 1954.

HAYTHORN, W. "The Influence of Individual Members on the Characteristics of Small Groups." *Journal of Abnormal and Social Psychology,* 1953, *48,* 276–284.

HOCH, P. E. and ZUBIN, J. *Depression.* New York: Grune & Stratton, 1954.

HEERMAN, E. F. "Univocal or Orthogonal Estimators of Orthogonal Factors." *Psychometrika,* 1963, *28,* 161–172.

HOGBEN, L. *Mathematics for the Million.* New York: Norton, 1937.

HOLLAND, J. L. "The Relation of the Vocational Preference Inventory to the 16 Personality Factor Questionnaire." *Journal of Applied Psychology,* 1960, *44,* 291–296.

HOLLANDER, E. P. "The Reliability of Peer Nominations Under Various Conditions of Administration." *Journal of Applied Psychology,* 1957, *41,* 85–90.

HOLT, N. F. "A 16 P.F. Profile for Prisoners Convicted of Drunk and Disorderly Behavior." *British Journal of Criminology,* 1965, *5,* 196–199.

HOLTZMANN, W. H. "Statistical Models for the Study of Change in the Single Case." In C. W. Harris (Ed.), *Problems in Measuring Change.* Madison: University of Wisconsin Press, 1963.

HOLTZMANN, W. H., and BITTERMAN, M. E. "A Factorial Study of Adjustment to Stress." *Journal of Abnormal Social Psychology,* 1956, *52,* 179–185.

HOLZBERG, J. D. "Projective Techniques." In I. A. Berg and L. A. Pennington (Eds.), *Rorschach Psychology.* New York: Wiley, 1960.

HORN, J. L. "Equations representing combinations of components in scoring variables." *Acta Psychologica,* 1963, *21,* 184–217.

HORN, J. L. "Second Order Factors in Questionnaire Data." *Educational and Psychological Measurement,* 1963, *23,* 117–134.

HORN, J. L. "A Note on the Estimation of Factor Scores." *Educational and Psychological Measurement,* 1964, *24,* 525–527.

HORN, J. L. "Motivation and Dynamic Calculus Concepts from Multivariate Experiment." In R. B. Cattell (Ed.), *Handbook of Multivariate Experimental Psychology.* Chicago: Rand McNally, 1966a.

HORN, J. L. *Short Period Fluctuations in Intelligence.* Denver: Denver Research Institute, 1966b.

HORN, J. L. Organization of Abilities and the Development of Intelligence. *Psychological Review,* 1968, *75,* 242–259.

HORN, J. L. "Structure of Intellect: Primary Abilities." In R. M. Dreger (Ed.), *Multivariate Personality Research.* Baton Rouge: Claitor's Publishing Division, 1972.

HORN, J. L. "Integration of concepts of reliability and standard error of measurement." *Educational and Psychological Measurement,* 1971, *31,* 57–74.

HORN, J. L. and CATTELL, R. B. "Vehicles, Ipsatization and the Multiple Method Measurement of Motivation." *Canadian Journal of Psychology,* 1965, *19,* 265–279.

HORN, J. L., WANBERG, K. W., and APPEL, M. "On the Internal Structure of the MMPI." *Multivariate Behavioral Research,* 1973, *8,* 131–172.

HORNEY, K. *Neurosis and Human Growth.* New York: Norton, 1950.

HORST, P. "Generalized Canonical Correlations." *Journal of Clinical Psychology,* Monograph Supplement 14, 1962.

HORST, P. *Psychological Measurement and Prediction.* Belmont, Calif.: Wadsworth, 1966.

HOWARD, K. I., and DIESENHAUS, H. "Personality Correlates of Change-Seeking Behavior." *Perceptual and Motor Skills,* 1965a, *21,* 655–664.

HOWARD, K. I., and DIESENHAUS, H. "16 P.F. Item Response Patterns as a Function of Repeated Testing." *Educational and Psychological Measurement,* 1965b, *25,* 365–579.

HOWARD, K. I., and DIESENHAUS, H. "Intro-Individual Variability, Response Set, and Response Uniqueness in a Personality Questionnaire." *Journal of Clinical Psychology,* 1965, *21* (4), 392–396.

HOWARTH, E. "An Item Analysis of the Eysenck Personality Inventory." *British Journal of Social and Clinical Psychology,* 1972, *11,* 162–174.

HOWARTH, E., and BROWNE, J. A. "Investigation of Personality Factors in a Canadian Context. I. Marker Structure in Personality Questionnaire Items." *Canadian Journal of Behavioral Science,* 1971a, *3,* 161–173.

HOWARTH, E., and BROWNE, J. A. "An Item Factor Analysis of the 16 P.F. Personality Questionnaire." *Personality: An International Journal,* 1971b, *2,* 117–139.

HOWARTH, E., and others. "An Item Analysis of Cattell's 16 P.F." *Canadian Journal of Behavioral Science,* 1972, *4* (1), 85–90.

HUMM, D. G., and WADSWORTH, G. W. "The Humm-Wadsworth Temperament Scale." *Personality Journal,* 1933, *12,* 314–323.

HUMPHREYS, L. G. "Criteria Research." In L. Carmichael and L. C. Mead (Eds.), *The Selection of Military Manpower: A Symposium.* Washington, D.C.: National Academy of Sciences—National Research Council, 1951.

HUMPHREYS, L. G. "Individual Differences." In C. P. Stone and D. W. Taylor (Eds.), *Annual Review of Psychology*. Stanford: Stanford Annual Review, 1952.

HUMPHREYS, L. G. "Note on the Multitrait-Multimethod Matrix." *Psychological Bulletin*, 1960, *57*, 86–88.

HUMPHREYS, L. G. *Implications of Group Differences for Test Interpretation*. Paper presented at the 1972 annual report on ETS Invitational Conference on Testings. Princeton: Educational Testings Service, 1973.

HUMPHREYS, L. G., TUCKER, L. R., and DACHLER, P. "Evaluating the Importance of Factors in Any Given Order of Factoring." *Multivariate Behavioral Research*, 1970, *5*, 209–215.

HUNDAL, P. S., SUDHAKAR, Y. P., and SIDHU, K. "Factor Analytical Study of Measures of Anxiety, Intelligence, and Academic Achievement." *Journal of Psychological Research*, 1972, *16* (1), 28–34.

HUNDLEBY, J. D. "The Construct Validity of a Scale of Acquiescence." *British Journal of Social and Clinical Psychology*, 1966, *5*, 290–298.

HUNDLEBY, J. D. "Structure of Personality: Surface and Source Traits." In R. M. Dreger (Ed.), *Multivariate Personality Research*. Baton Rouge: Claitor's Publishing Division, 1972.

HUNDLEBY, J. D. "The Measurement of Personality by Objective Tests." In Paul Kline (Ed.), *New Approaches in Psychological Measurement*. New York: Wiley, 1973.

HUNDLEBY, J. D. "The Factor Analytic Research Basis of the Adult O-A Personality Battery." In press, 1974.

HUNDLEBY, J. D., and CATTELL, R. B. The Adult *Objective Analytic Personality Factor Battery (The* AOA *Battery)*. Champaign, Ill.: Institute for Personality and Ability Testing, 1974.

HUNDLEBY, J. D., and CONNOR, W. H. "Interrelationships Between Personality Inventories: The 16 P.F., the MMPI, and the MPI." *Journal of Consulting and Clinical Psychology*, 1968, *32*, 152–157.

HUNDLEBY, J. D., PAWLIK, K., and CATTELL, R. B. *Personality Factors in Objective Test Devices*. San Diego: Knapp, 1965.

HUNT, J. M., EWING, T. N., LAFORGE, R., and GILBERT, W. M. "An Integrated Approach to Research on Therapeutic Counseling with Samples of Results." *Journal of Counseling Psychology*, 1959, *6*, 46–54.

HUSEK, T. R. "Acquiescence as a Response Set and as a Personality Characteristic." *Educational and Psychological Measurement*, 1961, *21*, 295–307.

INSTITUTE FOR PERSONALITY AND ABILITY TESTING. *Summary of 16 P.F. Data in the Clinical Area*. Information Bulletin No. 8. Champaign, Ill. IPAT, 1963.

ISHIKAWA, A. Translations of the HSPQ into Japanese. Report from Kansai University, Osaka, 1973.

JACKSON, C. W. Muscular strength, social adjustment and personality traits in five socio-economic groups. D.Pl. Thesis, Old Dominion University, Norfolk, Virginia, 1973.

JACKSON, D. N. *A Modern Strategy for Personality Assessment: The Personality*

Research Form. Research Bulletin No. 30. London: Department of Psychology, University of Western Ontario, 1966.

JACKSON, D. N. "Comments on 'Evaluation of Multi-Method Factor Analysis.'" *Psychological Bulletin,* 1971, *75,* 421–423.

JACKSON, D. N. "The High School Personality Questionnaire." In O. K. Buros (Ed.), *Seventh Mental Measurement Yearbook.* Highland Park, N.J.: Gryphon Press, 1972.

JACKSON, D. N., and LAY, C. "Homogeneous Dimensions of Personality Scale Content." *Multivariate Behavioral Research,* 1968, *3,* 321–338.

JACKSON, D. N., and MESSICK, S. "Response Styles and the Assessment of Psychopathology." In S. Messick and J. Ross (Eds.), *Measurement in Personality and Cognition.* New York: Wiley, 1962.

JACKSON, D. N., and MORF, M. E. *An Empirical Evaluation of Factor Reliability.* ETS Research Bulletin. Princeton: Educational Testing Service, 1971.

JACKSON, D. N., NEILL, A., and BROWN, B. *An Evaluation of Forced Choice Designs.* Princeton: Educational Testing Service, 1971.

JACKSON, D. N., and VOYCE, C. *A Threshold Theory for Personality Assessment.* Paper presented at the 12th annual conference of the Society of Multivaried Experimental Psychology. Fort Worth, November 9, 1972.

JACKSON, R. W. B., and FERGUSON, G. A. "A Functional Approach in Test Construction." *Educational and Psychological Measurement,* 1943, *3,* 23–28.

JANDELLI, C. L. "Un Profilo Maschile e un Profilo Femminile al 16 P.F. Test Forma A." *Bollettino di Psicologia Applicata,* 1963, *59–60,* 67–79.

JENKINS, T. E. "Measurement of the Primary Factors of the Total Personality." *Journal of Psychology,* 1962, *54,* 417–442.

JOHNSON, D., NEVILLE, C. W., and WORKMAN, S. N. "Field Independence and the Sixteen Personality Factor Questionnaire." *Perceptual and Motor Skills,* 1969, *28,* 670.

JÖRESKOG, K. G. "Testing a Simple Structure Hypothesis in Factor Analysis." *Psychometrika,* 1966, *31,* 165–178.

JÖRESKOG, K. G. "Simultaneous Factor Analysis in Several Populations." *Psychometrika,* 1971, *36,* 12–21.

JÖRESKOG, K. G., WARR, P. B., and LEE, R. E. "A Note on the Factorial Nature of the F and D Scales." *British Journal of Psychology,* 1969, *60,* 119–123.

JOSHI, M. C., and ROY, S. "Psychological Characteristics of Hypertension and Cardiac Cases." *Indian Psychological Review,* 1967, *4,* 62–67.

KAISER, H. F., HUNKA, S., and BIANCHINI, J. C. "Relating Factors Between Studies Based upon Different Individuals." *Multivariate Behavioral Research,* 1971, *6,* 409–422.

KAPOOR, S. D. "A Comparative Study of Sixteen Personality Factors at Banares and Punjab Universities." *Banares Hindu University Journal,* 1963, *9,* 163–165.

KARSON, S. "Validating Clinical Judgments with the 16 P.F. Test." *Journal of Clinical Psychology,* 1960, *16,* 394–397.

KARSON, S. "Second Order Personality Factors in Positive Mental Health." *Journal of Clinical Psychology,* 1961, *17,* 14–19.

KARSON, S. "Group Psychotherapy with Latency Age Boys." *International Journal of Group Psychotherapy,* 1965, *15,* 81–89.

KARSON, S. *Are There Source Trait Differences in Parents of Boys with Personality vs. Conduct Problems?* Paper presented at the annual meeting of the Midwestern Psychological Association. Chicago, May 1967.

KARSON, S. "Some Relations Between Personality Factors and Job Performance Ratings in Radar Controllers." *Aerospace Medicine,* 1969, *40,* 823–826.

KARSON, S. and HAUPT, T. D. "Second-Order Personality Factors in Parents of Child Guidance Clinic Patients." In R. B. Cattell (Ed.), *Progress in Clinical Psychology Through Multivariate Experimental Designs.* Fort Worth: Society of Multivariate Experimental Psychology, 1968.

KARSON, S., and O'DELL, J. "On the Validity of the 16 P.F." *Journal of Personality Assessment,* 1974. In press.

KARSON, S., and POOL, K. B. "Second Order Factors in Personality Measurement." *Journal of Consulting Psychology,* 1958, *22,* 299–303.

KARSON, S., and WIEDERSHINE, L. J. "An Objective Evaluation of Dynamically Oriented Group Psychotherapy." *International Journal of Group Psychotherapy,* 1961, *11,* 166–174.

KEAR–COLWELL, J. J. "Studies of the IPAT Neuroticism Scale Questionnaire (NSQ)." *British Journal of Social and Clinical Psychology,* 1965, *4,* 214–223.

KEAR–COLWELL, J. J. "Neuroticism (Cattell) and Its Relation to the Presence of Neurotic Symptomatology." *Multivariate Behavioral Research,* 1969, *4,* 223–234.

KEAR–COLWELL, J. J. "The B Factor Scale of the 16 P.F. as a Measure of Intelligence in Psychiatric Patients." *Journal of Clinical Psychology,* 1970, *26,* 477–479.

KELLY, E. L., and FISKE, D. W. *The Prediction of Performance in Clinical Psychology.* Ann Arbor: University of Michigan Press, 1951.

KILLIAN, L. R. *The Utility of Objective Test Personality Factors in Diagnosing Schizophrenia and the Character Disorders.* Unpublished masters thesis. Urbana: University of Illinois, 1965.

KLEIN, M. A. "A Contribution to the Psychogenesis of Manic-Depressive States." *International Journal of Psychoanalysis,* 1935, *16,* 145–194.

KLEIN, T. W. *A Second Order Analysis of the HSPQ.* Advance Publication No. 51. Boulder, Colo.: Institute for Research on Morality and Adjustment. In press.

KLEIN, T. W., and CATTELL, R. B. *Heritablities of HSPQ Personality Factors from Intra-Class Correlations on Twins and Sibs.* Paper presented at the annual meeting of the American Psychological Association. Hawaii, 1972. Advance Publication No. 52. Boulder, Colo.: Institute for Research on Morality and Adjustment, 1973.

KLEINMUNTZ, B. *Personality Measurement.* Homewood, Ill.: Dorsey, 1967.

KLINE, G. S. *Perception, Motives and Personality.* New York: Knopf, 1970.

KNAPP, R. R. "Objective Personality Test and Sociometric Correlates of Frequency of Sick Bay Visits." *Journal of Applied Psychology,* 1961, *45,* 104–110.

KNAPP, R. R. "The Validity of the Objective-Analytic Personality Test Battery in

Navy Settings." *Educational and Psychological Measurement,* 1962, *22,* 379–387.

KOCH, H. L. "A Factor Analysis of Some Measures of the Behavior of Preschool Children." *Journal of Genetic Psychology,* 1942, *27,* 257–287.

KRAEPELIN, E. *Manic Depressive Insanity and Paranoia.* Edinburgh: Livingston, 1921.

KRETSCHMER, E. *Körperbau und Charakter.* Berlin: Springer, 1921.

KRETSCHMER, E. *The Psychology of Men of Genius.* London: Kegan, 1932.

KRUG, S. E. *A Test of Cattell's Trait View Theory of Distortion in Questionnaires.* Unpublished doctoral dissertation. Urbana, Illinois: University of Illinois Library, 1968.

KRUG, S. E. *An Examination of Experimentally Induced Changes in Ergic Tension Level.* Unpublished doctoral dissertation. Urbana: University of Illinois, 1971a.

KRUG, S. E. *Personality Profile of Drug Addicts as Measured by the 16 Personality Factor Questionnaire.* Personality Profile No. 3. Champaign, Ill.: Institute for Personality and Ability Testing, March, 1971b.

KRUG, S. E. *Preliminary Criterion Evidence on the Clinical Analysis Questionnaire.* Information Bulletin No. 15. Champaign, Ill.: Institute for Personality and Ability Testing, 1971c.

KRUG, S. E. *Dimensions of personality Differences Among Occupational Groups.* Advance Publication 54. Boulder, Colo.: Institute for Research on Morality and Adjustment. In press.

KRUG, S. E., and CATTELL, R. B. "A Test of the Trait-View Theory of Distortion in Measurement of Personality by Questionnaire." *Educational and Psychological Measurement,* 1971, *31,* 721–734.

KRUG, S. E., and KULHAVY, R. "Personality Differences Across Regions of the United States." *Journal of Social Psychology,* 1973.

KUDER, G. F. *The Kuder Preference Record.* Chicago: Science Research Associates, 1953.

LACEY, J. I., and LACEY, B. C. "Verification and Extension of the Principle of Autonomic Response-Stereotypy." *American Journal of Psychology,* 1958, *71,* 50–73.

LAFORGE, R. "A Correlational Study of Two Personality Tests: The MMPI and Cattell 16 P.F." *Journal of Consulting Psychology,* 1962, *26,* 402–411.

LAVELY, C. D. *Non-Intellective Factors Relating to Academic Success in College or Withdrawal from College After One Year.* Unpublished masters thesis. Indiana, Pa.: Indiana State College, 1963.

LAWLEY, D. N., and MAXWELL, A. E. *Factor Analysis as a Statistical Method.* London: Butterworth, 1963.

LAZARUS, R. S., and OPTON E. M. "The Study of Psychological Stress." In C. D. Spielberger (Ed.). *Anxiety and Behavior.* New York: Academic, 1966.

LEBOVITS, B. J., and OSTFELD, A. M. "Personality, Defensiveness and Educational Achievement. II. The Cattell 16 P.F. Questionnaire." *Journal of Clinical Psychology,* 1970, *26,* 183–188.

LENTZ, F. F. "Generality and Specificity of Conservatism-Radicalism." *Journal of Educational Psychology,* 1938, *29,* 540–546.

LENTZ, F. F. "Personage Administration and Other Correlates of Conservatism-Radicalism." *Journal of Social Psychology,* 1939, *10,* 81–93.

LEVONIAN, E. "Personality Measurement with Items Selected from the 16 P.F. Questionnaire." *Educational and Psychological Measurement,* 1961, *21,* 937–946.

LIKERT, R. A. "A Technique for the Measurement of Attitudes." *Archives of Psychology,* 1932, No. 140.

LINDSLEY, D. B. "Emotion." In S. S. Stevens (Ed.), *Handbook of Experimental Psychology.* New York: Wiley, 1951.

LINDZEY, G., and HALL, C. S. *Theories of Personality.* New York: Wiley, 1965.

LINGOES, J. C. *New Computer Developments in Pattern Analysis and Nonmetric Techniques.* Computing Center Report No. 4. Ann Arbor: University of Michigan, 1965.

LLOYD, R. "Cross and Psychosis." *Faith and Freedom,* 1971, *24,* 1–40.

LOEHLIN, J. C. *Heredity, Environment, and Personality Inventory Items.* Paper presented at a meeting of the American Psychological Association. St. Louis, 1962.

LOEVINGER, J. "A Theory of Test Response." *Proceedings of the 1958 Invitational Conference on Test Problems.* Princeton: Educational Testing Service, 1959. Pp. 36–47.

LOEVINGER, O., GLESER, G. C., and DUBOIS, P. H. "Maximizing the Discriminatory Power of a Multiple Score Test." *Psychometrika,* 1953, *18,* 309–317.

LORD, F. M. "Elementary Models for Measuring Change." In C. W. Harris (Ed.), *Problems in Measuring Change.* Madison: University of Wisconsin Press, 1963.

LORD, F. M., and NOVICK, M. R. *Statistical Theories of Mental Test Scores.* Reading, Massachusetts: Addison-Wesley, 1960.

LORR, M. *Explorations in Typing Psychotics.* New York: Pergamon, 1966.

LORR, M., DASTON, P., and SMITH, I. R. "An Analysis of Mood States." *Educational and Psychological Measurement,* 1967, *27* (1), 89–96.

LORR, M., KLETT, C. J., MCNAIR, D. M., and LASKY, J. J. *Inpatient Multidimensional Scale Manual.* Palo Alto: Consulting Psychologists Press, 1962.

LURIA, A. R. *The Nature of Human Conflicts, or Emotion, Conflict and Will.* Translated by W. H. Gantt. New York: Liveright, 1932.

LYKKEN, D. G. "Multiple Factor Analysis of Personality Research." *Journal of Experimental Research in Personality,* 1971, *5,* 161–170.

LYNN, R. *Personality and National Character.* New York: Pergamon, 1971.

MAHRER, A. R. (Ed.). *New Approaches to Personality Classification.* New York: Columbia University Press, 1970.

MARSHALL, D., and CATTELL, R. B. *The Seven Scale Supplement to the 16 P.F.* Champaign, Ill.: Institute for Personality and Ability Testing, 1973.

MASLOW, A. H. "A Test for Dominance Feeling in College Women." *Journal of Social Psychology,* 1940, *12,* 255–270.

MASLOW, A. H. *Motivation and Personality.* New York: Harper, 1954.

MASSERMAN, J. H. *Behavior and Neurosis: An Experimental Psychoanalytic Approach to Psychological Principles.* Chicago: University of Chicago Press, 1943.

MCALLISTER, J. "Personality Profiles on the 16 P.F. and Diagnostic Categories." *Bulletin of the British Psychological Society,* 1966, *19* (63), 194.

MCCLAIN, E. W. "16 P.F. Scores and Success in Student Teaching." *Journal of Teacher Education,* 1968, *19,* 2532.

MCCLELLAND, D. C., ATKINSON, J. W., CLARK, R. A., and LOWELL, E. L. *The Achievement Motive.* New York: Appleton Century Crofts, 1953.

MCDONOUGH, M. R. *The Empirical Study of Character.* Studies in Psychology and Psychiatry. Washington, D.C.: Catholic University of America, 1929.

MCDOUGALL, W. *Ethics and Some Modern World Problems.* London: Methuen, 1924.

MCDOUGALL, W. *Energies of Men.* London: Methuen, 1932.

MCGAW, B., and JORESKOG, K. G. "Factorial Invariance of Ability Measures in Groups Differing in Intelligence and Socioeconomic States." *British Journal of Mathematical and Statistical Psychology,* 1971, *24,* 144–168.

MCNAIR, D. M., and LORR, M. "An Analysis of Mood in Neurotics." *Journal of Abnormal and Social Psychology,* 1964, *69,* 620–627.

MCQUITTY, L. L. "Item Selection for Configured Scoring." *Educational and Psychological Measurement,* 1961, *21,* 925–928.

MCQUITTY, L. L. "Rank-Order Typal Analysis." *Educational and Psychological Measurement,* 1963, *23,* 55–61.

MATHENY, A. P., JR. Personal communication with the associate director, Child Development Unit, Medical-Dental Research Building, University of Kentucky, Louisville, 1973.

MATTSSON, K. *Personality Factors Related to Student Teaching Effectiveness.* Unpublished paper. Mankato, Minn.: Mankato State College, December 1968.

MAURER, K. M. "Patterns of Behavior of Young Children as Revealed by a Factor Analysis of Trait 'Clusters.' " *Journal of Genetic Psychology,* 1941, *59,* 177–188.

MAY, D. R. *Psychiatric Syndrome Classifications Checked by Taxonome and Discriminant Functions on the Clinical Analysis Questionnaire.* Unpublished doctoral dissertation. Urbana: University of Illinois, 1971.

MAYESKE, G. W. *Some Associations of Music Preference and Dimensions of Personality.* Unpublished doctoral dissertation. Urbana: University of Illinois, 1962.

MEREDITH, G. M. "Observations on the Origins and Current Status of the Ego Assertive Personality Factor, U.I. 16." *Journal of Genetic Psychology,* 1967, *110,* 269–286.

MEREDITH, G. M. "Stereotypic Desirability Profiles for the 16 P.F. Questionnaire." *Psychological Reports,* 1968, *23,* 1173–1174.

MEREDITH, G., NESSELROADE, J. R., and CATTELL, R. B. *Questionnaire Items Correlating with Objective Test Factors.* Advance Publication No. 17. Urbana: Laboratory of Personality Analysis, University of Illinois, 1966.

MESCHIERI, L., and CATTELL, R. B. *The International, Cross Cultural Constancy of Personality Factors Examined on the 16 P.F.* 1. *Italian-American Relations.* Advanced Publication No. 12. Champaign, Ill.: Laboratory of Personality and Group Analysis, 1960.

MESSICK, S. J., and ROSS, J. (Eds.). *Measurement in Personality and Cognition.* New York: Wiley, 1962.

MICHAEL, W. B., BARTH, G., and KAISER, H. F. "Dimensions of Temperament in Three Groups of Music Teachers." *Psychological Reports,* 1961, *9,* 701–704.

MILL, J. S. *Utilitarianism.* London: Parker and Bourn, 1863.

MILL, J. S. *A System of Logic.* 9th edition. London: Longmans, 1875.

MISCHEL, W. *Personality and Measurement.* New York: Wiley, 1968.

MITCHELL, J. V., JR. "Statistical Relationships Between Score Categories of the 16 P.F. and CPI Inventories." *American Psychologist,* 1961, *16,* 386.

MITCHELL, J. V., JR. "A Comparison of the First and Second Order Dimensions of the 16 P.F. and CPI Inventories." *Journal of Social Psychology,* 1963, *61,* 151–166.

MITTLER, P. *The Study of Twins.* Baltimore: Penguin, 1971.

MOONEY, R. L. *Problem Check List, High School Form.* Columbus: Bureau of Educational Research, Ohio State University, 1941.

MOWRER, O. H. *Psychotherapy: Theory* and *Research.* New York: Ronald, 1953.

MOWRER, O. H. "Abnormal Reactions or Actions? An Autobiographical Answer." In J. Vernon (Ed.), *General Introduction to Psychology.* Dubuque: Brown, 1966.

MULAIK, S. A. "Are Personality Factors Raters' Conceptual Factors?" *Journal of Consulting Psychology,* 1964, *28,* 506–511.

MURRAY, H. A. "Historical Trends in Personality Research." In H. P. David and J. C. Brengelman (Eds.), *Perspective in Personality Research.* New York: Springer, 1960.

MURRAY, H. A., and others. *Explorations in Personality.* New York: Oxford, 1938.

MURTHY, H. N. "Clinical Use of the 16 P.F. Questionnaire." *Indian Journal of Psychology,* 1965, *40,* 7–11.

NAYLOR, J. C., and WHERRY, R. J. "The Use of Simulated Stimuli, Multiple Regression and the JAN Technique to Capture and Cluster the Policy of Raters." *Educational and Psychological Measurement,* 1965, *25,* 969–986.

NEBYLITSIN, V. D., and GRAY, J. A. *Biological Bases of Individual Behavior.* New York: Academic, 1972.

NEIL, F. *A Compendium of Duplicate and Opposite Pairs of Items.* Fort Worth: Texas Christian University IBR, 1972.

NEIL, J. A., and JACKSON, D. N. "An Evaluation of Item Selection Strategies in Personality Scale Construction." *Educational and Psychological Measurement,* 1970, *30,* 647–661.

NESSELROADE, J. R. *An Experimental Examination of Factorial Invariance with Different Rotation Methods and Indices of Matching.* Unpublished masters thesis. Urbana: University of Illinois, 1964.

NESSELROADE, J. R. *The Separation of State and Trait Factors by dR-Technique with Special Reference to Anxiety, Effort Stress, and Cortertia.* Unpublished doctoral dissertation. Urbana: University of Illinois, 1966.

NESSELROADE, J. R. "Application of Multivariate Strategies to Problems of Measuring and Structuring Long-Term Change." In J. R. Nesselroade and H. W. Reese (Eds.), *Life-Span Developmental Psychology: Research and Theory.* New York: Academic, 1973.

NESSELROADE, J. R., and BALTES, P. B. *Higher Order Convergence of Two Distinct*

Personality Systems: Cattell's HSPQ *and Jackson's* PRF. Paper presented at the 12th annual conference of the Society of Multivariate Experimental Psychology. Fort Worth, November 9, 1972.

NESSELROADE, J. R., and BARTSCH, T. W. "Multivariate Experimental Perspectives on the Construct Validity of the Trait-State Distinction." In R. B. Cattell and R. M. Dreger (Eds.), *Handbook of Modern Personality Theory.* New York: Appleton Century Crofts, 1973.

NESSELROADE, J. R., and CABLE, D. " 'Sometimes its OK to Factor Difference Scores'—The Separation of State and Trait Anxiety." *Multivariate Behavioral Research,* 1973.

NICHOLS, K. E. *Collation of Second and Third Order Studies of Personality Structure in the High School Period.* Advance Publication No. 55. Boulder, Colo.: Institute for Research on Morality and Adjustment, 1973a.

NICHOLS, R. C. "The National Merit Twin Study." In S. C. Vandenberg (Ed.), *Methods and Goals in Human Behavior Genetics.* New York: Academic, 1965.

NICHOLS, K. E., and CATTELL, R. B. *A Survey of Second Order Factor Structure in the HSPQ.* Advance Publication No. 57. Boulder, Colo.: Institute for Research on Morality and Adjustment, 1973a.

NORMAN, W. T. *Development of Self-Report Tests to Measure Personality Factors Identified from Peer Nominations.* USAF Technical Report No. 61-44, 1961.

NORMAN, W. T. "Toward an Adequate Taxonomy of Personality Attributes: Replicated Factor Structure in Peer Nomination Personality Ratings." *Journal of Abnormal and Social Psychology,* 1963, *66,* 574–583.

NORMAN, W. T. *2800 Personality Trait Descriptors: Normative Operating Characteristics for a University Population.* NFMH Grant No. MH 07195. Ann Arbor: University of Michigan, 1967a.

NORMAN, W. T. "Personality Measurement Faking and Detection: An Assessment Method for Use in Personnel Selection." In O. N. Jackson and M. Messick (Eds.), *Problems in Human Assessment.* New York: McGraw-Hill, 1967b.

NOVAKOWSKA, M. "Krytyczna Analiza Strategii Badawczej R. B. Cattella." *Przeglad Psychologiczny,* 1971, *1* (21), 13–33.

NOWLIS, V., and GREEN, R. F. *The Experimental Analysis of Mood.* Proceedings of the 15th International Congress of Psychology. Brussels, July–August 1957.

NUNNALLY, J. C. *Tests and Measurements: Assessment and Prediction.* New York: McGraw-Hill, 1959.

NUNNALLY, J. C. *Popular Conceptions of Mental Health.* New York: Holt, 1961.

NUNNALLY, J. C. *Psychometric Theory.* New York: McGraw-Hill, 1967.

NUNNALLY, J. C. *Introduction to Psychological Measurement.* New York: McGraw-Hill, 1970.

O'DELL, J. W. "Method for Detecting Random Answers on Personality Questionnaires." *Journal of Applied Psychology,* 1971, *55* (4), 380–383.

O'DELL, J. W., and KARSON, S. "Some relationships between the MMPI and 16 P.F." *Journal of Clinical Psychology,* 1969, *25,* 279–283.

O'HALLORAN, A. *An Investigation of Personality Factors Associated with Achieve-*

ment in Arithmetic and Reading. Unpublished masters thesis. Lafayette, Ind.: Purdue University, 1954.

OHNMACHT, T. W. "Note on the Validity of the 16 P.F. Measure of Field Independence." *Perception and Motivational Skills,* 1968, *27,* 564.

OSGOOD, C. E. "Studies on the Generality of Affective Meaning Systems." *American Psychologist,* 1962, *17,* 10–28.

OSTFELD, A. M., LEBOVITS, B. Z., SHEKELLE, R. B., and PAUL, O. "A Prospective Study of the Relationship between Personality and Coronary Heart Disease." *Journal of Chronic Disorders,* 1964, *17,* 265–276.

PASSINI, F. T., and NORMAN, W. T. "A Universal Conception of Personality Structure?" *Journal of Personality and Social Psychology,* 1966, *4,* 44–49.

PAWLIK, K. *Dimensionen des Verhaltens.* Bern: Huber, 1968.

PAWLIK, K., and CATTELL, R. B. "Third-Order Factors in Objective Personality Tests." *British Journal of Psychology,* 1964, *55,* 1–18.

PENMAN, A. S. Factors Influencing Learning and Problem Solving in Small Groups. Unpublished doctoral dissertation. Urbana, Illinois: University of Illinois Library, 1951.

PERVIN, L. A. *Personality: Theory, Assessment and Research.* New York: Wiley, 1970.

PETERSON, D. R. "The Age Generality of Personality Factors Derived from Ratings." *Educational and Psychological Measurement,* 1960, *20,* 461–474.

PETERSON, D. R. "Scope and Generality of Verbally Defined Personality Factors." *Psychological Review,* 1965, *72* (1), 48–59.

PETERSON, D. R., and CATTELL, R. B. "Personality Factors in Nursery School Children as Derived from Parent Ratings." *Journal of Clinical Psychology,* 1958, *14,* 346–355.

PETERSON, D. R., and CATTELL, R. B. "Personality Factors in Nursery School Children as Derived from Teacher Ratings." *Journal of Consulting Psychology,* 1959, *23,* 562.

PHILIP, A. E. "Personality and Attempted Suicide: Traits Related to a Prior History of Suicidal Attempts." *Applied Social Studies,* 1970, *2,* 35–39.

PHILIP, A. E. Cross-cultural stability of second-order factors in the 16 PF *British Journal of Social and Clinical Psychology,* 1972, Vol. II, Part 3, 276–283.

PHILLIPS, J. D., and DELHEES, K. H. *A Personality Analysis of Drug Addicts by the 16 Personality Factor Questionnaire and Evaluation of Influence of Rehabilitation.* Corona, Calif.: California Rehabilitation Center, 1968.

PIERSON, G. R. "A Refinement in the Use of SMAT as a Predictor of School Achievement in Delinquent Boys." *Educational and Psychological Measurement,* 1964, *24,* 929–934.

PIERSON, G. R. "A Specification Equation for Predicting Treatment Responses." *Journal of Social Psychology,* 1965, *65,* 59–62.

PIERSON, G. R., BARTON, V., and HEY, G. "SMAT Motivation Factors as Predictors of Academic Achievement of Delinquent Boys." *Journal of Psychology,* 1964, *57,* 243–249.

PIERSON, G. R., CATTELL, R. B., and PIERCE, J. "A Demonstration by the HSPQ of the Nature of the Personality Changes Produced by Institutionalization of Delinquents." *Journal of Social Psychology,* 1966, *70,* 229–239.

PIERSON, G. R., and KELLY, R. F. "Anxiety, Extraversion, and Personality Idiosyncrasy in Delinquency." *Journal of Psychology,* 1963, *56,* 441–445.

PIESZKO, H. A. *Global Perceptiveness as a Process Common to Sensitization-Regression and the Factors of Independence, Comentive Superego and Asthenia.* Unpublished masters thesis. Urbana: University of Illinois, 1967.

PINSKA, C., and SAUNDERS, D. R. *Analytic Rotation to Simple Structure. II. Extension to an Oblique Solution.* Research Bulletin 54-31. Princeton: Educational Testing Service, 1954.

PORTER, R. B., CATTELL, R. B., and SCHAIE, C. W. *The Children's Personality Questionnaire.* Champaign, Ill.: Institute for Personality and Ability Testing, 1959, 1974.

PORTER, R. B., CATTELL, R. B., PORTER, A., and SCHAIE, K. W. *Handbook for the Children's Personality Questionnaire.* Champaign, Ill.: Institute for Personality and Ability Testing, 1966, 1974.

PUMFREY, P. D., and WARD, I. "A Four-Year Followup of Maladjusted and Normal Children." *Bulletin of the British Psychological Society,* 1971, *24,* 83.

REMMERS, H. H., and SHIMBERG, B. *SRA Youth Inventory, Form S.* Chicago: Science Research Associates, 1956–1960.

RHYMER, R. M. *An Exploratory Application of P-Technique to Personality Traits.* Unpublished masters thesis. Urbana: University of Illinois, 1947.

RICAN, P. Report on Factor Structure of the Czech Translation of the 16 PF. Psychology Institute, University of Prague, 1968.

RICAN, P., HEINZL, Z., and JANONSKOVA, N. "Dimenz ionalita Cattellova Osobnostniho Dotazniku." *Czechoslovenska Psychology,* 1970, *9,* 1–9.

RICKELS, K., and CATTELL, R. B. "The Clinical Factor Validity and Trueness of the IPAT Verbal Objective Batteries for Anxiety and Regression." *Journal of Clinical Psychology,* 1965, *21,* 257–264.

RICKELS, K., CATTELL, R. B., MACAFEE, A., and HESBACHER, P. "Drug Response and Important External Events in the Patient's Life." *Diseases of the Nervous System,* 1965, *26,* 782–786.

RICKELS, K., CATTELL, R. B., WEISE, C., GRAY, B., YEE, R., MULLIN, A., and AARONSON, H. G. "Controlled Psychopharmacological Research in Private Psychiatric Practice." *Psychopharmacologia,* 1966, *9,* 288–306.

RIMLAND, B. *Infantile Autism.* New York: Appleton Century Crofts, 1964.

RIMM, D. "Cost Efficiency and Test Prediction." *Journal of Consulting Psychology,* 1963, *27,* 89–91.

ROBACK, A. A. *Psychology of Character.* London: Kegan Paul, 1927.

ROFF, M. "A Factorial Study of Tests in the Perceptual Area." *Psychometric Monograph,* 1953, *8.*

ROGERS, C. R. *Measuring Personality Adjustment in Children 9–13 Years of Age.* Teachers College Contributions to Education No. 458. New York: Columbia University Press, 1931.

ROGERS, T. B. "The Process of Respoding to Personality Items: A Theory and Some Research." *Multivariate Behavioral Research,* 1971, *6,* 1–63.

RORER, L. G. "The Great Response Style Myth." *Psychological Bulletin,* 1965, *63,* 129–150.

RORER, L. G. "The 16 P.F. Questionnaire." In O. K. Buros (Ed.), *Seventh Mental Measurement Yearbook*. Highland Park, N.J.: Gryphon Press, 1972.

RORER, L. G., and GOLDBERG, L. R. "Acquiescence in the MMPI." *Educational and Psychological Measurement,* 1965, *25* (3), 801–817.

ROSS, J. "Factor Analysis and Levels of Measurement in Psychology." In S. Messick and J. Ross (Eds.), *Measurement in Personality and Cognition.* New York: Wiley, 1962.

ROSS, J. "The Relation Between Test and Personality Factors." *Psychological Review,* 1963, *70* (5), 432–443.

ROTHMAN, A. I., and FLOWERS, J. F. "Personality Correlates of First-Year Medical School Achievement." *Journal of Medical Education,* 1970, *45,* 901–905.

ROTTER, J. B. "Generalized Expectancies for Internal Versus External Control of Reinforcement." *Psychological Monographs: General and Applied,* 1966, *80* (1), 1–28.

ROYCE, J. R. "Factors as Theoretical Constructs." *American Psychologist,* 1963, *18,* 522–528.

ROYO, D. "Sensibilité du HSPQ aux Influences Culturelles." *Review de Psychologie Appliquée,* 1967, *17,* 193–210.

RUMMEL, R. J. *Applied Factor Analysis.* Evanston, Ill.: Northwestern University Press, 1970.

RUSSELL, J. *Relationship Between College Freshmen Withdrawal and Certain Crucial Personality and Study Factors.* Unpublished doctoral dissertation. Los Angeles: University of Southern California, 1969.

RYAN, F. J. Cold turkey in Greenfield, Iowa: a follow up study. In W. J. Dunn (Ed.) Smoking behavior; motives and incentives N. Y. Wiley, 1973.

SANKAR, D. V. S. *Schizophrenia, Current Concepts and Research.* Hicksville, N.Y.: PJD Publications, 1969.

SARASON, S. B. "The Measurement of Anxiety in Children: Some Questions and Problems." In C. D. Spielberger (Ed.), *Anxiety and Behavior.* New York: Academic, 1966.

SAVILLE, P. *British Standardization of the 16 P.F. Norms for Forms A & B.* Windsor, England: National Foundation of Educational Research, 1972.

SAVILLE, P., and FINLAYSON, L. *The British Standardization of the High School Personality Questionnaire.* Windsor, England: National Foundation of Educational Research, 1973.

SCHAIE, K. W. "On the Equivalence of Questionnaire and Rating Data." *Psychological Reports,* 1962, *10* (2), 521–522.

SCHAIE, K. W. "Year-by-year Changes in Personality from Six to Eighteen Years." *Multivariate Behavioral Research,* 1966, *1,* 293–305.

SCHAIE, K. W., and CATTELL, R. B. *Upper and Lower Boundary Alignment of Personality Factors Measured by the Child Personality Questionnaire.* Advance Publication No. 60. Boulder, Colo.: Institute for Research on Morality and Adjustment. In preparation.

SCHAIE, K. W., PORTER, R. B., and CATTELL, R. B. *A Check on Personality Structure at the 8–12 Year Level by the CPQ.* Advance Publication No. 61. Boulder, Colorado: Institute for Research on Morality and Adjustment. In preparation.

SCHAIE, K. W., and STROTHER, C. R. "The Effect of Time and Cohort Differences on the Interpretation of Age Changes in Cognitive Behavior." *Multivariate Behavioral Research,* 1968a, *3,* 259–294.

SCHAIE, K. W., and STROTHER, C. R. "A Cross-Sequential Study of Age Changes in Cognitive Behavior." *Psychological Bulletin,* 1968b, *68.*

SCHEIER, I. H. "Confirmation of Objective Test Factors and Their Relation to Other Variables." *Journal of Mental Science,* 1958, *104,* 608–624.

SCHEIER, I. H. *The Eight-Parallel Form Anxiety Battery.* Champaign, Ill.: Institute for Personality and Ability Testing, 1959.

SCHEIER, I. H. *Recent Data on IPAT Anxiety Tests.* Information Bulletin No. 13. Champaign, Ill.: Institute for Personality and Ability Testing, 1967.

SCHEIER, I. H. *Interpreting the 16 PF Profile: Some Case Studies.* IPAT Special Publication. Champaign, Ill.: Institute for Personality and Ability Testing, August, 1968a.

SCHEIER, I. H. *Airline Hostesses as Measured by the 16 Personality Factor Test.* Personality Profile No. 2. Champaign, Ill.: Institute for Personality and Ability Testing, September, 1968b.

SCHEIER, I. H., and CATTELL, R. B. "Confirmation of Objective Test Factors and Assessment of Their Relation to Questionnaire Factors: A Factor Analysis of 113 Rating, Questionnaire and Objective Test Measurements of Personality." *Journal of Mental Science,* 1958, *104,* 608–624.

SCHMID, J., and LEIMAN, J. M. "The Development of Hierarchical Factor Solutions." *Psychometrika,* 1957, *22,* 53–62.

SCHMIDT, L. R. "Differential Diagnosis mit Hilfe Objectiver Persönlichkeitstests." *Diagnostica,* 1972.

SCHNEEWIND, K. A., and CATTELL, R. B. "Zum Problem der Faktoridentifikation: Verteilungen und Vertrauensintervalle von Kongruenzkoeffizienten für Persönlichkeitsfaktoren im Bereich Objektiv-Analytischer Tests. *Psychologische Beiträge,* 1970, *12,* 214–226.

SCHNEEWIND, K. A., and SCHRODER, G. *Report on the Factorization and Standardization of the German Translation of the 16 P.F.* Champaign, Ill.: Institute for Personality and Ability Testing, 1974.

SCHUERGER, J. M., and CATTELL, R. B. *The High School O-A Battery.* Champaign, Ill.: Institute for Personality and Ability Testing, 1973.

SCHUERGER, J. M., DIELMAN, T. E., and CATTELL, R. B. "Objective-Analytic Personality Factors (U.I. 16, 17, 19, and 20) as Correlates of School Achievement." *Personality,* 1970, *1* (2), 95–101.

SCOFIELD, R. W., and SUN, CHIN-WAN. "A Comparative Study of the Differential Effect upon Personality of Chinese and American Child Training Practices." *Journal of Social Psychology,* 1960, *52,* 221–224.

SELLS, S. B. *Essentials of Psychology.* New York: Ronald, 1962.

SELLS, S. B. *Stimulus Determinants of Behavior.* New York: Ronald, 1963.

SELLS, S. B., DEMAREE, R. B., and WILL, D. P. *A Taxonomic Investigation of Personality: Conjoint Factor Structure of Guilford and Cattell Trait Markers.* Mimeographed report on Project No. OE5-0072. Washington, D.C.: Office of Education, Department of Health, Education, and Welfare, 1968.

SELLS, S. B., DEMAREE, R. B., and WILL, D. P. "Dimensions of Personality: 1. Conjoint

Factor Structure of Guilford and Cattell Trait Markers." *Multivariate Behavioral Research,* 1970, *4,* 391–422.

SEWARD, G. H. *Sex and the Social Order.* New York: McGraw-Hill, 1946.

SHAPIRO, M. B., NEWFIELD, J. L., and POST, T. "Experimental Study of Depressive Illness." *Psychological Reports,* 1962, *10,* 590.

SHEKELLE, R. B., and OSTFELD, A. M. "Psychometric Evaluation in Cardiovascular Epidemiology." *Annal of the New York Academy of Science,* 1965, *126,* 696–705.

SHIELDS, J. "Personality Differences and Neurotic Traits in Normal Twin School Children: A Study in Psychiatric Genetics." *Eugenics Review,* 1953, *45,* 213–246.

SHIELDS, J. *Monozygotic Twins Brought Up Together and Apart.* New York: Oxford University Press, 1962.

SHNEIDMAN, E. S. "Projective Techniques." In B. B. Wolman (Ed.), *Handbook of Clinical Psychology.* New York: McGraw-Hill, 1965.

SHOSTRUM, E. L. "An Inventory for the Measurement of Self-Actualization." *Educational and Psychological Measurement,* 1964, *24* (2), 207–218.

SHRADER, R. R., and CATTELL, R. B. *The High School Anxiety Scale, Trait and State.* Champaign, Ill.: Institute for Personality and Ability Testing. In press.

SIEGEL, P. V., and HAYNES, H. C. *Clinical Experience with Psychological Testing of Air Traffic Controllers.* Paper presented at the International Meeting on Air Space Medicine. Atlantic City, 1972.

SIGNORI, E. J., REMPEL, H., and PICKFORD, J. H. "Multivariate Relations Between Spouses' Trait Scores on the Guilford-Zimmerman Temperament Survey." *Psychological Reports,* 1968, *22,* 103–106.

SINHA, D. "Position Effect in the Readministration of an Anxiety Scale." *Journal of General Psychology,* 1964, *70,* 305–309.

SMITH, R. G. *A Factorial Study of Attitude Toward the Negro.* Unpublished Doctoral dissertation. Urbana: University of Illinois, 1950.

SOKAL, R. R. "A Comparison of Five Tests for Completeness of Factor Extraction." *Transactions of the Kansas Academy of Science,* 1959, 62, 141–152.

SOKAL, R. R., and SNEATH, P. H. *Principles of Numerical Taxonomy.* San Francisco: Freeman, 1964.

SPEARMAN, C. *The Abilities of Man.* London: Macmillan, 1927.

SPENGLER, O. *The Decline of the West.* Abridged edition. New York: Knopf, 1962.

SPIELBERGER, C. D. *Anxiety and Behavior.* New York: Academic, 1966.

SPIELBERGER, C. D. *Anxiety: Current trends in Theory and Research.* New York: Academic, 1972.

SPIELBERGER, C. D., GORSUCH, D. L., and LUSHENE, R. E. *Manual for the State-Trait Anxiety Inventory.* Palo Alto: Consulting Psychologists Press, 1970.

SPILKA, B., HORN, J. L., and LANGENDERFER, L. "Social Desirabilities Among Measures of Social Desirability." *Educational and Psychological Measurement,* 1966, *26* (1), 111–120.

STAFFORD, R. E. "New Techniques in Analyzing Parent-Child Test Scores for Evidence of Hereditary Components." In S. G. Vandenberg (Ed.), *Methods and Goals in Human Behavior Genetics.* New York: Academic, 1965.

STANLEY, J. C., and WANG, M. D. "Weighting Test Items and Test-Item Options:

An Overview of the Analytical and Empirical Literature." *Educational and Psychological Measurement,* 1970, *30,* 21–35.

START, K. B. "The Relation of Teaching Ability to Measures of Personality." *British Journal of Educational Psychology,* 1966, *36,* 158–165.

START, K. B. "Rater-Ratee Personality in the Assessment of Teaching Ability." *British Journal of Educational Psychology,* 1968, *38,* 14–28.

STEPHENSON, W. *The study of Behavior: Q-Technique and Its Methodology.* Chicago: University of Chicago Press, 1953.

STRICKER, L. J. *Response Styles and 16 P.F. Higher Order Factors.* ETS Research Bulletin RB-73-8. Princeton: Educational Testing Service, 1973a.

STRICKER, L. J. *Personality Research from Factor Structure and Response Style Involvement.* ETS Research Bulletin No. 23. Princeton, New Jersey: Educational Testing Service, 1973b.

STRICKER, L. J., JACOBS, P. I., and KOGAN, N. *Trait Interrelations in Implicit Personality Theories and Questionnaire Data.* ETS Research Bulletin. Princeton: Educational Testing Service, 1972.

STRONG, E. K., JR. *Vocational Interests of Men and Women.* Stanford: Stanford University Press, 1943.

SWENEY, A. B. "Objective Measurement of Strength of Dynamic Structure Factors." In R. B. Cattell and F. W. Warburton (Eds.), *Objective Personality and Motivation Tests. A Theoretical Introduction and Practical Compendium.* Urbana: University of Illinois Press, 1967.

SWENEY, A. B., CATTELL, R. B., and KRUG, S. E. *School Motivation Analysis Test.* Champaign. Ill.: Institute for Personality and Ability Testing, 1970.

TAMKIN, A. S., and SONKIN, N. "Personality Factors in Psychogenic Somatic Complaints." *Newsletter for Research in Psychology,* 1966, *8,* 20–21.

TAMKIN, A. S., and SONKIN, N. "The Use of Psychological Tests in Differential Diagnosis." *Psychological Reports,* 1969, *24,* 590.

TATRO, D. F. *The Interpretation of Objectively Measured Personality Factors in Terms of Clinical Data and Concepts.* Unpublished doctoral dissertation. Urbana: University of Illinois, 1967.

TATSUOKA, M. M. *Specification Equations for Counselor Effectiveness.* Personality Profile No. 1a. Champaign, Ill.: Institute for Personality and Ability Testing, Fall, 1968.

TATSUOKA, M. M. *Discriminant Analysis: The Study of Group Differences.* Selected Topics in Advanced Statistics, No. 6. Champaign, Ill.: Institute for Personality and Ability Testing, 1970.

TATSUOKA, M. M. *What is Job Relevance?* Champaign, Ill.: Institute for Personality and Ability Testing, 1973.

TATSUOKA, M. M., and CATTELL, R. B. "Linear Equations for Estimating a Person's Occupational Adjustment, Based on Information on Occupational Profiles." *The British Journal of Educational Psychology,* 1970, *40,* 324–334.

TERMAN, L. M., and MERRILL, M. A. *Stanford-Binet Intelligence Scale.* Boston: Houghton Mifflin, 1960.

THAYER, R. E. "Activation States as Assessed by Verbal Report and Four Psychophysiological Variables." *Psychophysiology,* 1970, 7 (1), 86–94.

THOMSON, G. H. *The Factorial Analysis of Human Ability*. London: University of London Press, 1939.

THORNDIKE, R. L., and HAGEN, E. *Measurement and Evaluation in Psychology and Education*. New York: Wiley, 1955.

THURSTONE, L. L. "The Absolute Zero in Intelligence Measurement." *Psychological Review*, 1928, *35*, 175–197.

THURSTONE, L. L. *The Vectors of the Mind*. Chicago. University of Chicago Press, 1937.

THURSTONE, L. L. *Primary Mental Abilities*. Chicago: University of Chicago Press, 1938.

THURSTONE, L. L. *Multiple Factor Analysis*. Chicago: University of Chicago Press, 1947.

THURSTONE, L. L. *Thurstone Temperament Schedule: Examiner's Manual*. Chicago: Science Research Associates, 1950.

THURSTONE, L. L., and CHAVE, E. J. *The Measurement of Attitude*. Chicago: University of Chicago Press, 1929.

TIMM, U. "Reliabilität und Faktorenstruktur von Cattell's 16 P.F. Test bei einer Deutschen Stichprobe." *Zeitschrift für Experimentelle und Angewandte Psychologie*, 1968, *15*, 354–373.

TOLLEFSON, D. L. *Differential Responses to Humor and Their Relation to Personality and Motivation Measures*. Unpublished doctoral dissertation. Urbana: University of Illinois, 1961.

TORGERSON, W. S. *Theory and Methods of Scaling*. New York: Wiley, 1958.

TRYON, C. M. *Cluster Analysis*. Chicago: University of Chicago Press, 1939.

TRYON, R. C. "A Comparative Cluster of Variables and Individuals in the MMPI." *Multivariate Behavioral Research*, 1968, *3*, 115–144.

TSUJIOKA, B., and CATTELL, R. B. "Constancy and Difference in Personality Structure and Mean Profile, in the Questionnaire Medium, from Applying the 16 P.F. Test in America and Japan." *British Journal of Social and Clinical Psychology*, 1965a, *4*, 287–297.

TSUJIOKA, B., and CATTELL, R. B. "A Cross-Cultural Comparison of Second-Stratum Questionnaire Personality Factor Structures—Anxiety and Extraversion—in America and Japan." *Journal of Social Psychology*, 1965b, *65*, 205–219.

TSUSHIMA, Y. *Failure Stress in Examinations Related to Anxiety Inventory Scores*. Unpublished masters thesis. Urbana: University of Illinois, 1957.

TUCKER, L. R. "The Objective Definition of Simple Structure in Linear Factor Analysis." *Psychometrika*, 1955, *20*, 209–225.

TUCKER, L. R. "Formal Models for a Central Prediction System." *Psychometry Monographs*, 1963, *10*.

TUCKER, L. R. "Learning Theory and Multivariate Experiment: Illustration by Determination of Generalized Learning Curves." In R. B. Cattell (Ed.), *Handbook of Multivariate Experimental Psychology*. Chicago: Rand McNally, 1966.

TUCKER, L. R. "Relations of Factor Score Estimates to Their Use." *Psychometrika*, 1971, *36*, 427–436.

TUDDENHAM, R. D. "Soldier Intelligence in World War I and II." *American Psychologist*, 1948, *3*, 54–56.

TUPES, E. C. *Relationships Between Behavior Trait Ratings by Peers and Later Officer Performance of* USAF *Officer Candidate School Graduates.* Report No. AFPTRC-TN-57-125 (ASTIA Doc. No. 134357). Lackland AFB, Texas: USAF Personnel and Training Research Center, 1957.

TUPES, E. C., and CRISTAL, R. C. *Stability of Personality-Trait Rating Factors Obtained Under Diverse Conditions.* USAF, WACD, Technical Note, No. 58-61. Lackland AFB, Texas: USAF Personnel and Training Research Center, 1958.

TUPES, E. C., and CRISTAL, R. C. *Recurrent Personality Factors Based on Trait Ratings.* USAF, ASD Technical Report No. 61–97, 1–40. Lackland AFB, Texas: USAF Personnel and Training Research Center, May 1961.

TYLER, F. T. "A Factorial Analysis of Fifteen MMPI Scales." *Journal of Consulting Psychology,* 1951, *15,* 451–456.

UBERLA, K. *Faktorenanalyse.* New York: Springer, 1968.

UHR, L., and MILLER, J. G. *Drugs and Behavior.* New York: Wiley, 1960.

VANDENBERG, S. G. "The Hereditary Abilities Study: Hereditary Components in a Psychological Test Battery." *American Journal of Human Genetics,* 1962, *14,* 220–237.

VANDENBERG, S. G. *Methods and Goals in Human Behavior Genetics.* New York: Academic, 1965.

VAN EGEREN, L. F. *Experimental Determination by P-Technique of Functional Unities of Depression and Other Psychological States.* Unpublished masters thesis. Urbana: University of Illinois, 1963.

VAUGHAN, D. "On the technical standards of ten representative factor analyses purporting to decide personality theories." *Journal of Behavioral Science* (South Africa), In press.

VAUGHAN, D., and BURDSAL, C. *A Third Check on the Factor Structure of the HSPQ.* Advance Publication No. 62. Boulder, Colo.: Institute for Research on Morality and Adjustment. In preparation.

VAUGHAN, D., and CATTELL, R. B. *The Search for Common Personality Factors in Questionnaire and Objective Test Media.* Advance Publication No. 63. Boulder, Colo.: Institute for Research on Morality and Adjustment, 1973.

VAUGHAN, D., and CATTELL, R. B. *The* HSOAQ*—High School Objective Analytic Questionnaire.* Champaign, Ill.: Institute for Personality and Ability Testing. In preparation.

VERNON, P. E. "The Rorschach Inkblot Test, II." *British Journal of Medical Psychology,* 1933, *13,* 179–205.

VERNON, P. E. *Personality Assessment: A Critical Survey.* New York: Wiley, 1964.

VIDAL, A. *BG8 Diagnostic Psychologique a Compte Rendu Programme sur Ordinqteur.* Paris: Centre de Psychologie Appliquée, 1972.

WACKWITZ, I. H., and HORN, J. L. "On Obtaining the Best Estimates of Factor Scores Within an Ideal Simple Structure." *Multivariate Behavioral Research,* 1971, *6,* 389–408.

WALKER, D. A. "Answer Patterns and Score Scatter in Tests and Examinations." *British Journal of Psychology,* 1940, *30,* 248–260.

WALKER, W. L. "A Preliminary Investigation of Personality Change in Depressed

Patients Following ECT." *Australian Journal of Psychology,* 1966, *18,* 239–243.

WALTON, H. J. "Personality as a Determinant in the Form of Alcoholism." *British Journal of Psychiatry,* 1968, *114,* 761–766.

WARBURTON, F. W., BUTCHER, H. J., and FORREST, G. M. "Predicting Student Performance in a University Department of Education." *British Journal of Educational Psychology,* 1963, *33,* 68–79.

WARDELL, D. *Cognitive-Affective Linkages and the Problem of Style.* Advance Publication 117A. Edmonton, Canada: Center for Advanced Study in Theoretical Psychology, 1973.

WATERS, L. K. "A Note on the 'Fakability' of Forced-Choice Scales." *Personnel Psychology,* 1965, *18* (2), 187–191.

WECKOWICZ, T. E., CROPLEY, A., and MUIR, W. "An Attempt to Replicate the Results of a Factor-Analytic Study in Depressed Patients." *Journal of Clinical Psychology,* 1971, *27,* 30–31.

WECKOWICZ, T. E., MUIR, W., and CROPLEY, A. "Factor Analysis of the Beck Inventory of Depression." *Journal of Consulting Psychology,* 1967, *31,* 23–28.

WENGER, M. "Interrelations Among Some Physiological Variables." *Psychological Bulletin,* 1940, *37,* 466.

WENIG, P. *The Relative Roles of Naive, Artistic, Cognitive, and Press Compatibility Misperception and Ego Defense Operations in Tests of Misperception.* Unpublished masters thesis. Urbana: University of Illinois, 1952.

WESSMAN, A. E., and RICKS, D. F. *Mood and Personality.* New York: Holt, 1966.

WHERRY, R. J., and GAYLORD, R. H. "Factor Pattern of Test Items and Tests as a Function of the Correlation Coefficient: Content, Difficulty, and Constant Error Factors." *Psychometrika,* 1944, *9,* 237–244.

WHITE, K. "Anxiety, Extraversion-Introversion, and Divergent Thinking Ability." *Journal of Creative Behavior,* 1968, *2,* 119–127.

WHITE, W. F. "Personality and Cognitive Learning Among Alcoholics with Different Intervals of Sobriety." *Psychological Reports,* 1965, *16,* 1125–1140.

WIGGINS, J. S. "Definitions of Social Desirability and Acquiescence in Personality Inventories." In S. Messick and J. Ross (Eds.), *Measurement in Personality and Cognition.* New York: Wiley, 1962a.

WIGGINS, J. S. "Strategy, Method and Stylistic Variance in the MMPI." *Psychological Bulletin,* 1962b, *59,* 224–242.

WIGGINS, J. S. "Convergences among Stylistic Response Measures from Objective Personality Tests." *Educational and Psychological Measurement,* 1964, *24,* 551–562.

WIGGINS, J. S. "Personality Structure." *Annual Review of Psychology,* 1968, *19,* 293–350.

WIGGINS, J. S. *Personality and Prediction: Principles of Personality Assessment.* London: Addison-Wesley, 1973.

WILDE, G. J. S. "Trait Description and Measurement by Personality Questionnaires." In R. B. Cattell and R. M. Dreger (Eds.), *Handbook of Modern Personality Theory.* New York: Appleton Century, 1974.

WILLIAMS, H. V. "A Factor Analysis of Berne's 'Social Behavior Patterns in Young Children.'" *Journal of Experimental Education,* 1935, *4,* 142–146.

WILLIAMS, H. V. "A P-Technique Study of Personality Factors in the Psychosomatic Areas." *Microfilm Abstracts,* 1950, *9,* 177–178.

WILLIAMS, H. V. "A Determination of Psychosomatic Functional Unities in Personality by Means of P-Technique." *Journal of Social Psychology,* 1954, *39,* 25–45.

WILLIAMS, J. R. "A Test of the Validity of P-Technique in the Measurement of *nique: A Test of Validity.* Unpublished doctoral dissertation. Urbana: University of Illinois, 1958.

WILLIAMS, J. R. "A Test of the Validity of P-Technique in the Measurement of Internal Conflict." *Journal of Personality,* 1959, *27,* 418–437.

WITKIN, H. A. *Psychological Differentiation: Studies of Development.* New York: Wiley, 1962.

WITTENBORN, J. R. *Manual: Wittenborn Psychiatric Rating Scales.* New York: Psychological Corporation, 1955.

WOODWORTH, R. S. *Experimental Psychology.* New York: Holt, 1938.

WRIGHT, C. E. *Relations Between Normative and Ipsative Measures of Personality.* Unpublished doctoral dissertation. Seattle: University of Washington, 1957.

WRIGHT, S. *Some Psychological and Physiological Characteristics of Certain Academic Underachievers.* Unpublished doctoral dissertation. Los Angeles: University of California, 1954.

YAMAGUCHI, K. *The Use of the Japanese 16 PF.* Advance Publication No. 50. Boulder, Colo.: Institute for Research on Morality and Adjustment. In preparation.

YOUNG, P. T. *Emotion in Man and Animal.* New York: Wiley, 1943.

YULE, C. U. "Why We Sometimes Get Nonsense Correlations Between Time Series." *Journal of the Royal Statistical Association,* 1926, *89,* 1–64.

ZAVALA, A. "Development of the Forced Choice Rating Technique." *Psychological Bulletin,* 1965, *63,* 117–124.

Index